CAN'T GET NO

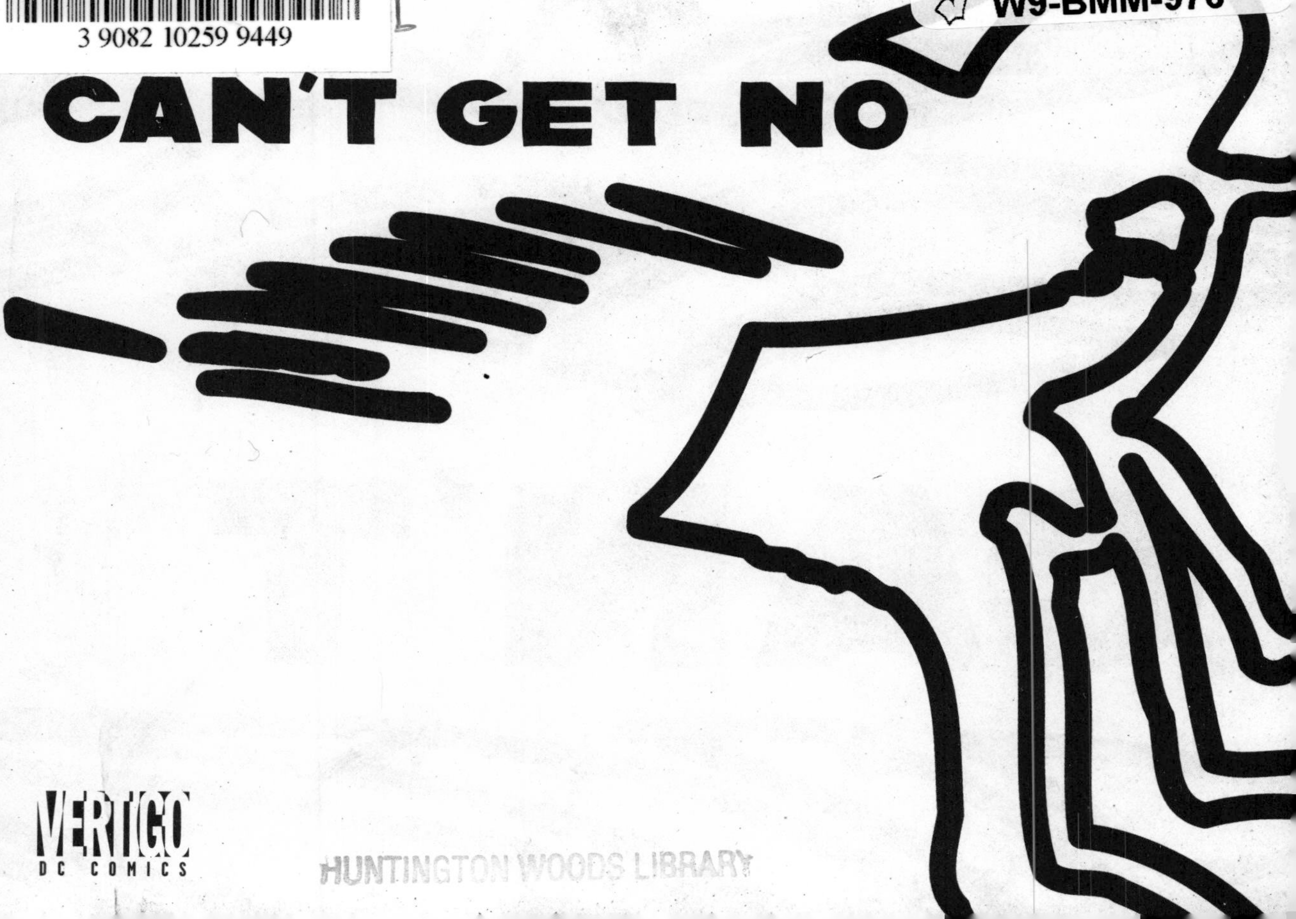

VERTIGO
DC COMICS

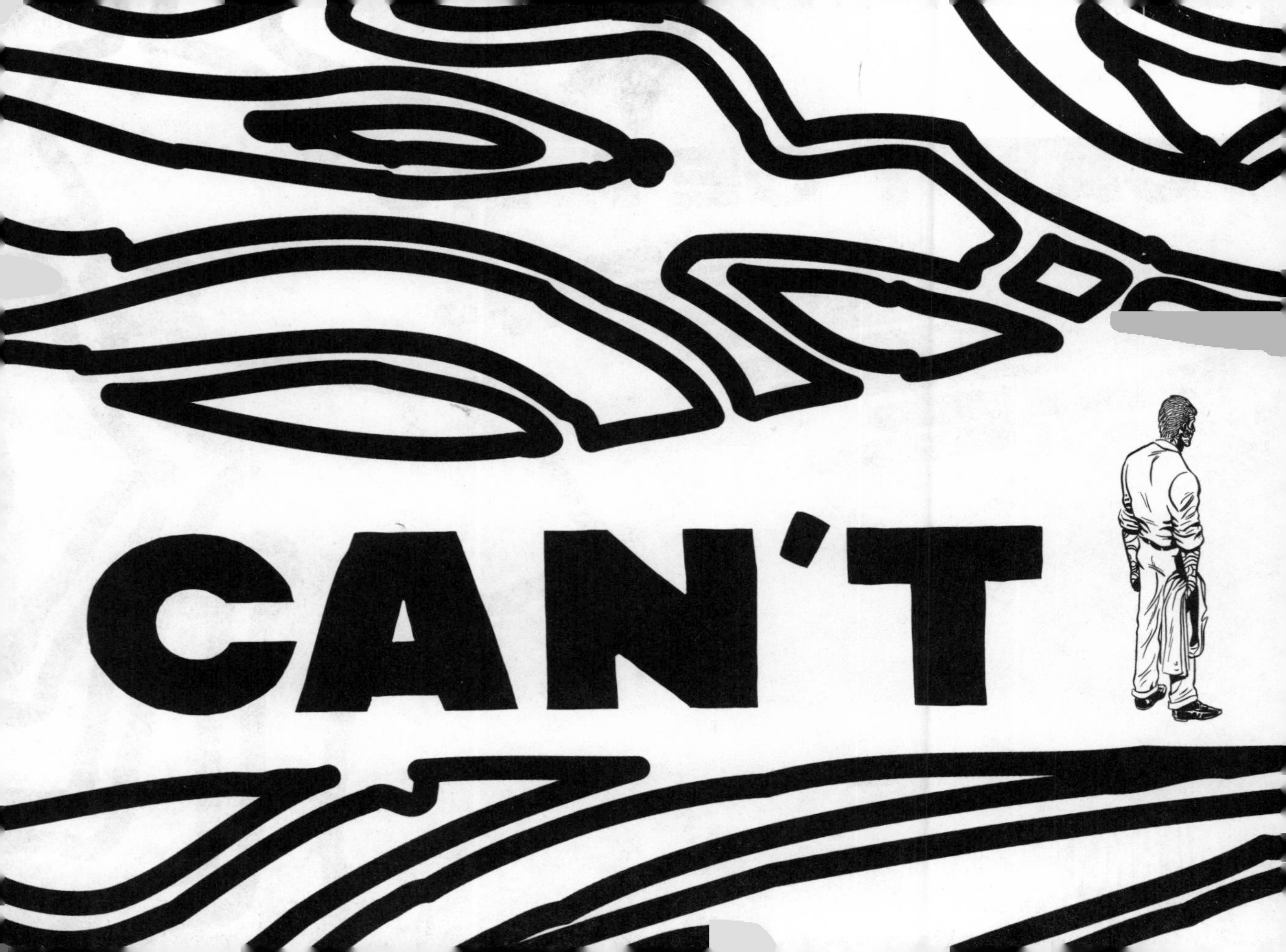
CAN'T

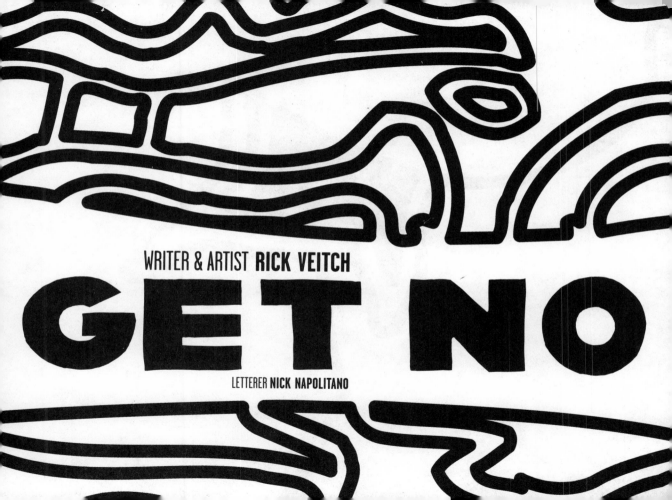

WRITER & ARTIST **RICK VEITCH**

GET NO

LETTERER **NICK NAPOLITANO**

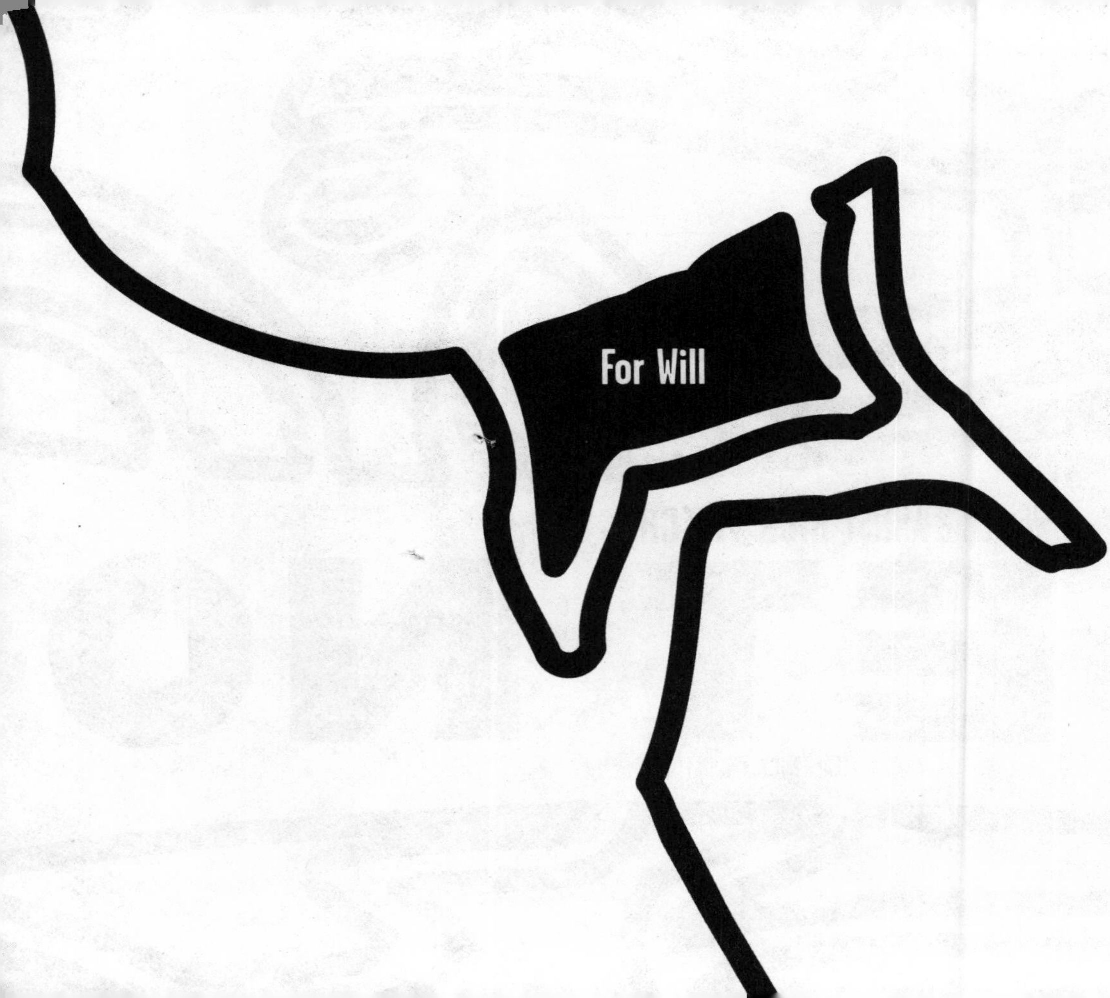

For Will

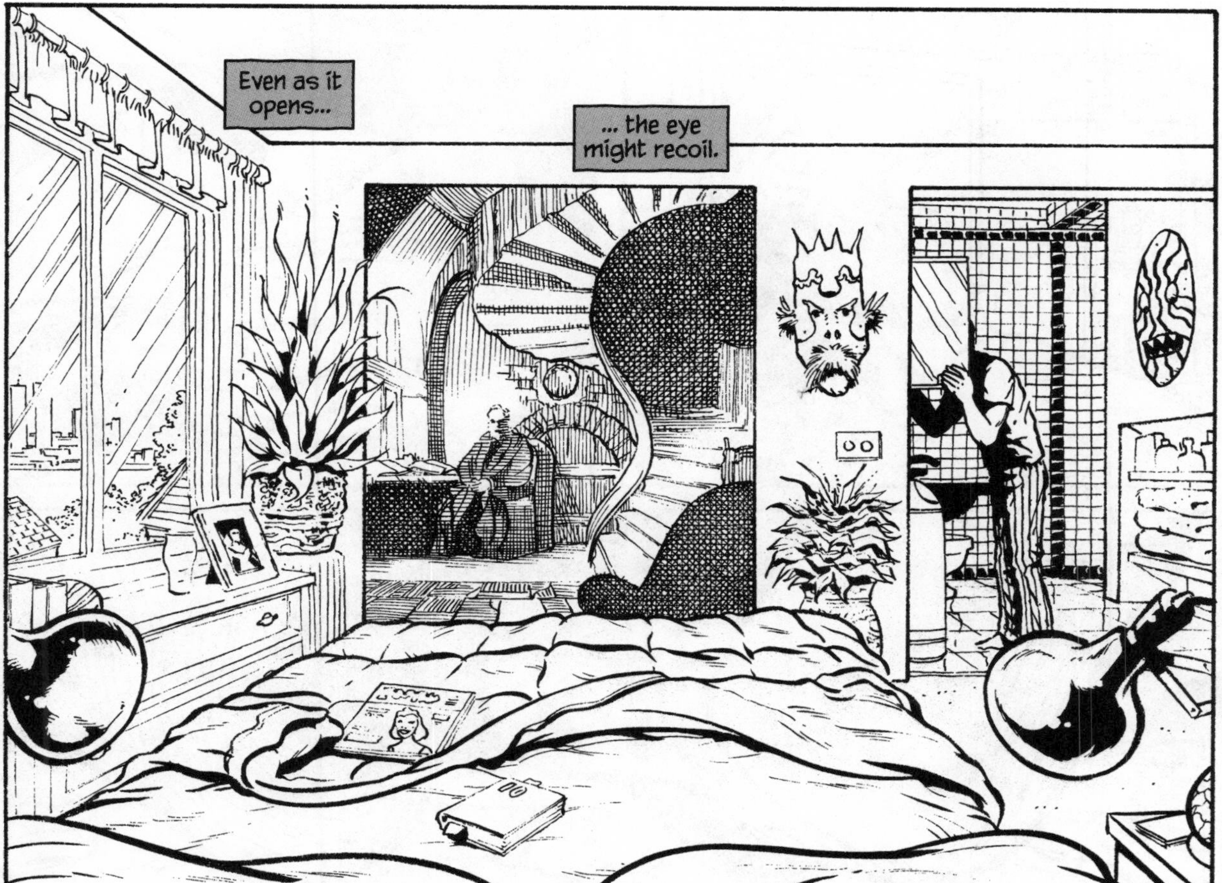
Even as it opens...
... the eye might recoil.

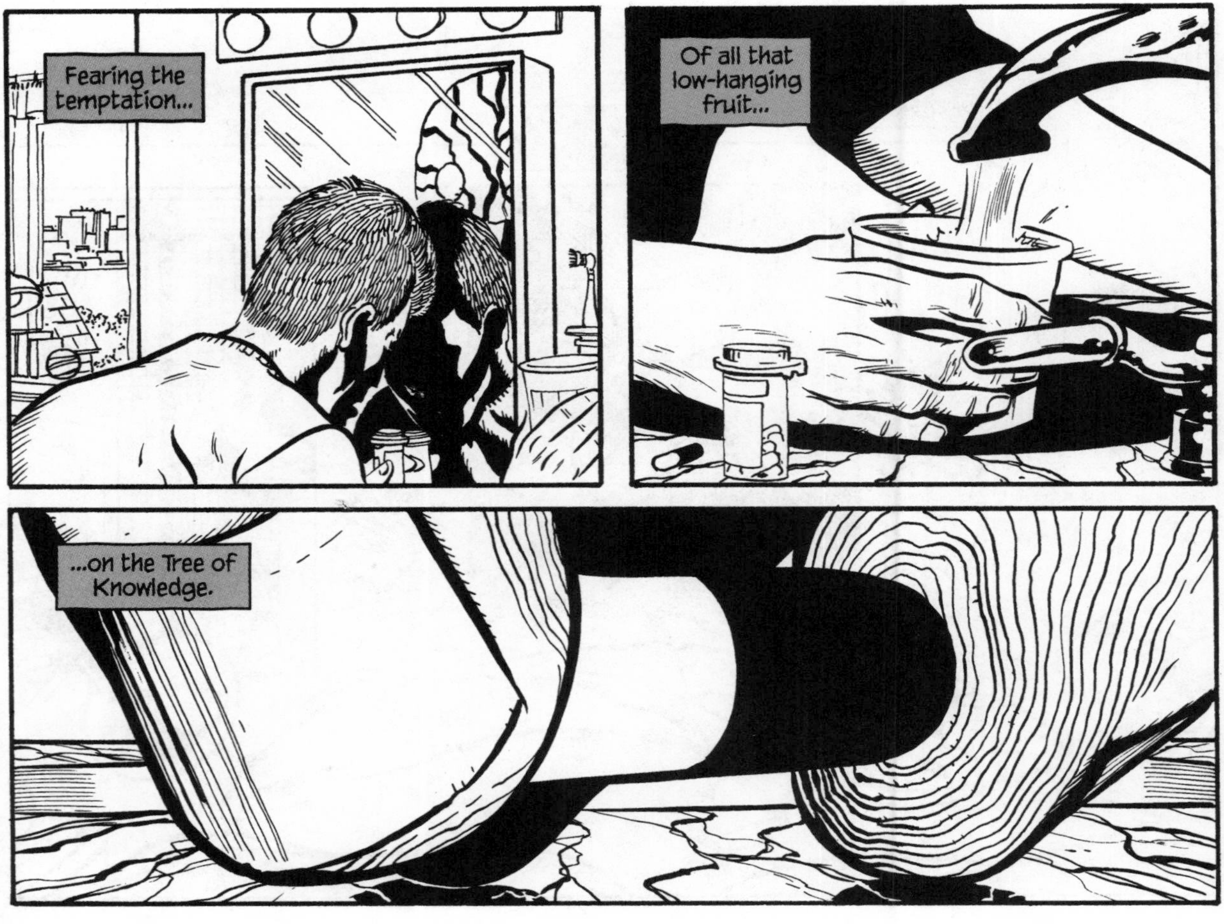
Fearing the temptation...
Of all that low-hanging fruit...
...on the Tree of Knowledge.

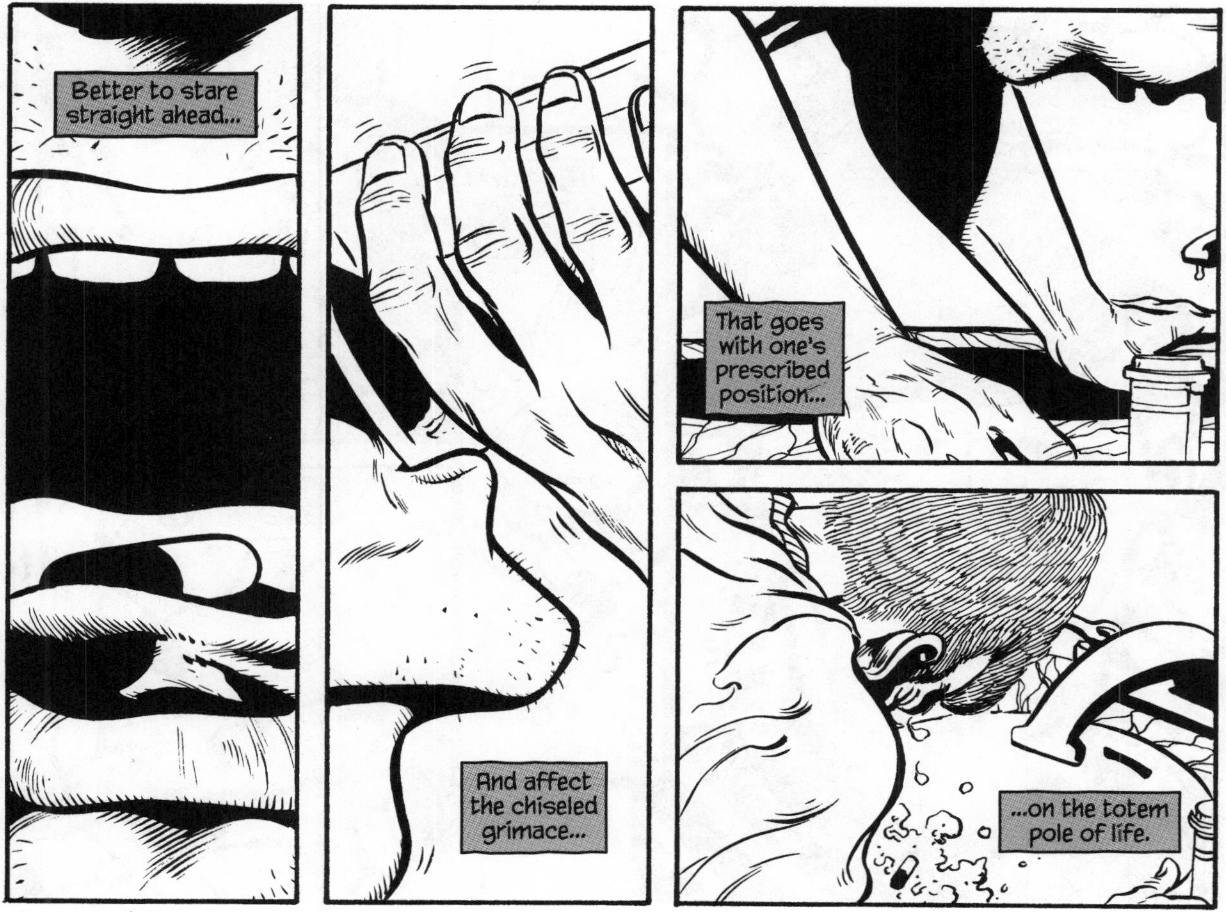
Better to stare straight ahead...
And affect the chiseled grimace...
That goes with one's prescribed position...
...on the totem pole of life.

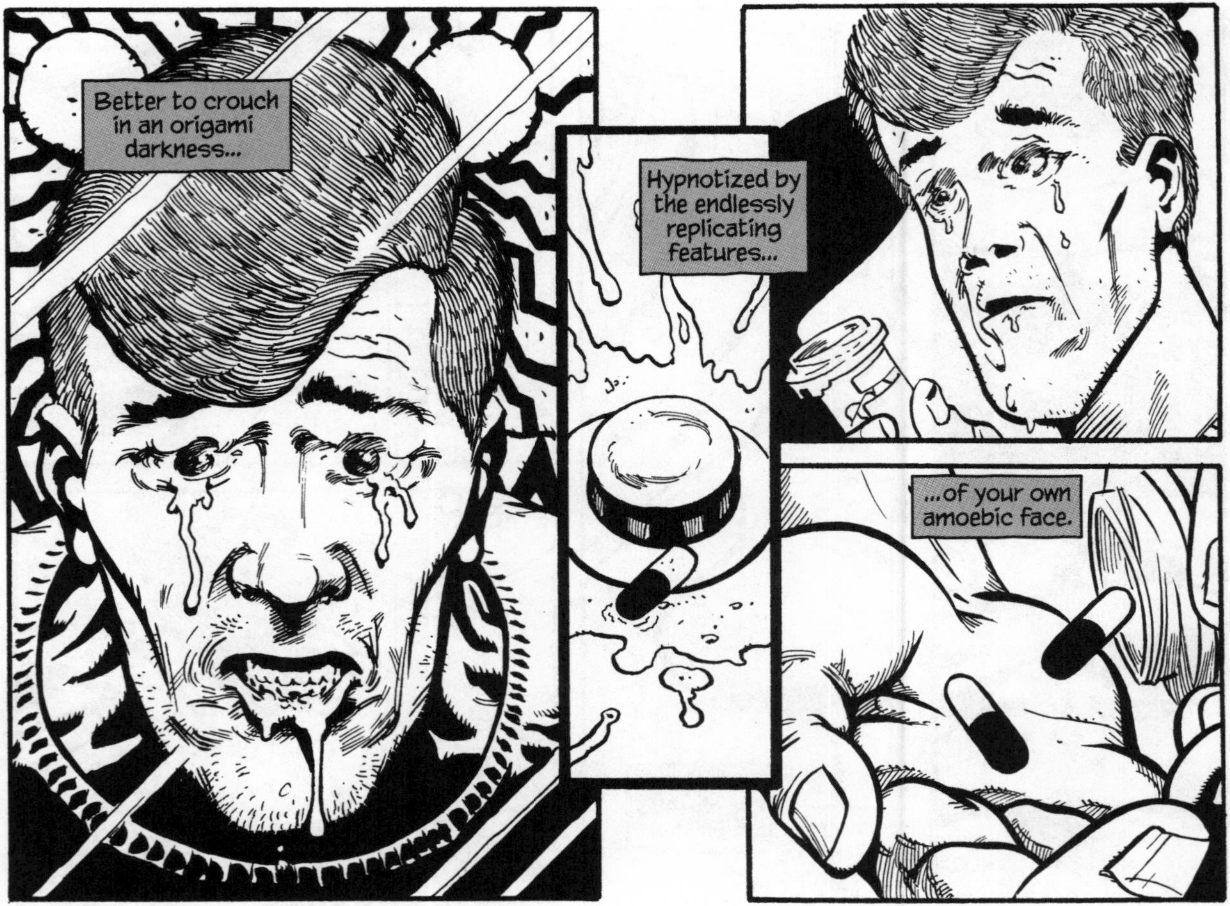
Better to crouch in an origami darkness...
Hypnotized by the endlessly replicating features...
...of your own amoebic face.

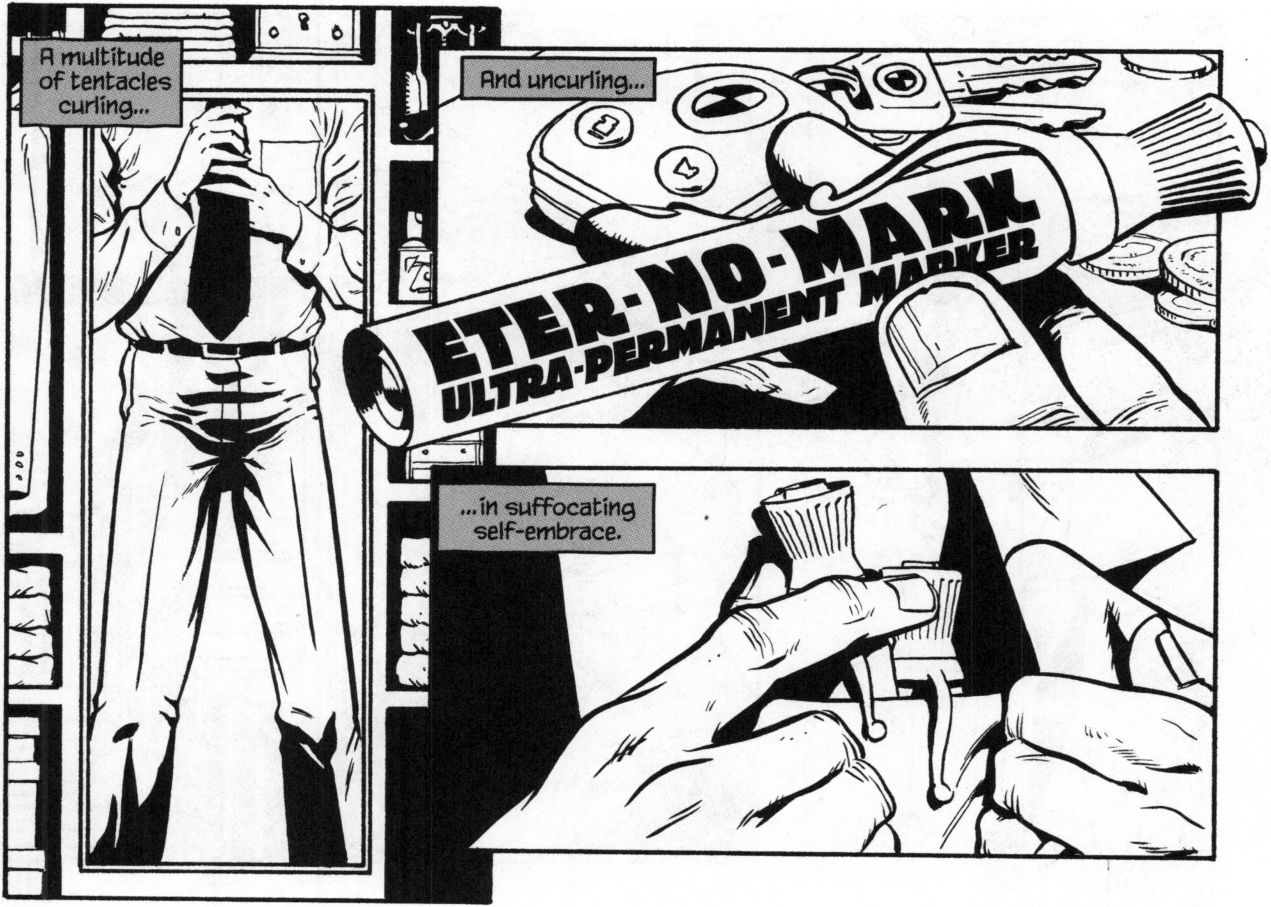
A multitude of tentacles curling...
And uncurling...
ETER-NO-MARK
ULTRA-PERMANENT MARKER
...in suffocating self-embrace.

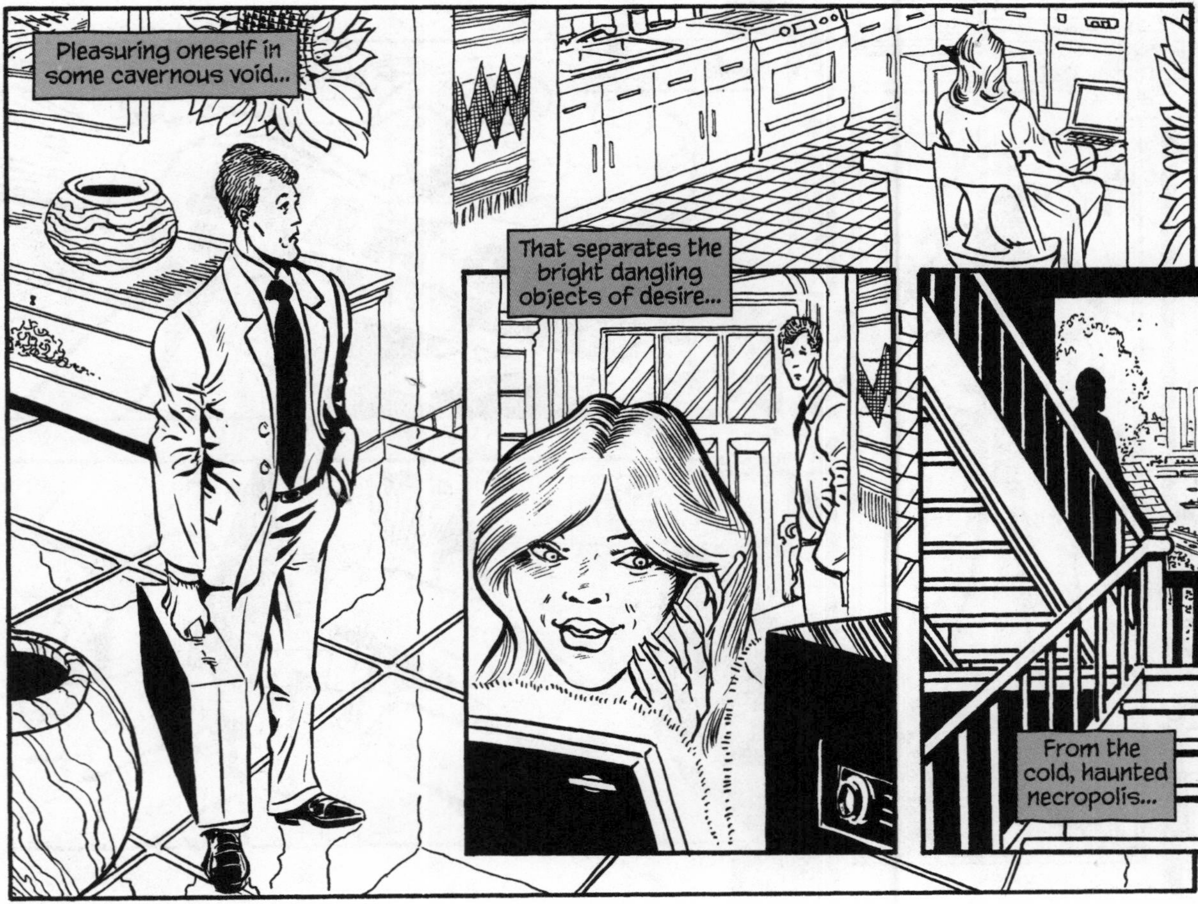
Pleasuring oneself in some cavernous void...
That separates the bright dangling objects of desire...
From the cold, haunted necropolis...

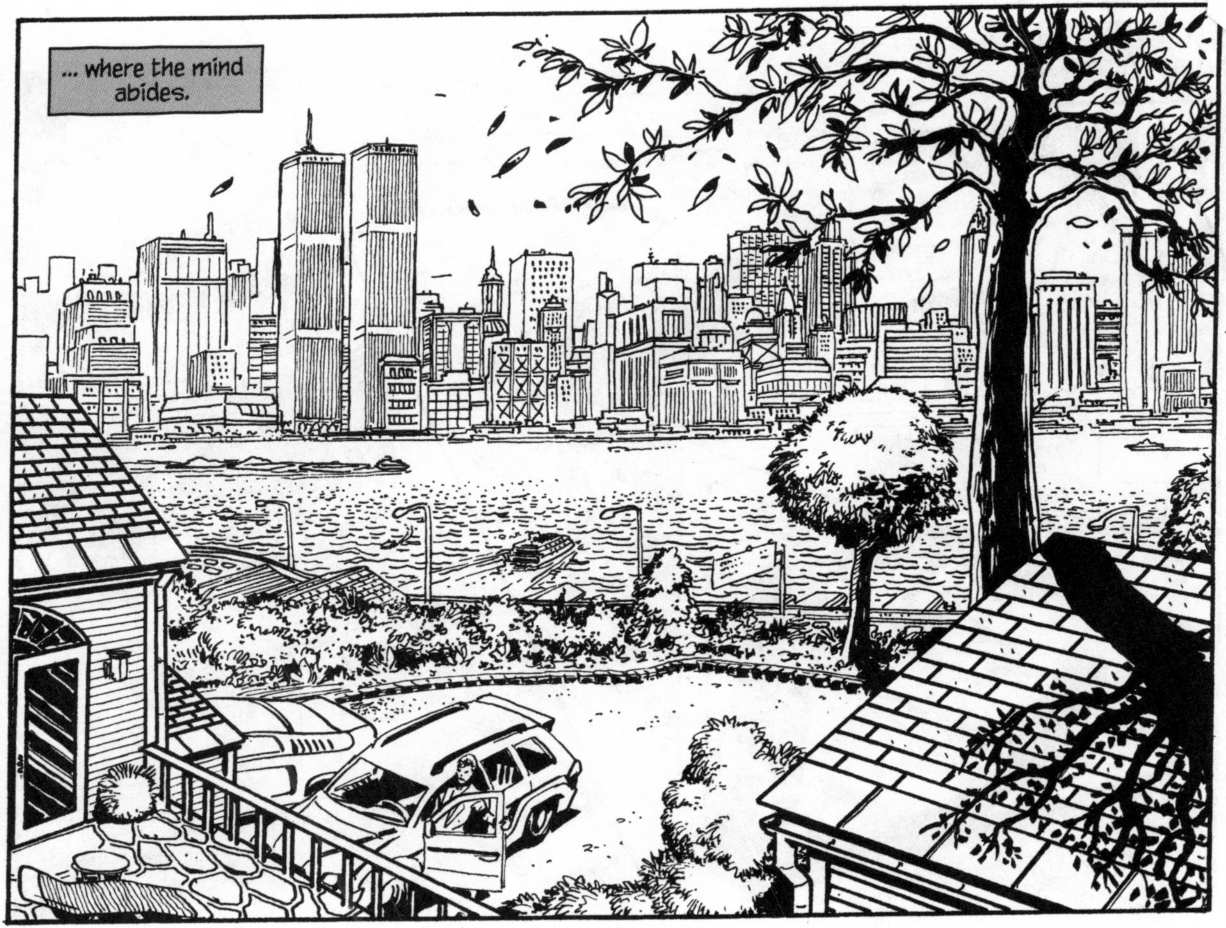
... where the mind abides.

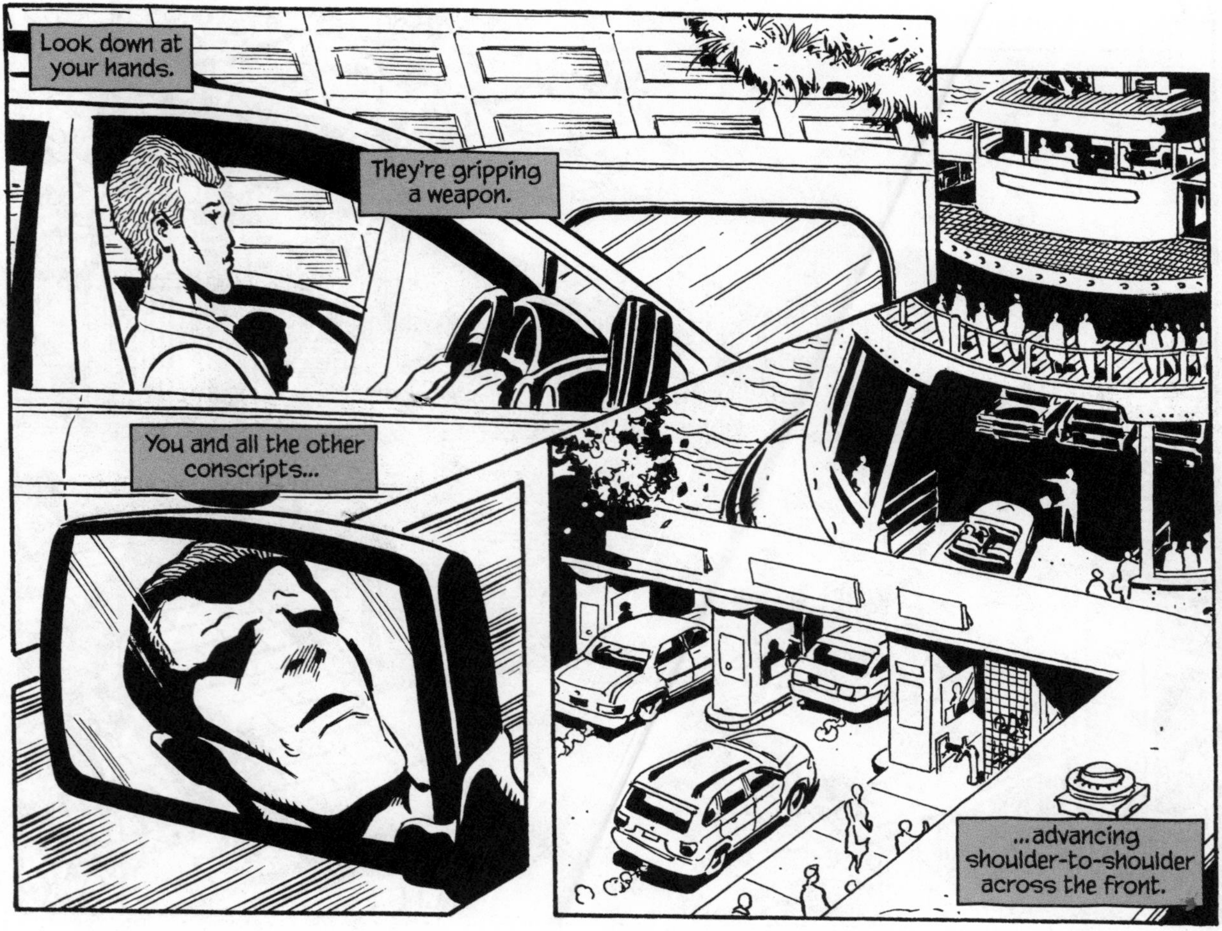
Look down at your hands.
They're gripping a weapon.
You and all the other conscripts...
...advancing shoulder-to-shoulder across the front.

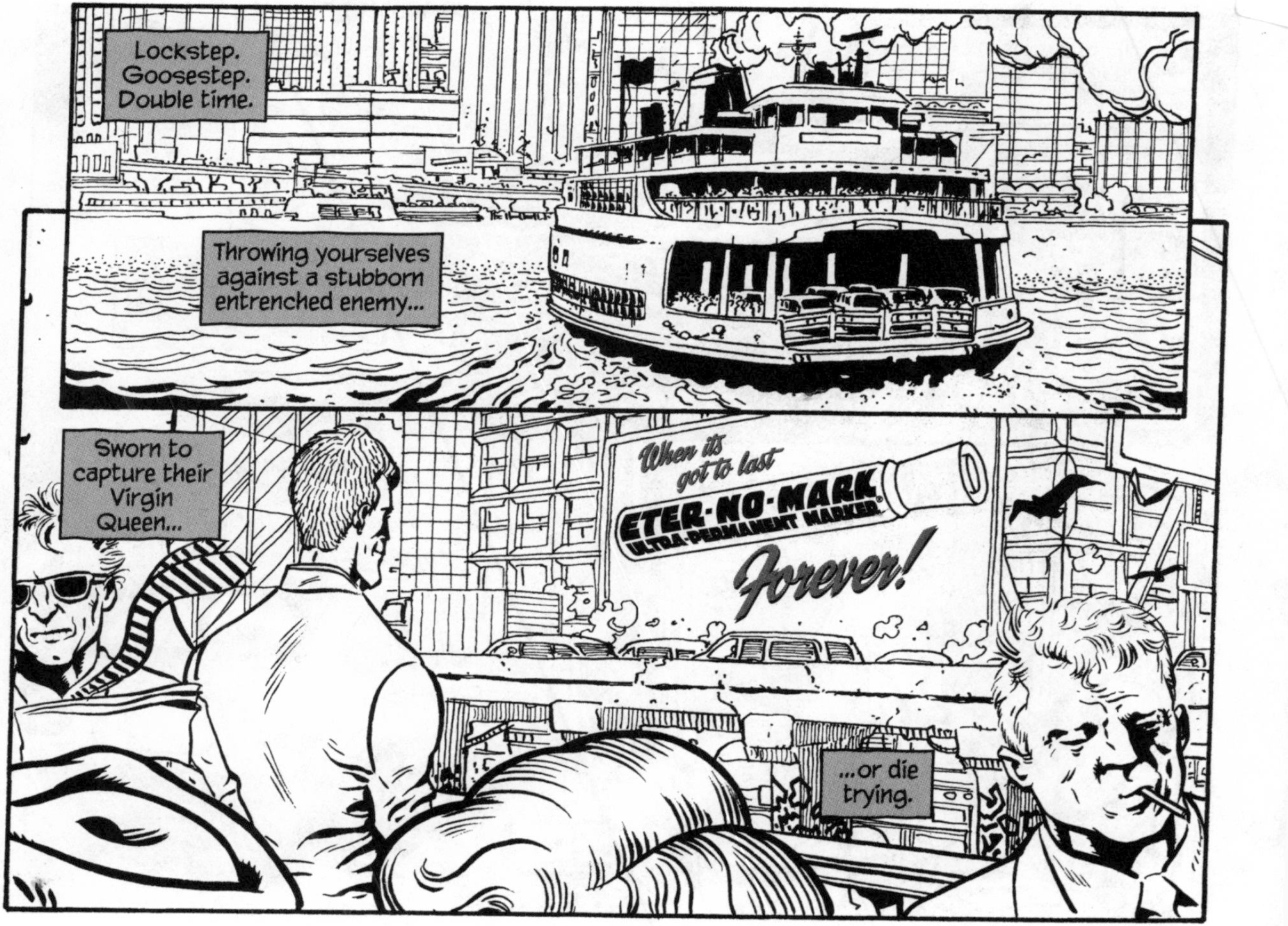
Lockstep. Goosestep. Double time.
Throwing yourselves against a stubborn entrenched enemy...
Sworn to capture their Virgin Queen...
When its got to last
ETER-NO-MARK
ULTRA-PERMANENT MARKER
Forever!
...or die trying.

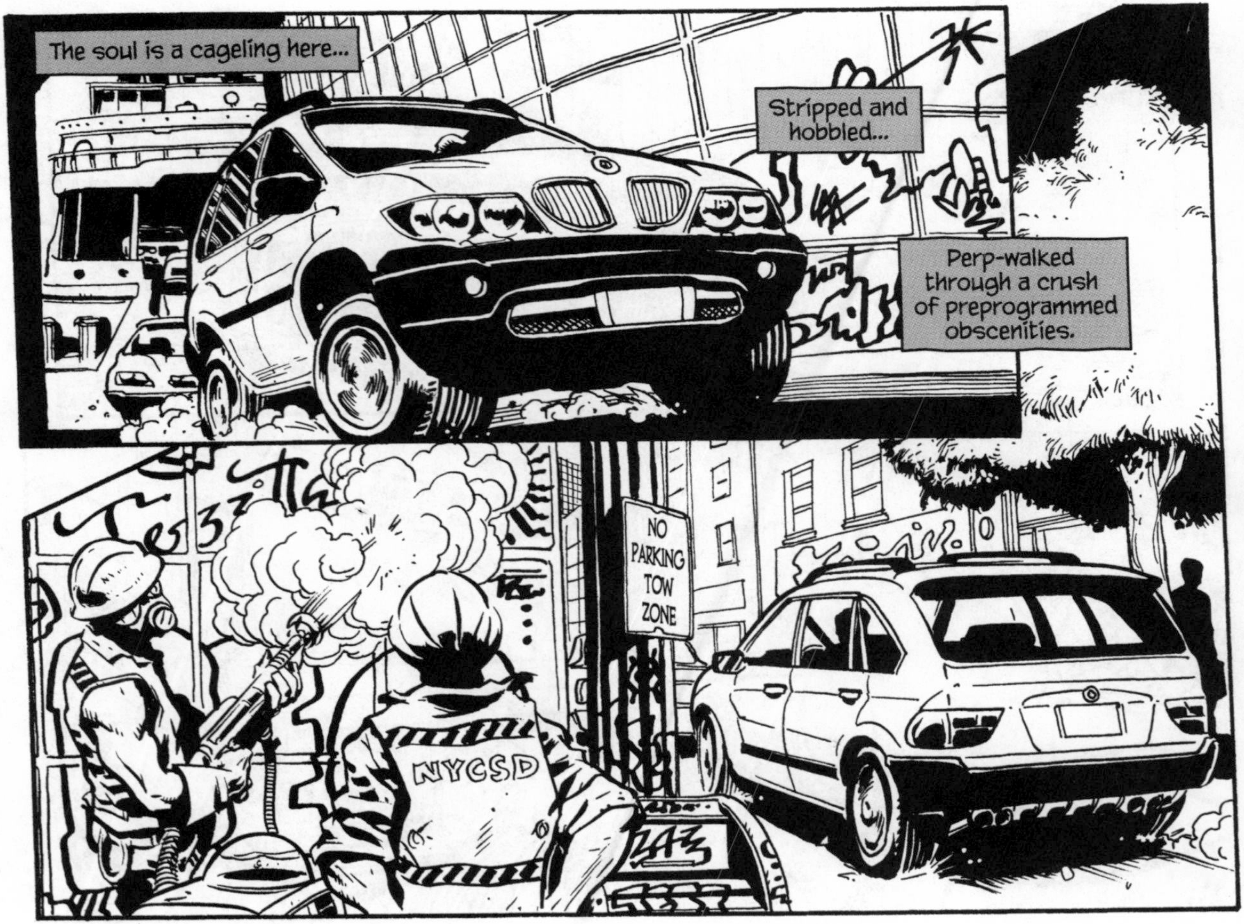

The soul is a cageling here...
Stripped and hobbled...
Perp-walked through a crush of preprogrammed obscenities.
NO PARKING TOW ZONE
NYCSD

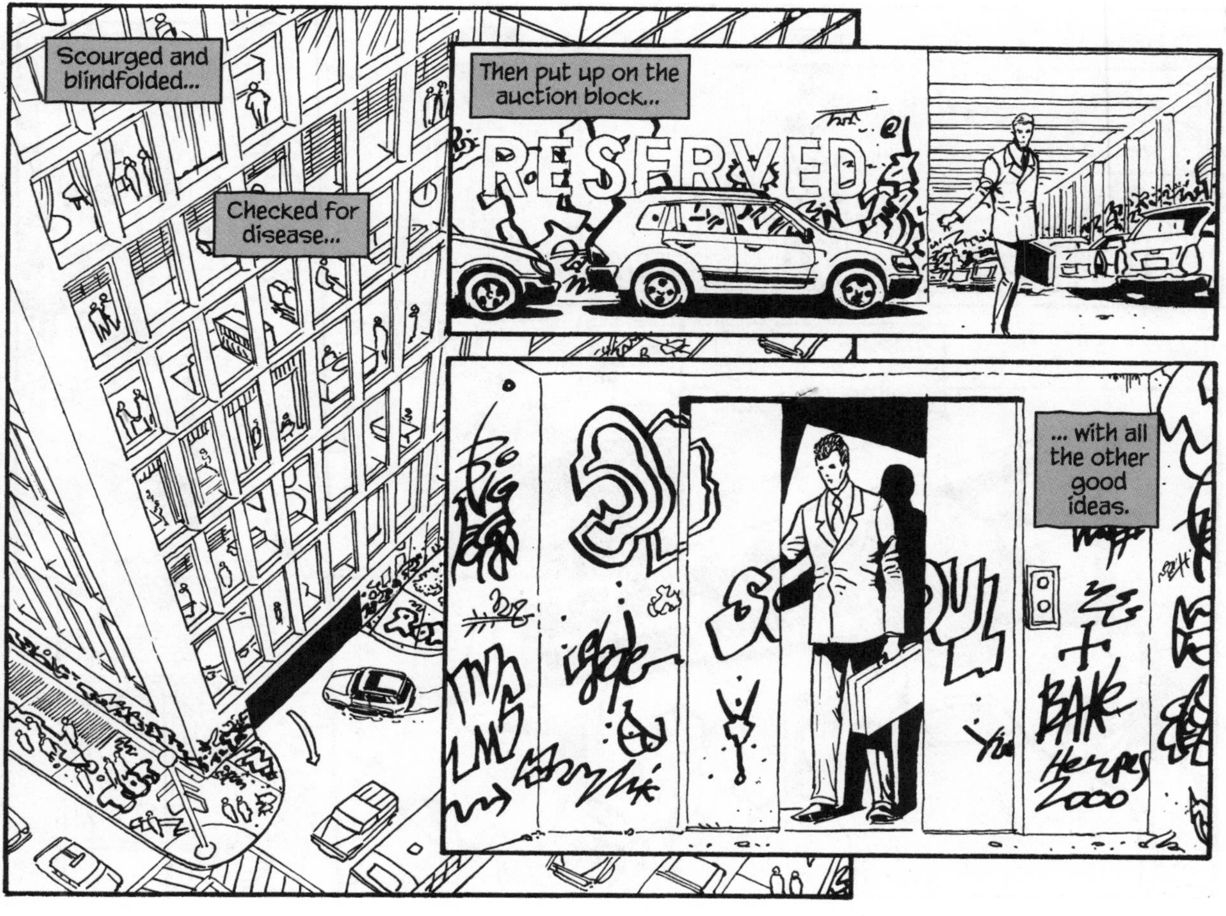
Scourged and blindfolded...
Checked for disease...
Then put up on the auction block...
RESERVED
... with all the other good ideas.

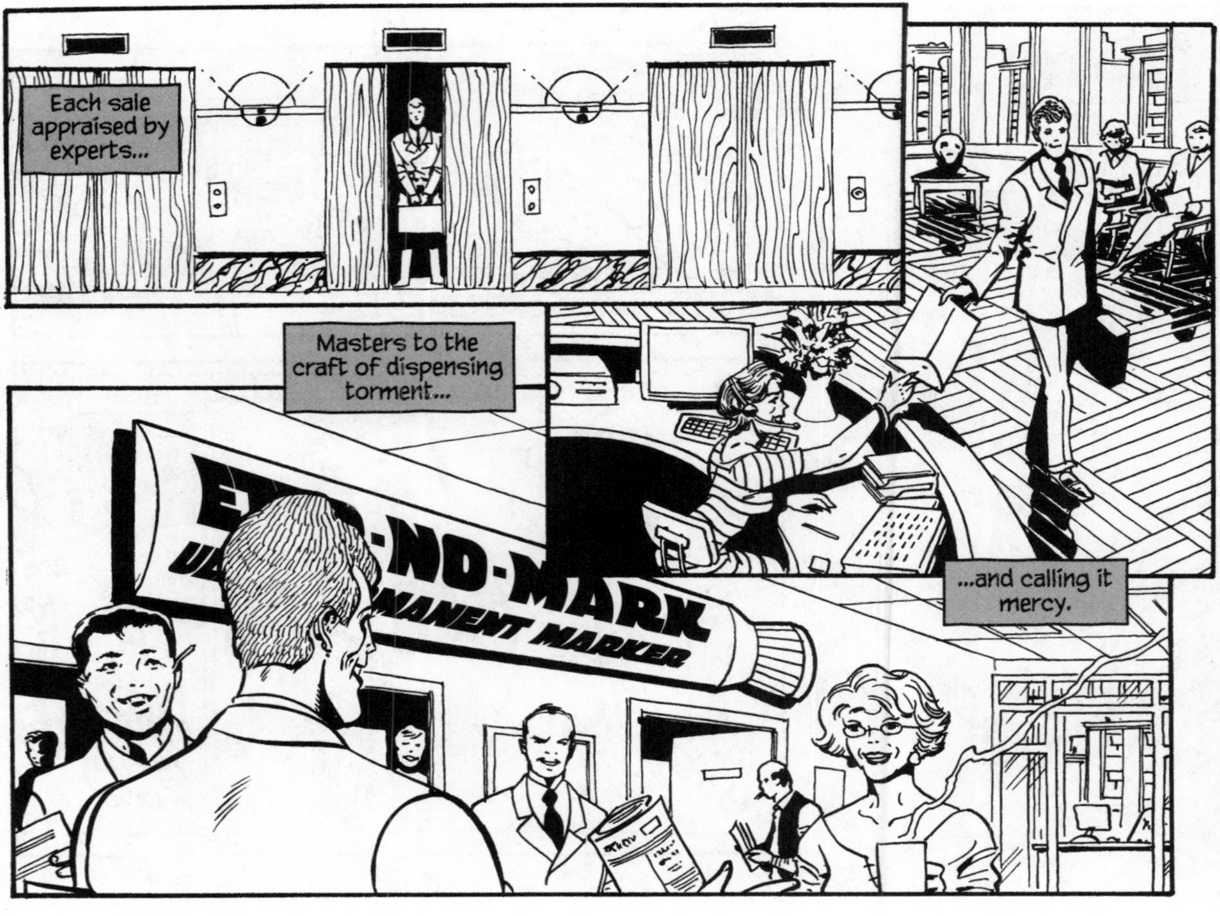
Each sale appraised by experts...
Masters to the craft of dispensing torment...
...and calling it mercy.

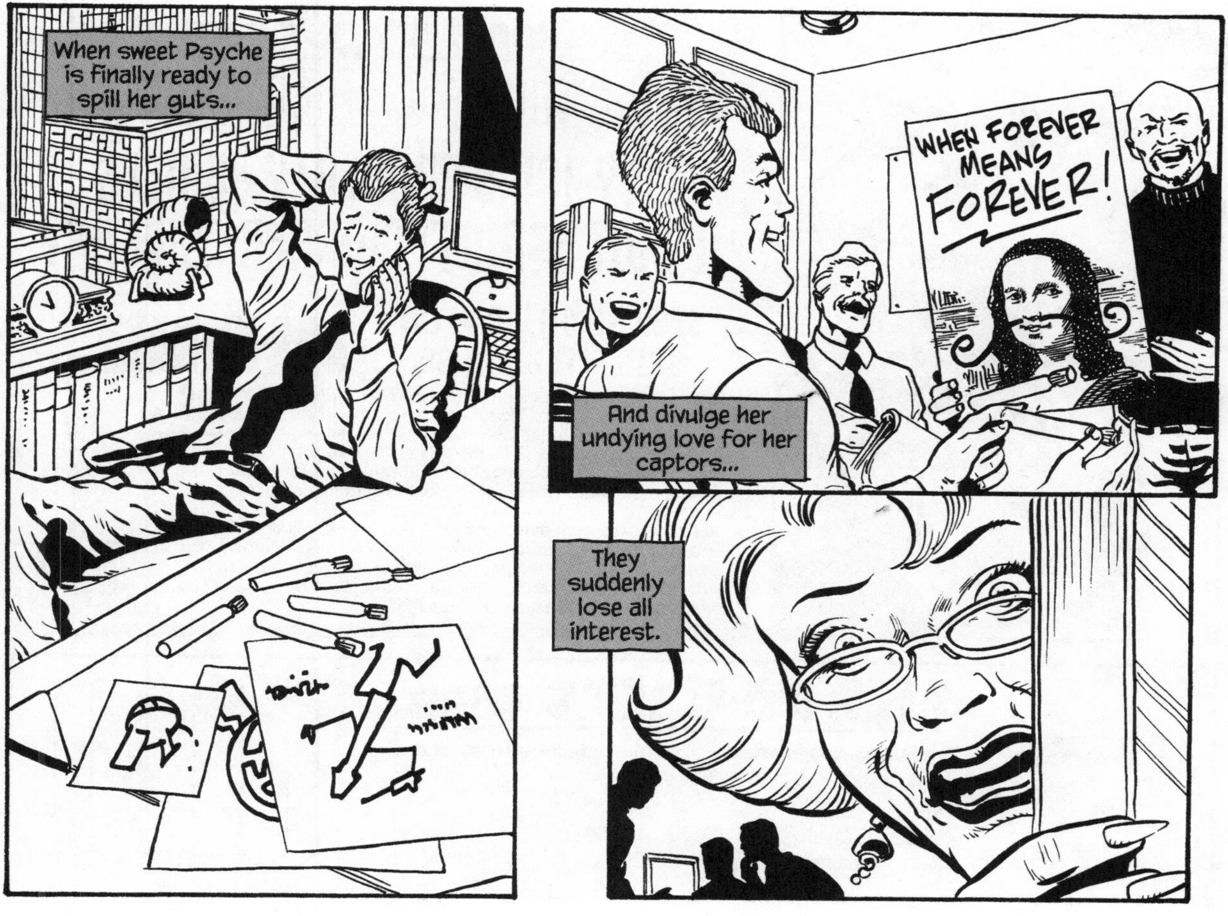
When sweet Psyche is finally ready to spill her guts...
WHEN FOREVER MEANS FOREVER!
And divulge her undying love for her captors...
They suddenly lose all interest.

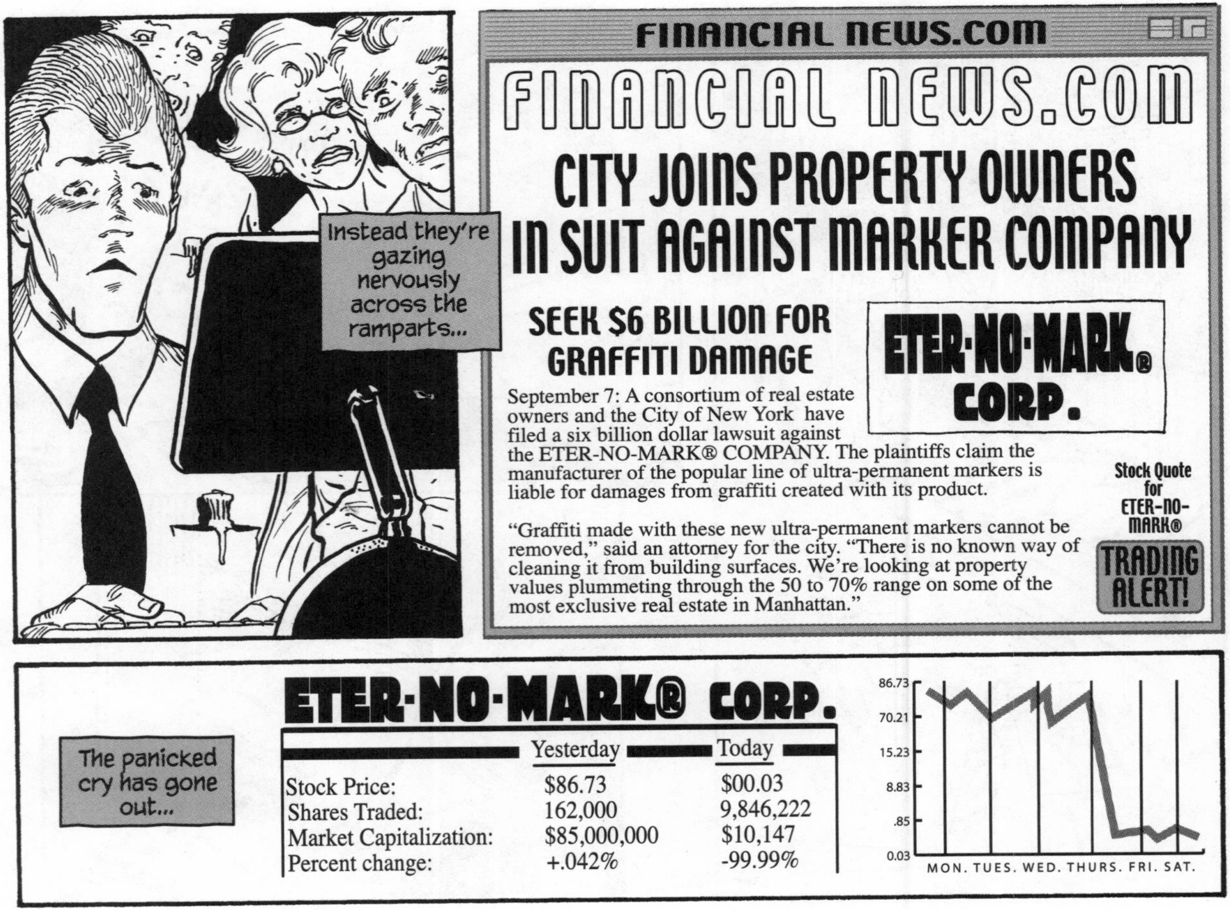
Instead they're gazing nervously across the ramparts...
FINANCIAL NEWS.COM
FINANCIAL NEWS.COM
CITY JOINS PROPERTY OWNERS IN SUIT AGAINST MARKER COMPANY
SEEK $6 BILLION FOR GRAFFITI DAMAGE
ETER-NO-MARK® CORP.
September 7: A consortium of real estate owners and the City of New York have filed a six billion dollar lawsuit against the ETER-NO-MARK® COMPANY. The plaintiffs claim the manufacturer of the popular line of ultra-permanent markers is liable for damages from graffiti created with its product.
"Graffiti made with these new ultra-permanent markers cannot be removed," said an attorney for the city. "There is no known way of cleaning it from building surfaces. We're looking at property values plummeting through the 50 to 70% range on some of the most exclusive real estate in Manhattan."
Stock Quote for ETER-NO-MARK®
TRADING ALERT!
The panicked cry has gone out...
ETER-NO-MARK® CORP.
Yesterday
Today
Stock Price: $86.73 $00.03
Shares Traded: 162,000 9,846,222
Market Capitalization: $85,000,000 $10,147
Percent change: +.042% -99.99%
86.73
70.21
15.23
8.83
.85
0.03
MON. TUES. WED. THURS. FRI. SAT.

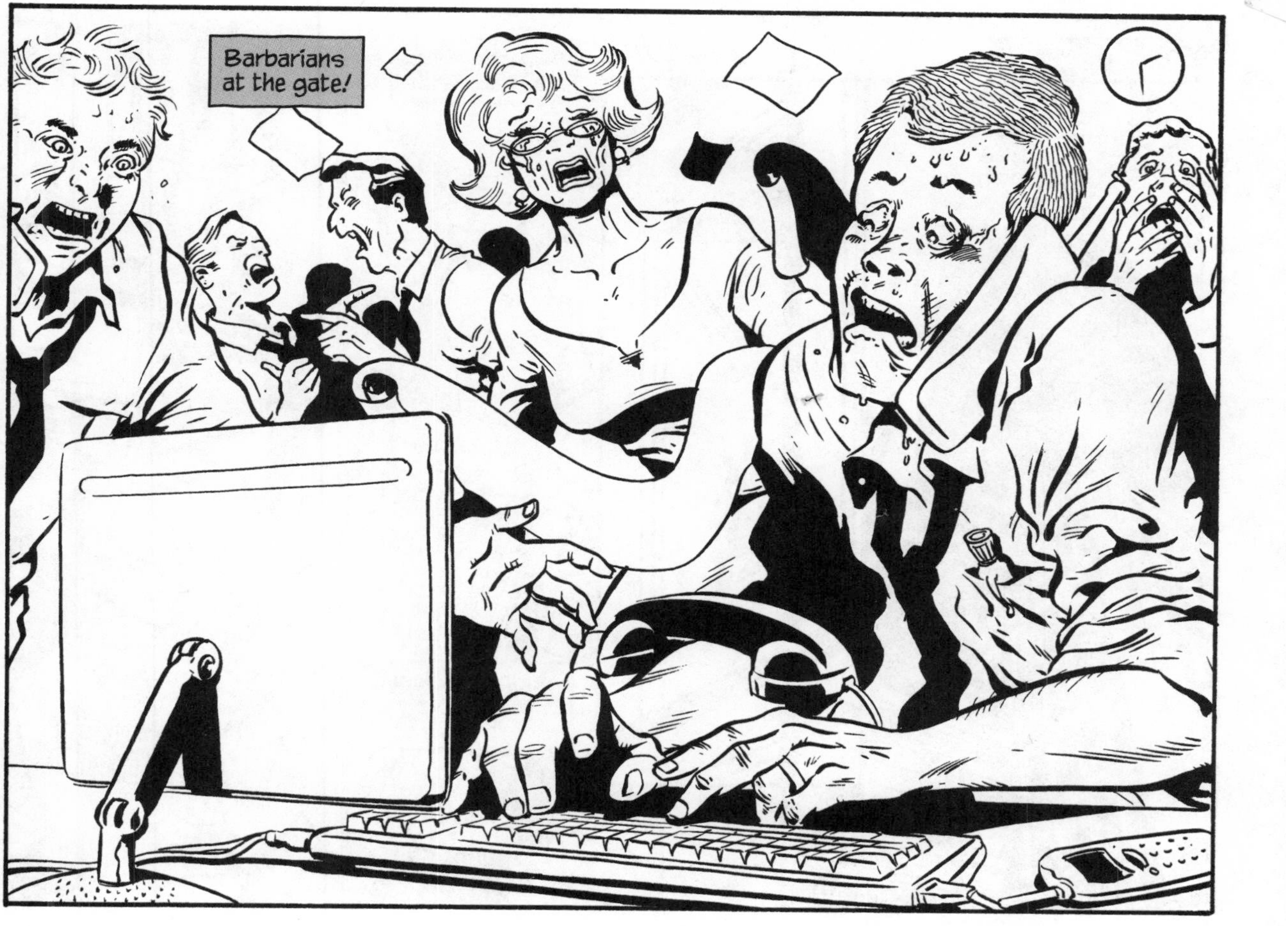
Barbarians at the gate!

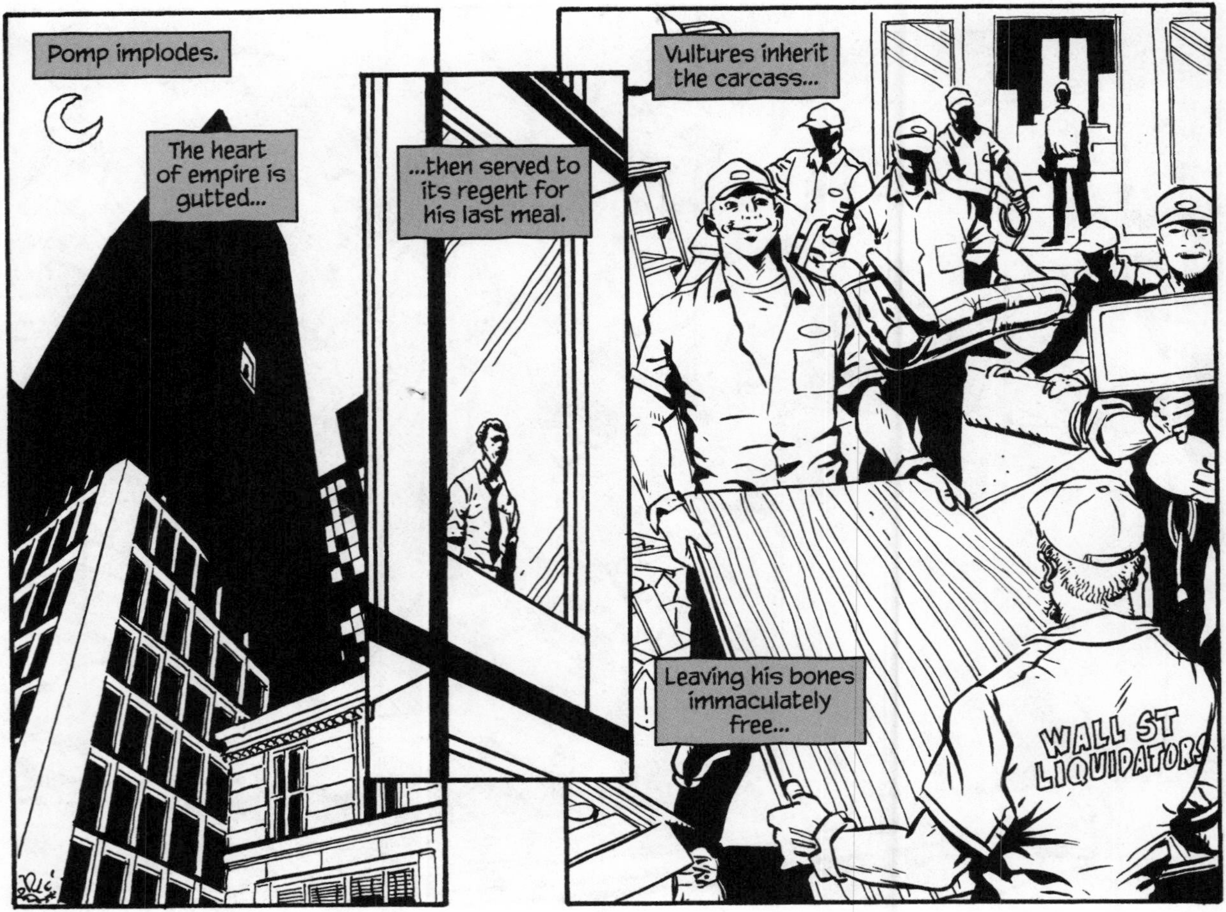
Pomp implodes.
The heart of empire is gutted...
...then served to its regent for his last meal.
Vultures inherit the carcass...
Leaving his bones immaculately free...
WALL ST LIQUIDATORS

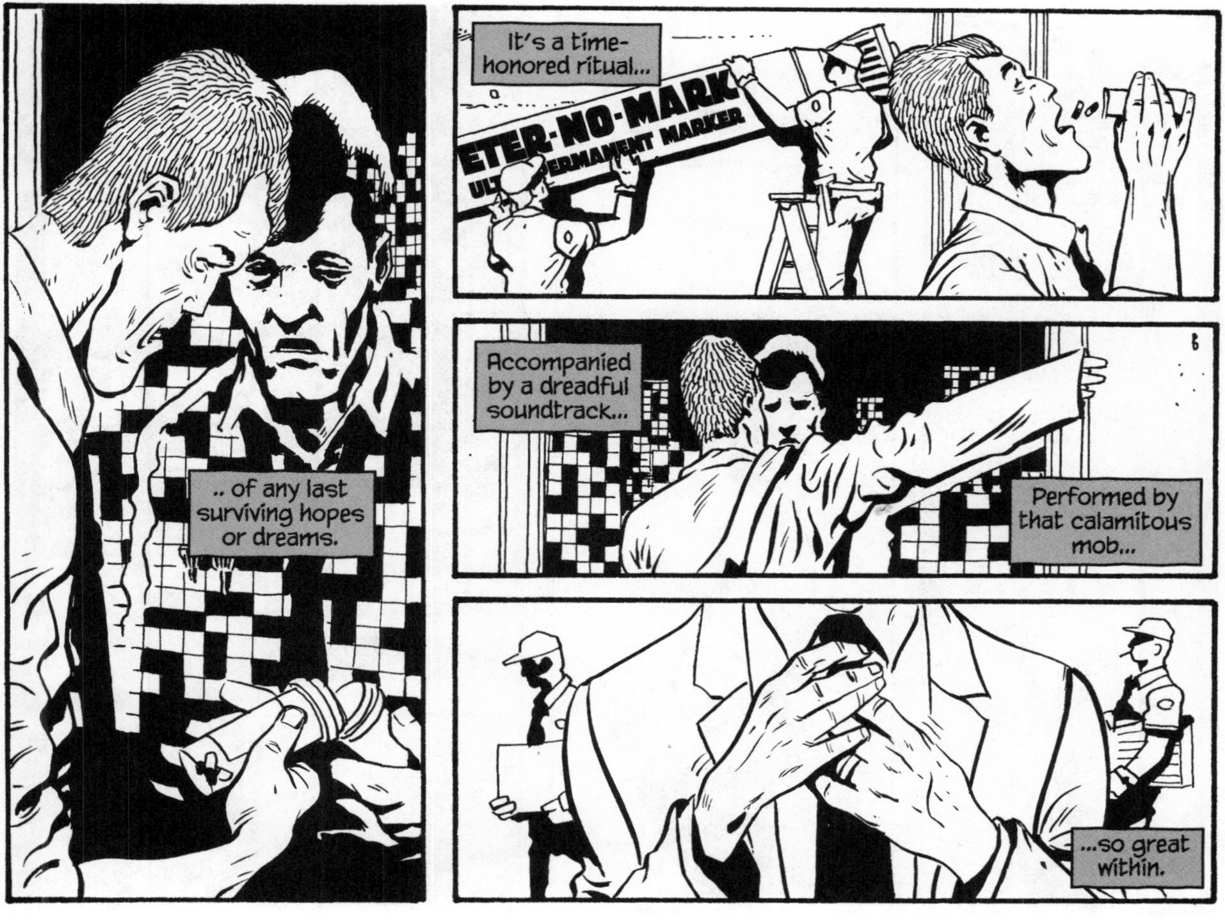
.. of any last surviving hopes or dreams.
It's a time-honored ritual...
ETER-NO-MARK
ULT ERMANENT MARKER
Accompanied by a dreadful soundtrack...
Performed by that calamitous mob...
...so great within.

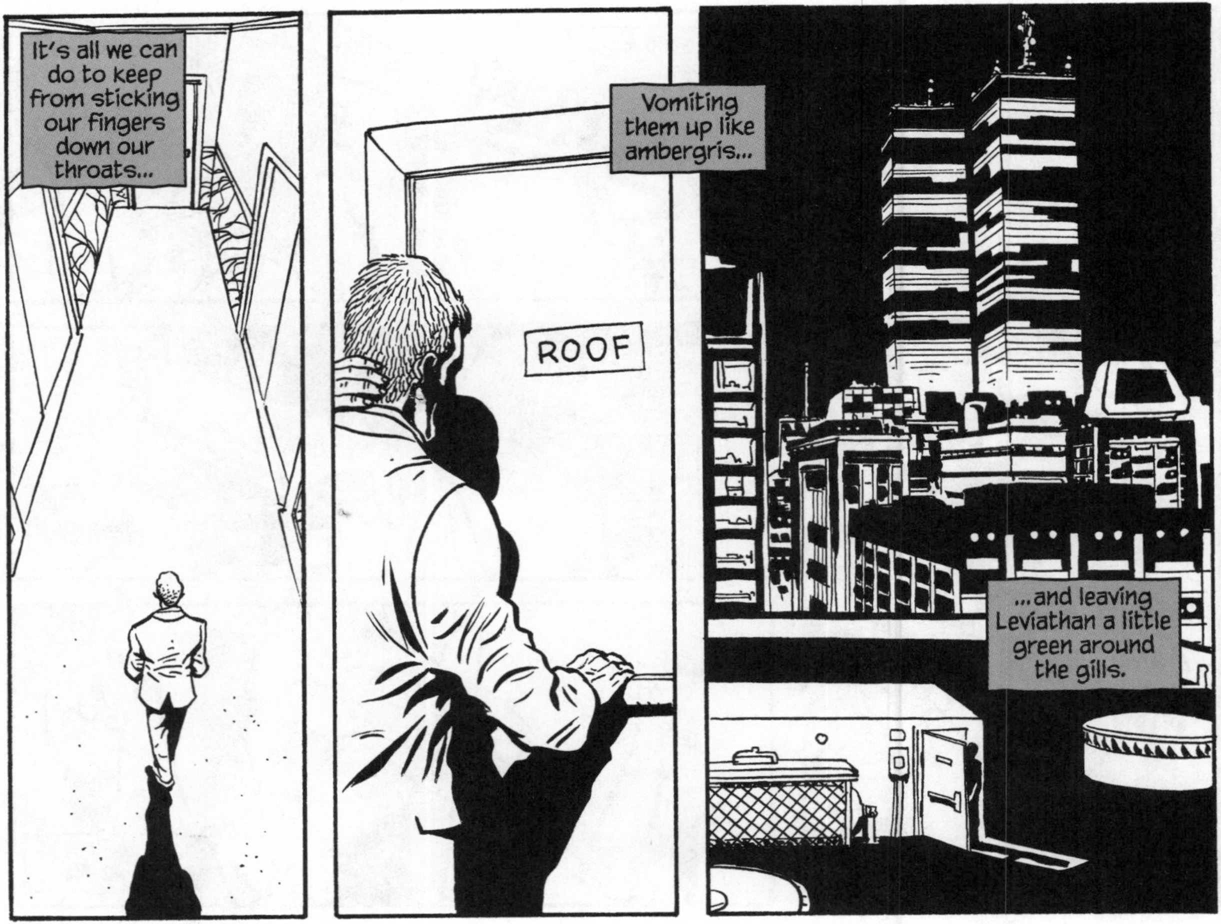
It's all we can do to keep from sticking our fingers down our throats...
Vomiting them up like ambergris...
ROOF
...and leaving Leviathan a little green around the gills.

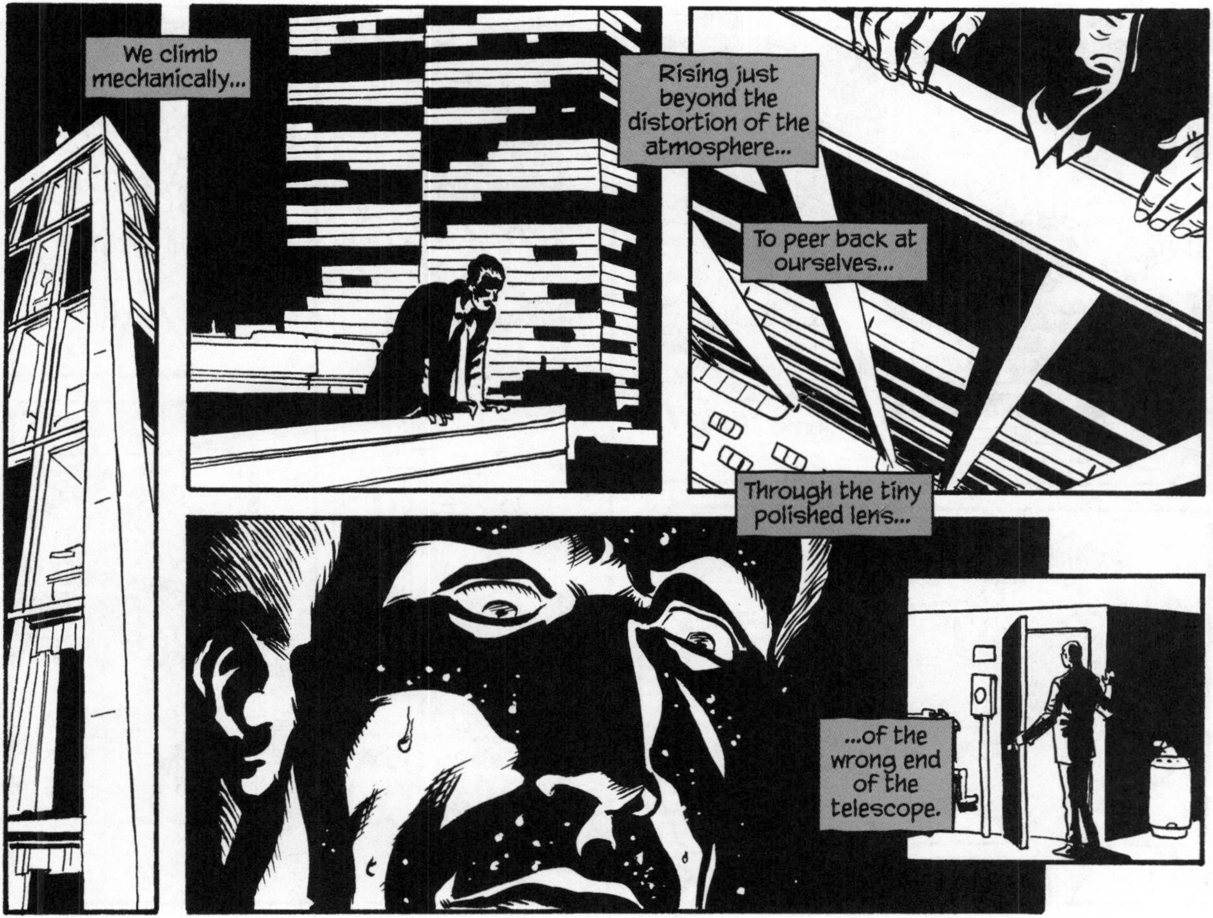
We climb mechanically...
Rising just beyond the distortion of the atmosphere...
To peer back at ourselves...
Through the tiny polished lens...
...of the wrong end of the telescope.

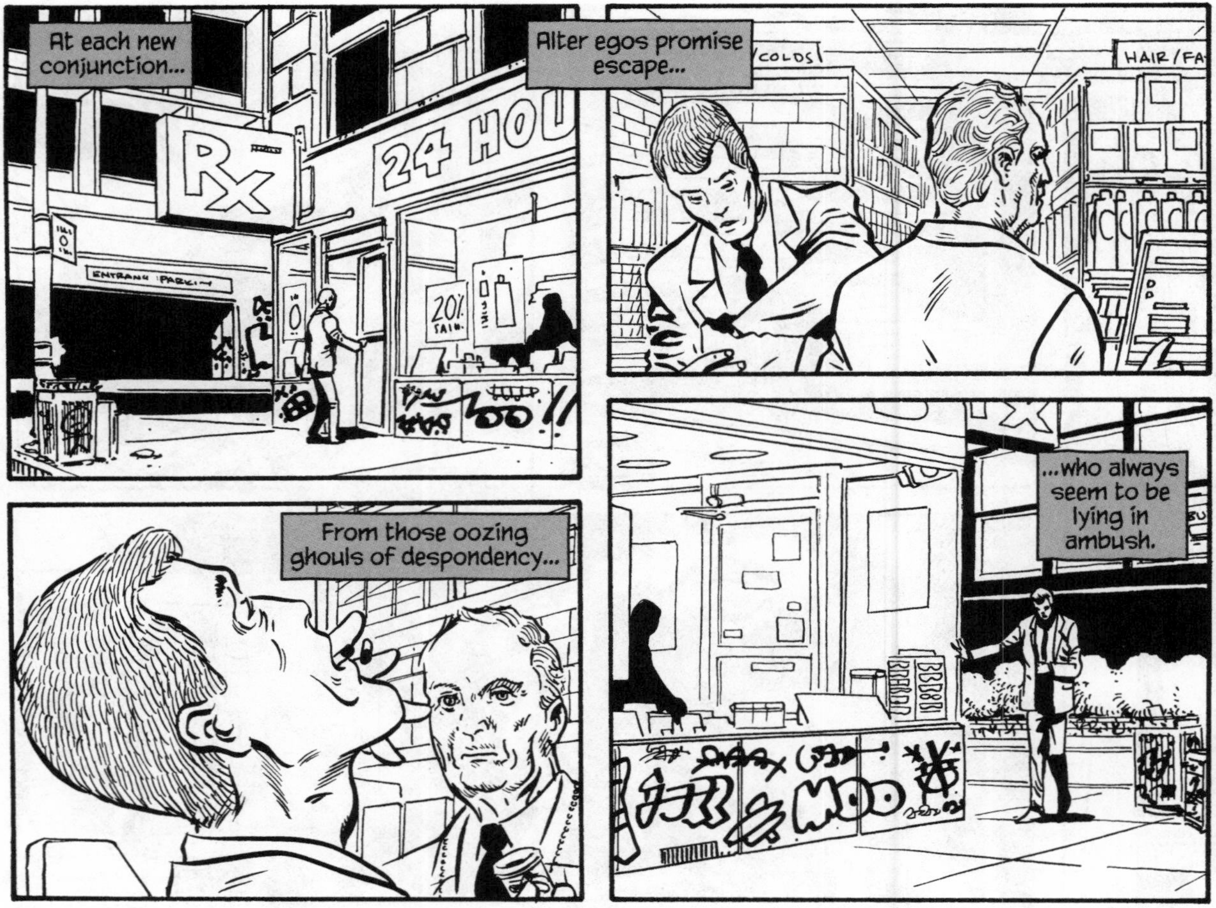
At each new conjunction...
Alter egos promise escape...
From those oozing ghouls of despondency...
...who always seem to be lying in ambush.

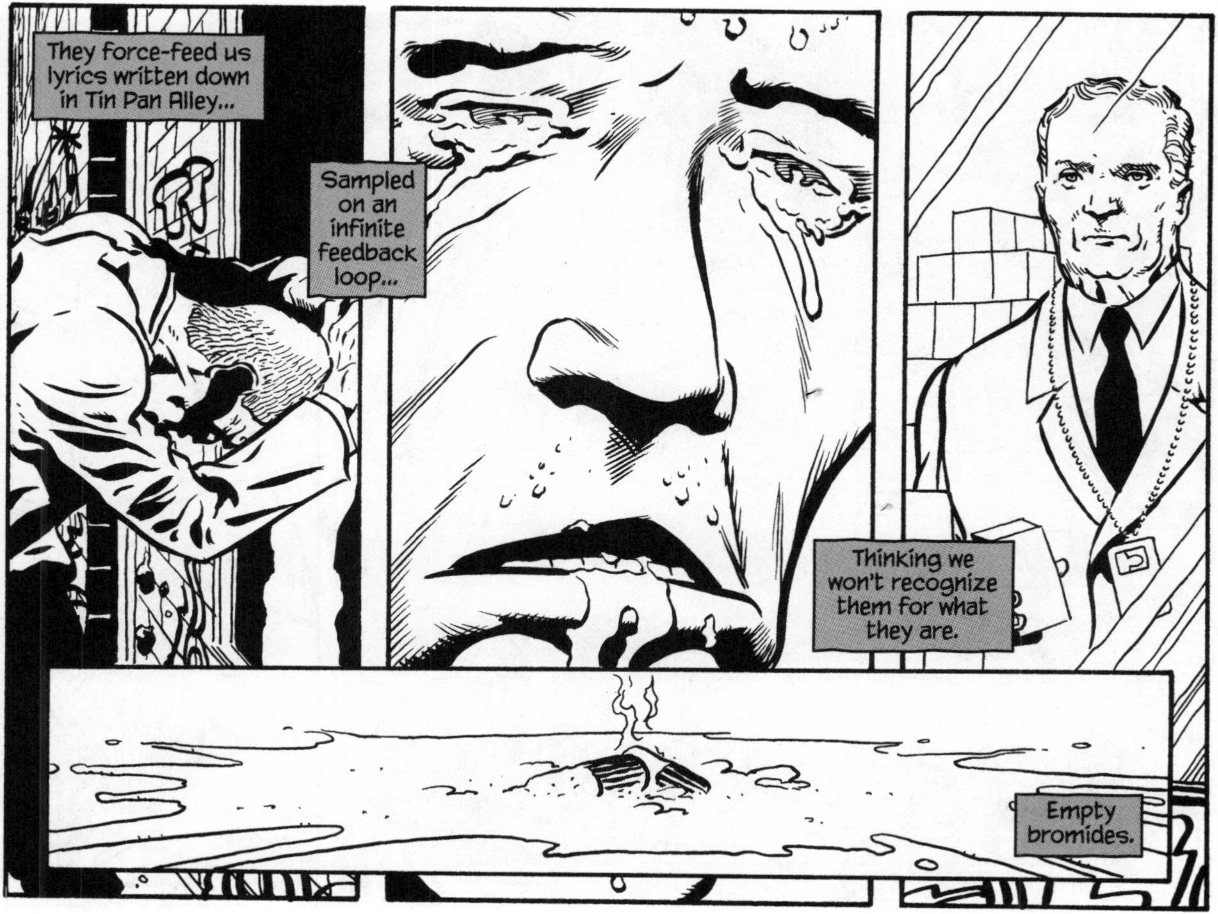
They force-feed us lyrics written down in Tin Pan Alley...
Sampled on an infinite feedback loop...
Thinking we won't recognize them for what they are.
Empty bromides.

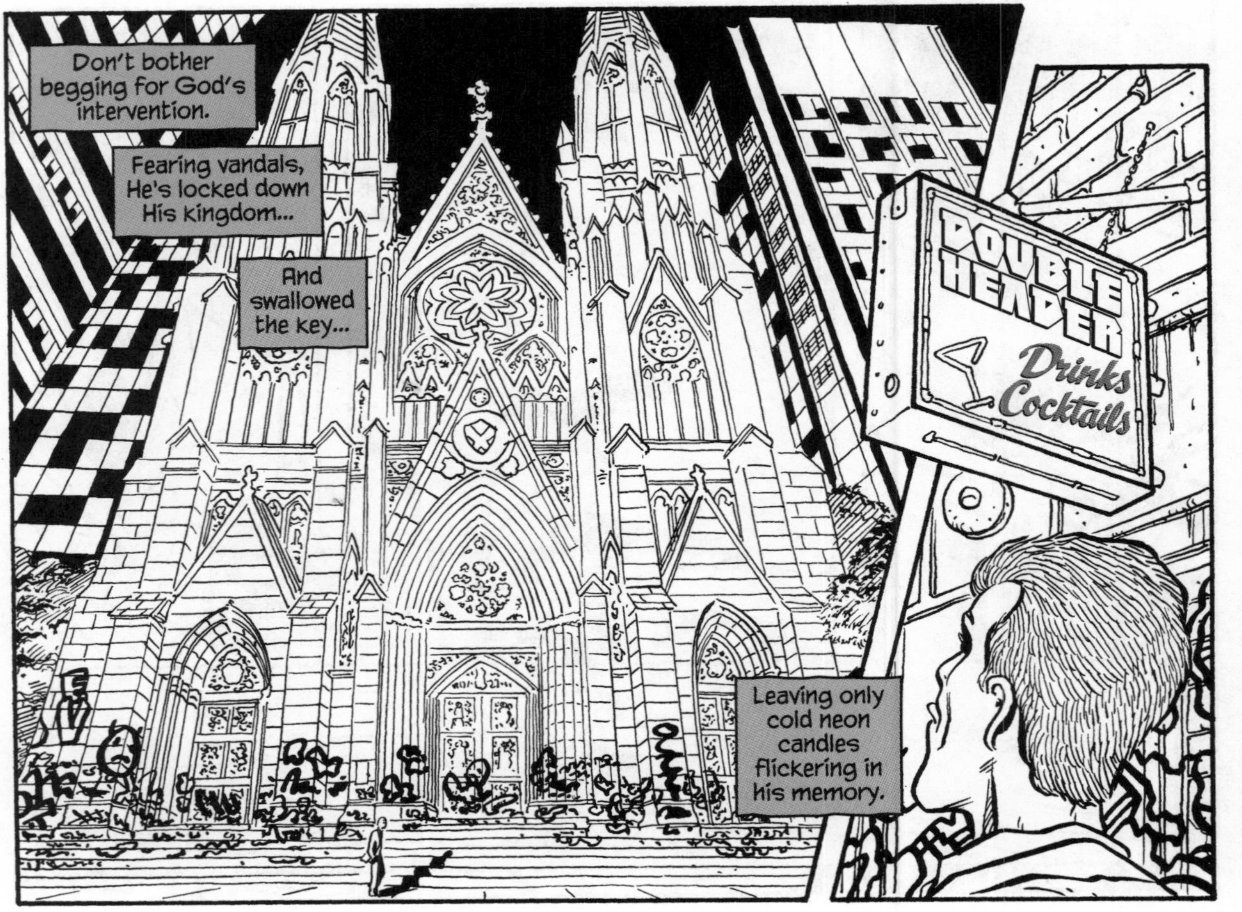

Don't bother begging for God's intervention.
Fearing vandals, He's locked down His kingdom...
And swallowed the key...
DOUBLE HEADER
Drinks Cocktails
Leaving only cold neon candles flickering in his memory.

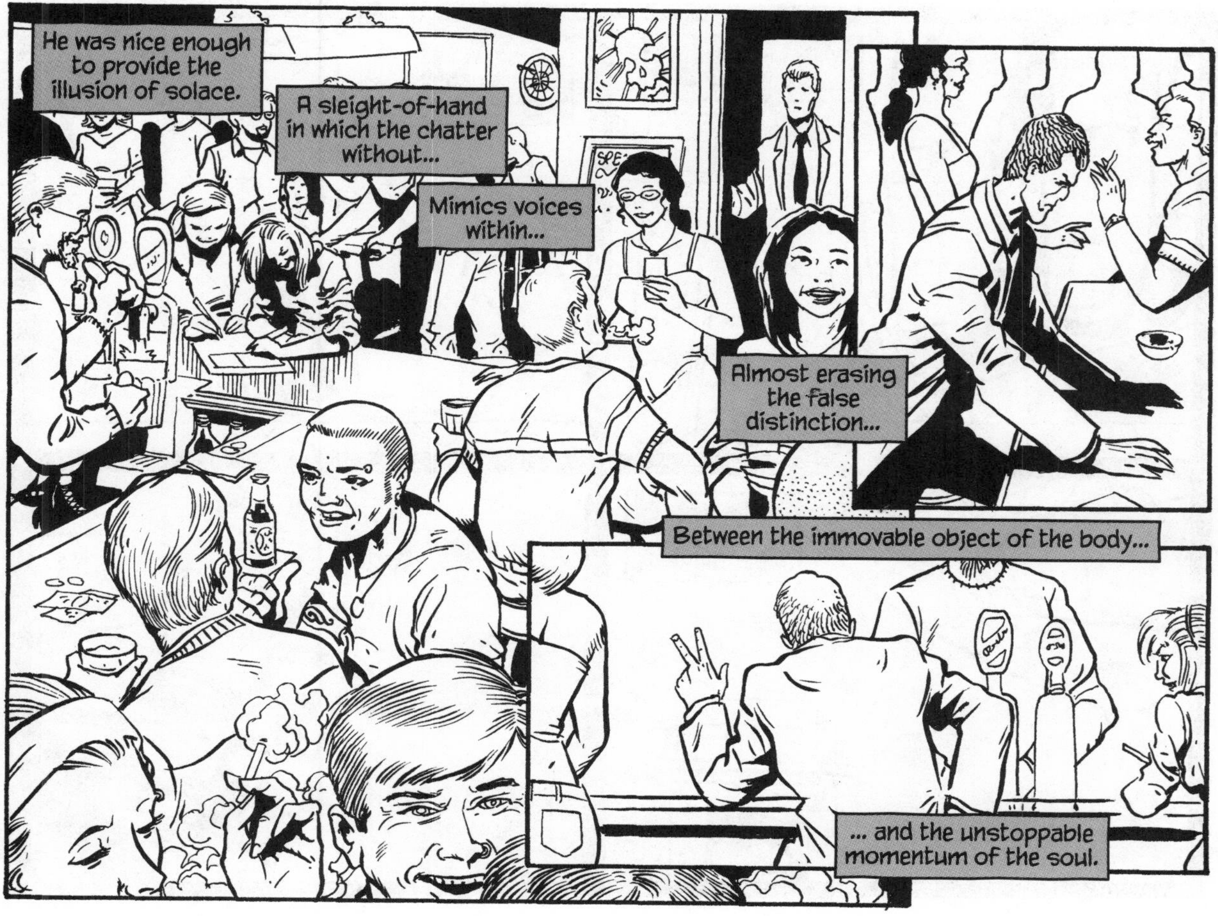
He was nice enough to provide the illusion of solace.
A sleight-of-hand in which the chatter without...
Mimics voices within...
Almost erasing the false distinction...
Between the immovable object of the body...
... and the unstoppable momentum of the soul.

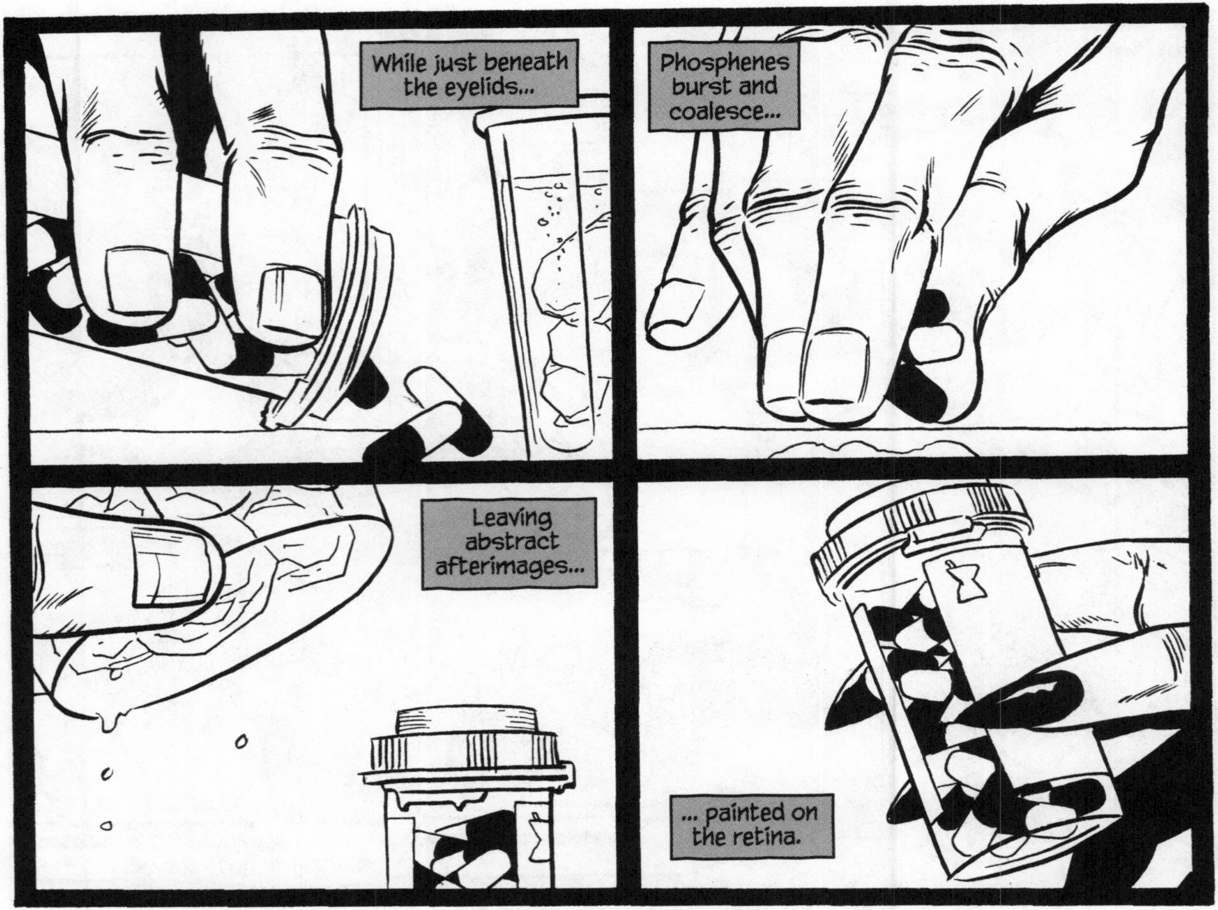
While just beneath the eyelids...
Phosphenes burst and coalesce...
Leaving abstract afterimages...
... painted on the retina.

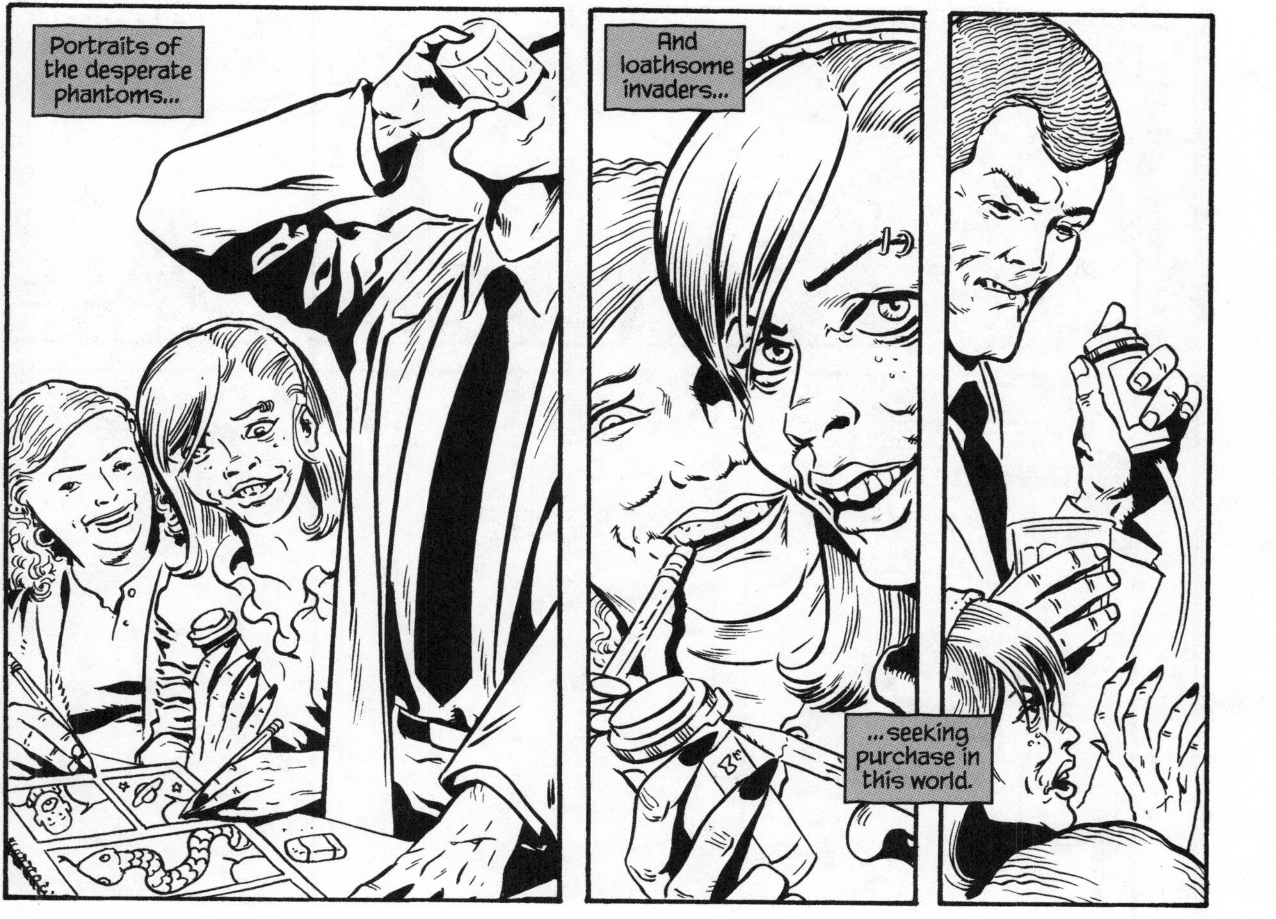
Portraits of the desperate phantoms...
And loathsome invaders...
...seeking purchase in this world.

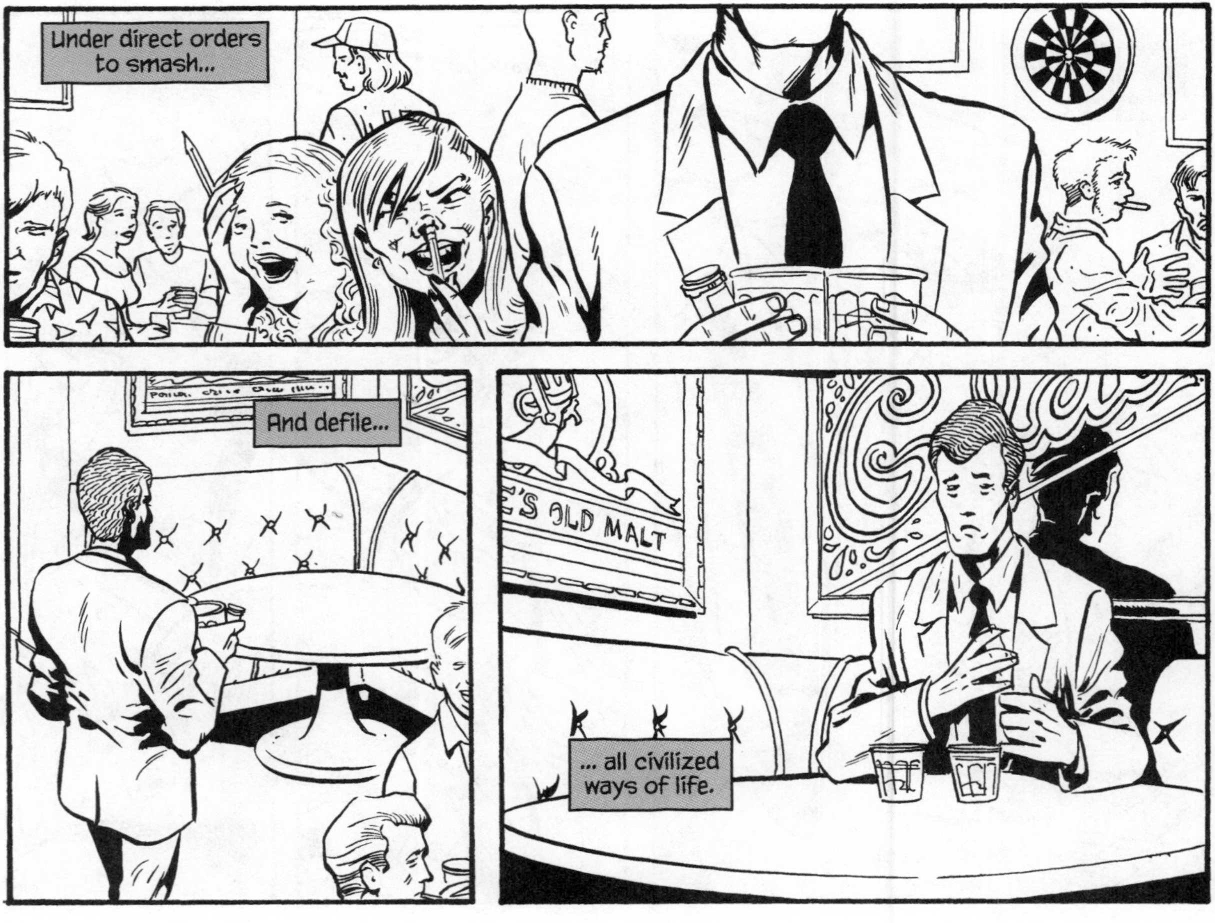
Under direct orders to smash...
And defile...
'S OLD MALT
... all civilized ways of life.

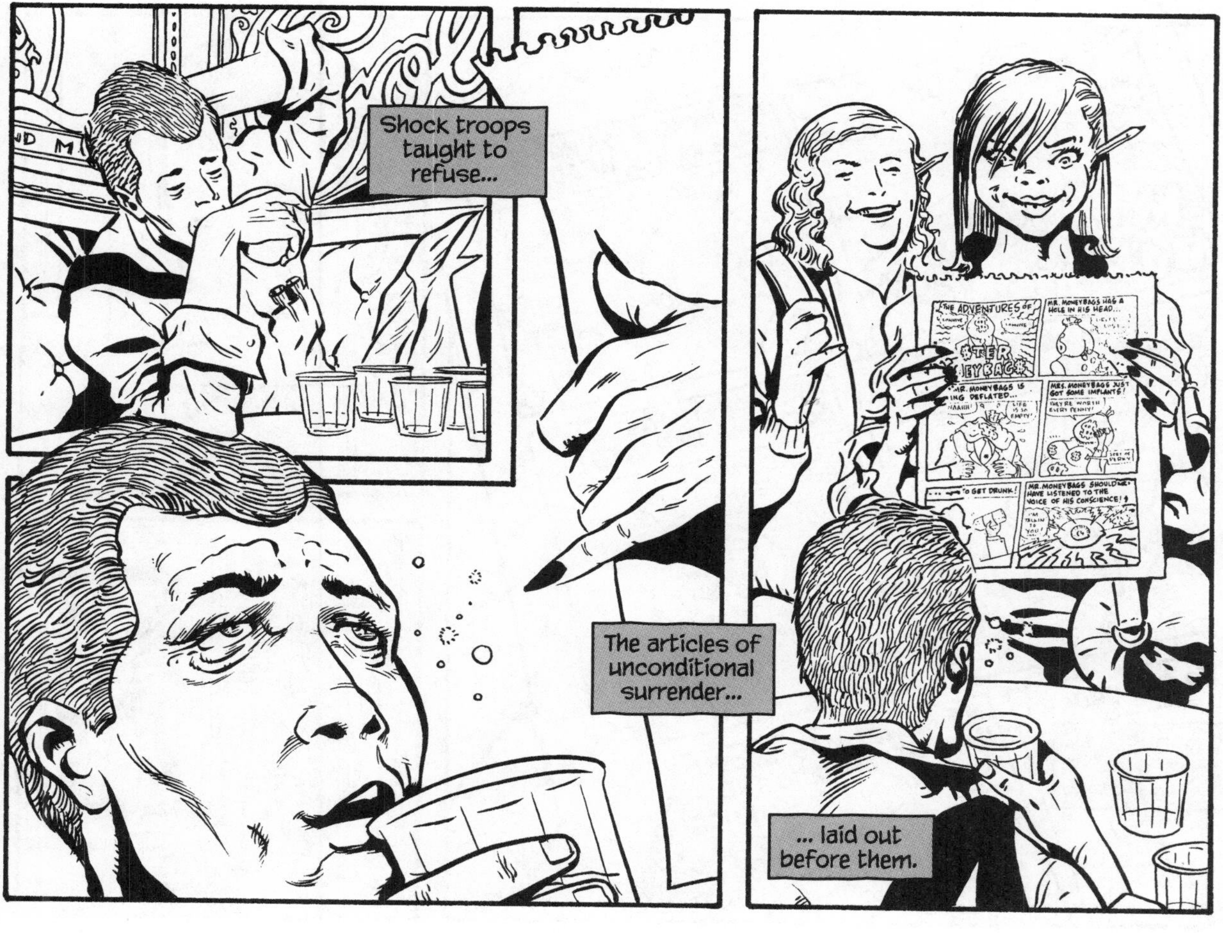
Shock troops taught to refuse...
THE ADVENTURES OF
MR. MONEYBAGS HAS A HOLE IN HIS HEAD...
LIFE IS SO EMPTY!
MRS. MONEYBAGS JUST GOT SOME IMPLANTS!
THEY'RE WORTH EVERY PENNY!
MR. MONEYBAGS SHOULD HAVE LISTENED TO THE VOICE OF HIS CONSCIENCE!
I'M TALKIN TO YOU!
The articles of unconditional surrender...
... laid out before them.

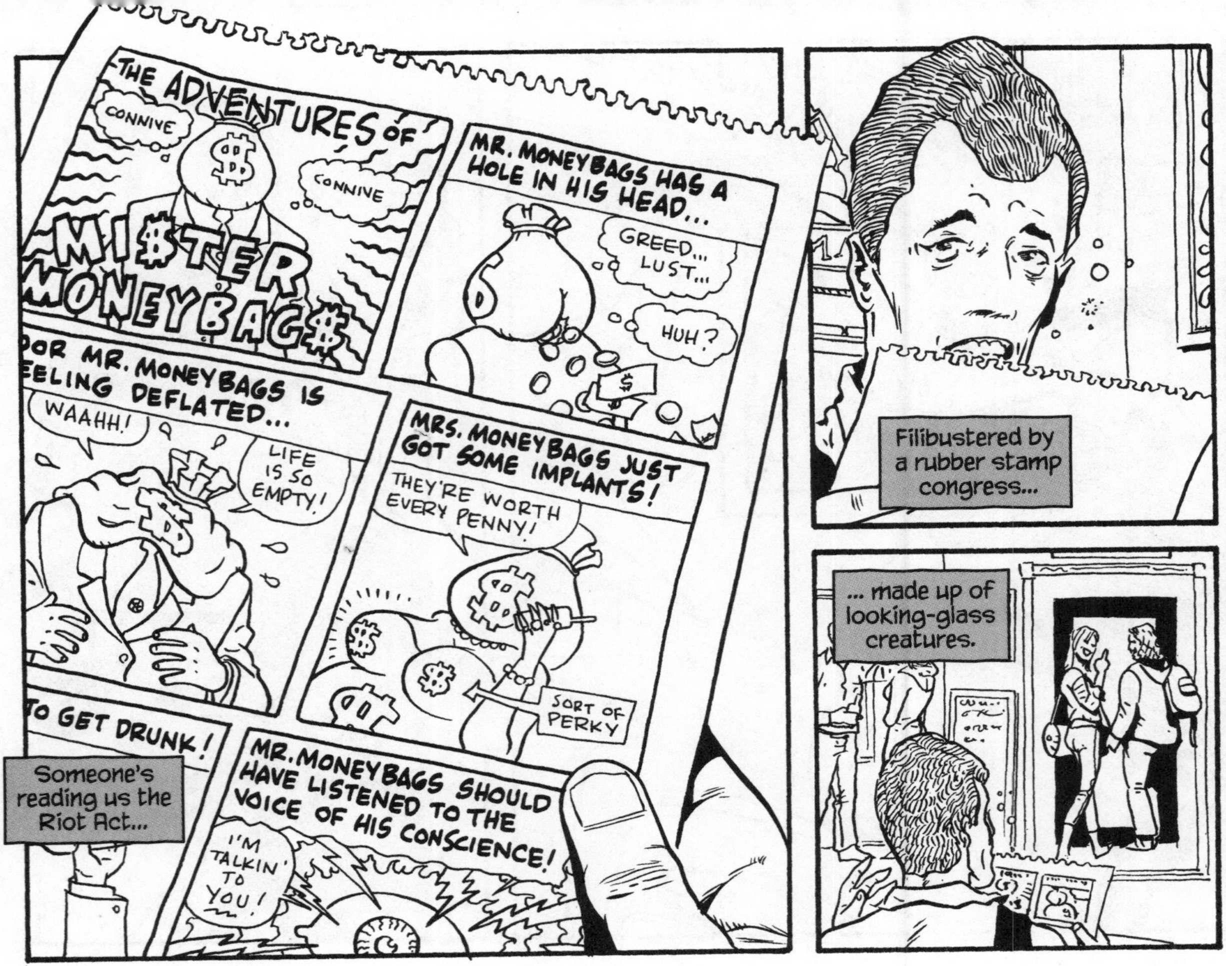
THE ADVENTURES OF
CONNIVE
CONNIVE
MI$TER MONEYBAG$
MR. MONEYBAGS HAS A HOLE IN HIS HEAD...
GREED... LUST...
HUH?
OOR MR. MONEYBAGS IS EELING DEFLATED...
WAAHH!
LIFE IS SO EMPTY!
MRS. MONEYBAGS JUST GOT SOME IMPLANTS!
THEY'RE WORTH EVERY PENNY!
SORT OF PERKY
TO GET DRUNK!
MR. MONEYBAGS SHOULD HAVE LISTENED TO THE VOICE OF HIS CONSCIENCE!
I'M TALKIN' TO YOU!
Someone's reading us the Riot Act...
Filibustered by a rubber stamp congress...
... made up of looking-glass creatures.

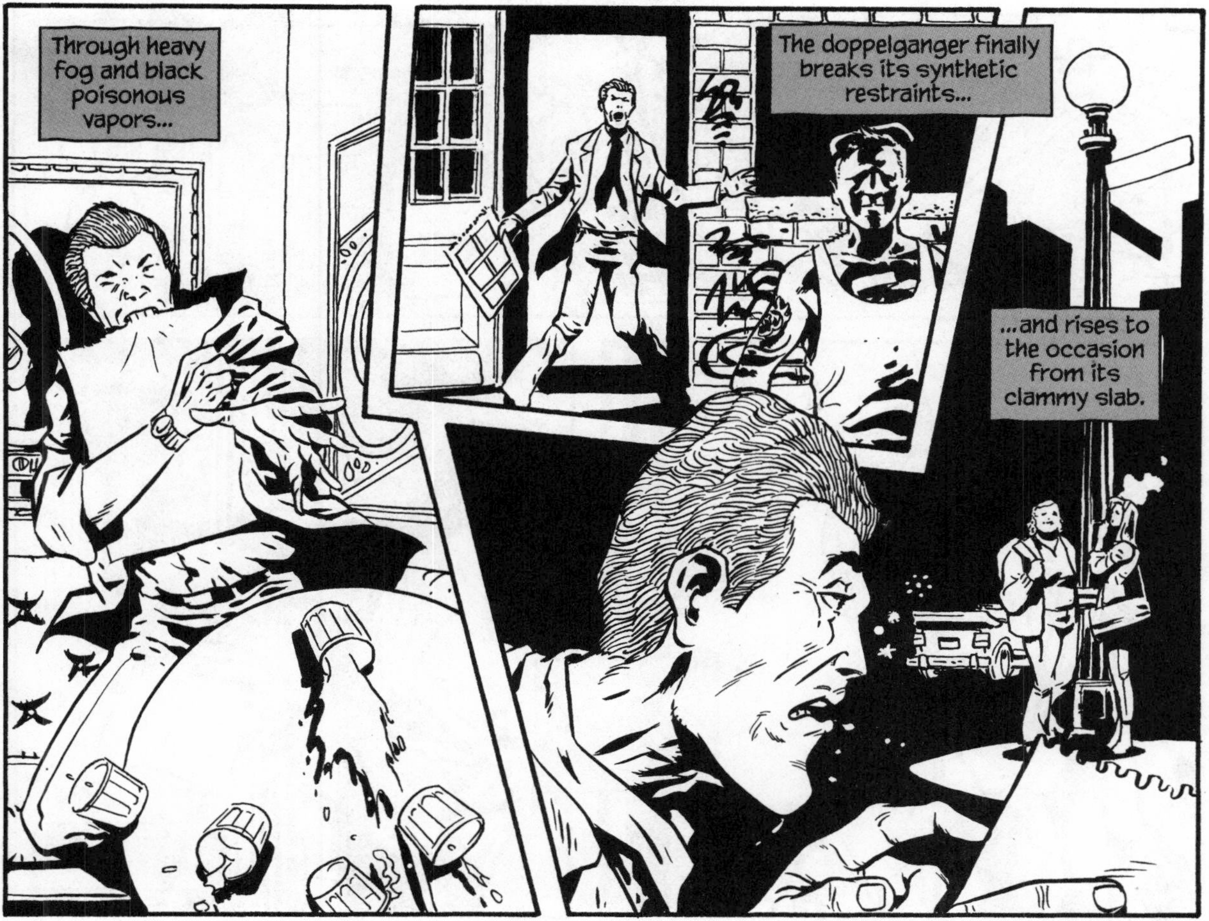
Through heavy fog and black poisonous vapors...
The doppelganger finally breaks its synthetic restraints...
...and rises to the occasion from its clammy slab.

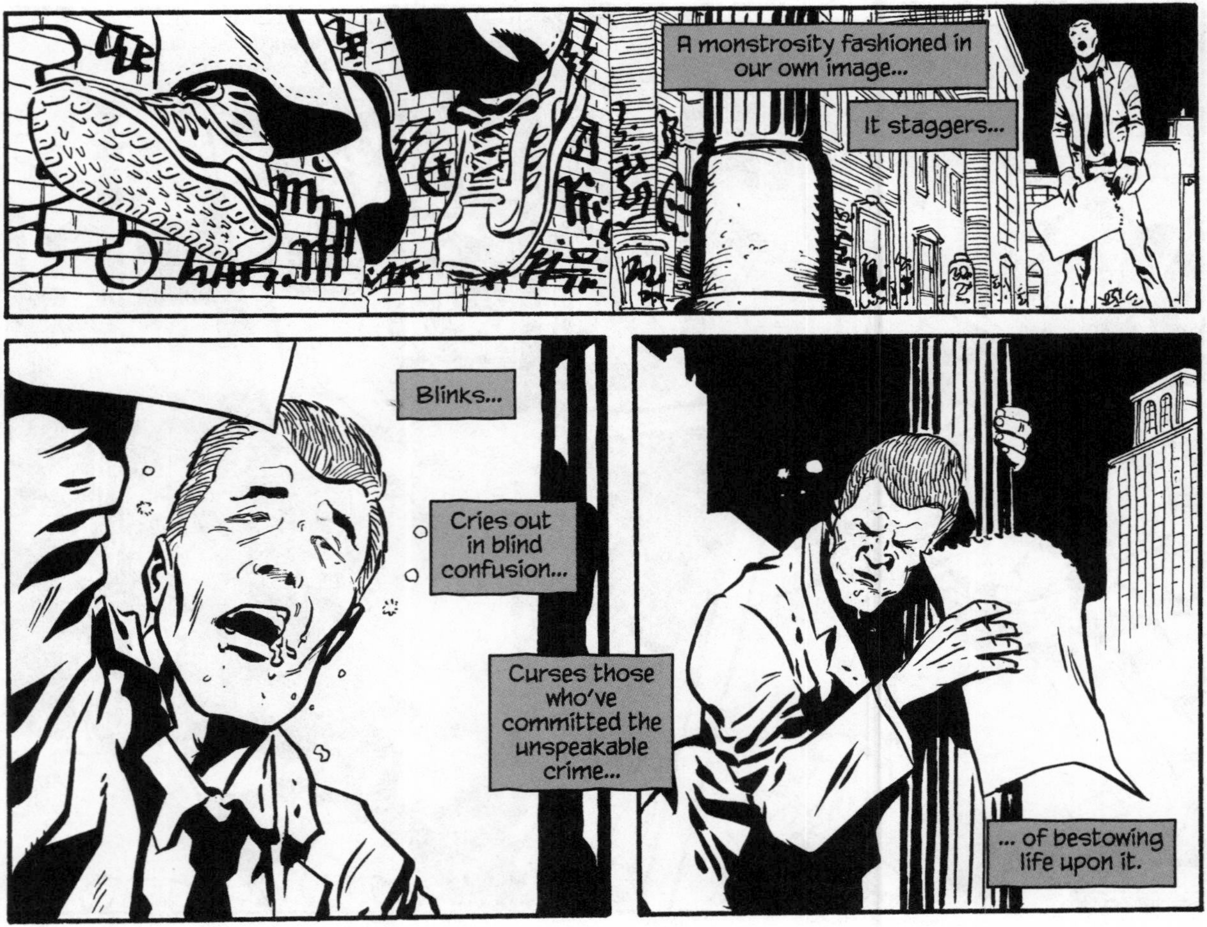

A monstrosity fashioned in our own image...
It staggers...
Blinks...
Cries out in blind confusion...
Curses those who've committed the unspeakable crime...
... of bestowing life upon it.

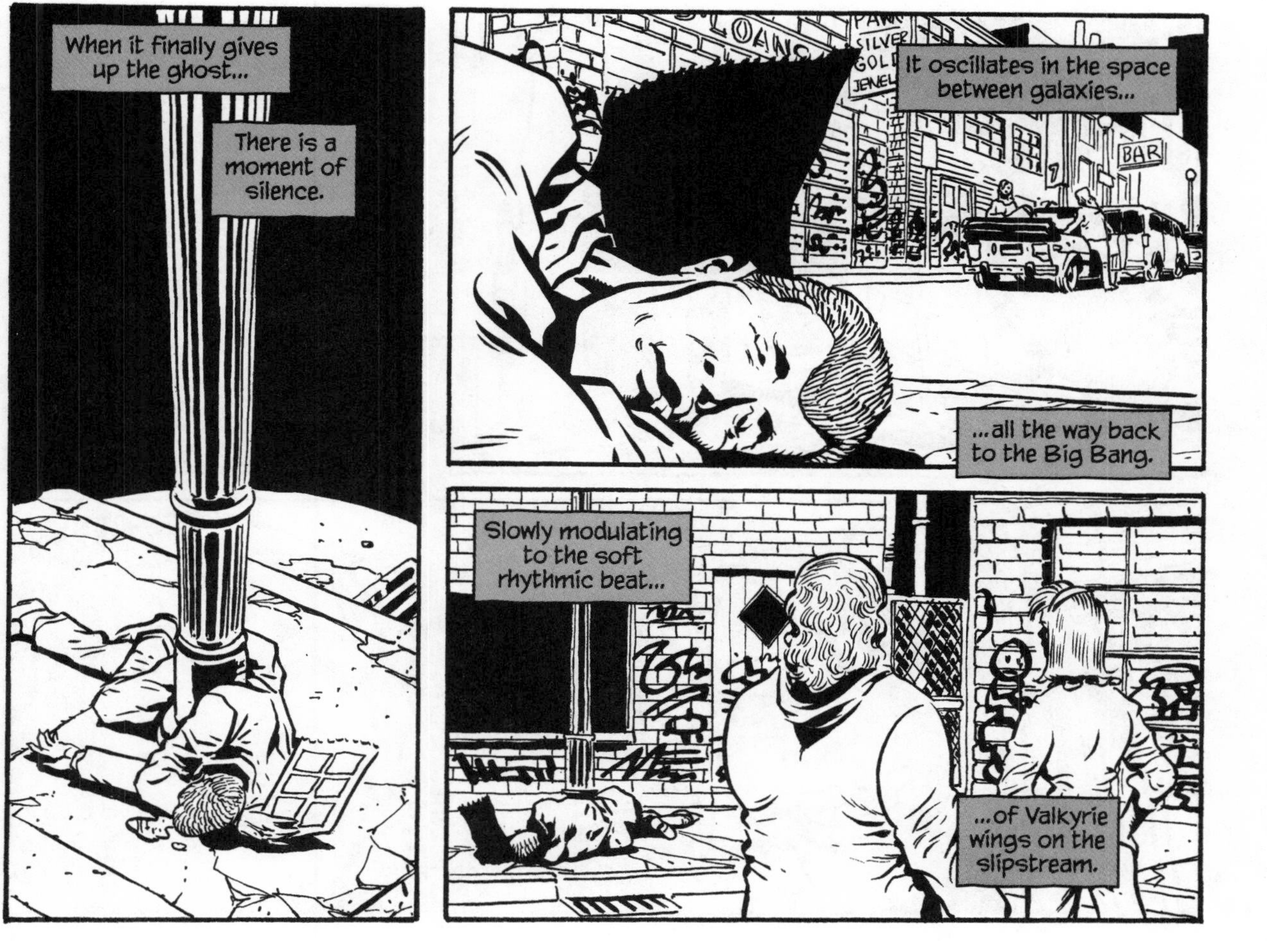
When it finally gives up the ghost...
There is a moment of silence.
It oscillates in the space between galaxies...
...all the way back to the Big Bang.
Slowly modulating to the soft rhythmic beat...
...of Valkyrie wings on the slipstream.
LOANS
PAWN
SILVER
GOLD
JEWEL
BAR

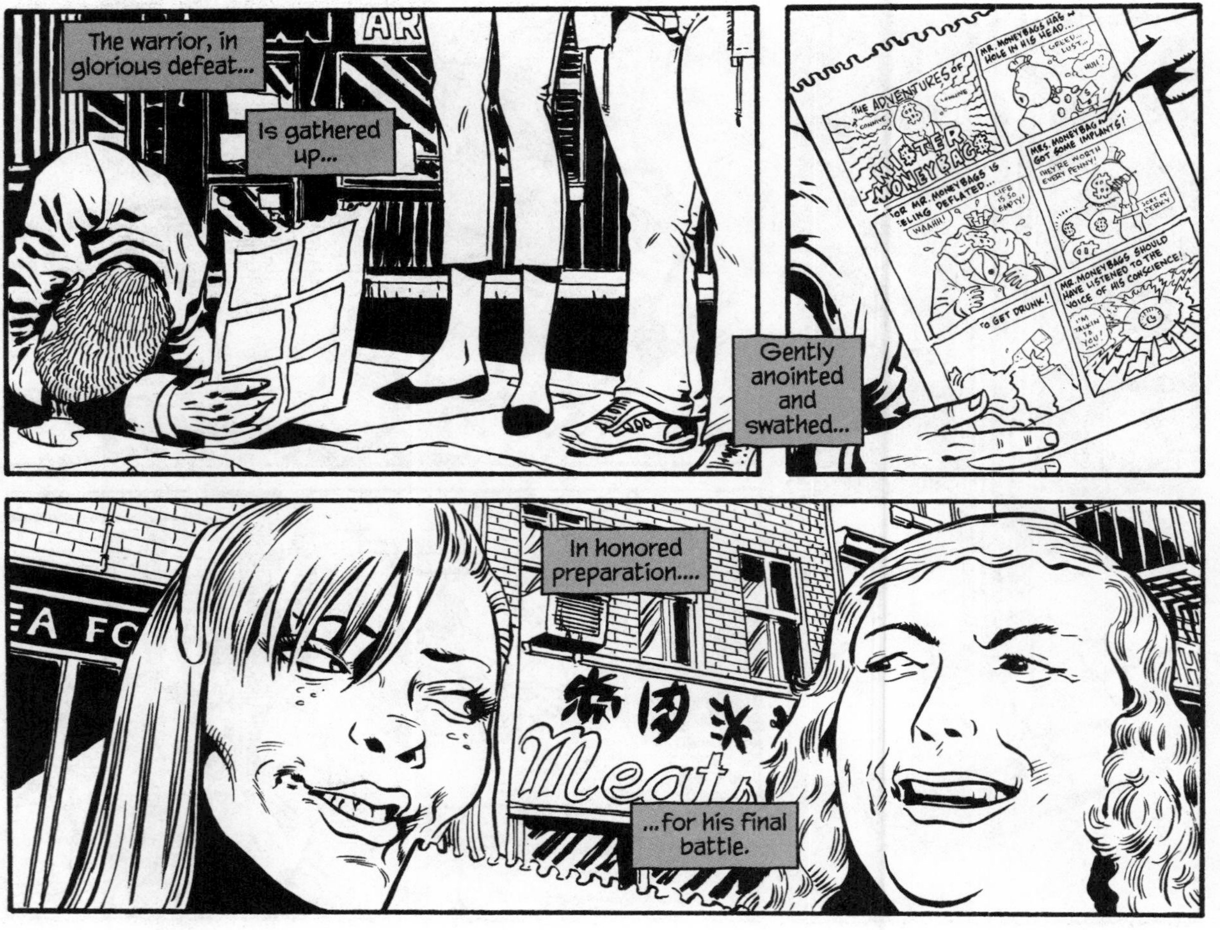
The warrior, in glorious defeat...
Is gathered up...
THE ADVENTURES OF MI$TER MONEYBAG$
CONNIVE
CONNIVE
MR. MONEYBAGS HAS A HOLE IN HIS HEAD...
HUH?
MRS. MONEYBAGS GOT SOME IMPLANTS!
THEY'RE WORTH EVERY PENNY!
FOR MR. MONEYBAGS IS FEELING DEFLATED...
WAAHH!
LIFE IS SO EMPTY!
TO GET DRUNK!
MR. MONEYBAGS SHOULD HAVE LISTENED TO THE VOICE OF HIS CONSCIENCE!
I'M TALKIN' TO YOU!
Gently anointed and swathed...
In honored preparation....
...for his final battle.

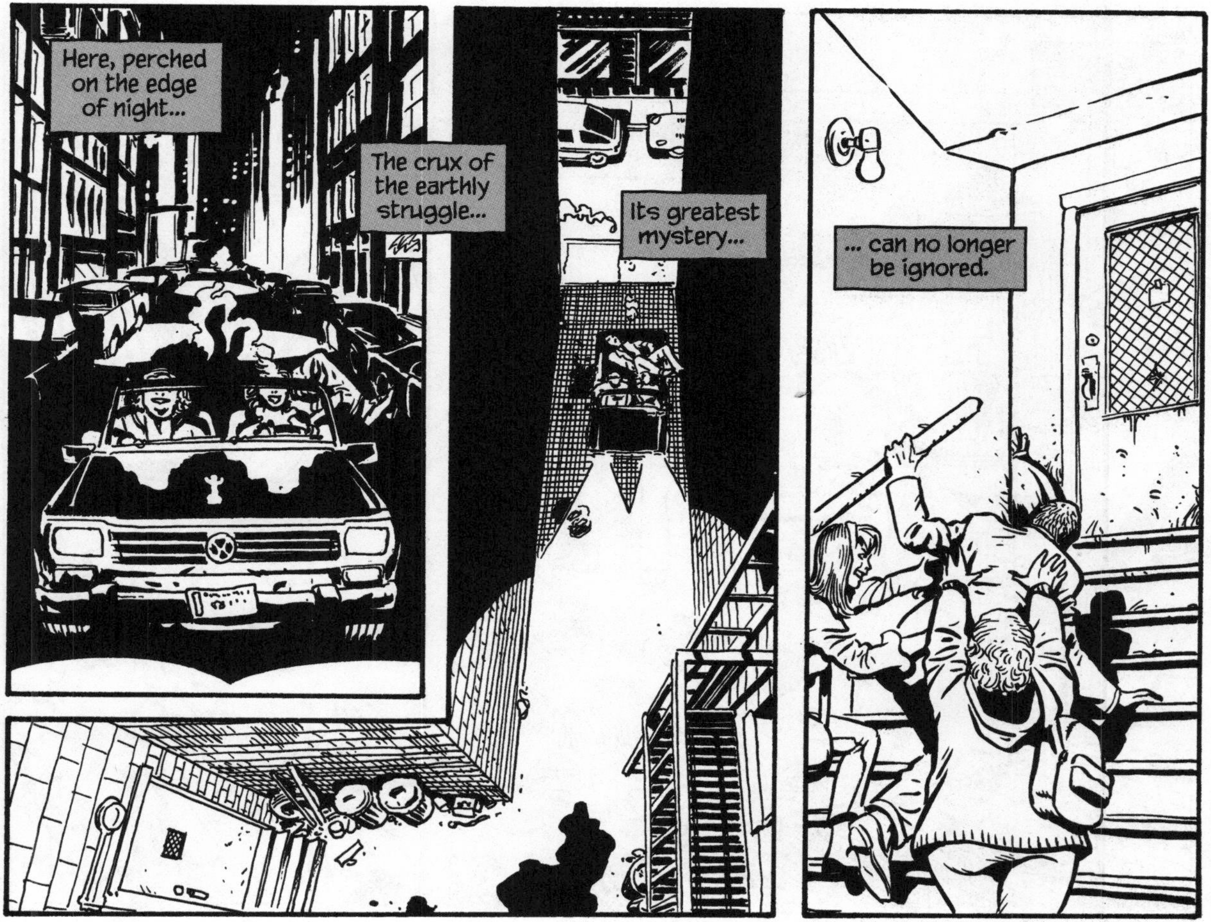
Here, perched on the edge of night...
The crux of the earthly struggle...
Its greatest mystery...
... can no longer be ignored.

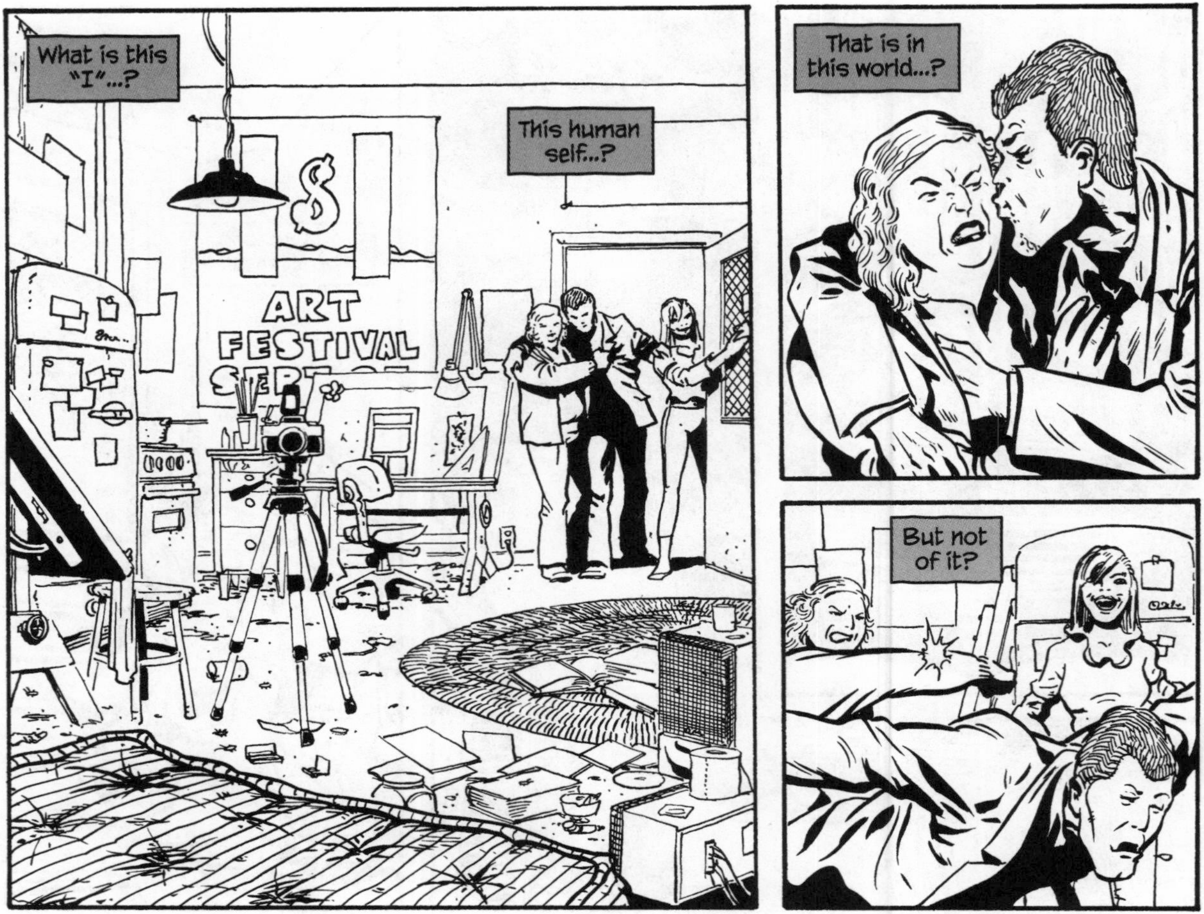
What is this "I"...?
ART
FESTIVAL
This human self...?
That is in this world...?
But not of it?

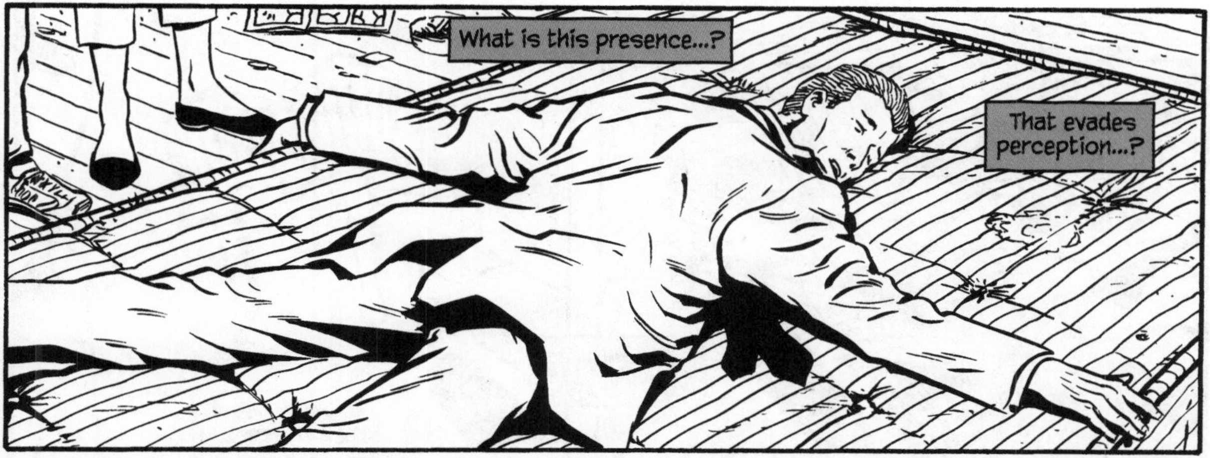
What is this presence...?
That evades perception...?

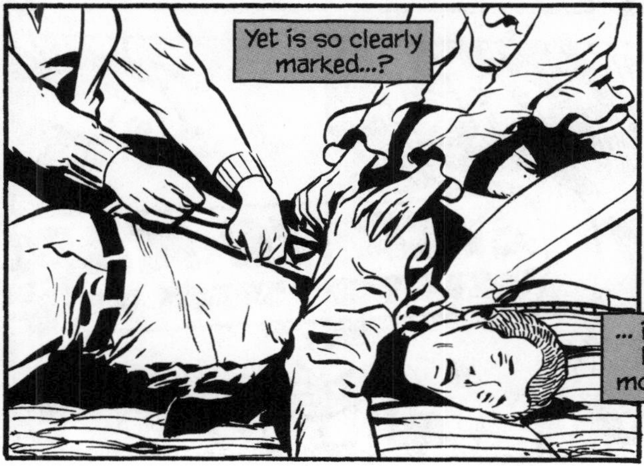
Yet is so clearly marked...?
... in every living moment?

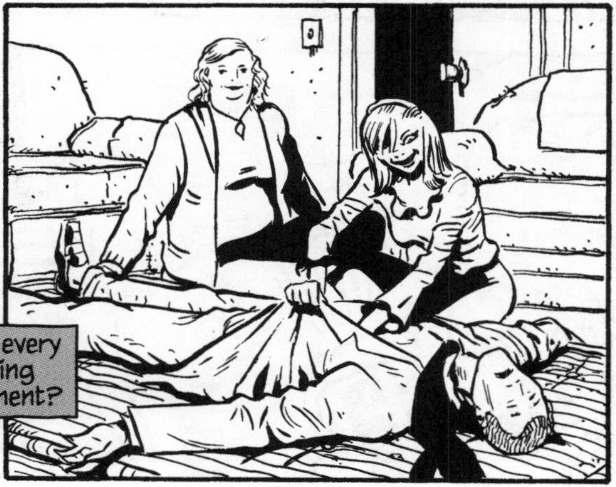

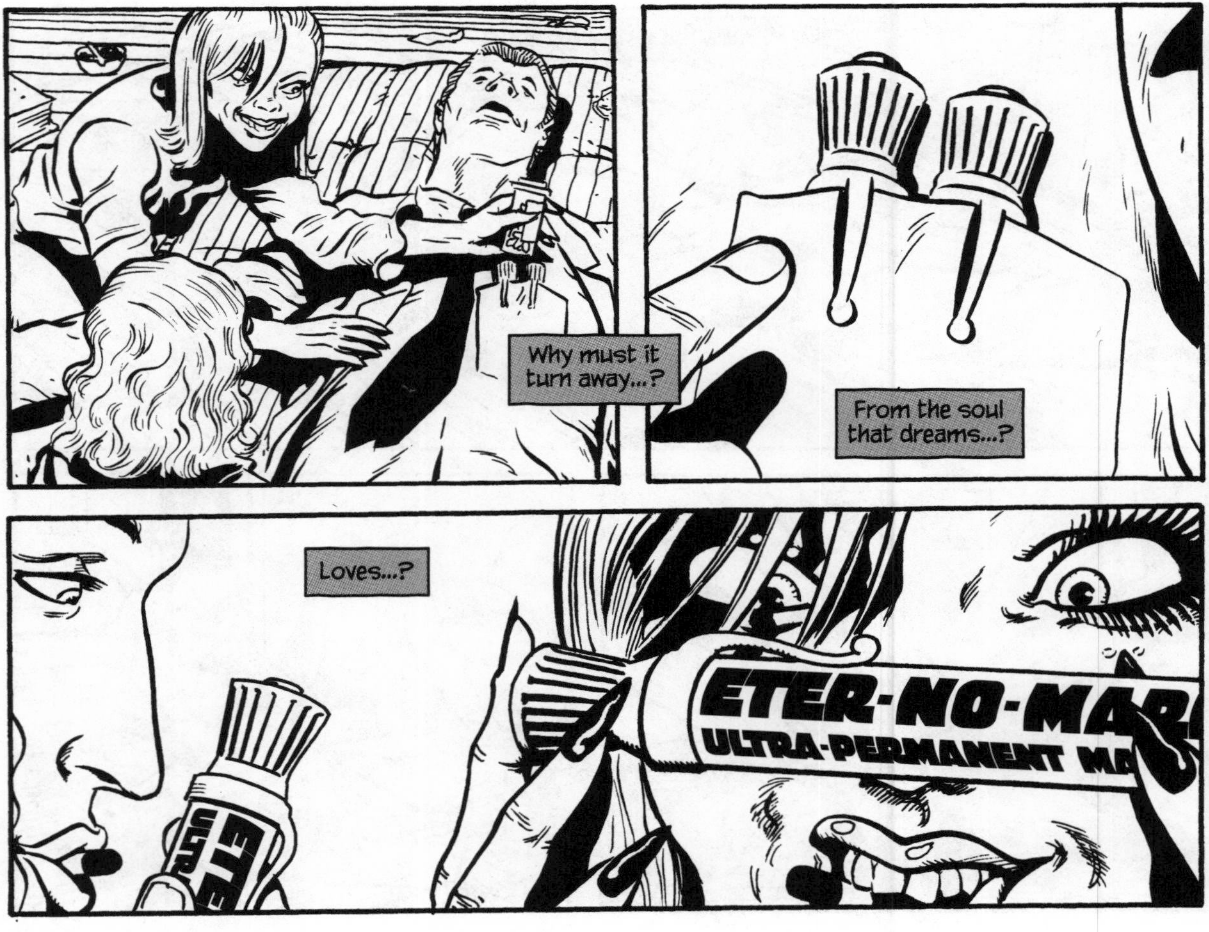
Why must it turn away...?
From the soul that dreams...?
Loves...?

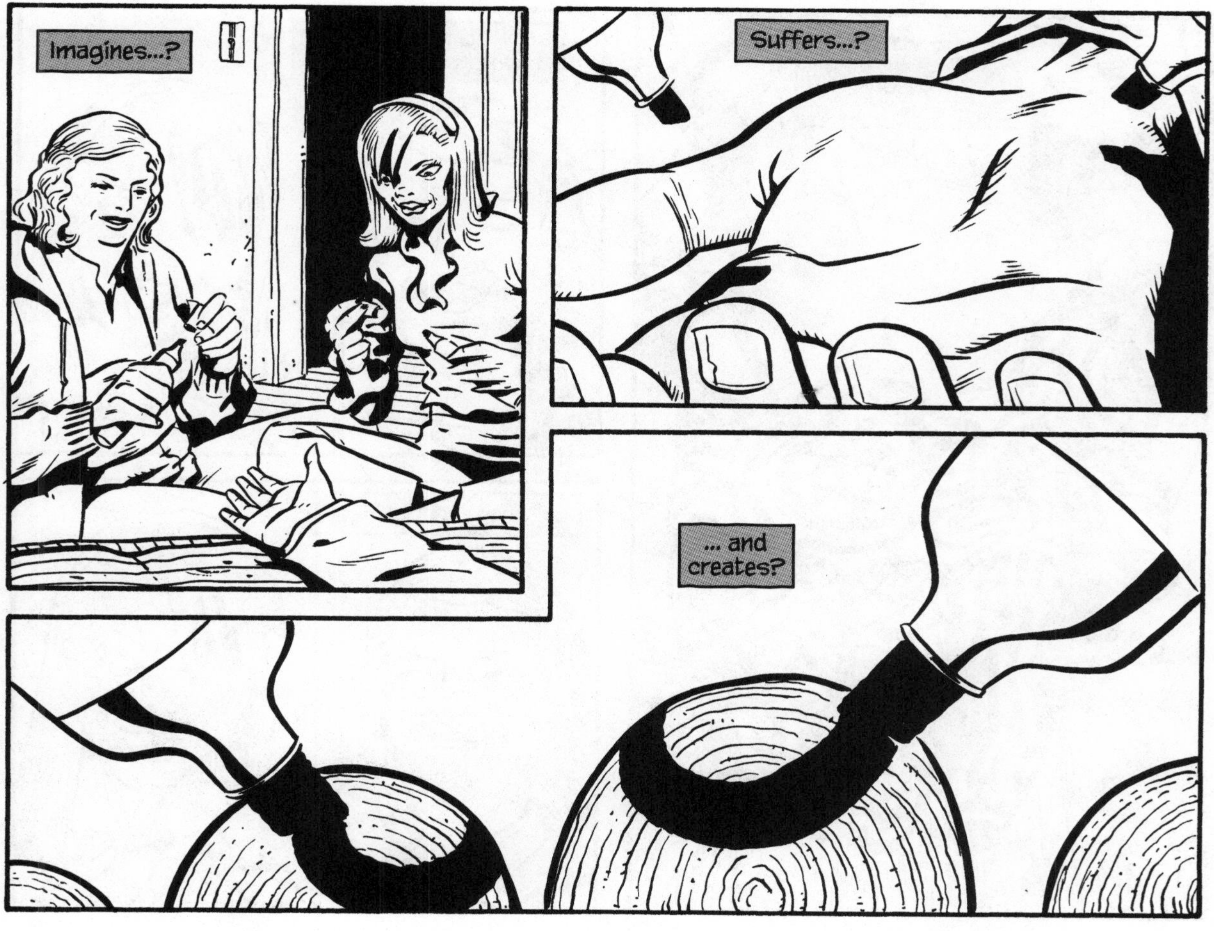
Imagines...?
Suffers...?
... and creates?

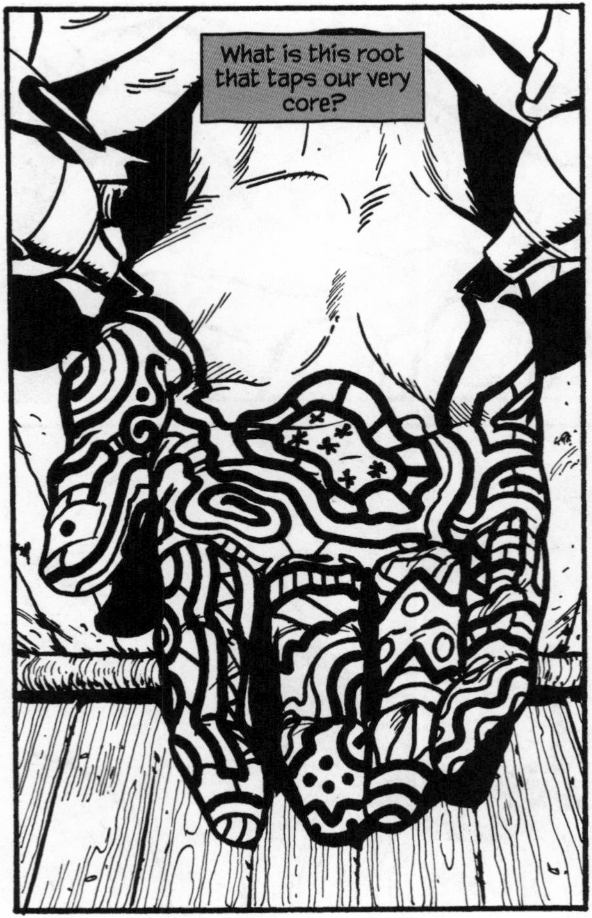
What is this root that taps our very core?

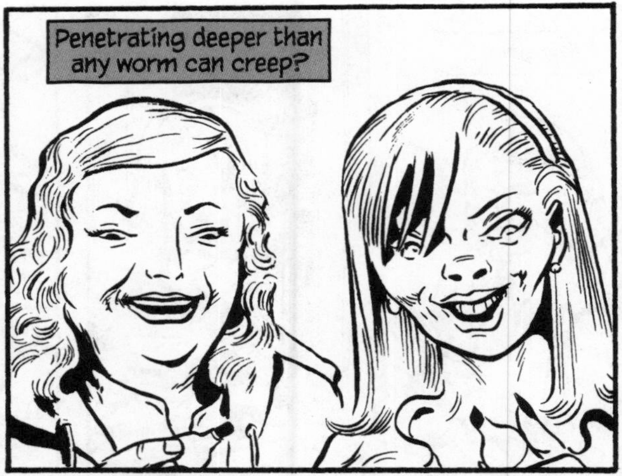
Penetrating deeper than any worm can creep?

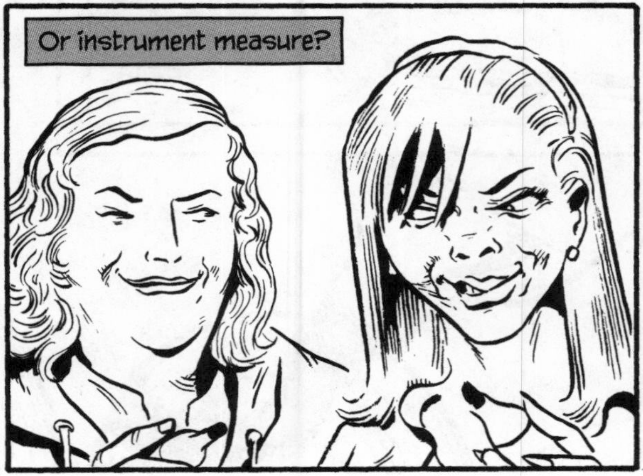
Or instrument measure?

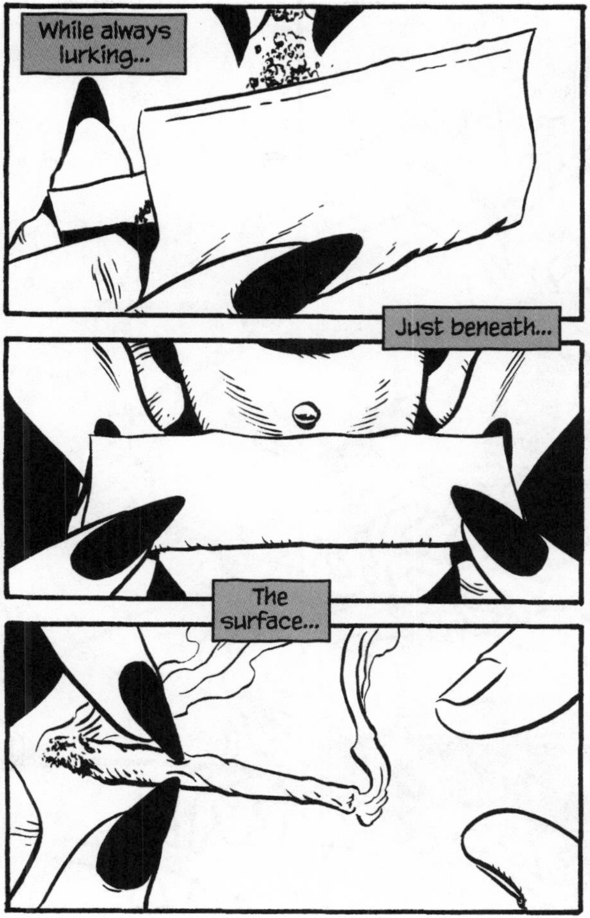
While always lurking...
Just beneath...
The surface...
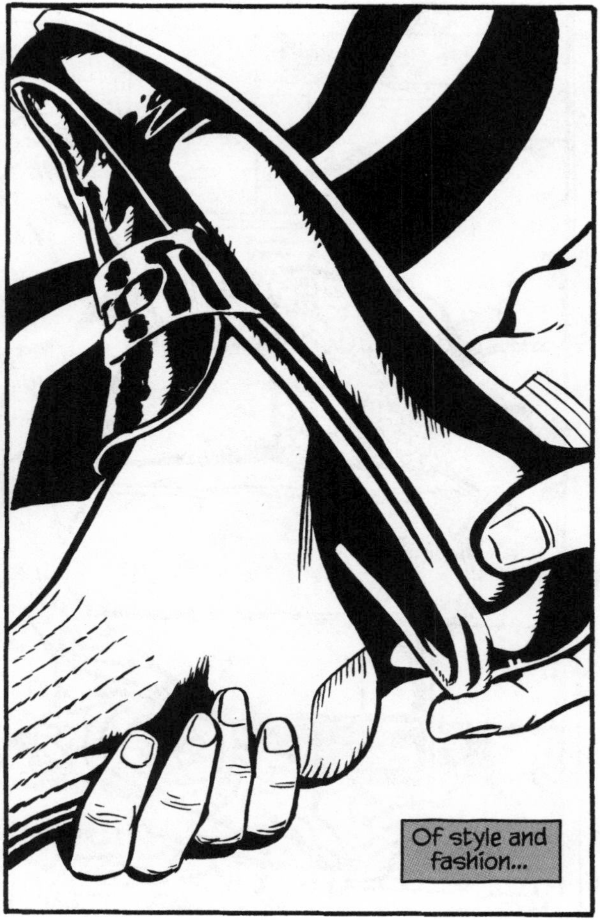
Of style and fashion...

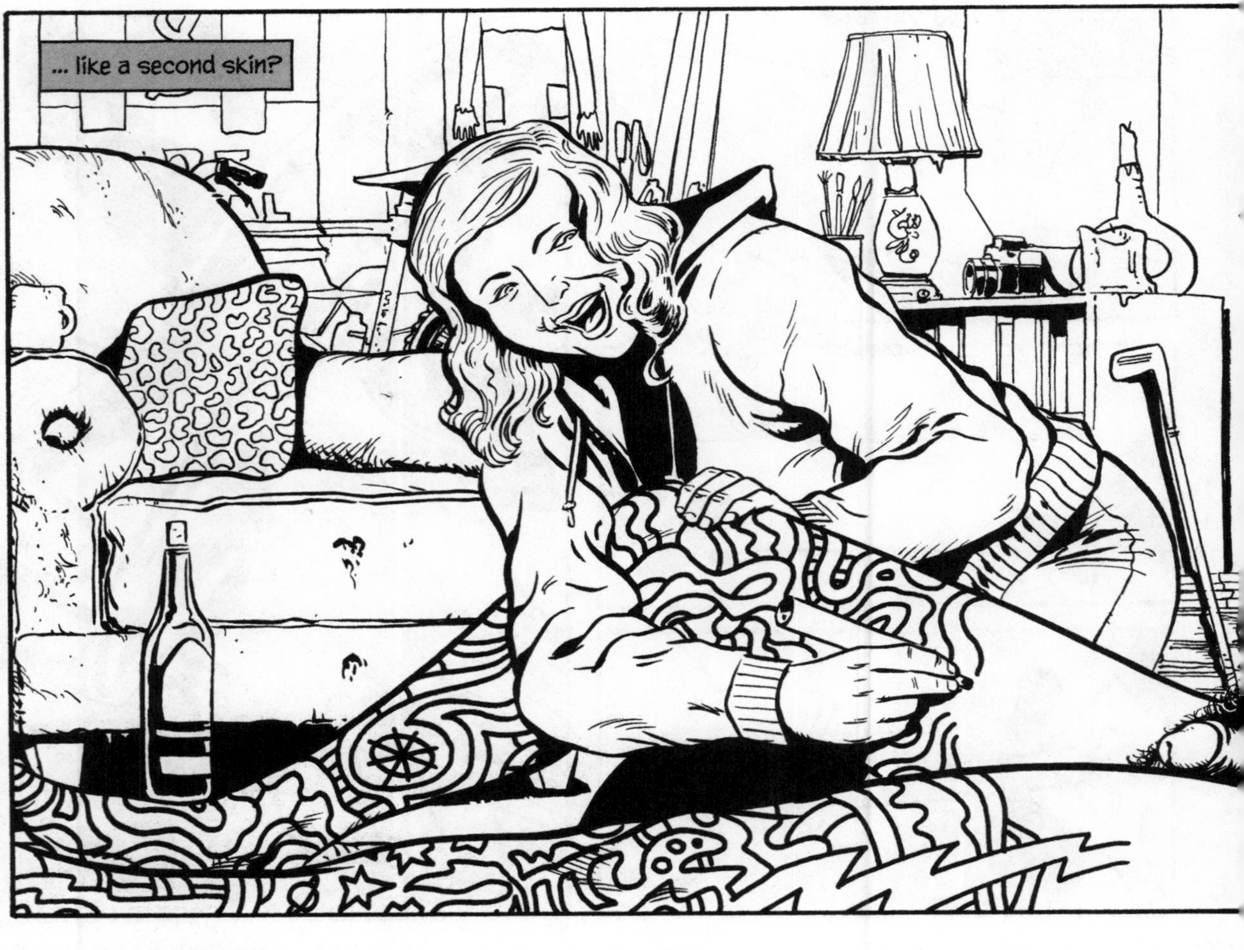
... like a second skin?

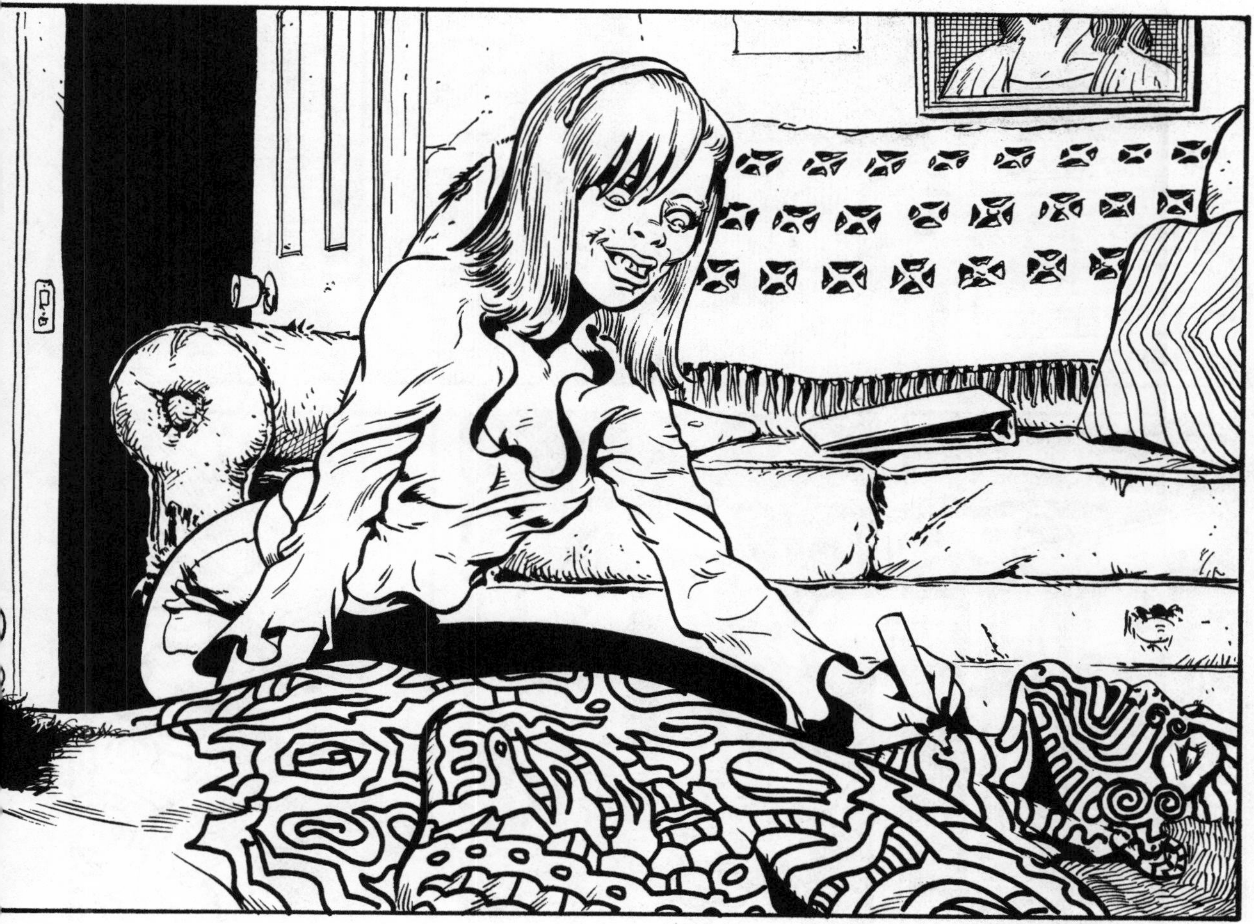

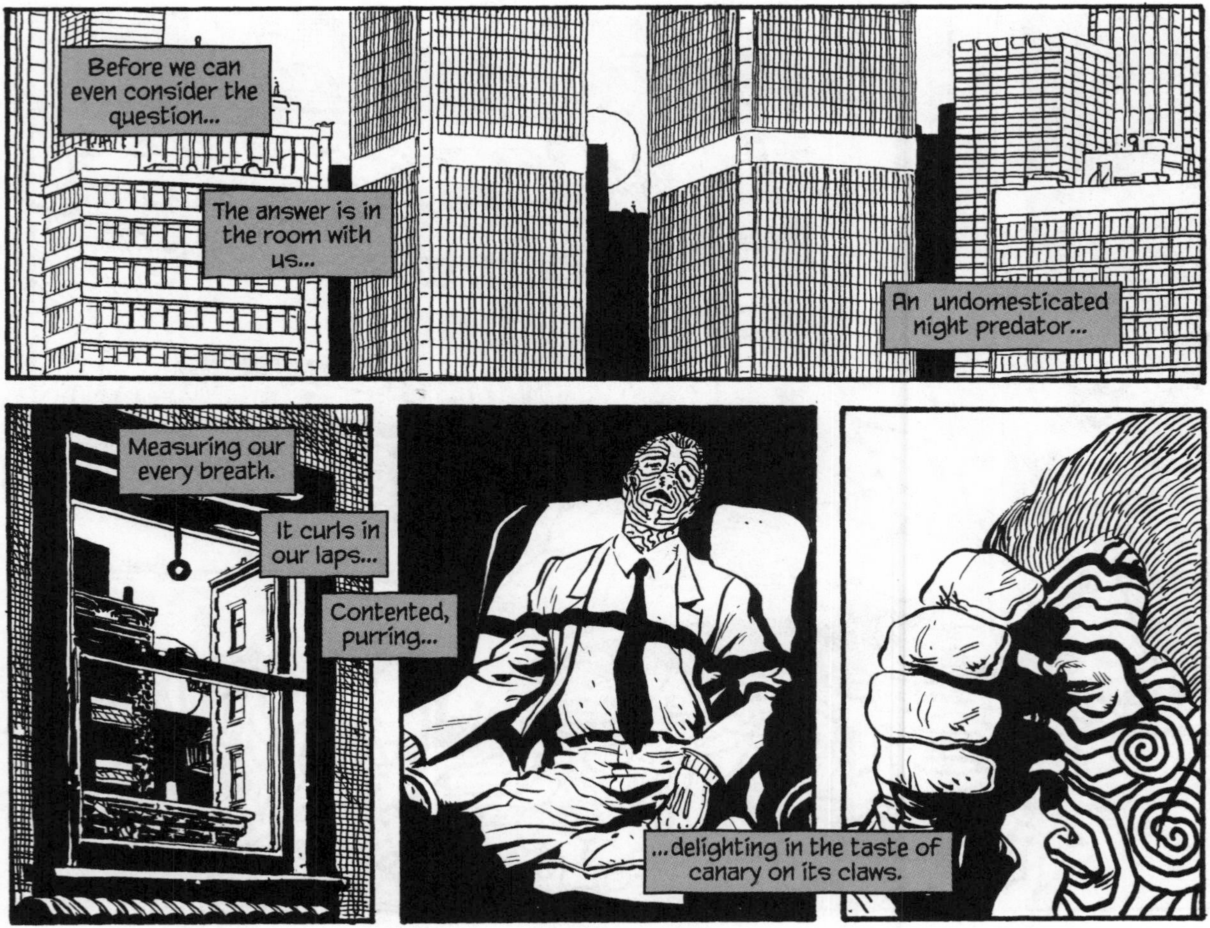
Before we can even consider the question...
The answer is in the room with us...
An undomesticated night predator...
Measuring our every breath.
It curls in our laps...
Contented, purring...
...delighting in the taste of canary on its claws.

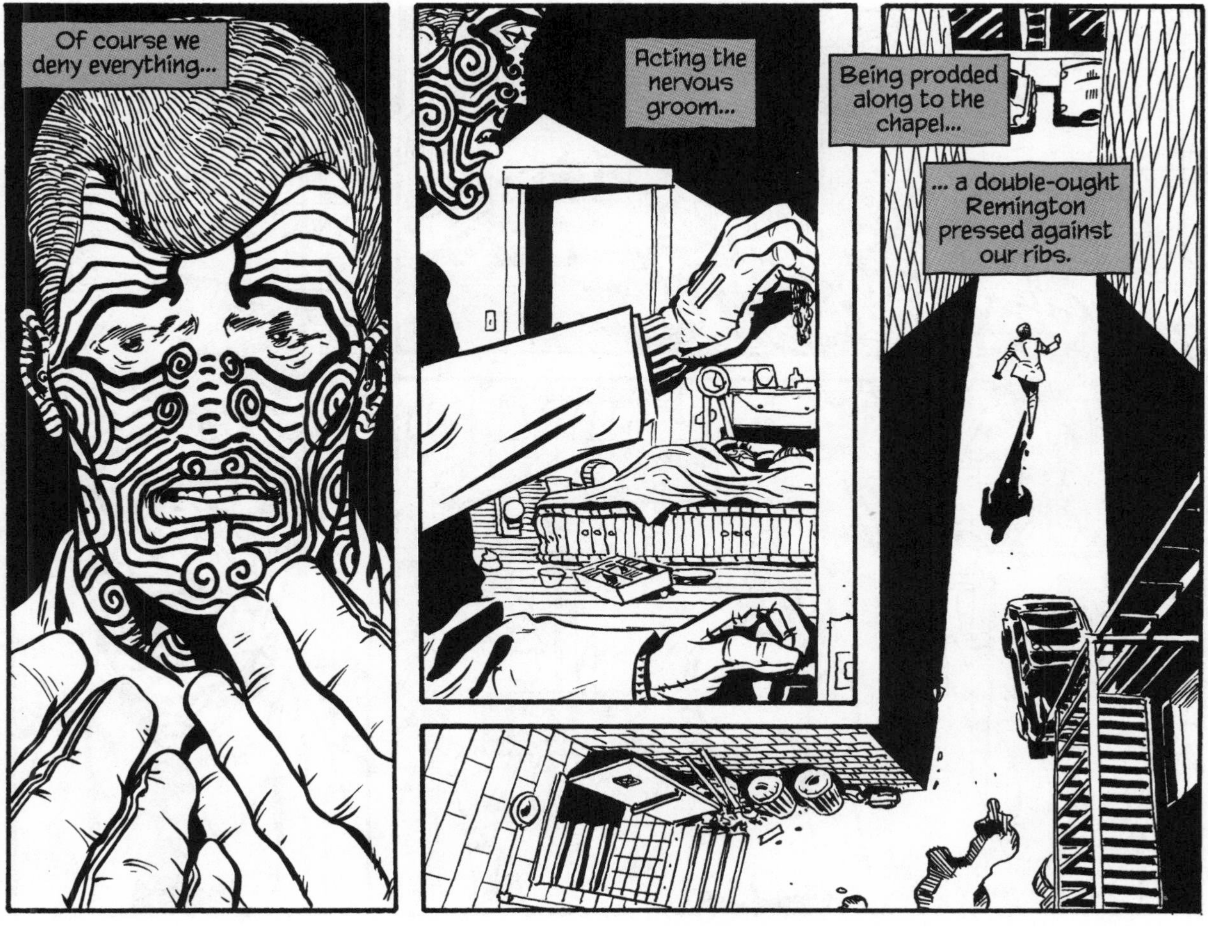
Of course we deny everything...
Acting the nervous groom...
Being prodded along to the chapel...
... a double-ought Remington pressed against our ribs.

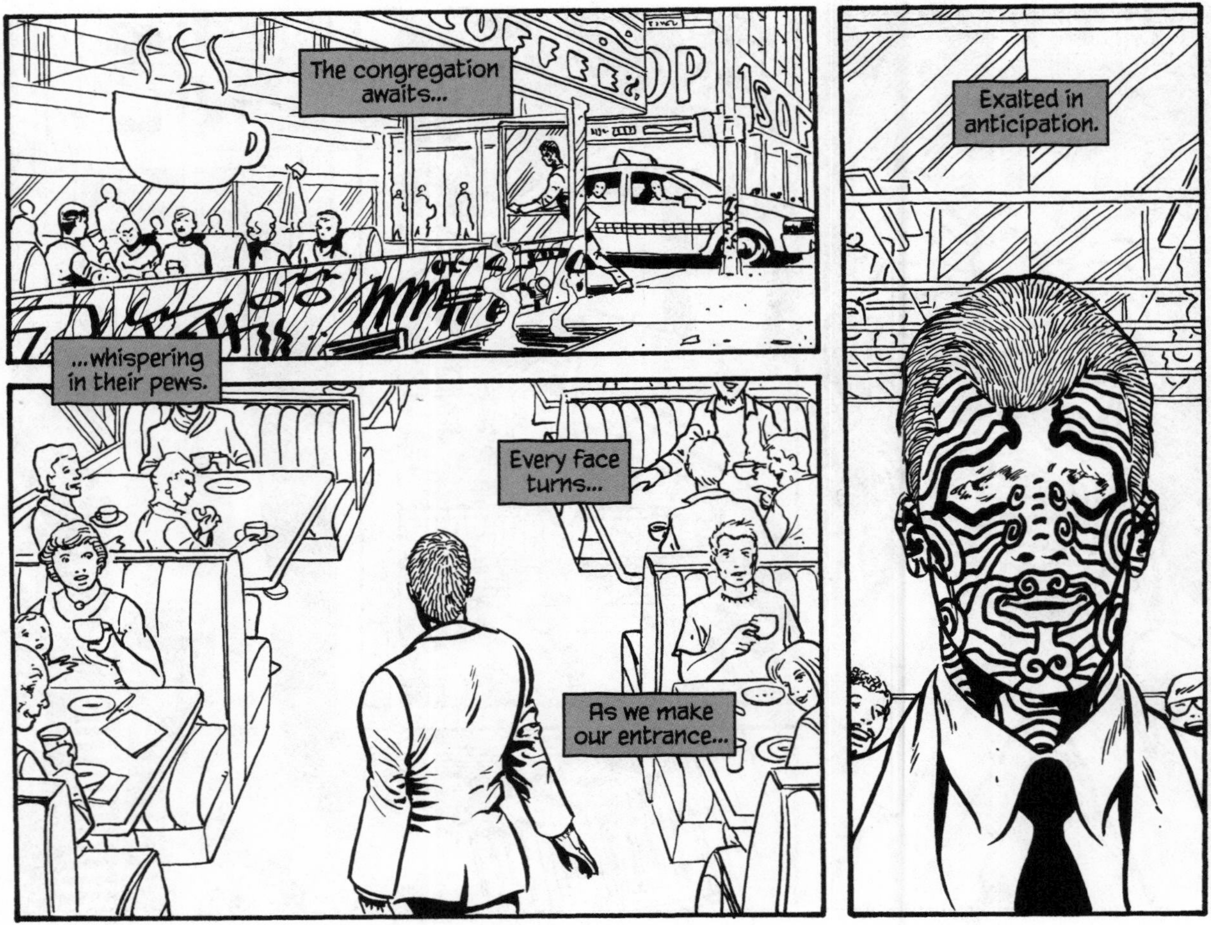

The congregation awaits...
...whispering in their pews.
Every face turns...
As we make our entrance...
Exalted in anticipation.

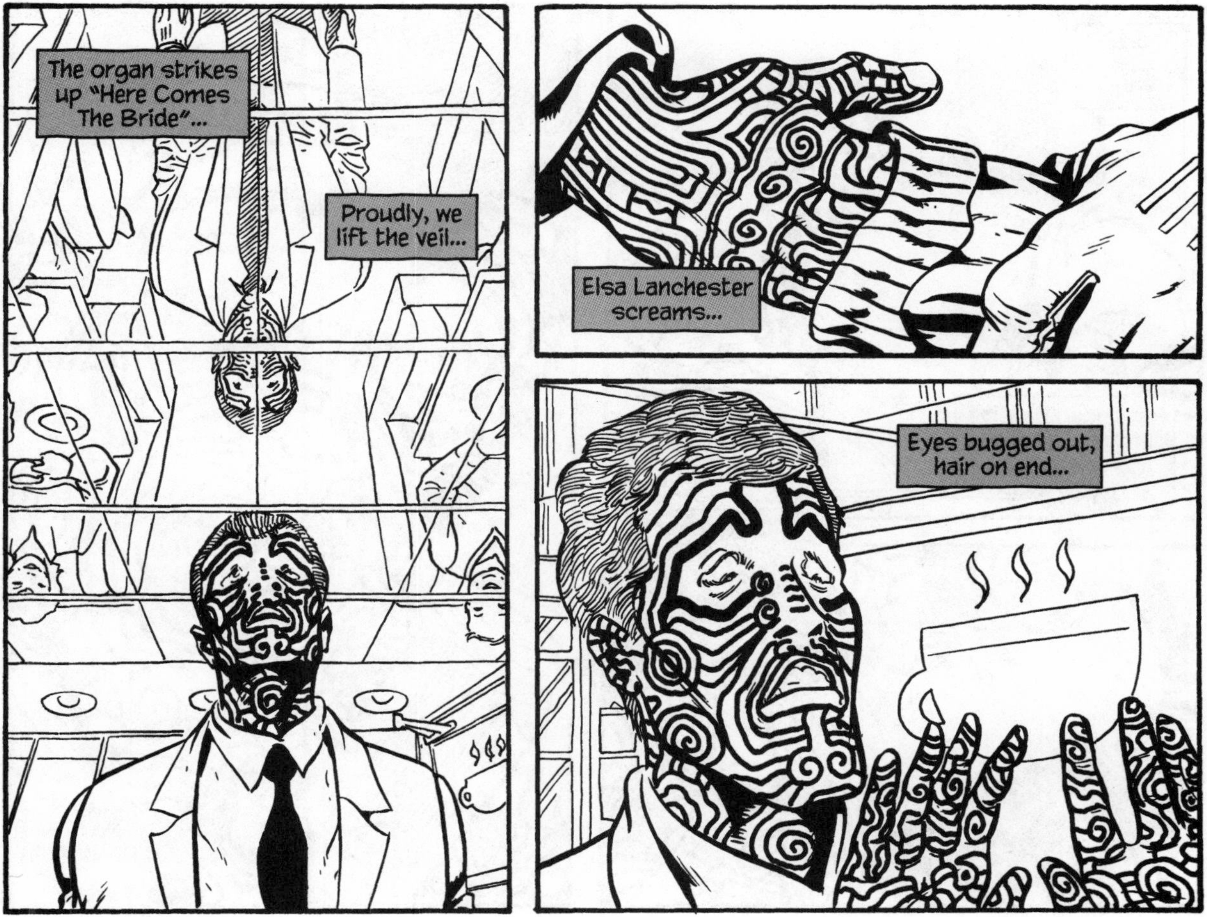
The organ strikes up "Here Comes The Bride"...
Proudly, we lift the veil...
Elsa Lanchester screams...
Eyes bugged out, hair on end...

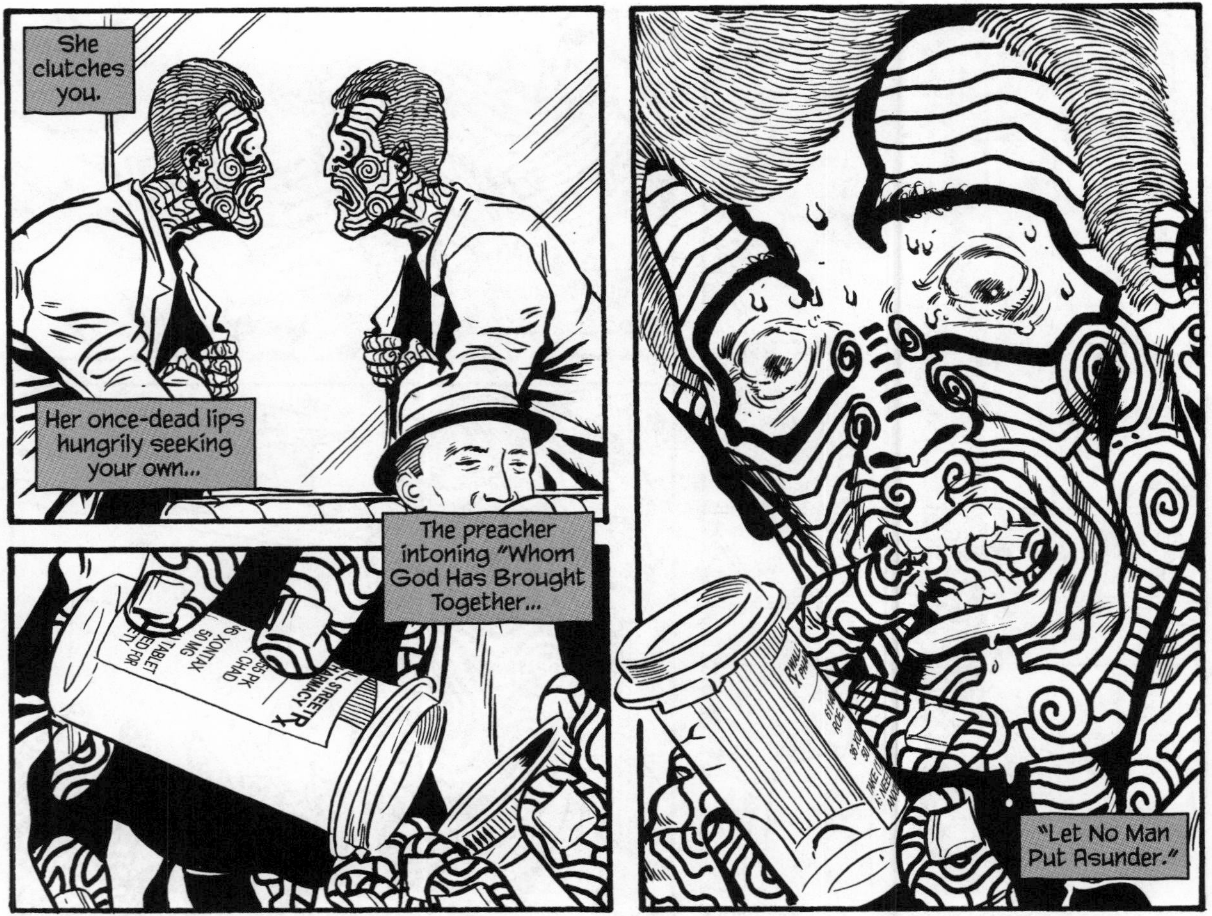
She clutches you.
Her once-dead lips hungrily seeking your own...
The preacher intoning "Whom God Has Brought Together...
"Let No Man Put Asunder."

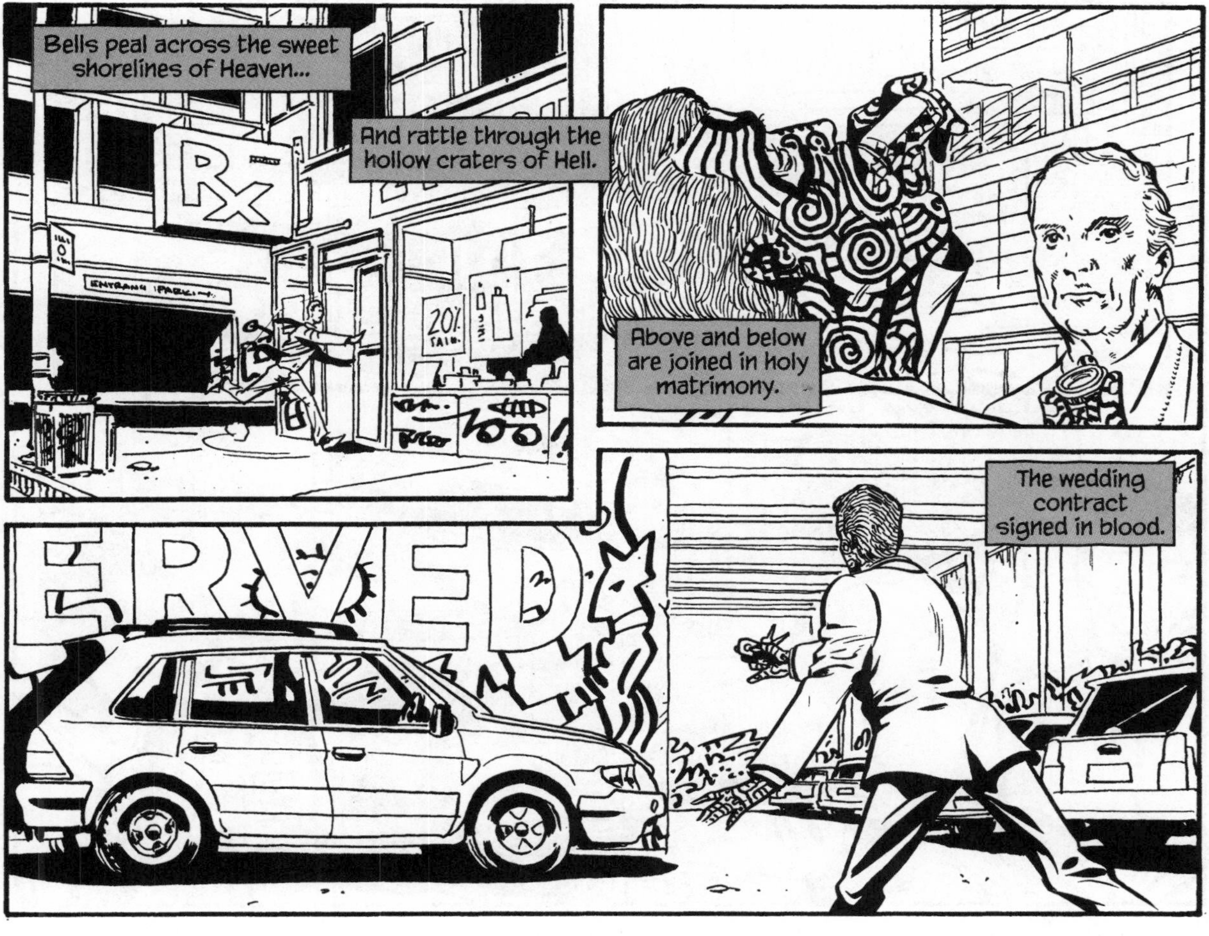
Bells peal across the sweet shorelines of Heaven...
And rattle through the hollow craters of Hell.
Rx
Above and below are joined in holy matrimony.
The wedding contract signed in blood.
ERVED

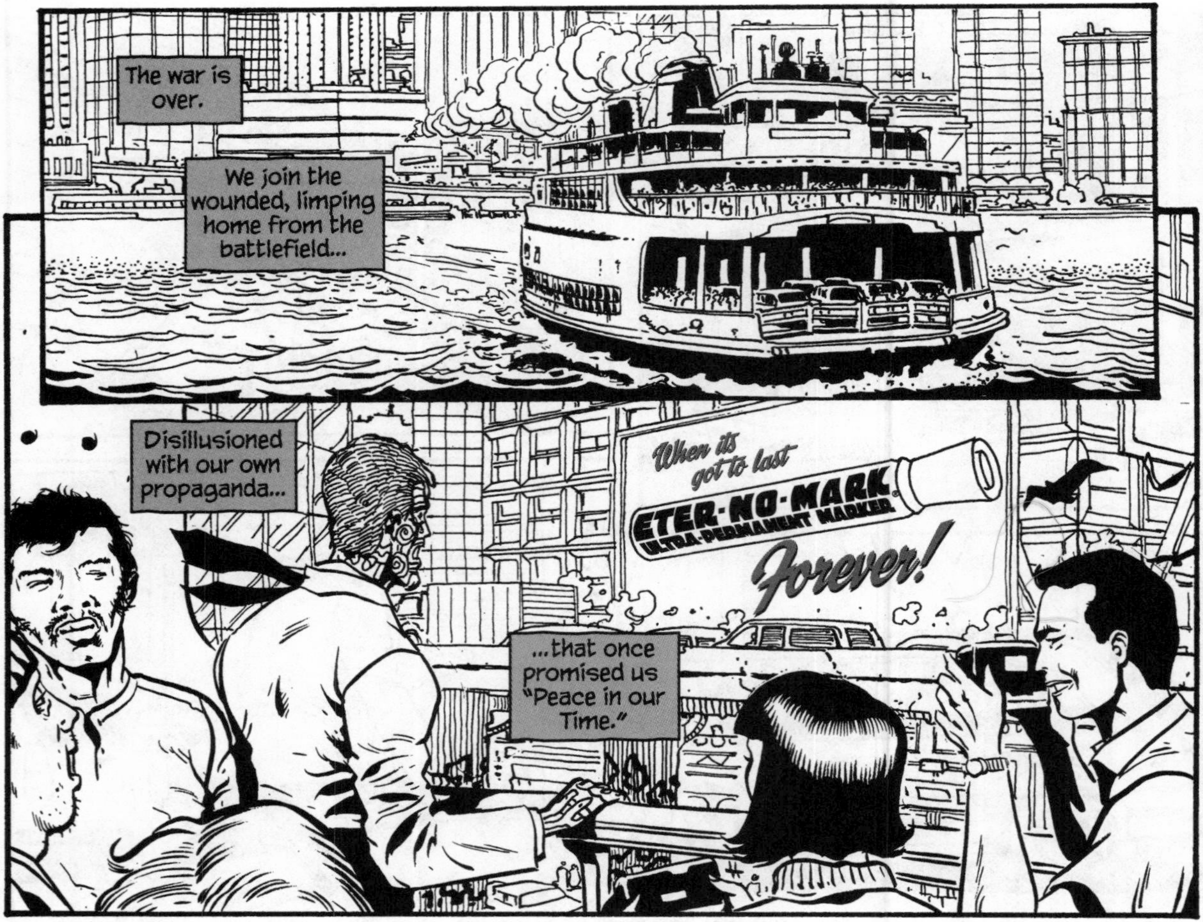

The war is over.
We join the wounded, limping home from the battlefield...
Disillusioned with our own propaganda...
When its got to last
ETER-NO-MARK
ULTRA-PERMANENT MARKER
Forever!
...that once promised us "Peace in our Time."

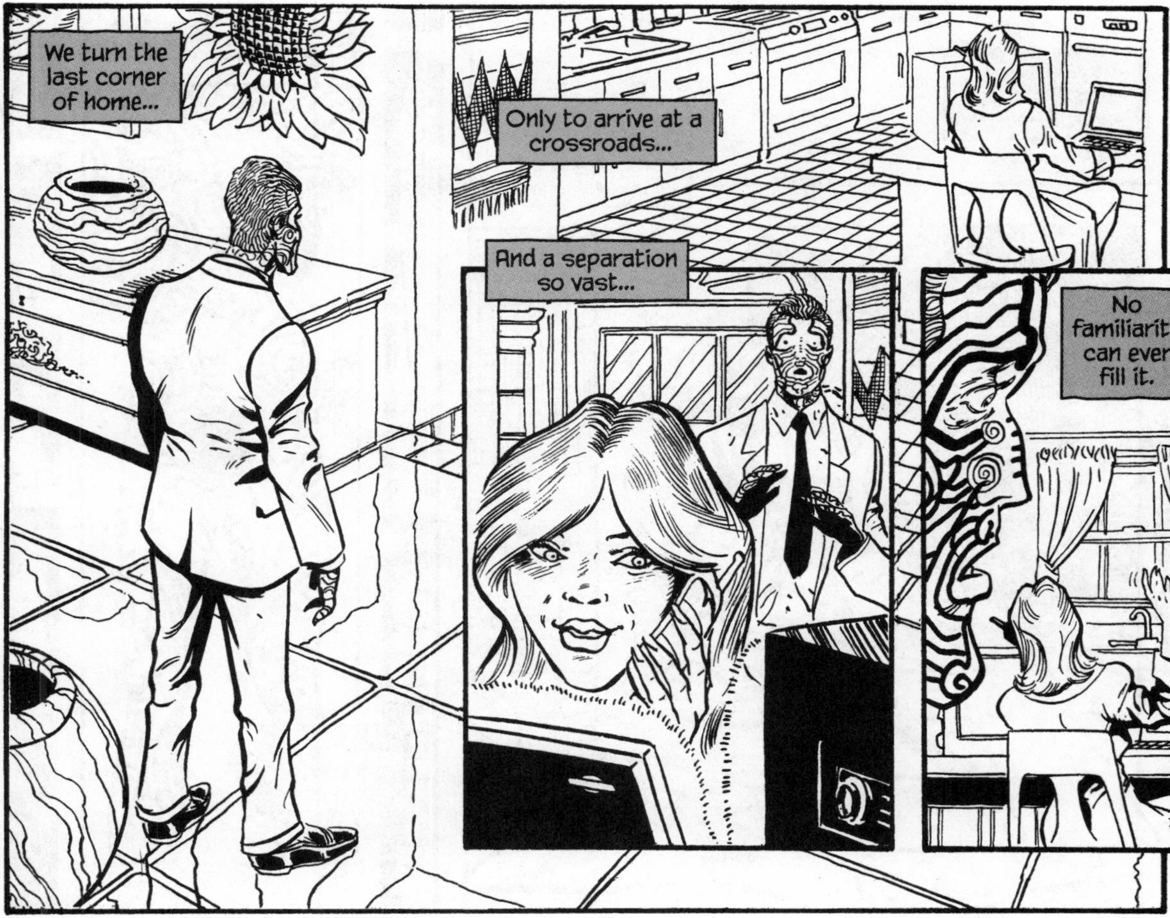
We turn the last corner of home...
Only to arrive at a crossroads...
And a separation so vast...
No familiarity can ever fill it.

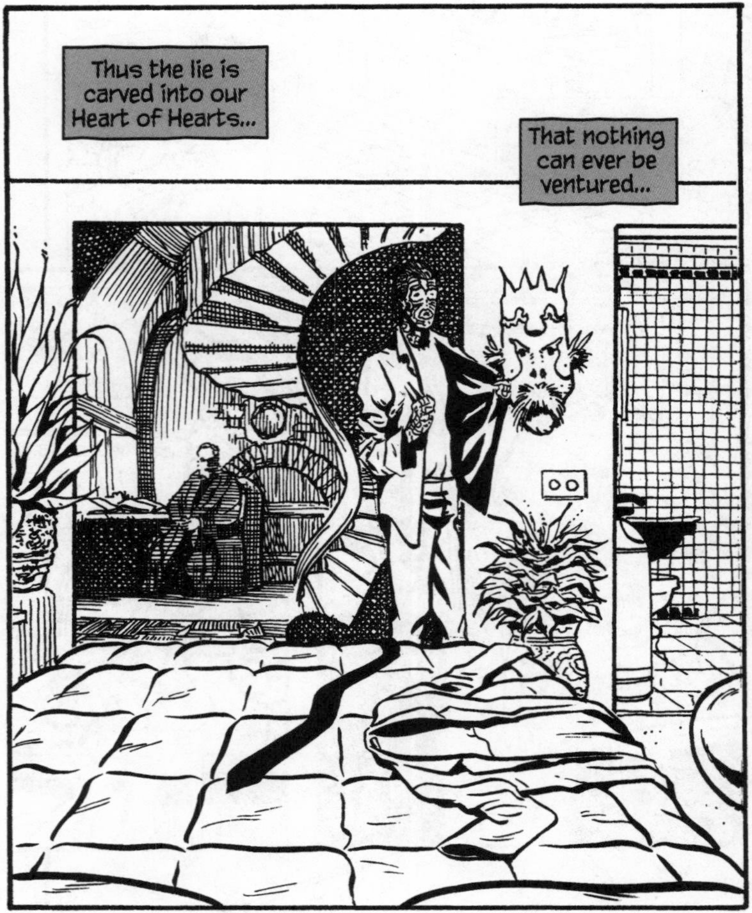
Thus the lie is carved into our Heart of Hearts...
That nothing can ever be ventured...

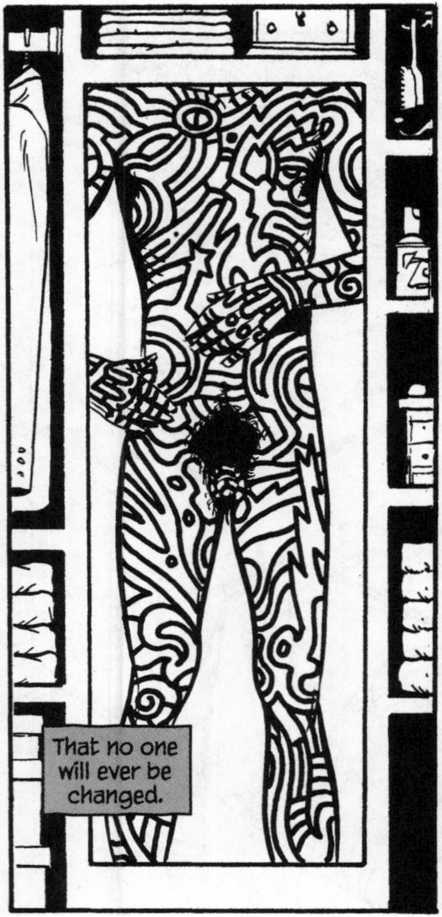
That no one will ever be changed.

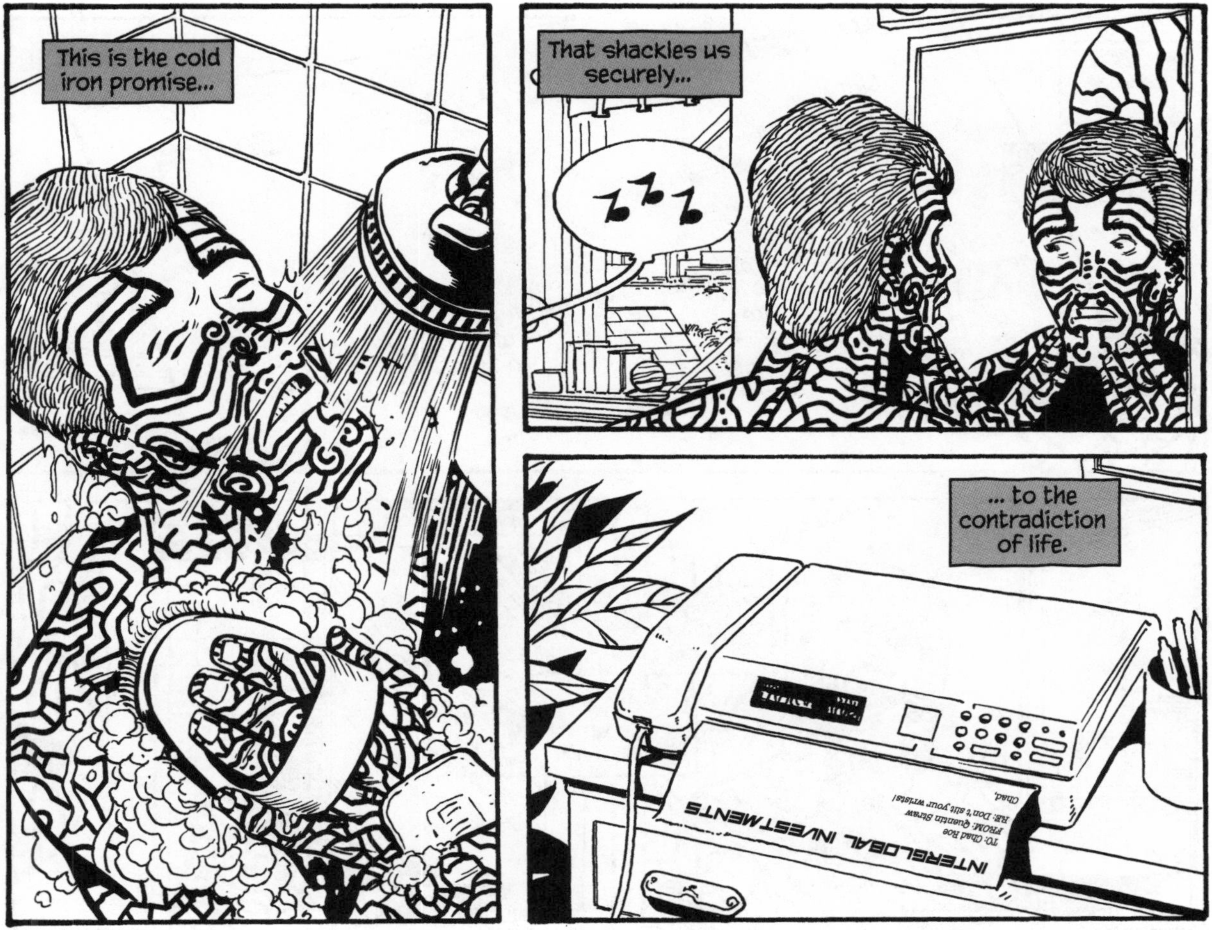
This is the cold iron promise...
That shackles us securely...
ZZZ
... to the contradiction of life.
INTERGLOBAL INVESTMENTS
TO: Chad Roe
FROM: Quentin Straw
RE: Don't slit your wrists!
Chad,

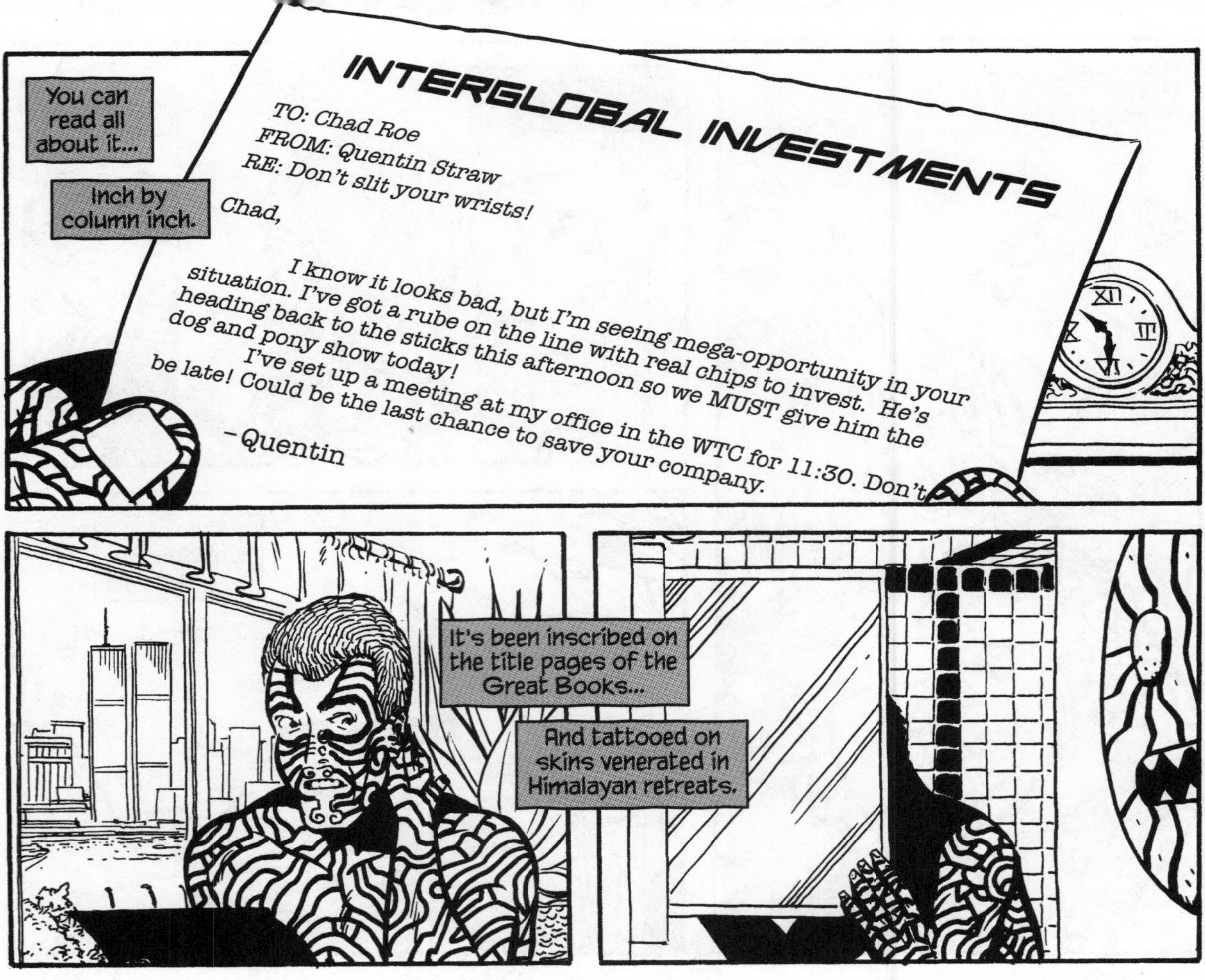

You can read all about it...
Inch by column inch.
INTERGLOBAL INVESTMENTS
TO: Chad Roe
FROM: Quentin Straw
RE: Don't slit your wrists!
Chad,
I know it looks bad, but I'm seeing mega-opportunity in your situation. I've got a rube on the line with real chips to invest. He's heading back to the sticks this afternoon so we MUST give him the dog and pony show today!
I've set up a meeting at my office in the WTC for 11:30. Don't be late! Could be the last chance to save your company.
–Quentin
It's been inscribed on the title pages of the Great Books...
And tattooed on skins venerated in Himalayan retreats.

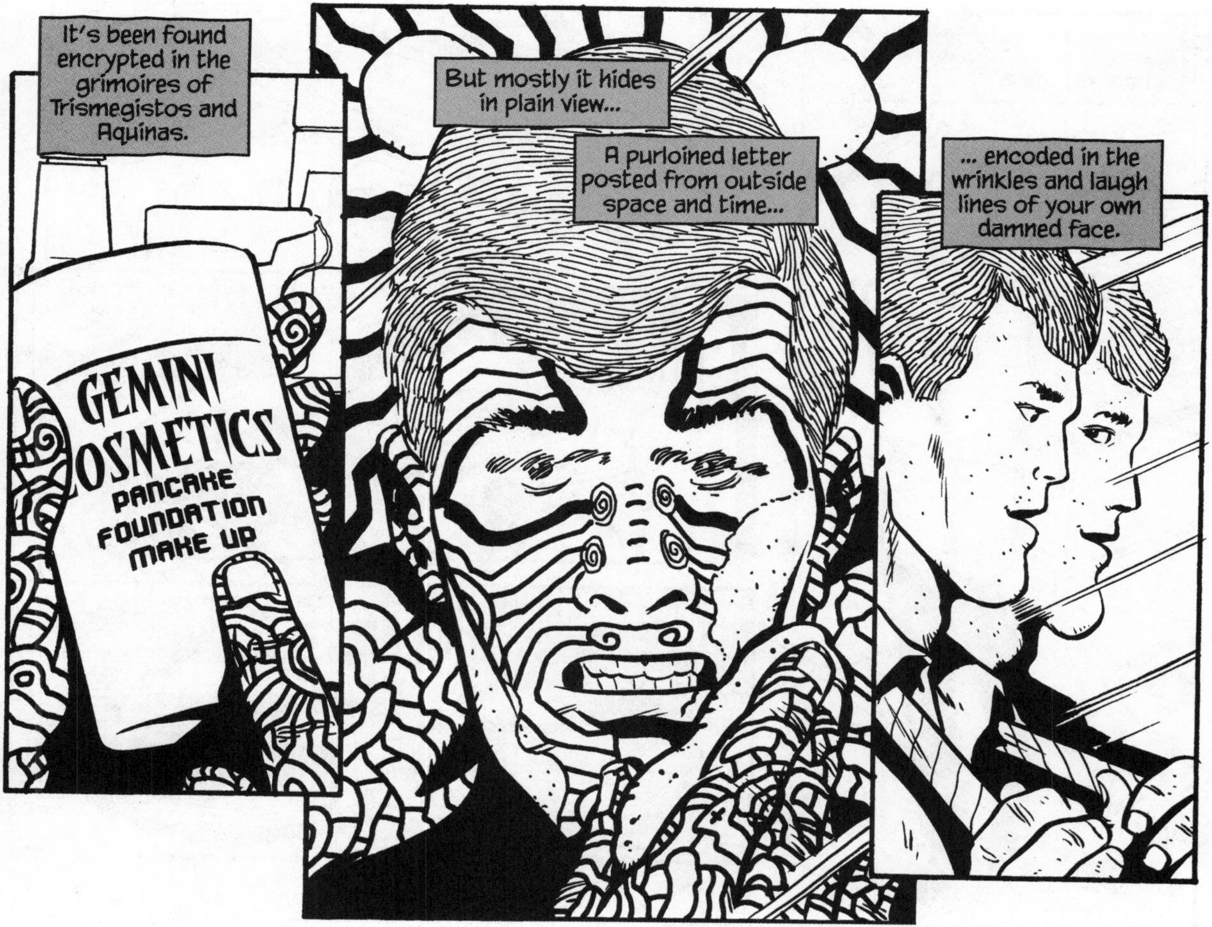
It's been found encrypted in the grimoires of Trismegistos and Aquinas.
GEMINI COSMETICS
PANCAKE FOUNDATION MAKE UP
But mostly it hides in plain view...
A purloined letter posted from outside space and time...
... encoded in the wrinkles and laugh lines of your own damned face.

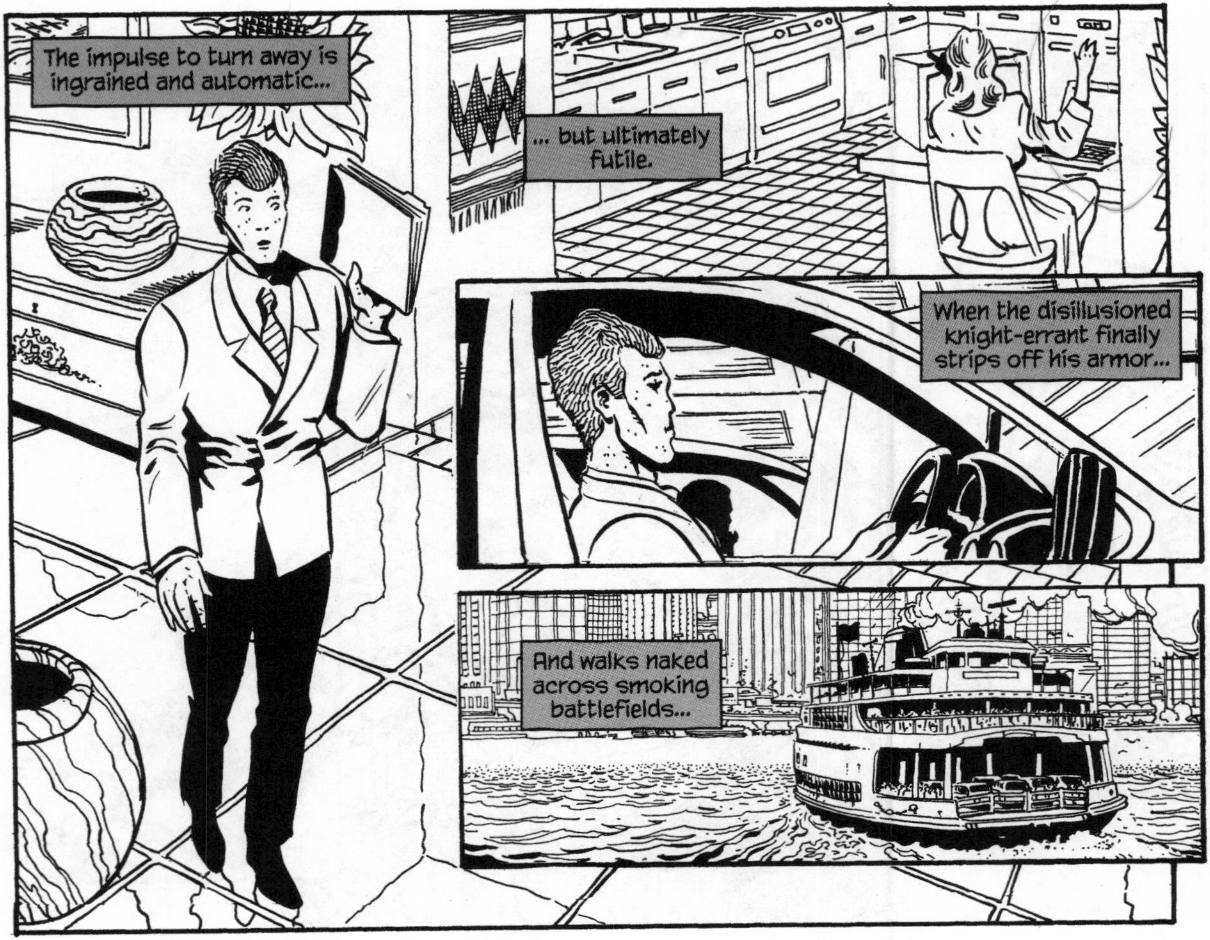
The impulse to turn away is ingrained and automatic...
... but ultimately futile.
When the disillusioned knight-errant finally strips off his armor...
And walks naked across smoking battlefields...

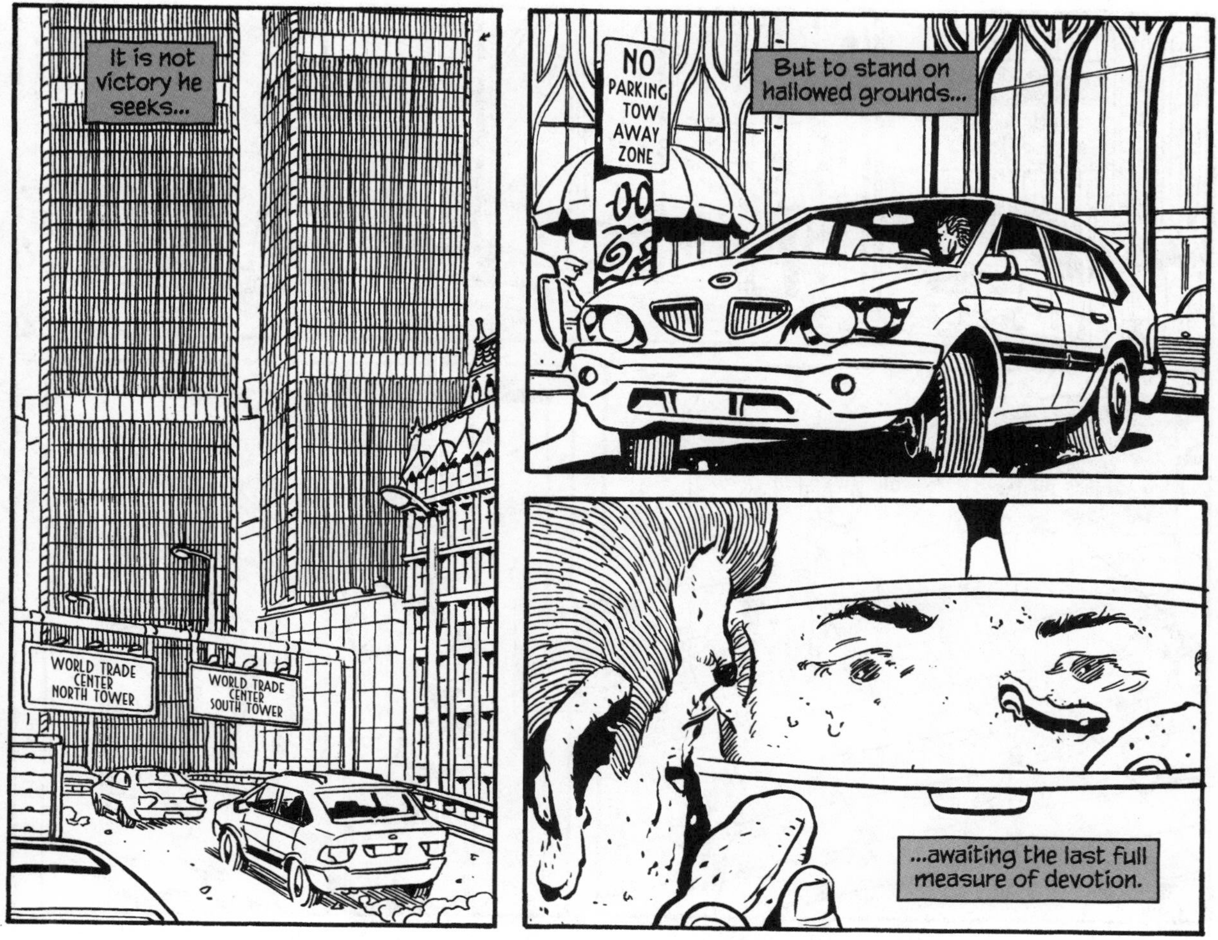
It is not victory he seeks...
WORLD TRADE CENTER NORTH TOWER
WORLD TRADE CENTER SOUTH TOWER
NO PARKING TOW AWAY ZONE
But to stand on hallowed grounds...
...awaiting the last full measure of devotion.

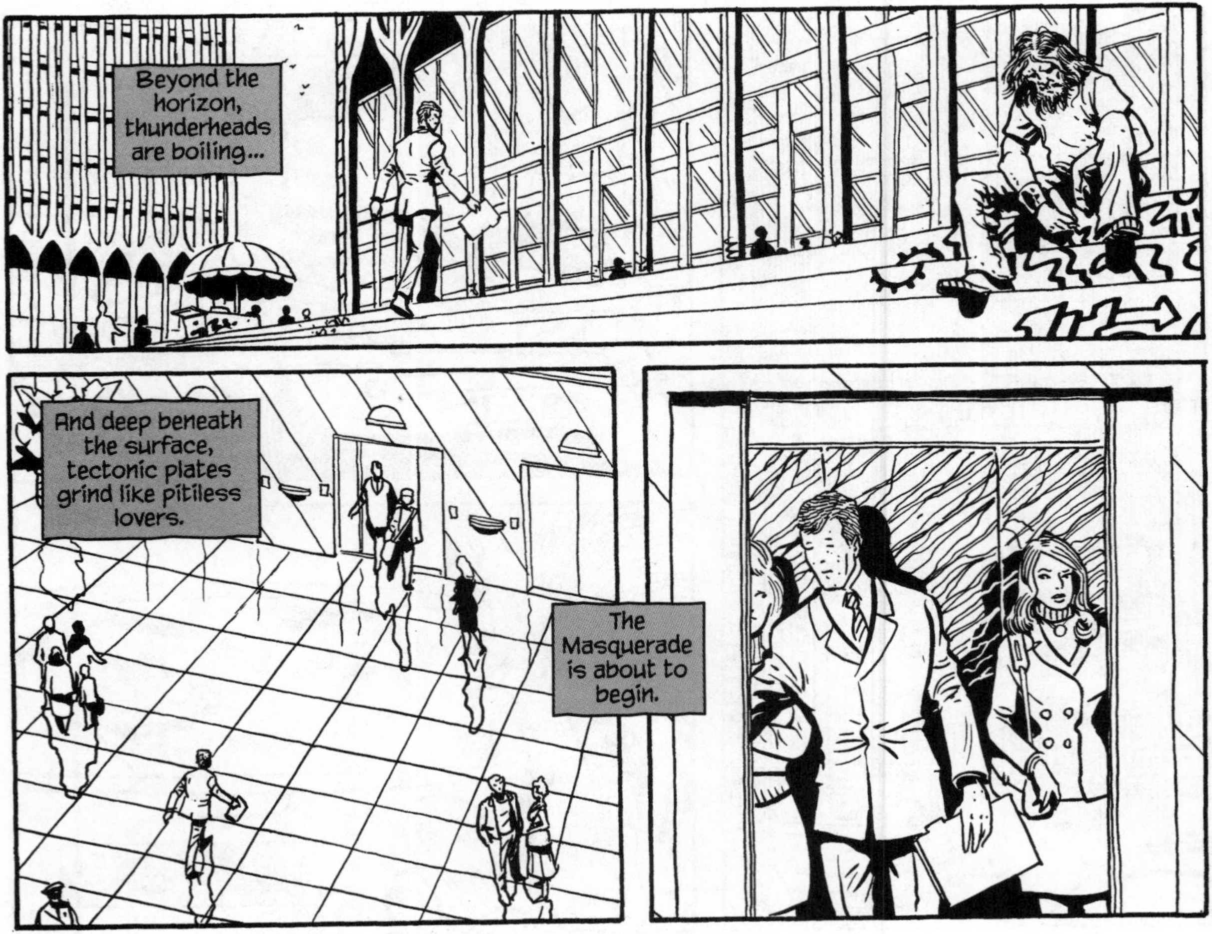
Beyond the horizon, thunderheads are boiling...
And deep beneath the surface, tectonic plates grind like pitiless lovers.
The Masquerade is about to begin.

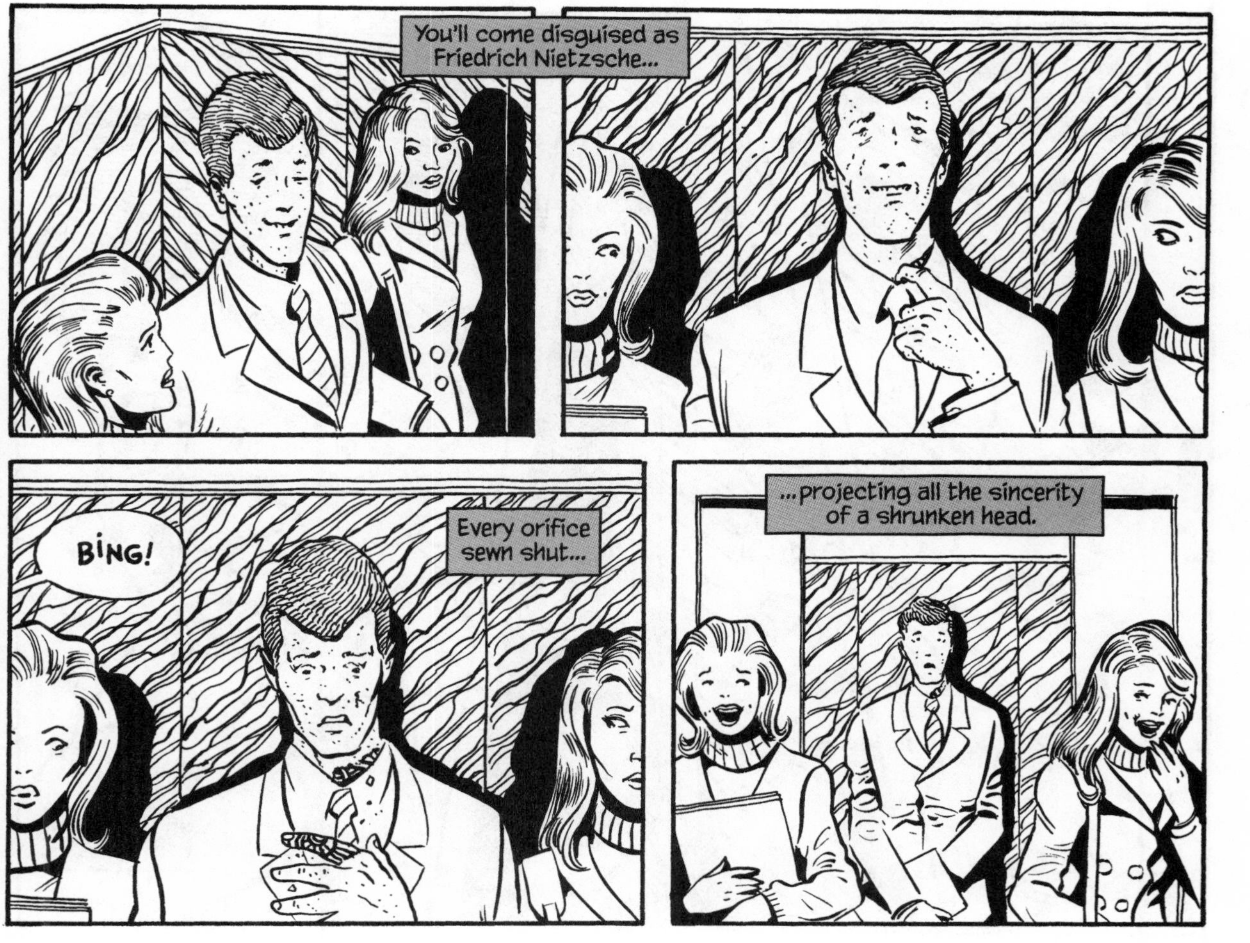
You'll come disguised as Friedrich Nietzsche...
BING!
Every orifice sewn shut...
...projecting all the sincerity of a shrunken head.

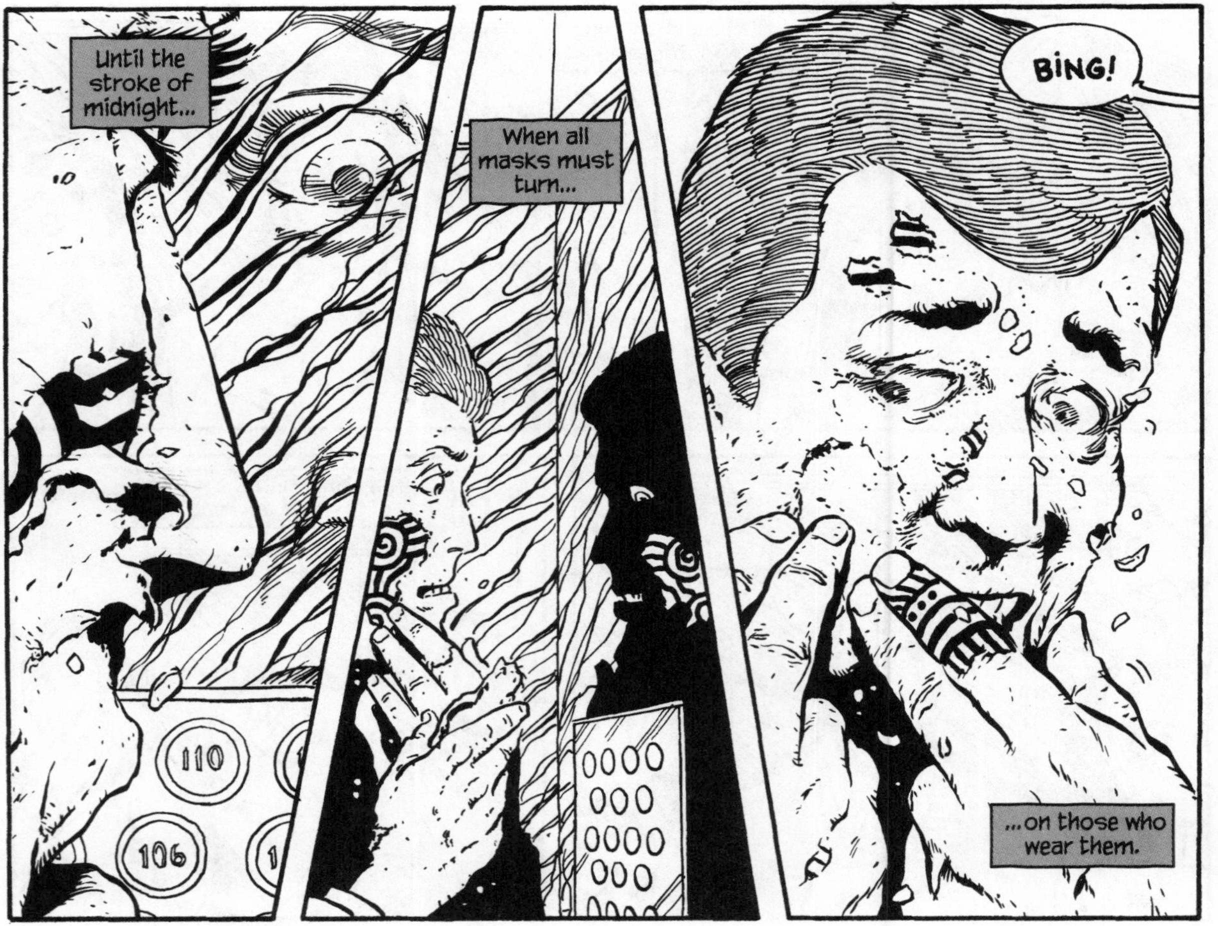
Until the stroke of midnight...
When all masks must turn...
BING!
...on those who wear them.

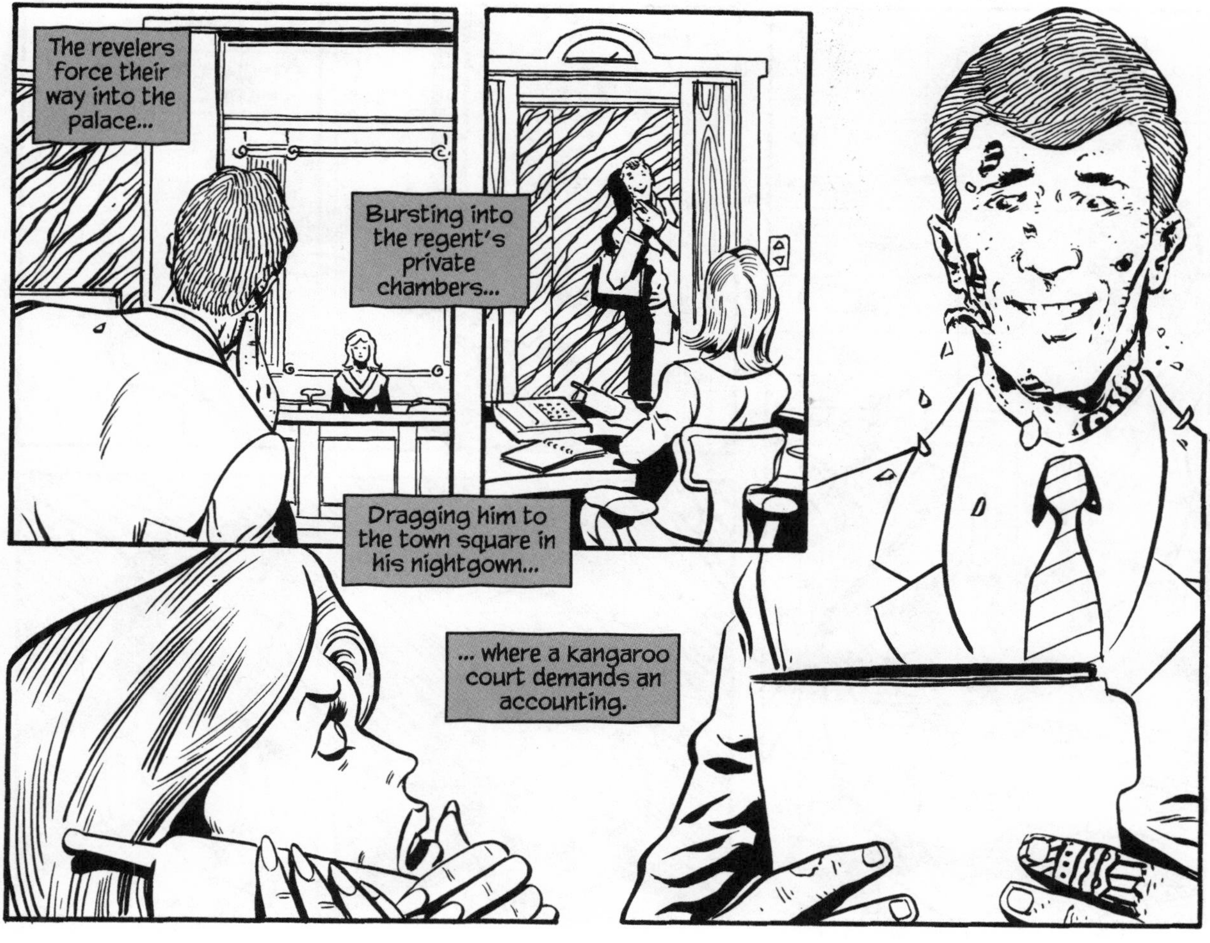
The revelers force their way into the palace...
Bursting into the regent's private chambers...
Dragging him to the town square in his nightgown...
... where a kangaroo court demands an accounting.

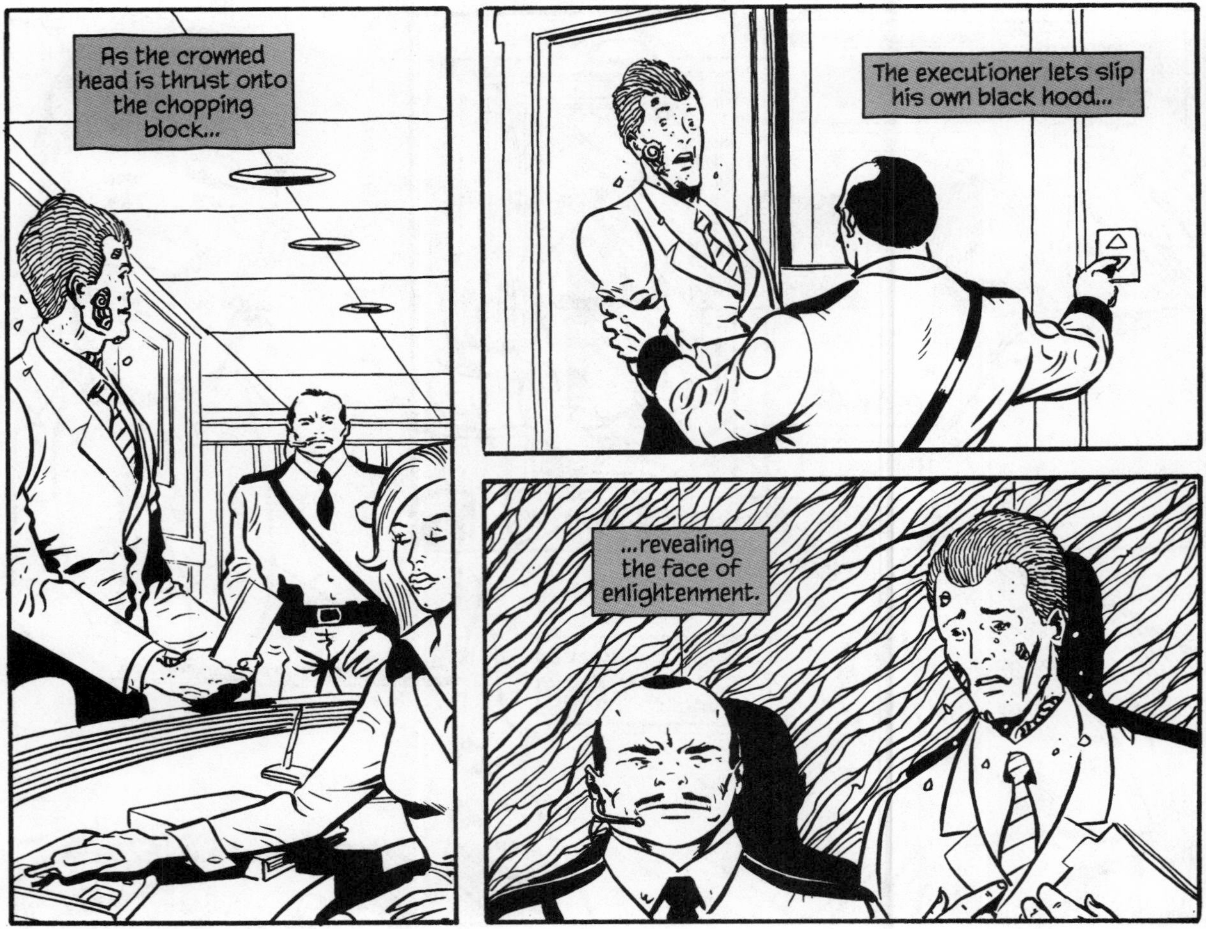
As the crowned head is thrust onto the chopping block...
The executioner lets slip his own black hood...
...revealing the face of enlightenment.

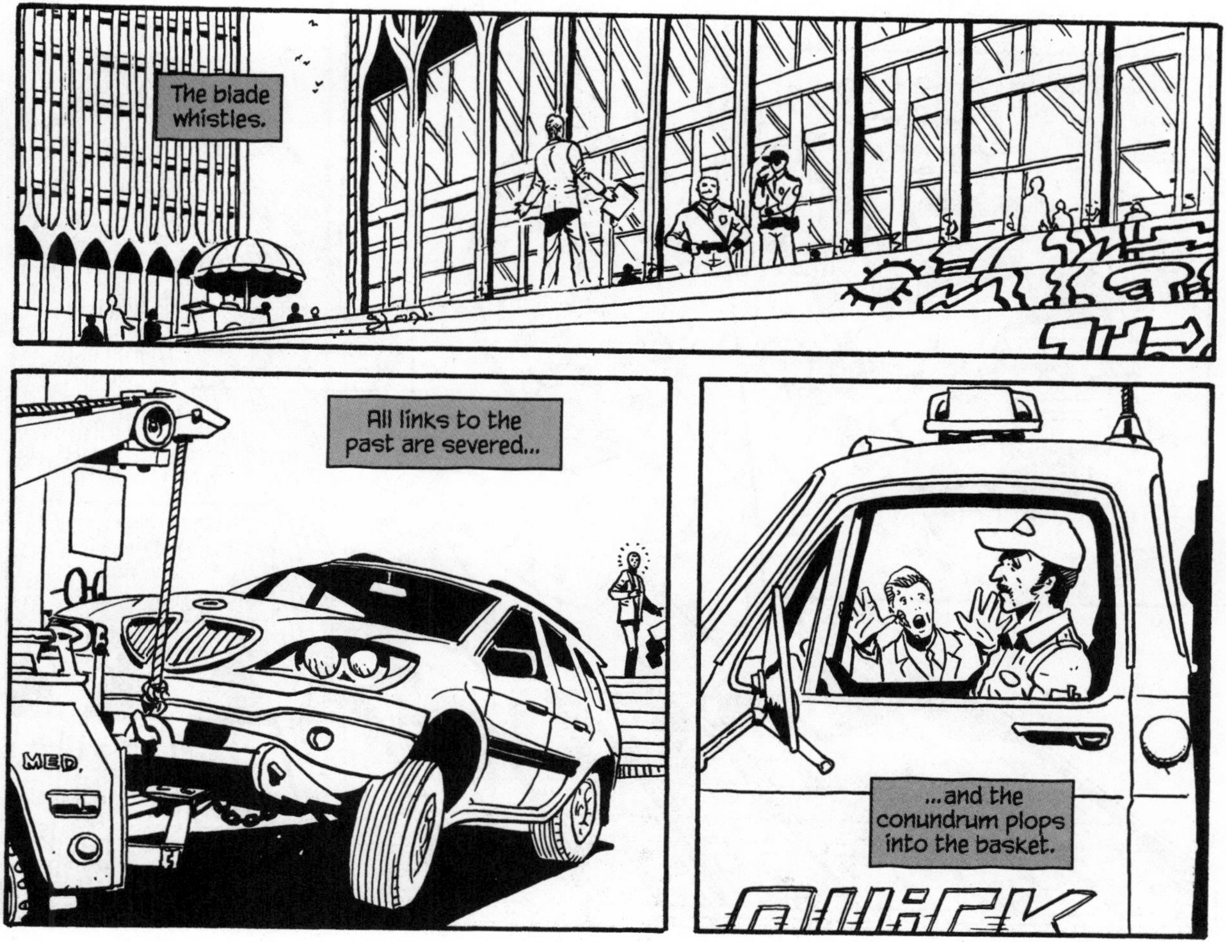
The blade whistles.
All links to the past are severed...
...and the conundrum plops into the basket.

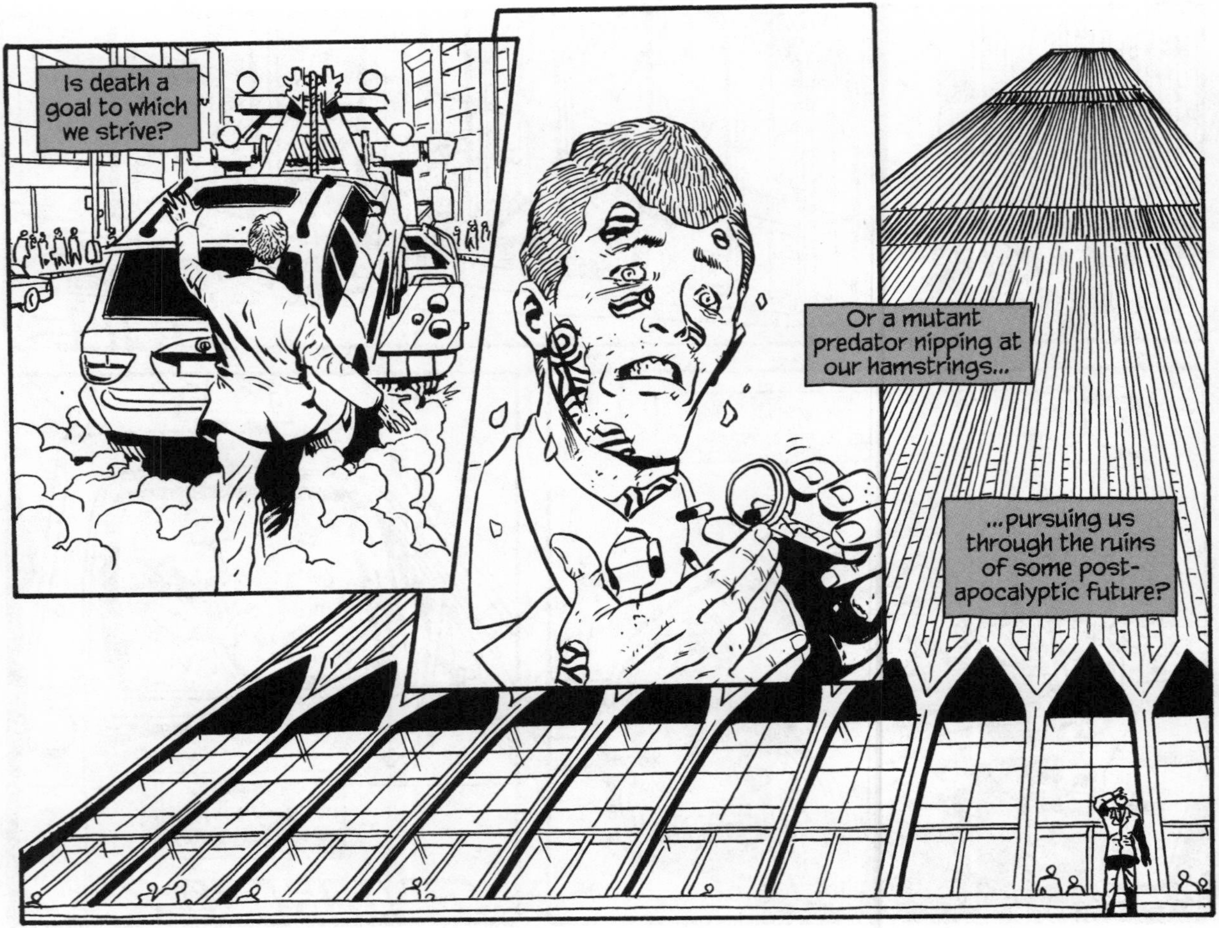
Is death a goal to which we strive?
Or a mutant predator nipping at our hamstrings...
...pursuing us through the ruins of some post-apocalyptic future?

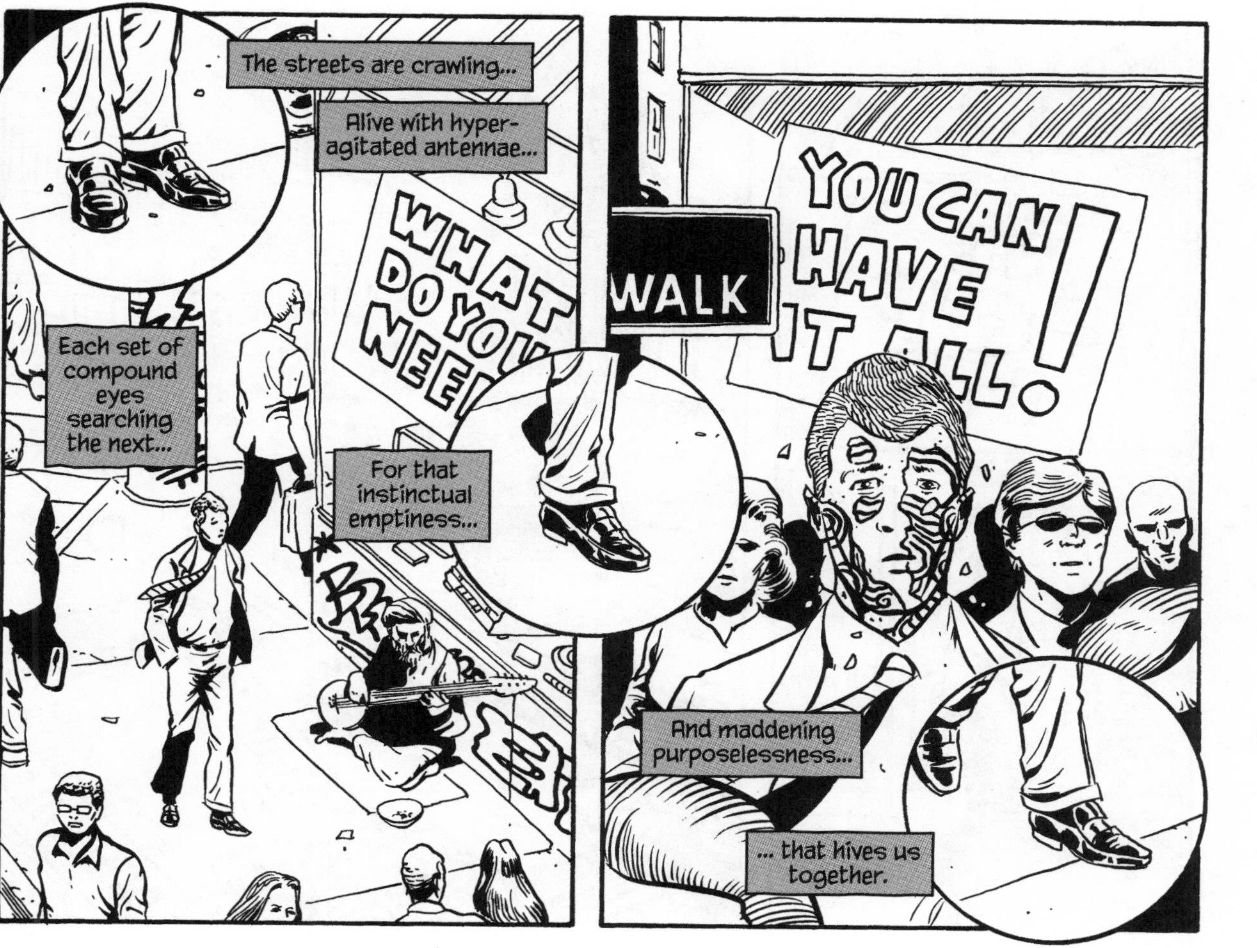
The streets are crawling...
Alive with hyper-agitated antennae...
Each set of compound eyes searching the next...
WHAT DO YOU NEE
For that instinctual emptiness...
WALK
YOU CAN HAVE IT ALL!
And maddening purposelessness...
... that hives us together.

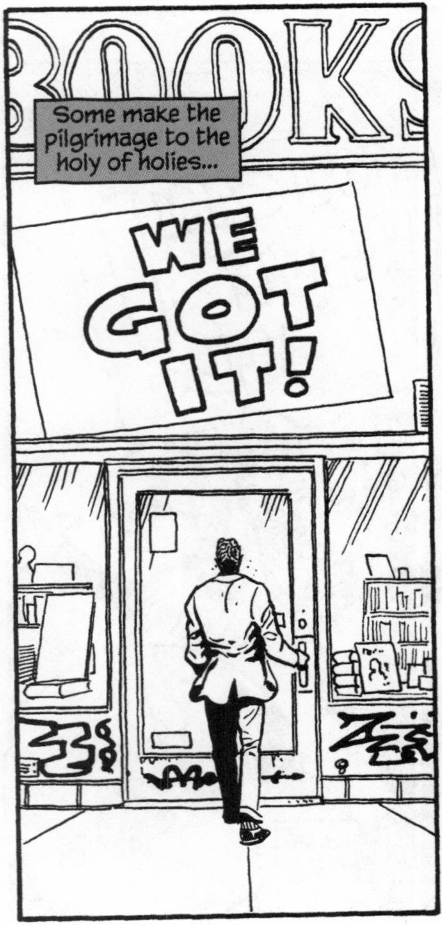
BOOKS
Some make the pilgrimage to the holy of holies...
WE GOT IT!

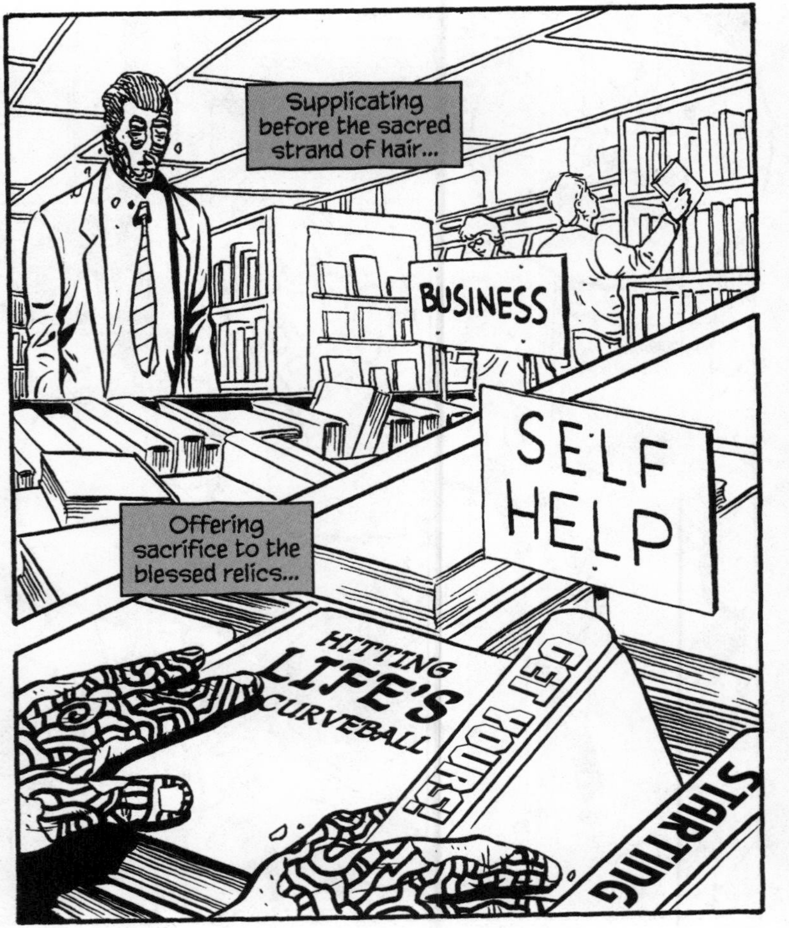
Supplicating before the sacred strand of hair...
BUSINESS
SELF HELP
Offering sacrifice to the blessed relics...
HITTING LIFE'S CURVEBALL
GET YOURS!
STARTING

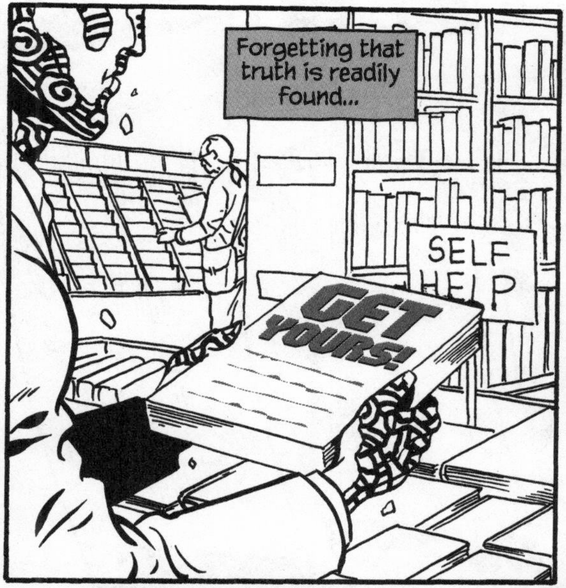
Forgetting that truth is readily found...
SELF HELP
GET YOURS!

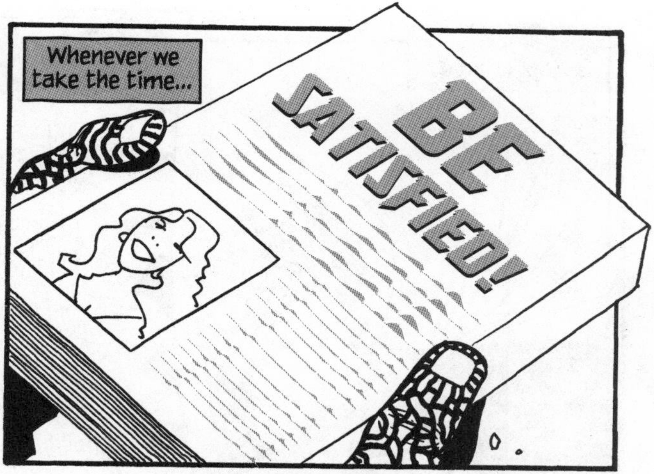
Whenever we take the time...
BE SATISFIED!

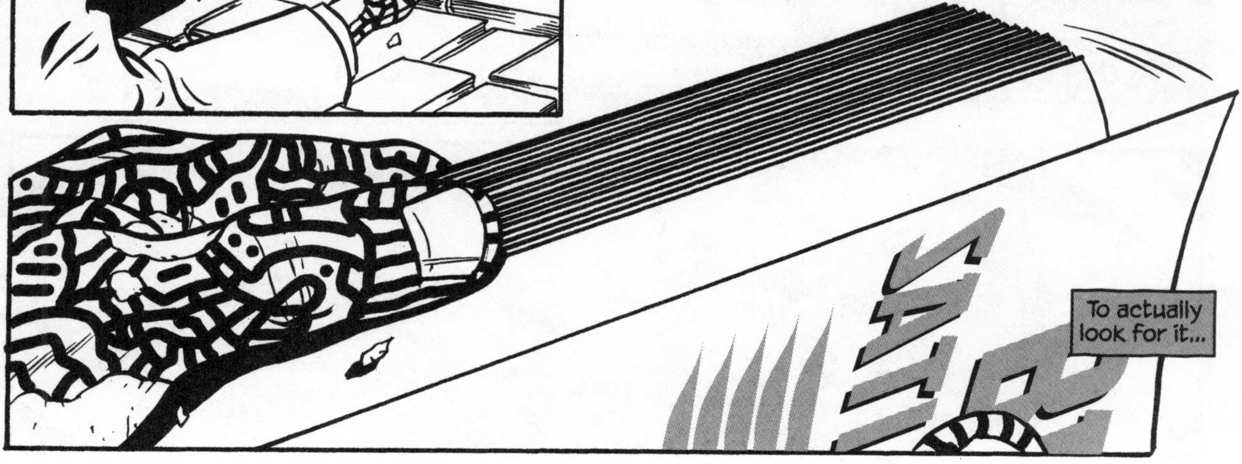
To actually look for it...

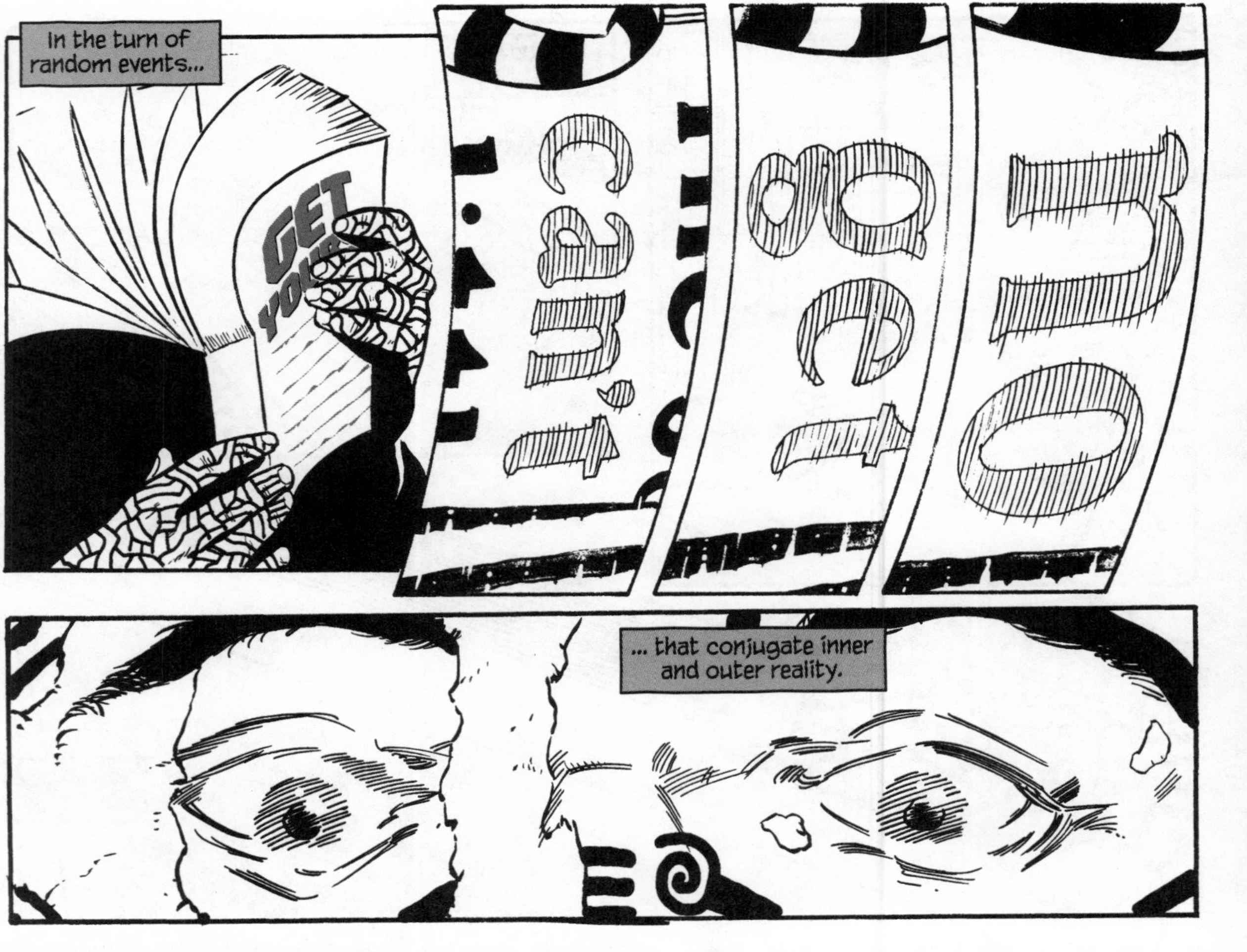
In the turn of random events...
GET YOU
... that conjugate inner and outer reality.

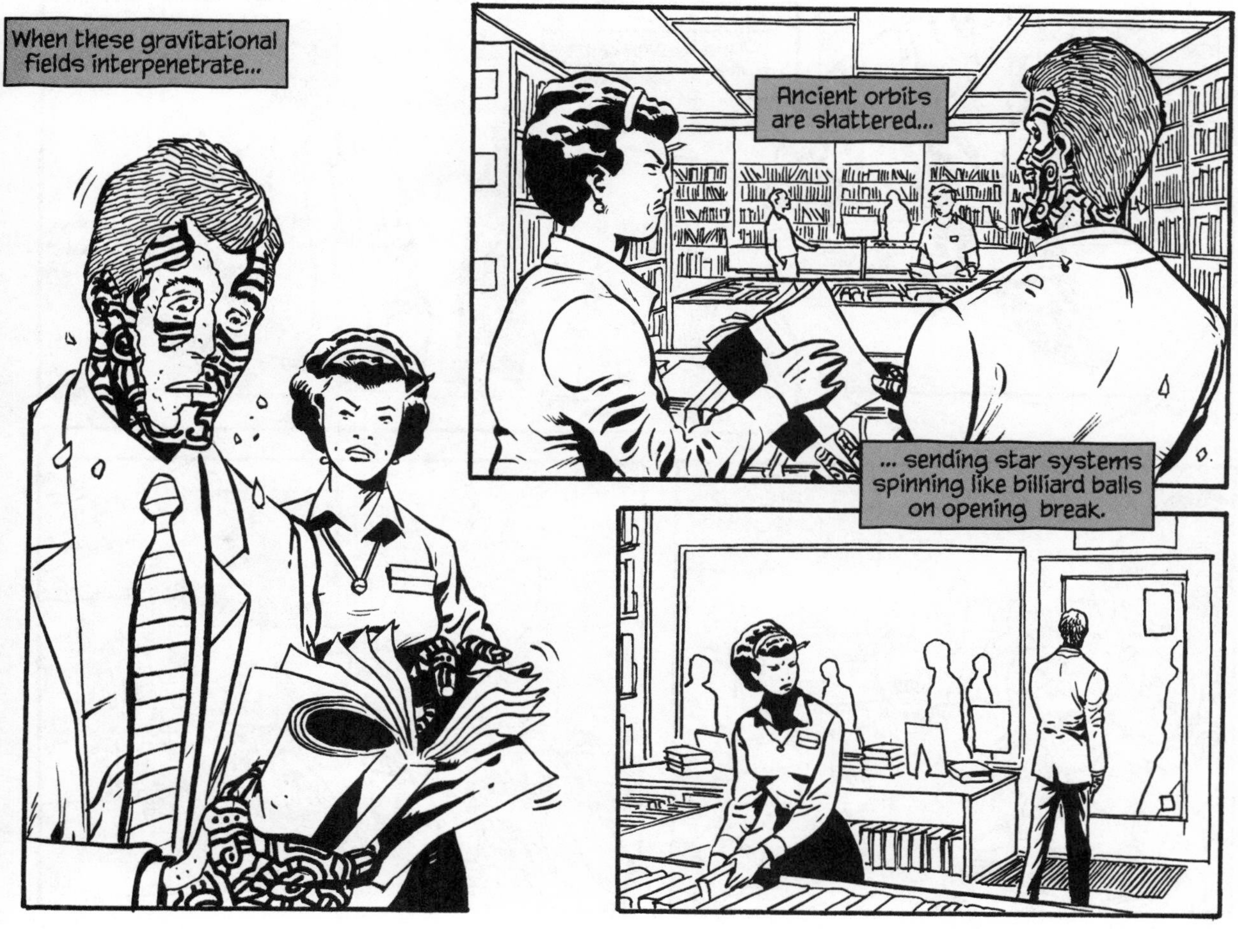

When these gravitational fields interpenetrate...
Ancient orbits are shattered...
... sending star systems spinning like billiard balls on opening break.

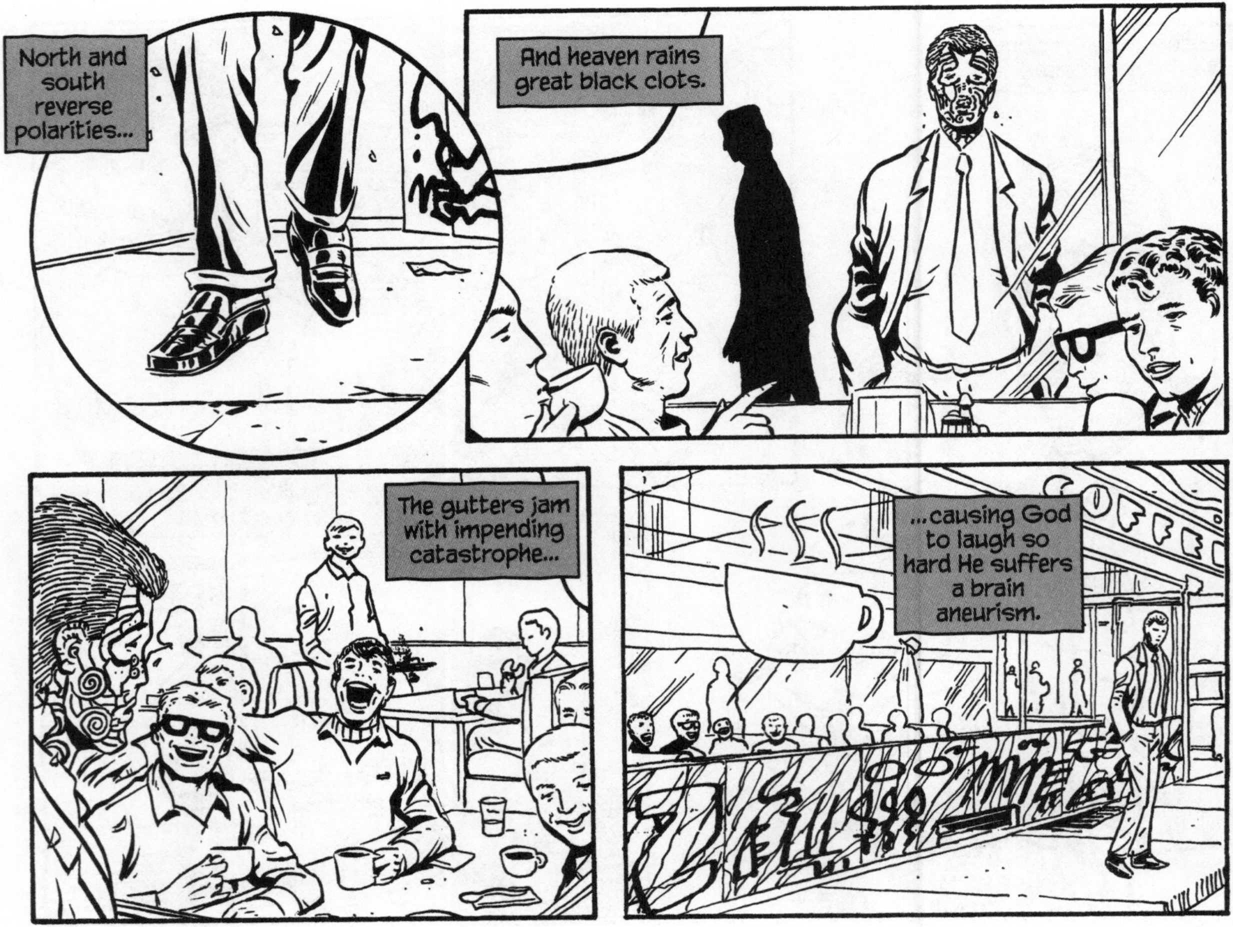
North and south reverse polarities...
And heaven rains great black clots.
The gutters jam with impending catastrophe...
...causing God to laugh so hard He suffers a brain aneurism.

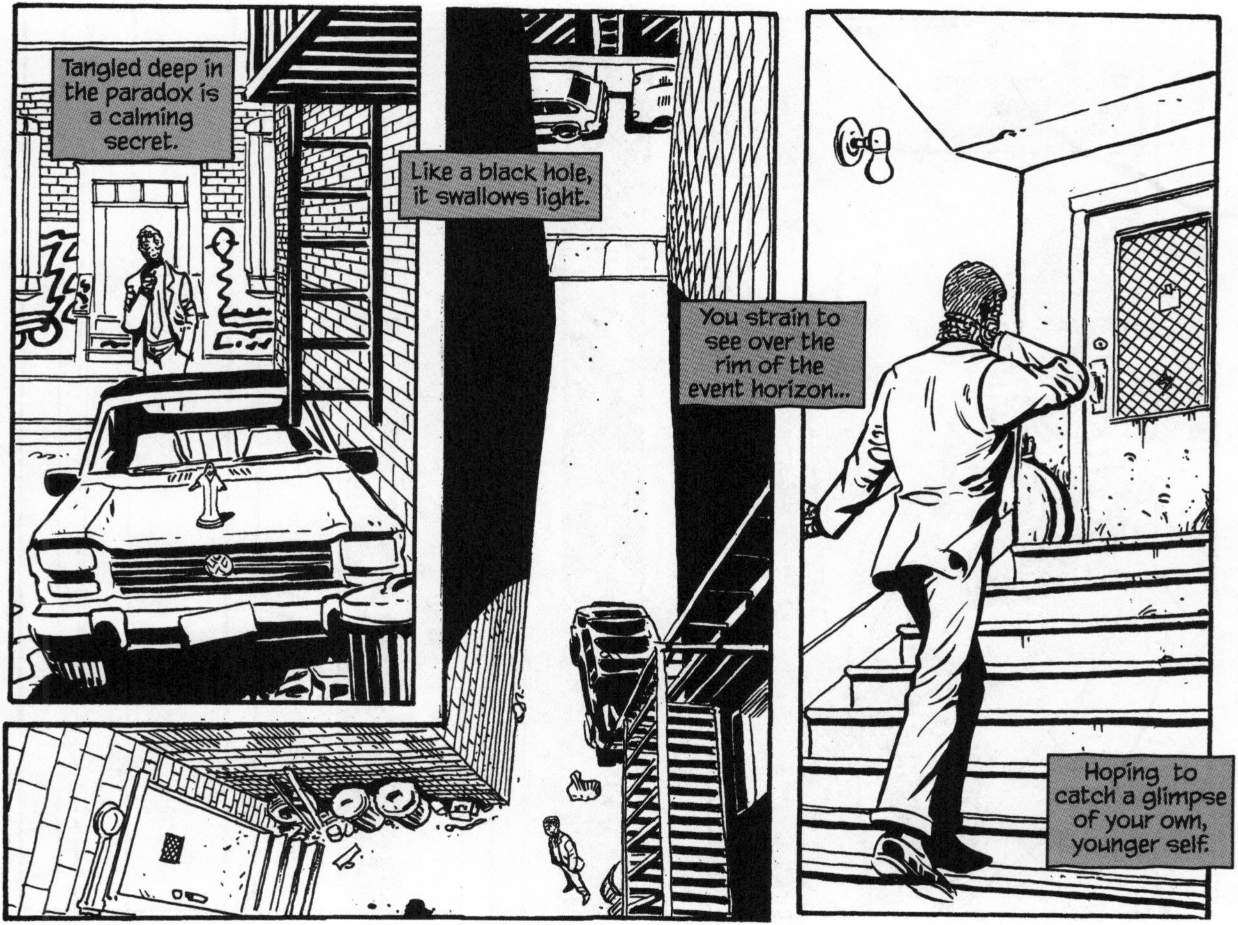
Tangled deep in the paradox is a calming secret.
Like a black hole, it swallows light.
You strain to see over the rim of the event horizon...
Hoping to catch a glimpse of your own, younger self.

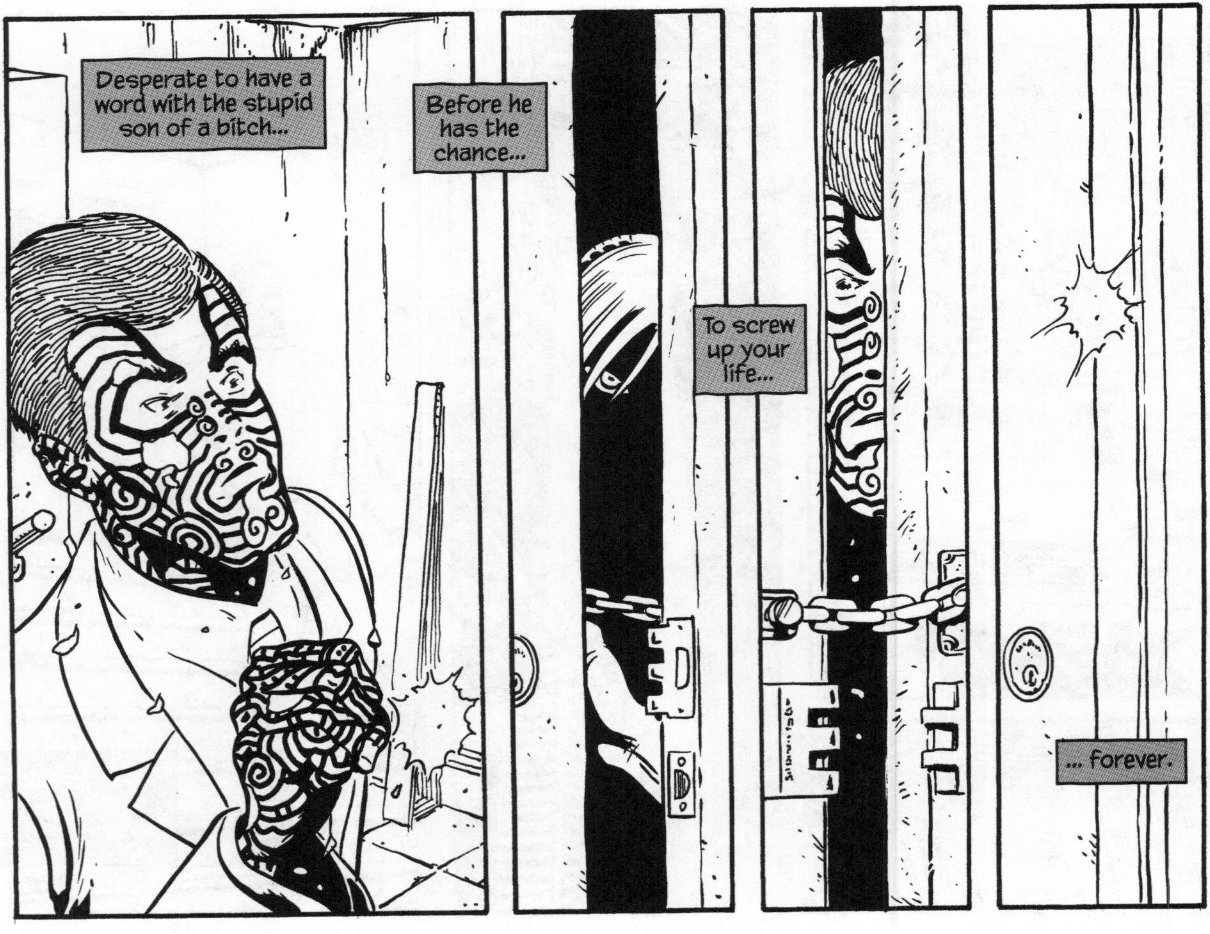
Desperate to have a word with the stupid son of a bitch...
Before he has the chance...
To screw up your life...
... forever.

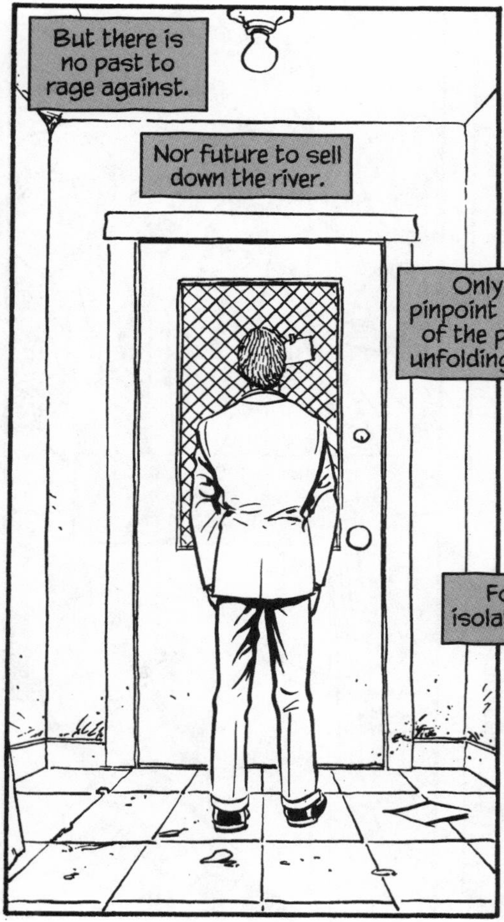
But there is no past to rage against.
Nor future to sell down the river.
Only the pinpoint present of the perfect unfolding divine.

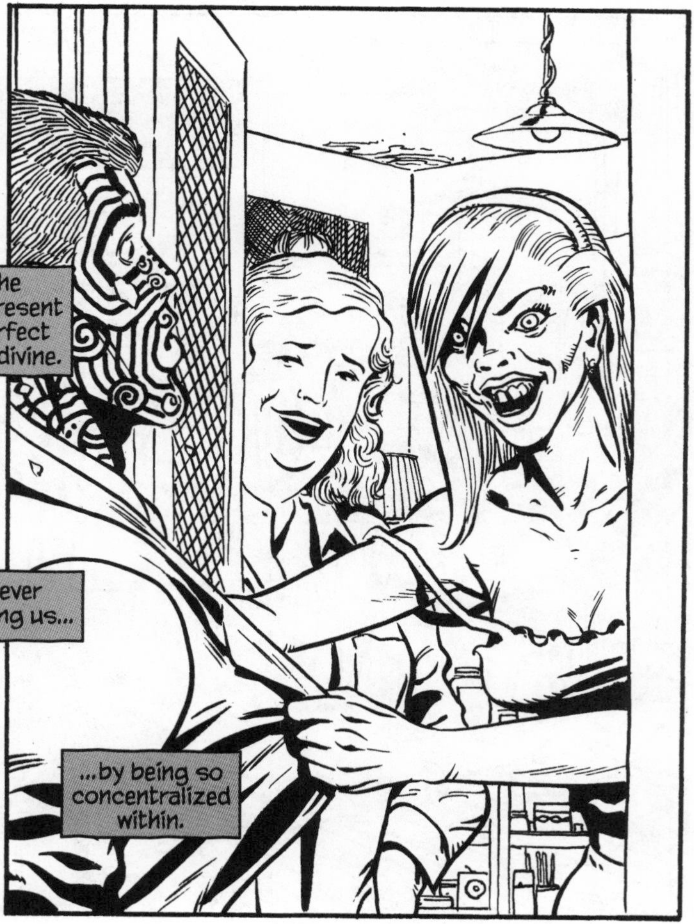
Forever isolating us...
...by being so concentralized within.

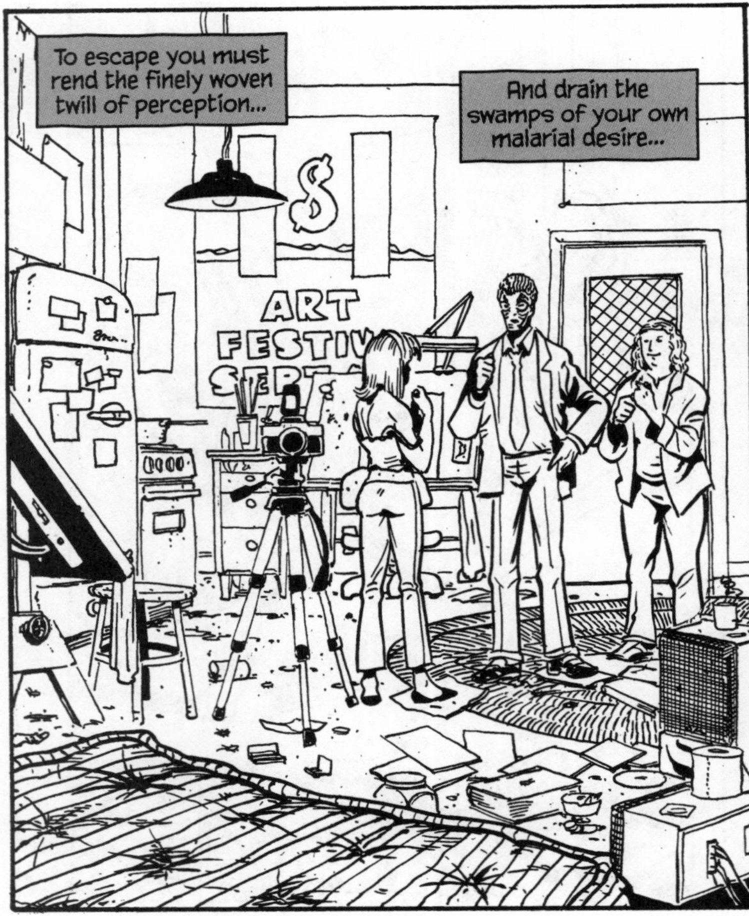
To escape you must rend the finely woven twill of perception...
And drain the swamps of your own malarial desire...
ART

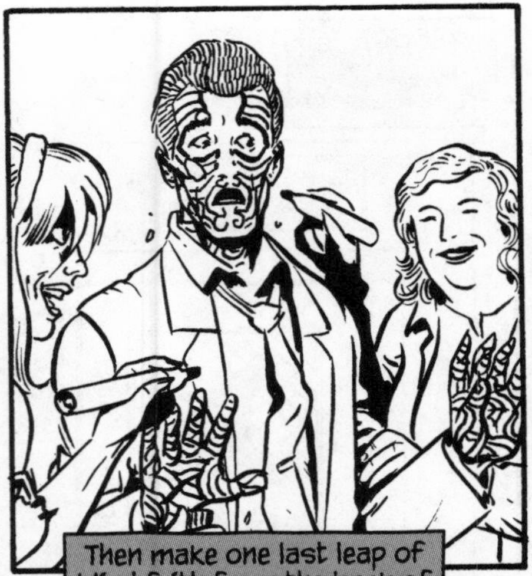

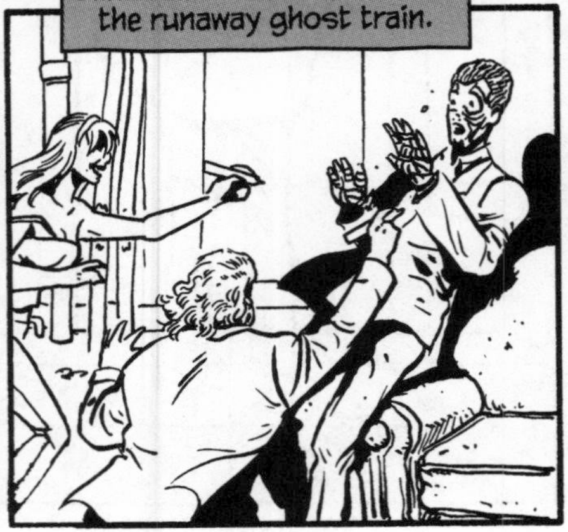
Then make one last leap of blind faith from the back of the runaway ghost train.

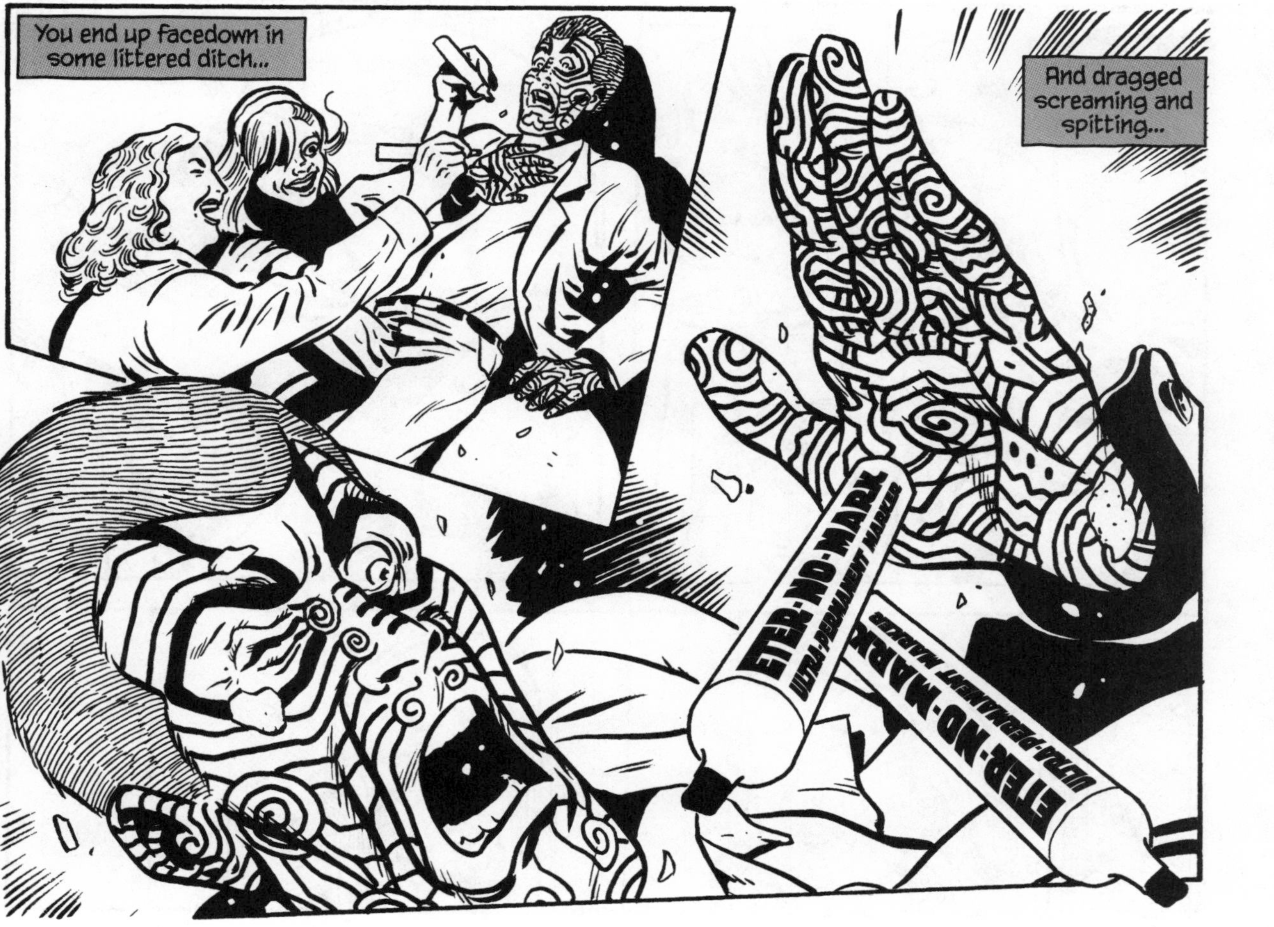
You end up facedown in some littered ditch...
And dragged screaming and spitting...
ETER-NO-MARK
ULTRA-PERMANENT MARKER
ETER-NO-MARK
ULTRA-PERMANENT MARKER

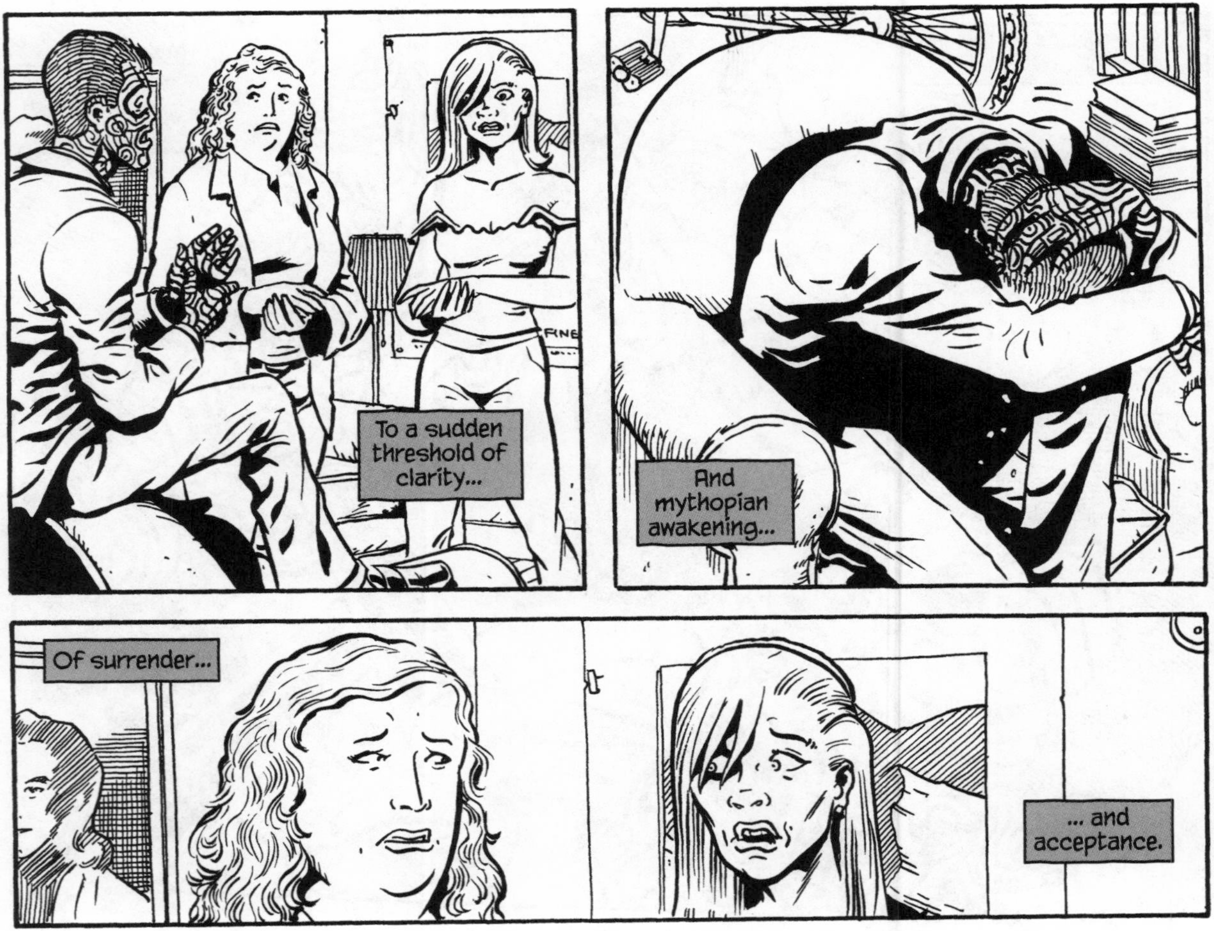
To a sudden threshold of clarity...
And mythopian awakening...
Of surrender...
... and acceptance.

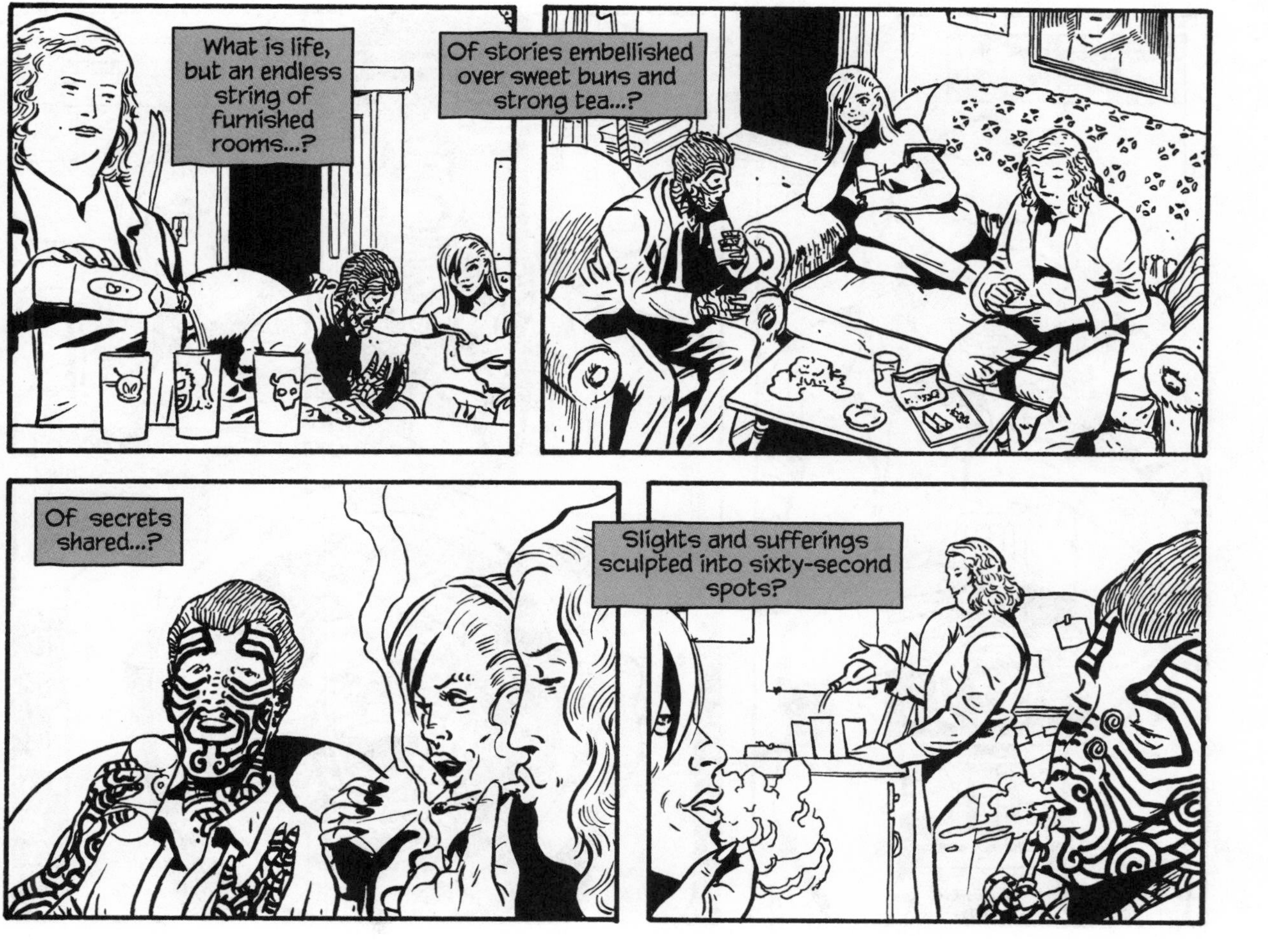
What is life, but an endless string of furnished rooms...?
Of stories embellished over sweet buns and strong tea...?
Of secrets shared...?
Slights and sufferings sculpted into sixty-second spots?

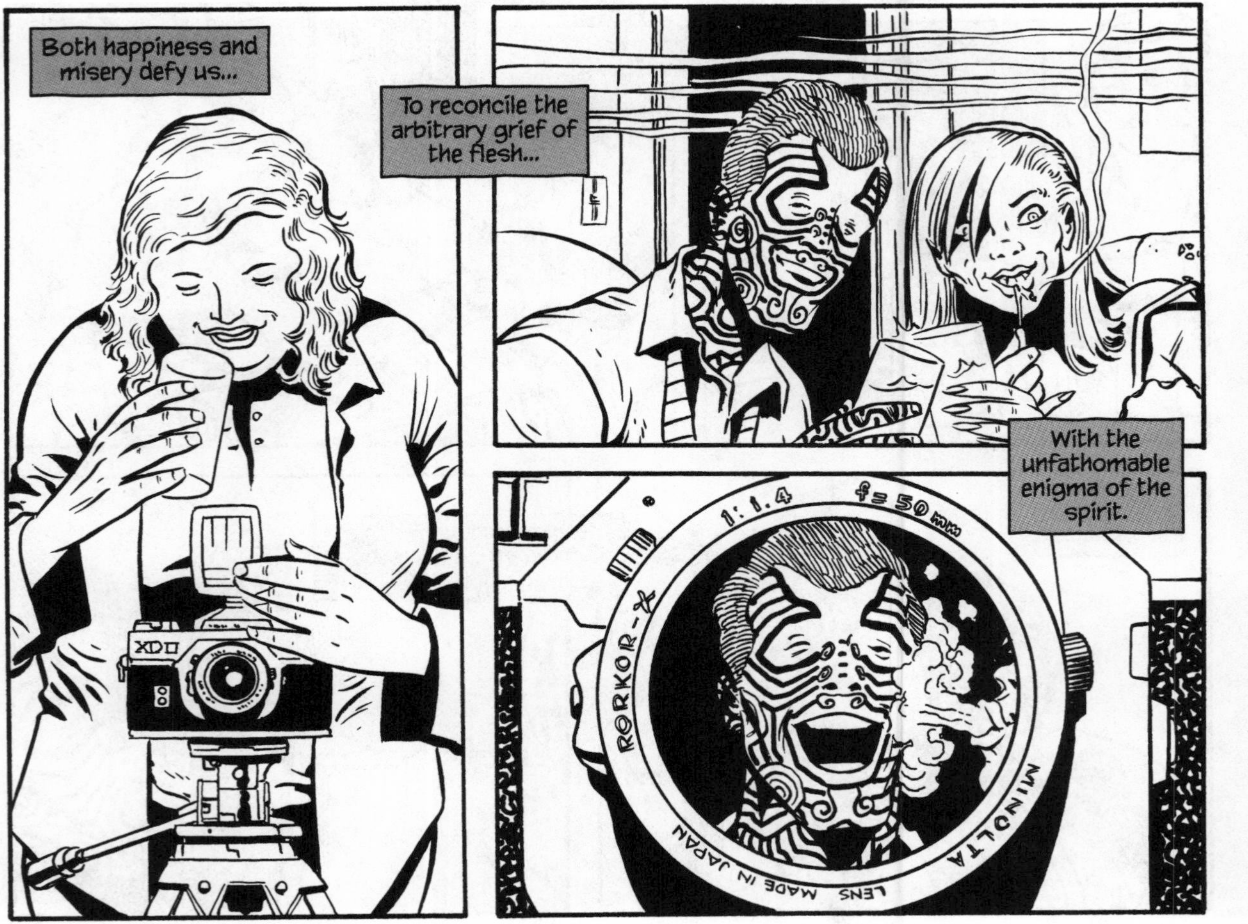
Both happiness and misery defy us...
To reconcile the arbitrary grief of the flesh...
With the unfathomable enigma of the spirit.
1:1.4 f=50mm
MINOLTA
LENS MADE IN JAPAN

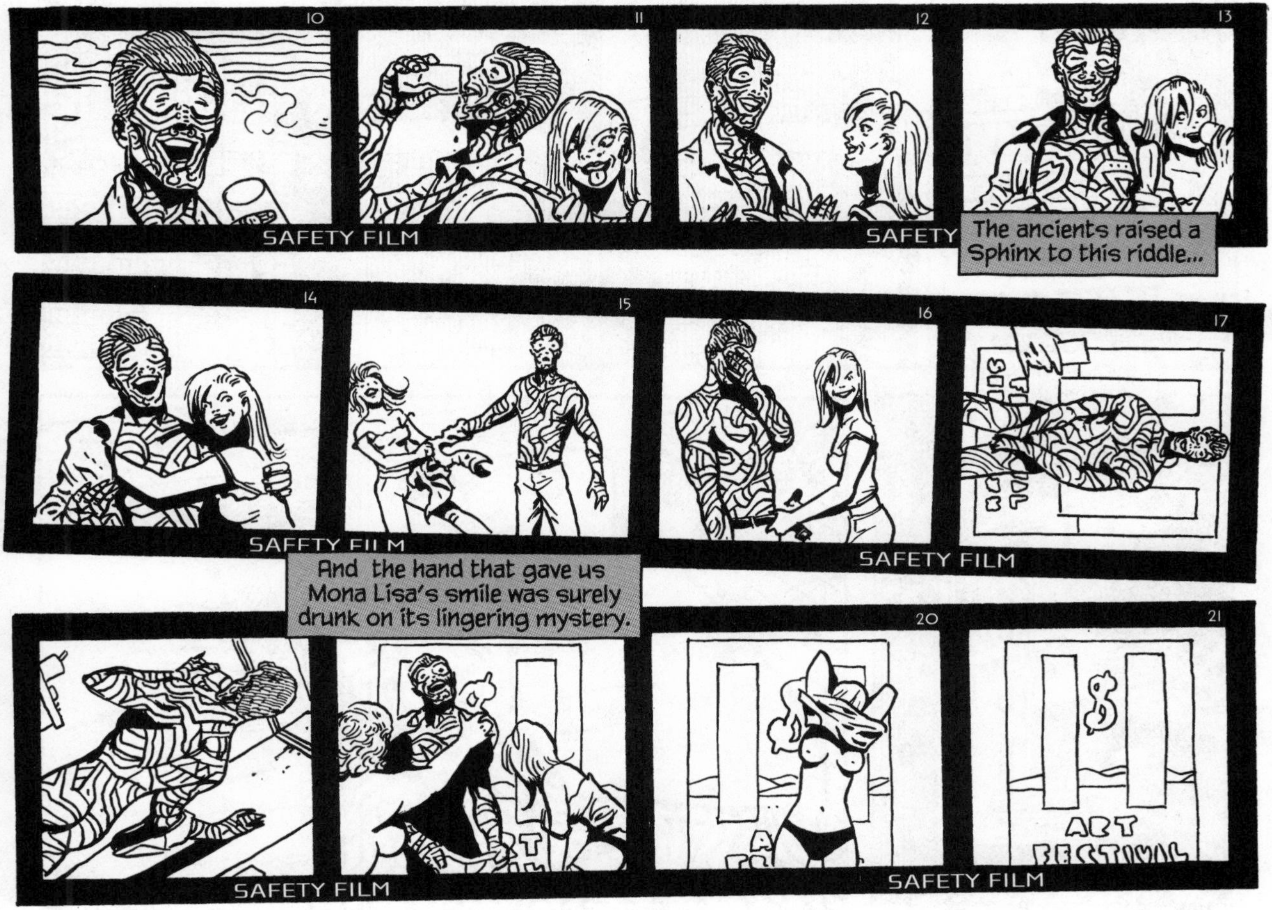
10
11
12
13
SAFETY FILM
SAFETY
The ancients raised a Sphinx to this riddle...
14
15
16
17
SAFETY FILM
SAFETY FILM
And the hand that gave us Mona Lisa's smile was surely drunk on its lingering mystery.
20
21
ART FESTIVAL
SAFETY FILM
SAFETY FILM

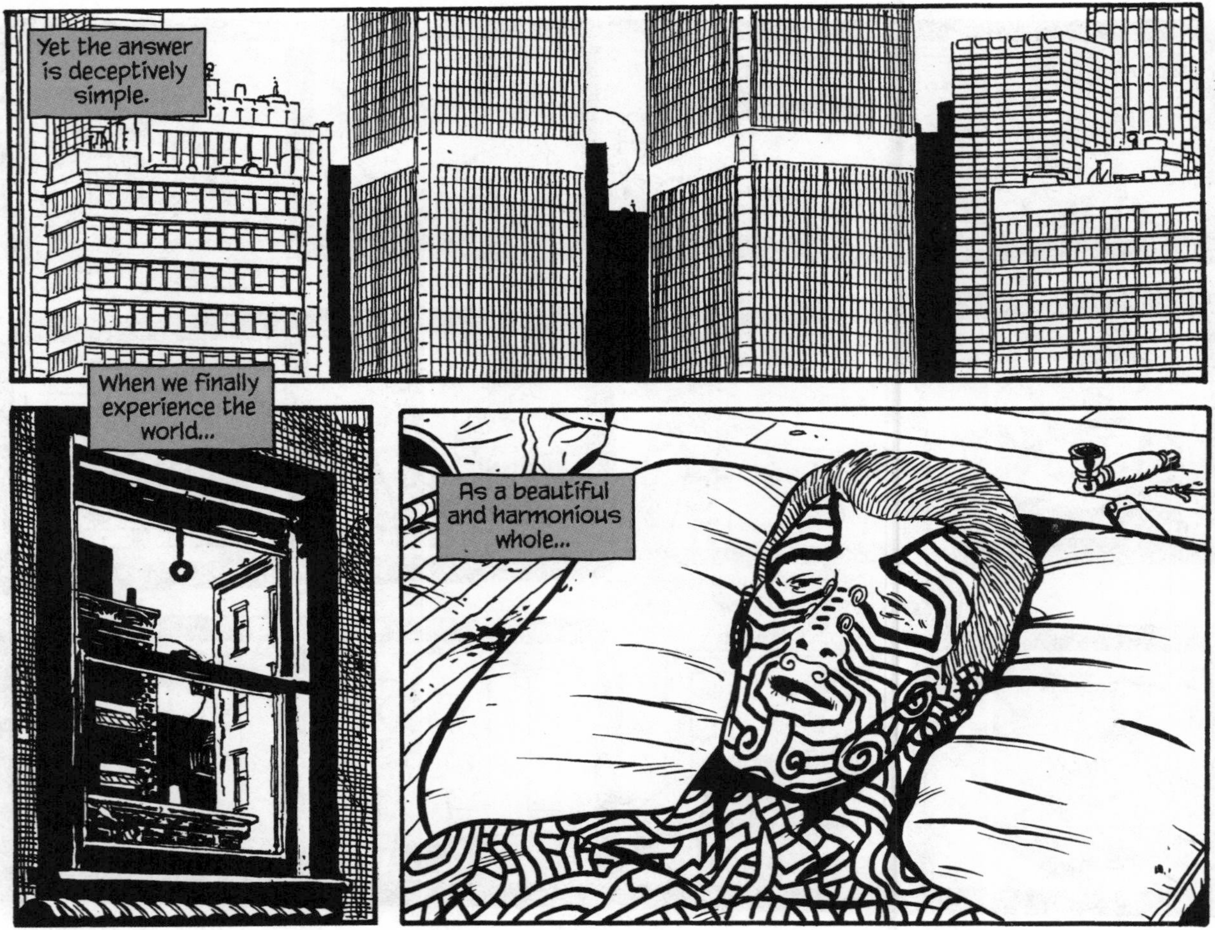
Yet the answer is deceptively simple.
When we finally experience the world...
As a beautiful and harmonious whole...

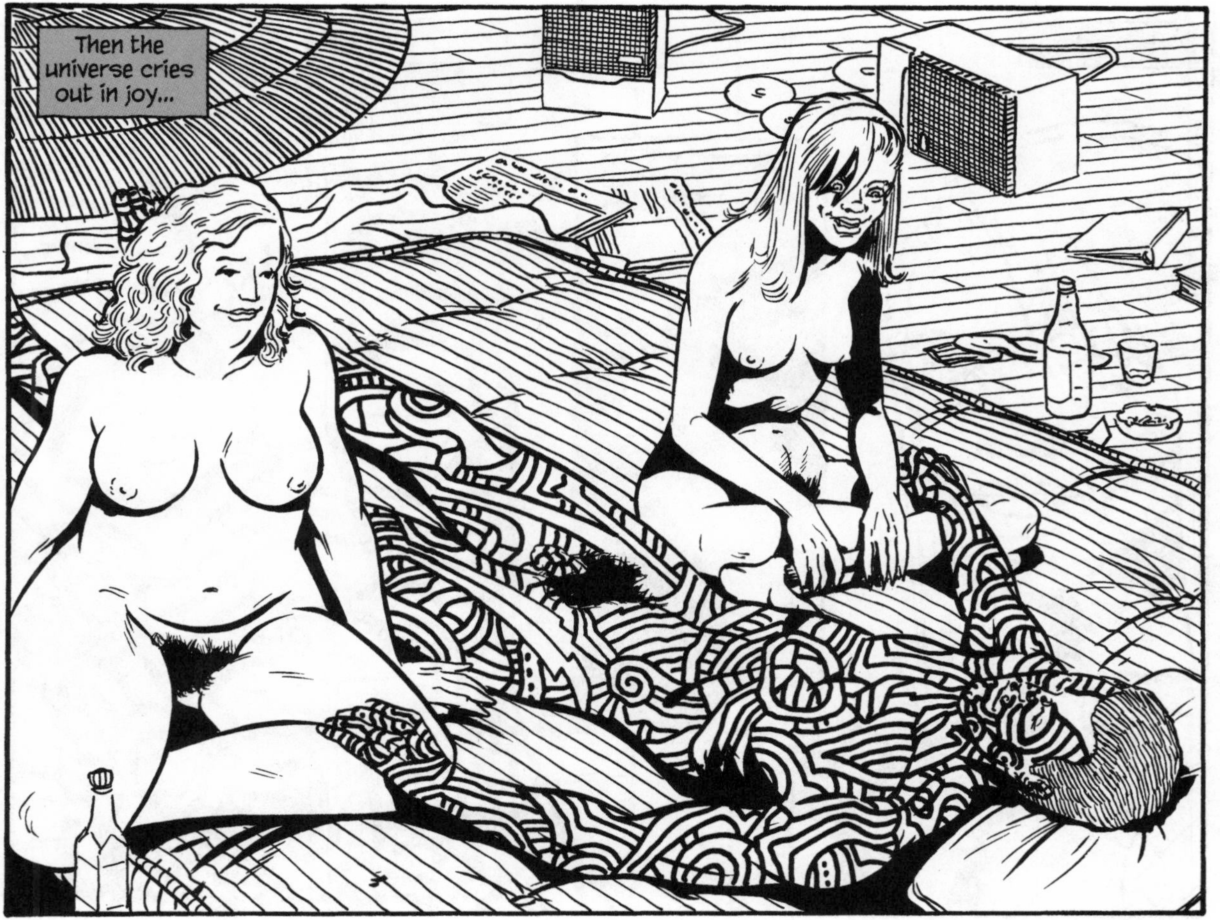
Then the universe cries out in joy...

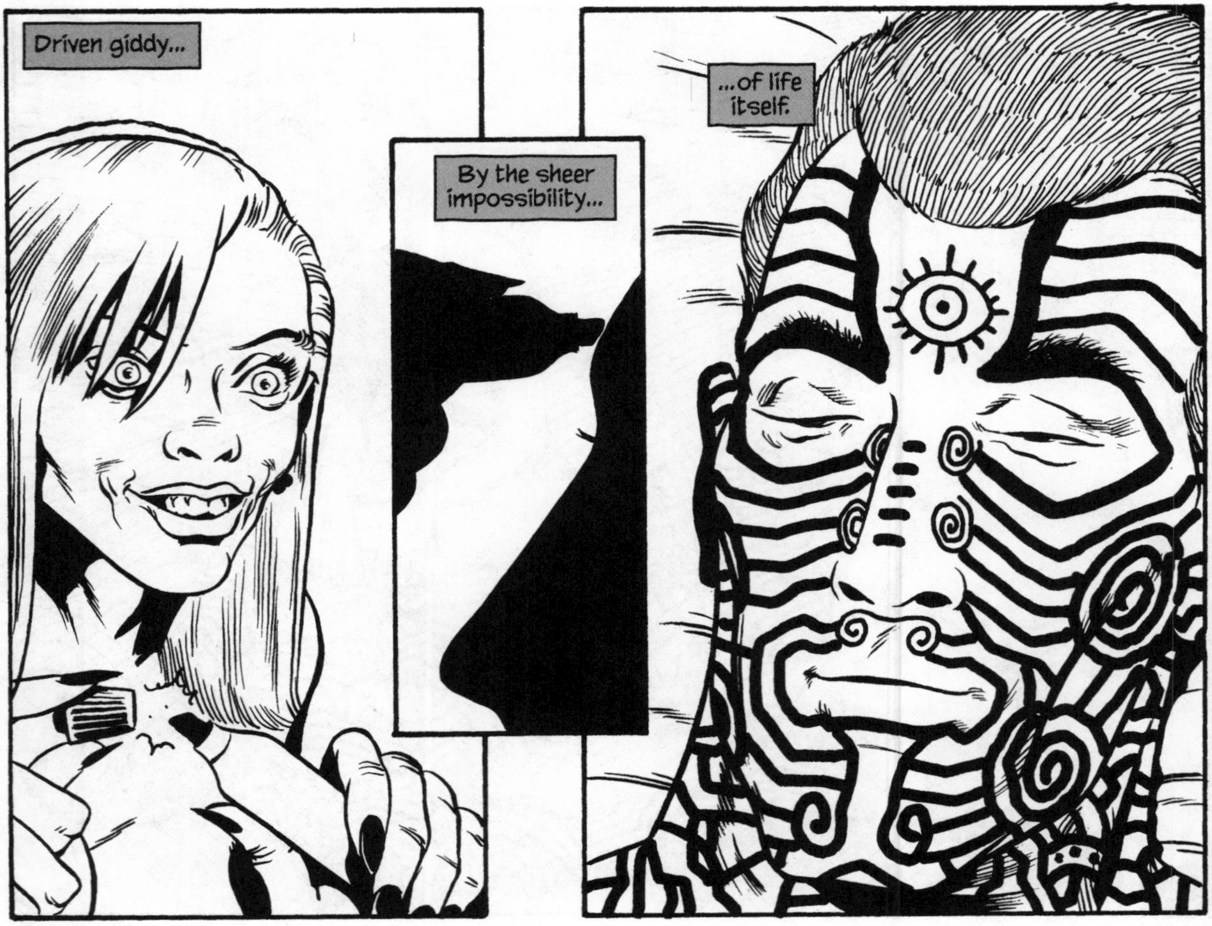
Driven giddy...
By the sheer impossibility...
...of life itself.

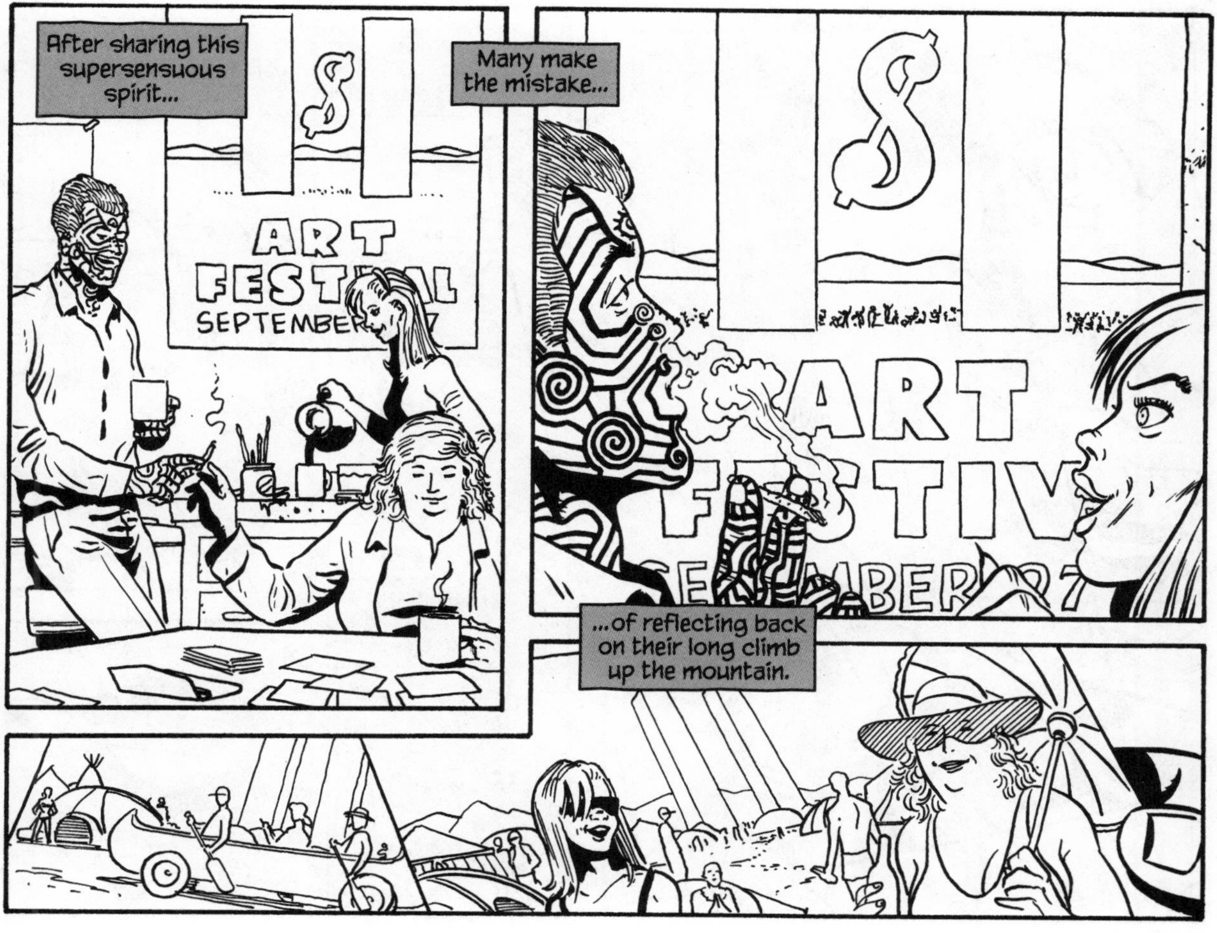
After sharing this supersensuous spirit...
ART FESTIVAL SEPTEMBER
Many make the mistake...
ART FESTIV
...of reflecting back on their long climb up the mountain.

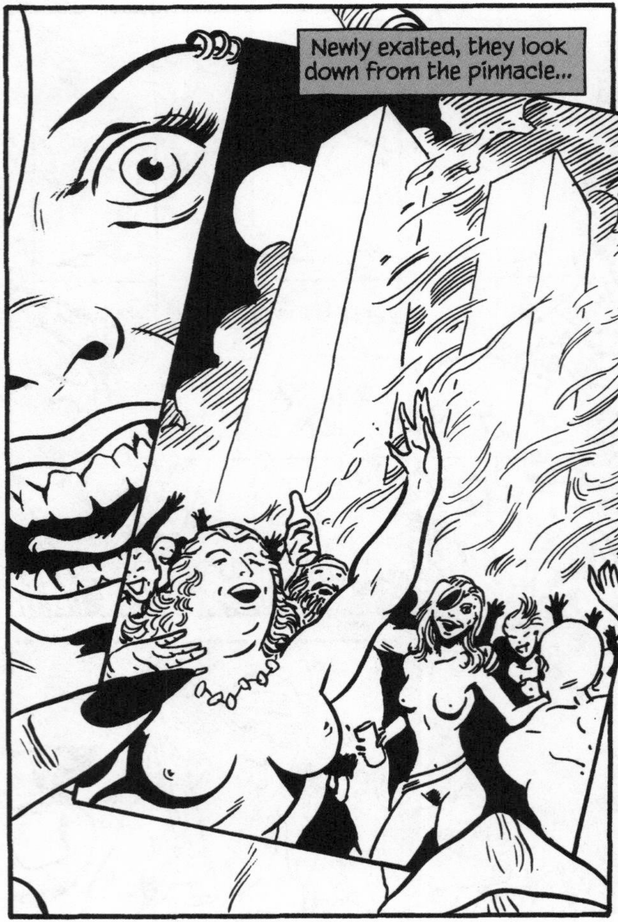
Newly exalted, they look down from the pinnacle...

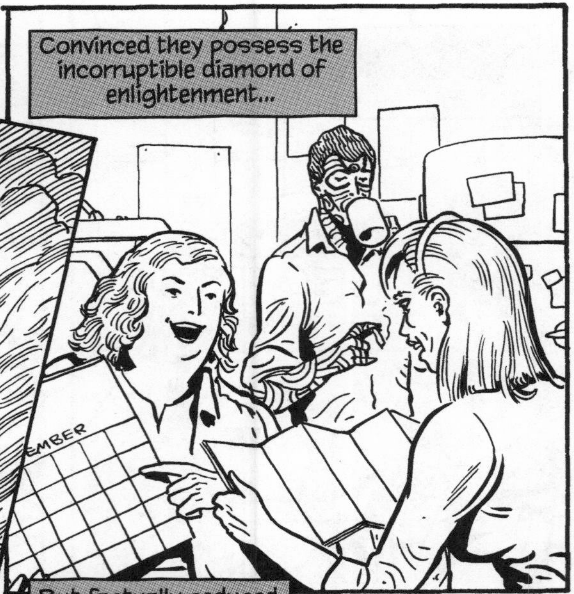
Convinced they possess the incorruptible diamond of enlightenment...

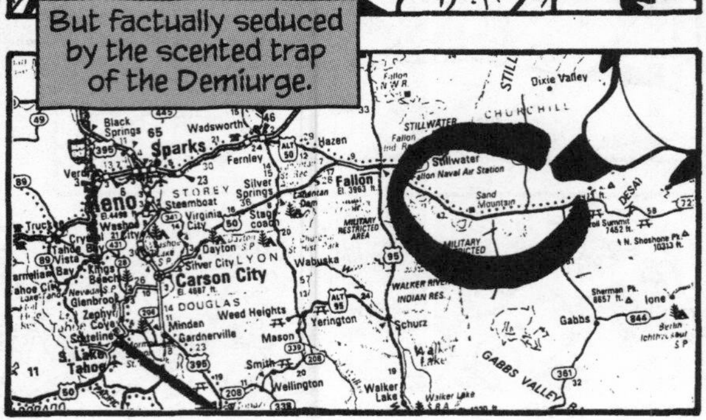
But factually seduced by the scented trap of the Demiurge.
Sparks
Reno
Carson City
Fallon
Wadsworth
Fernley
Hazen
Stillwater
Dixie Valley
CHURCHILL
STOREY
LYON
DOUGLAS
Virginia City
Silver Springs
Silver City
Dayton
Minden
Gardnerville
Yerington
Wabuska
Weed Heights
Mason
Smith
Wellington
Schurz
Walker Lake
Gabbs
Ione
GABBS VALLEY
Black Springs

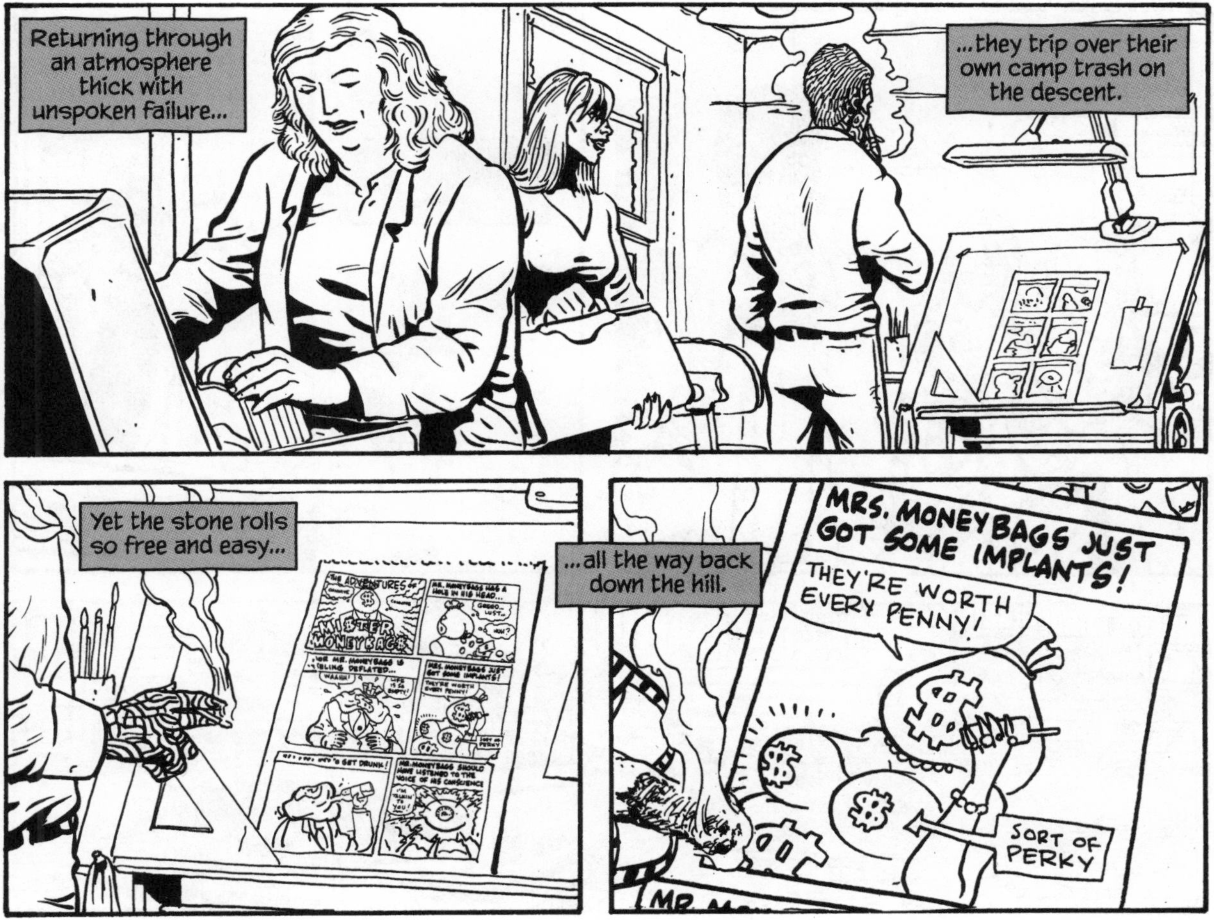

Returning through an atmosphere thick with unspoken failure...
...they trip over their own camp trash on the descent.
Yet the stone rolls so free and easy...
...all the way back down the hill.
MRS. MONEYBAGS JUST GOT SOME IMPLANTS!
THEY'RE WORTH EVERY PENNY!
SORT OF PERKY

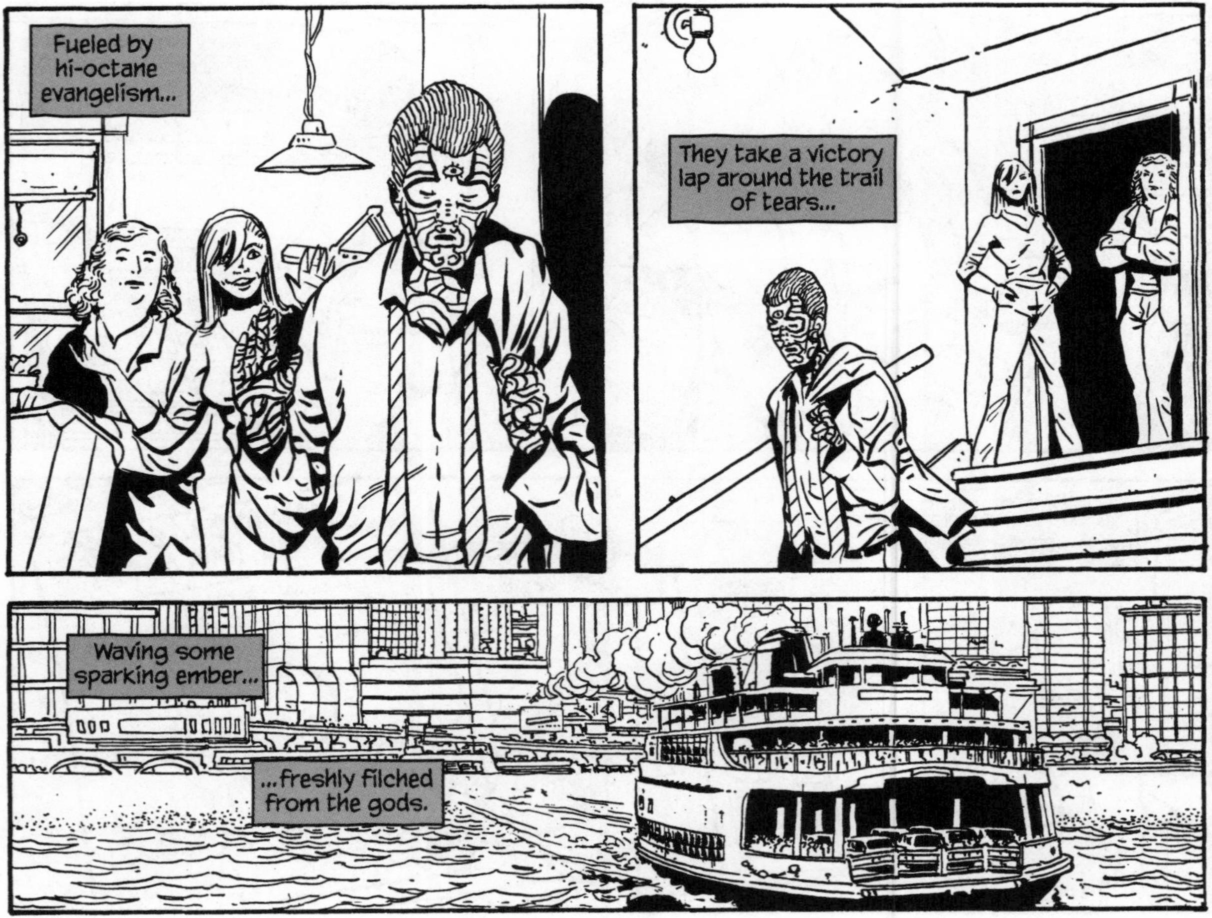
Fueled by hi-octane evangelism...
They take a victory lap around the trail of tears...
Waving some sparking ember...
...freshly filched from the gods.

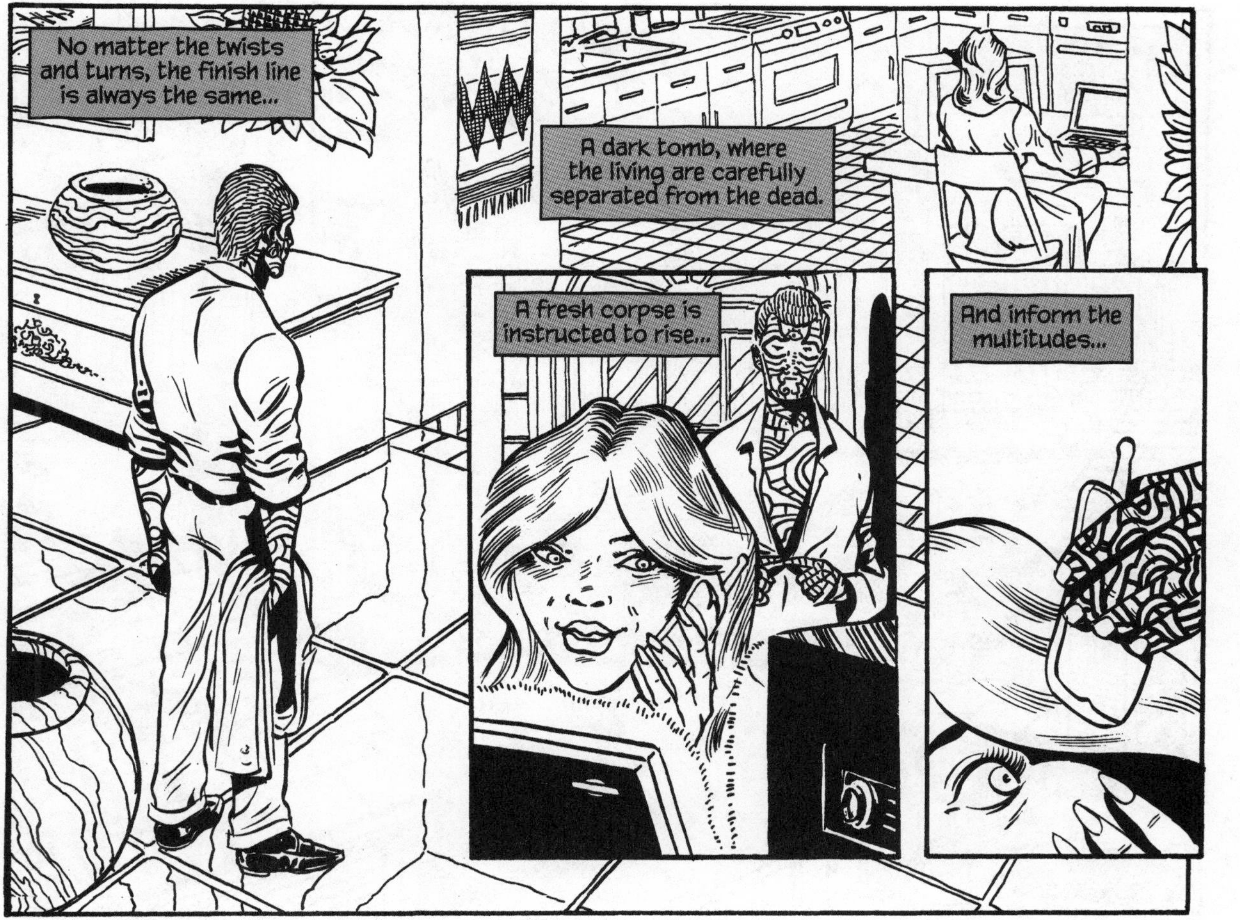
No matter the twists and turns, the finish line is always the same...
A dark tomb, where the living are carefully separated from the dead.
A fresh corpse is instructed to rise...
And inform the multitudes...

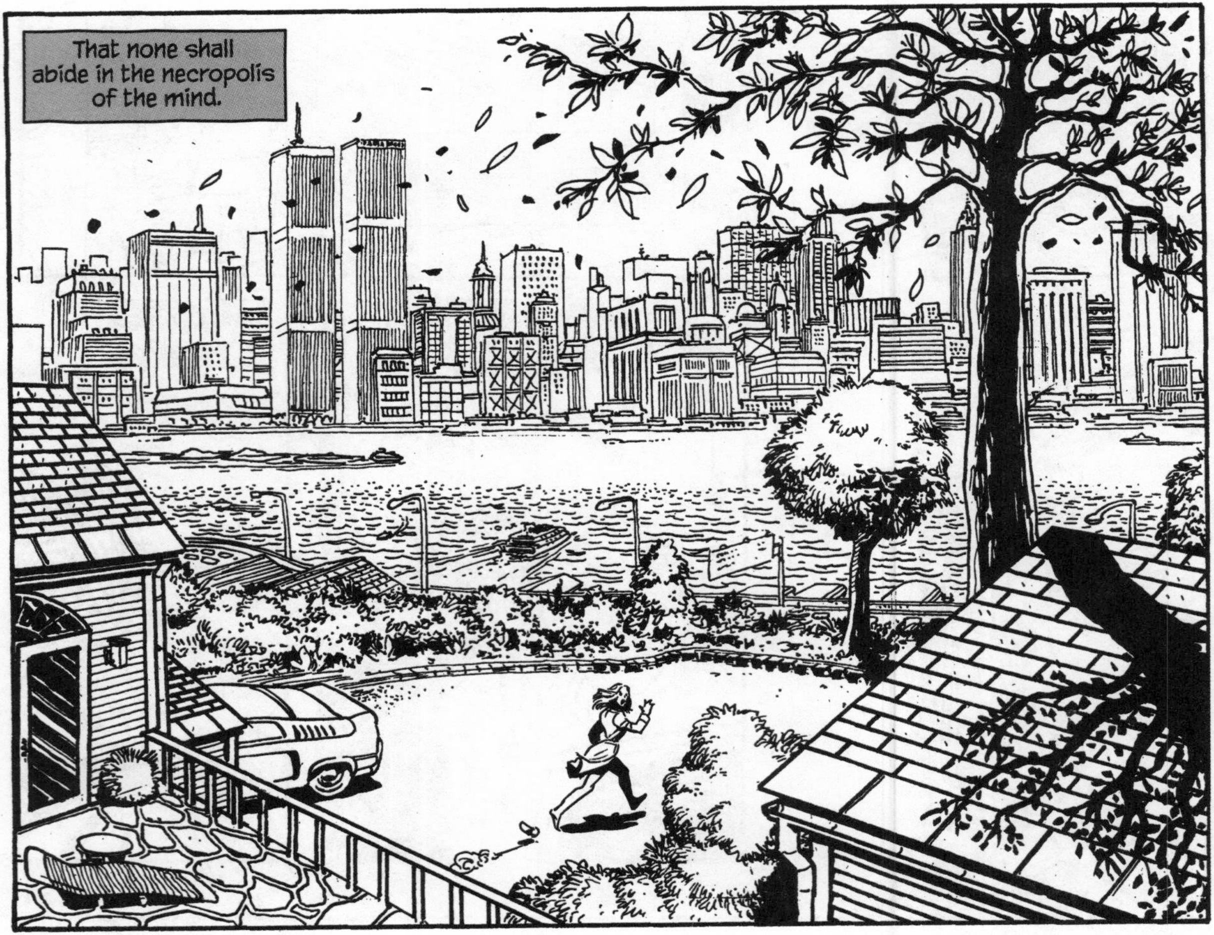
That none shall abide in the necropolis of the mind.

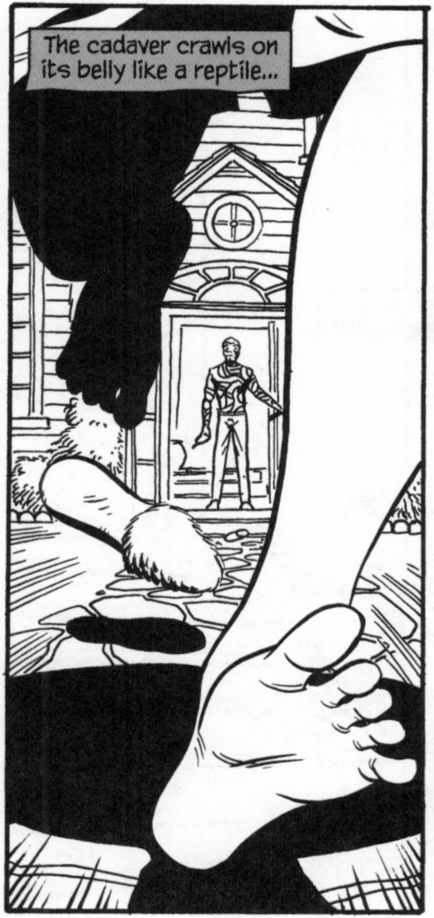
The cadaver crawls on its belly like a reptile...

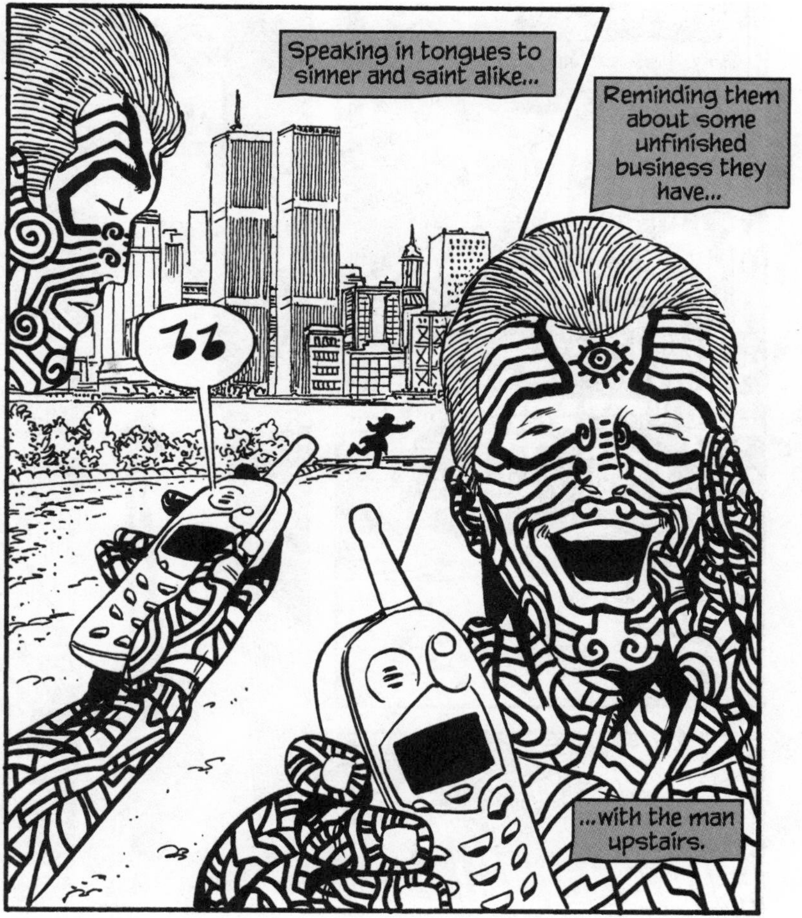
Speaking in tongues to sinner and saint alike...
Reminding them about some unfinished business they have...
...with the man upstairs.

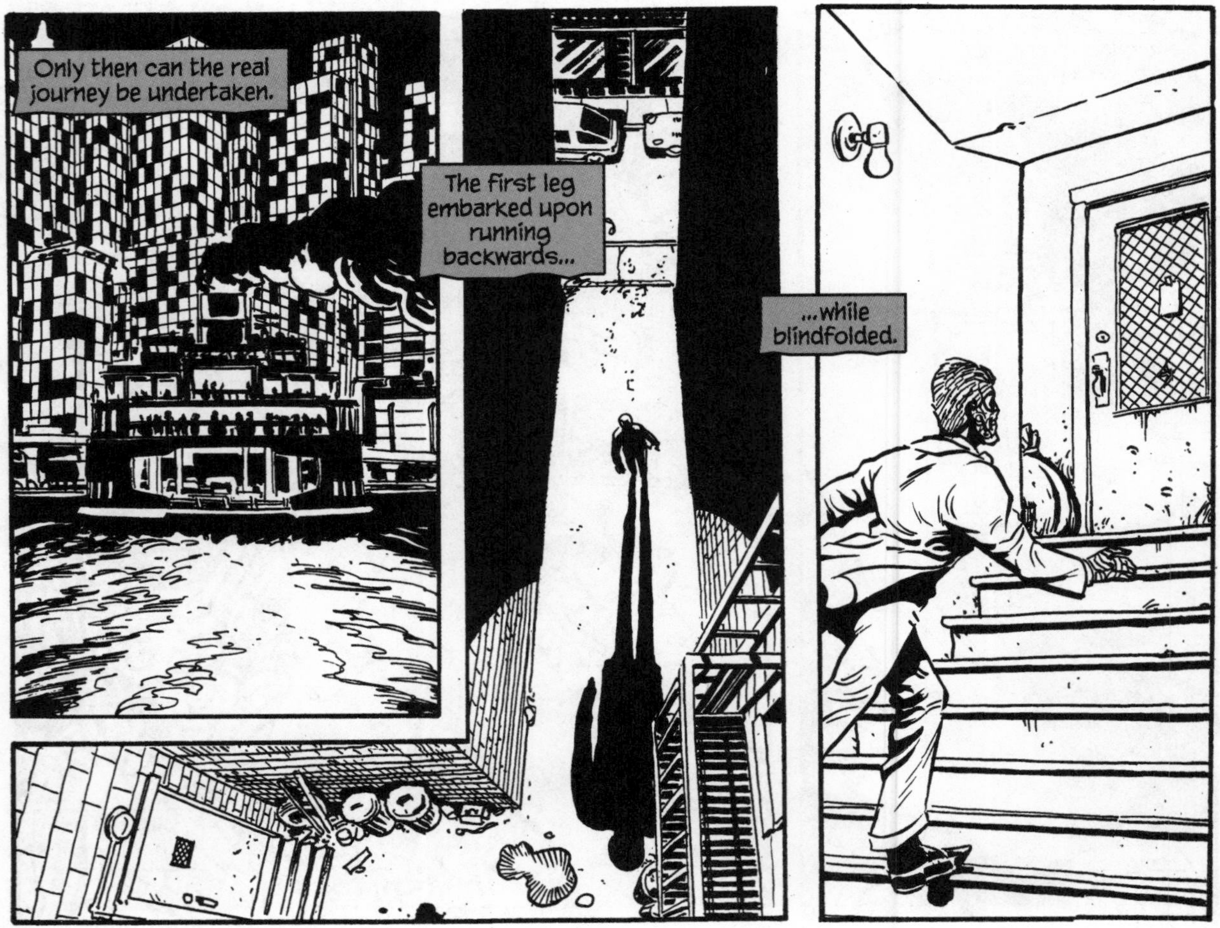
Only then can the real journey be undertaken.
The first leg embarked upon running backwards...
...while blindfolded.

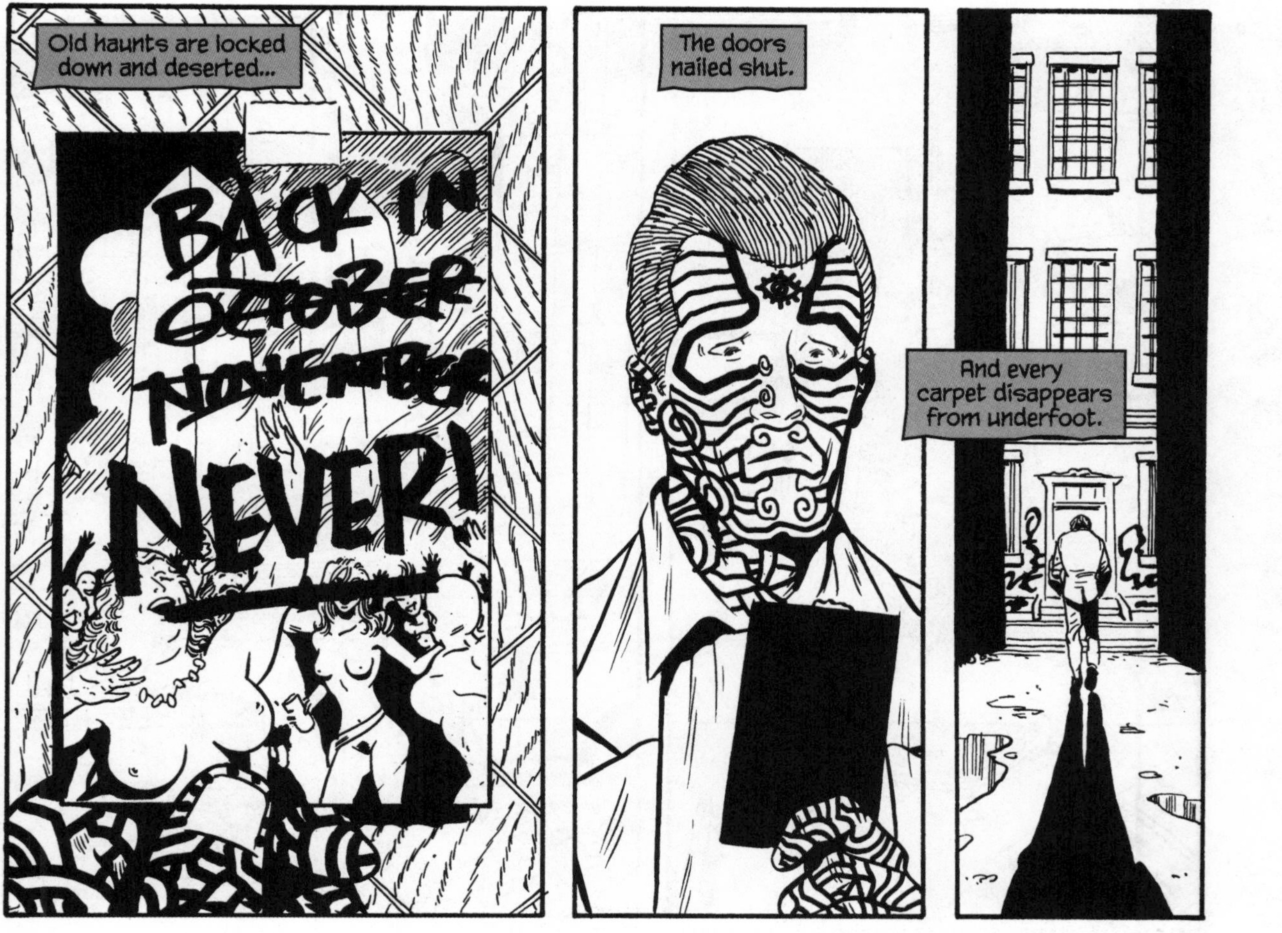
Old haunts are locked down and deserted...
BACK IN
OCTOBER
NOVEMBER
NEVER!
The doors nailed shut.
And every carpet disappears from underfoot.

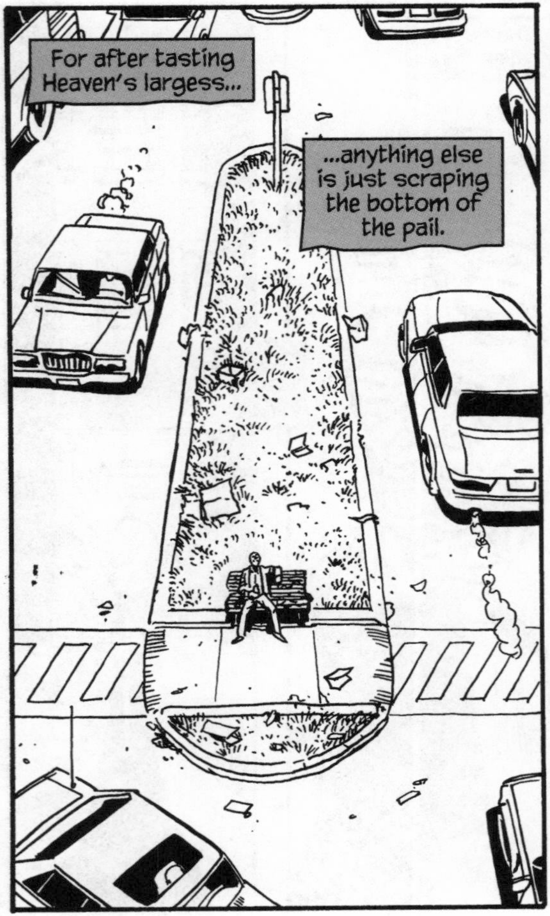
For after tasting Heaven's largess...
...anything else is just scraping the bottom of the pail.

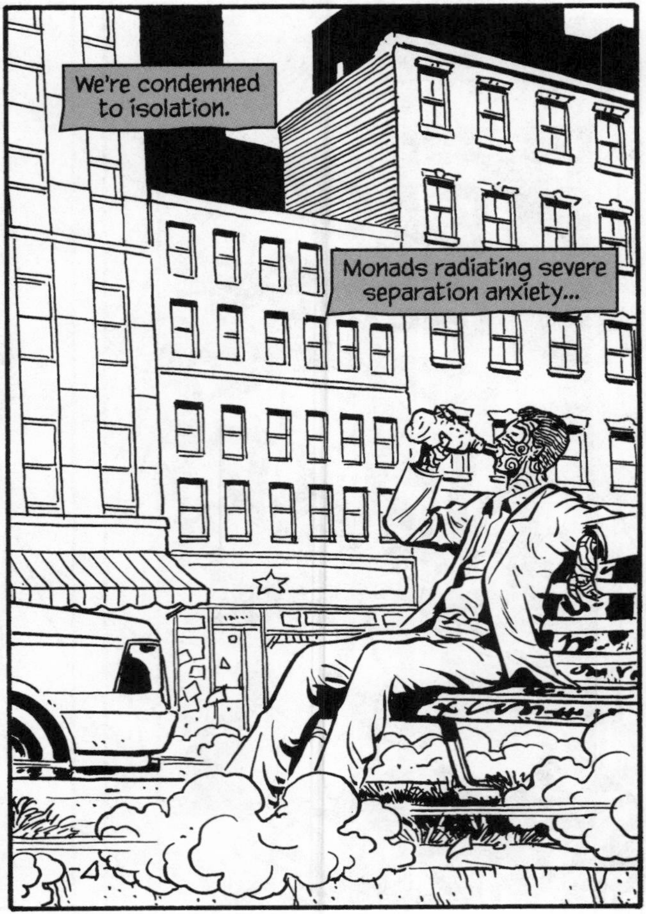
We're condemned to isolation.
Monads radiating severe separation anxiety...

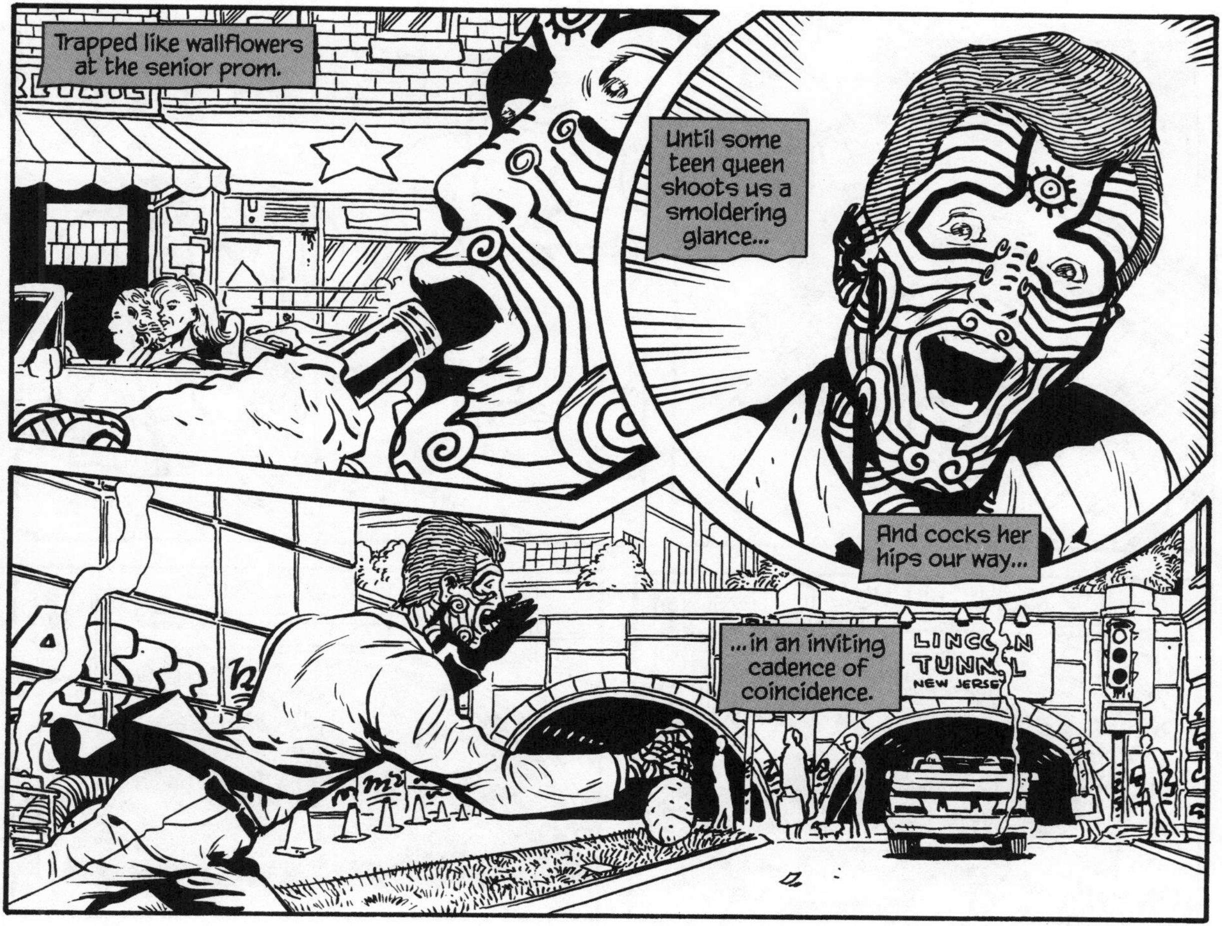
Trapped like wallflowers at the senior prom.
Until some teen queen shoots us a smoldering glance...
And cocks her hips our way...
...in an inviting cadence of coincidence.
NEW JERSEY

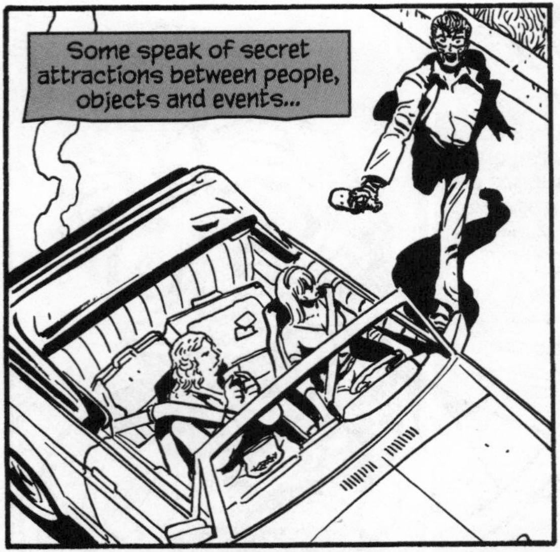
Some speak of secret attractions between people, objects and events...

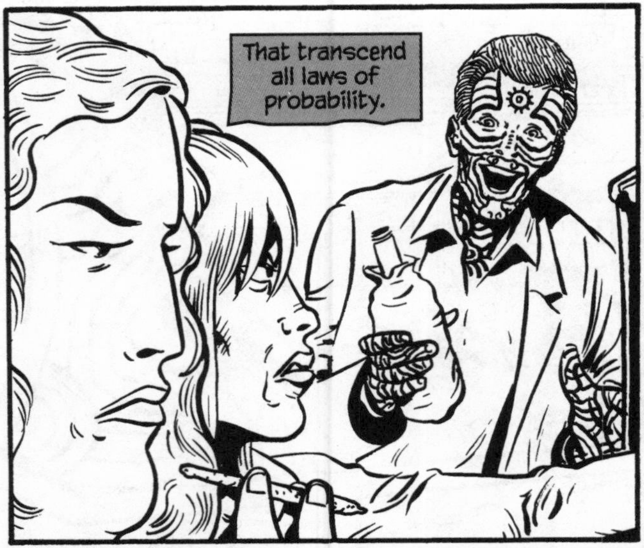
That transcend all laws of probability.

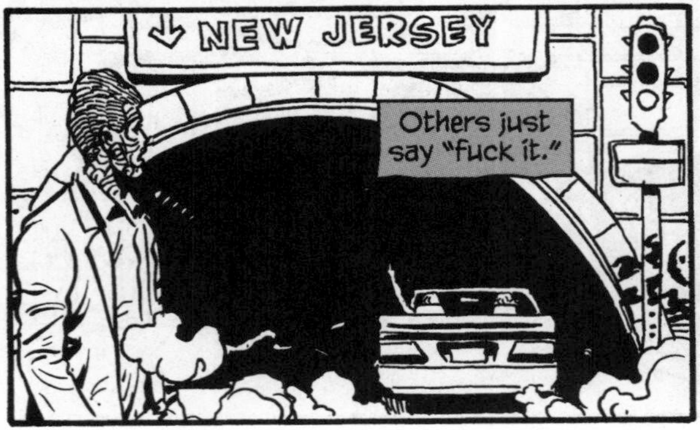
NEW JERSEY
Others just say "fuck it."

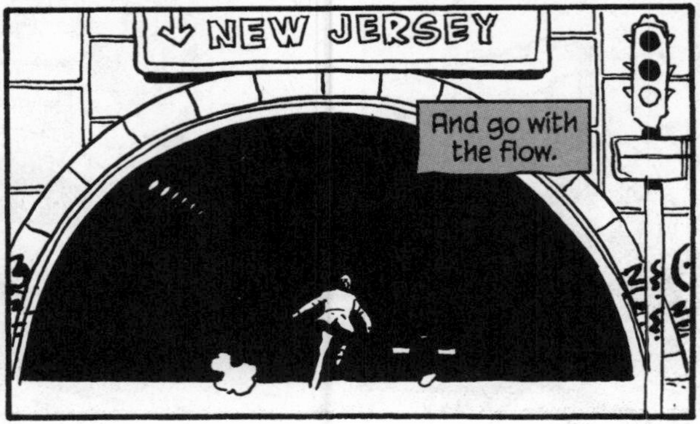
NEW JERSEY
And go with the flow.

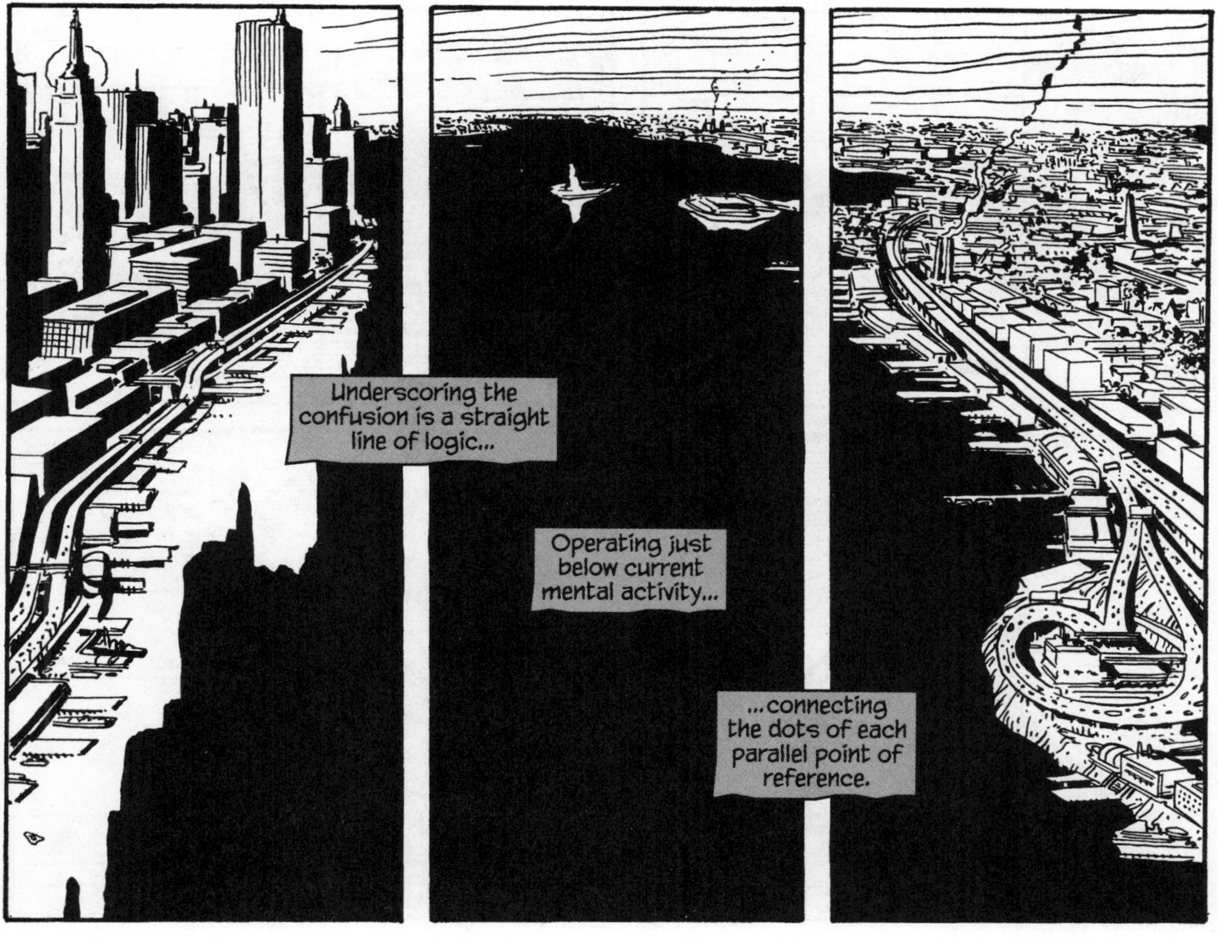

Underscoring the confusion is a straight line of logic...
Operating just below current mental activity...
...connecting the dots of each parallel point of reference.

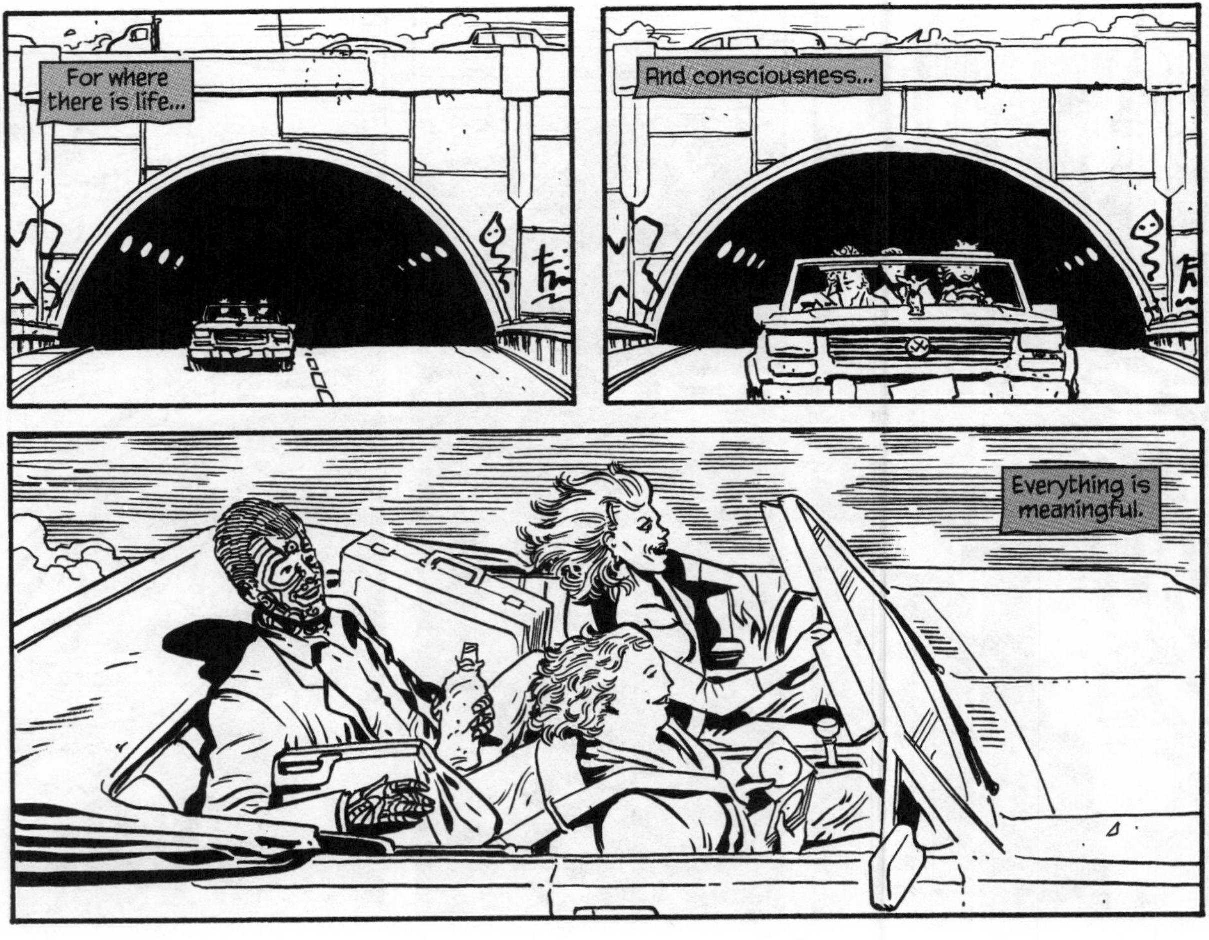
For where there is life...
And consciousness...
Everything is meaningful.

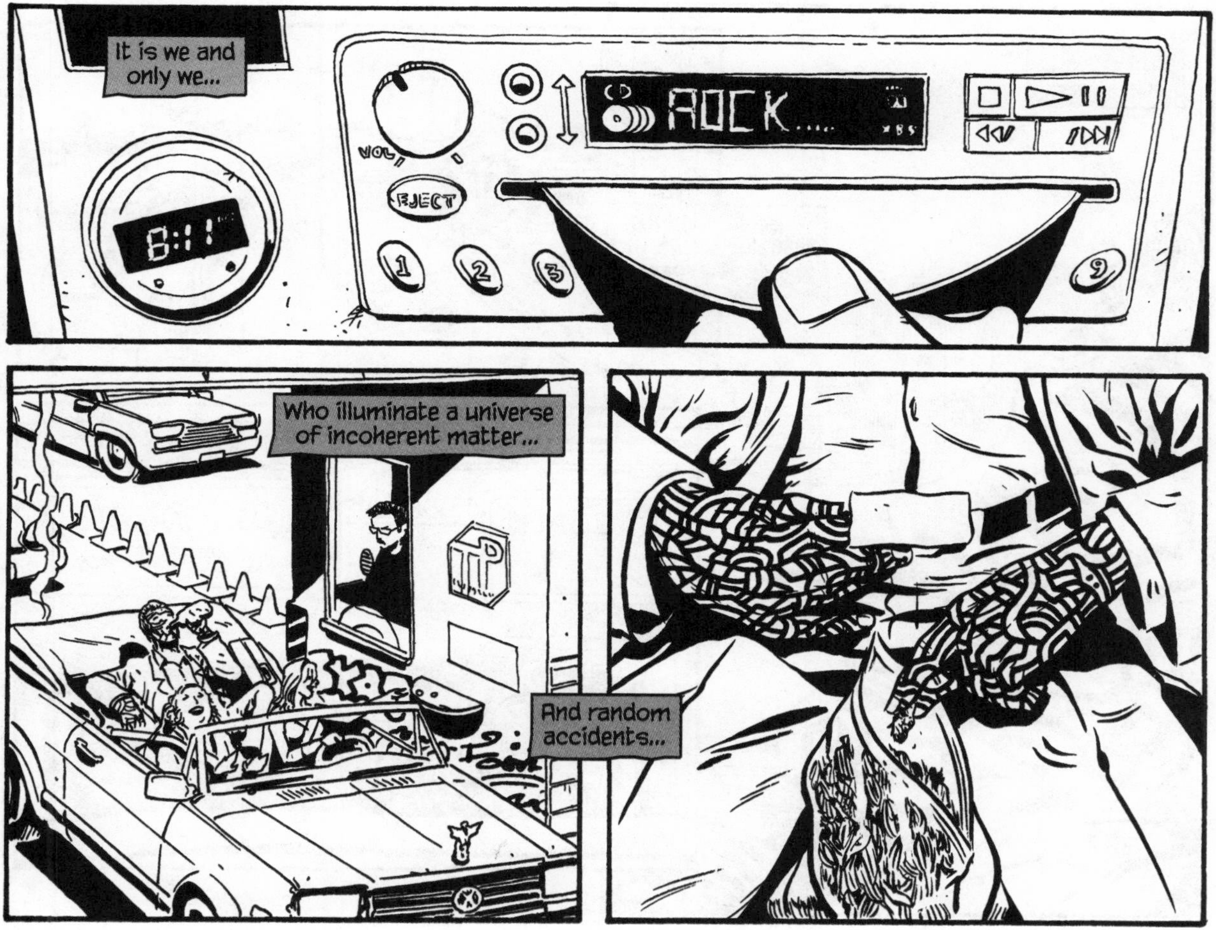
It is we and only we...
ROCK....
VOL
EJECT
Who illuminate a universe of incoherent matter...
And random accidents...

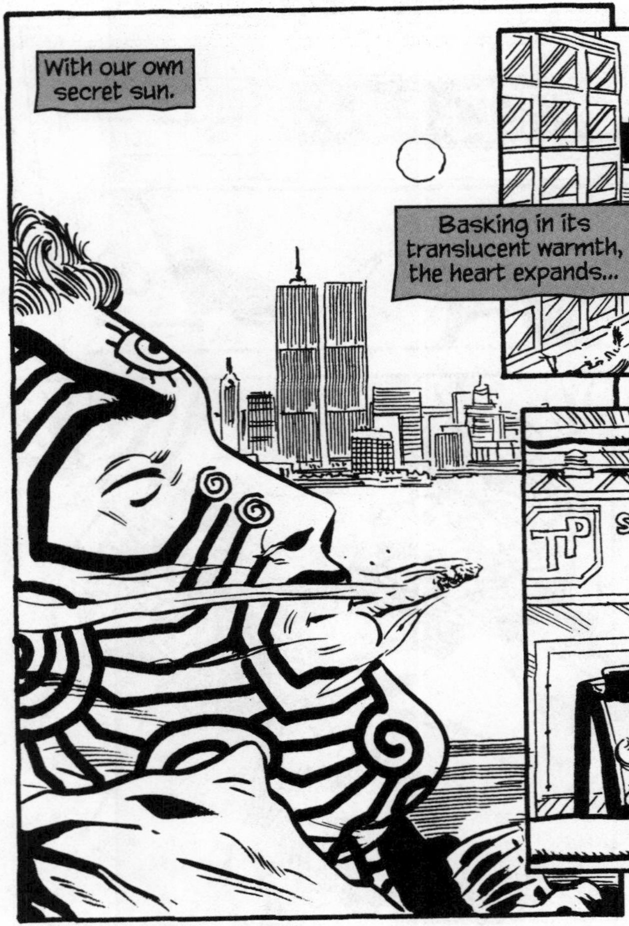
With our own secret sun.

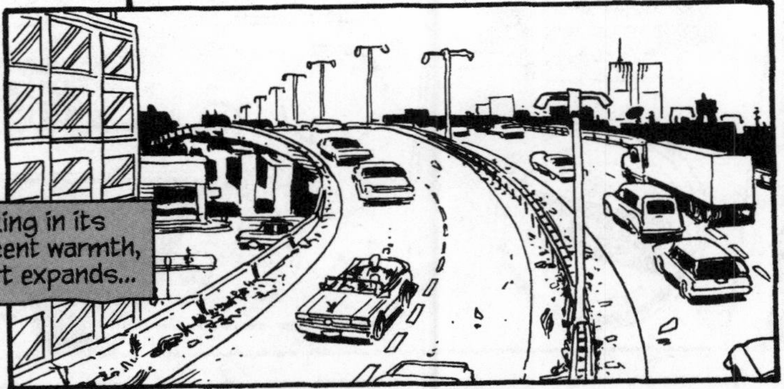
Basking in its translucent warmth, the heart expands...

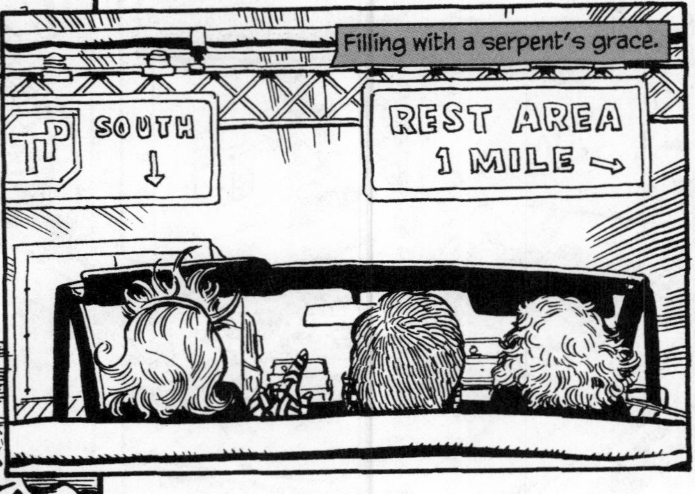
Filling with a serpent's grace.
TP
SOUTH
REST AREA
1 MILE

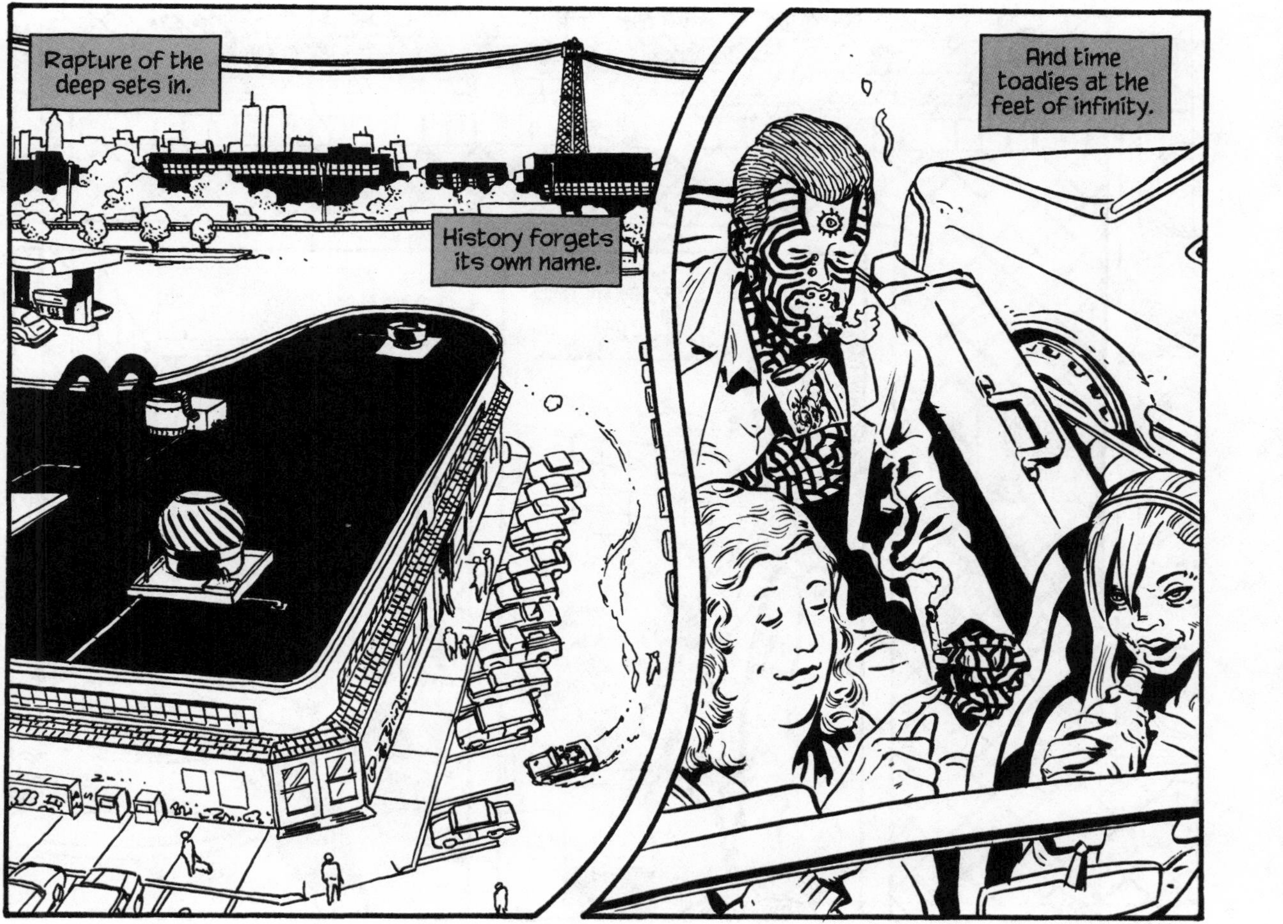
Rapture of the deep sets in.
History forgets its own name.
And time toadies at the feet of infinity.

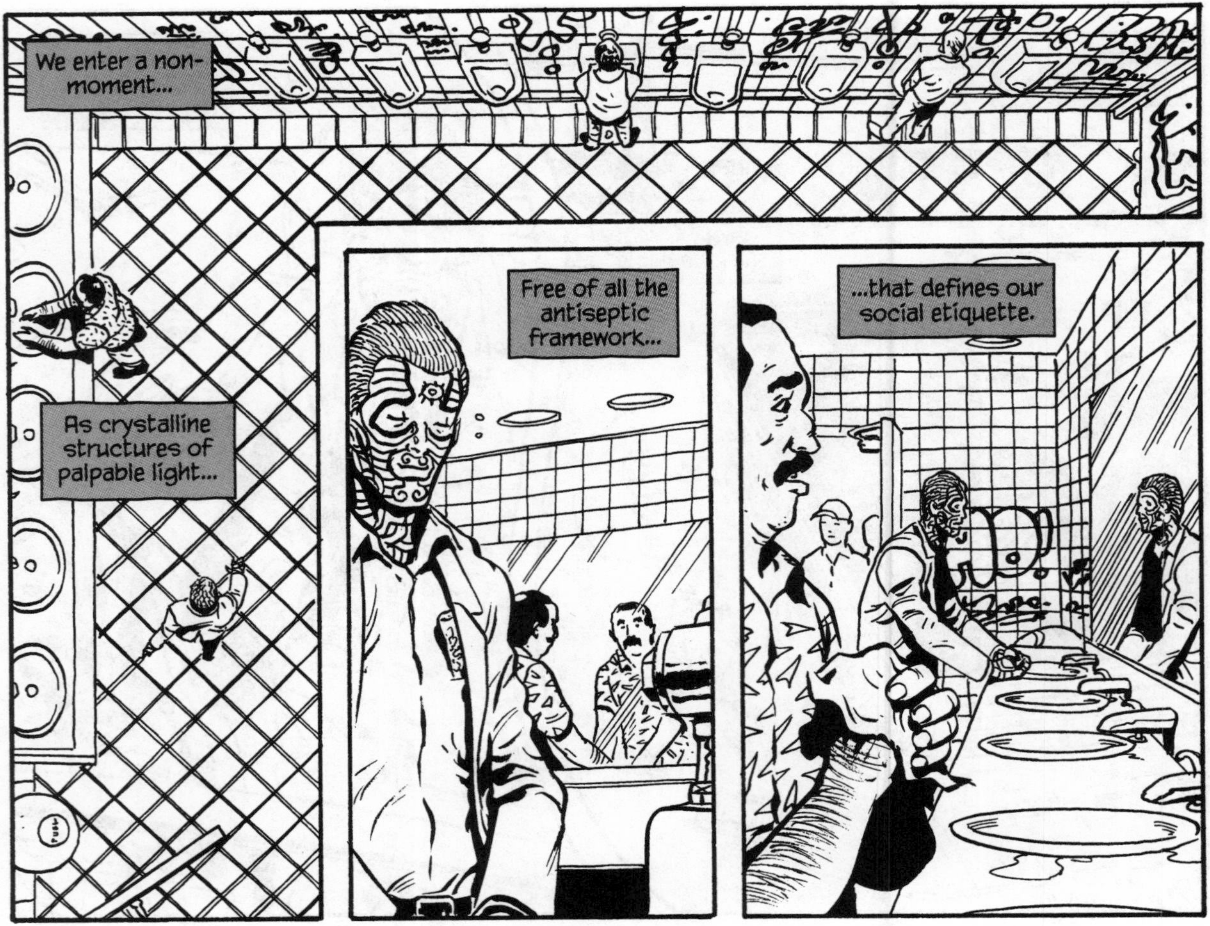
We enter a non-moment...
As crystalline structures of palpable light...
Free of all the antiseptic framework...
...that defines our social etiquette.
PUSH

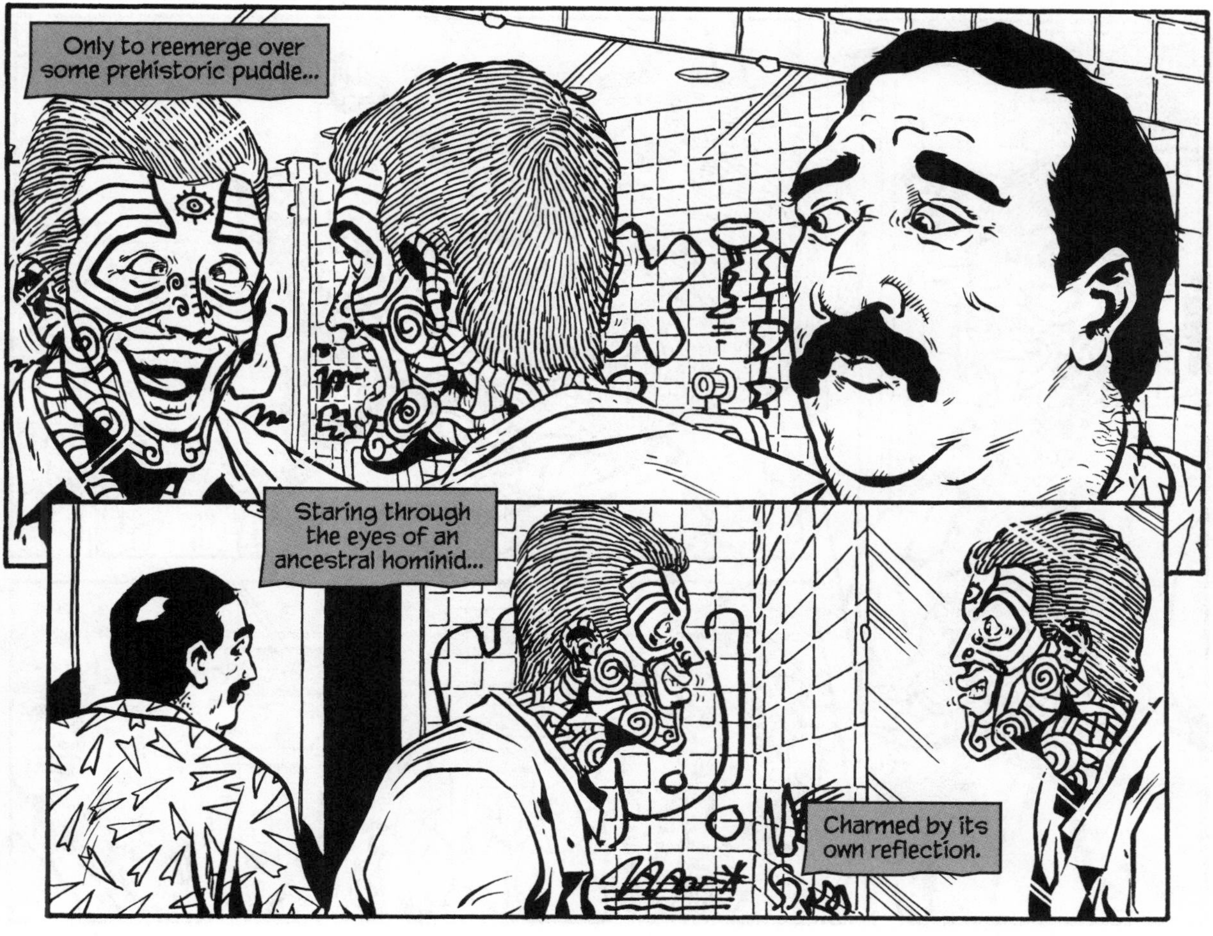
Only to reemerge over some prehistoric puddle...
Staring through the eyes of an ancestral hominid...
Charmed by its own reflection.

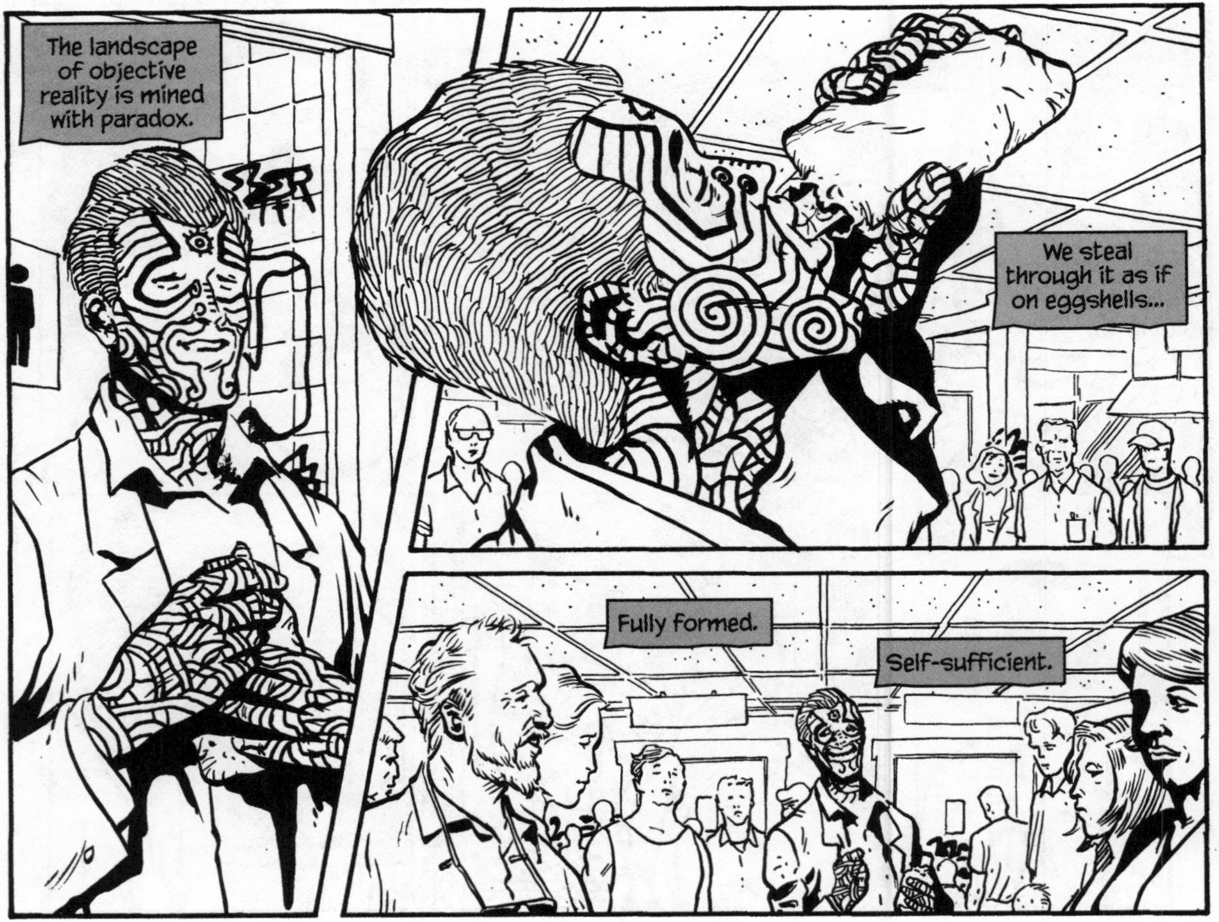
The landscape of objective reality is mined with paradox.
We steal through it as if on eggshells...
Fully formed.
Self-sufficient.

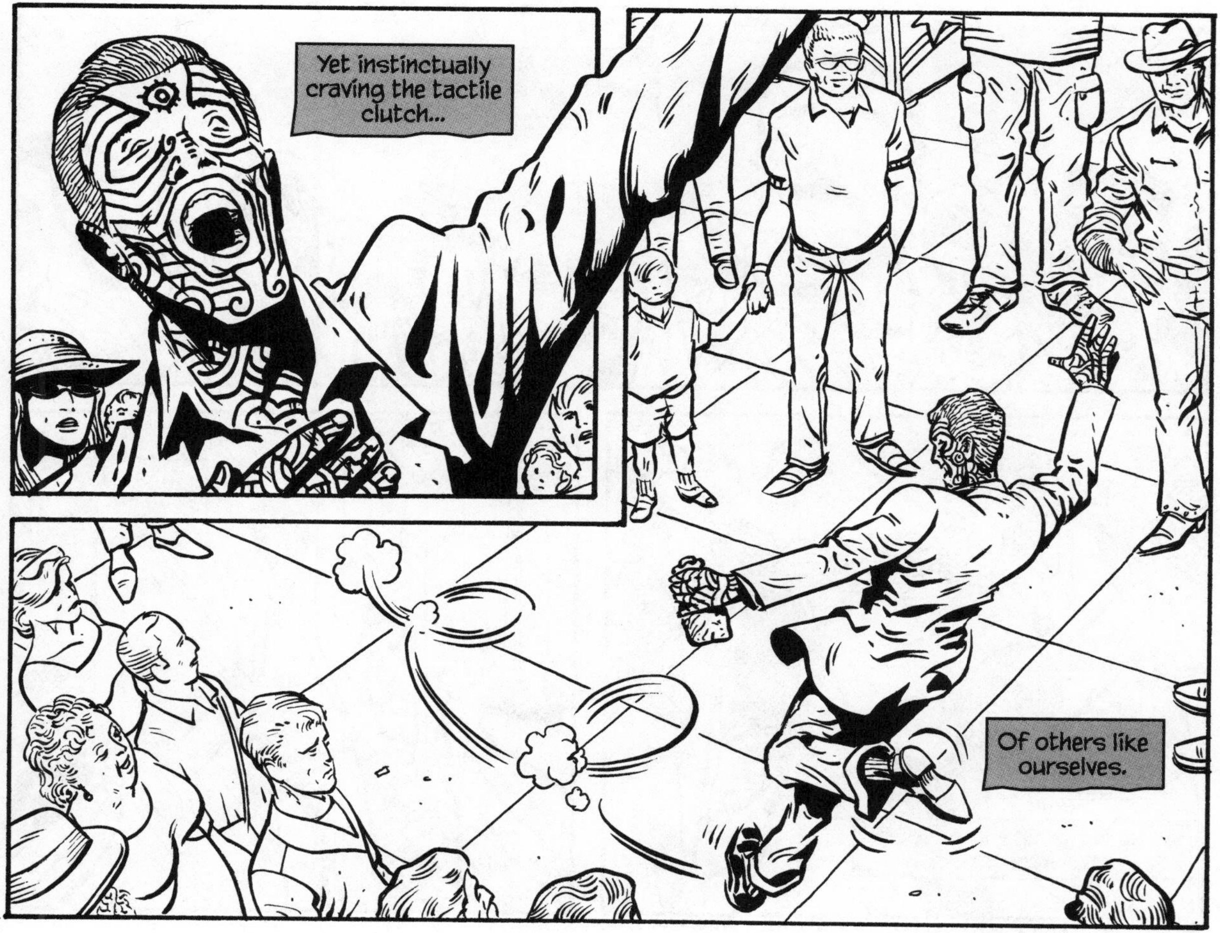
Yet instinctually craving the tactile clutch...
Of others like ourselves.

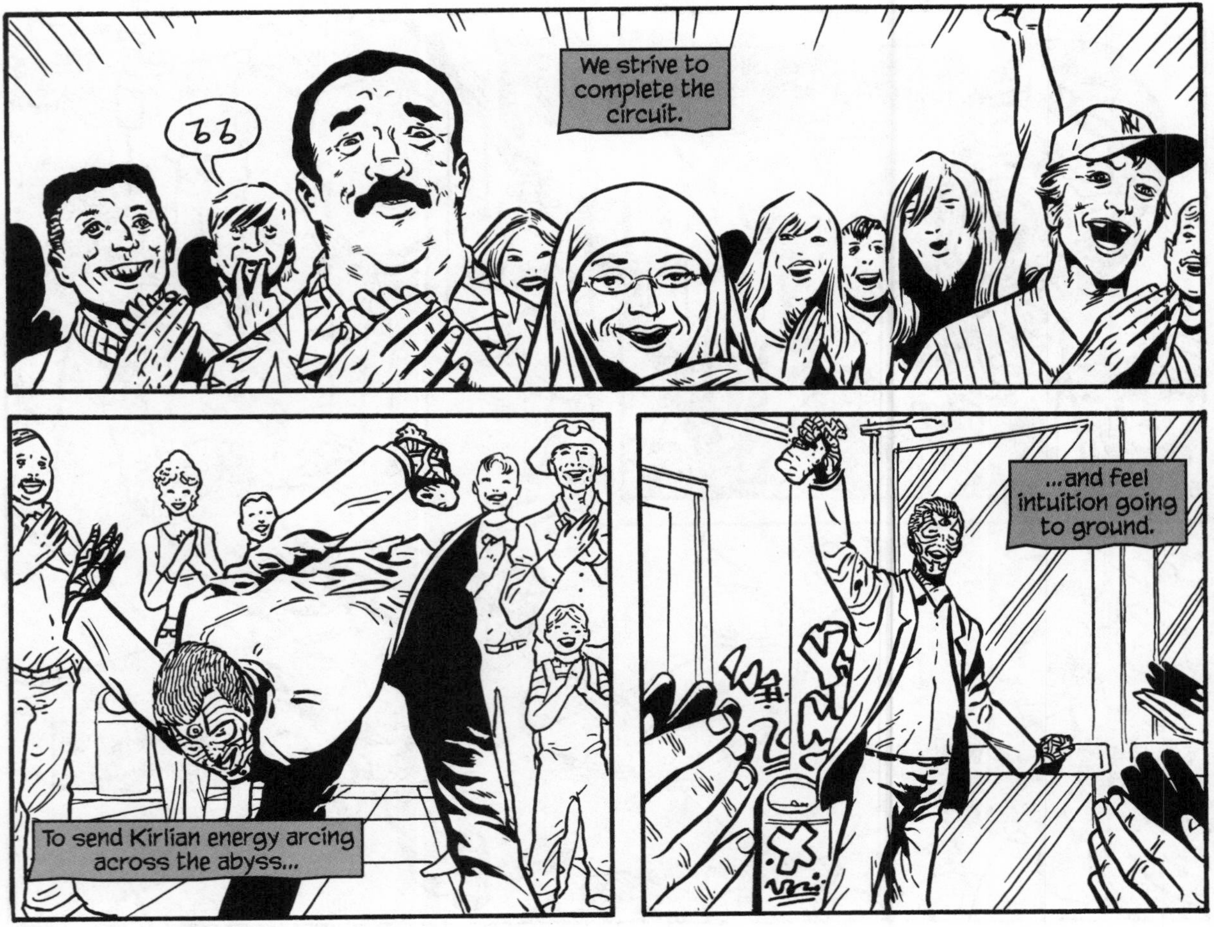
We strive to complete the circuit.
To send Kirlian energy arcing across the abyss...
...and feel intuition going to ground.

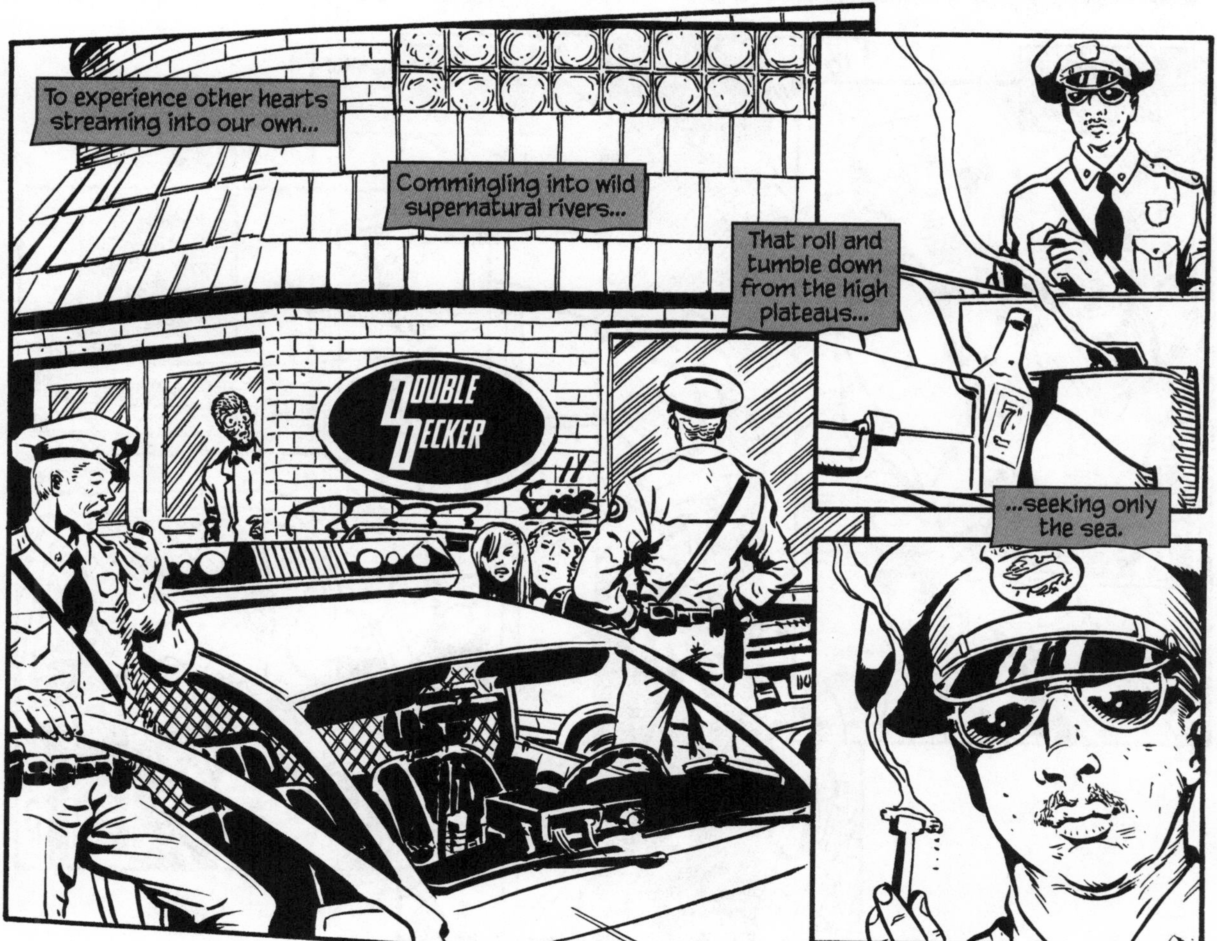
To experience other hearts streaming into our own...
Commingling into wild supernatural rivers...
That roll and tumble down from the high plateaus...
DOUBLE DECKER
...seeking only the sea.

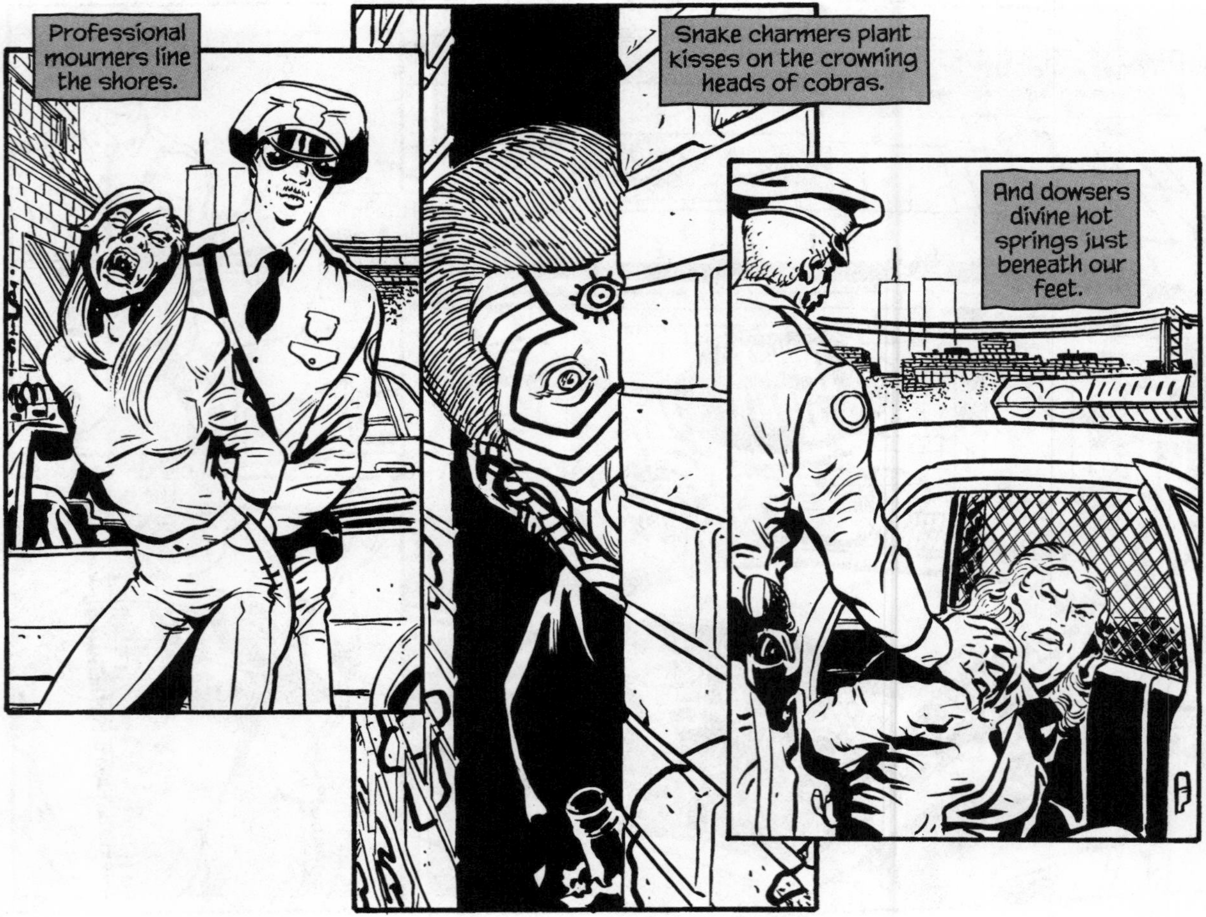
Professional mourners line the shores.
Snake charmers plant kisses on the crowning heads of cobras.
And dowsers divine hot springs just beneath our feet.

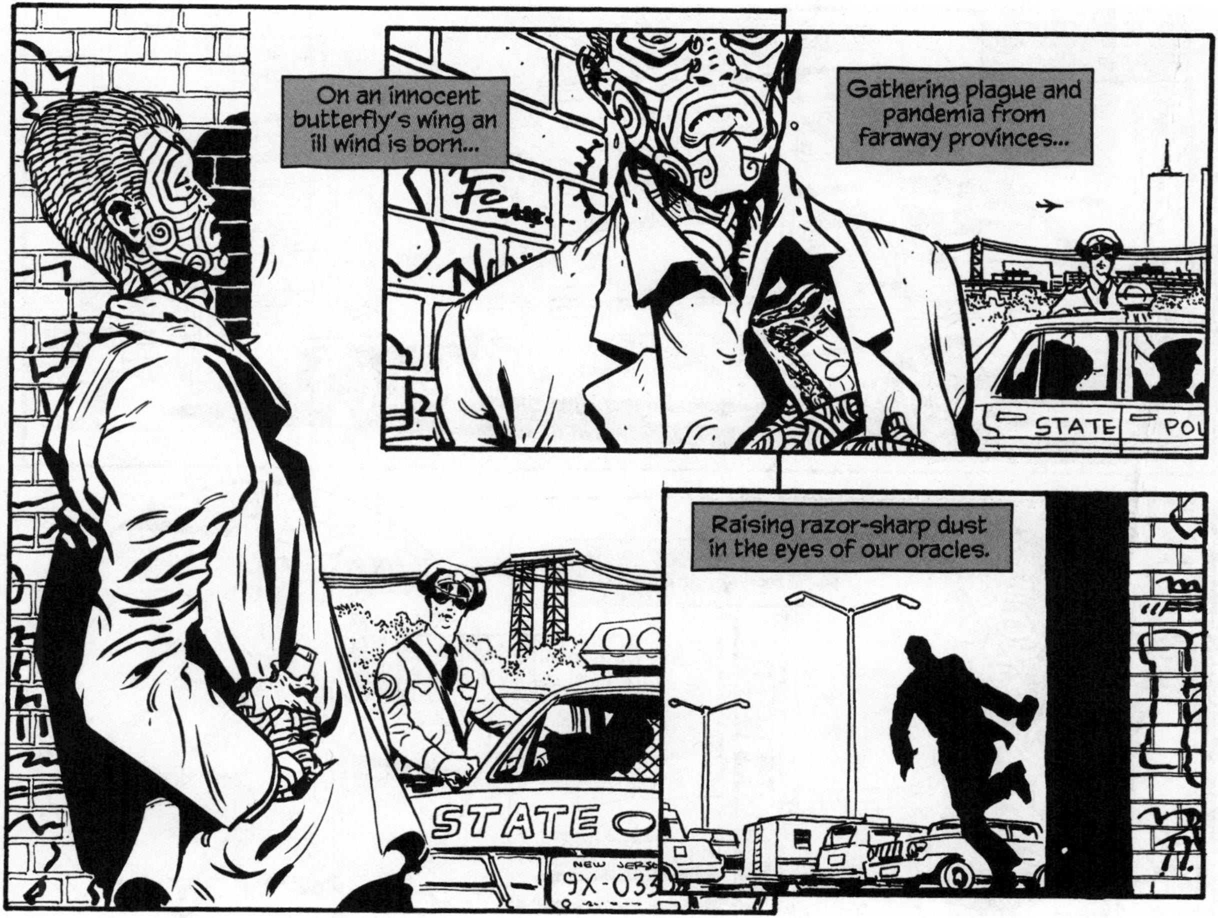
On an innocent butterfly's wing an ill wind is born...
Gathering plague and pandemia from faraway provinces...
STATE POL
Raising razor-sharp dust in the eyes of our oracles.
STATE
NEW JERS
9X-033

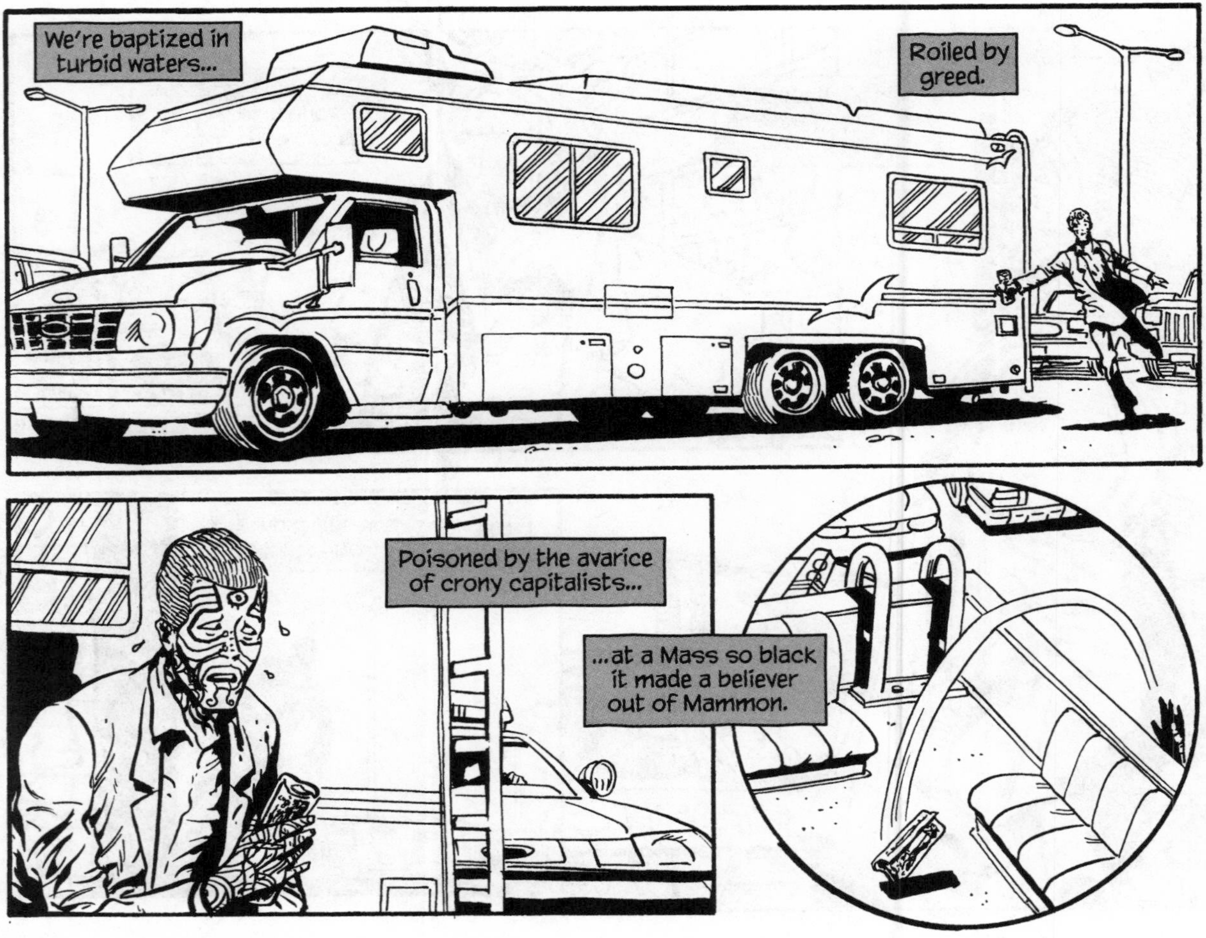
We're baptized in turbid waters...
Roiled by greed.
Poisoned by the avarice of crony capitalists...
...at a Mass so black it made a believer out of Mammon.

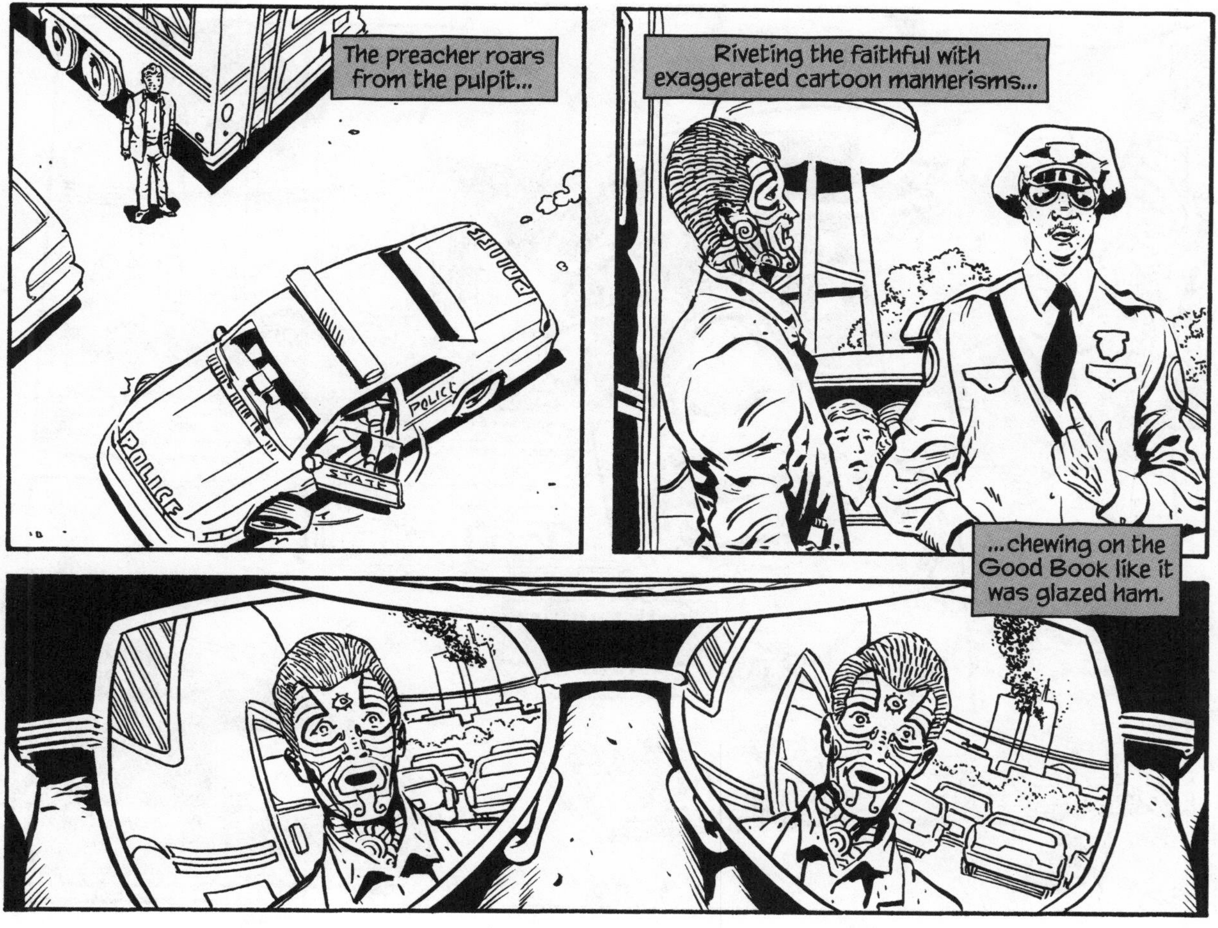
The preacher roars from the pulpit...
POLICE
POLICE
POLICE
STATE
Riveting the faithful with exaggerated cartoon mannerisms...
...chewing on the Good Book like it was glazed ham.

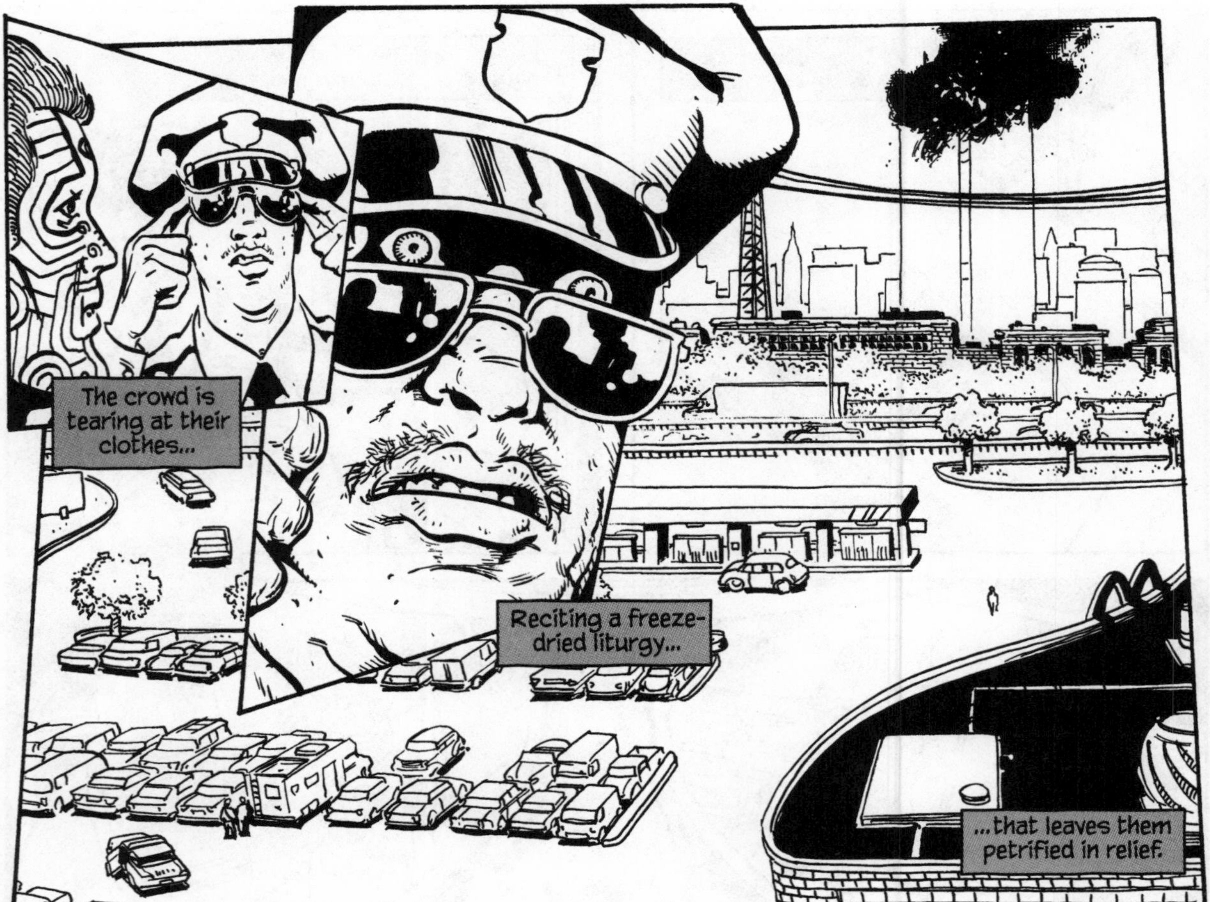
The crowd is tearing at their clothes...
Reciting a freeze-dried liturgy...
...that leaves them petrified in relief.

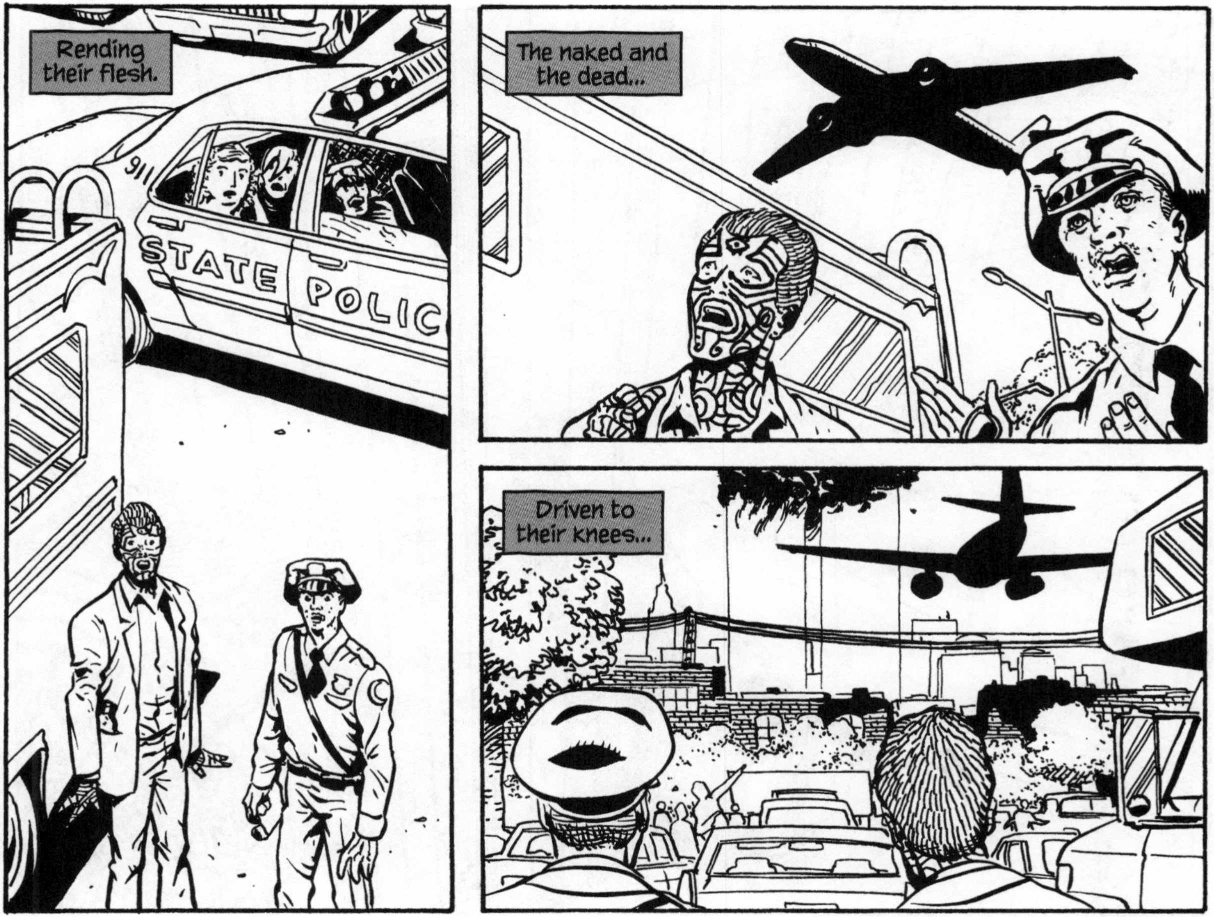
Rending their flesh.
911
STATE POLIC
The naked and the dead...
Driven to their knees...

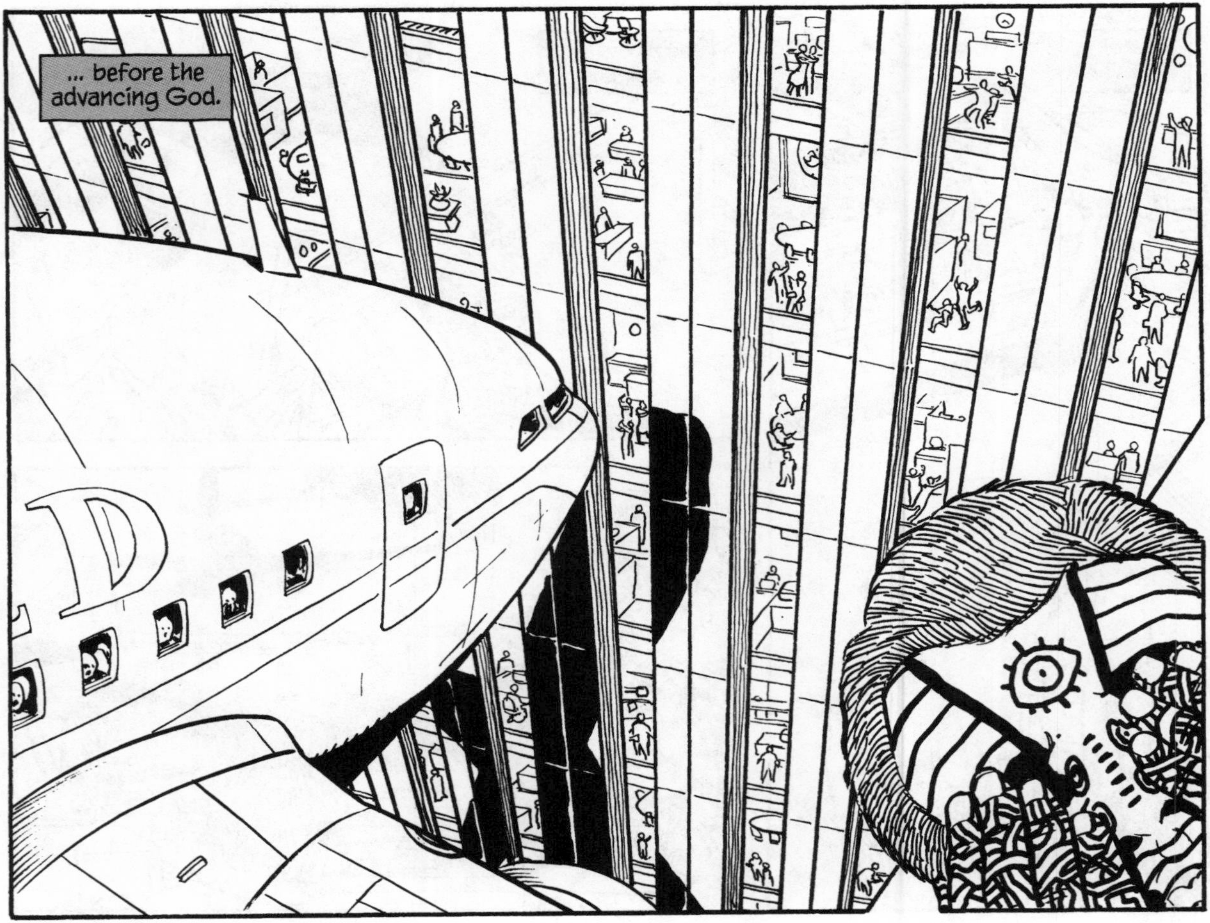
... before the advancing God.

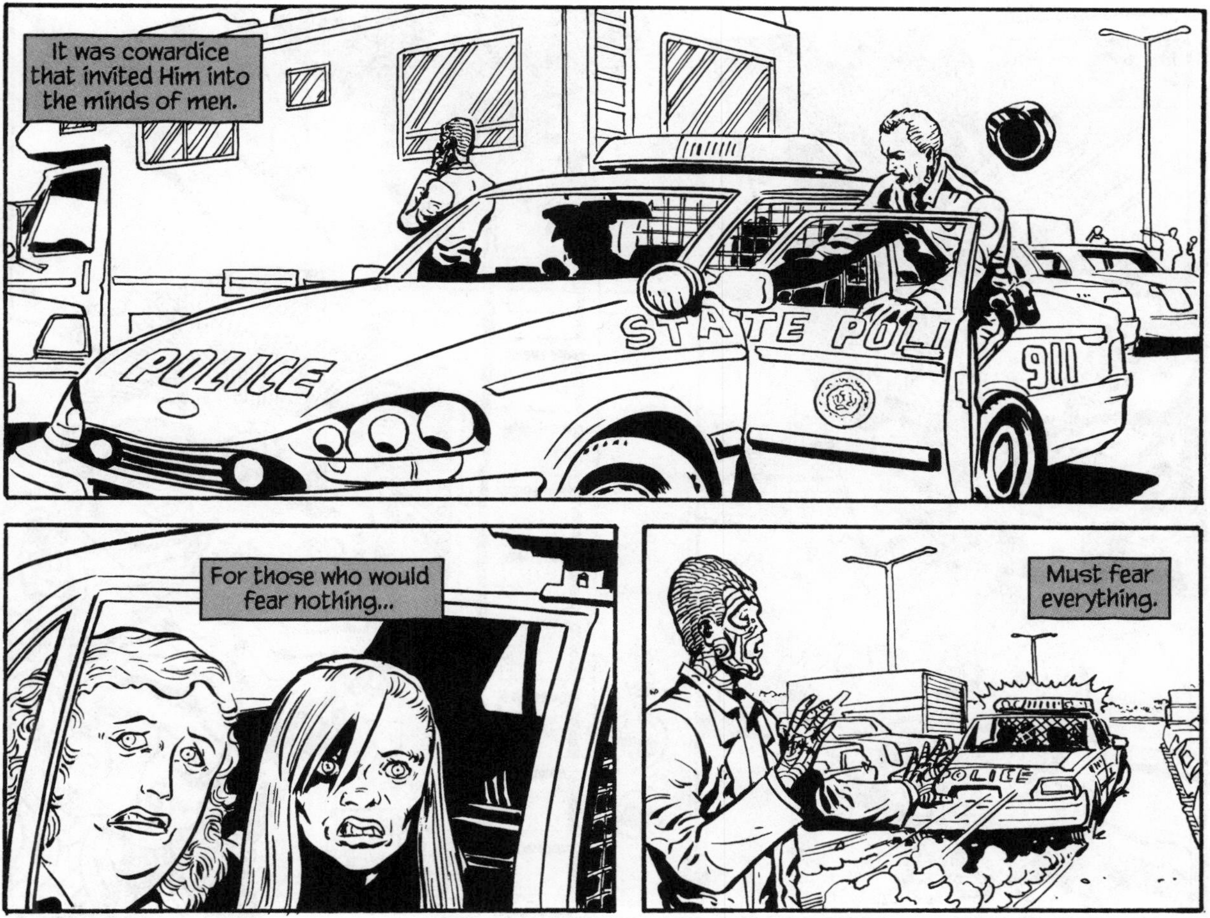
It was cowardice that invited Him into the minds of men.
POLICE
STATE POLI
911
For those who would fear nothing...
Must fear everything.
POLICE

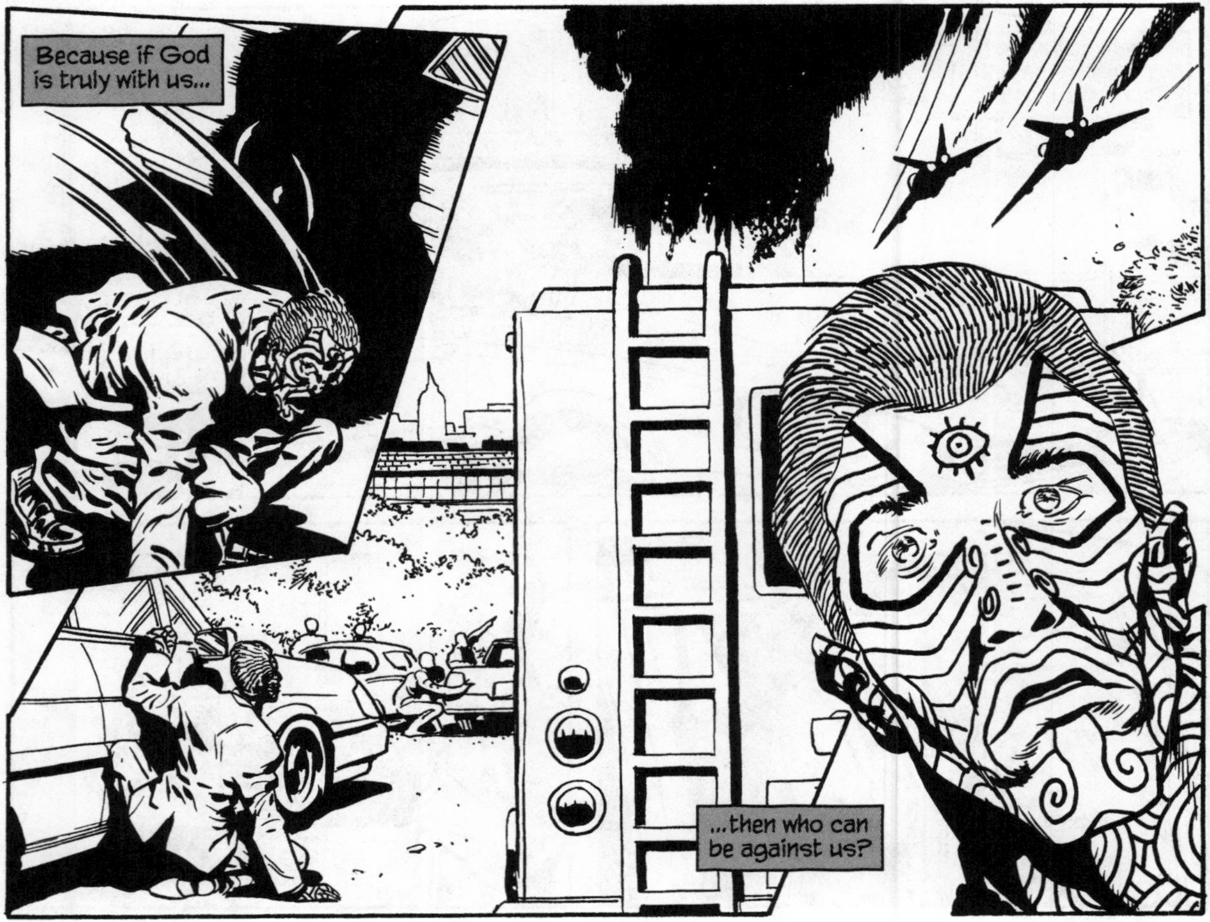
Because if God is truly with us...
...then who can be against us?

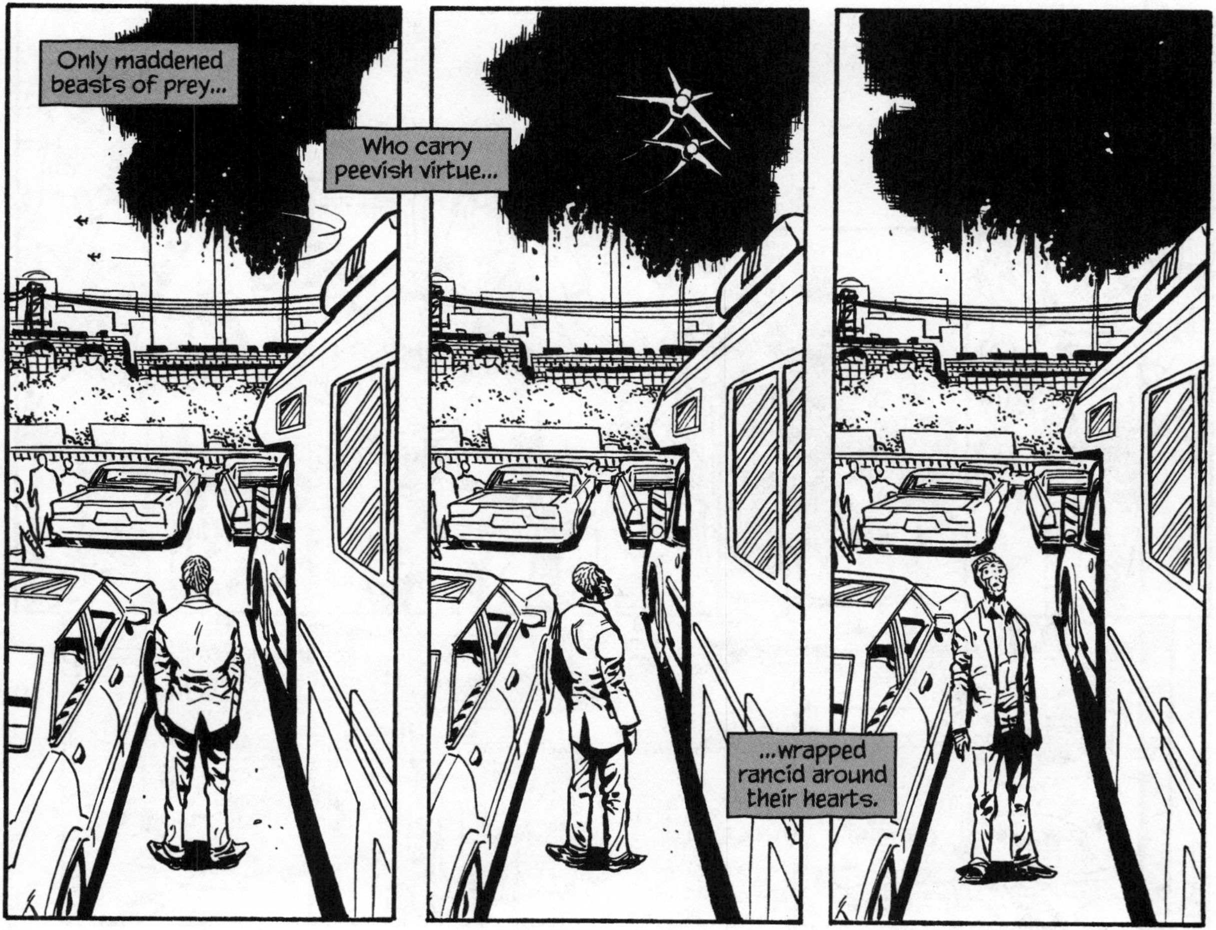
Only maddened beasts of prey...
Who carry peevish virtue...
...wrapped rancid around their hearts.

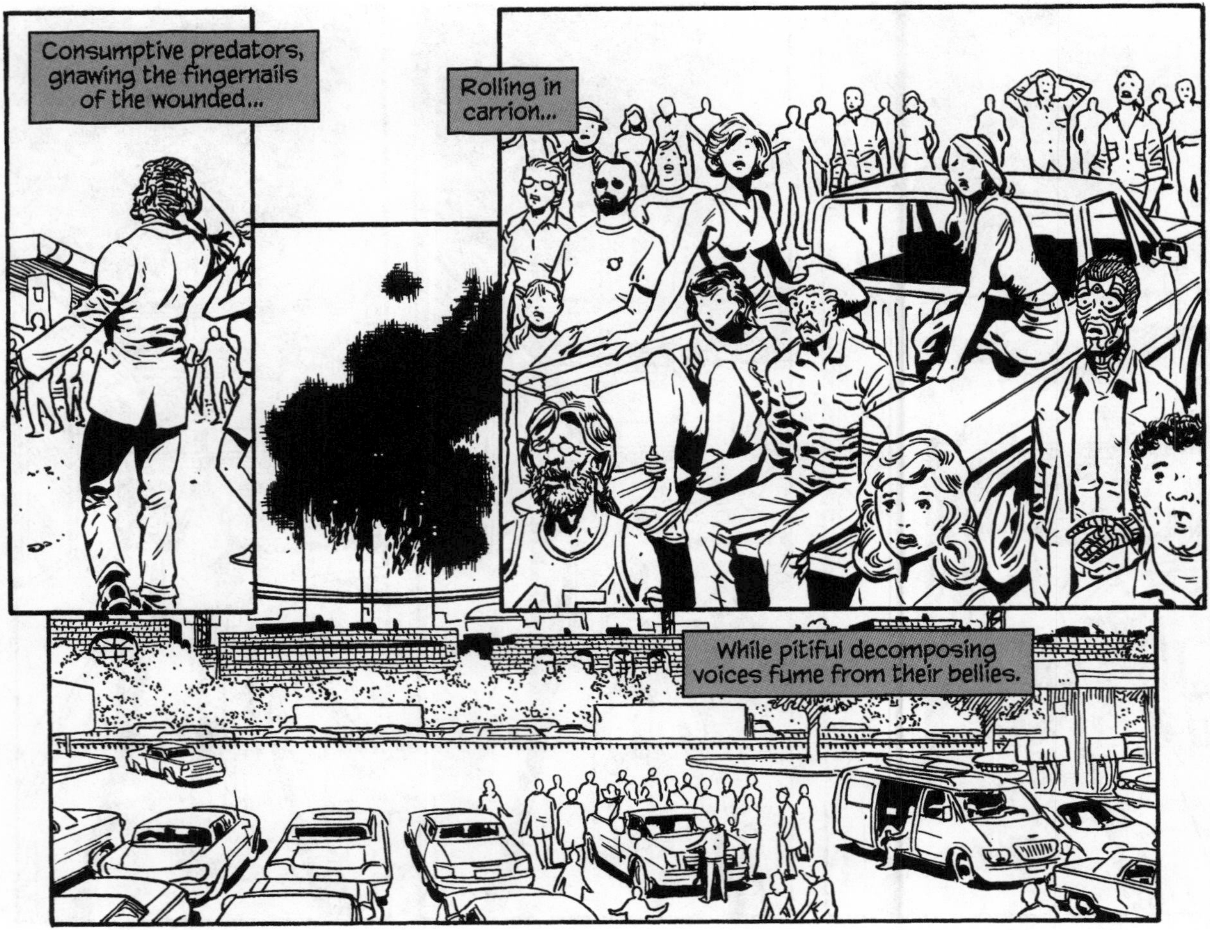
Consumptive predators, gnawing the fingernails of the wounded...
Rolling in carrion...
While pitiful decomposing voices fume from their bellies.

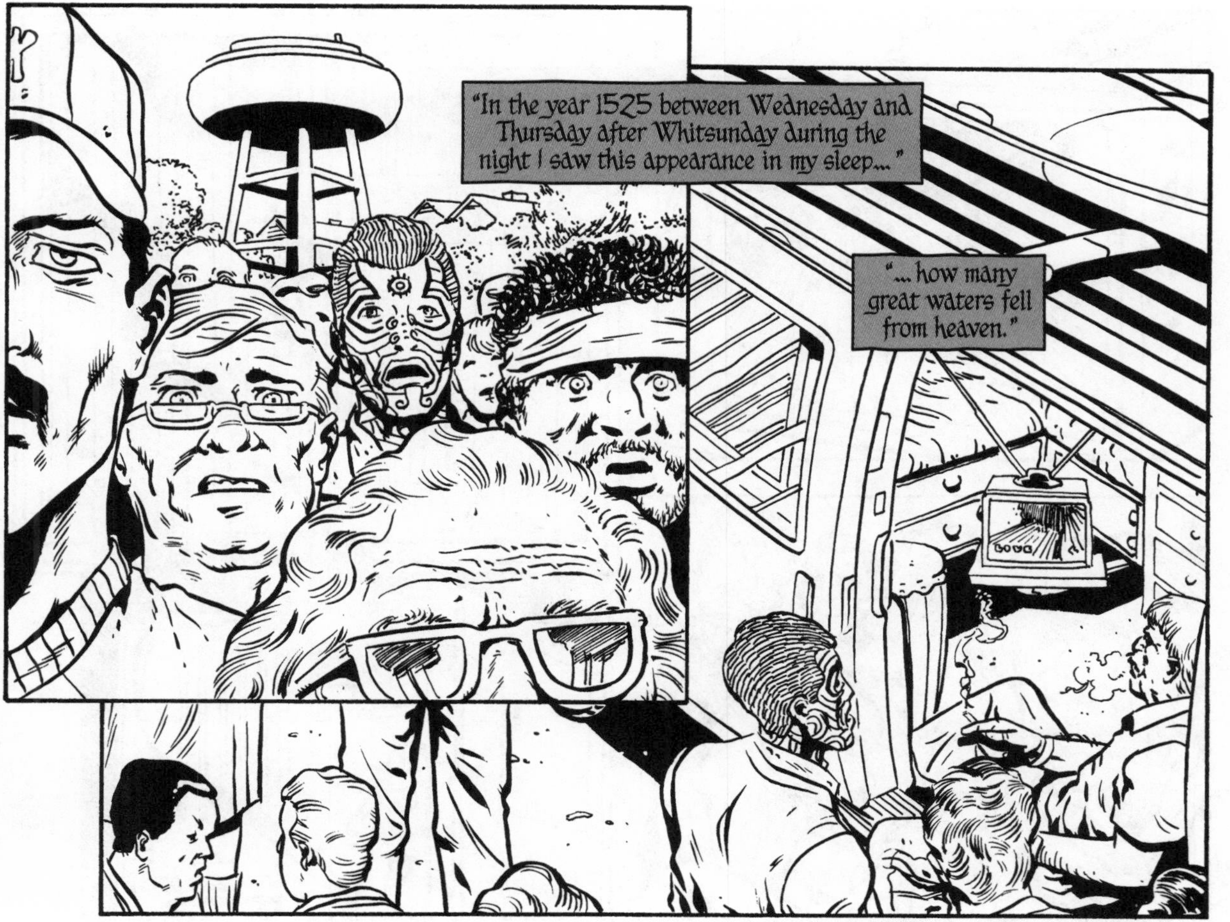
"In the year 1525 between Wednesday and Thursday after Whitsunday during the night I saw this appearance in my sleep..."
"... how many great waters fell from heaven."

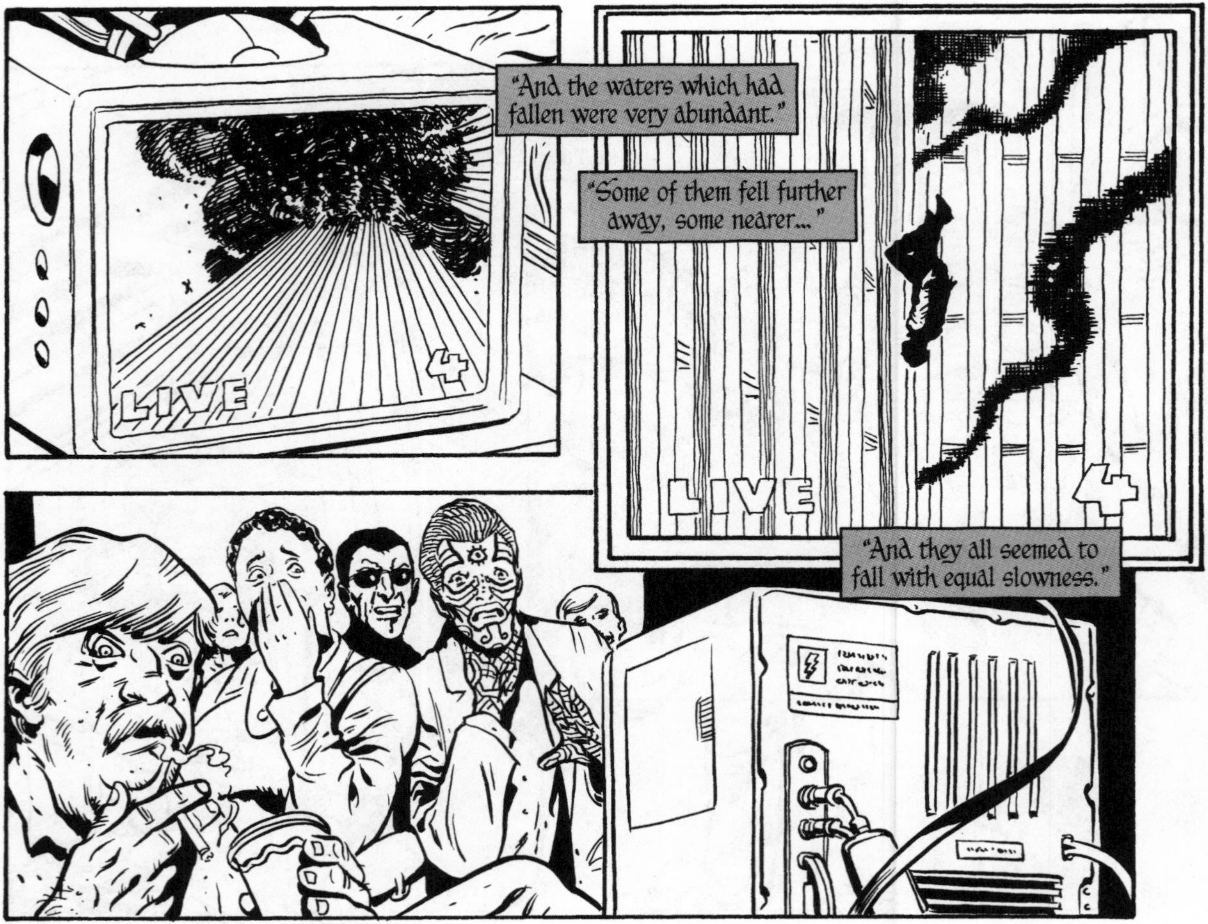
"And the waters which had fallen were very abundant."
LIVE
4
"Some of them fell further away, some nearer..."
LIVE
4
"And they all seemed to fall with equal slowness."

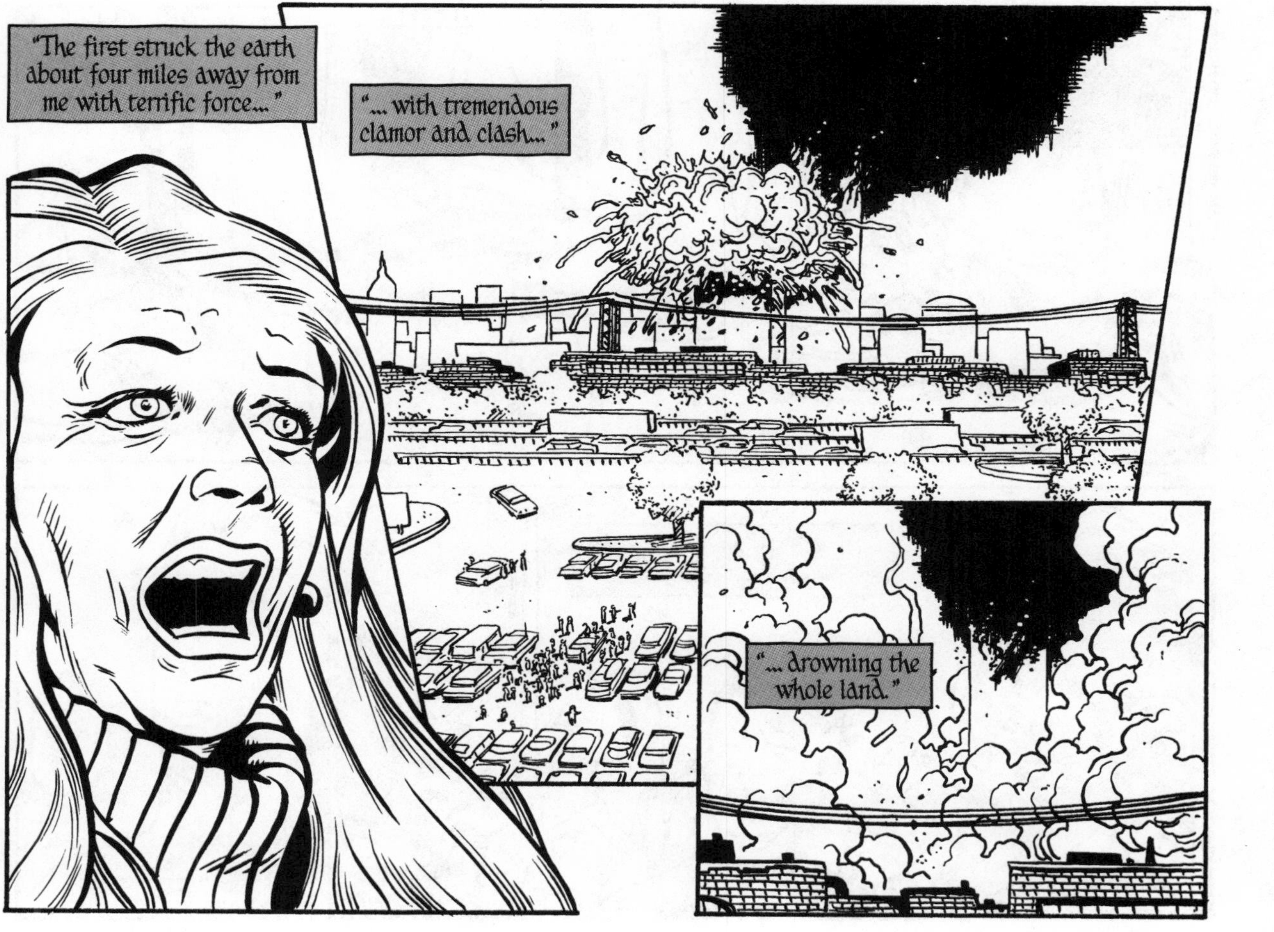
"The first struck the earth about four miles away from me with terrific force..."
"... with tremendous clamor and clash..."
"... drowning the whole land."

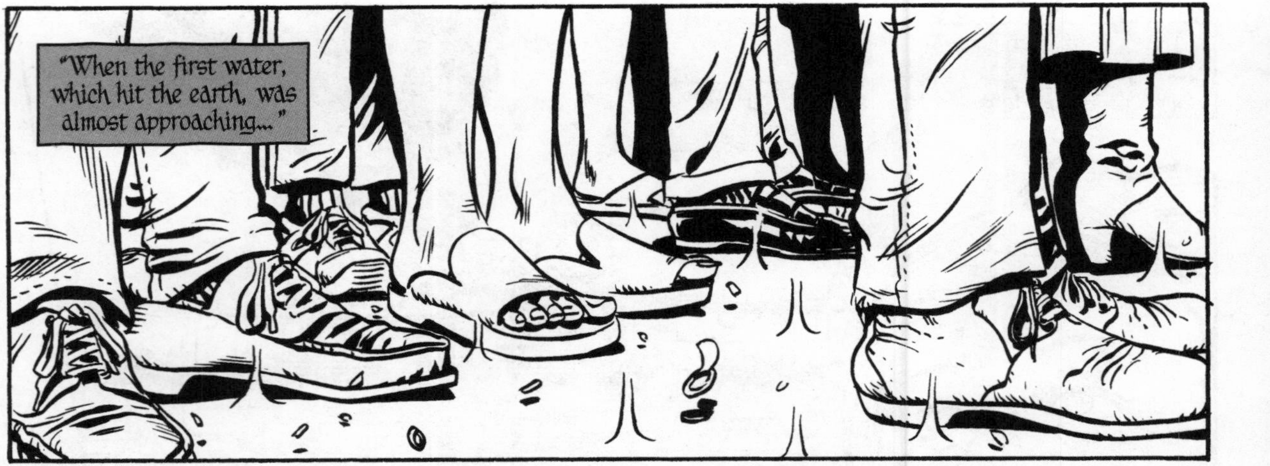
"When the first water, which hit the earth, was almost approaching..."

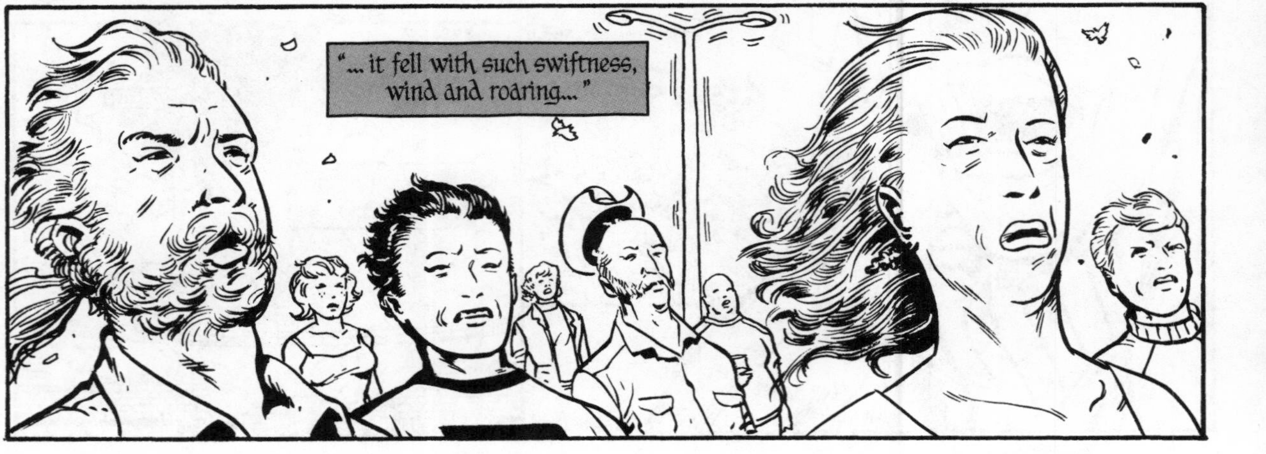
"... it fell with such swiftness, wind and roaring..."

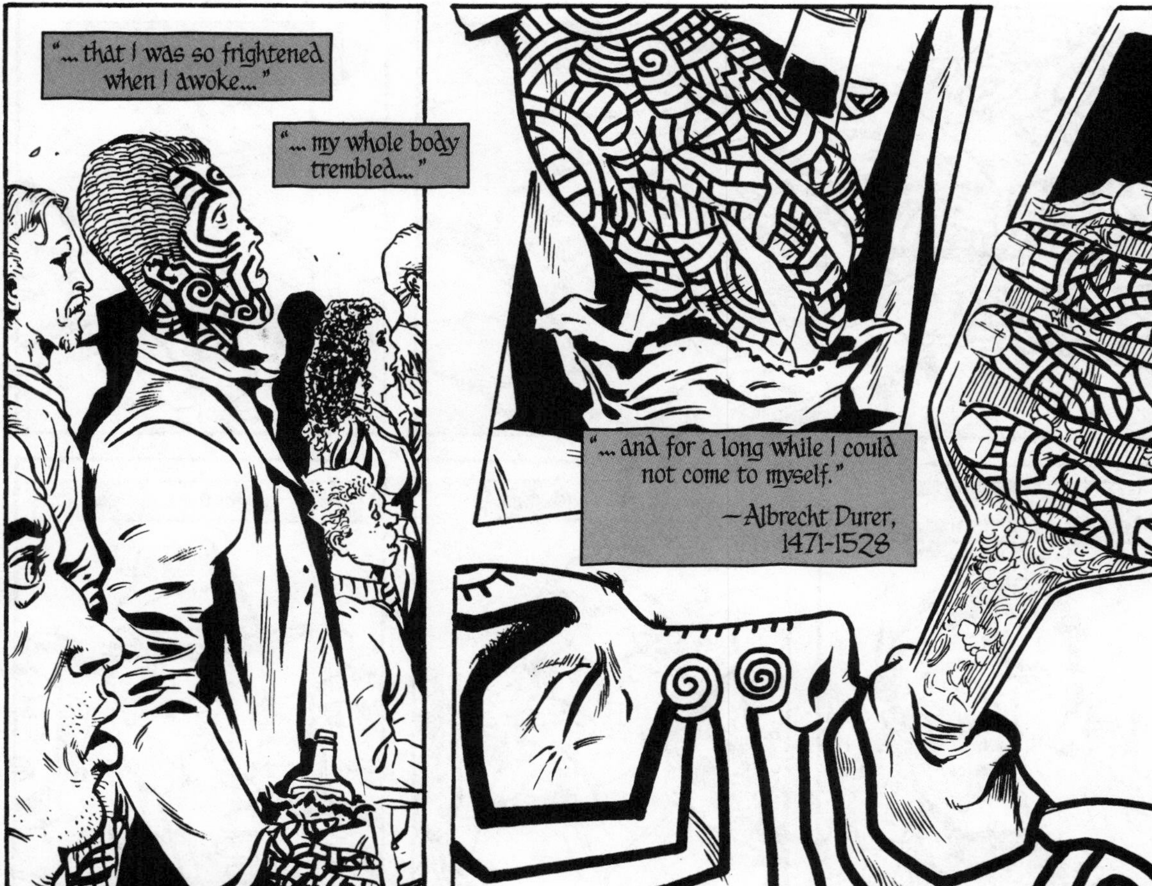
"... that I was so frightened when I awoke..."
"... my whole body trembled..."
"... and for a long while I could not come to myself."
—Albrecht Durer, 1471-1528

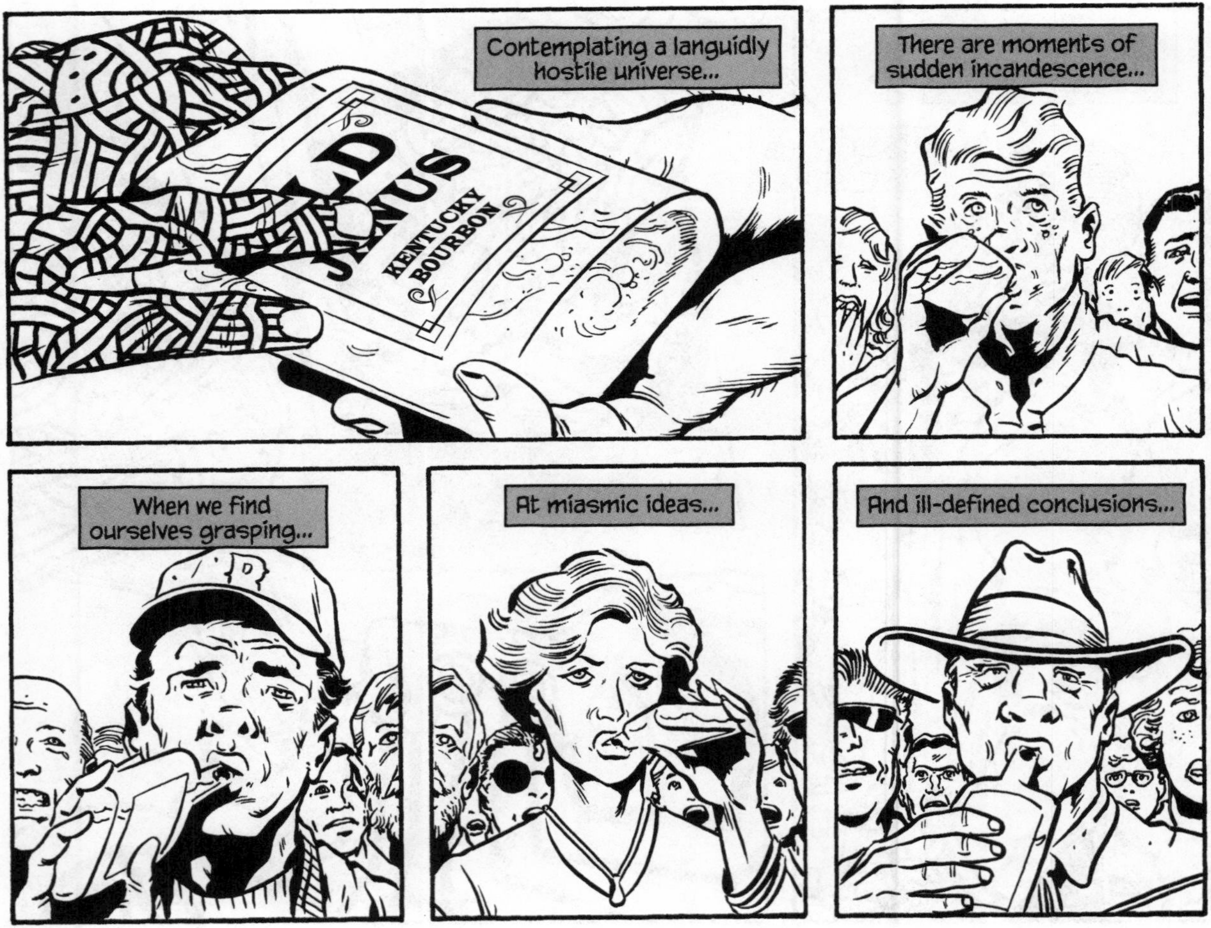
Contemplating a languidly hostile universe...
JD JANUS
KENTUCKY BOURBON
There are moments of sudden incandescence...
When we find ourselves grasping...
At miasmic ideas...
And ill-defined conclusions...

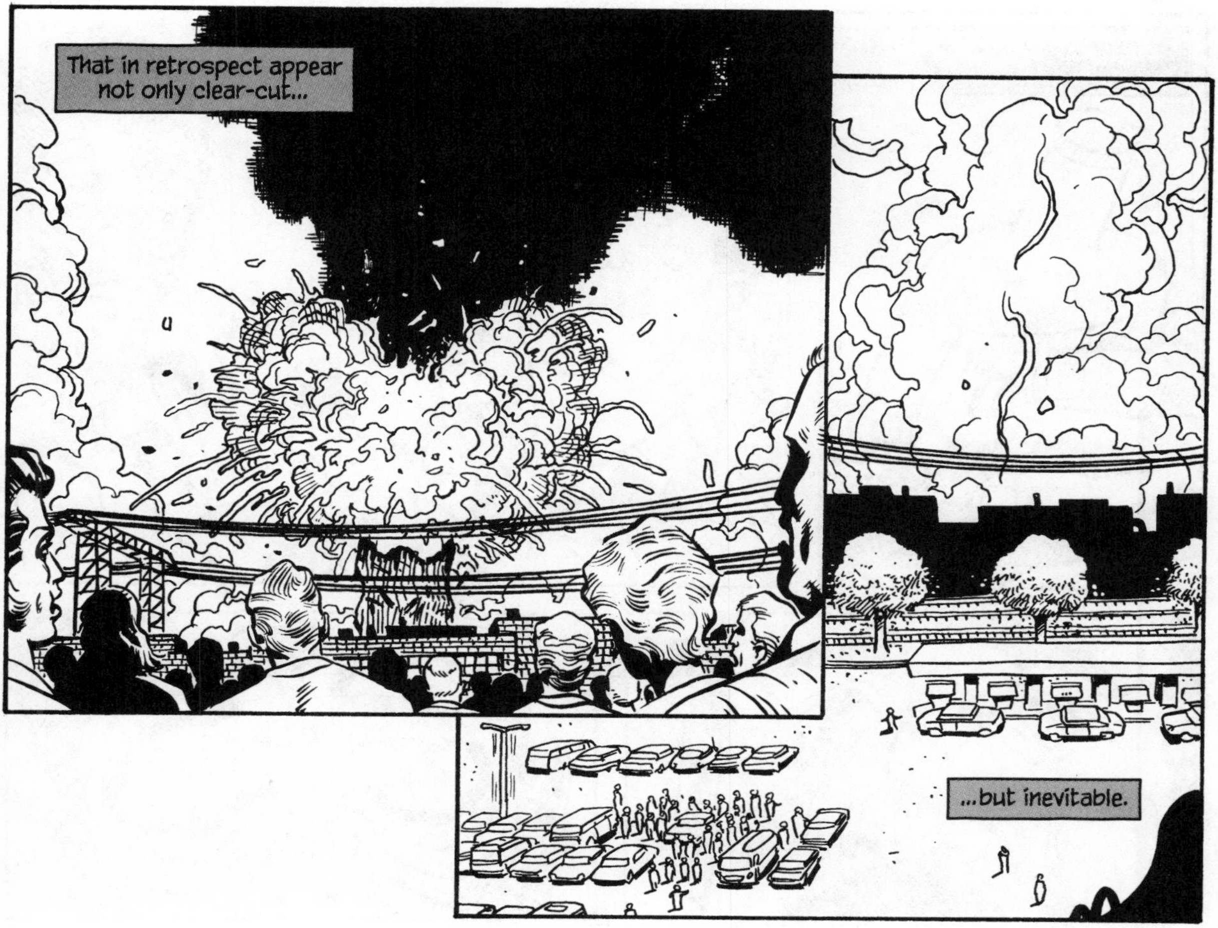
That in retrospect appear not only clear-cut...
...but inevitable.

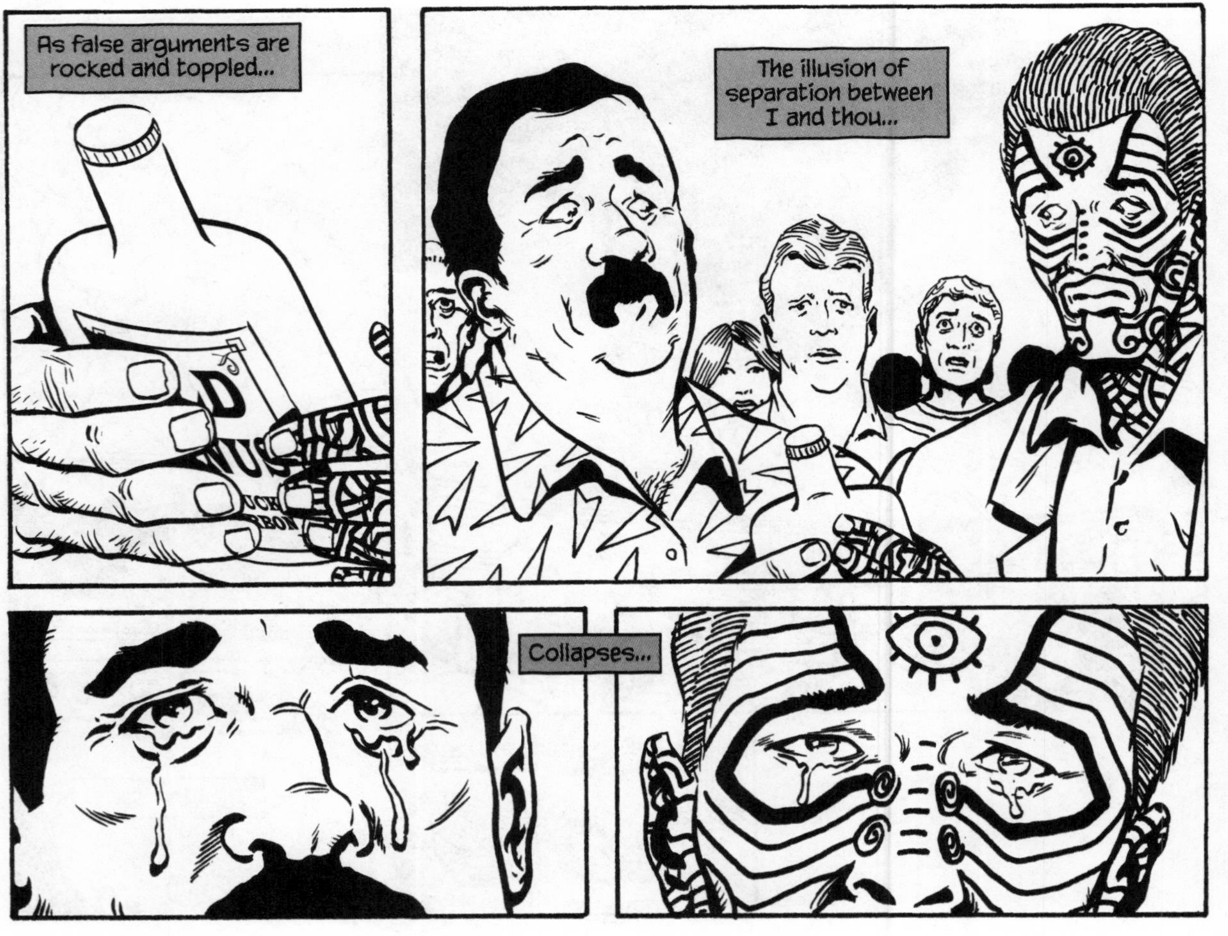
As false arguments are rocked and toppled...
The illusion of separation between I and thou...
Collapses...

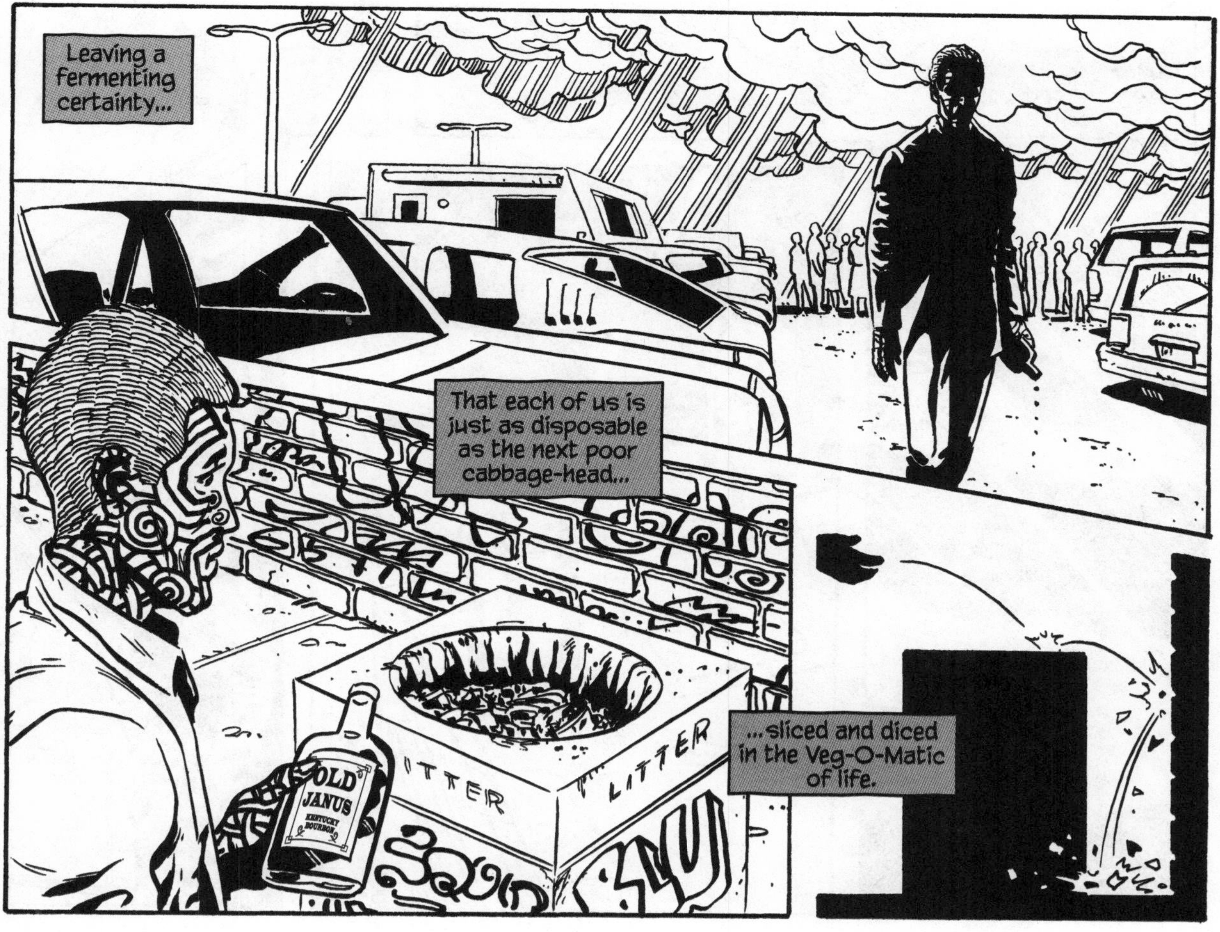
Leaving a fermenting certainty...
That each of us is just as disposable as the next poor cabbage-head...
...sliced and diced in the Veg-O-Matic of life.
OLD JANUS KENTUCKY BOURBON
LITTER
LITTER

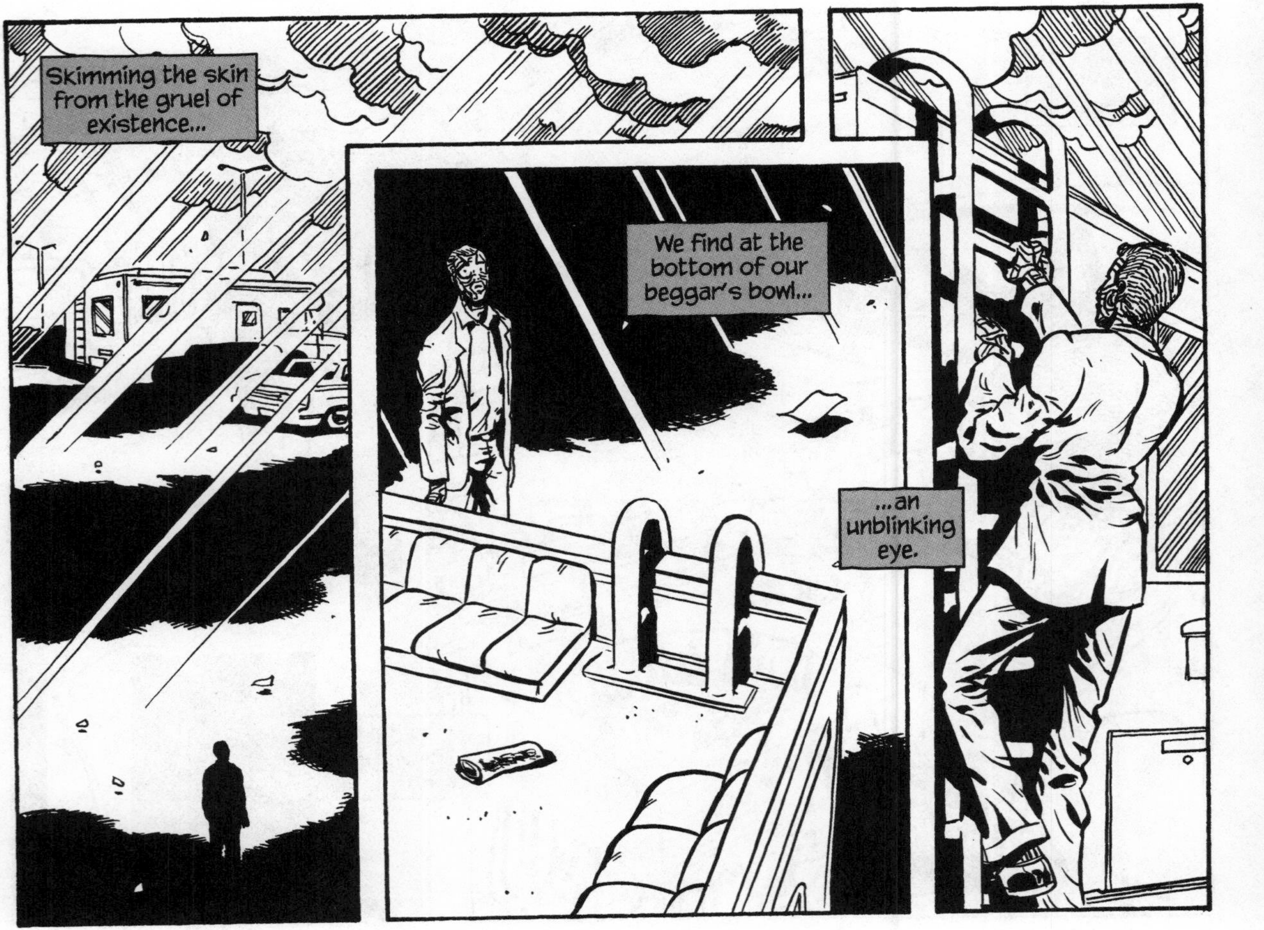
Skimming the skin from the gruel of existence...
We find at the bottom of our beggar's bowl...
...an unblinking eye.

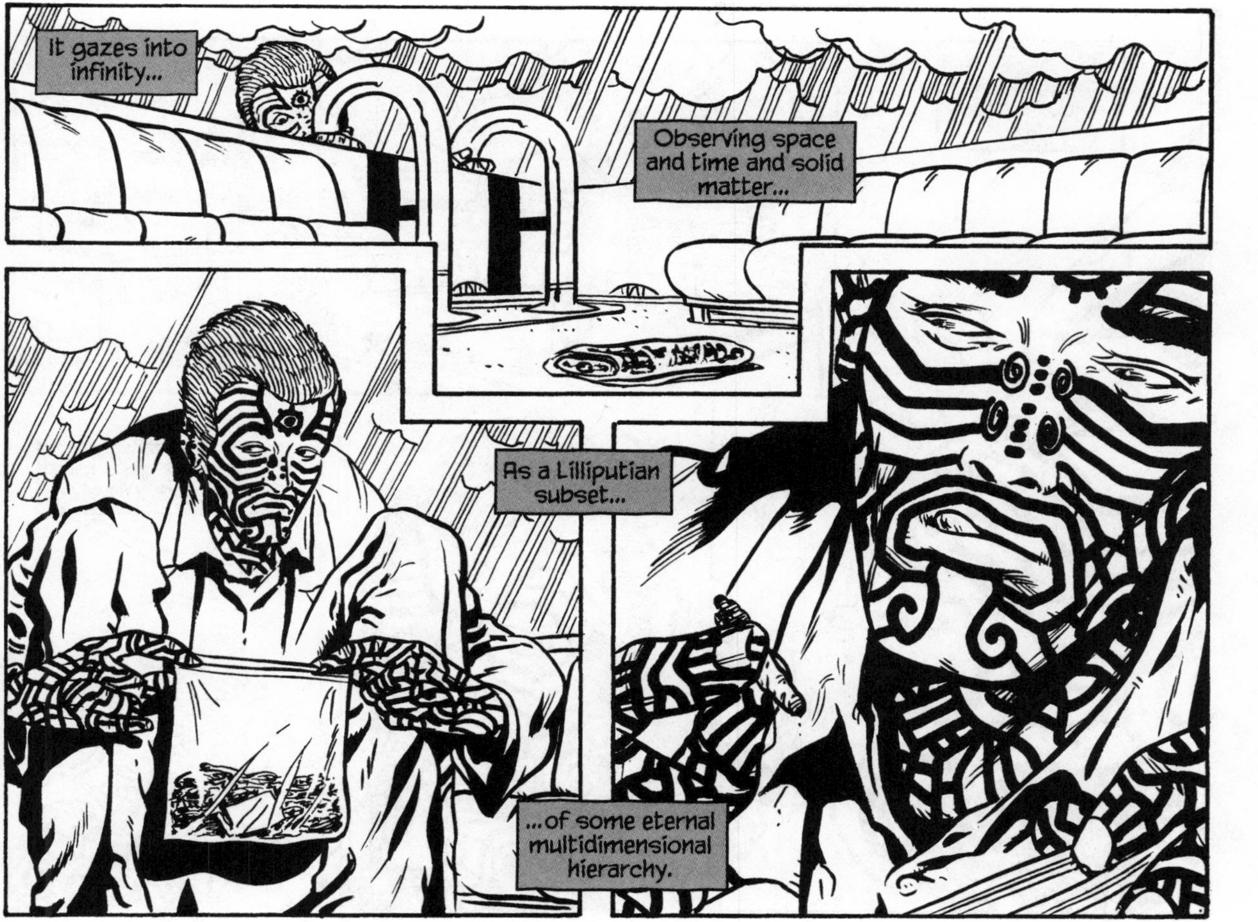
It gazes into infinity...
Observing space and time and solid matter...
As a Lilliputian subset...
...of some eternal multidimensional hierarchy.

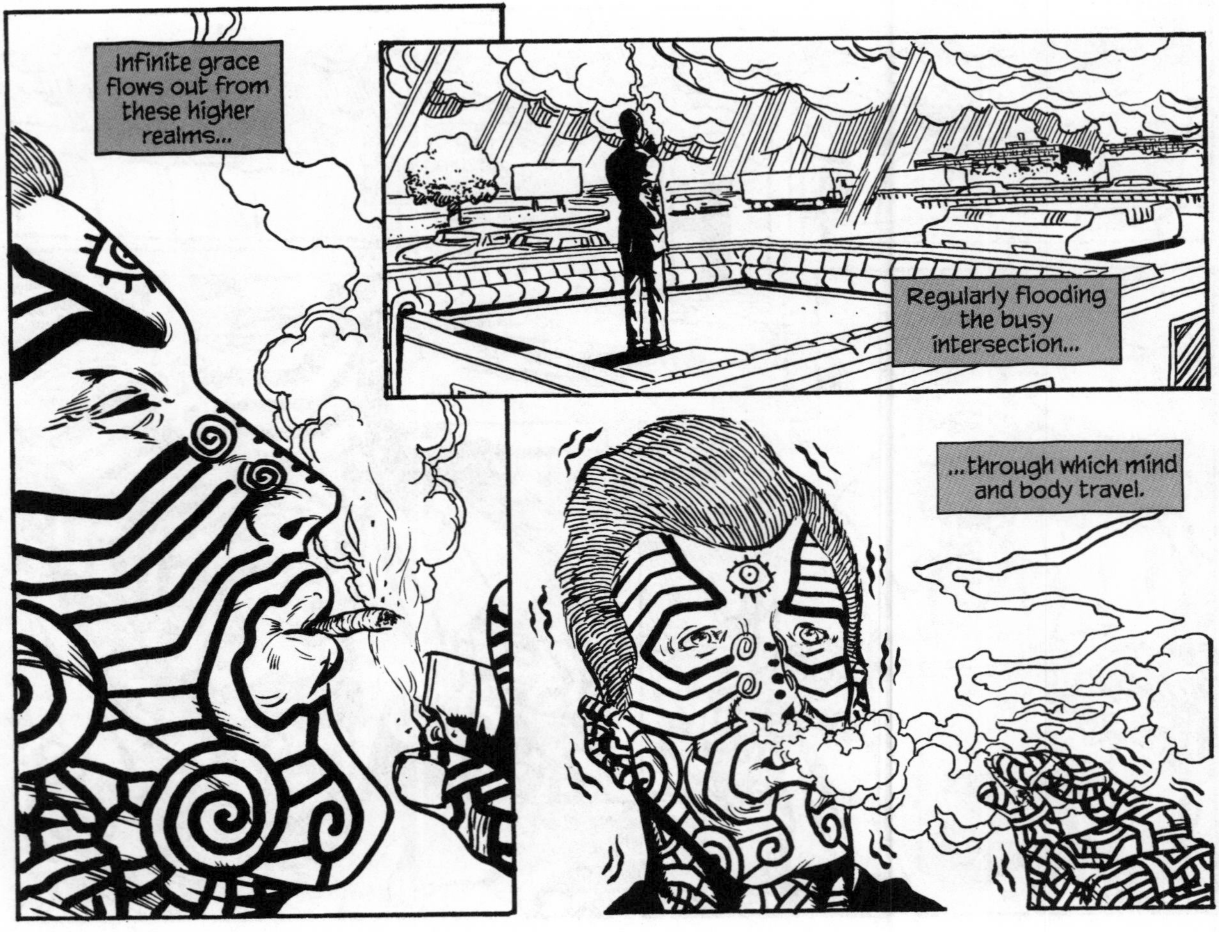
Infinite grace flows out from these higher realms...
Regularly flooding the busy intersection...
...through which mind and body travel.

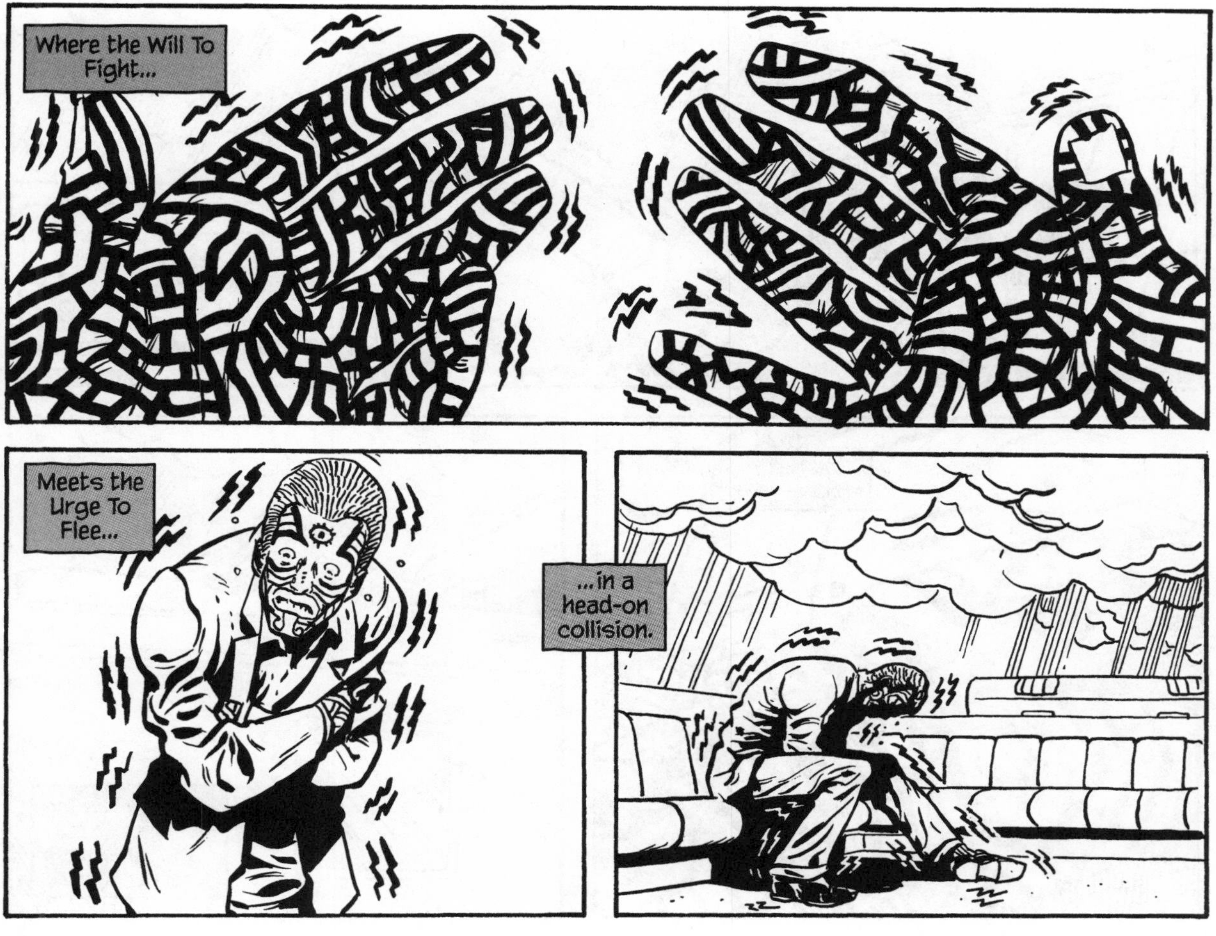
Where the Will To Fight...
Meets the Urge To Flee...
...in a head-on collision.

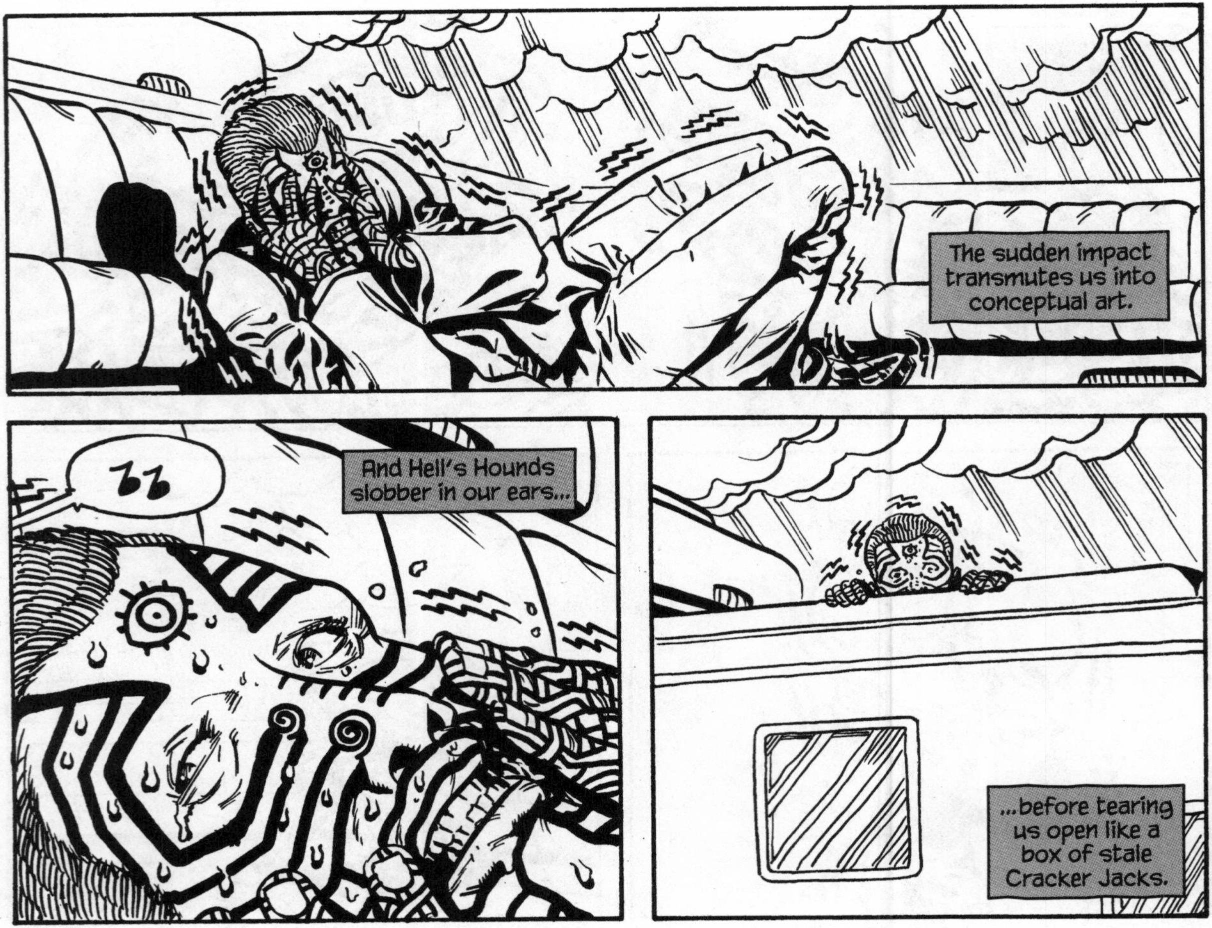
The sudden impact transmutes us into conceptual art.
ZZ
And Hell's Hounds slobber in our ears...
...before tearing us open like a box of stale Cracker Jacks.

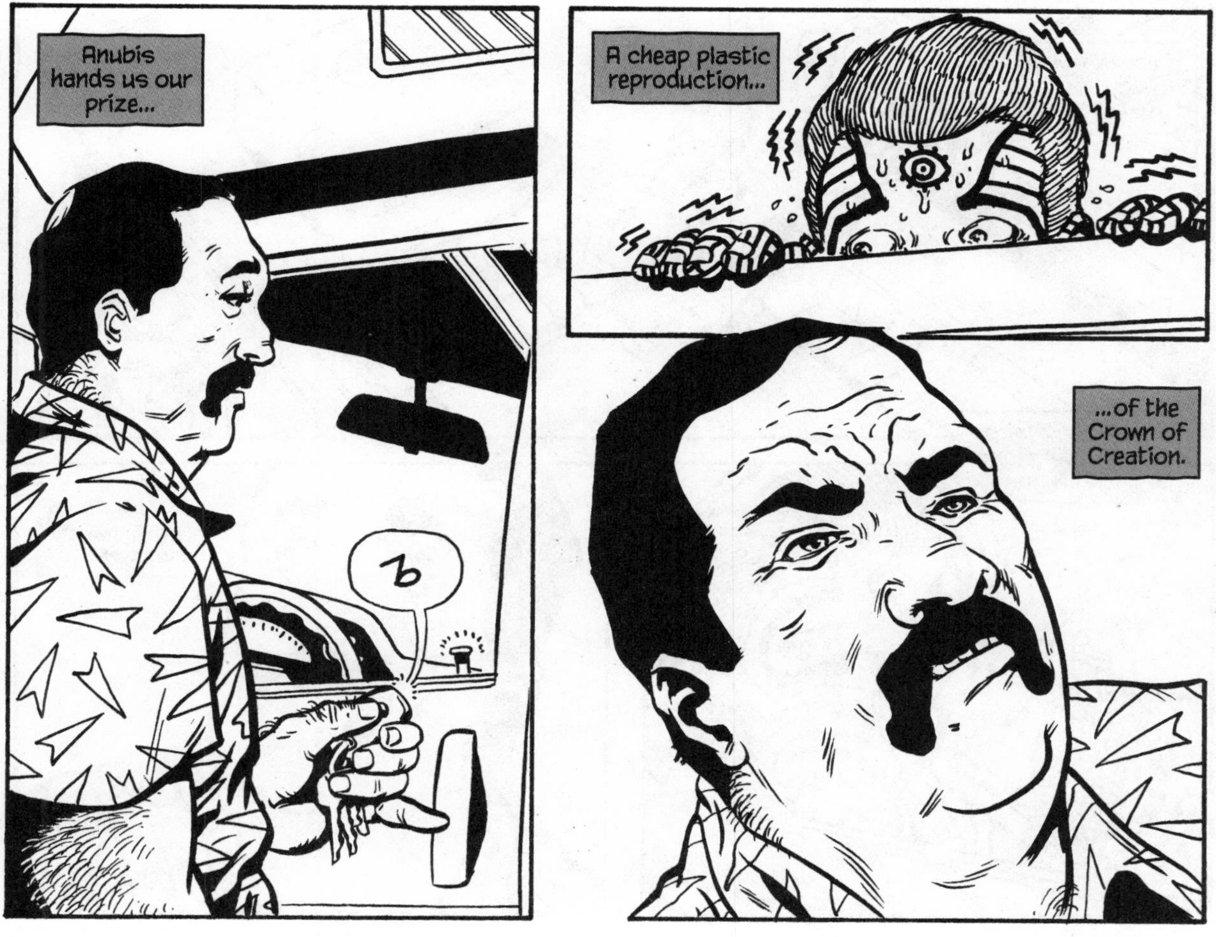
Anubis hands us our prize...
A cheap plastic reproduction...
...of the Crown of Creation.

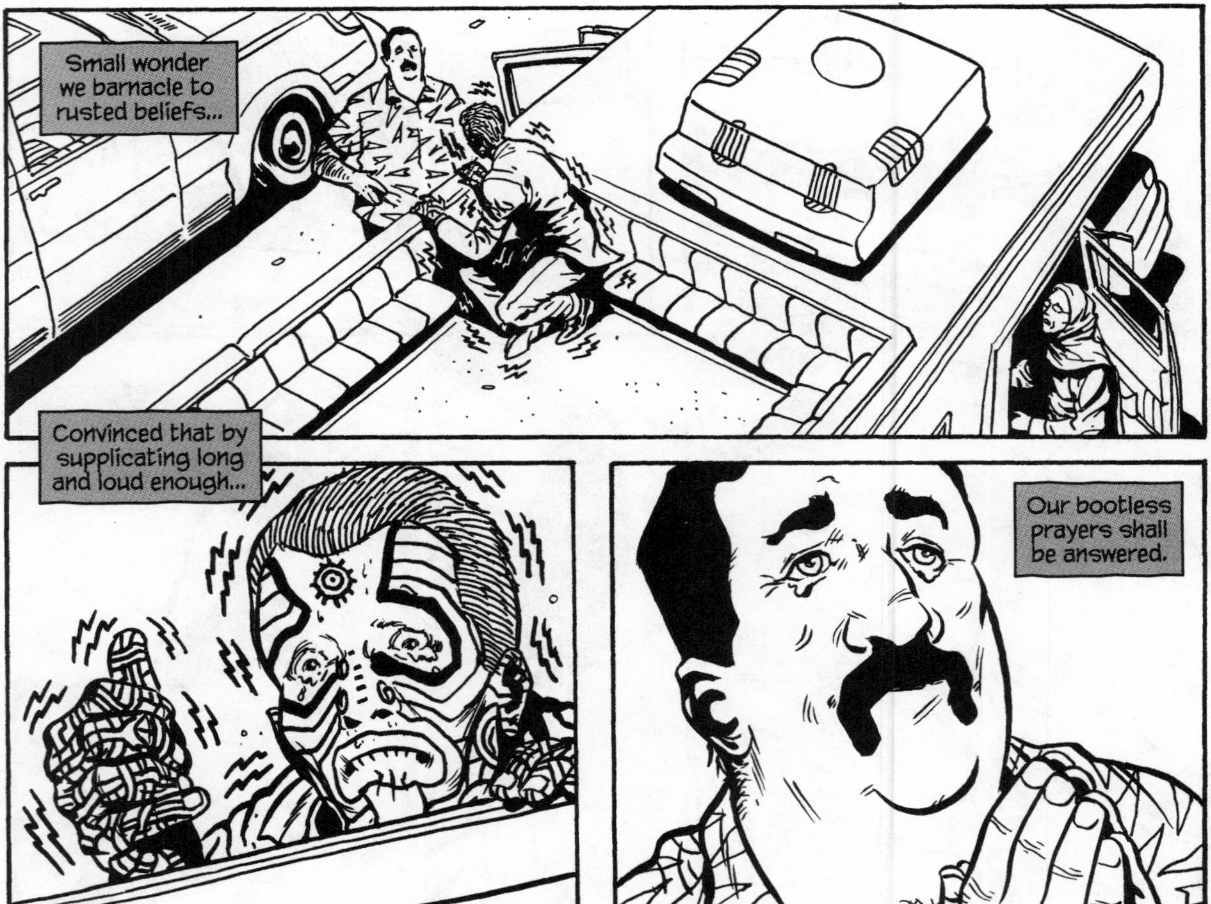
Small wonder we barnacle to rusted beliefs...
Convinced that by supplicating long and loud enough...
Our bootless prayers shall be answered.

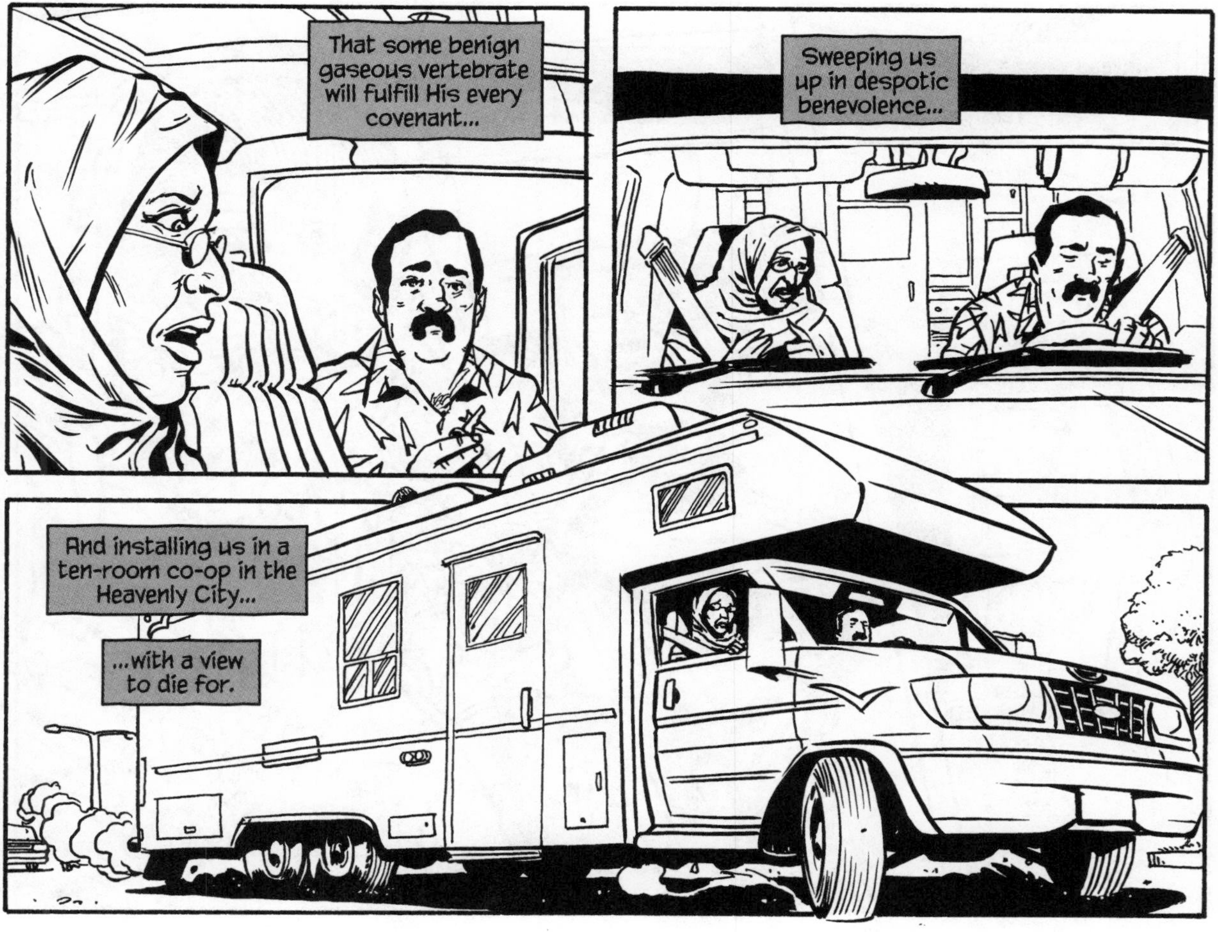
That some benign gaseous vertebrate will fulfill His every covenant...
Sweeping us up in despotic benevolence...
And installing us in a ten-room co-op in the Heavenly City...
...with a view to die for.

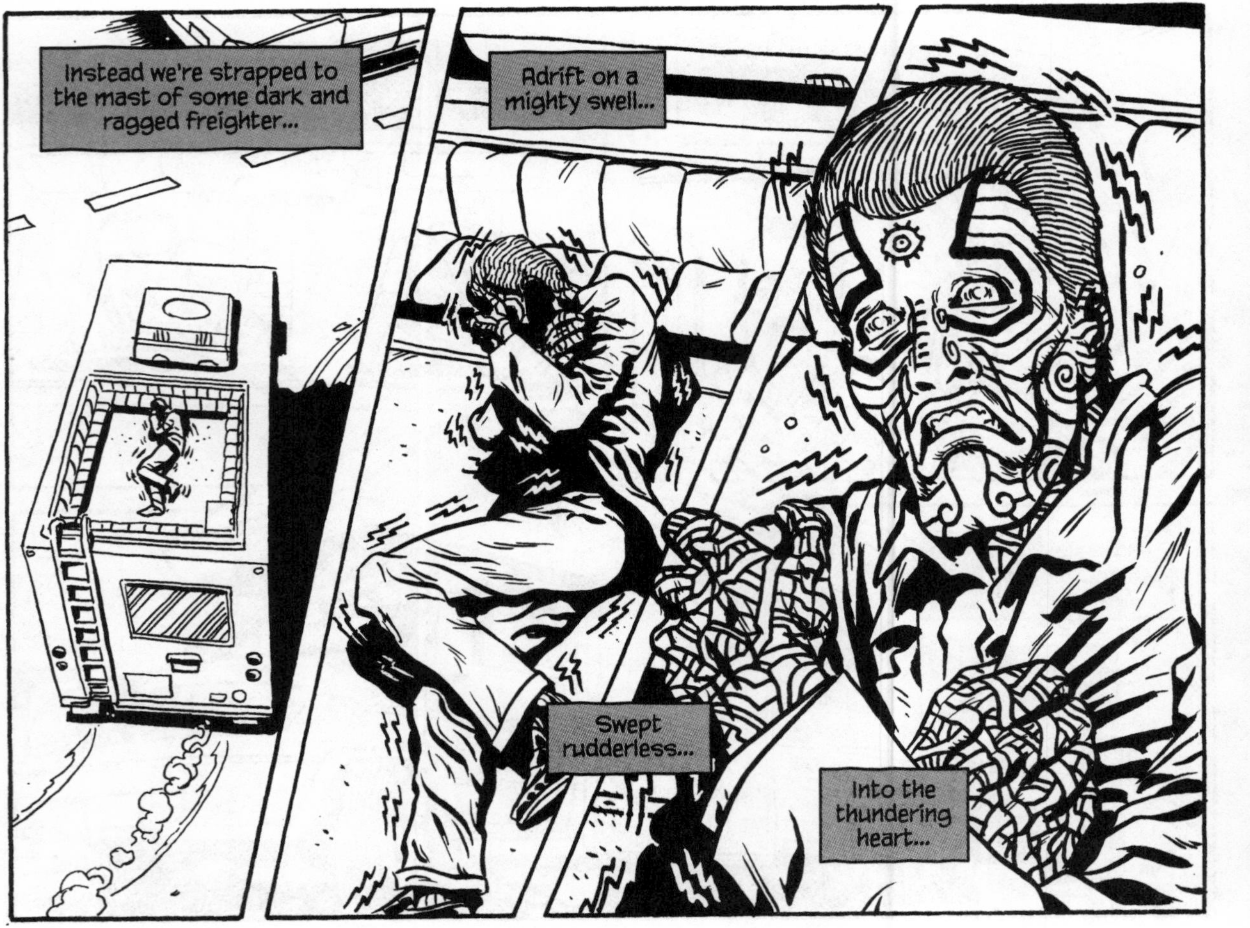
Instead we're strapped to the mast of some dark and ragged freighter...
Adrift on a mighty swell...
Swept rudderless...
Into the thundering heart...

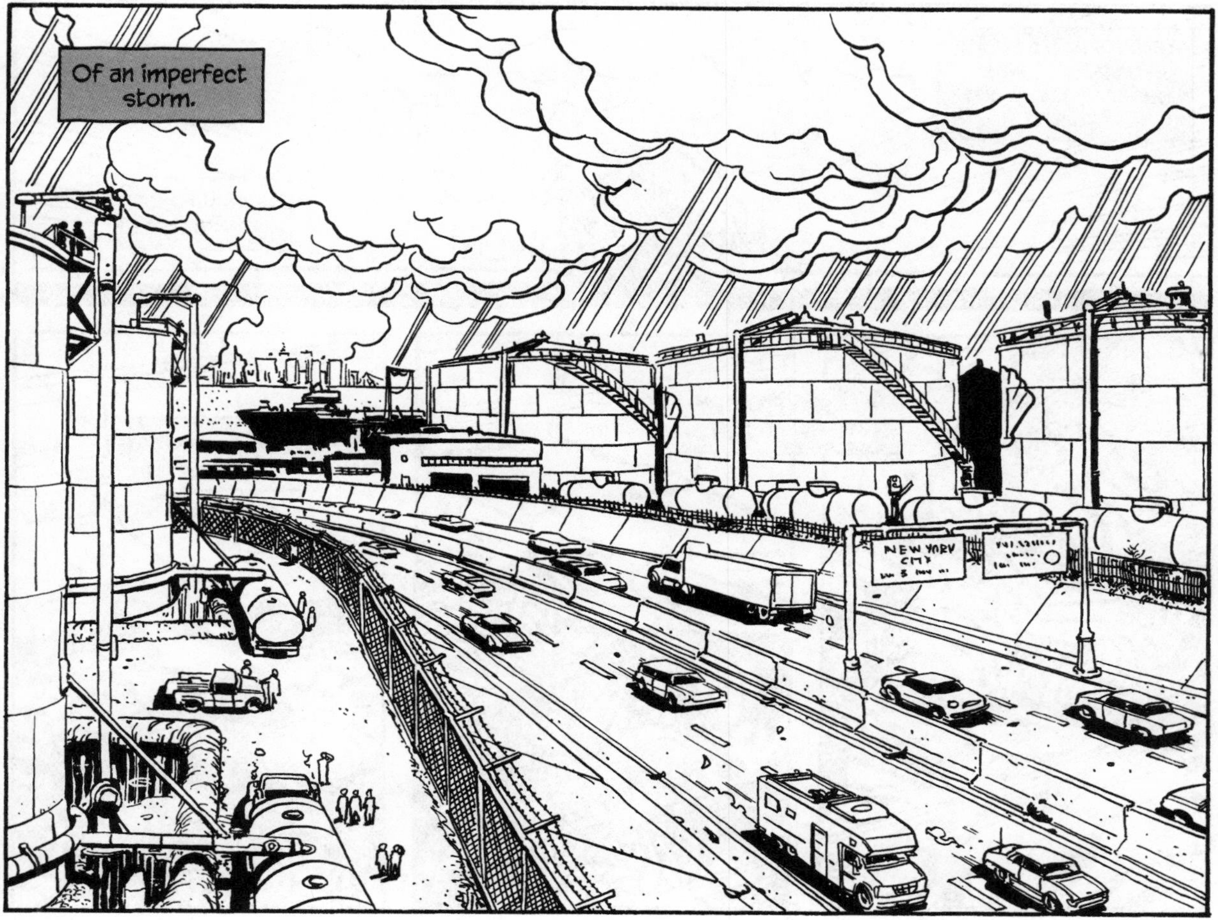
Of an imperfect storm.

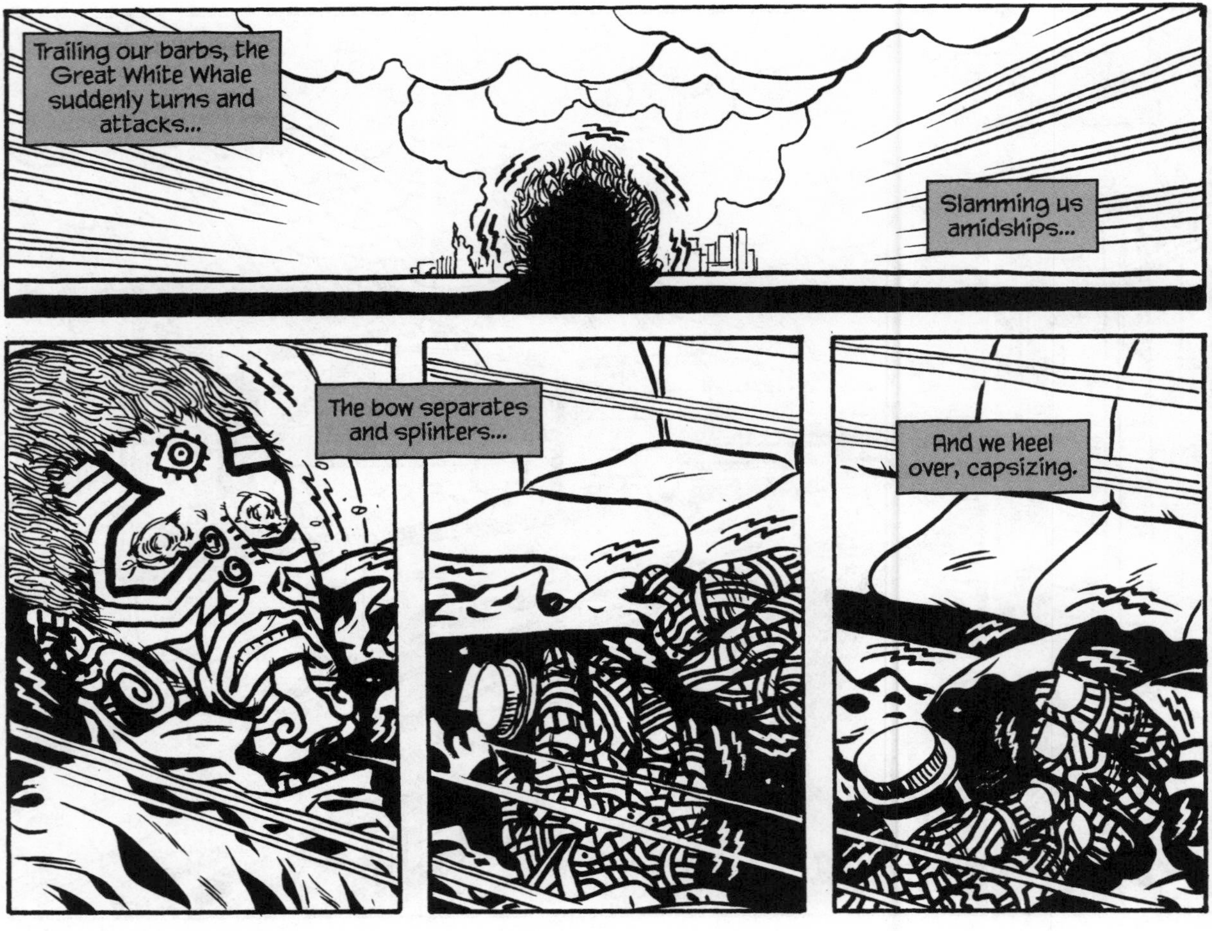
Trailing our barbs, the Great White Whale suddenly turns and attacks...
Slamming us amidships...
The bow separates and splinters...
And we heel over, capsizing.

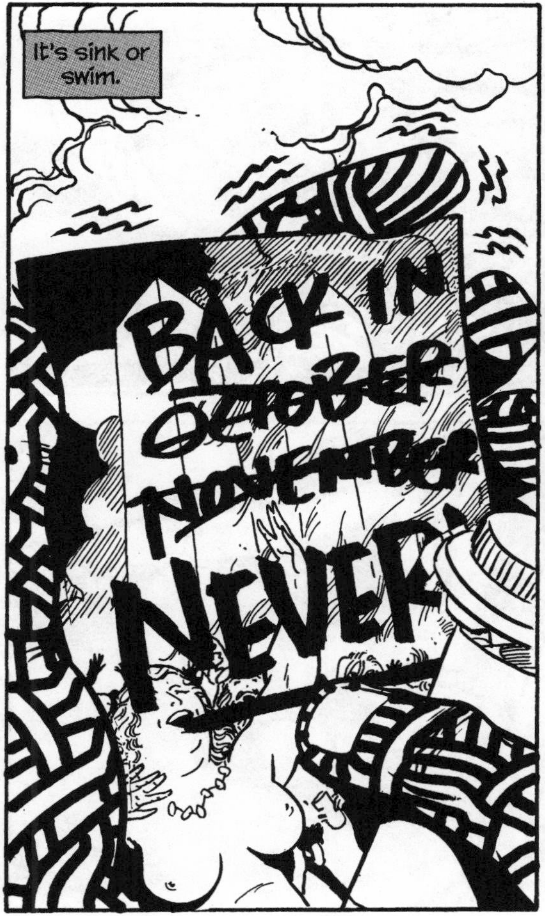
It's sink or swim.
BACK IN OCTOBER NOVEMBER NEVER

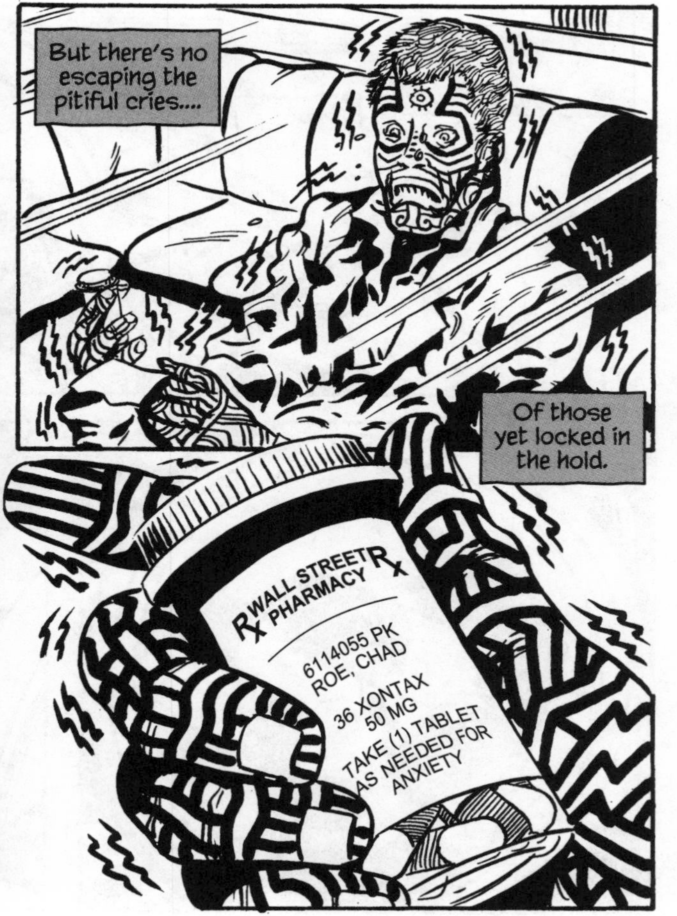
But there's no escaping the pitiful cries....
Of those yet locked in the hold.
WALL STREET PHARMACY
6114055 PK
ROE, CHAD
36 XONTAX
50 MG
TAKE (1) TABLET AS NEEDED FOR ANXIETY

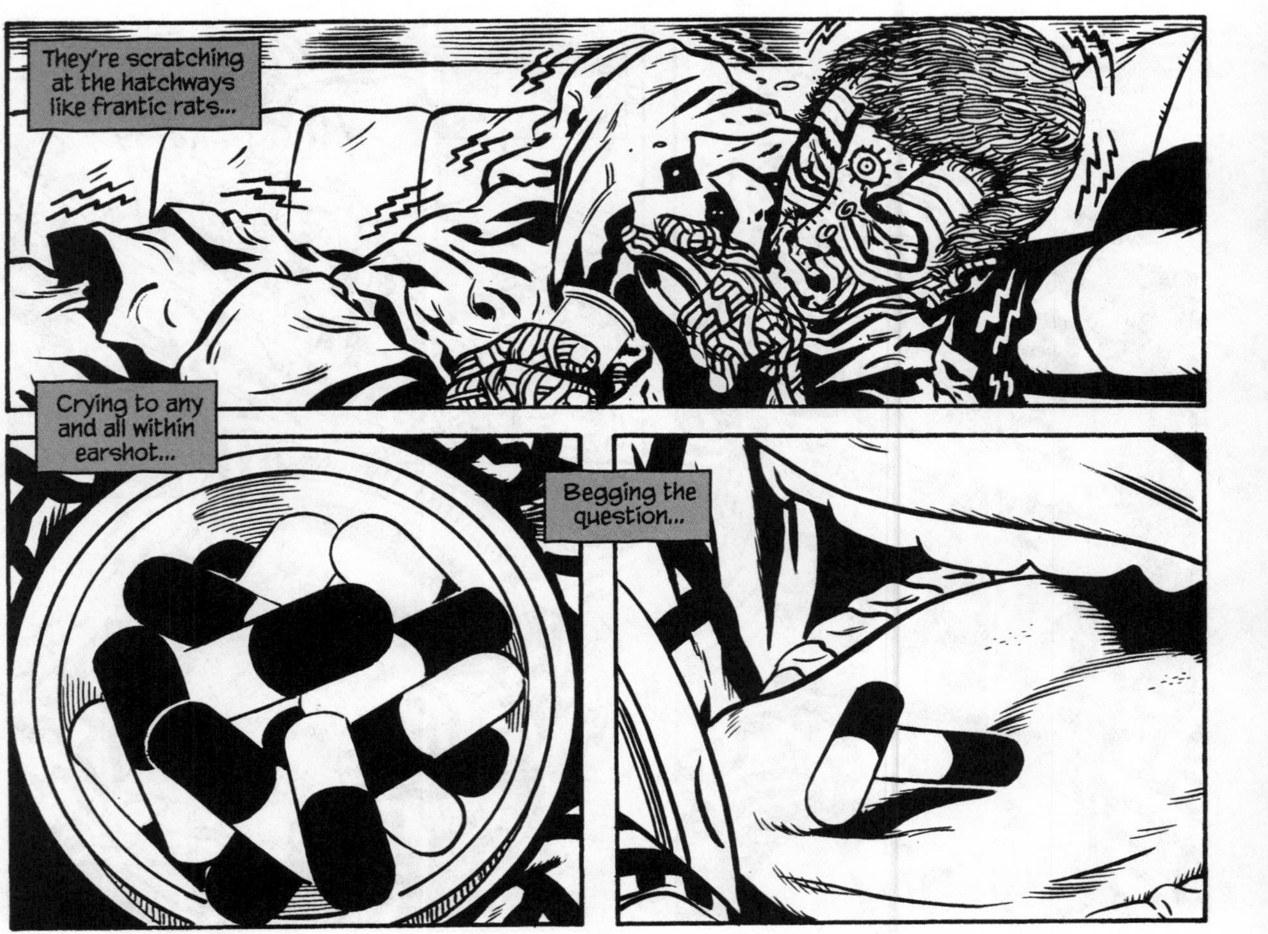
They're scratching at the hatchways like frantic rats...
Crying to any and all within earshot...
Begging the question...

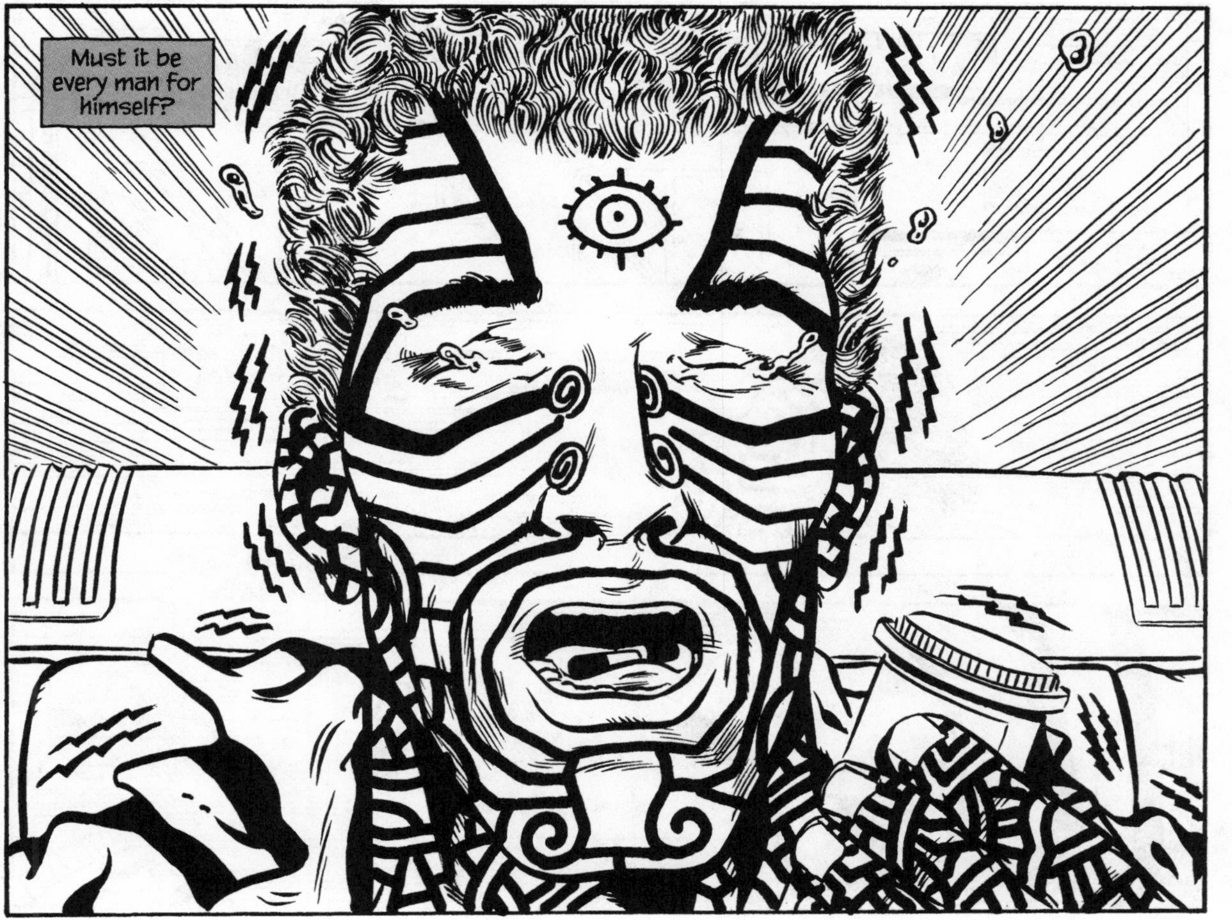
Must it be every man for himself?

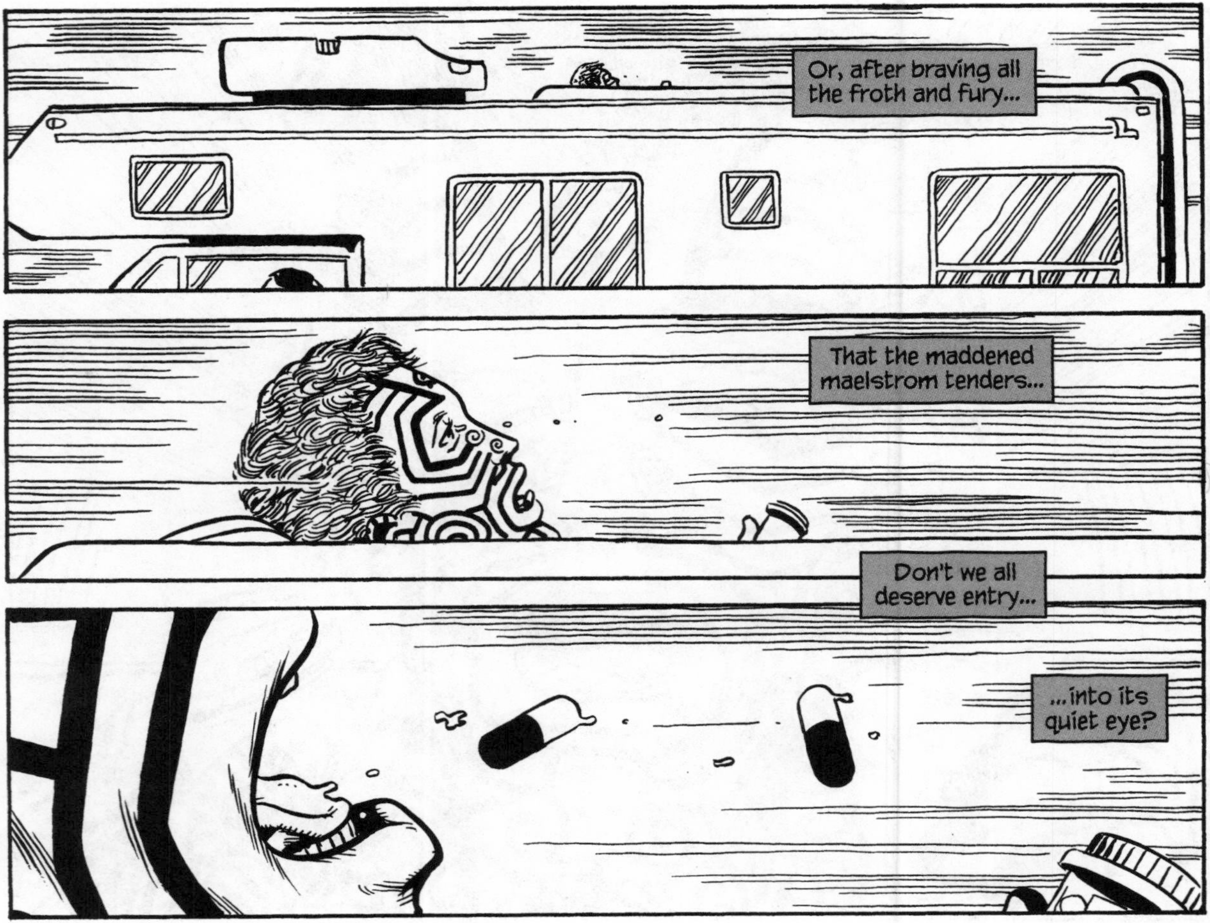
Or, after braving all the froth and fury...
That the maddened maelstrom tenders...
Don't we all deserve entry...
...into its quiet eye?

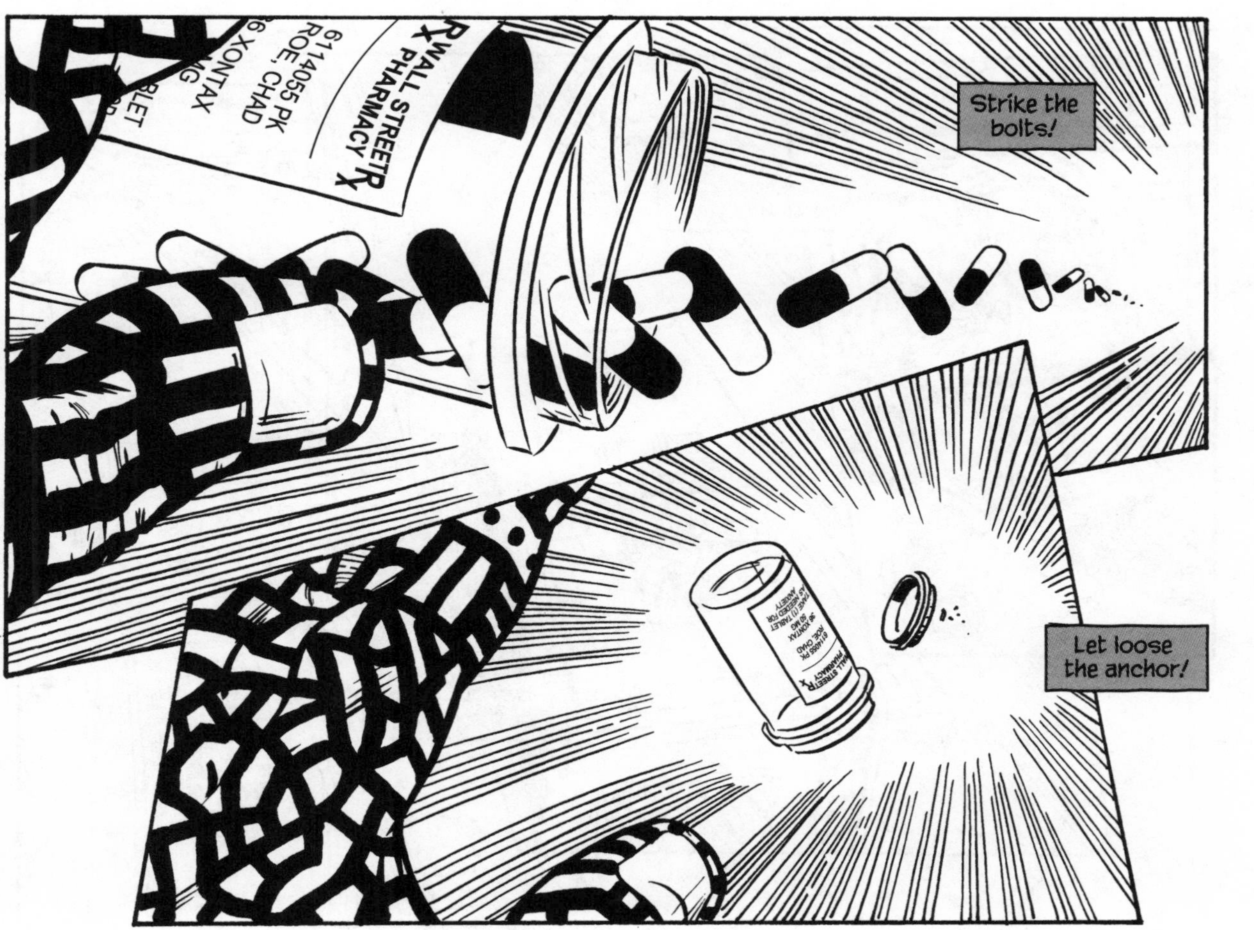
WALL STREET
PHARMACY
61-14055 PK
ROE, CHAD
Strike the bolts!
Let loose the anchor!

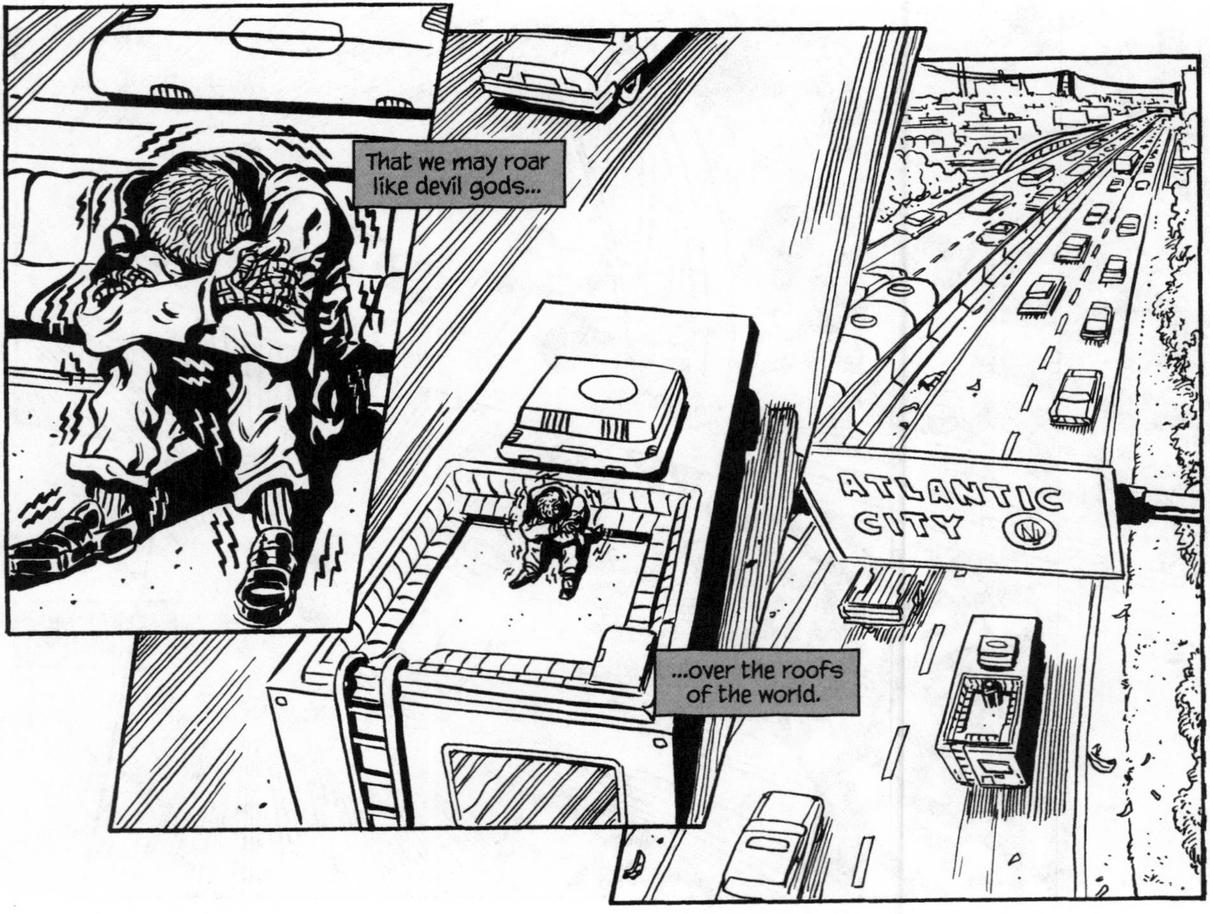
That we may roar like devil gods...
ATLANTIC CITY
...over the roofs of the world.

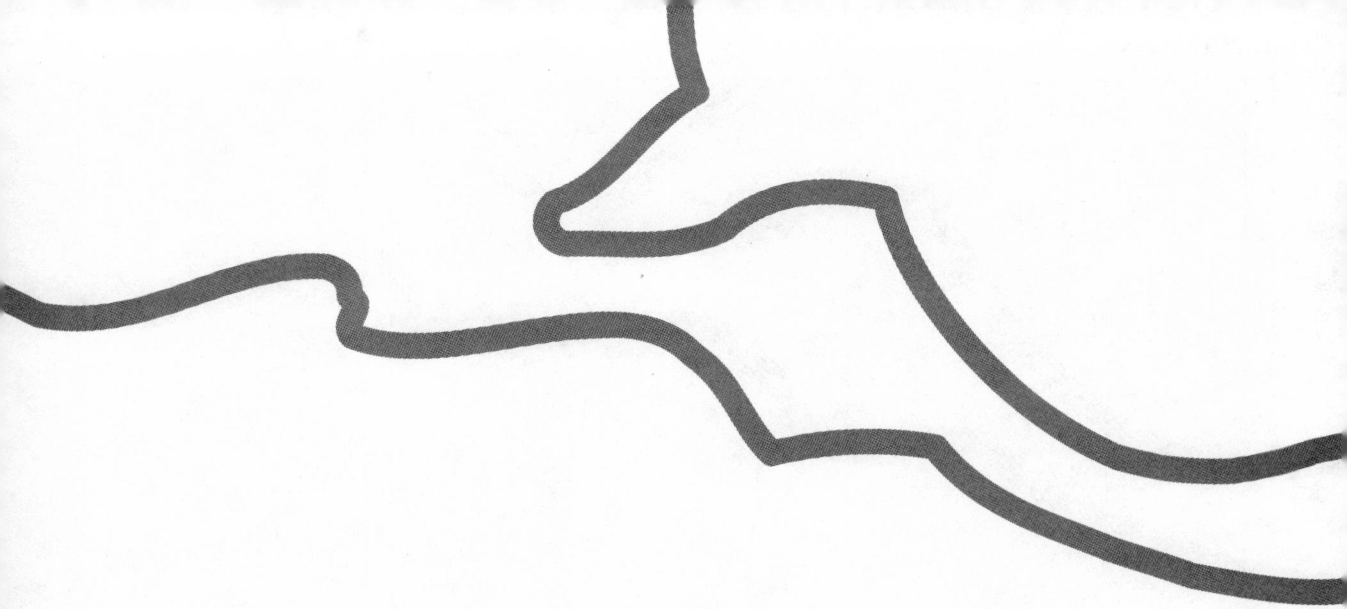

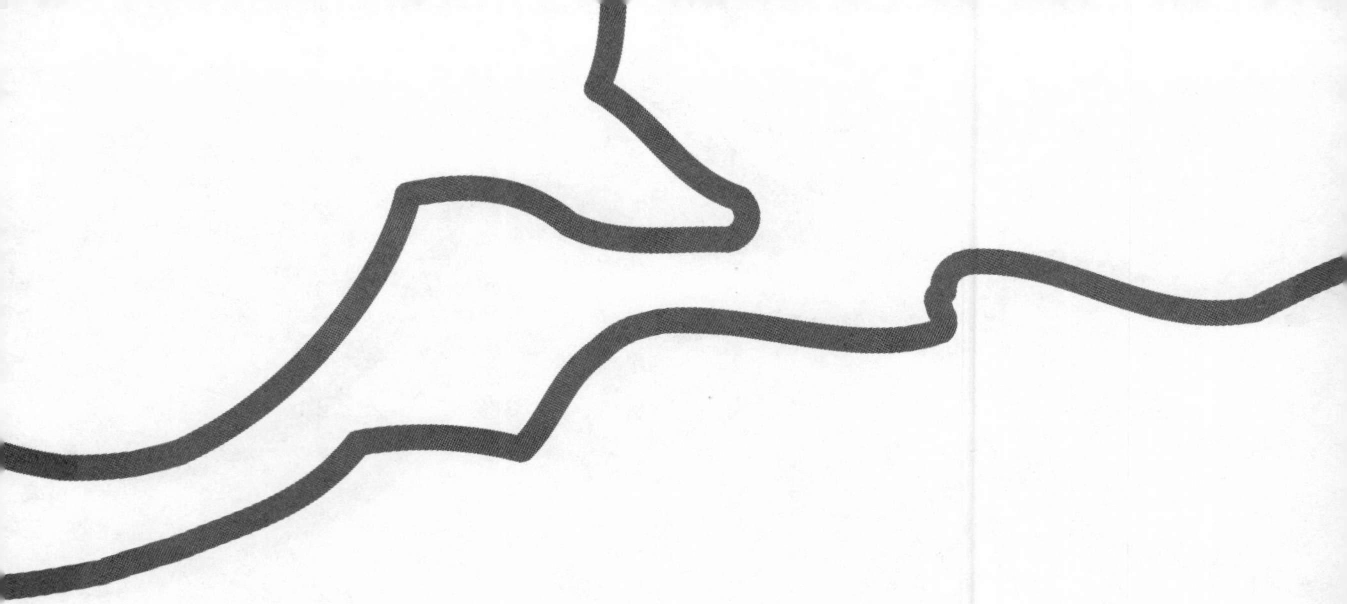

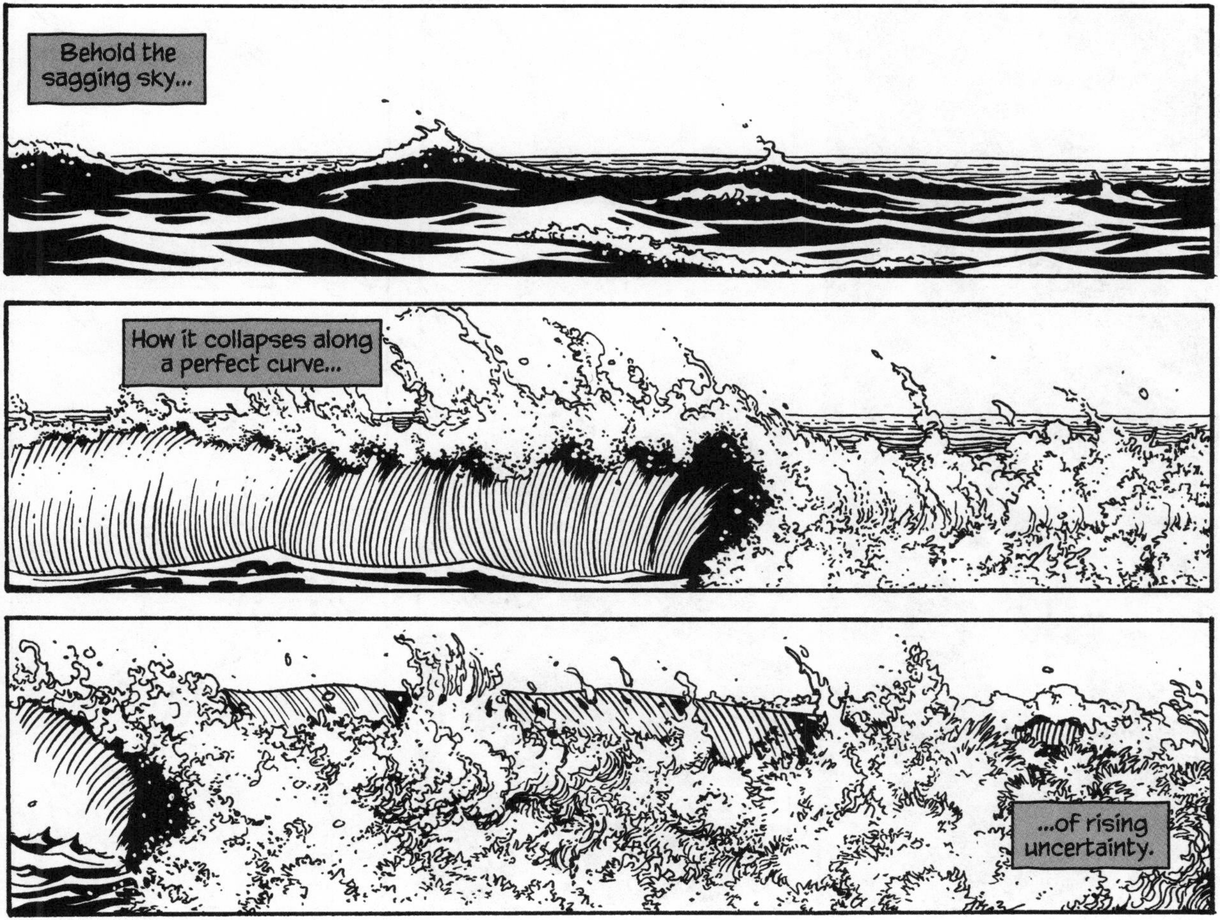
Behold the sagging sky...
How it collapses along a perfect curve...
...of rising uncertainty.

Subatomic yeast is fermenting...

Possibility is kneaded like ropy dough.

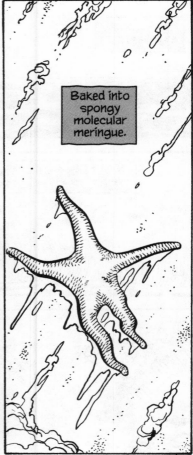

Baked into spongy molecular meringue.

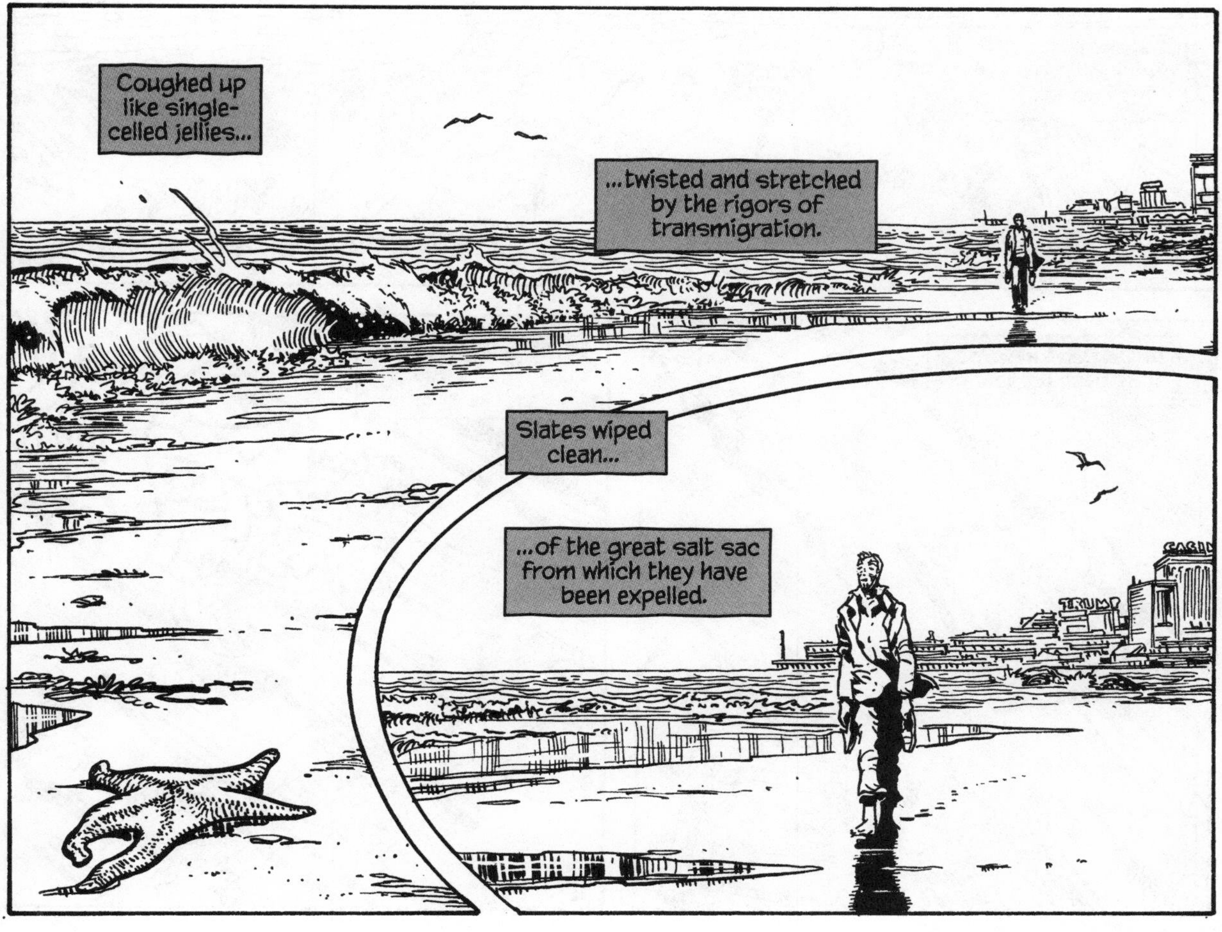
Coughed up like single-celled jellies...
...twisted and stretched by the rigors of transmigration.
Slates wiped clean...
...of the great salt sac from which they have been expelled.

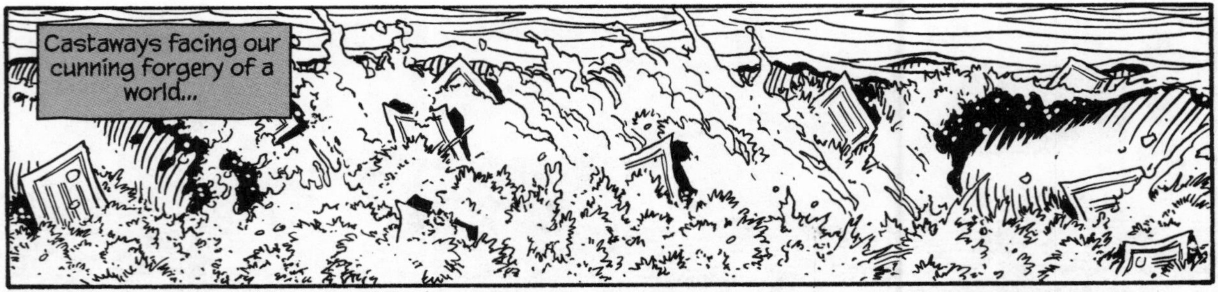
Castaways facing our cunning forgery of a world...

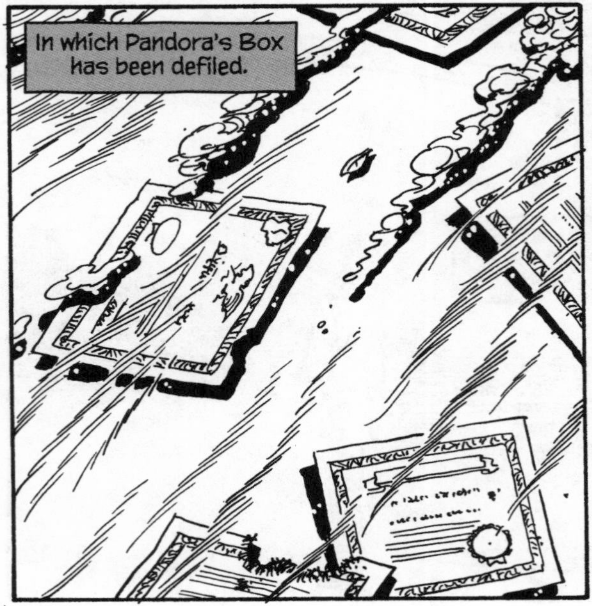
In which Pandora's Box has been defiled.

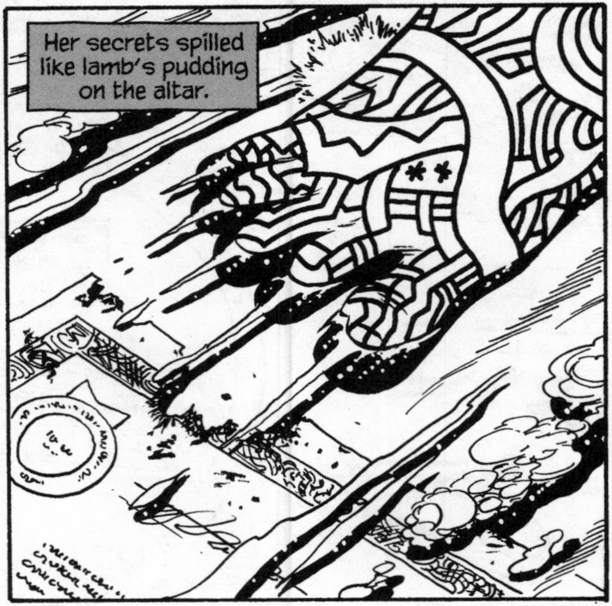
Her secrets spilled like lamb's pudding on the altar.

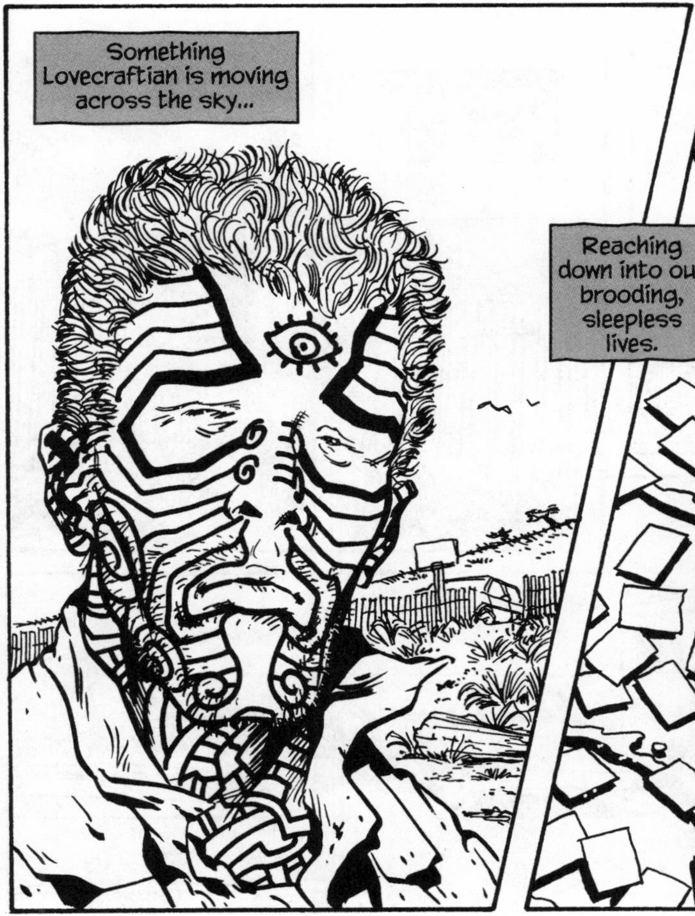
Something Lovecraftian is moving across the sky...

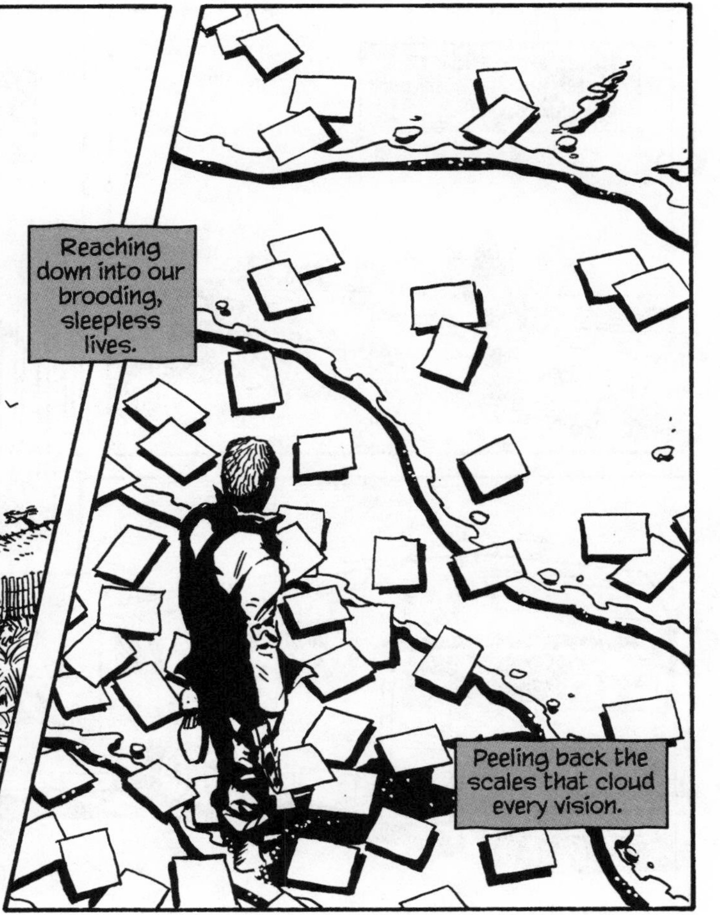
Reaching down into our brooding, sleepless lives.
Peeling back the scales that cloud every vision.

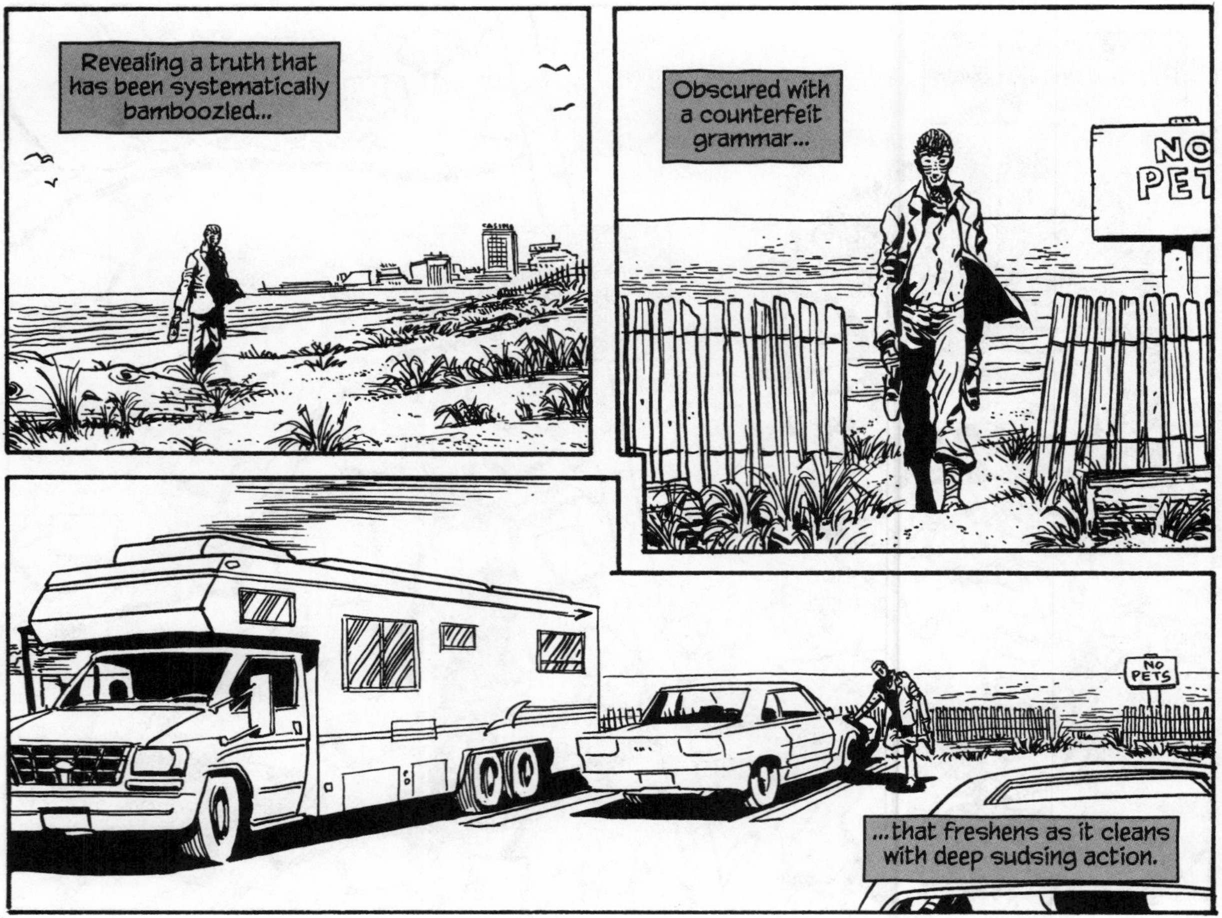
Revealing a truth that has been systematically bamboozled...
Obscured with a counterfeit grammar...
NO PETS
CASINO
NO PETS
...that freshens as it cleans with deep sudsing action.

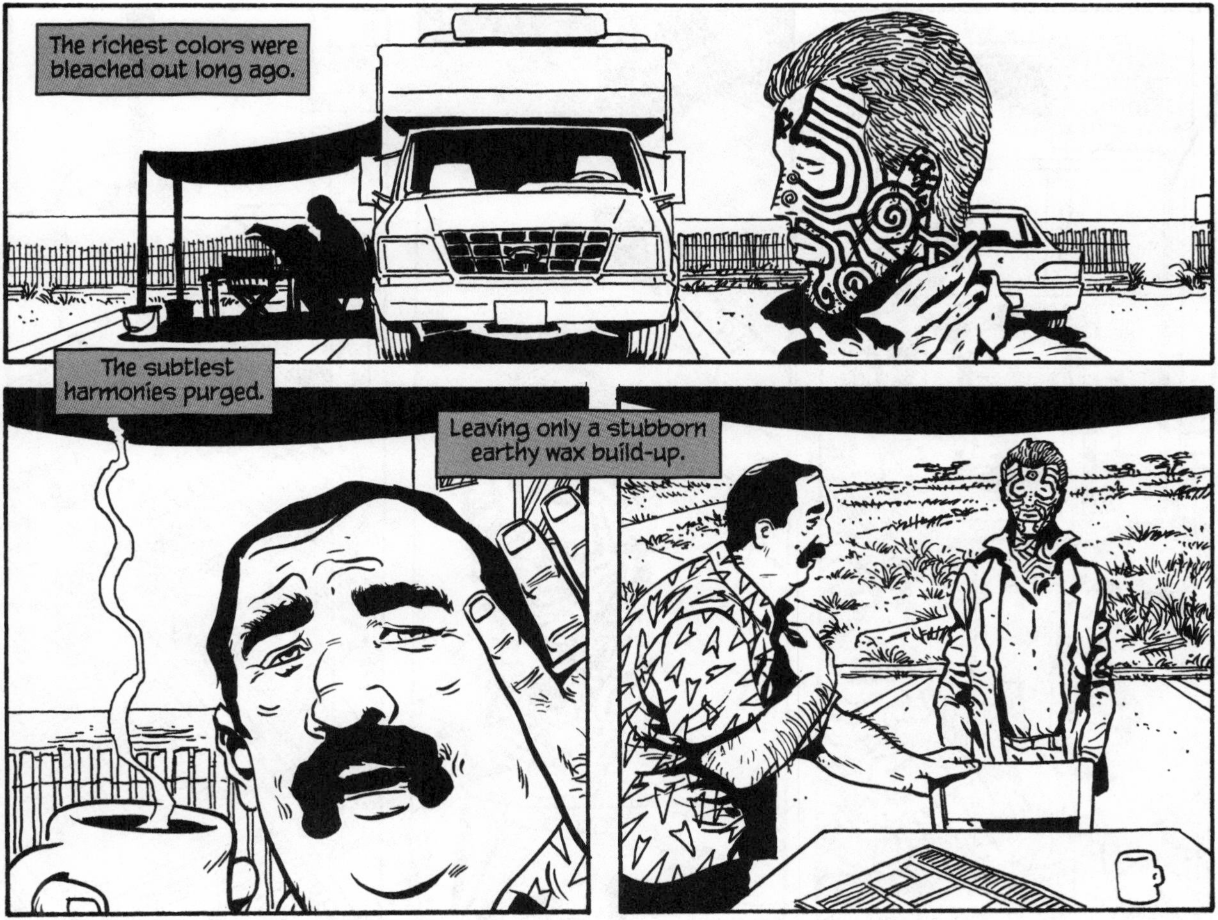
The richest colors were bleached out long ago.
The subtlest harmonies purged.
Leaving only a stubborn earthy wax build-up.

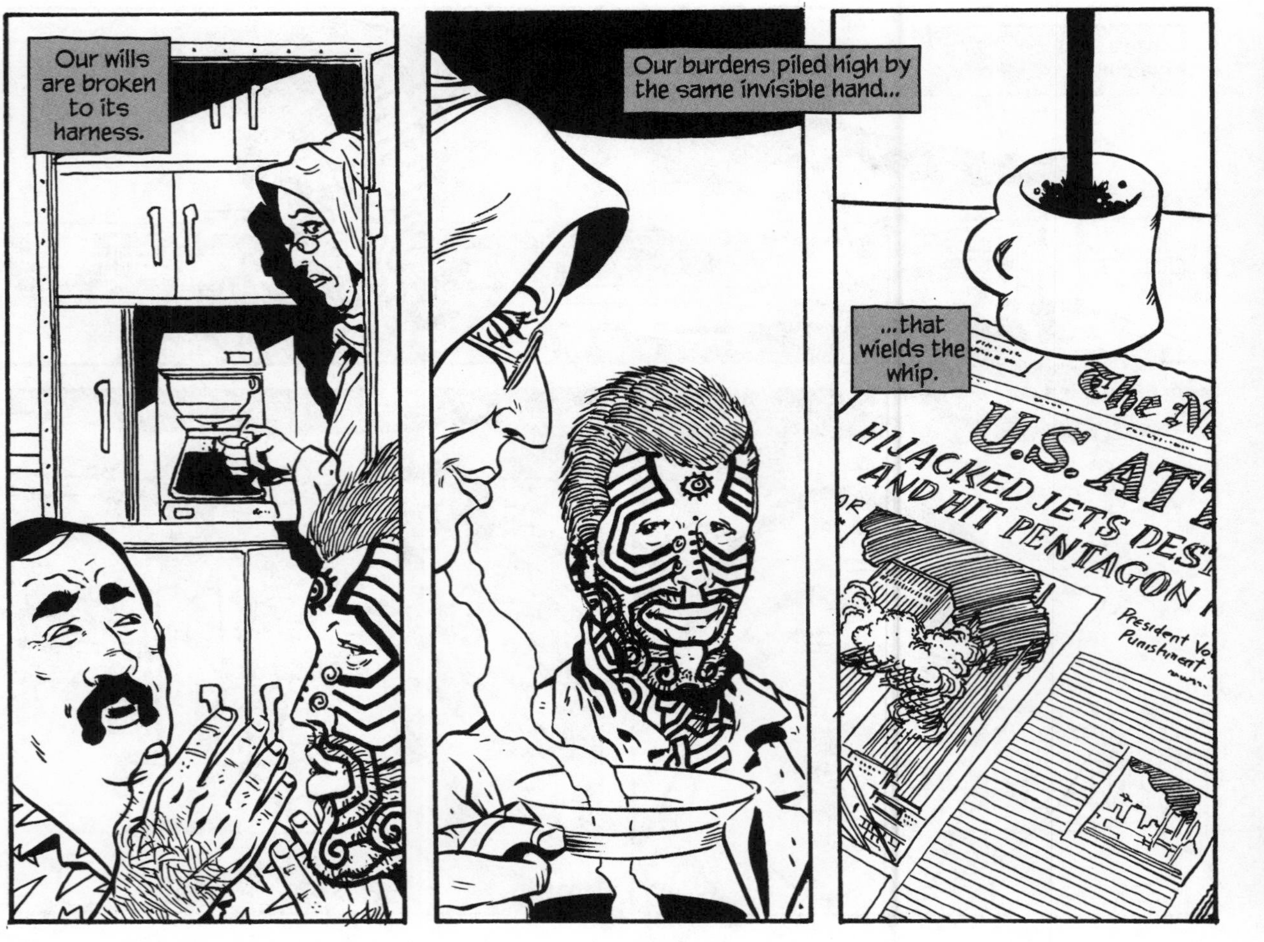
Our wills are broken to its harness.
Our burdens piled high by the same invisible hand...
...that wields the whip.
U.S.
HIJACKED JETS
AND HIT PENTAGON
President
Punishment

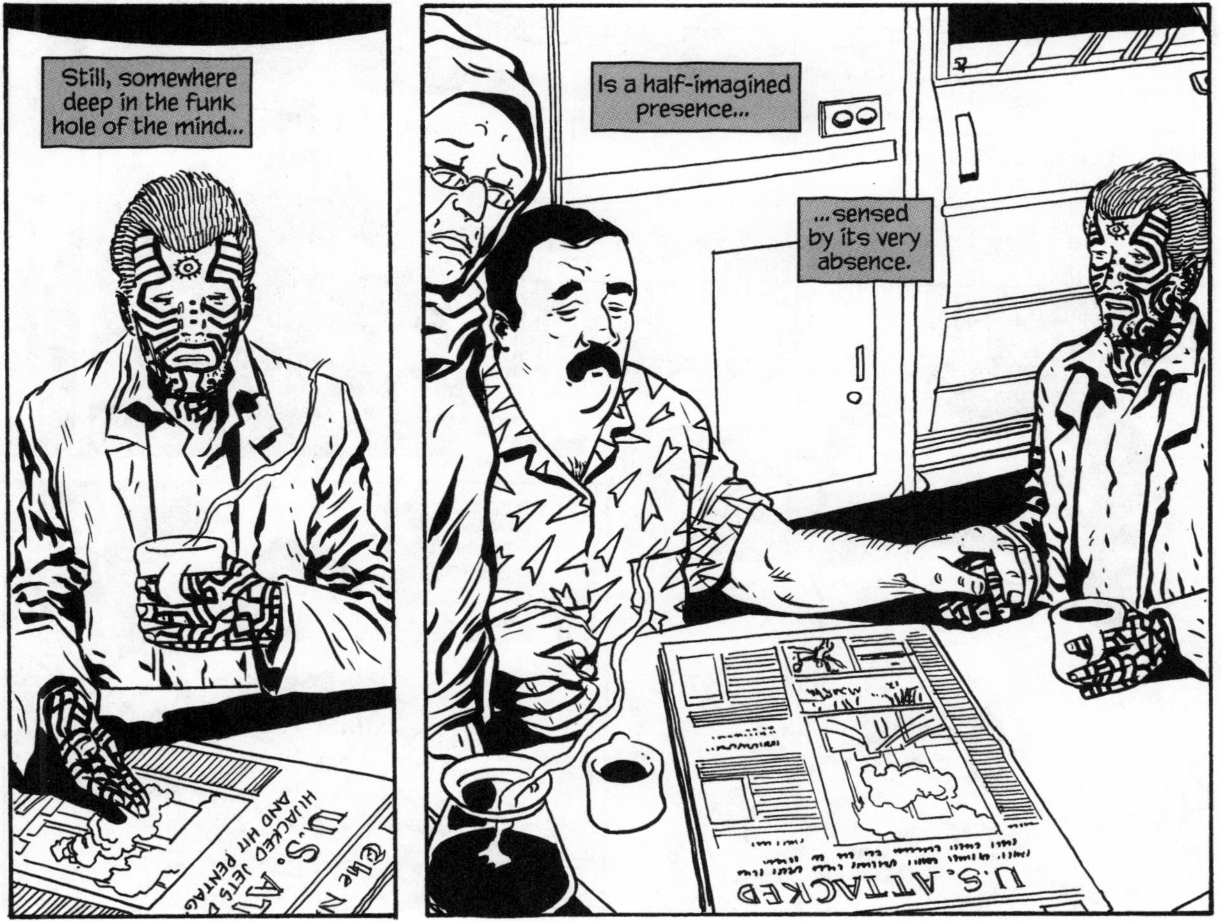
Still, somewhere deep in the funk hole of the mind...
Is a half-imagined presence...
...sensed by its very absence.
U.S. ATTACKED

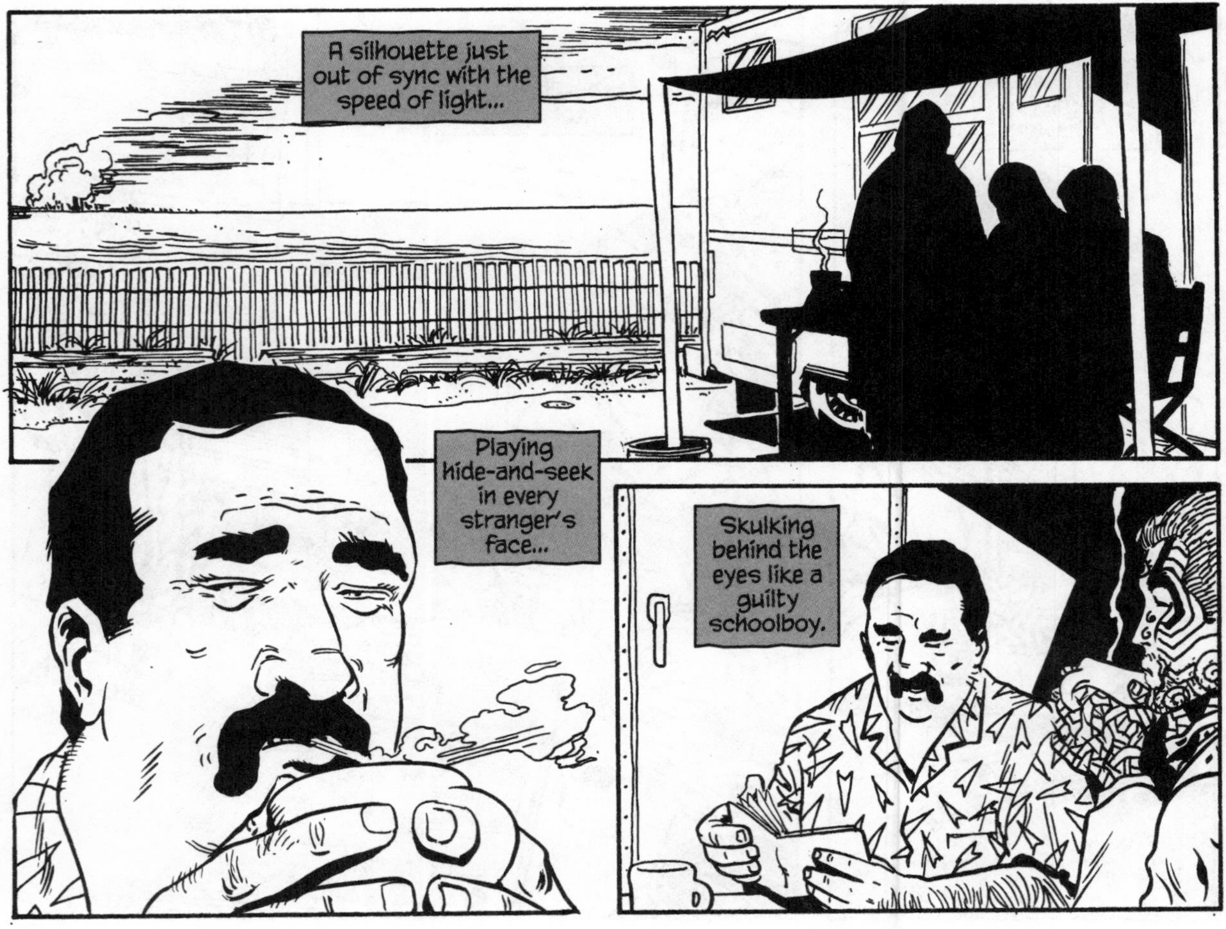
A silhouette just out of sync with the speed of light...
Playing hide-and-seek in every stranger's face...
Skulking behind the eyes like a guilty schoolboy.

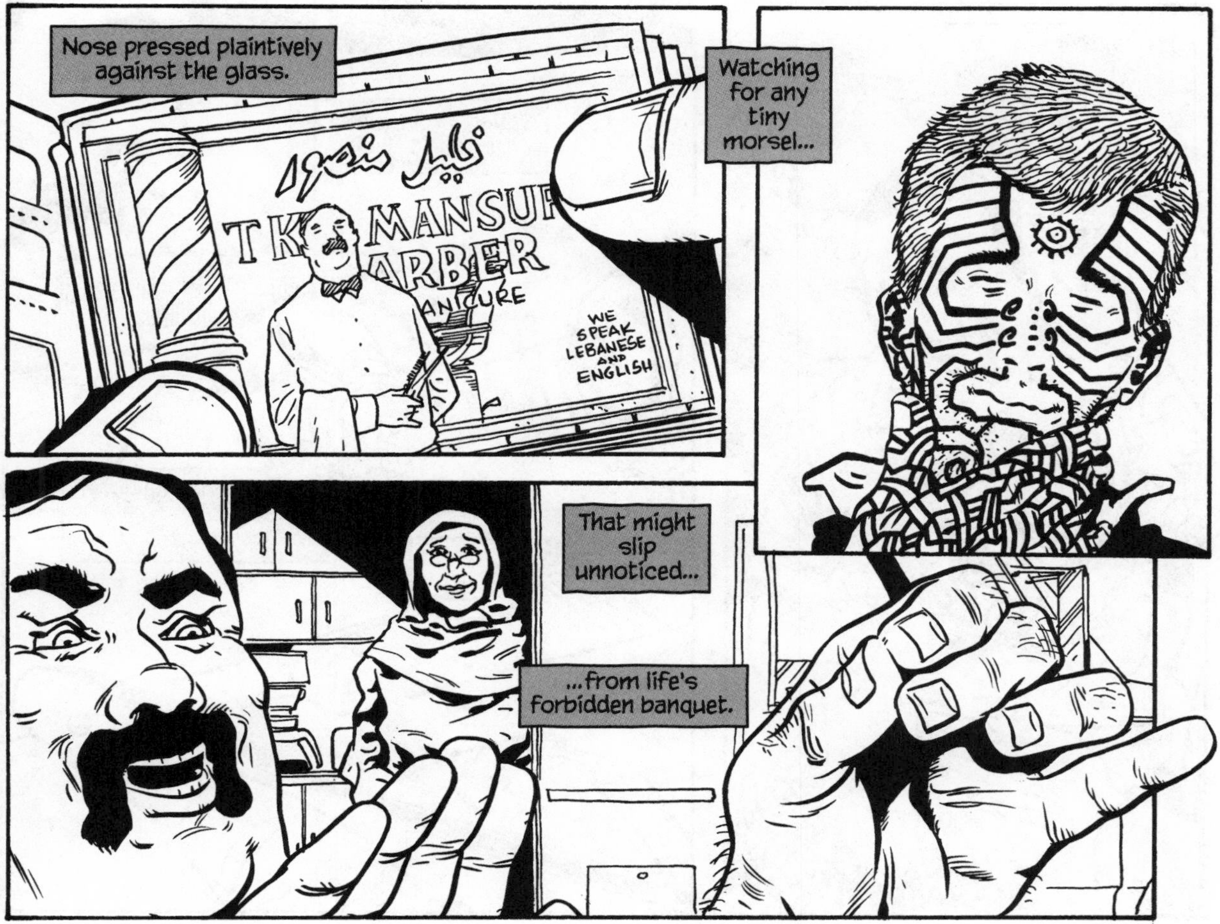
Nose pressed plaintively against the glass.
WE SPEAK LEBANESE AND ENGLISH
Watching for any tiny morsel...
That might slip unnoticed...
...from life's forbidden banquet.

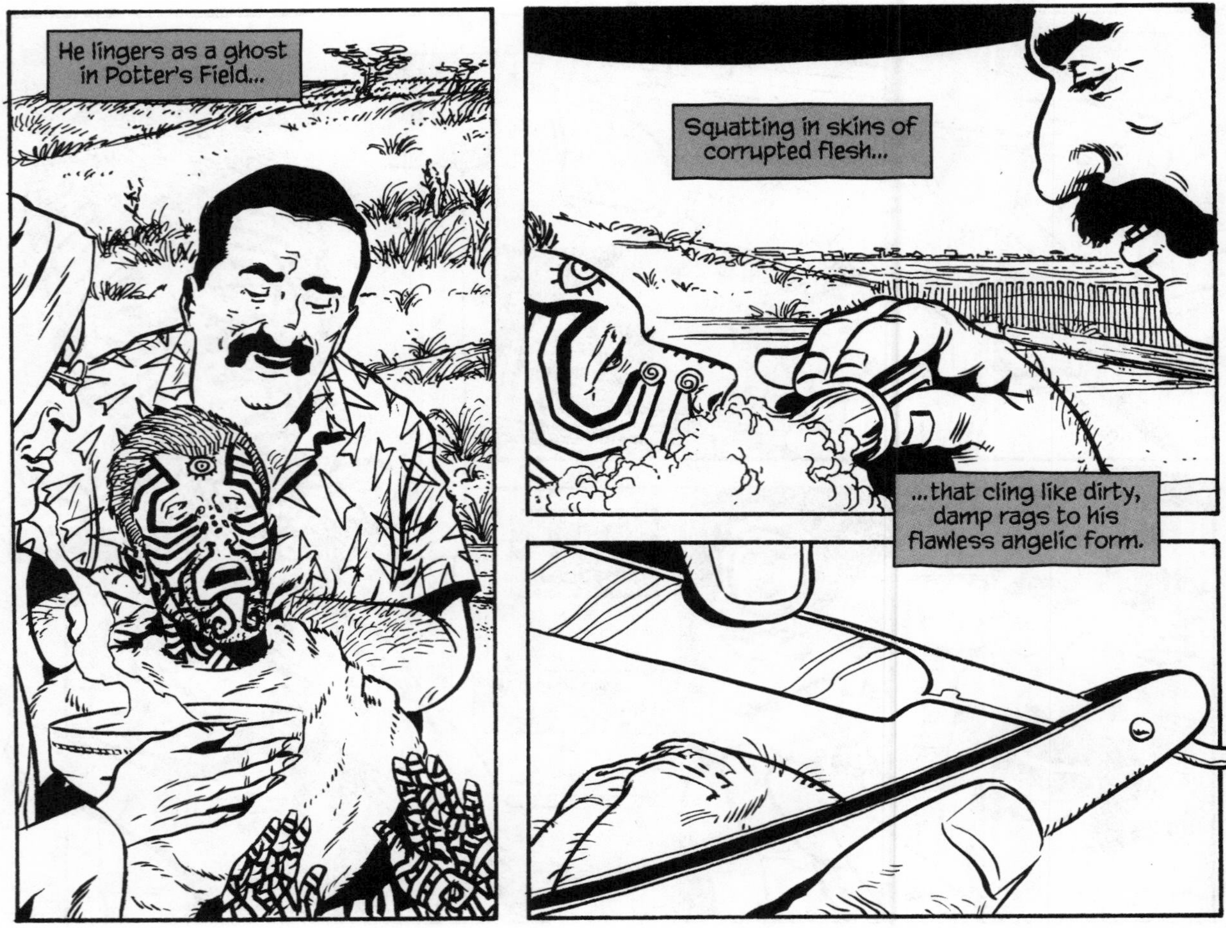
He lingers as a ghost in Potter's Field...
Squatting in skins of corrupted flesh...
...that cling like dirty, damp rags to his flawless angelic form.

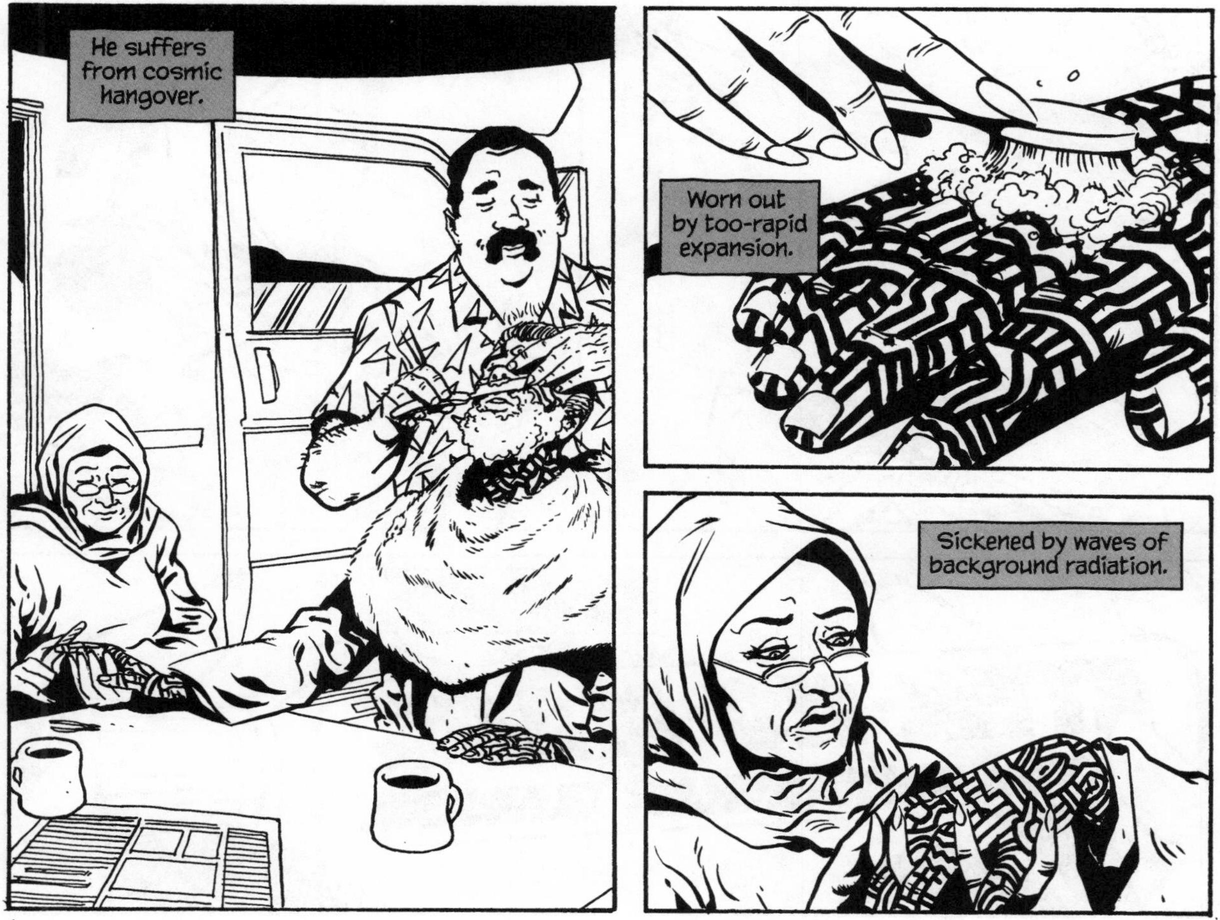
He suffers from cosmic hangover.
Worn out by too-rapid expansion.
Sickened by waves of background radiation.

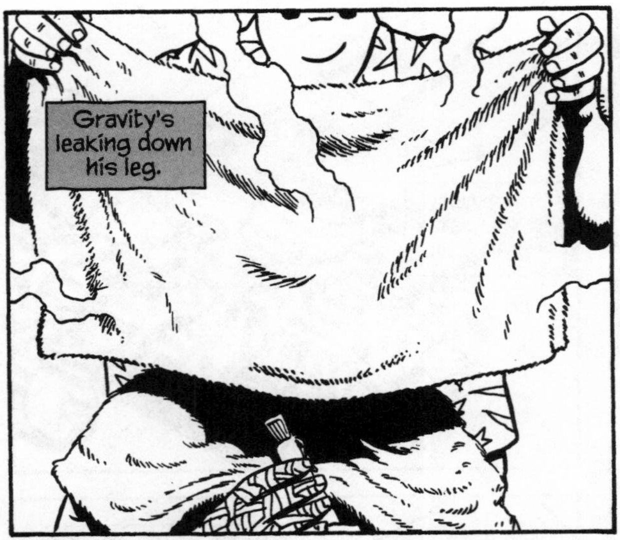
Gravity's leaking down his leg.

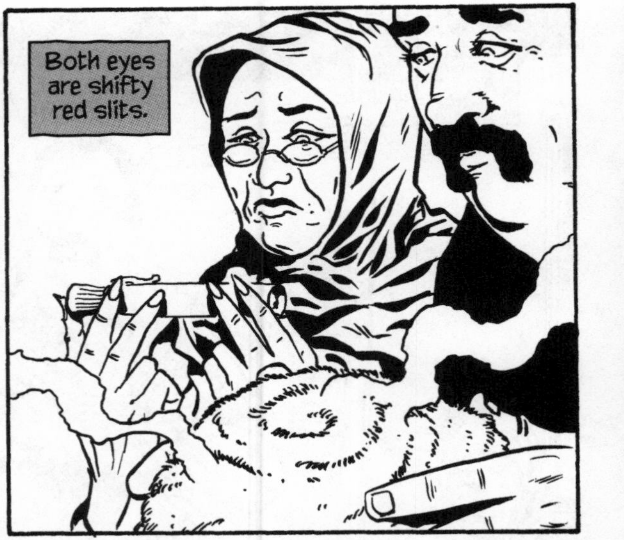
Both eyes are shifty red slits.

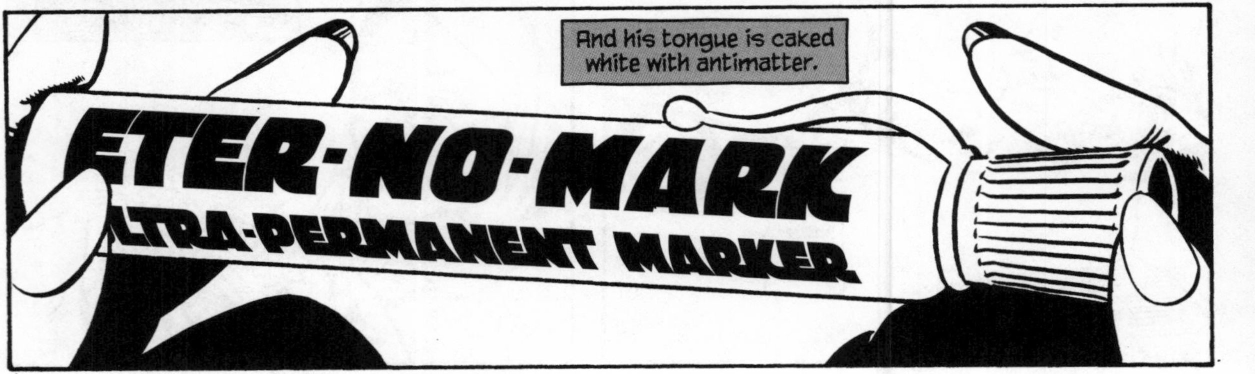
And his tongue is caked white with antimatter.
ETER-NO-MARK
LTRA-PERMANENT MARKER

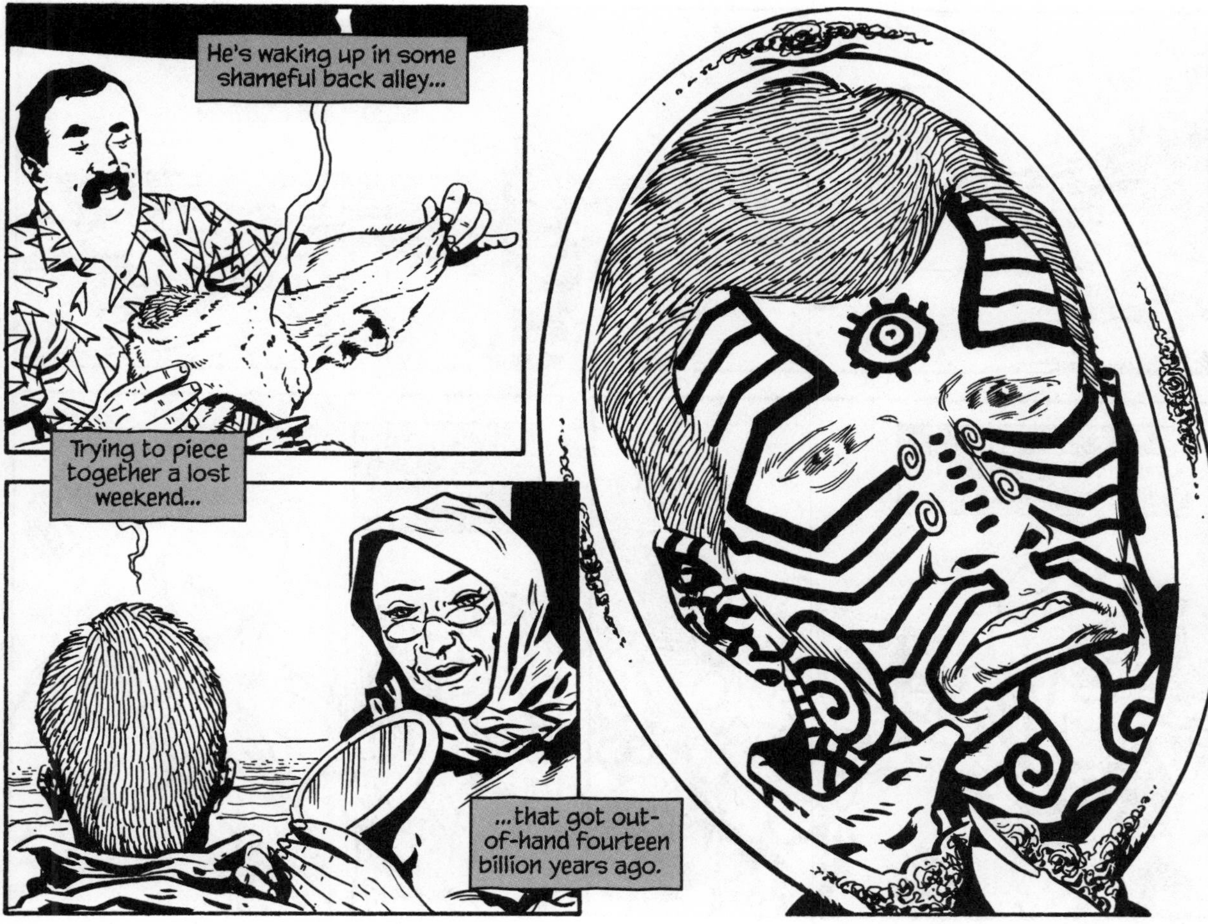
He's waking up in some shameful back alley...
Trying to piece together a lost weekend...
...that got out-of-hand fourteen billion years ago.

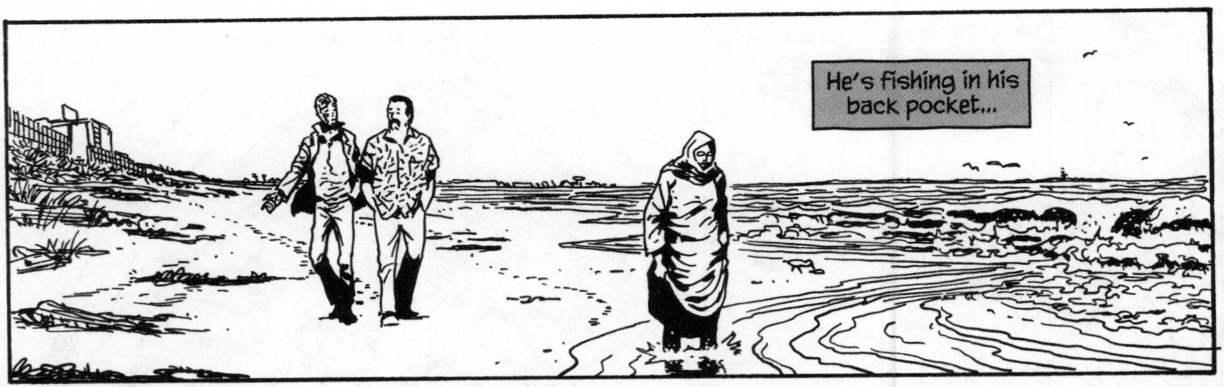
He's fishing in his back pocket...

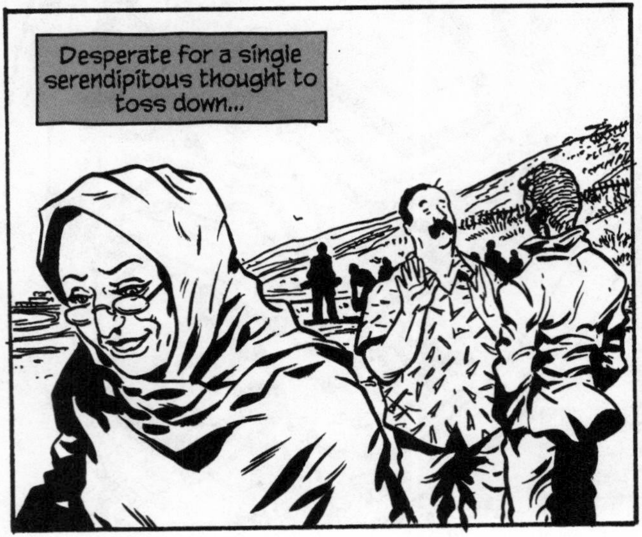
Desperate for a single serendipitous thought to toss down...

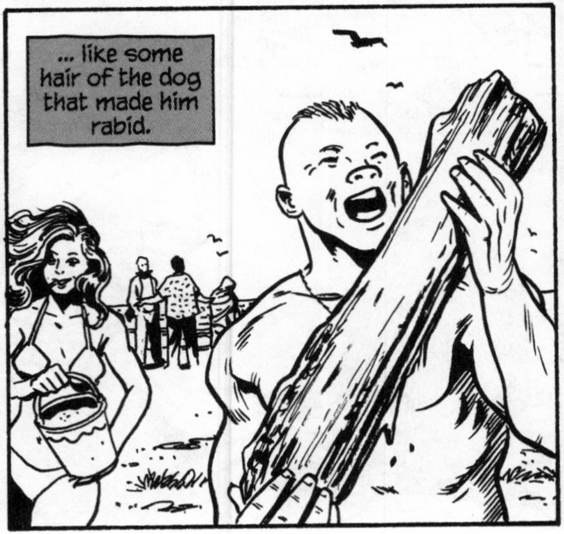
... like some hair of the dog that made him rabid.

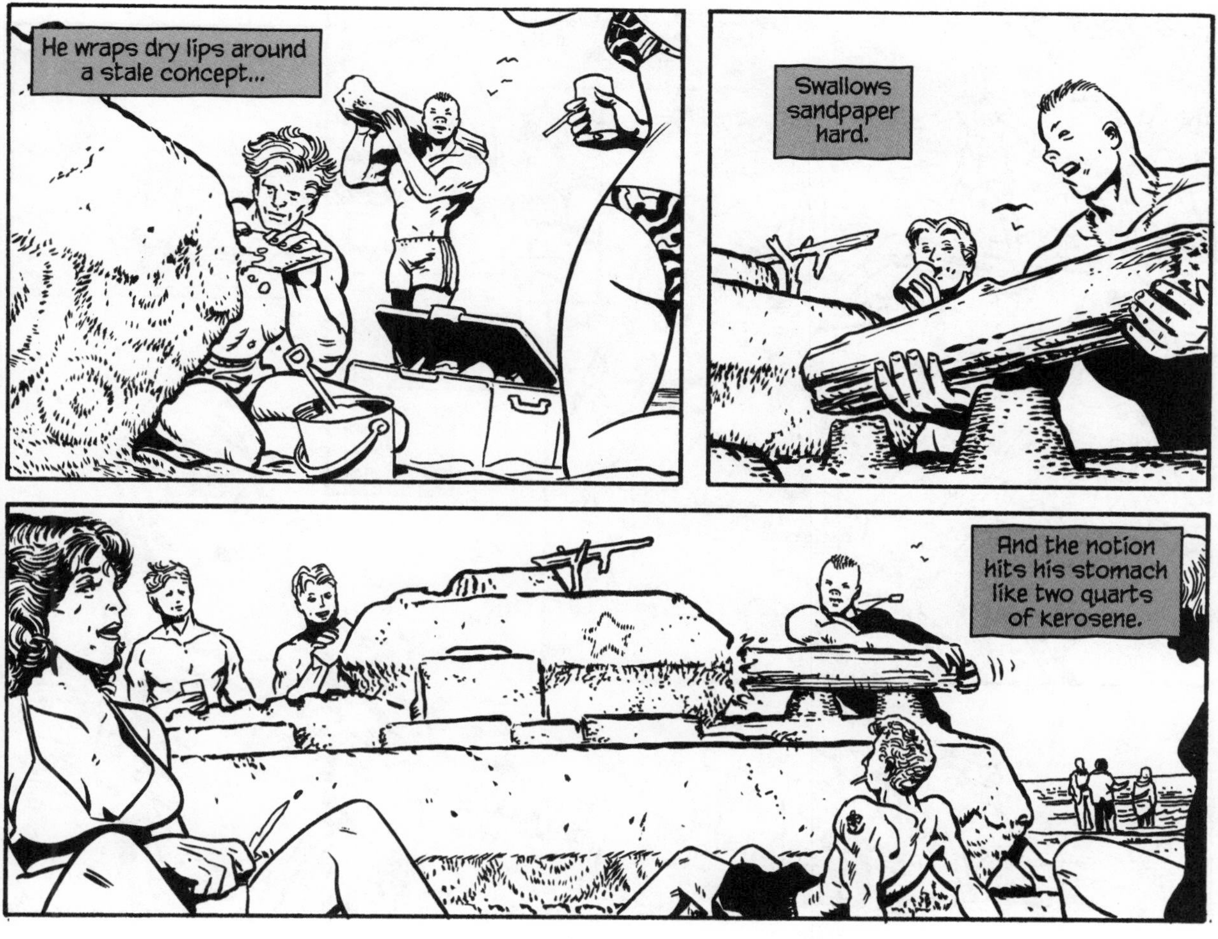
He wraps dry lips around a stale concept...
Swallows sandpaper hard.
And the notion hits his stomach like two quarts of kerosene.

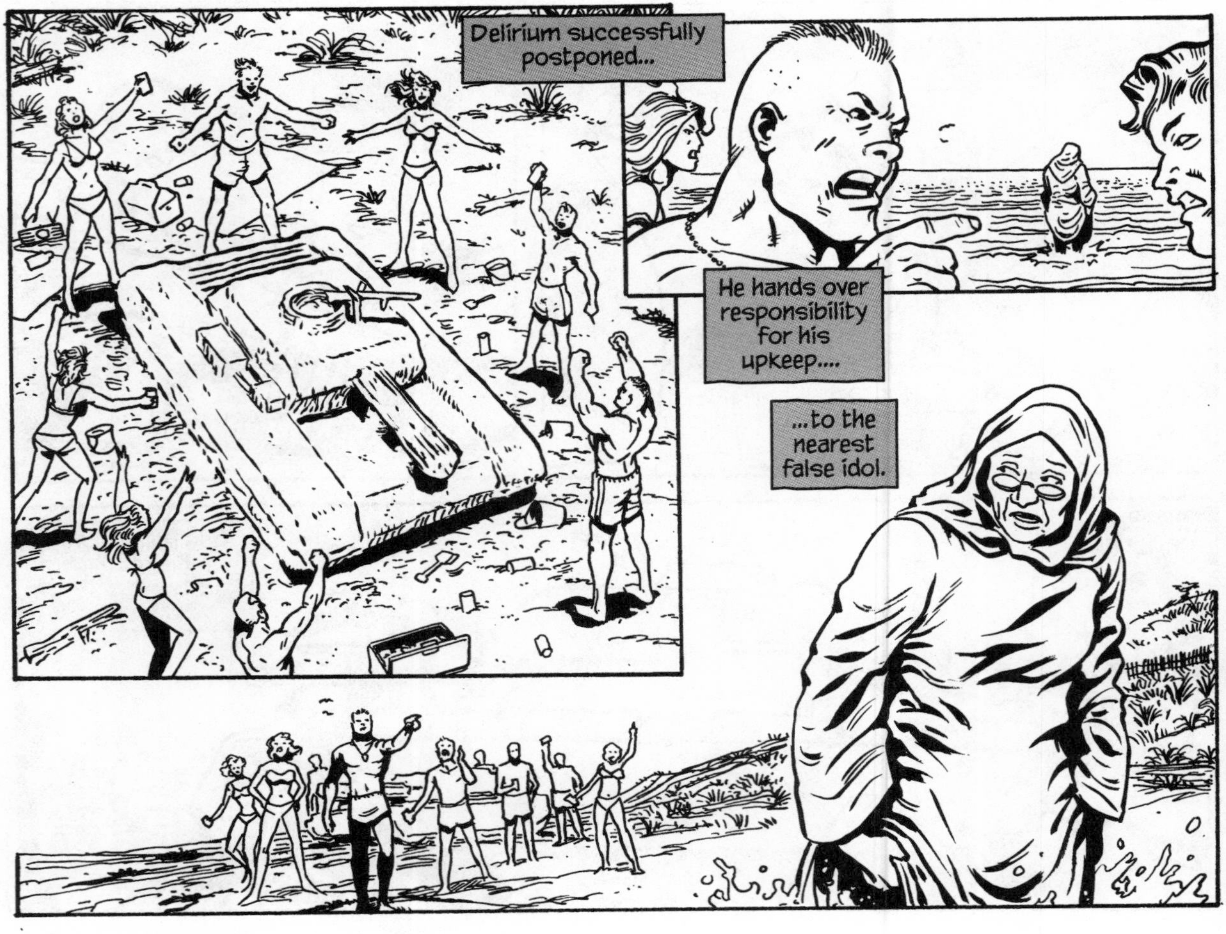
Delirium successfully postponed...
He hands over responsibility for his upkeep....
...to the nearest false idol.

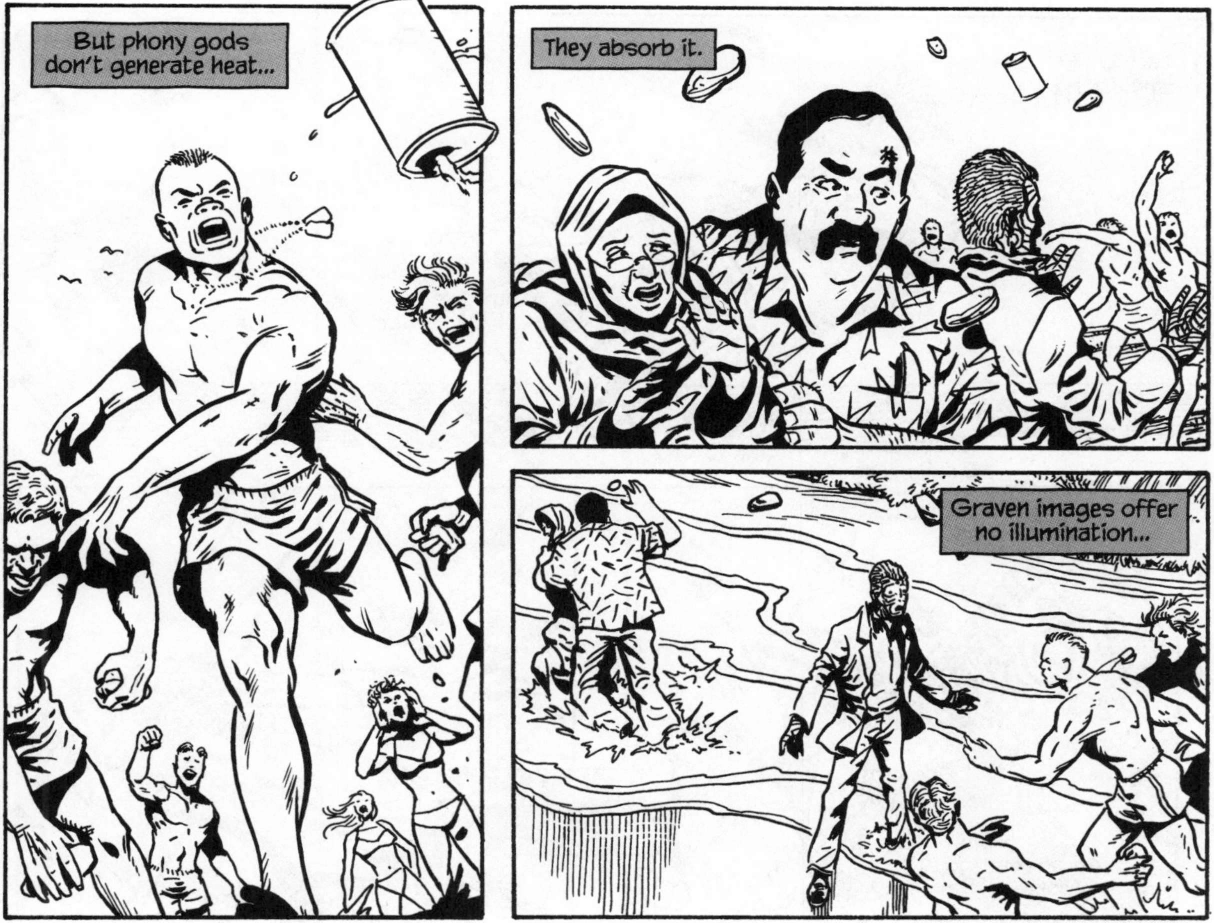
But phony gods don't generate heat...
They absorb it.
Graven images offer no illumination...

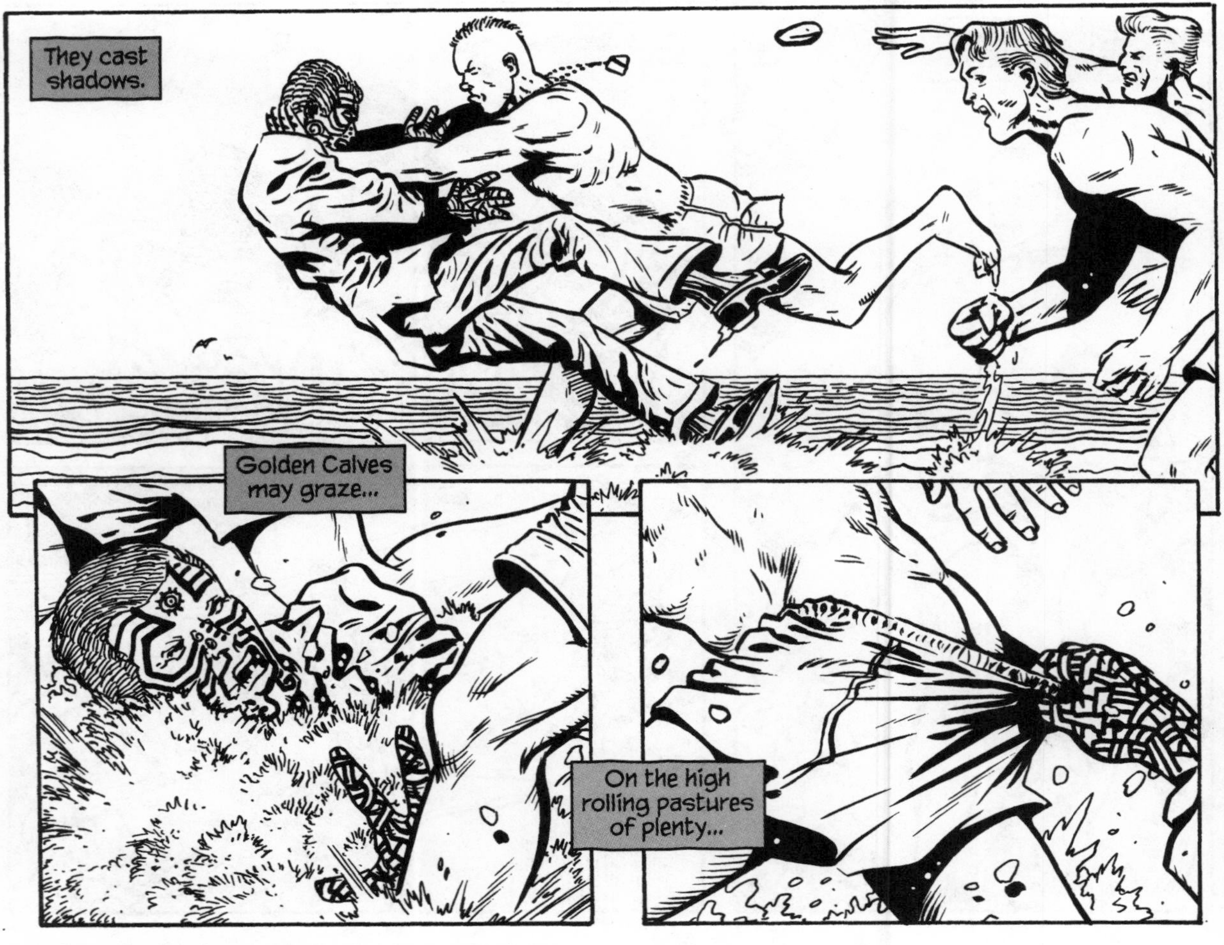
They cast shadows.
Golden Calves may graze...
On the high rolling pastures of plenty...

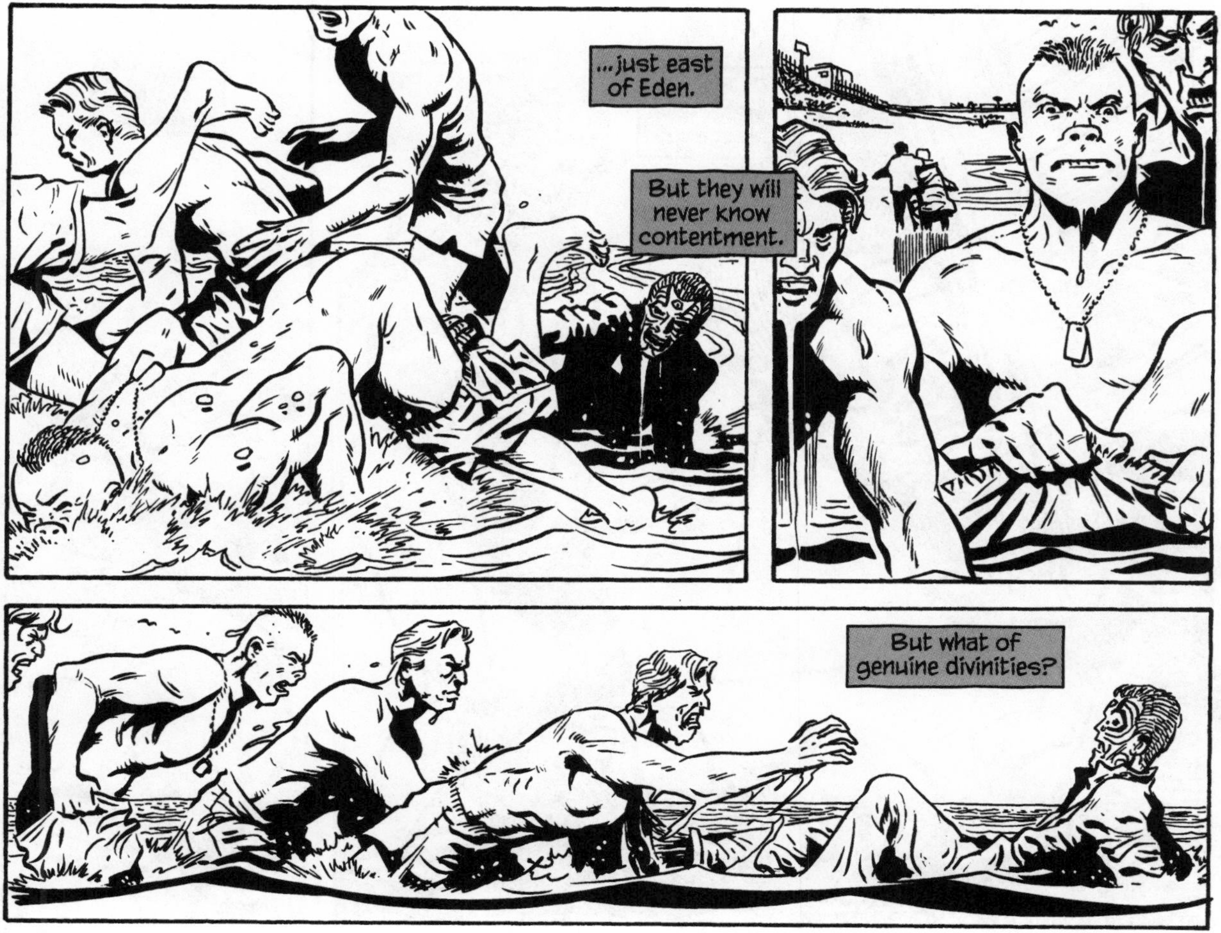
...just east of Eden.
But they will never know contentment.
But what of genuine divinities?

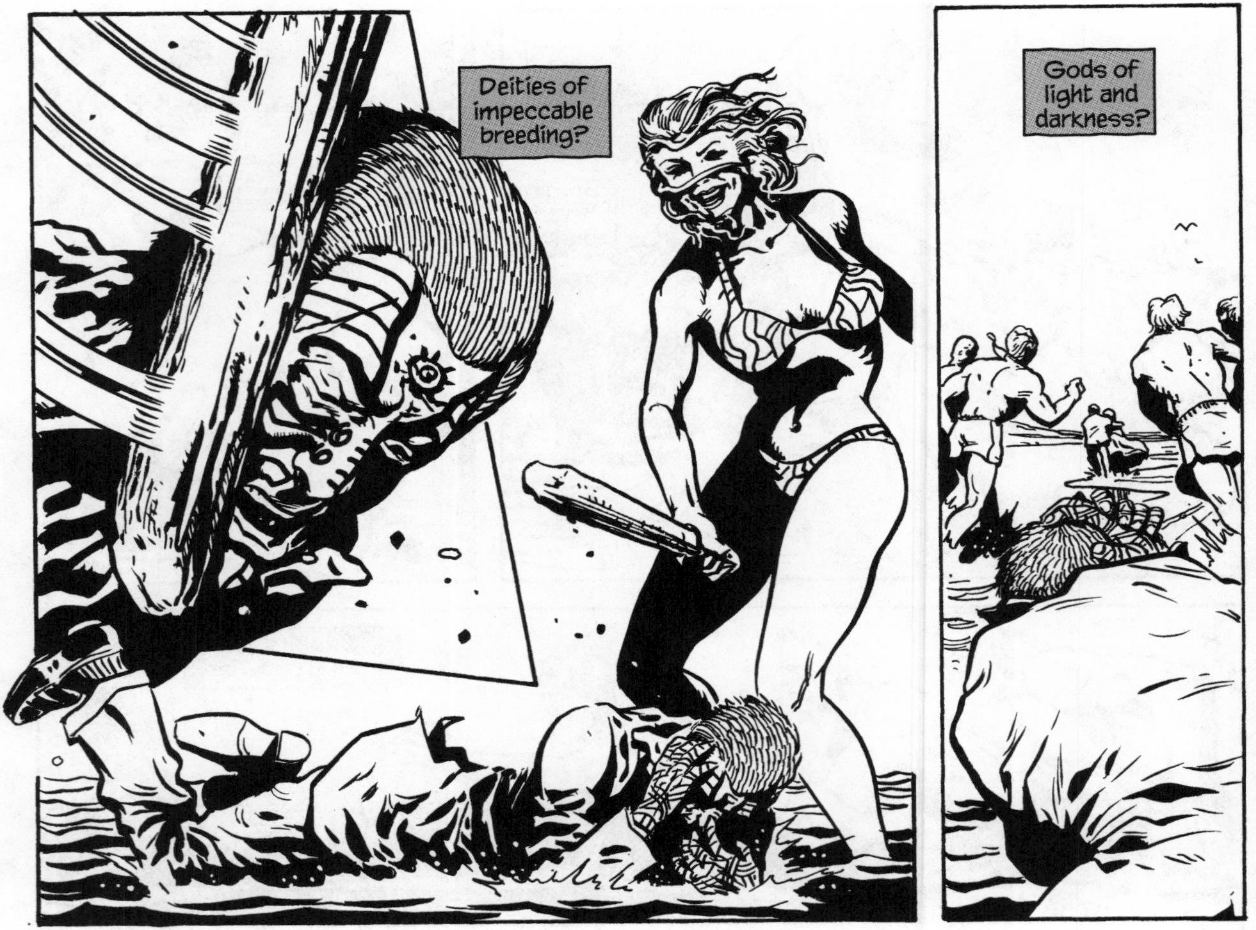
Deities of impeccable breeding?
Gods of light and darkness?

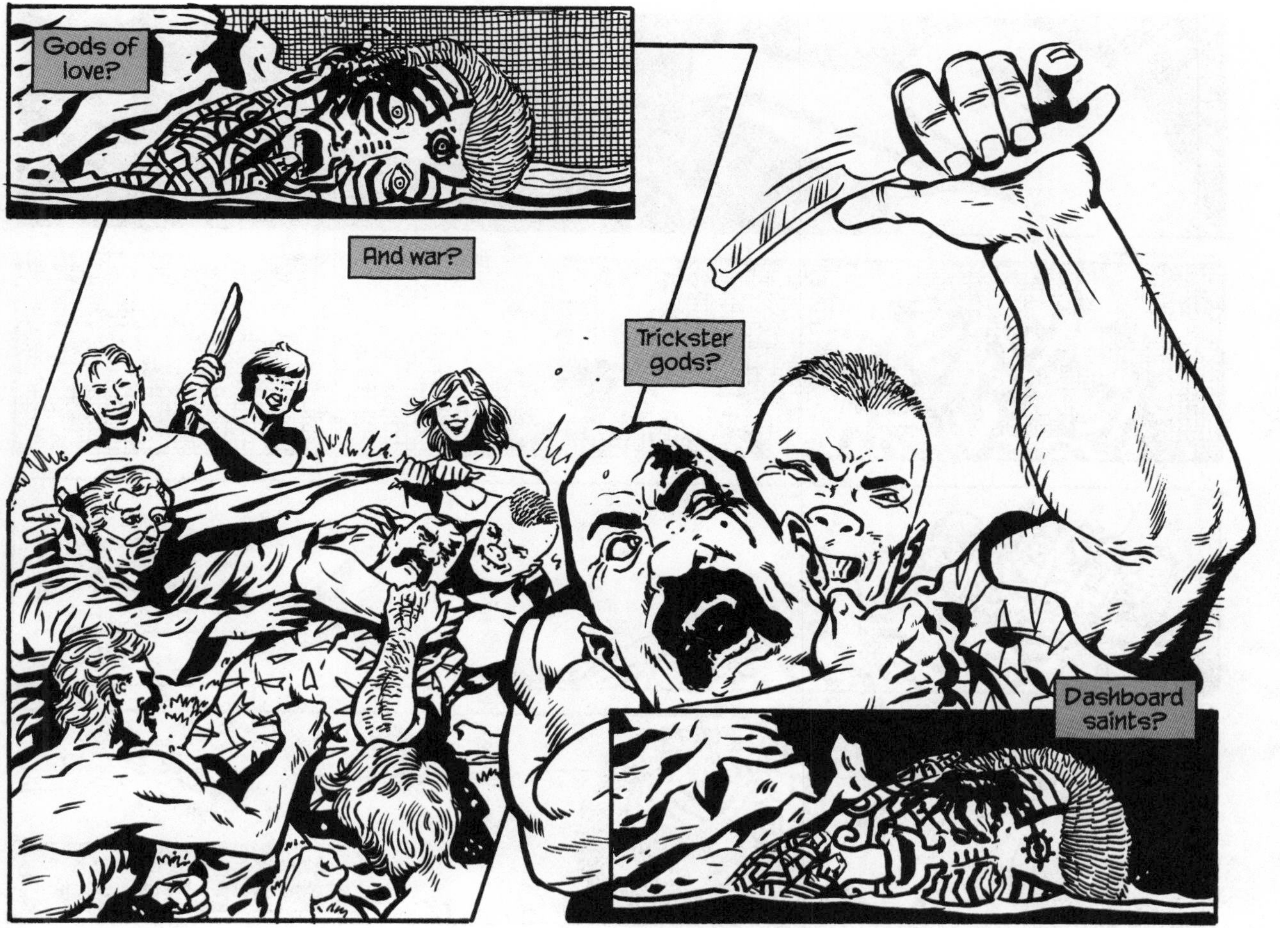
Gods of love?
And war?
Trickster gods?
Dashboard saints?

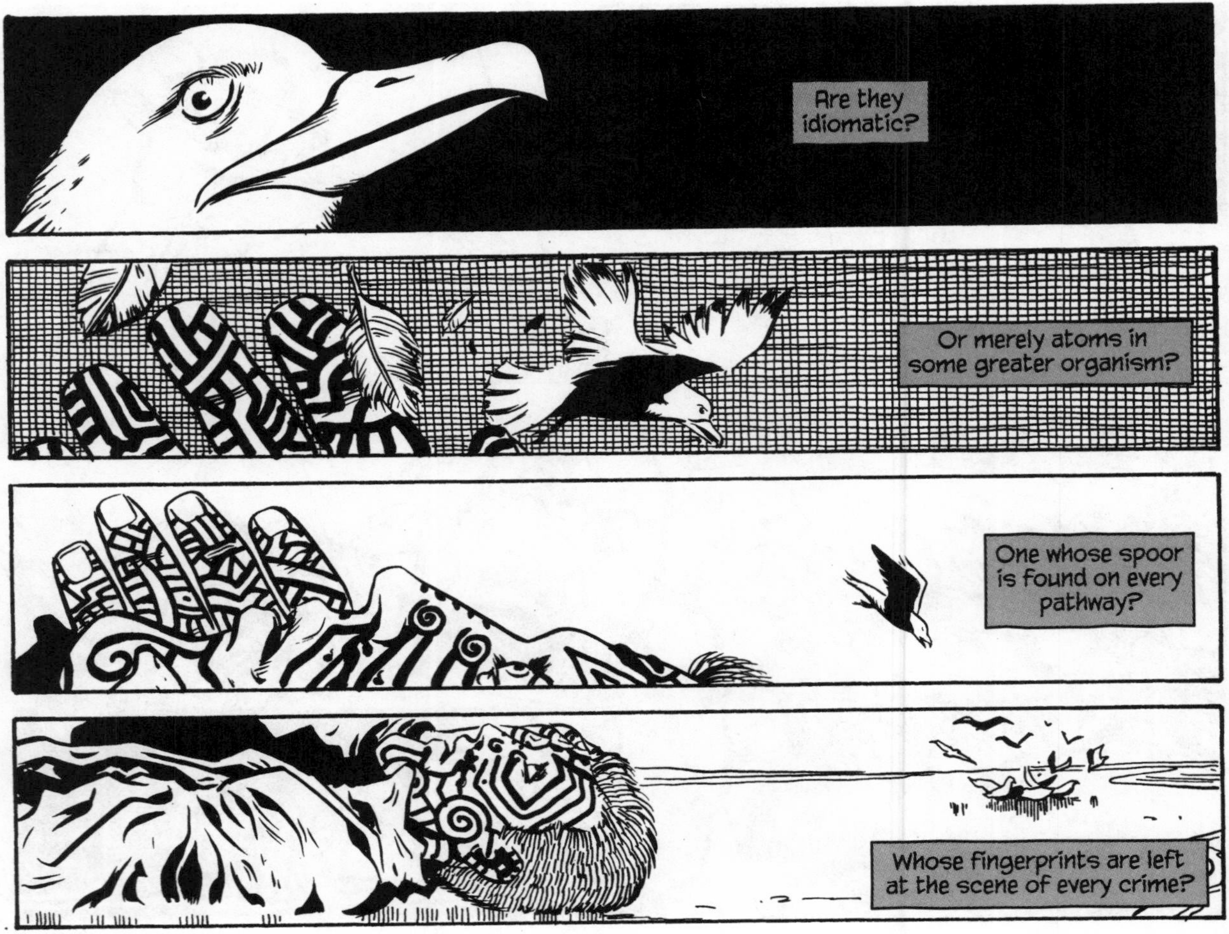

Are they idiomatic?
Or merely atoms in some greater organism?
One whose spoor is found on every pathway?
Whose fingerprints are left at the scene of every crime?

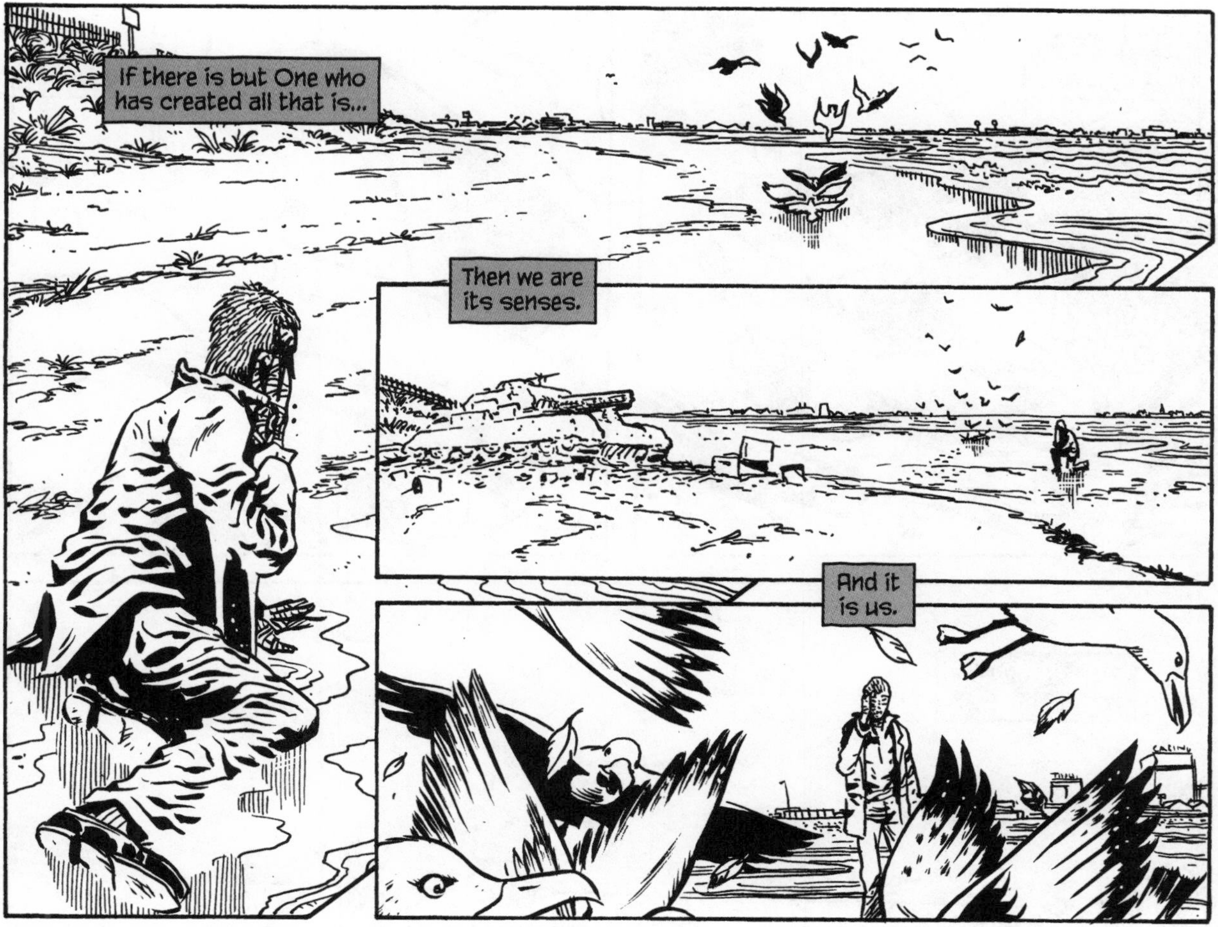
If there is but One who has created all that is...
Then we are its senses.
And it is us.

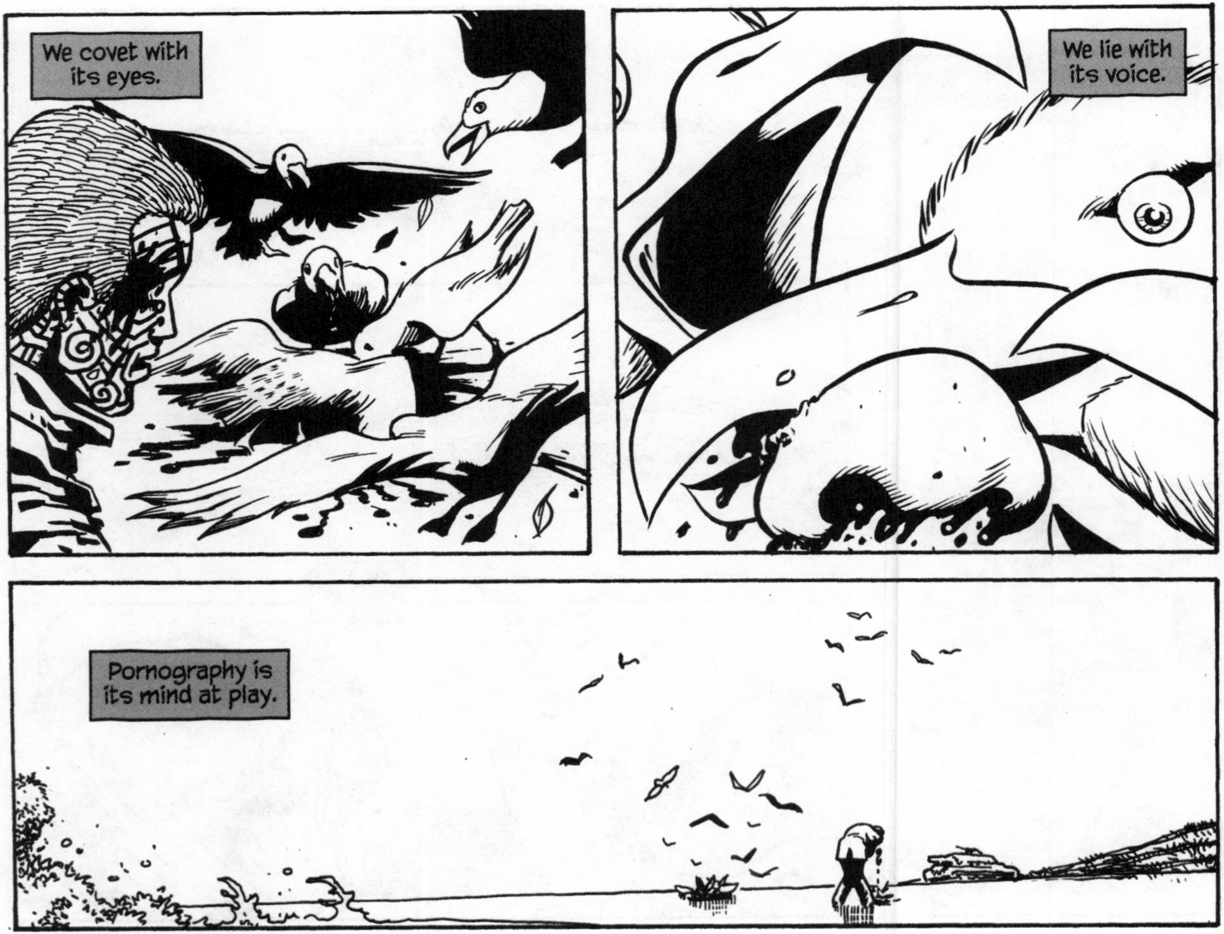
We covet with its eyes.
We lie with its voice.
Pornography is its mind at play.

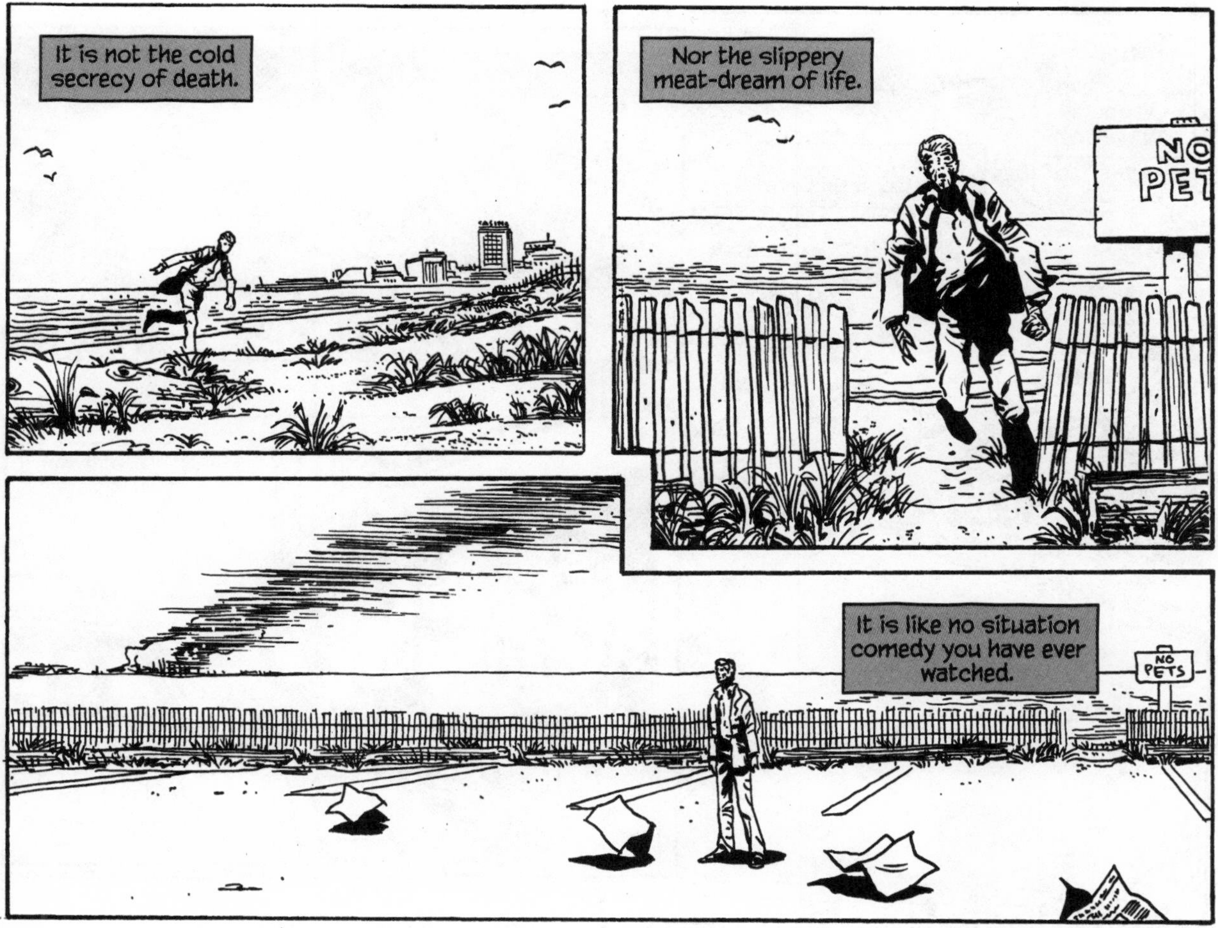
It is not the cold secrecy of death.
Nor the slippery meat-dream of life.
NO PET
It is like no situation comedy you have ever watched.
NO PETS

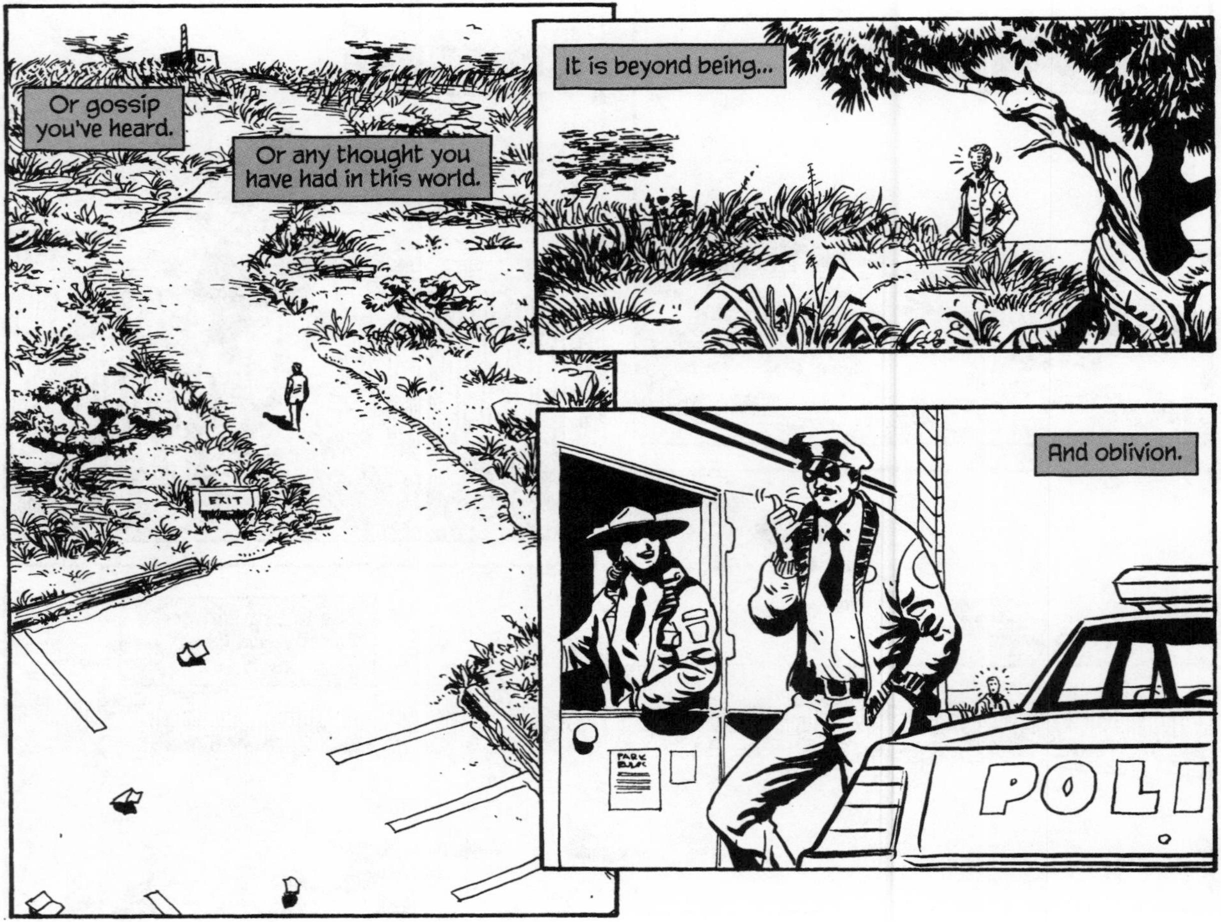
Or gossip you've heard.
Or any thought you have had in this world.
EXIT
It is beyond being...
And oblivion.
POLI

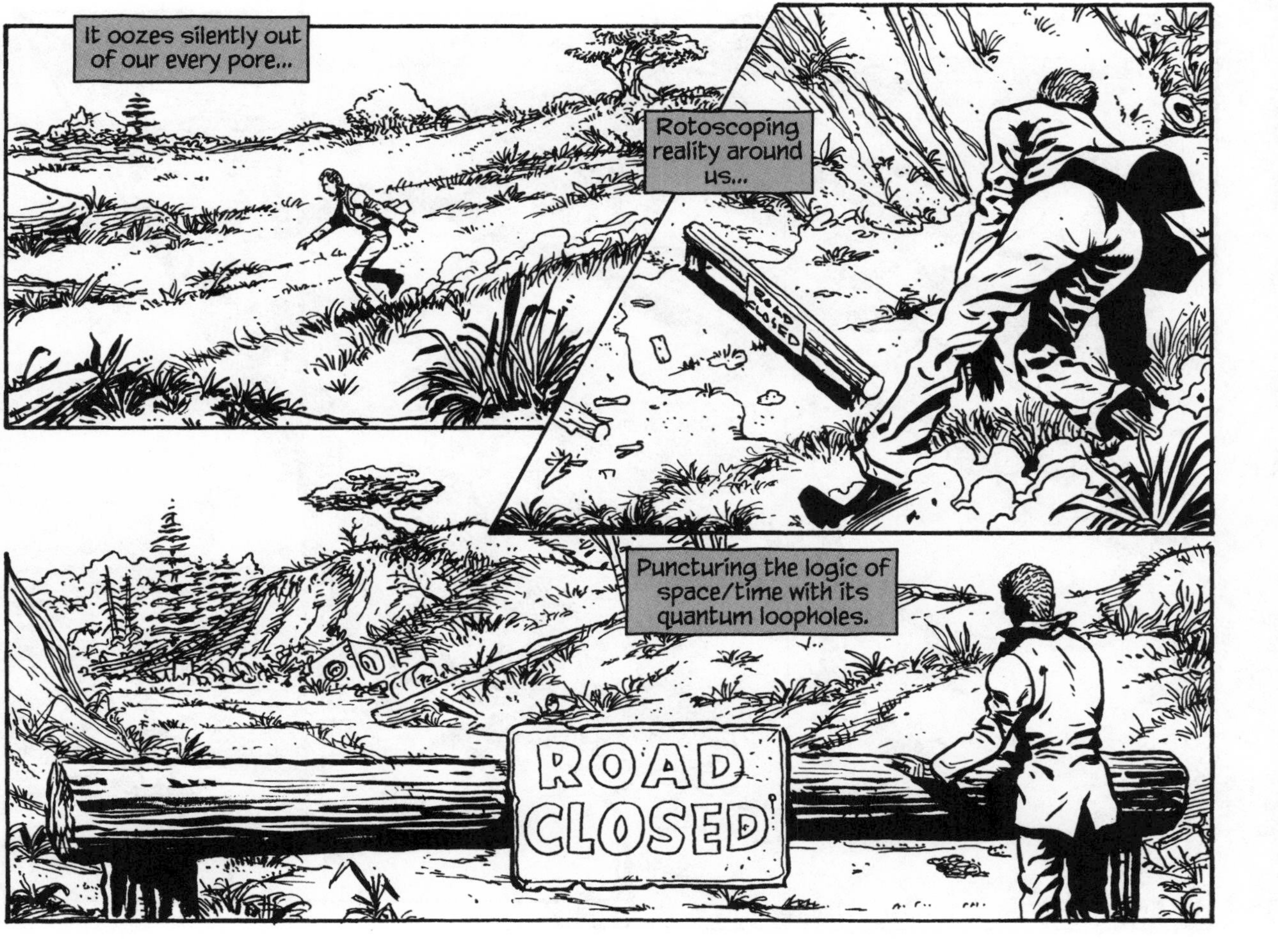
It oozes silently out of our every pore...
Rotoscoping reality around us...
ROAD CLOSED
Puncturing the logic of space/time with its quantum loopholes.
ROAD CLOSED

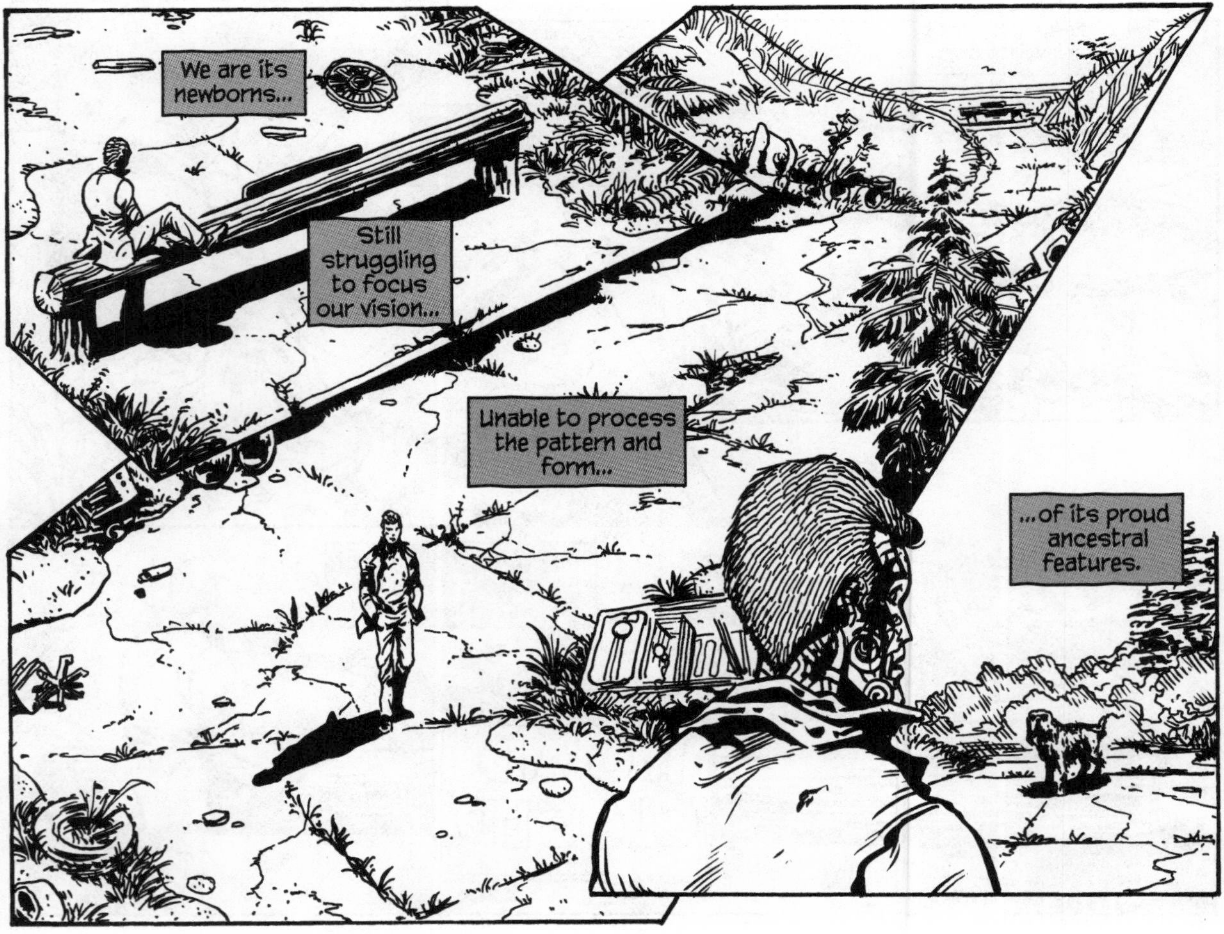

We are its newborns...
Still struggling to focus our vision...
Unable to process the pattern and form...
...of its proud ancestral features.

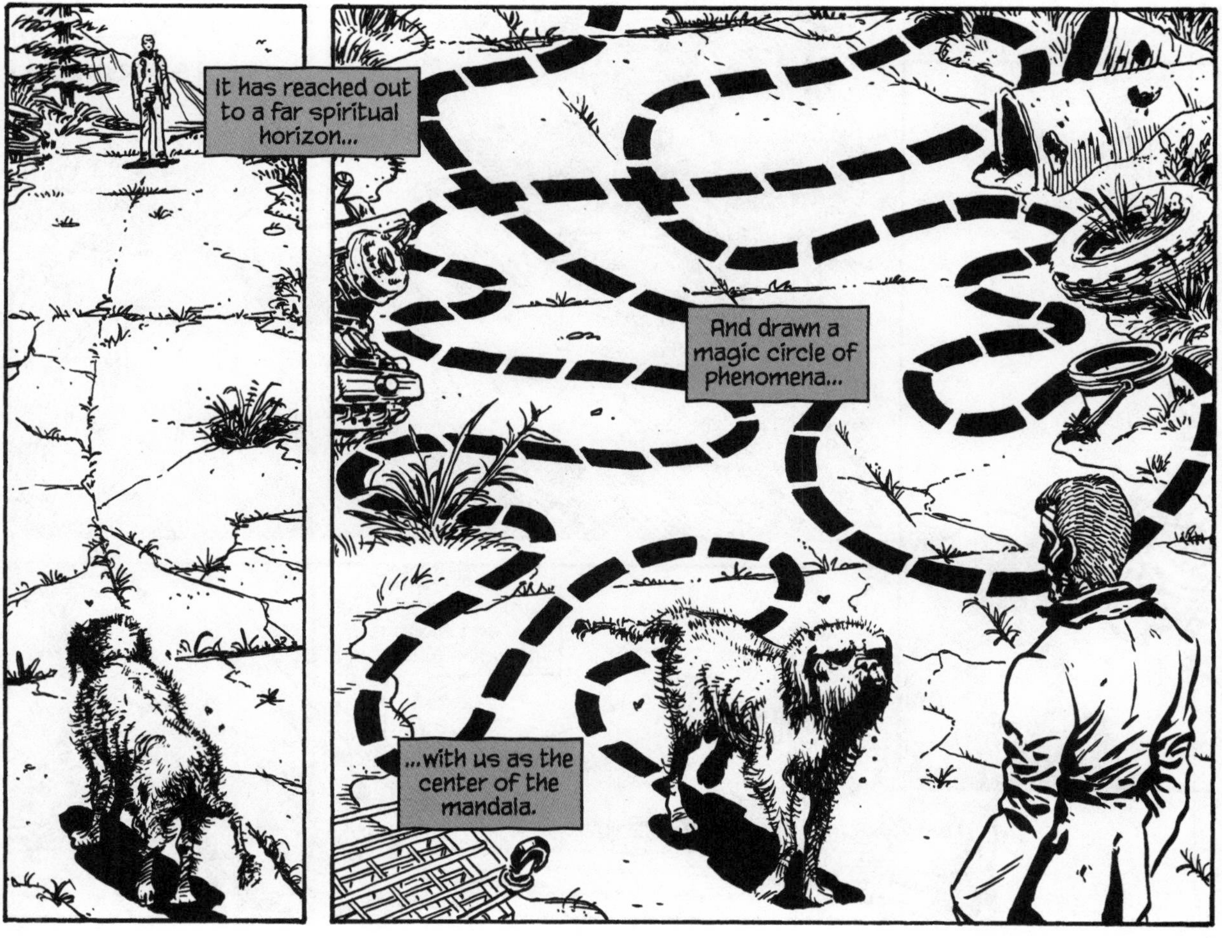
It has reached out to a far spiritual horizon...
And drawn a magic circle of phenomena...
...with us as the center of the mandala.

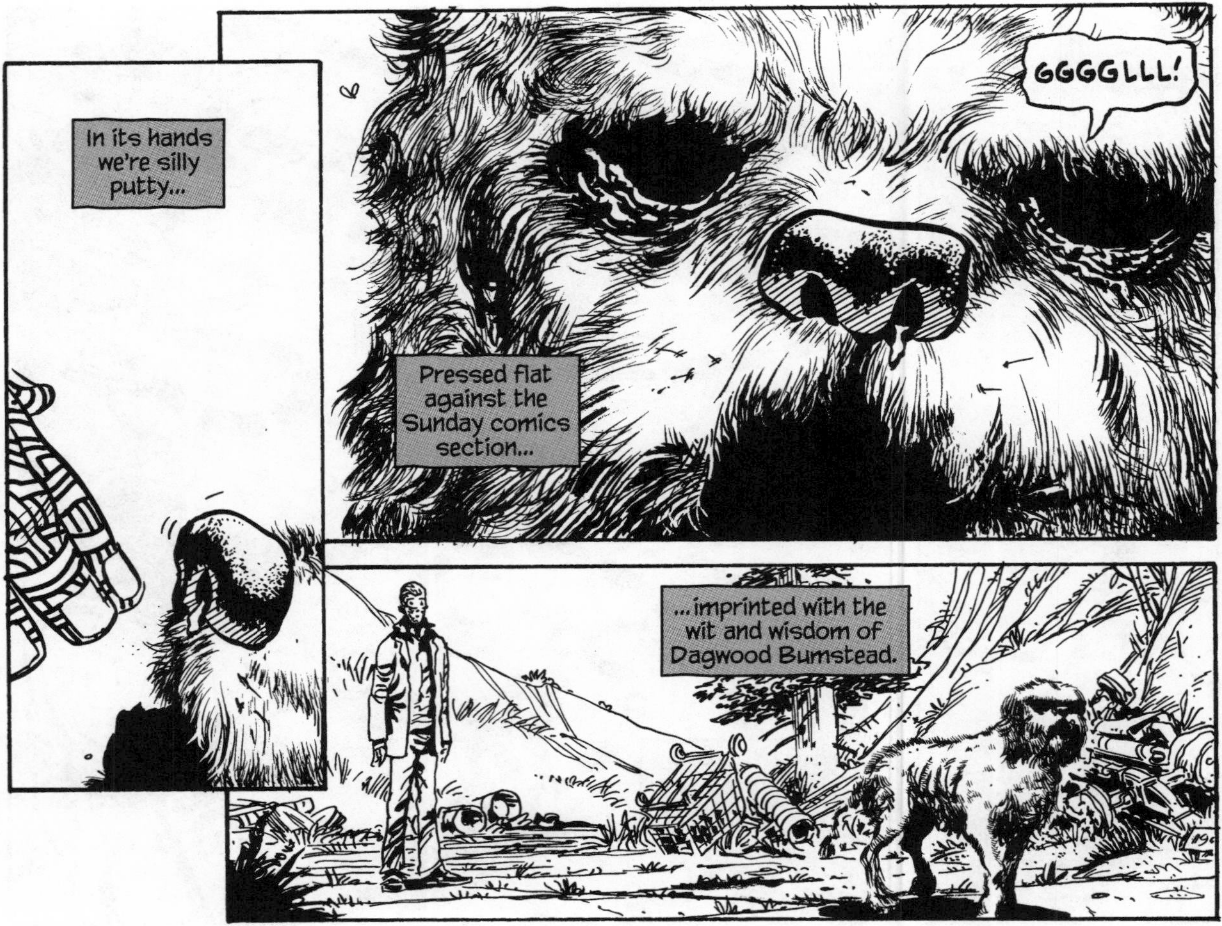
In its hands we're silly putty...
GGGGLLL!
Pressed flat against the Sunday comics section...
...imprinted with the wit and wisdom of Dagwood Bumstead.

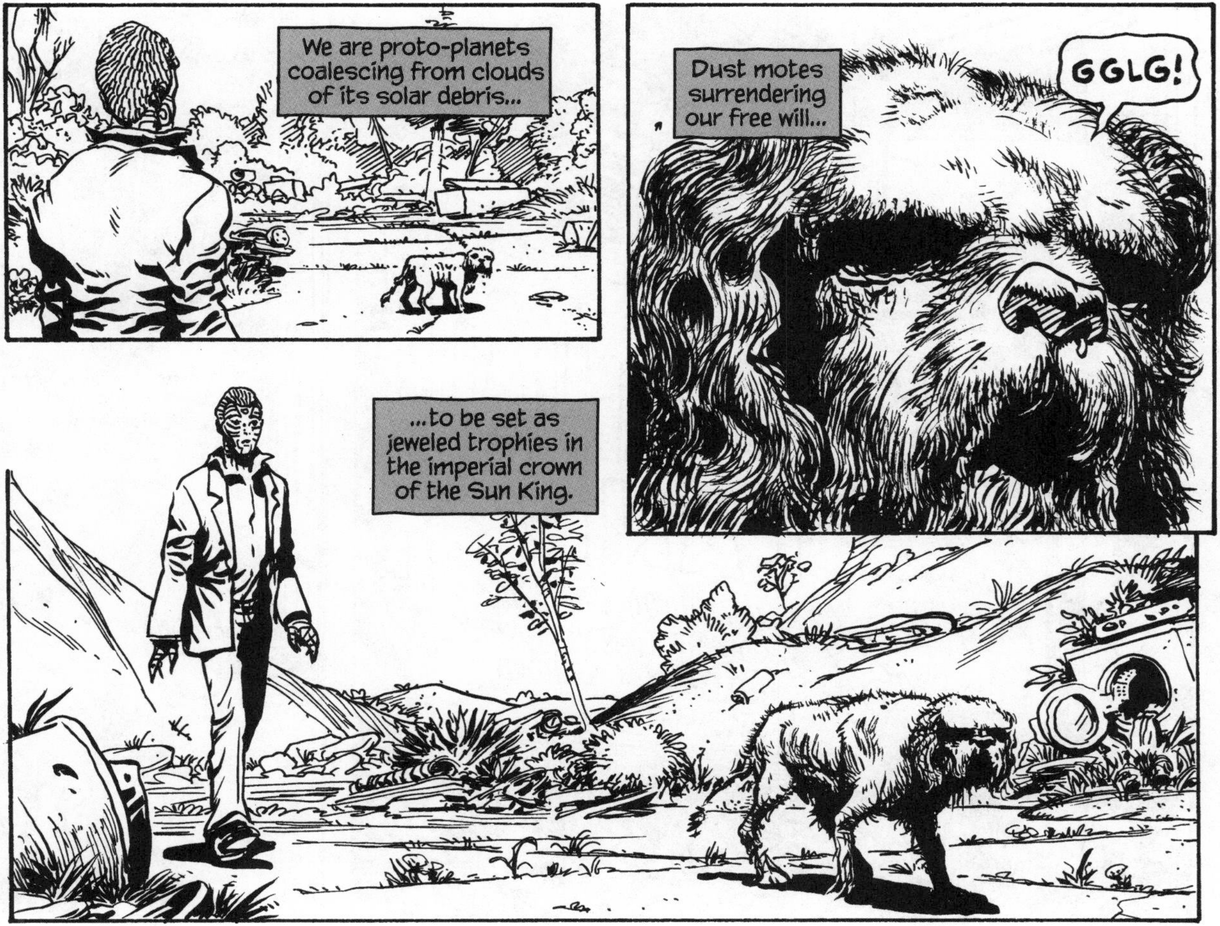
We are proto-planets coalescing from clouds of its solar debris...
Dust motes surrendering our free will...
GGLG!
...to be set as jeweled trophies in the imperial crown of the Sun King.

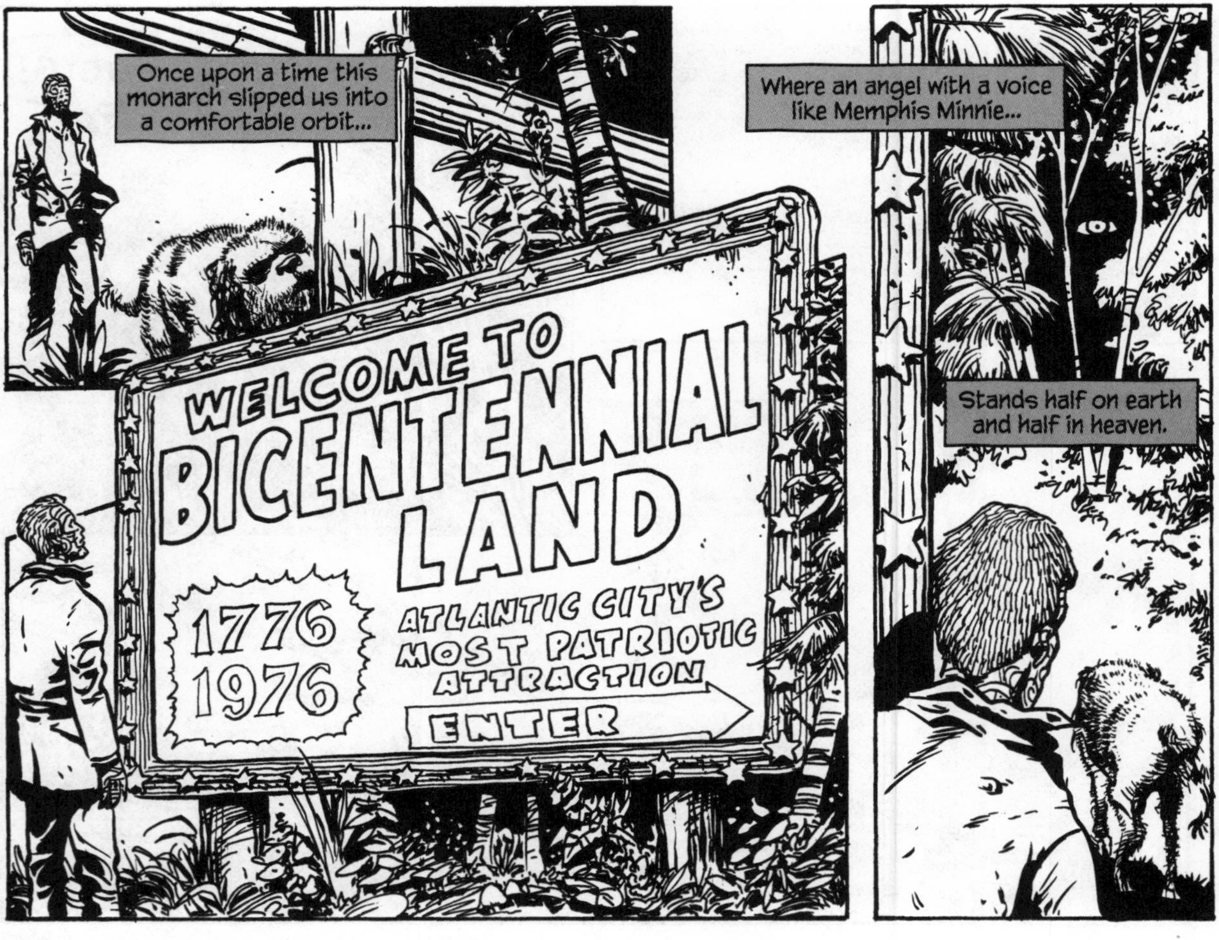
Once upon a time this monarch slipped us into a comfortable orbit...
WELCOME TO
BICENTENNIAL LAND
1776 1976
ATLANTIC CITY'S MOST PATRIOTIC ATTRACTION
ENTER
Where an angel with a voice like Memphis Minnie...
Stands half on earth and half in heaven.

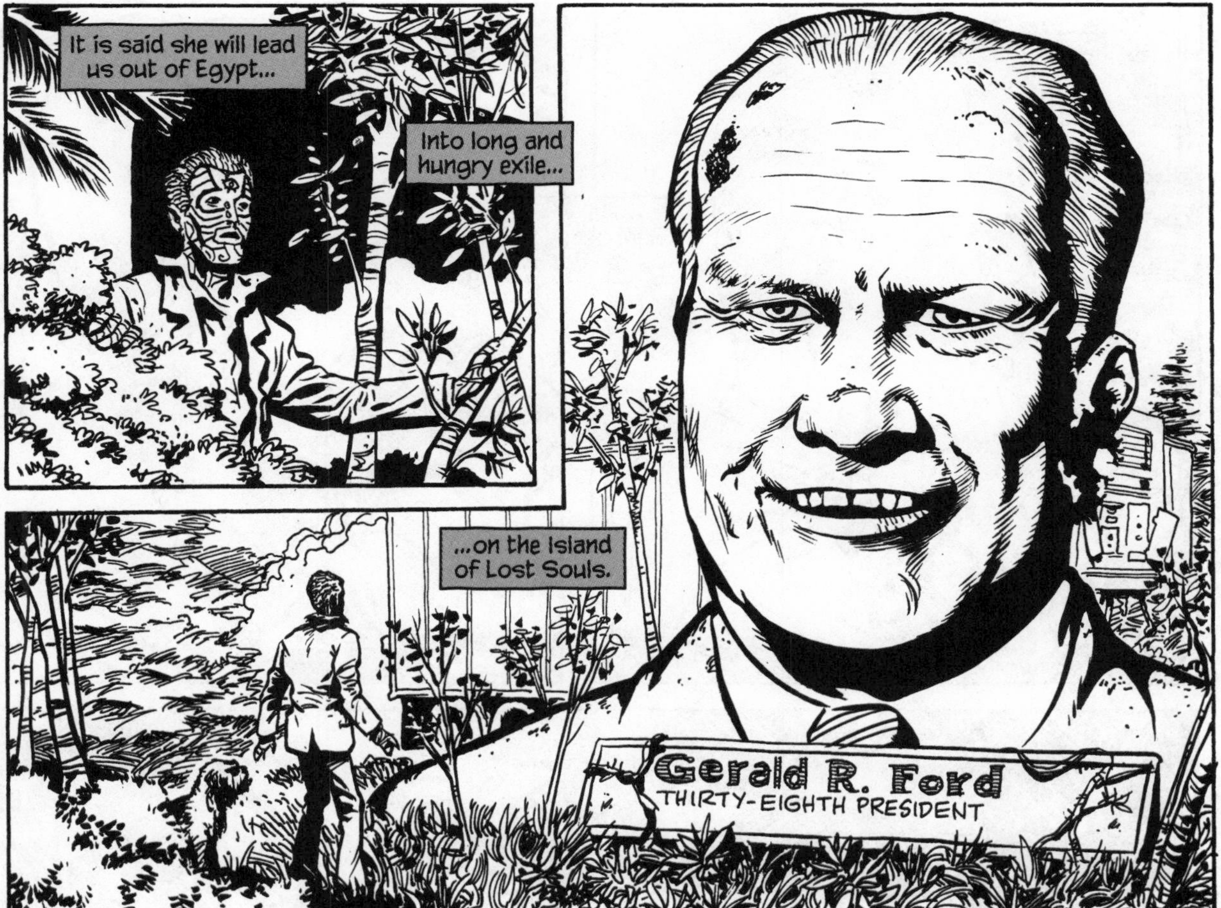
It is said she will lead us out of Egypt...
Into long and hungry exile...
...on the Island of Lost Souls.
Gerald R. Ford
THIRTY-EIGHTH PRESIDENT

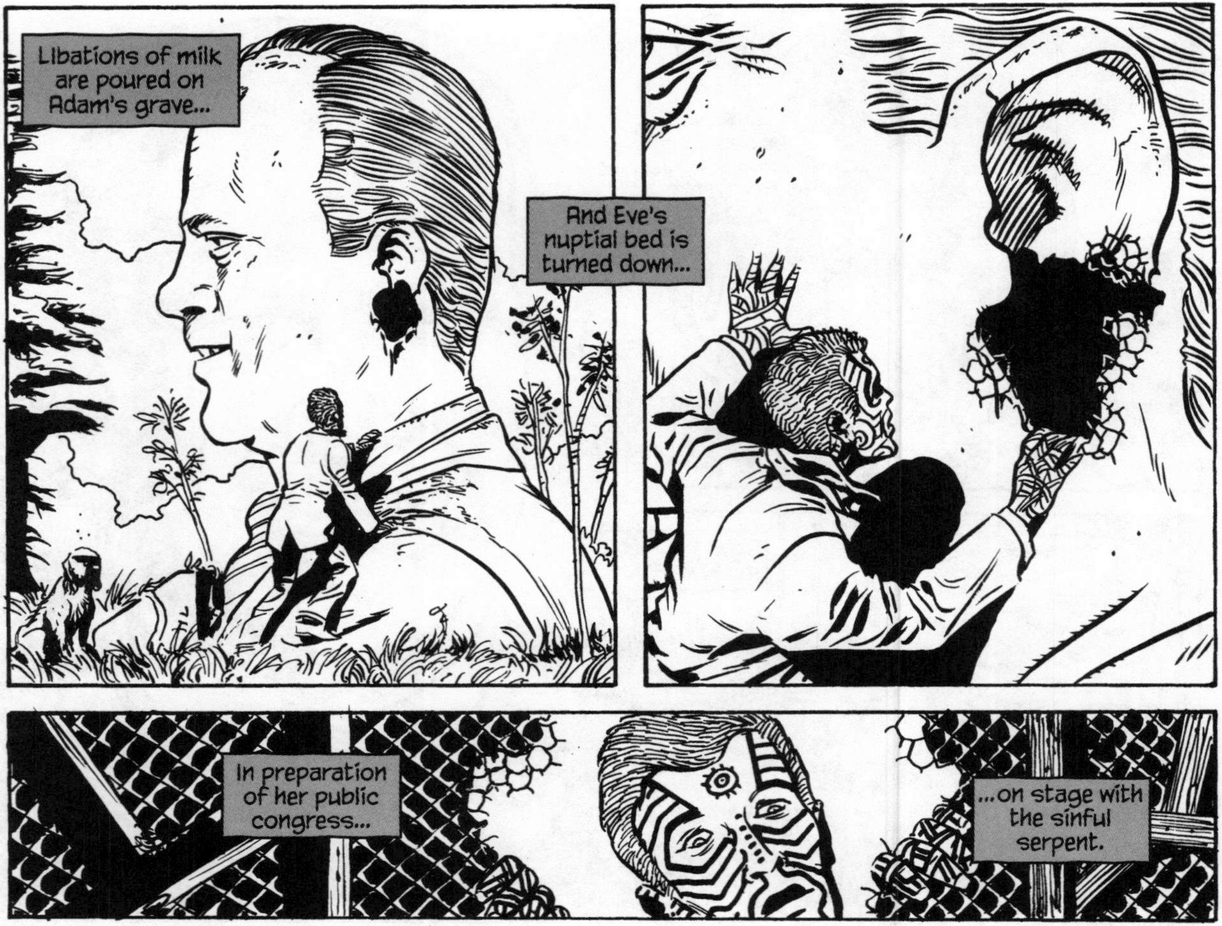
Libations of milk are poured on Adam's grave...
And Eve's nuptial bed is turned down...
In preparation of her public congress...
...on stage with the sinful serpent.

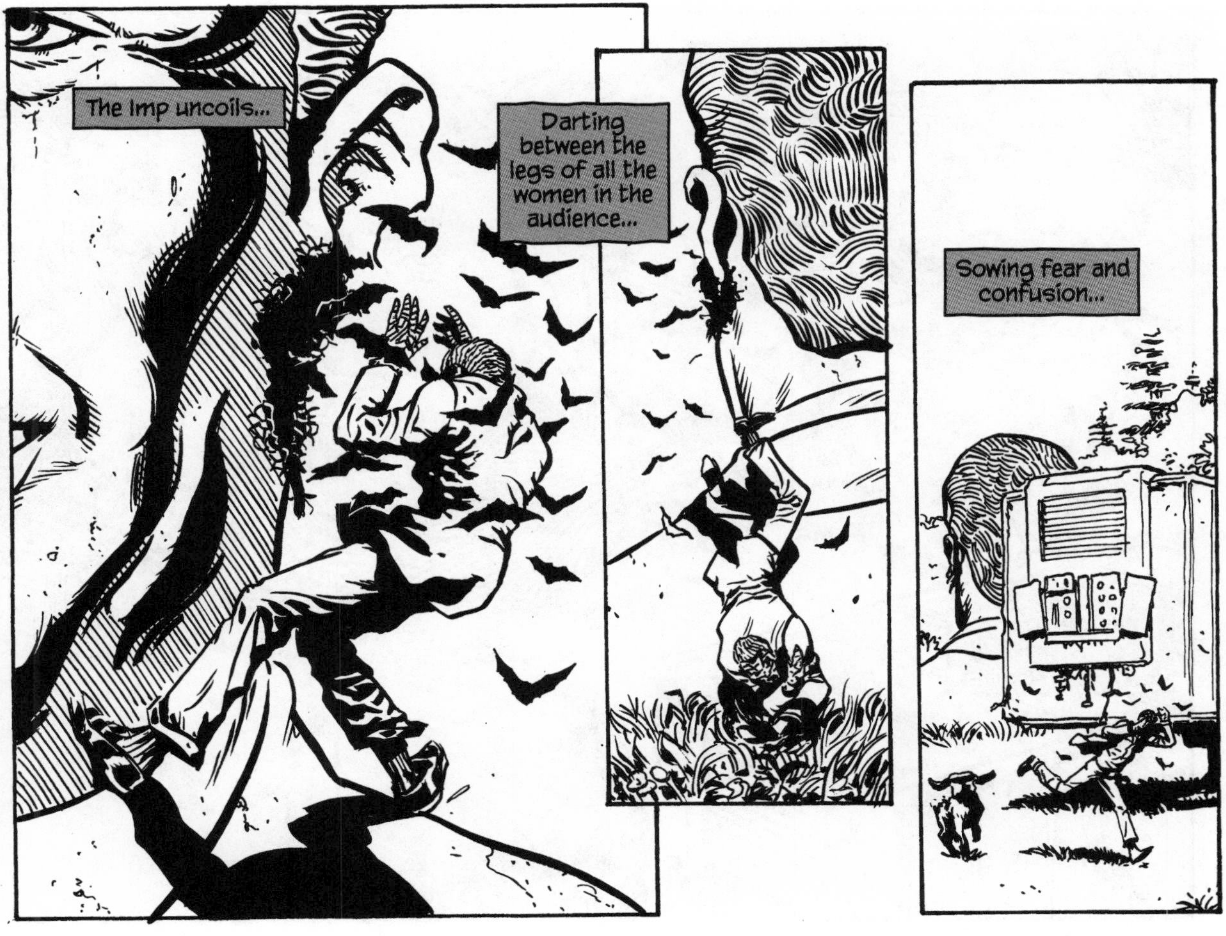
The Imp uncoils...
Darting between the legs of all the women in the audience...
Sowing fear and confusion...

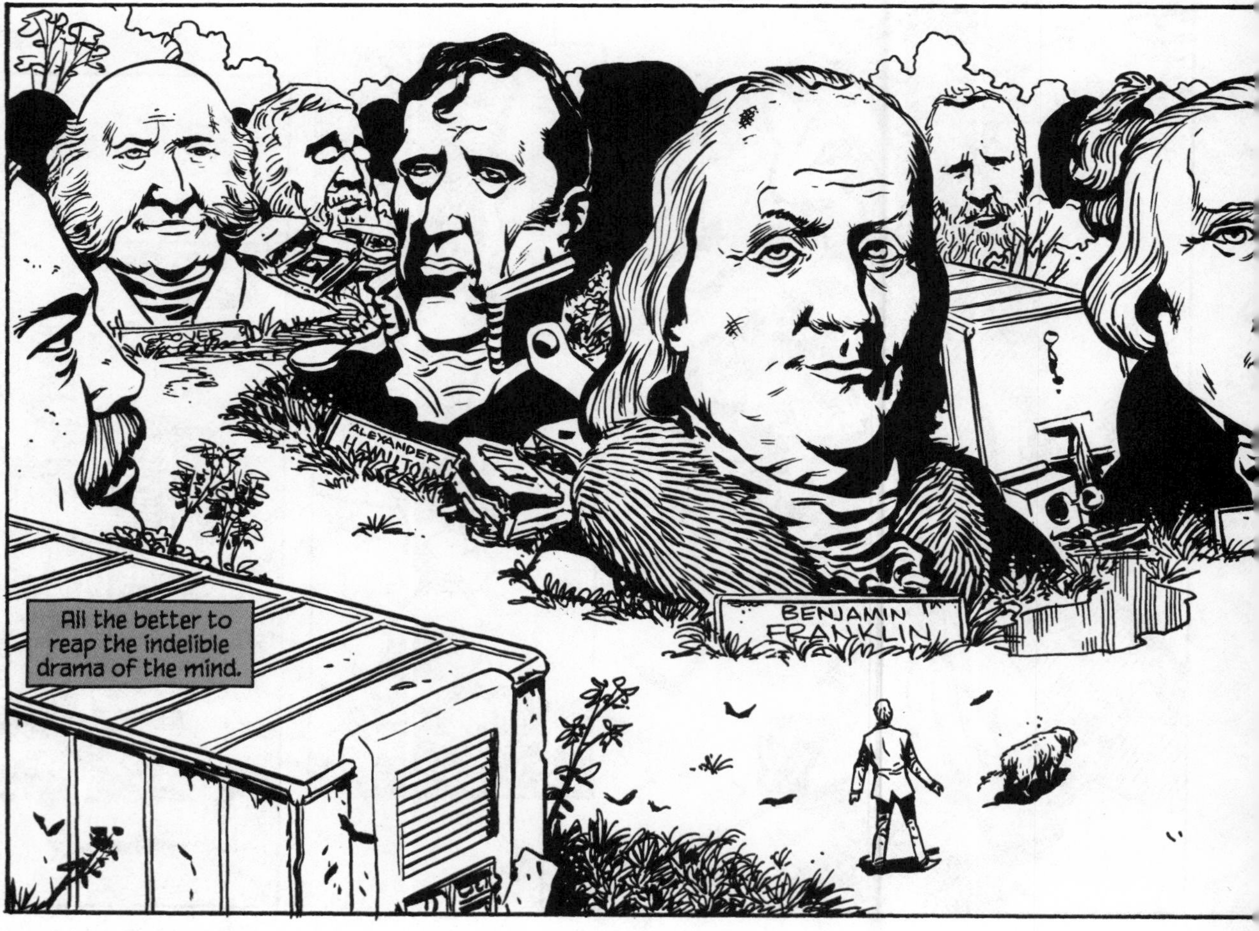
GROVER
ALEXANDER HAMILTON
BENJAMIN FRANKLIN
All the better to reap the indelible drama of the mind.

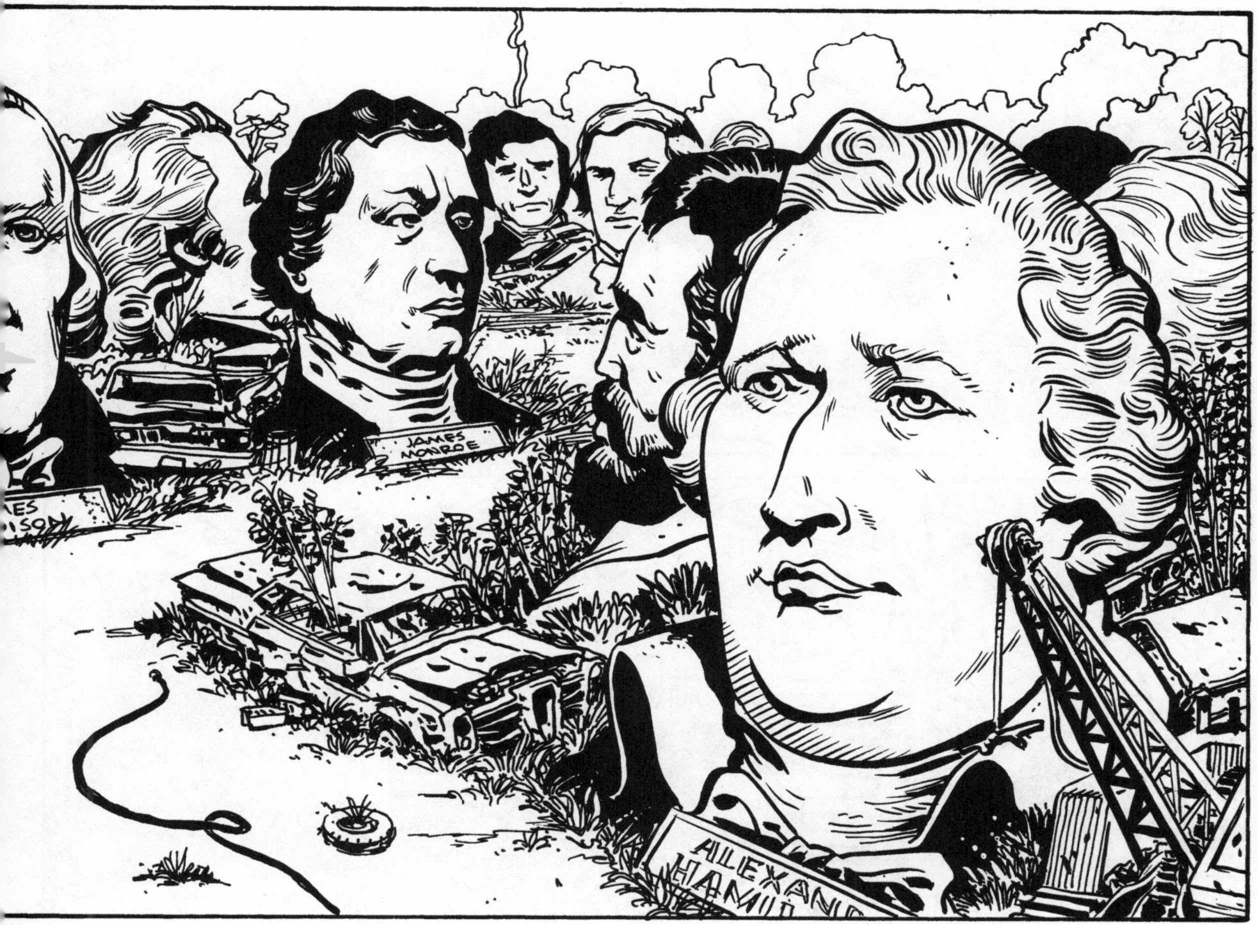

JAMES MONROE
ALEXAND
HAMIL

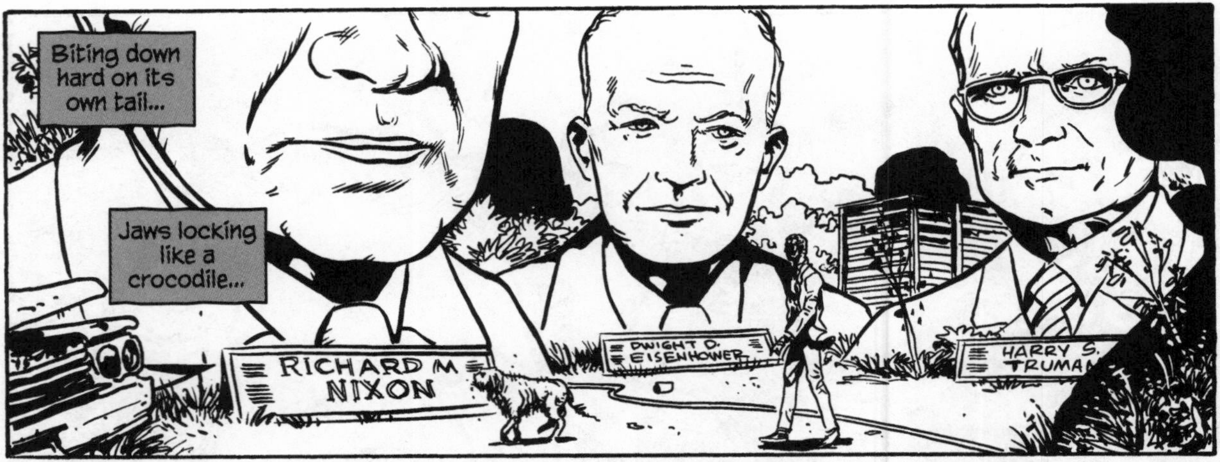
Biting down hard on its own tail...
Jaws locking like a crocodile...
RICHARD M NIXON
DWIGHT D. EISENHOWER
HARRY S. TRUMA

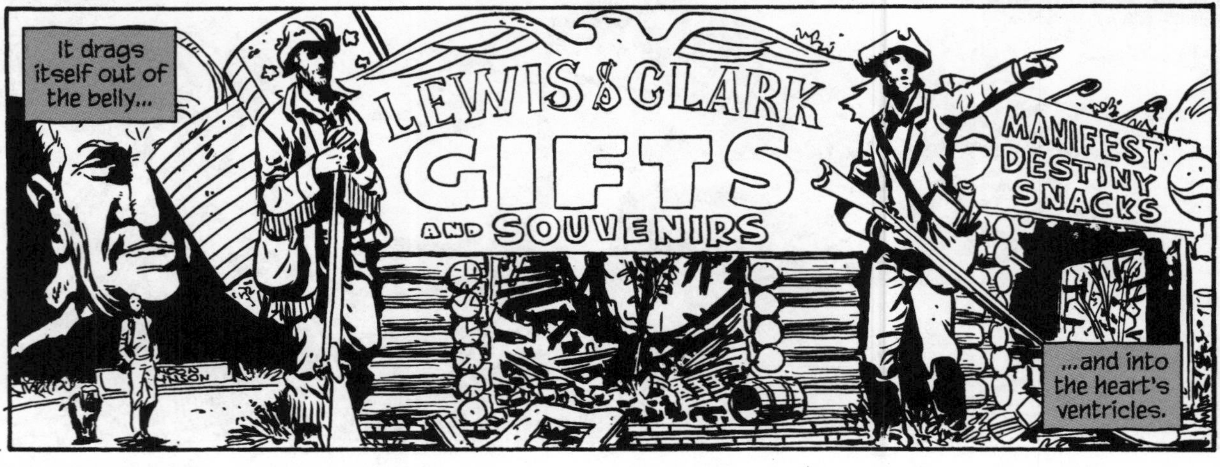
It drags itself out of the belly...
LEWIS & CLARK
GIFTS
AND SOUVENIRS
MANIFEST DESTINY SNACKS
...and into the heart's ventricles.

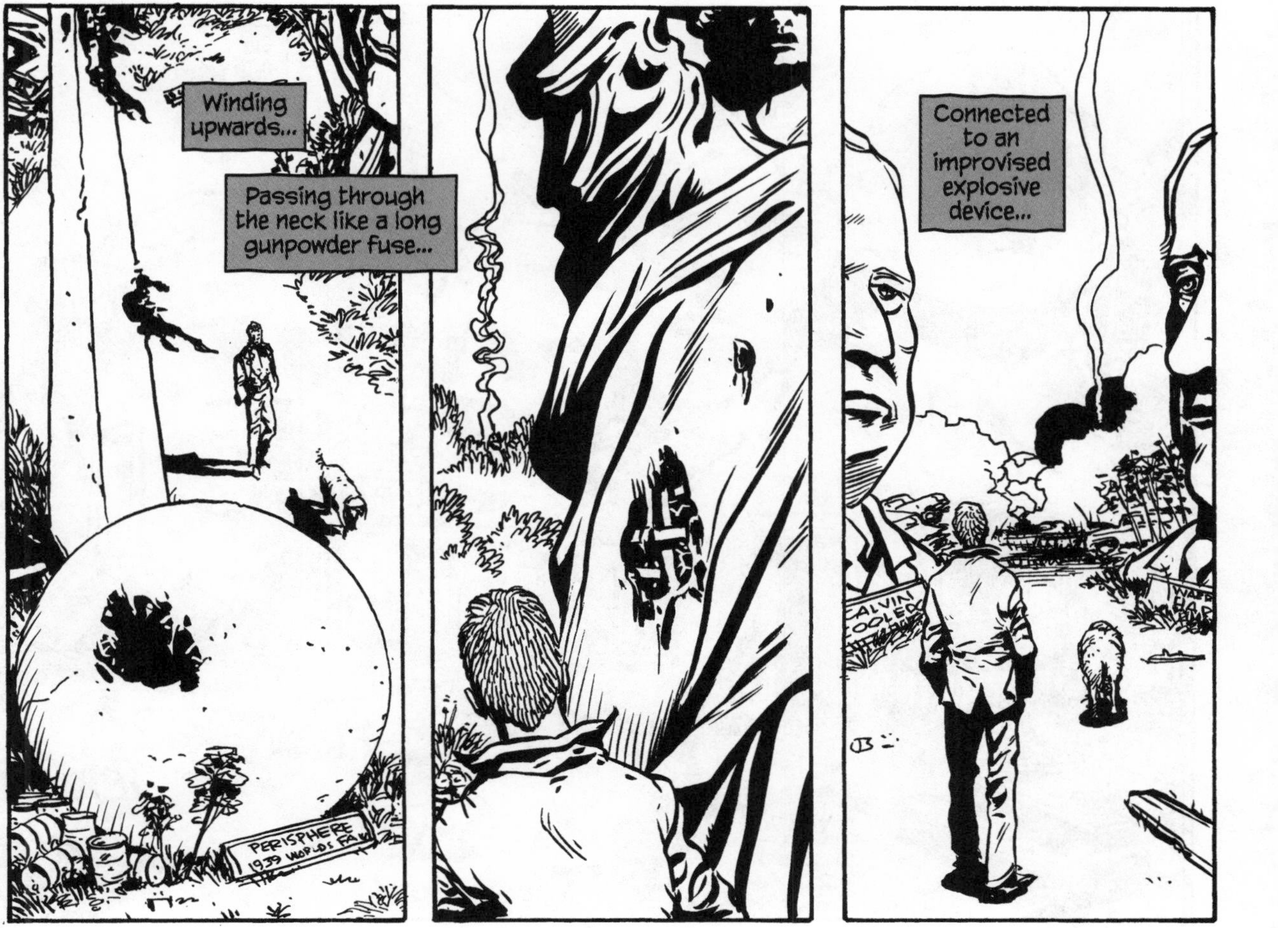

Winding upwards...
Passing through the neck like a long gunpowder fuse...
PERISPHERE
1939 WORLDS FA
Connected to an improvised explosive device...

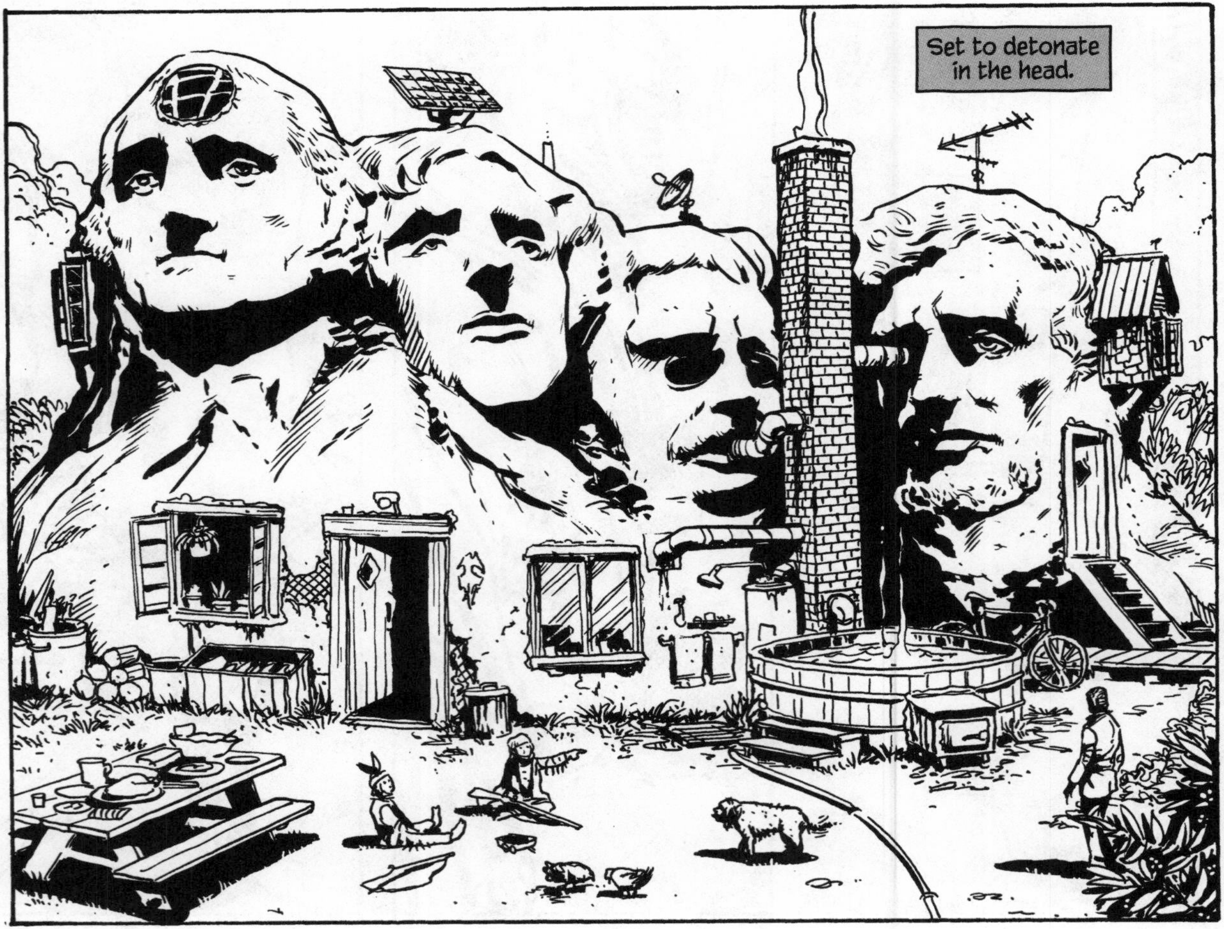
Set to detonate in the head.

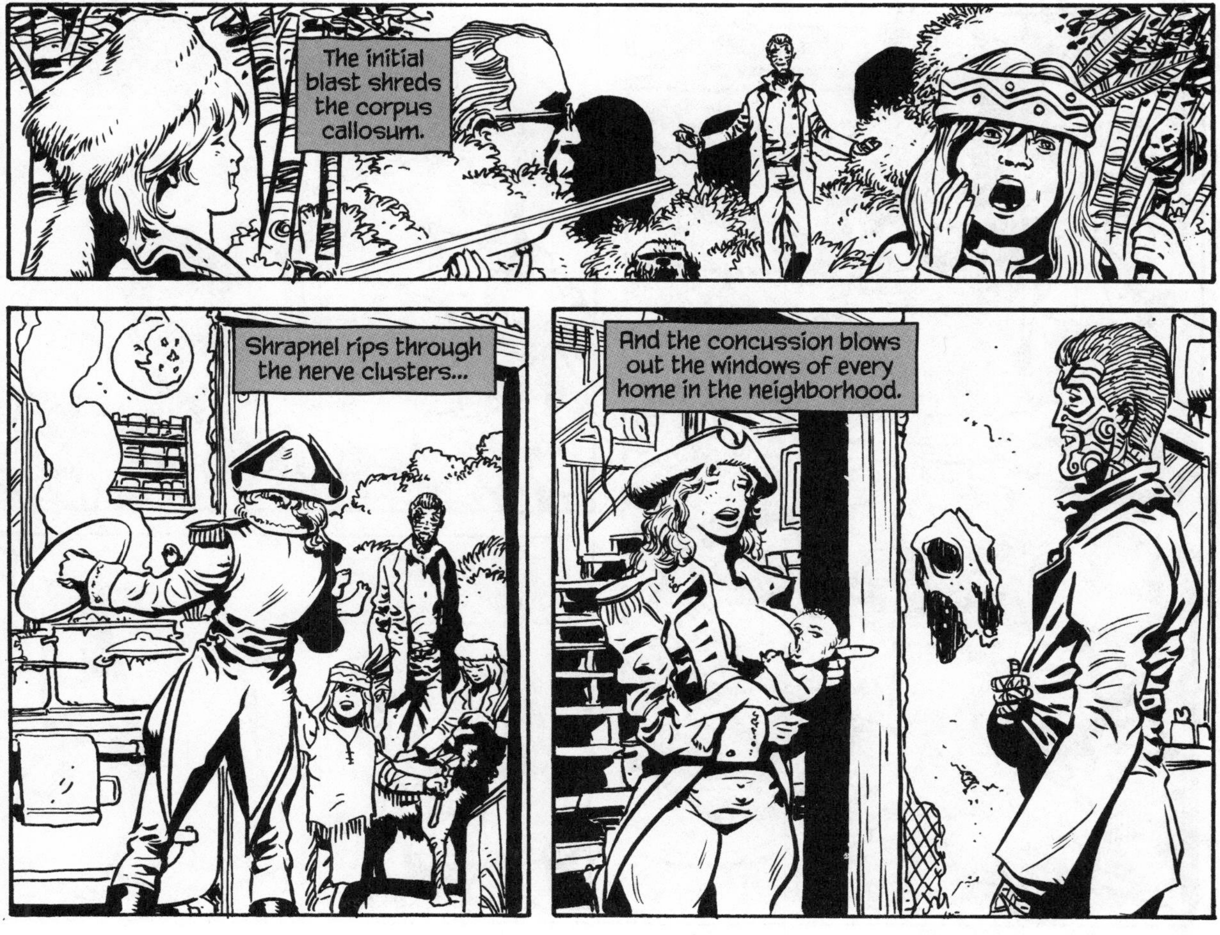
The initial blast shreds the corpus callosum.
Shrapnel rips through the nerve clusters...
And the concussion blows out the windows of every home in the neighborhood.

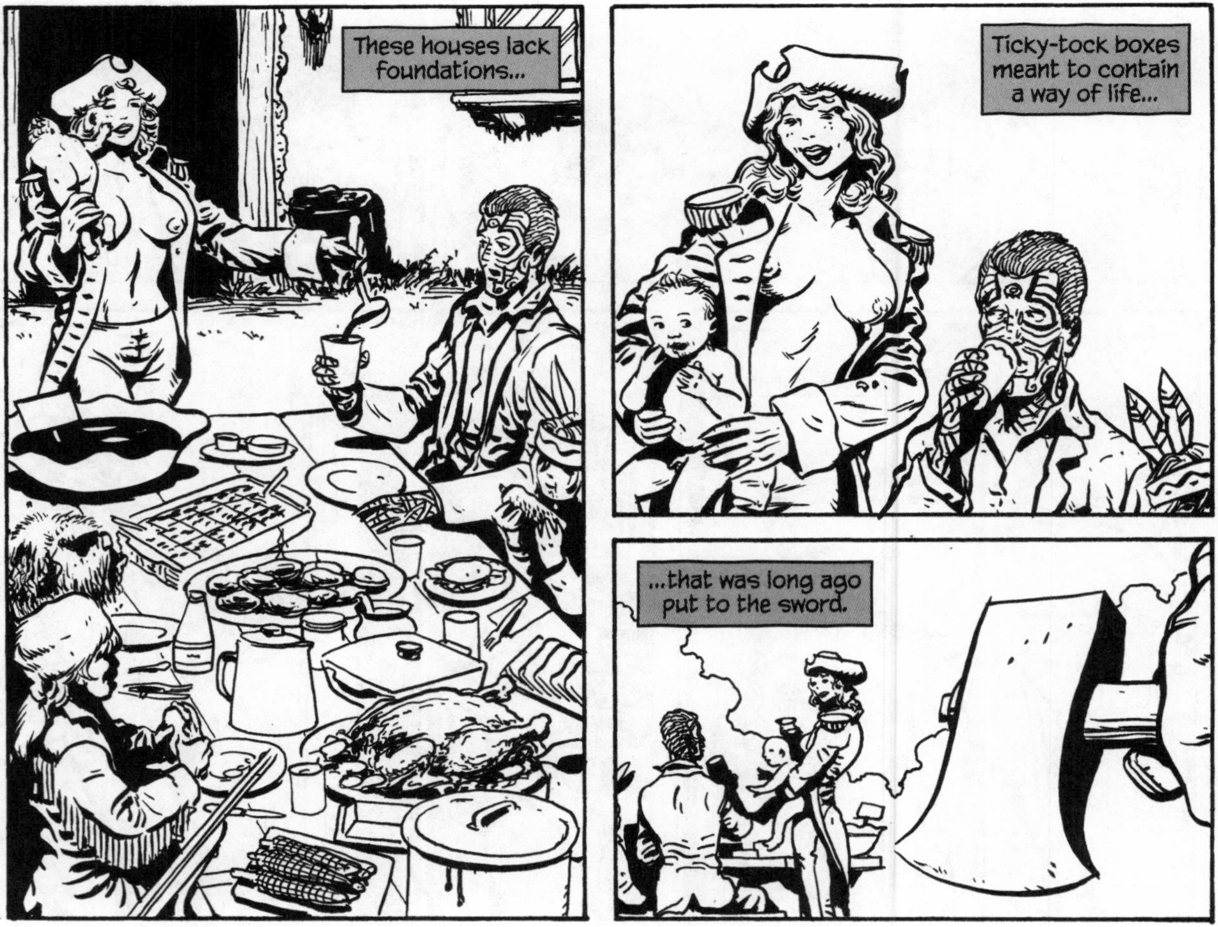
These houses lack foundations...
Ticky-tock boxes meant to contain a way of life...
...that was long ago put to the sword.

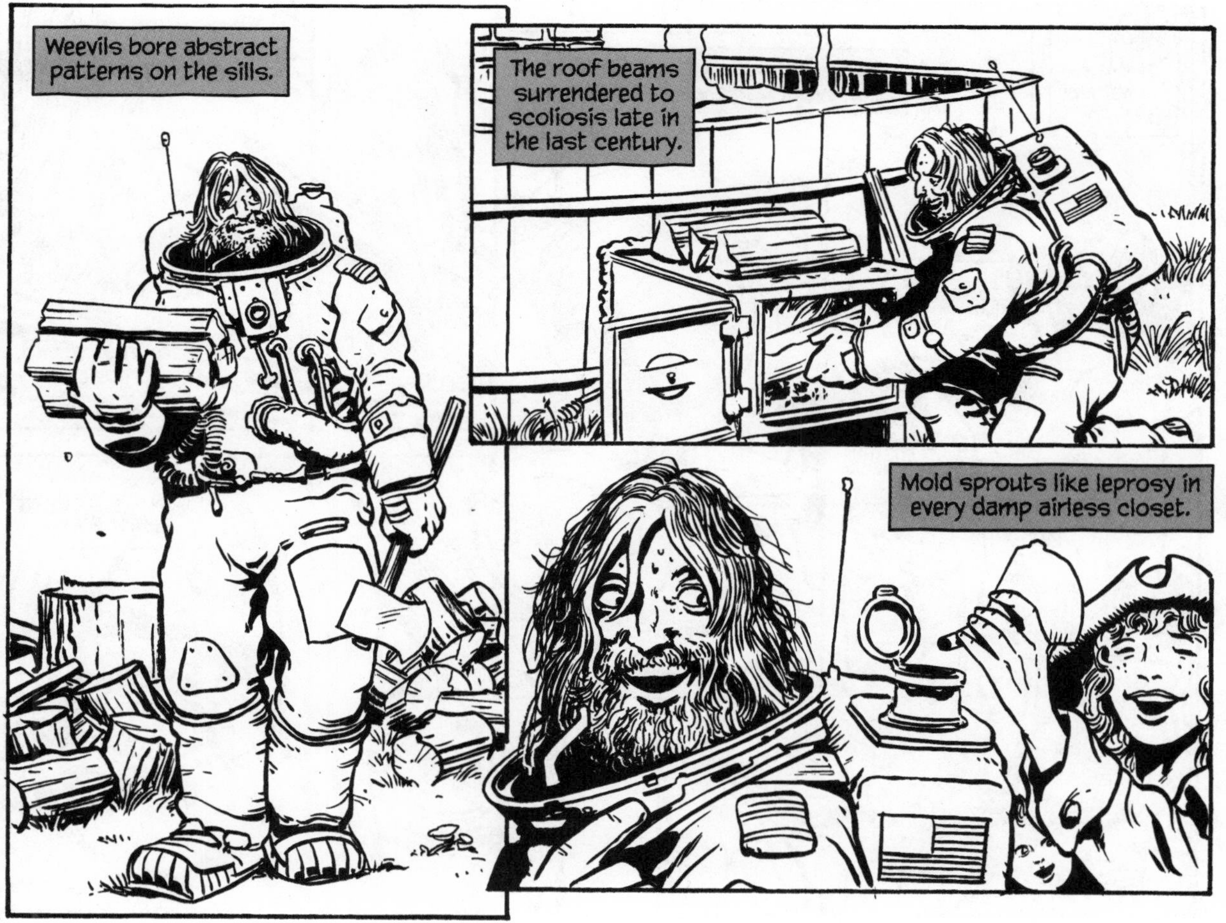
Weevils bore abstract patterns on the sills.
The roof beams surrendered to scoliosis late in the last century.
Mold sprouts like leprosy in every damp airless closet.

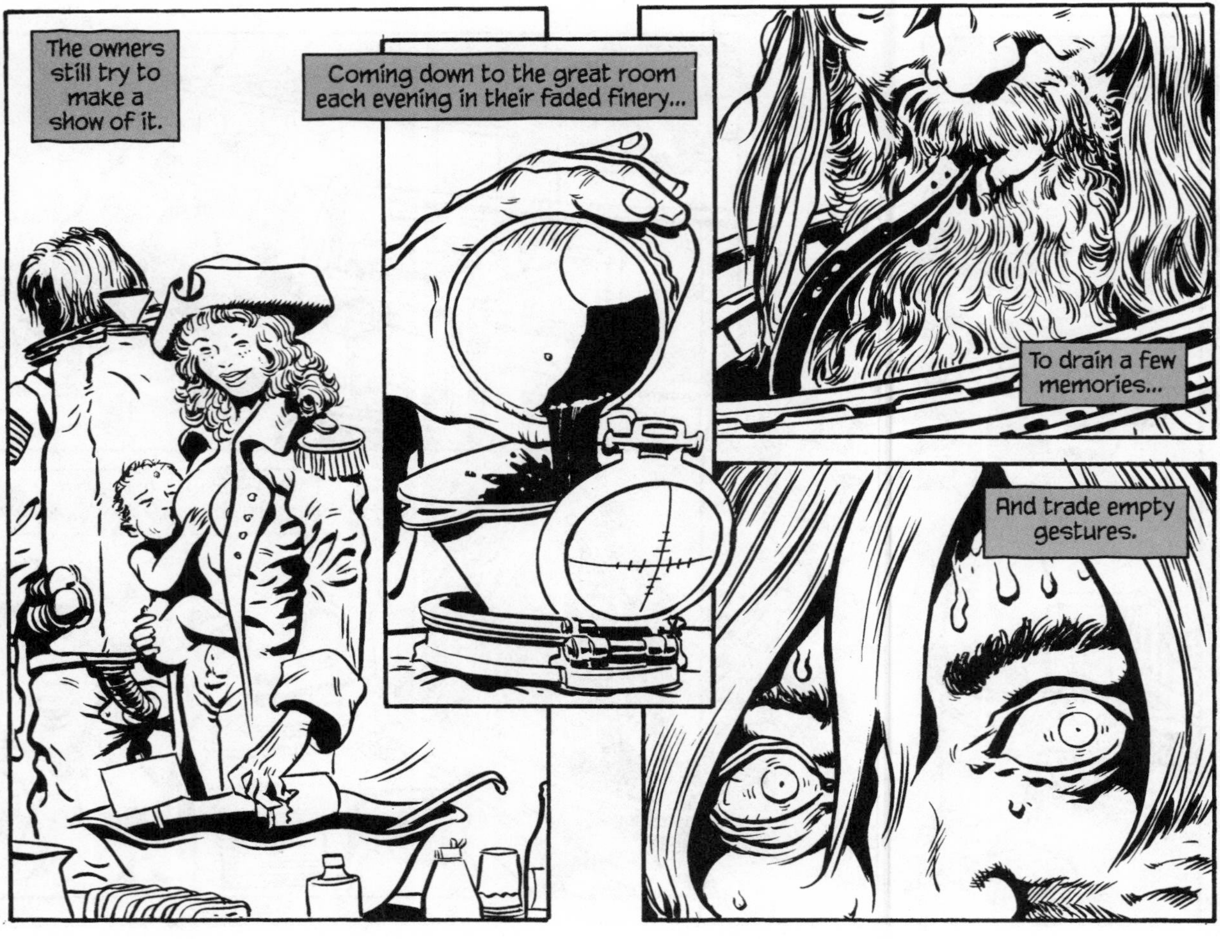
The owners still try to make a show of it.
Coming down to the great room each evening in their faded finery...
To drain a few memories...
And trade empty gestures.

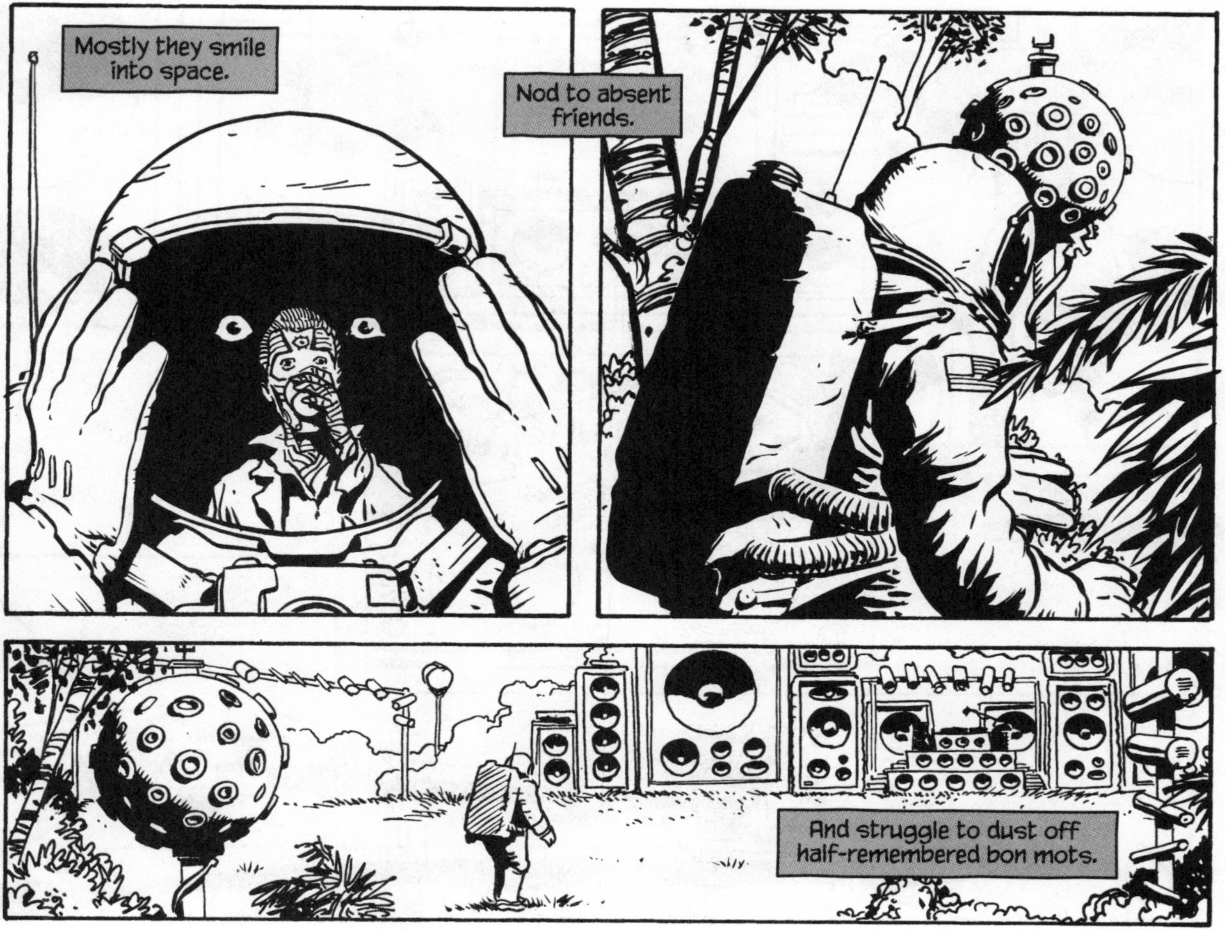
Mostly they smile into space.
Nod to absent friends.
And struggle to dust off half-remembered bon mots.

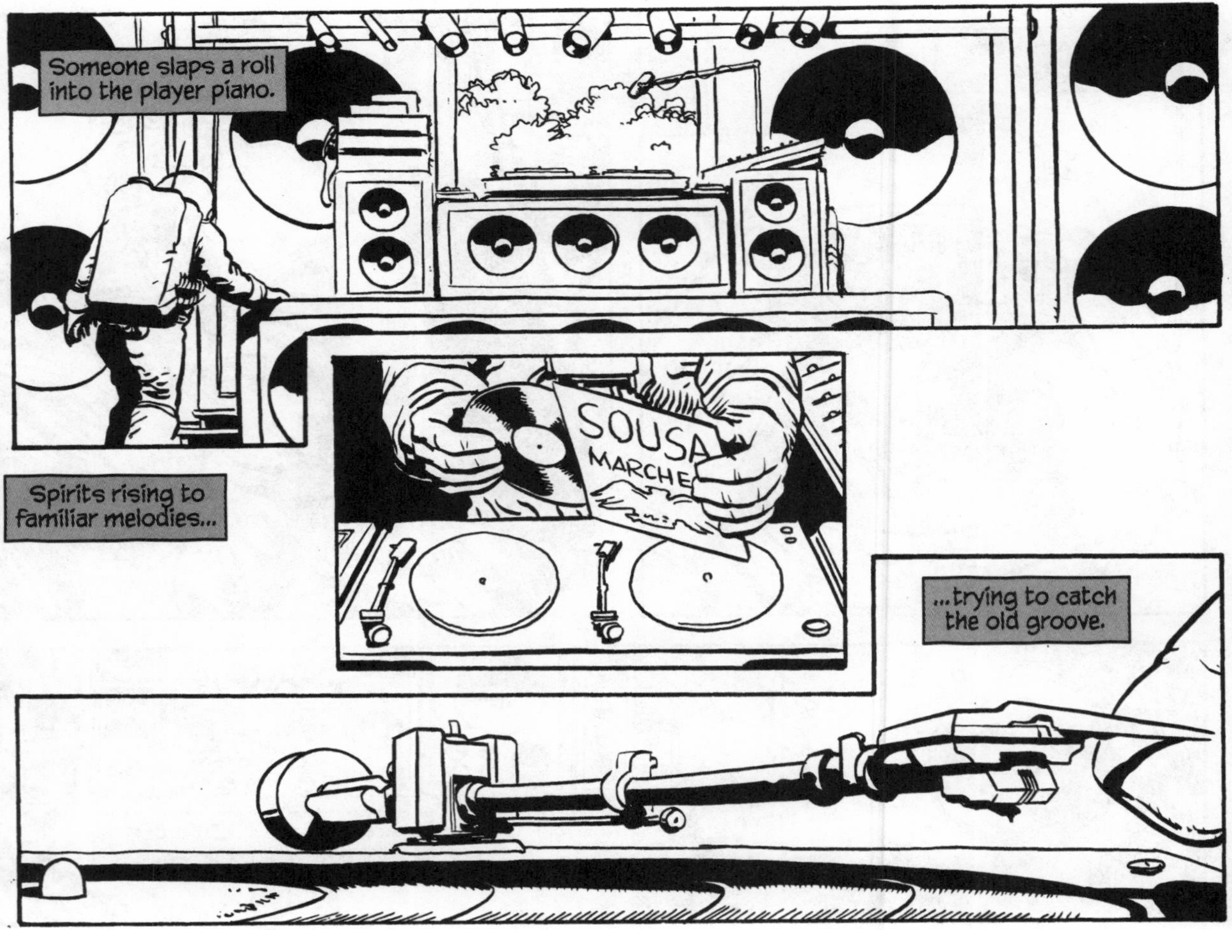

Someone slaps a roll into the player piano.
SOUSA MARCHE
Spirits rising to familiar melodies...
...trying to catch the old groove.

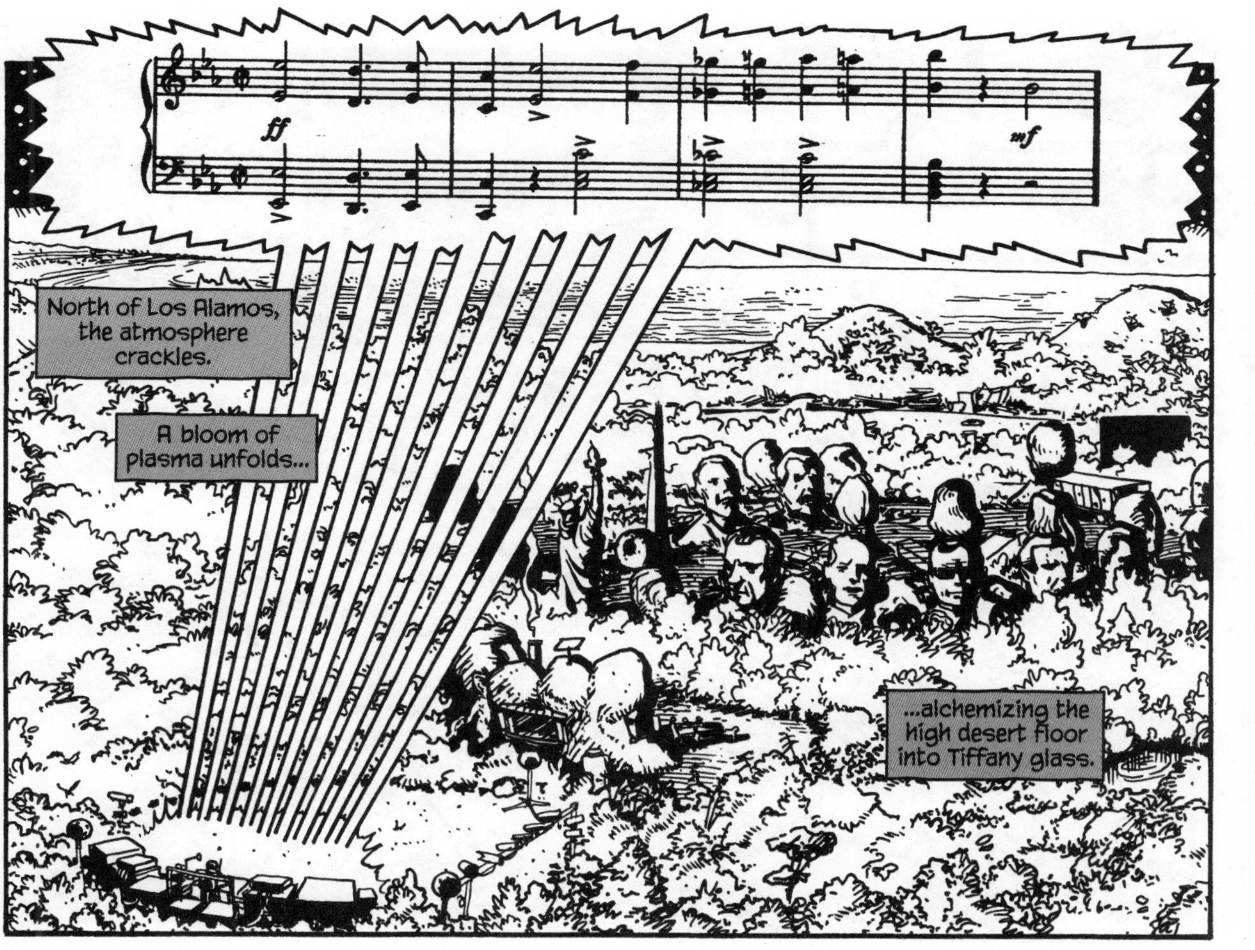
ff
mf
North of Los Alamos, the atmosphere crackles.
A bloom of plasma unfolds...
...alchemizing the high desert floor into Tiffany glass.

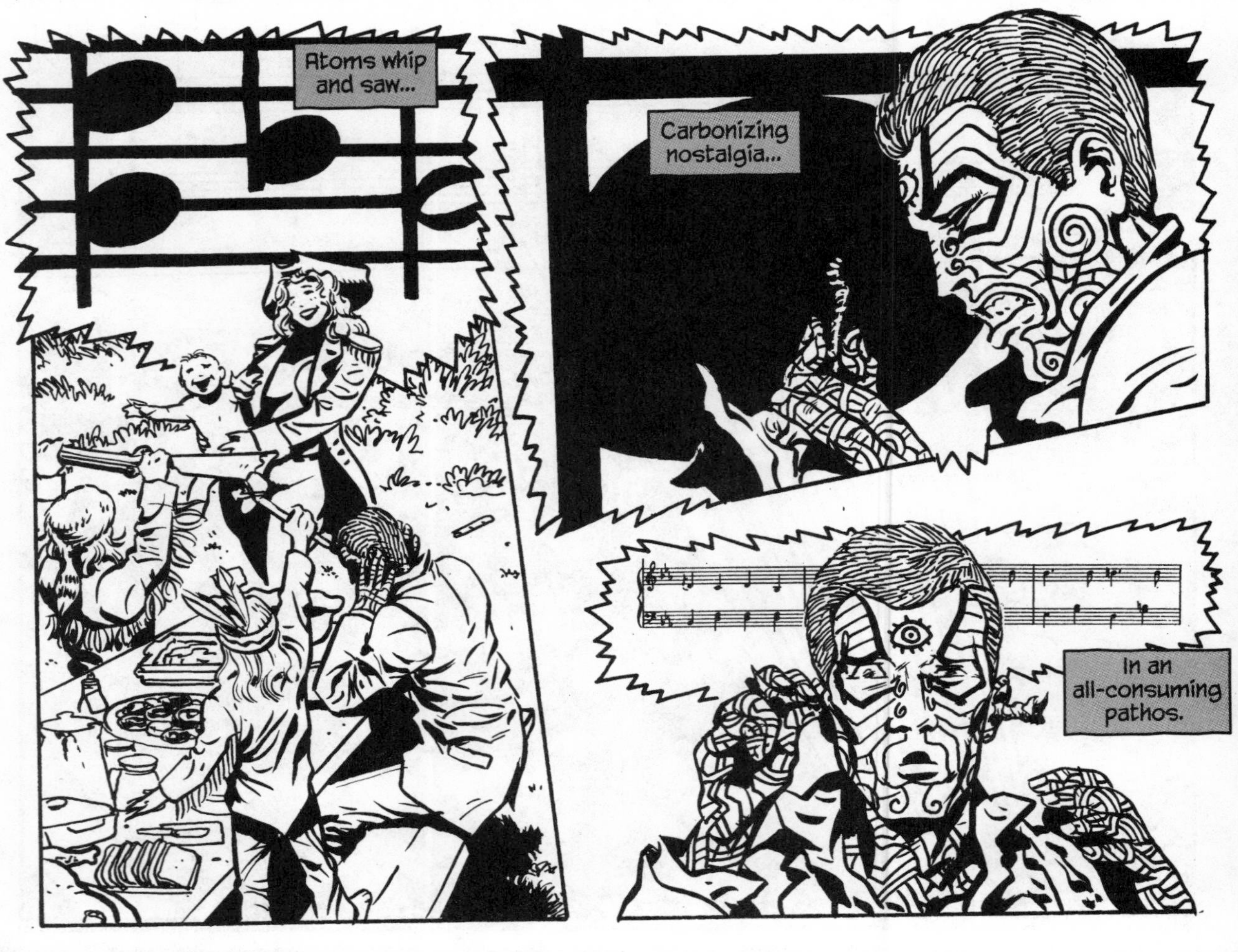
Atoms whip and saw...
Carbonizing nostalgia...
In an all-consuming pathos.

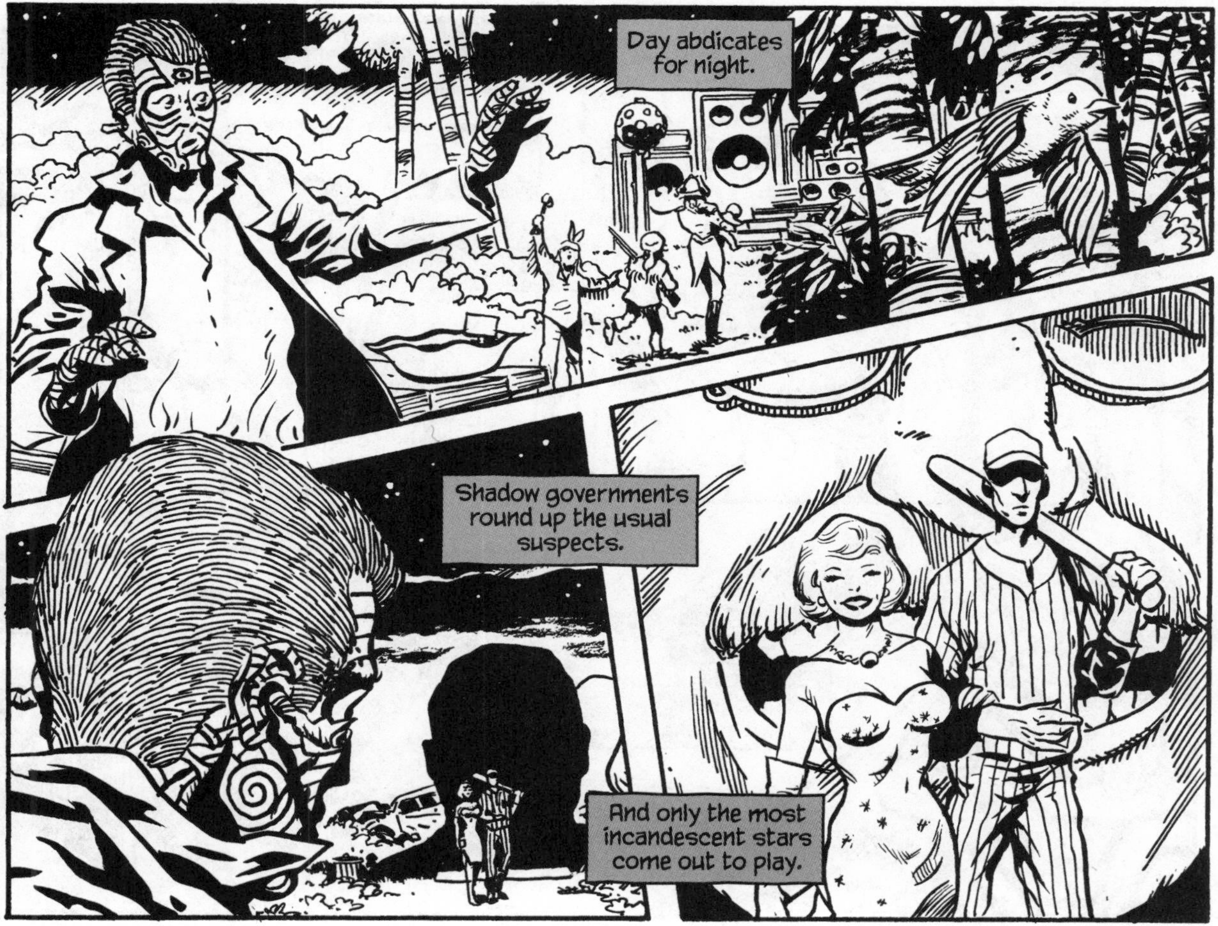
Day abdicates for night.
Shadow governments round up the usual suspects.
And only the most incandescent stars come out to play.

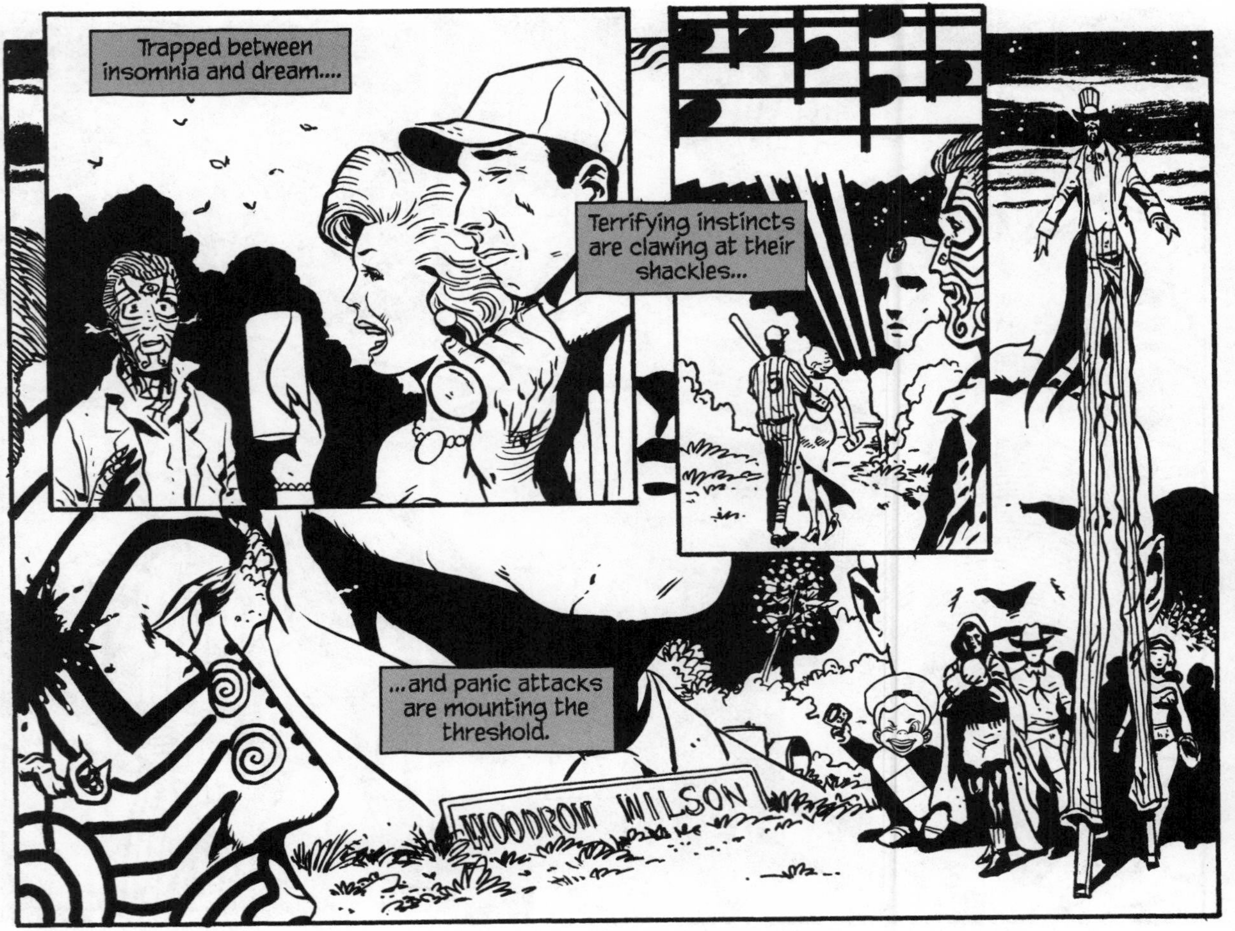
Trapped between insomnia and dream....
Terrifying instincts are clawing at their shackles...
...and panic attacks are mounting the threshold.
WOODROW WILSON

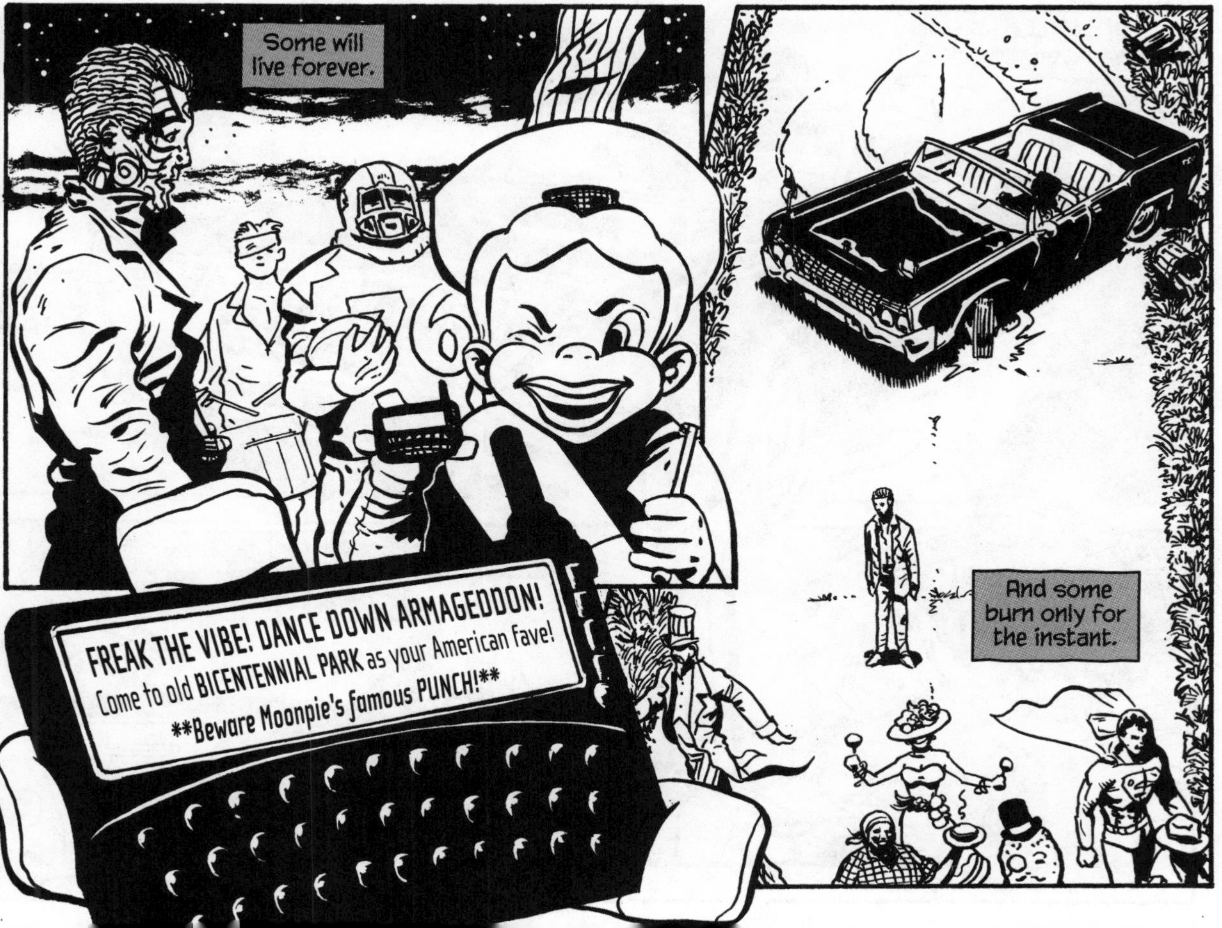
Some will live forever.
FREAK THE VIBE! DANCE DOWN ARMAGEDDON!
Come to old BICENTENNIAL PARK as your American fave!
Beware Moonpie's famous PUNCH!
And some burn only for the instant.

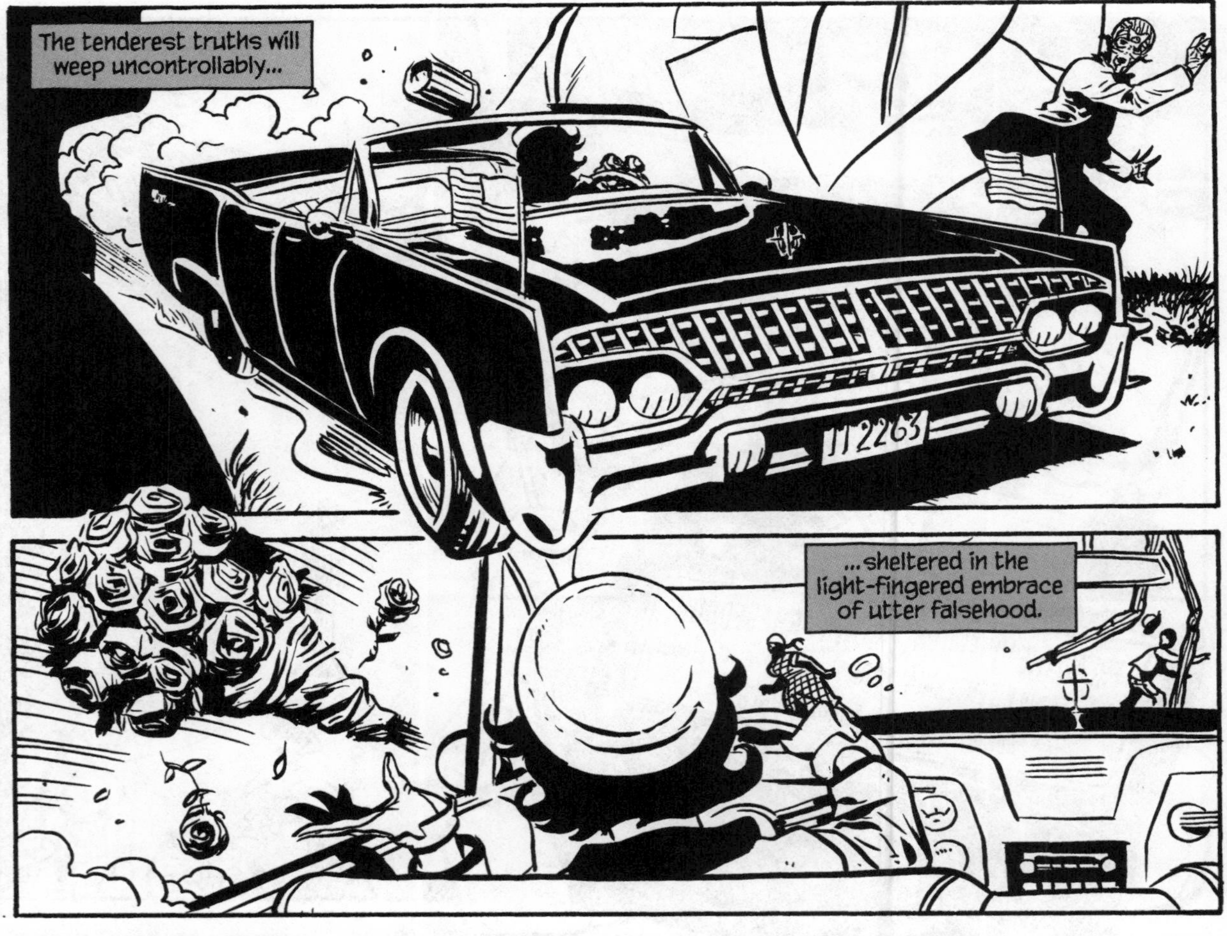
The tenderest truths will weep uncontrollably...
JJ 2263
...sheltered in the light-fingered embrace of utter falsehood.

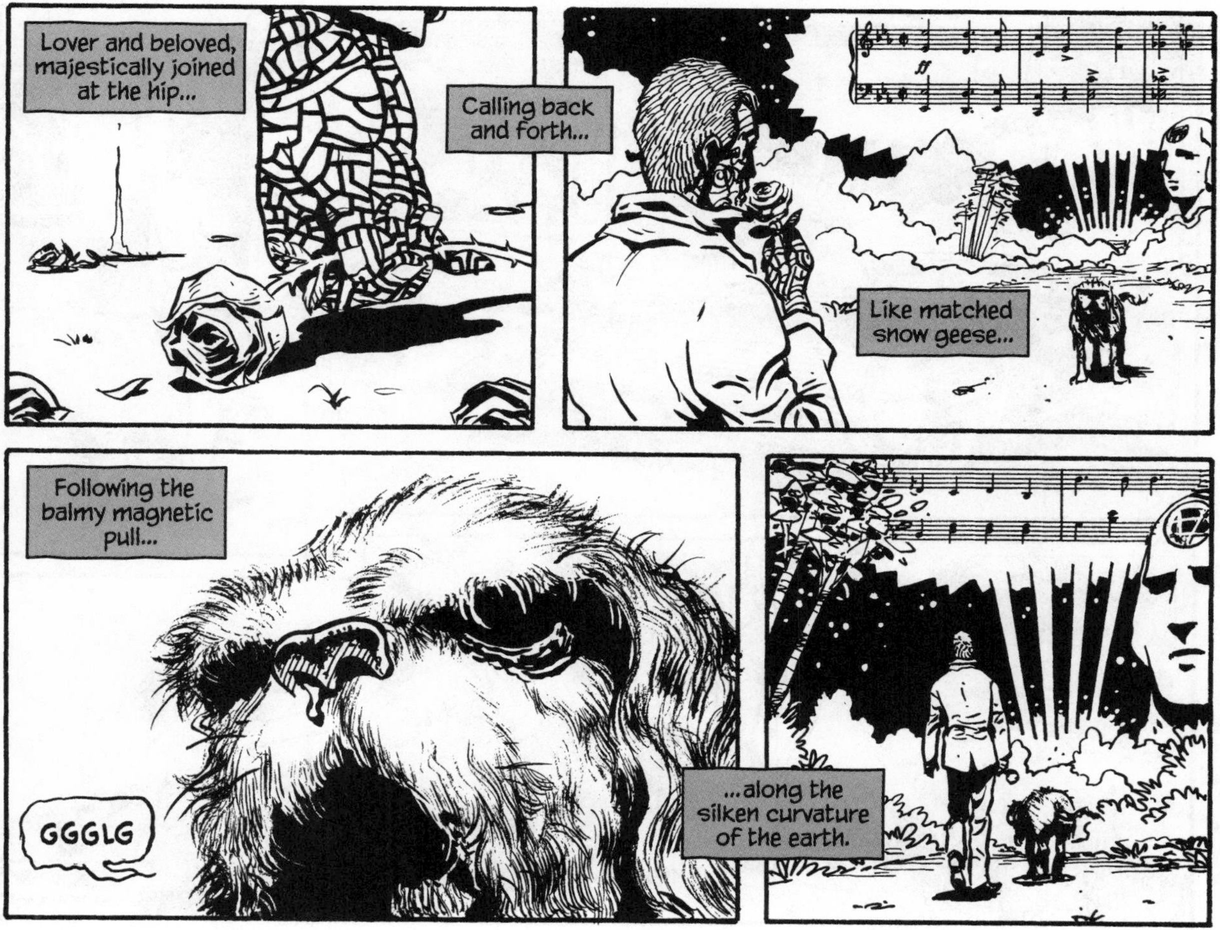
Lover and beloved, majestically joined at the hip...
Calling back and forth...
Like matched snow geese...
Following the balmy magnetic pull...
GGGLG
...along the silken curvature of the earth.

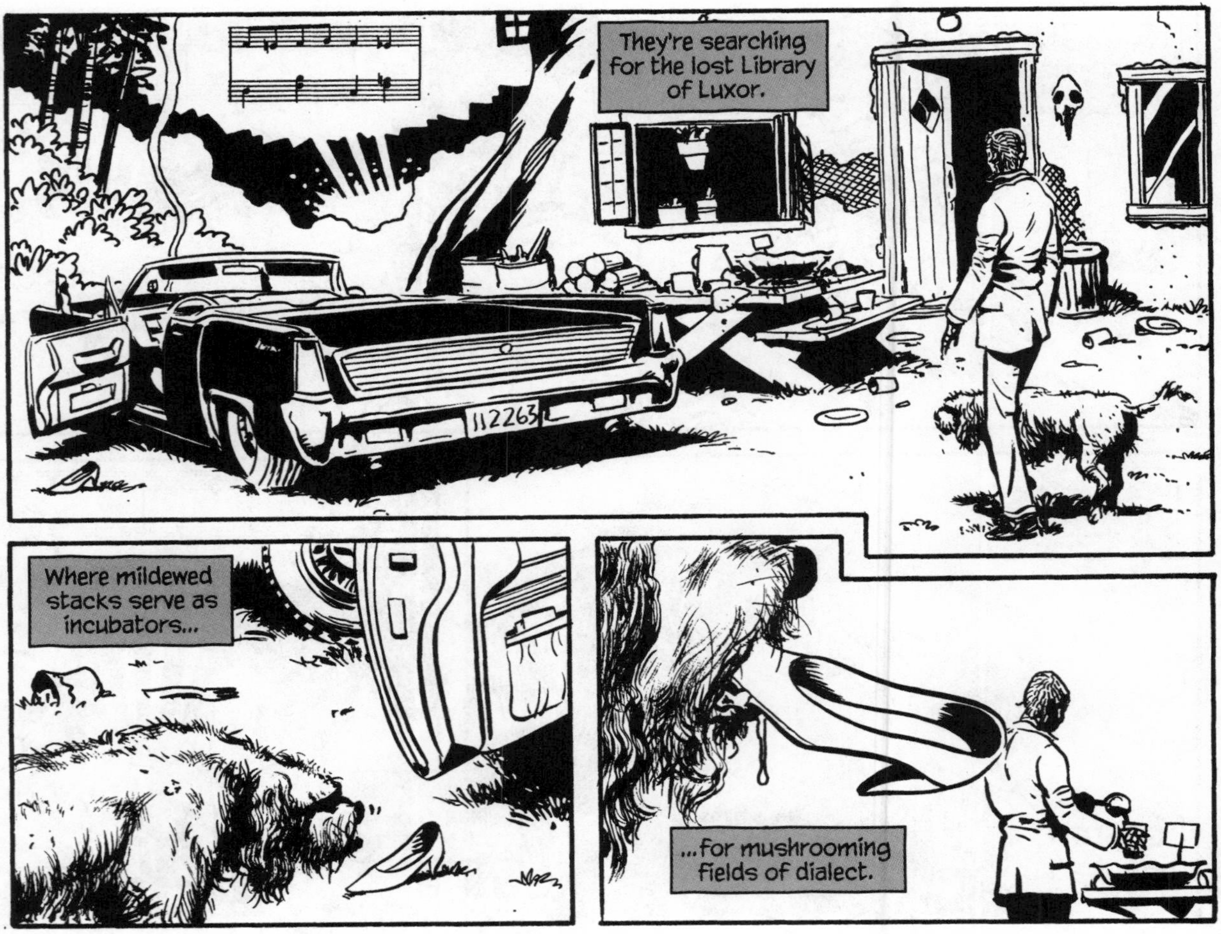
They're searching for the lost Library of Luxor.
JJ2263
Where mildewed stacks serve as incubators...
...for mushrooming fields of dialect.

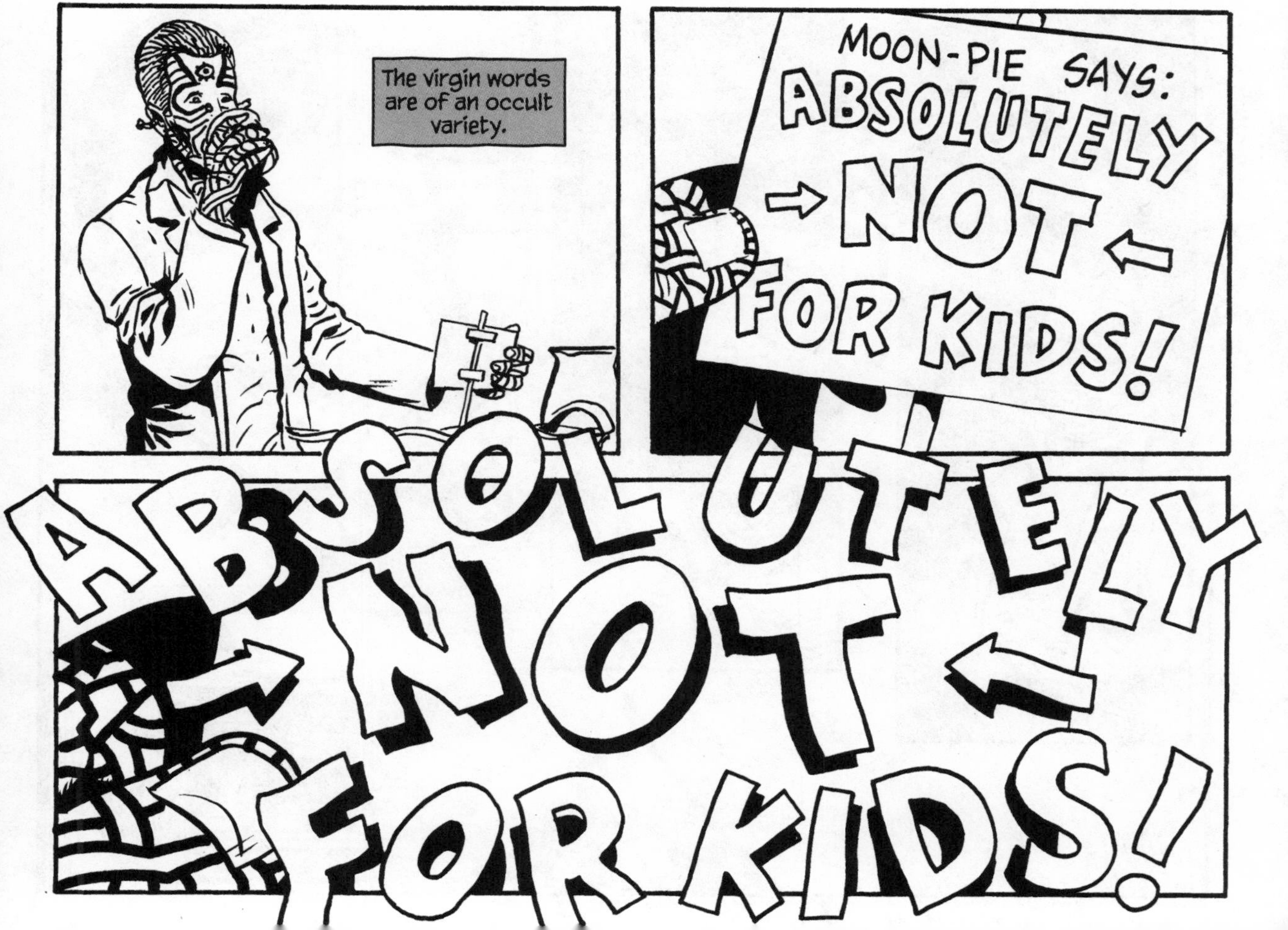
The virgin words are of an occult variety.
MOON-PIE SAYS: ABSOLUTELY NOT FOR KIDS!
ABSOLUTELY NOT FOR KIDS!

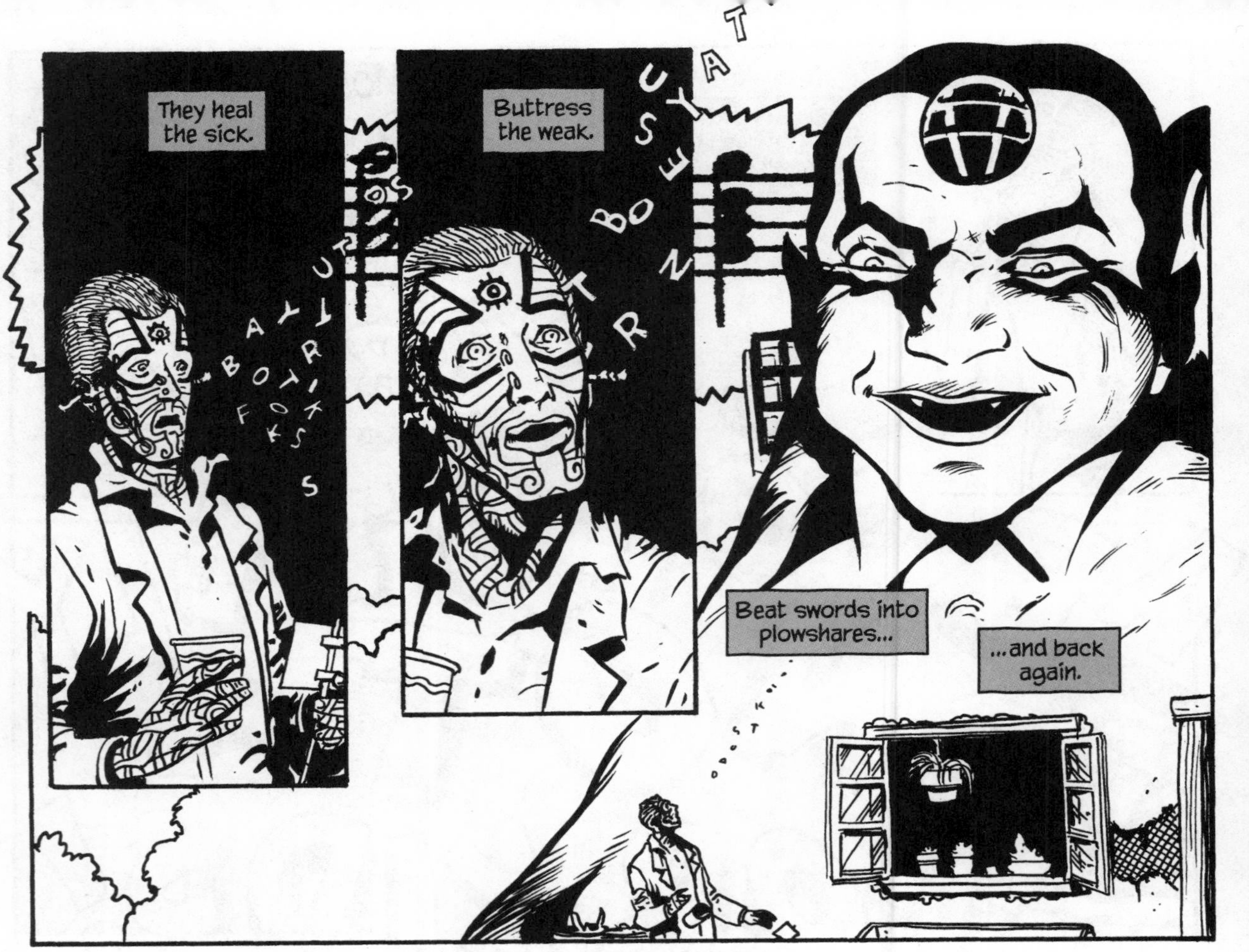
They heal the sick.
Buttress the weak.
Beat swords into plowshares...
...and back again.

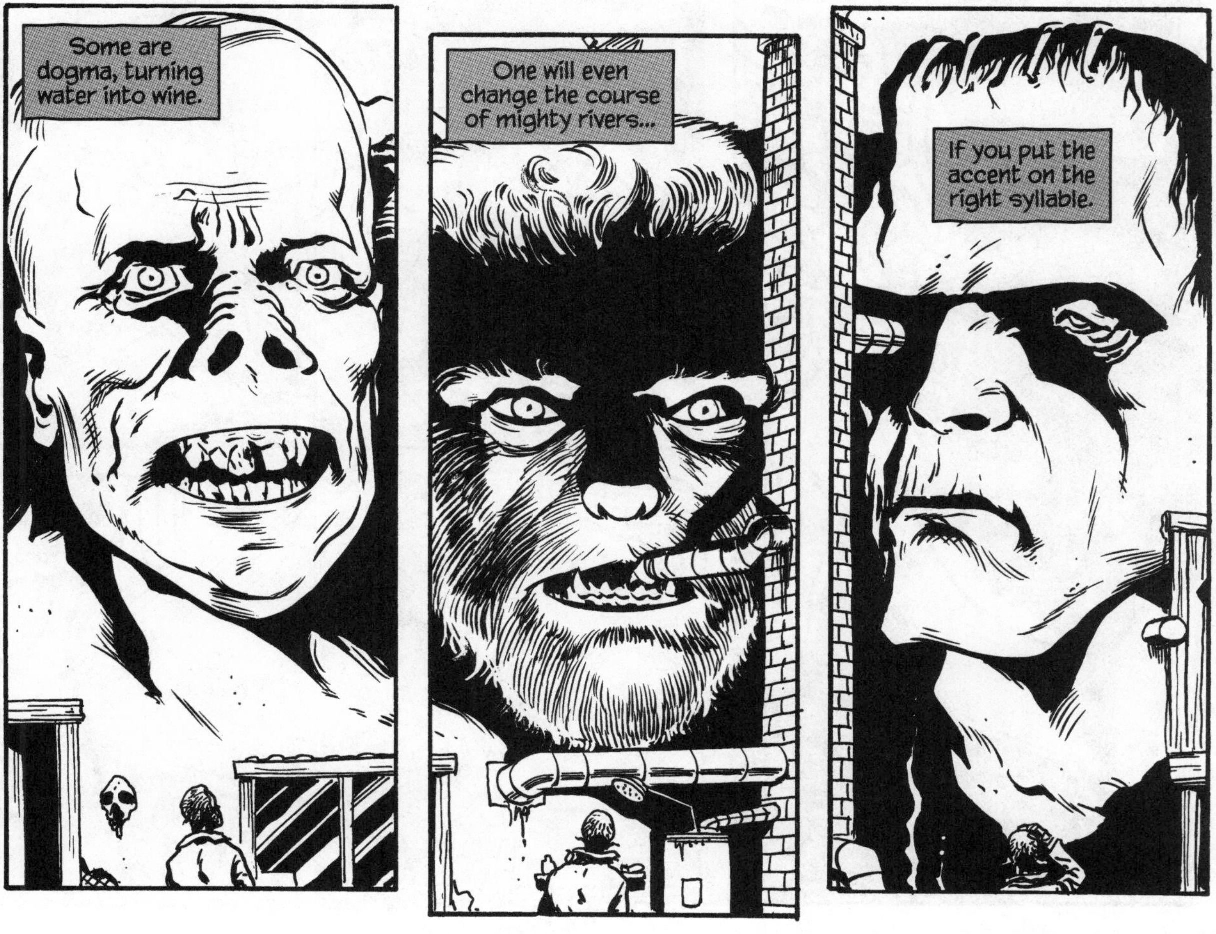
Some are dogma, turning water into wine.
One will even change the course of mighty rivers...
If you put the accent on the right syllable.

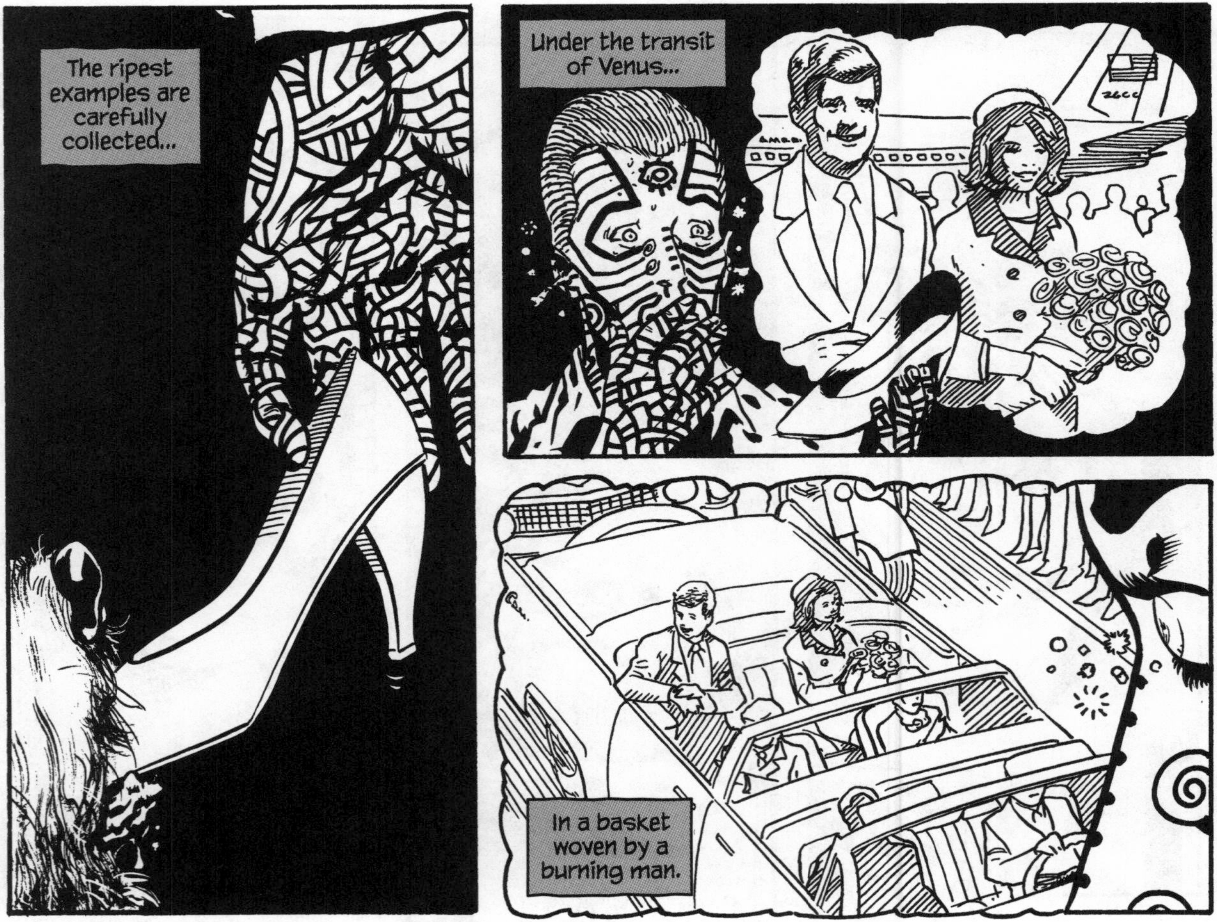
The ripest examples are carefully collected...
Under the transit of Venus...
In a basket woven by a burning man.

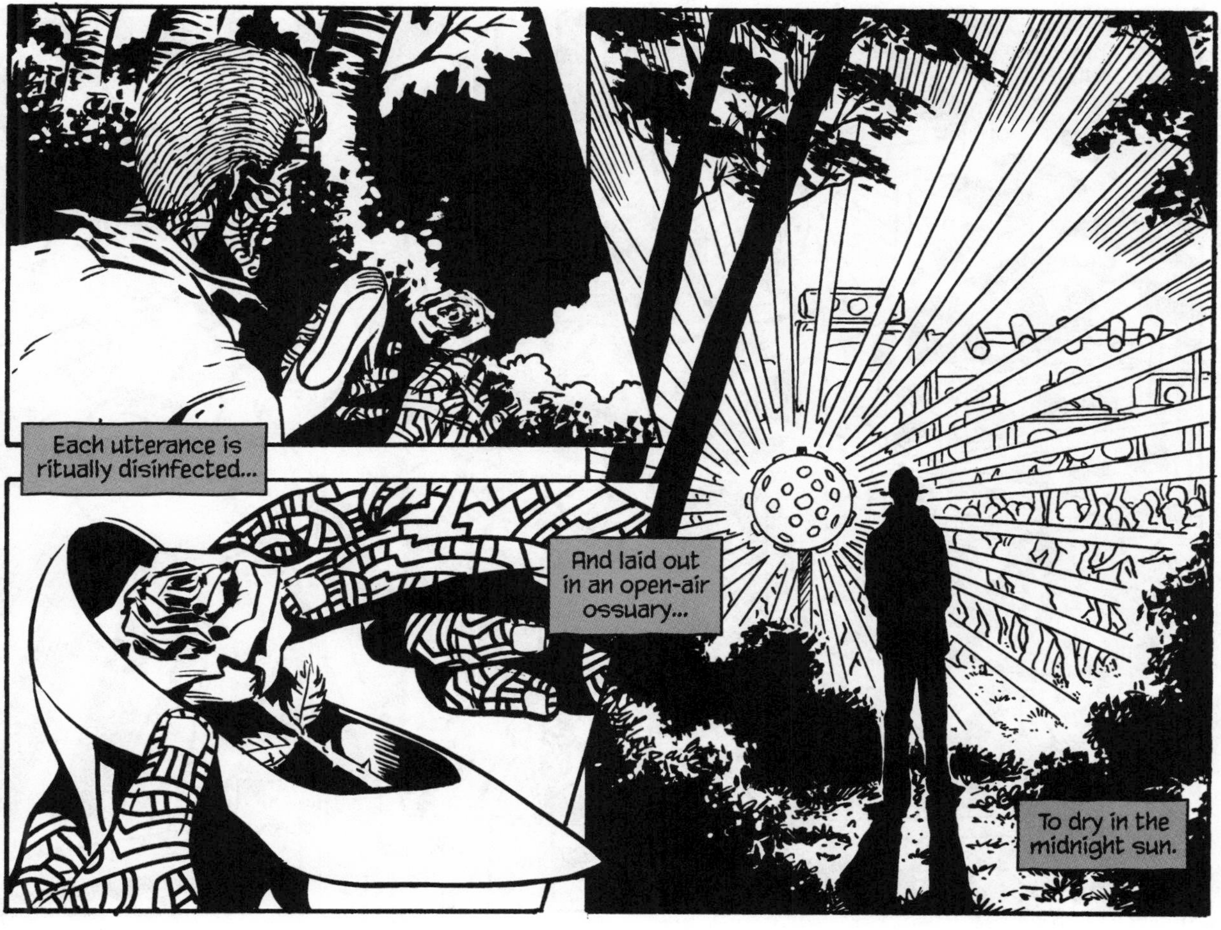
Each utterance is ritually disinfected...
And laid out in an open-air ossuary...
To dry in the midnight sun.

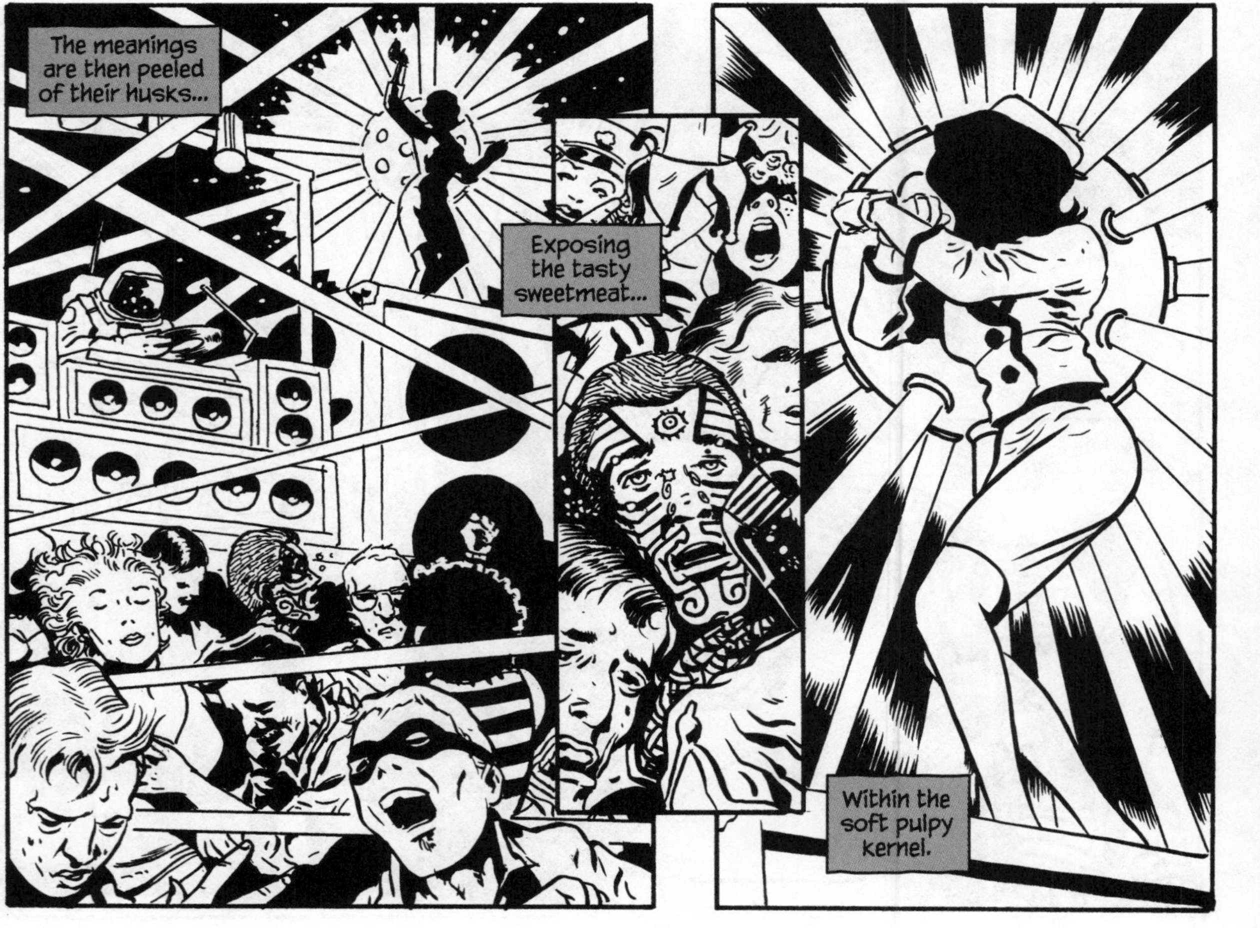

The meanings are then peeled of their husks...
Exposing the tasty sweetmeat...
Within the soft pulpy kernel.

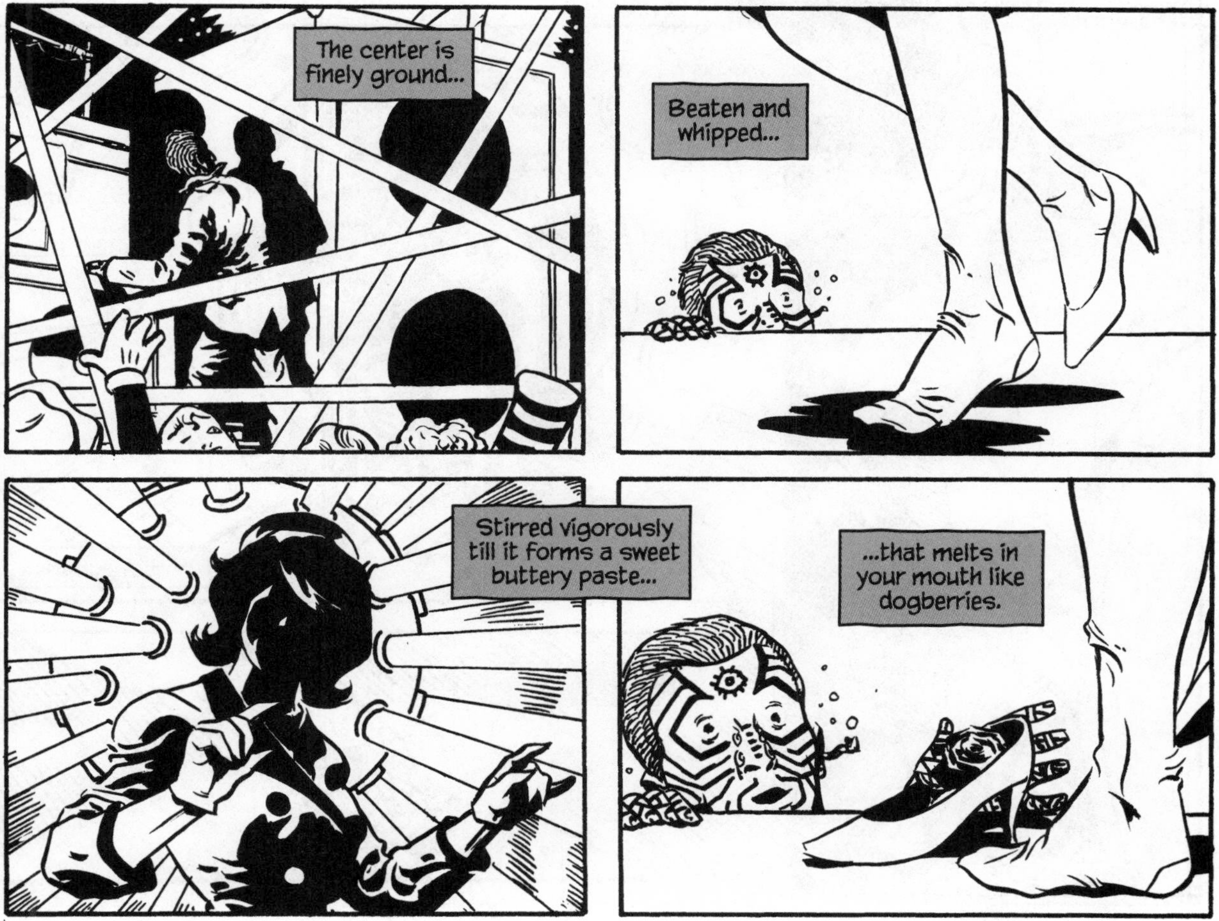
The center is finely ground...
Beaten and whipped...
Stirred vigorously till it forms a sweet buttery paste...
...that melts in your mouth like dogberries.

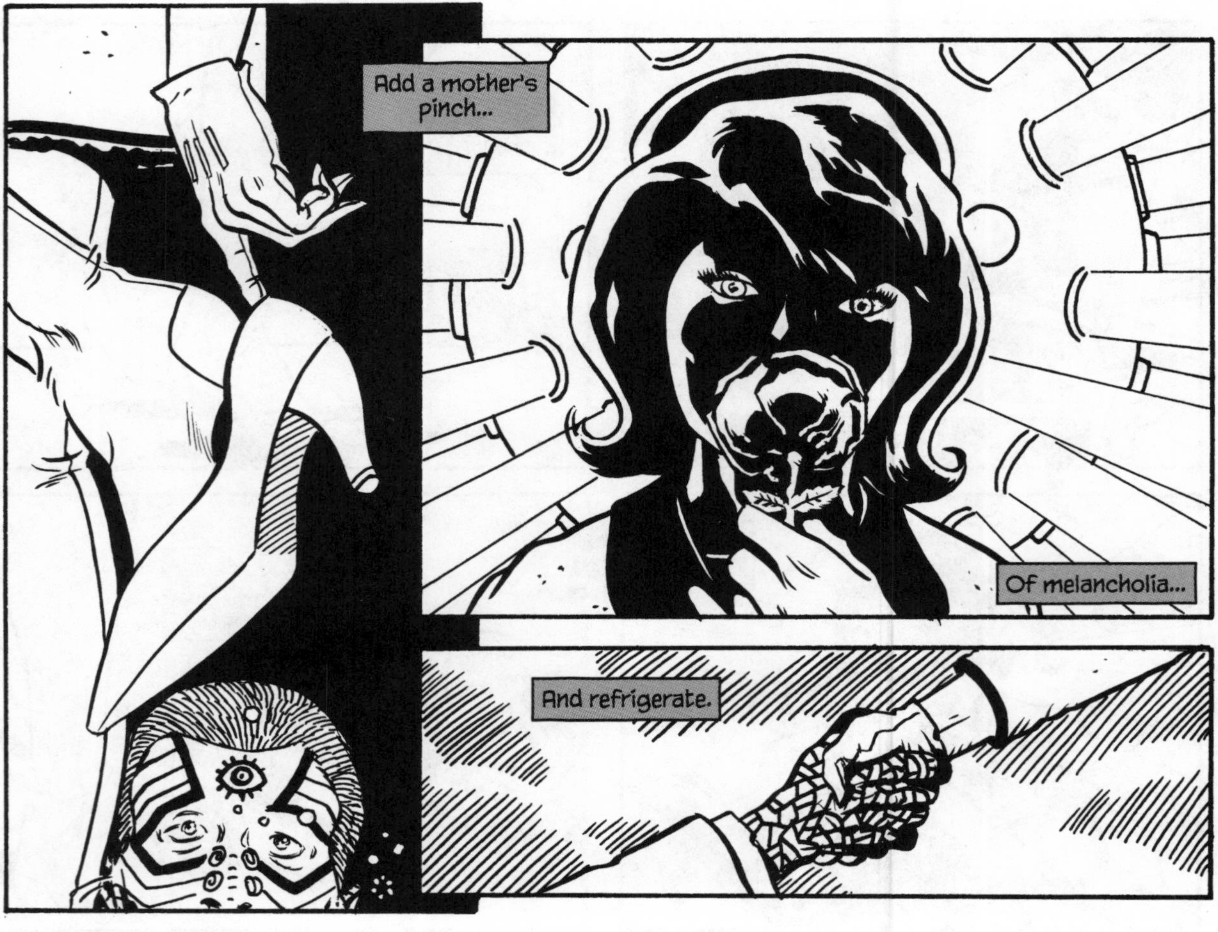
Add a mother's pinch...
Of melancholia...
And refrigerate.

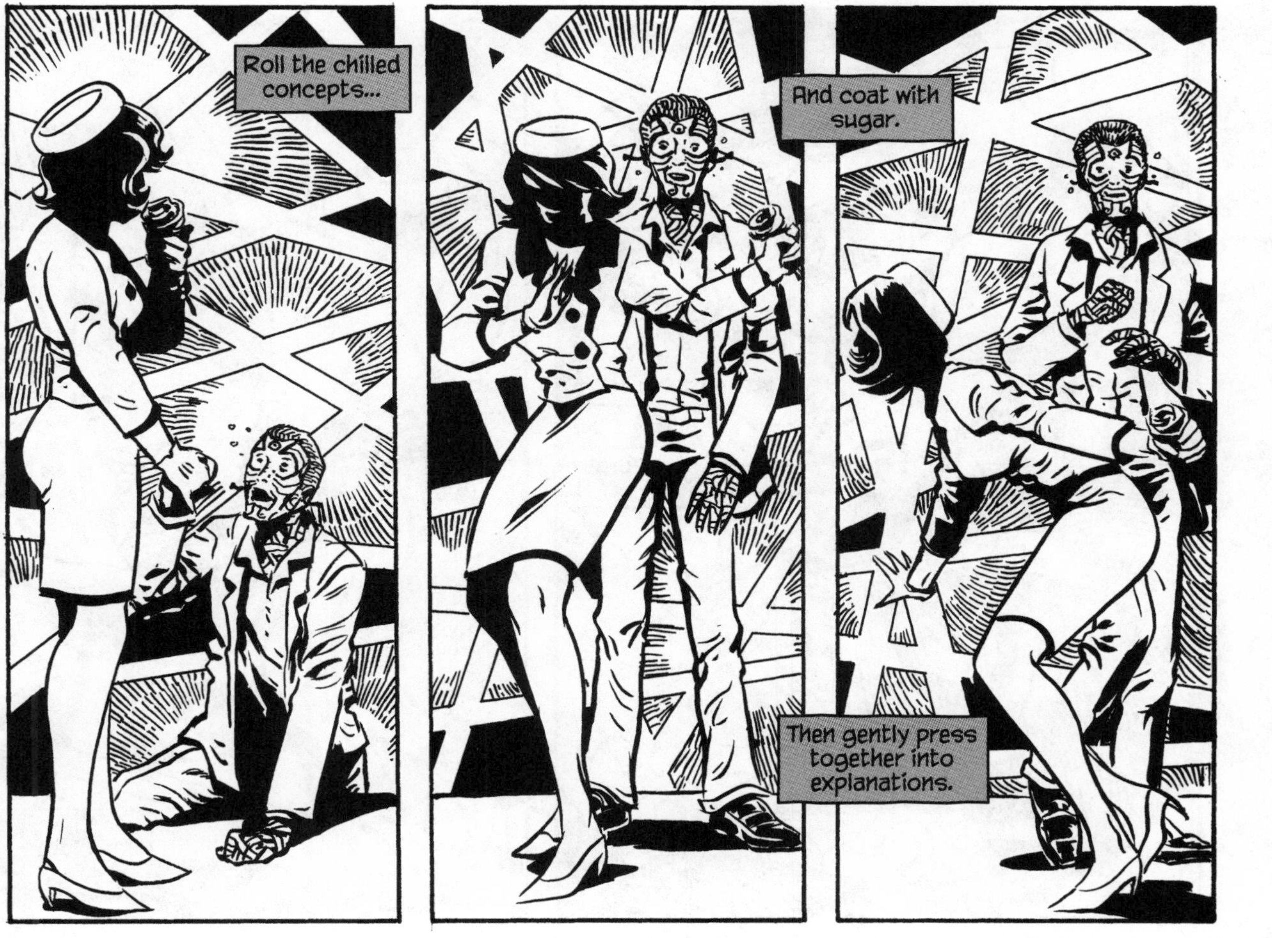
Roll the chilled concepts...
And coat with sugar.
Then gently press together into explanations.

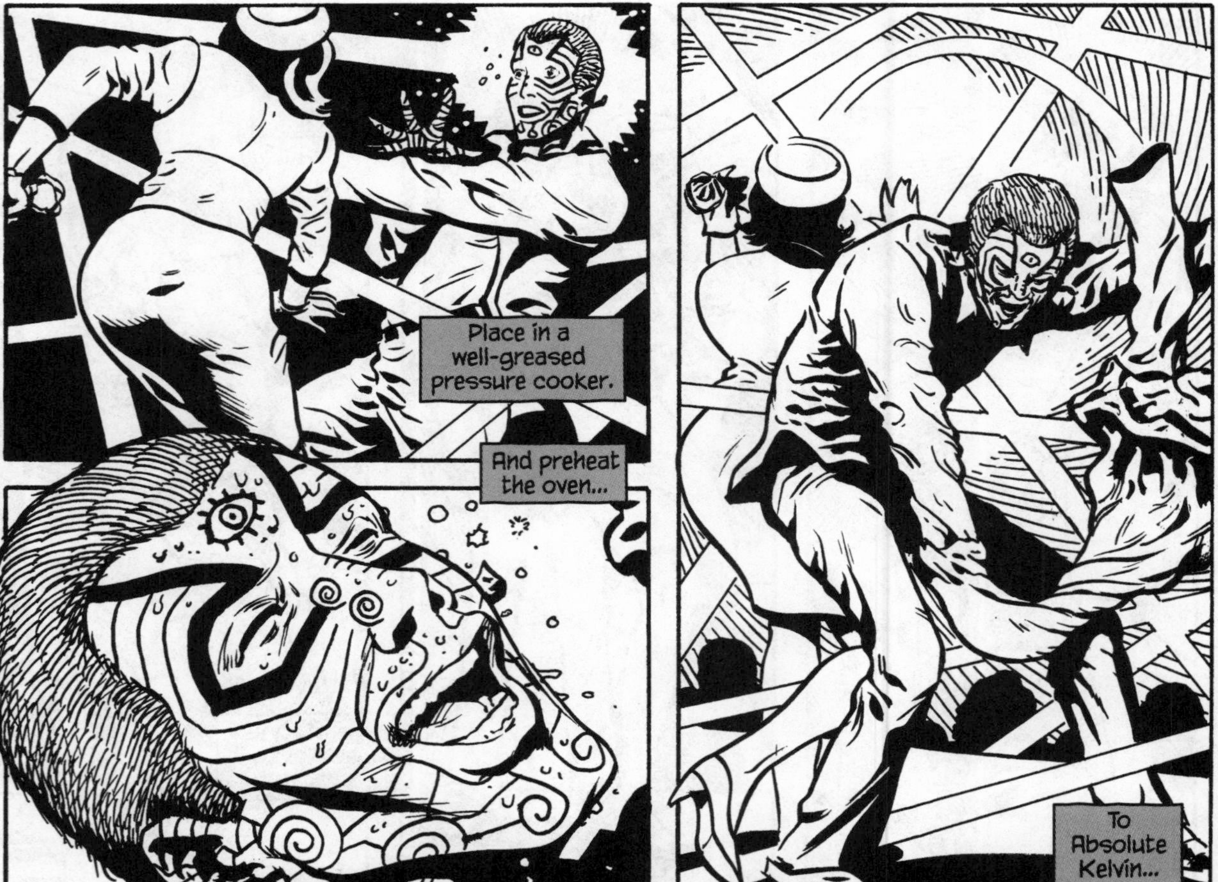
Place in a well-greased pressure cooker.
And preheat the oven...
To Absolute Kelvin...

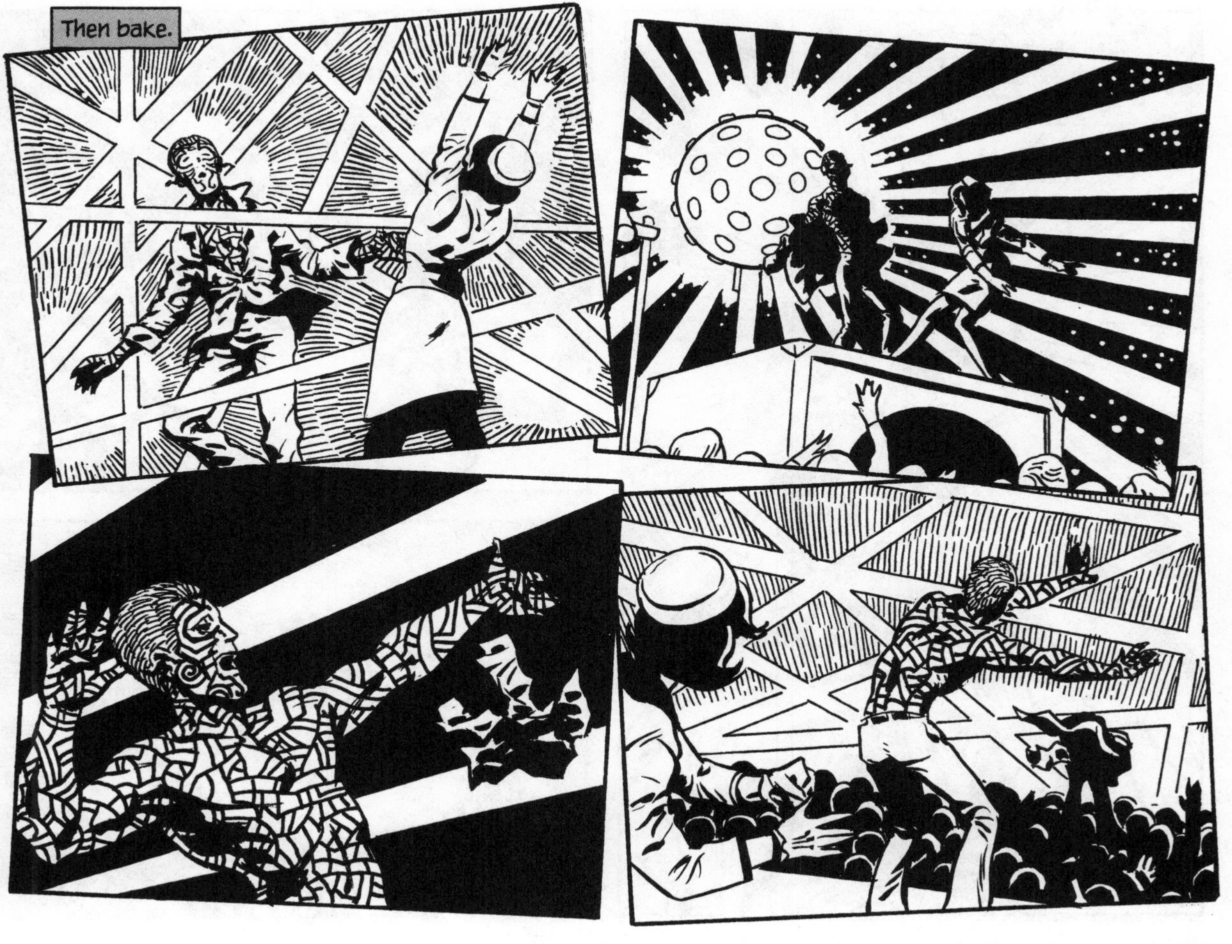
Then bake.

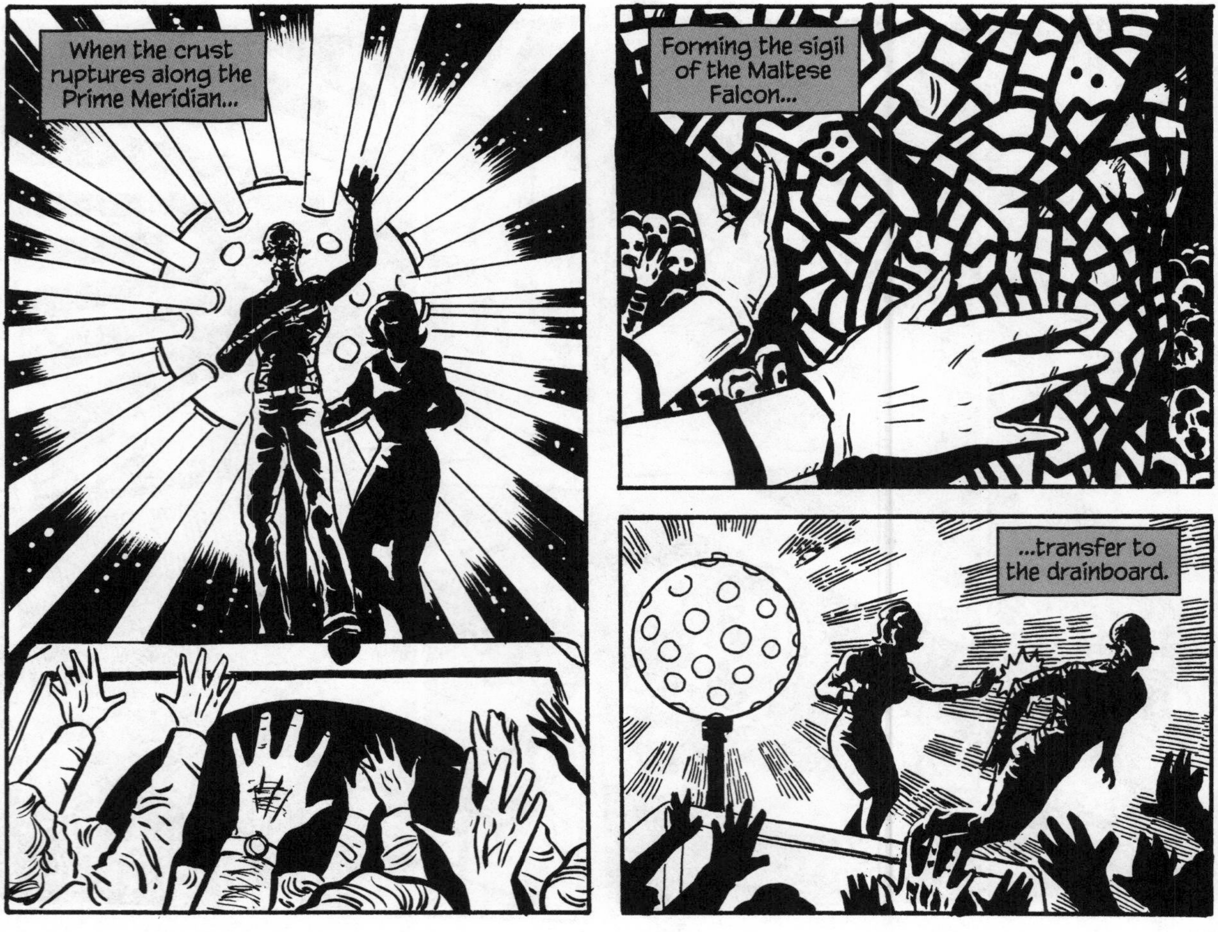
When the crust ruptures along the Prime Meridian...
Forming the sigil of the Maltese Falcon...
...transfer to the drainboard.

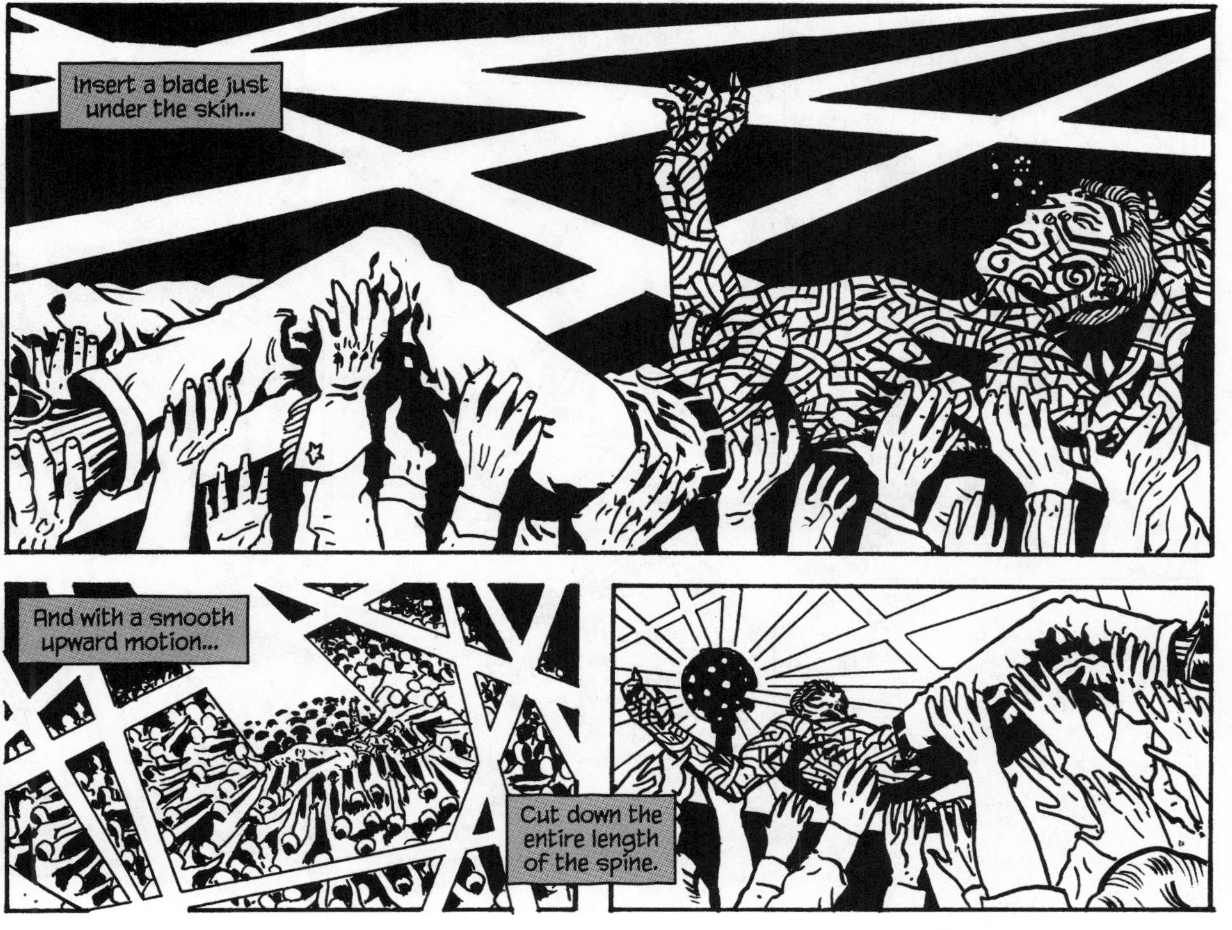

Insert a blade just under the skin...
And with a smooth upward motion...
Cut down the entire length of the spine.

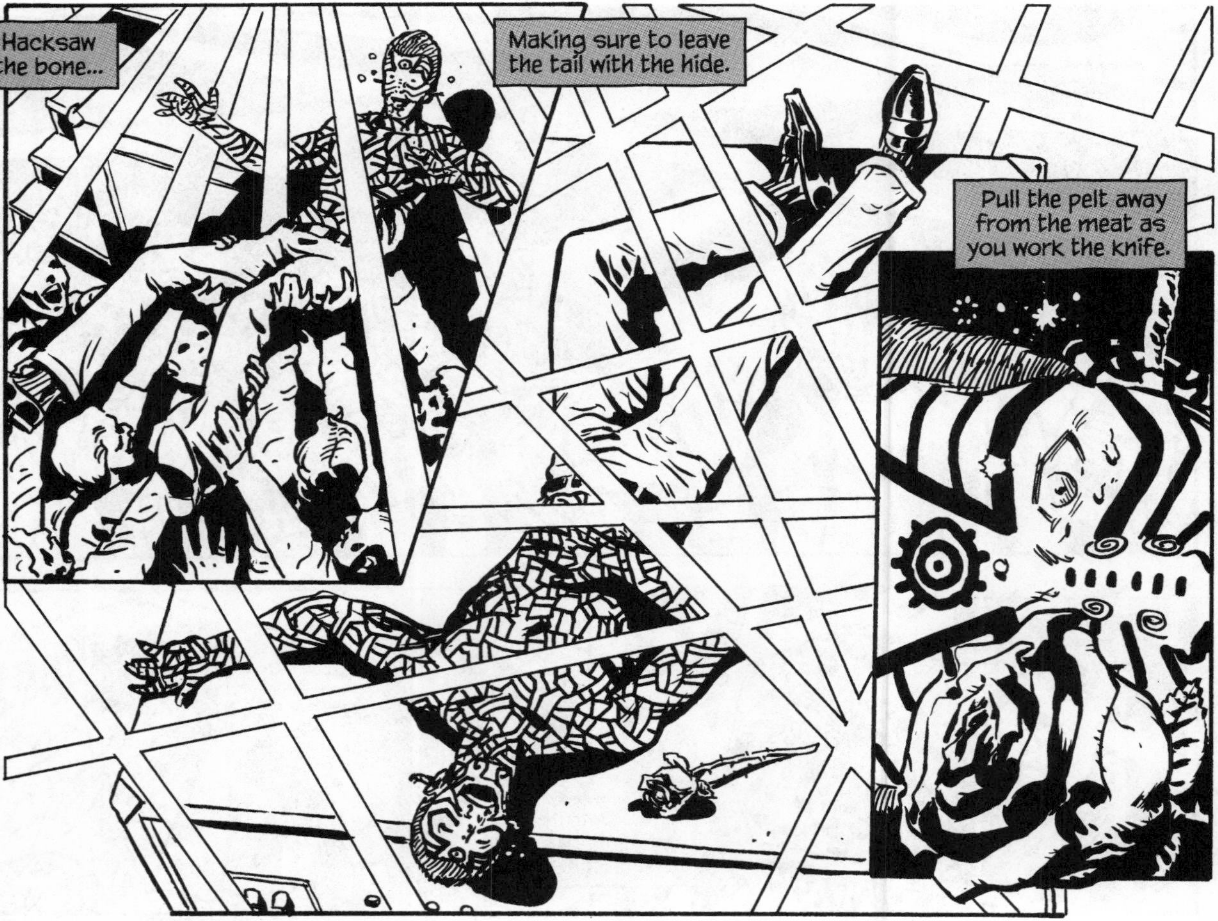
Hacksaw the bone...
Making sure to leave the tail with the hide.
Pull the pelt away from the meat as you work the knife.

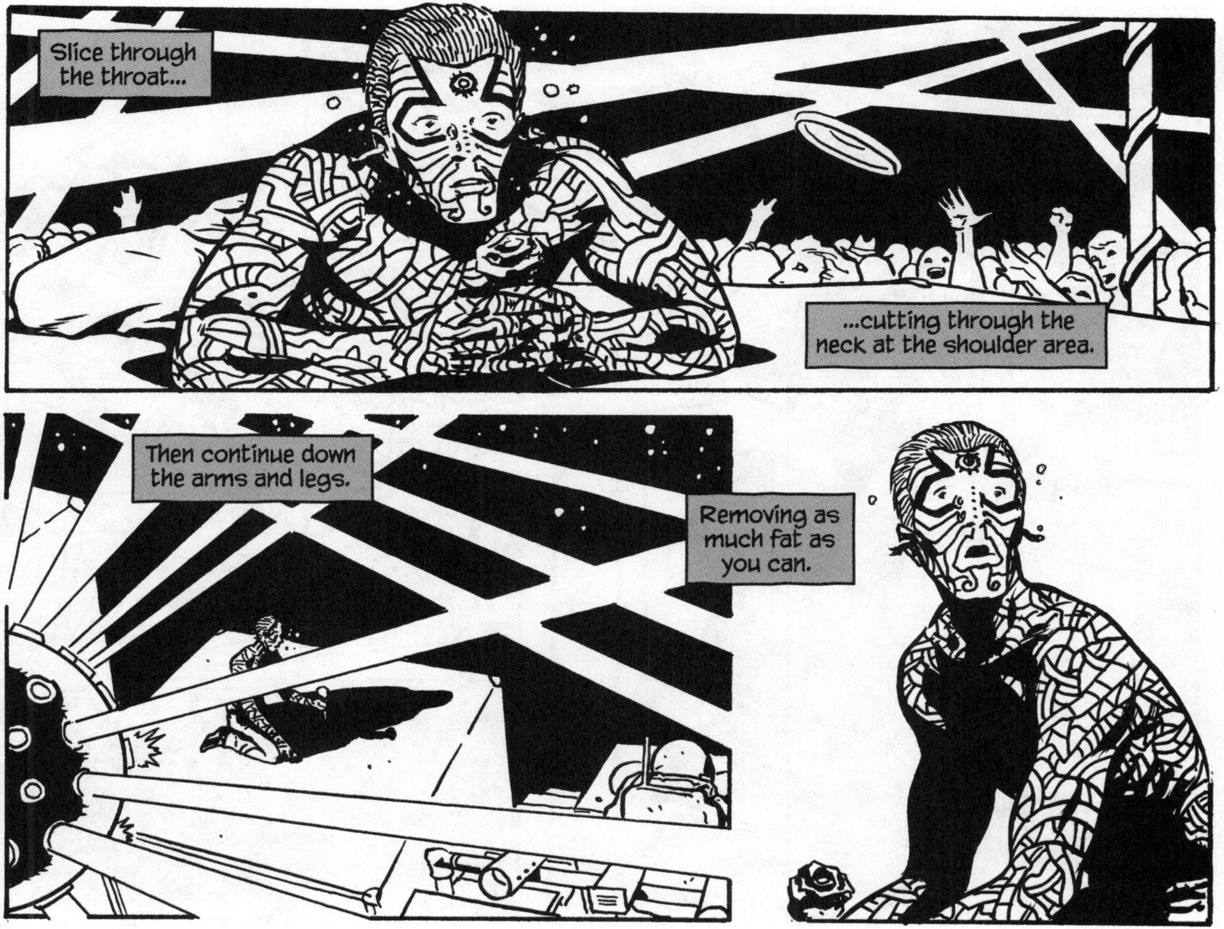

Slice through the throat...
...cutting through the neck at the shoulder area.
Then continue down the arms and legs.
Removing as much fat as you can.

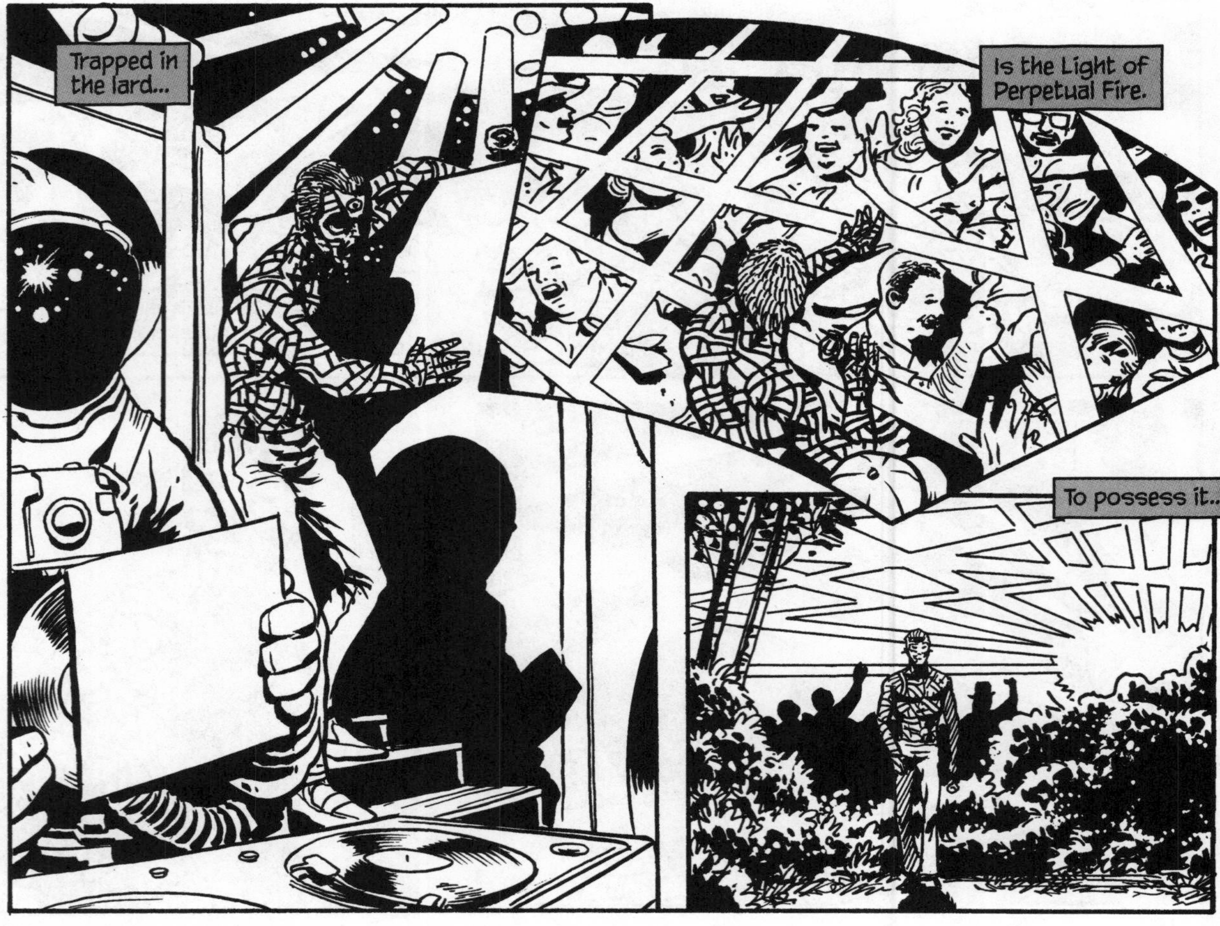
Trapped in the lard...
Is the Light of Perpetual Fire.
To possess it...

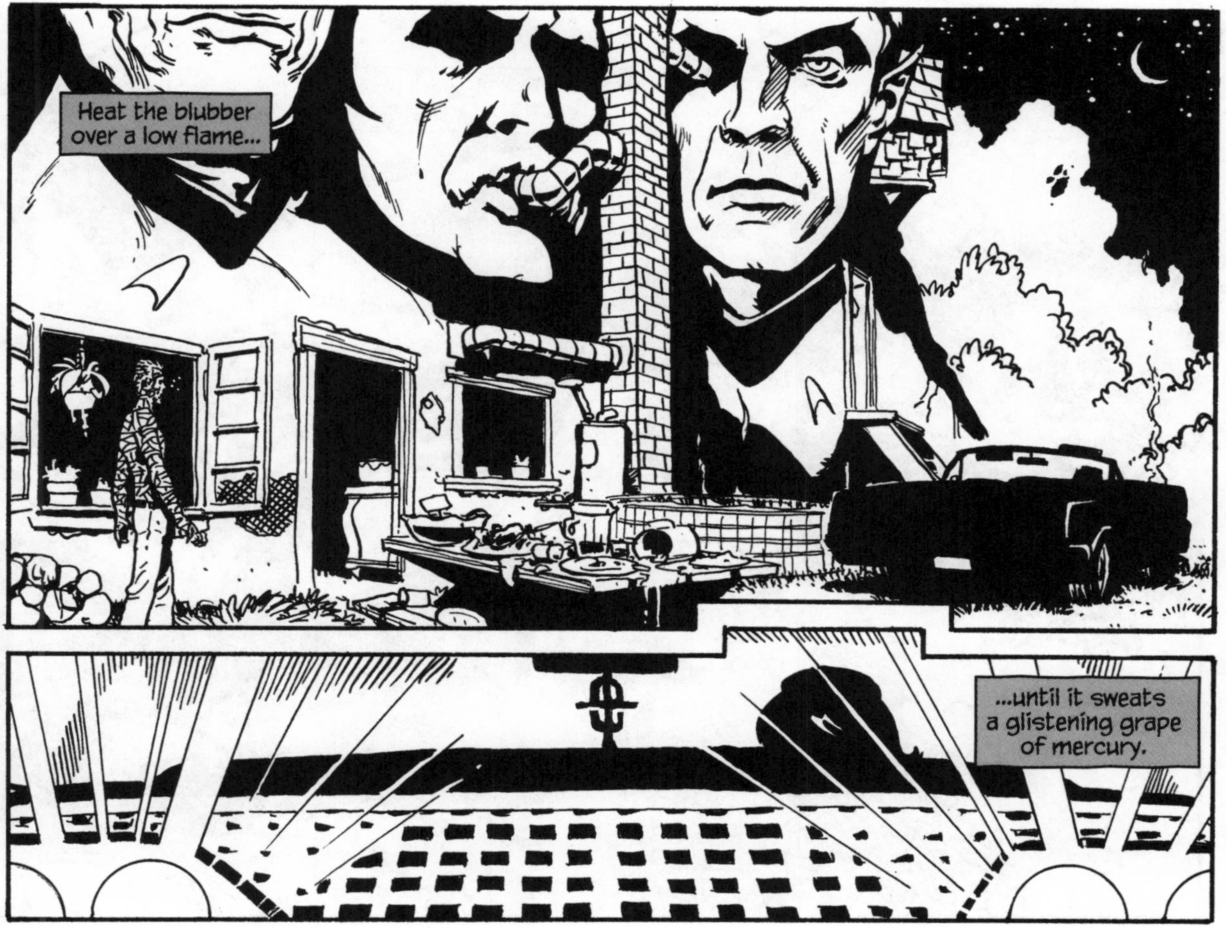
Heat the blubber over a low flame...
...until it sweats a glistening grape of mercury.

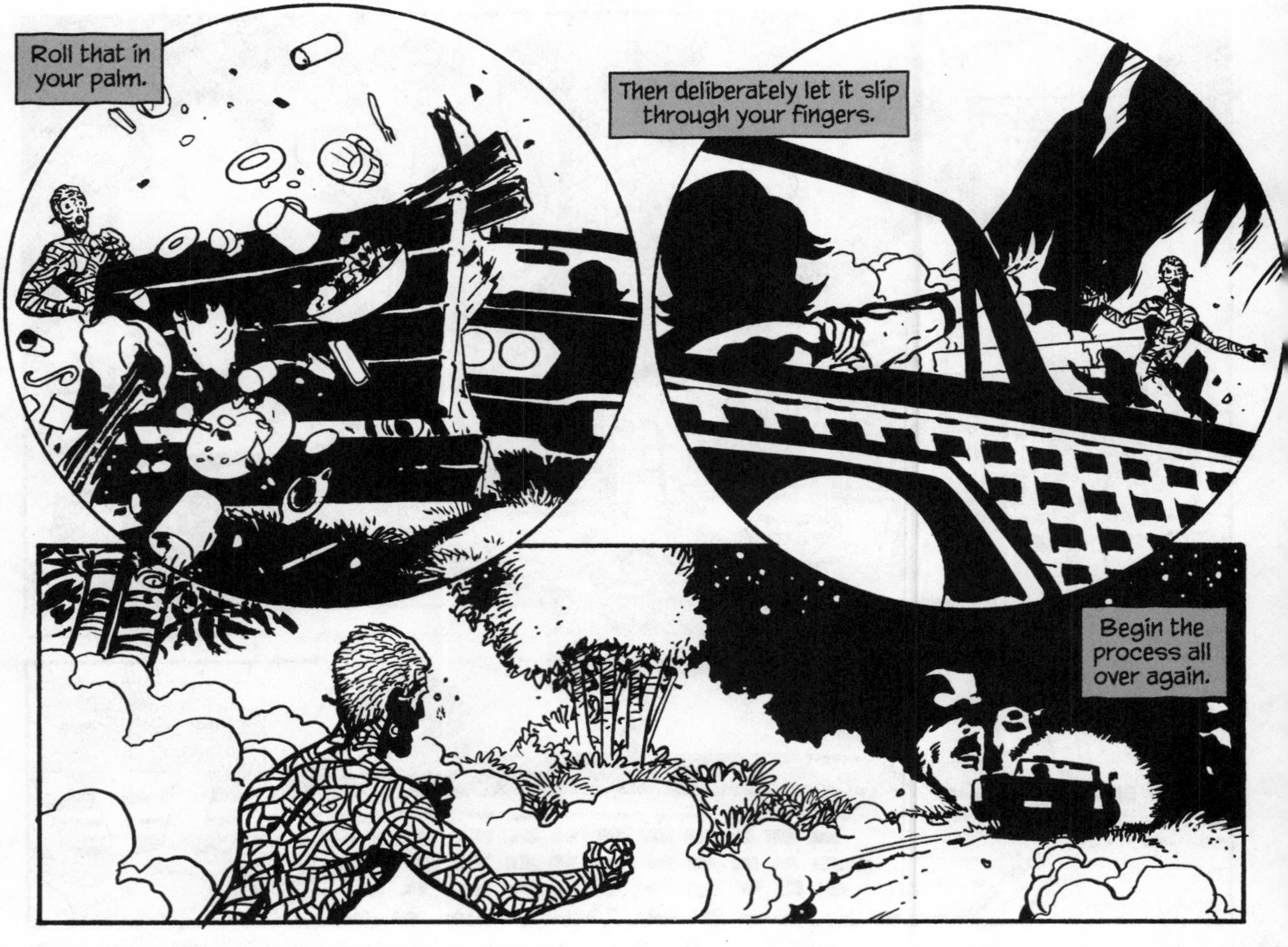
Roll that in your palm.
Then deliberately let it slip through your fingers.
Begin the process all over again.

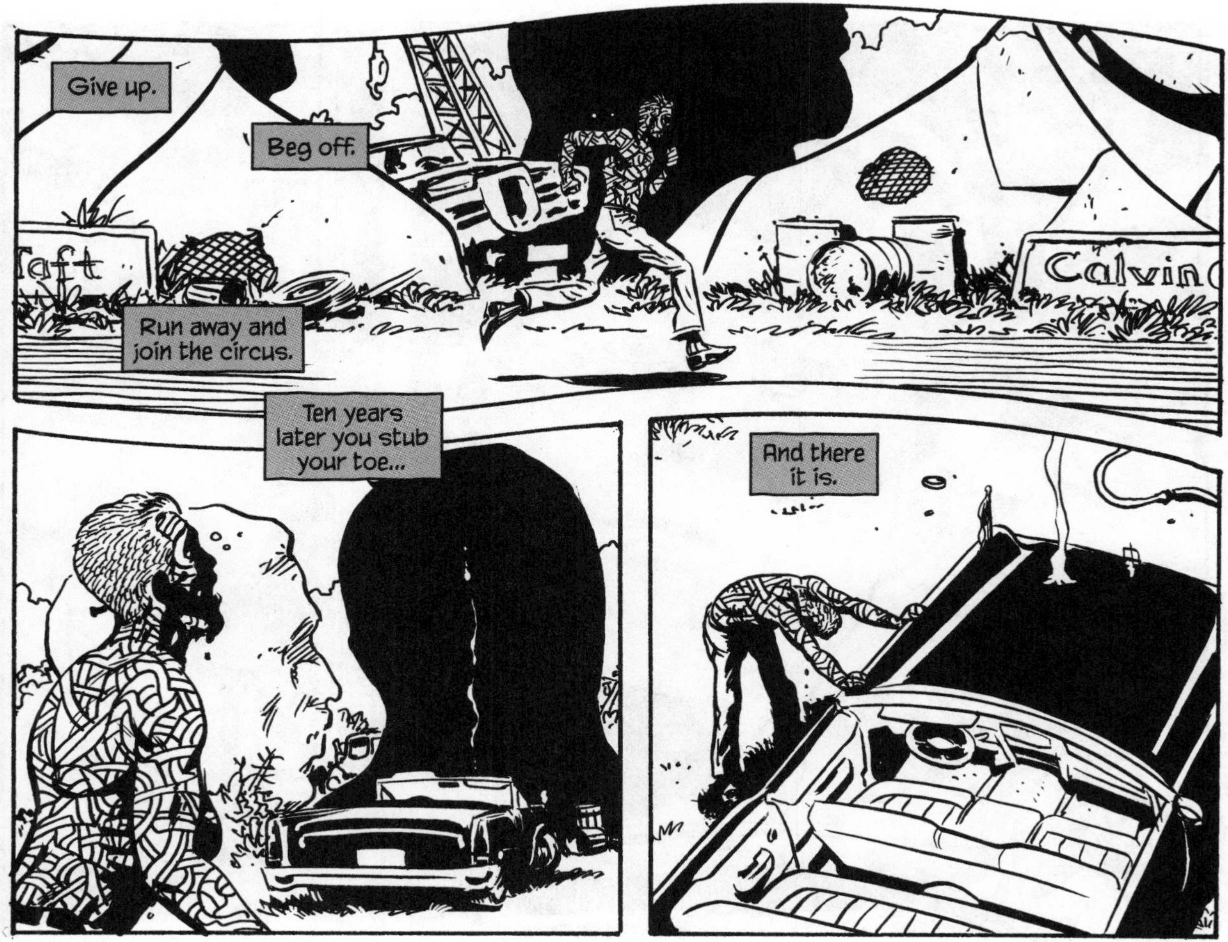
Give up.
Beg off.
Taft
Calvin
Run away and join the circus.
Ten years later you stub your toe...
And there it is.

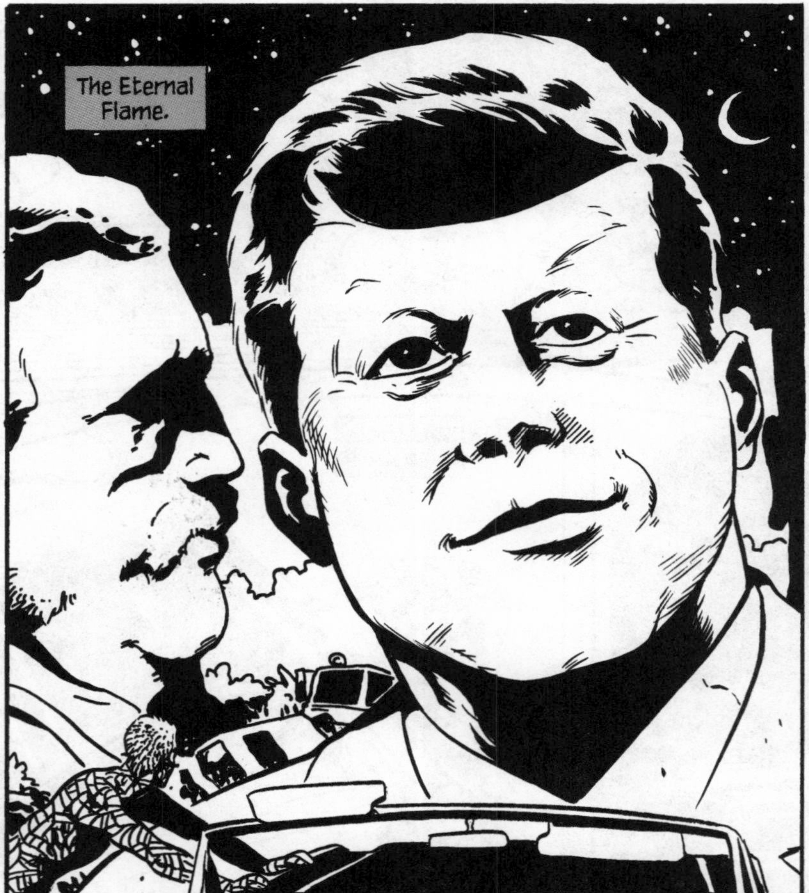
The Eternal Flame.

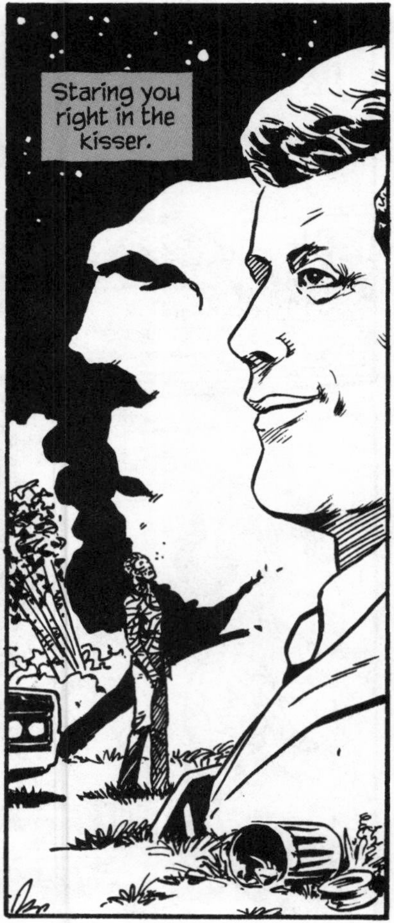
Staring you right in the kisser.

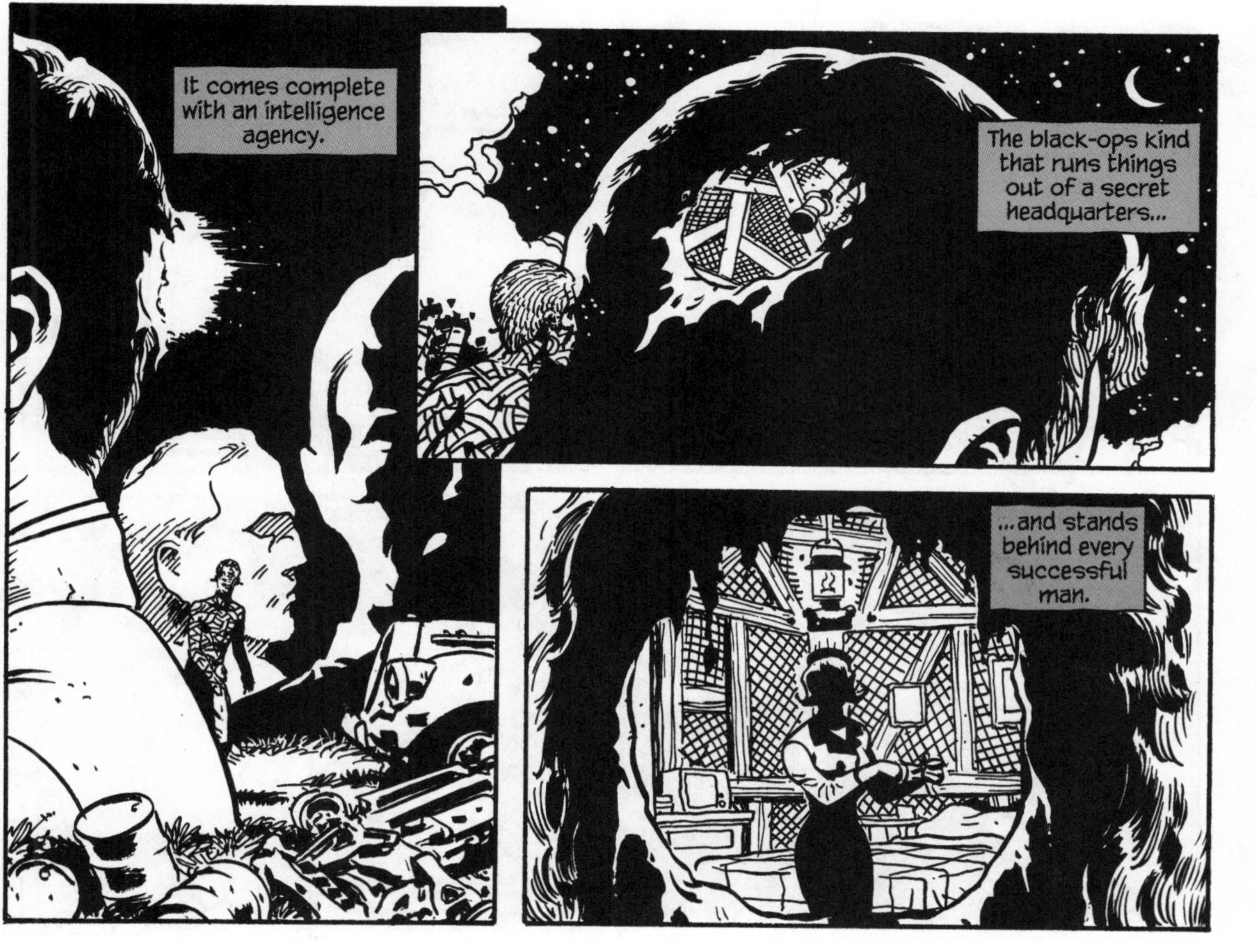
It comes complete with an intelligence agency.
The black-ops kind that runs things out of a secret headquarters...
...and stands behind every successful man.

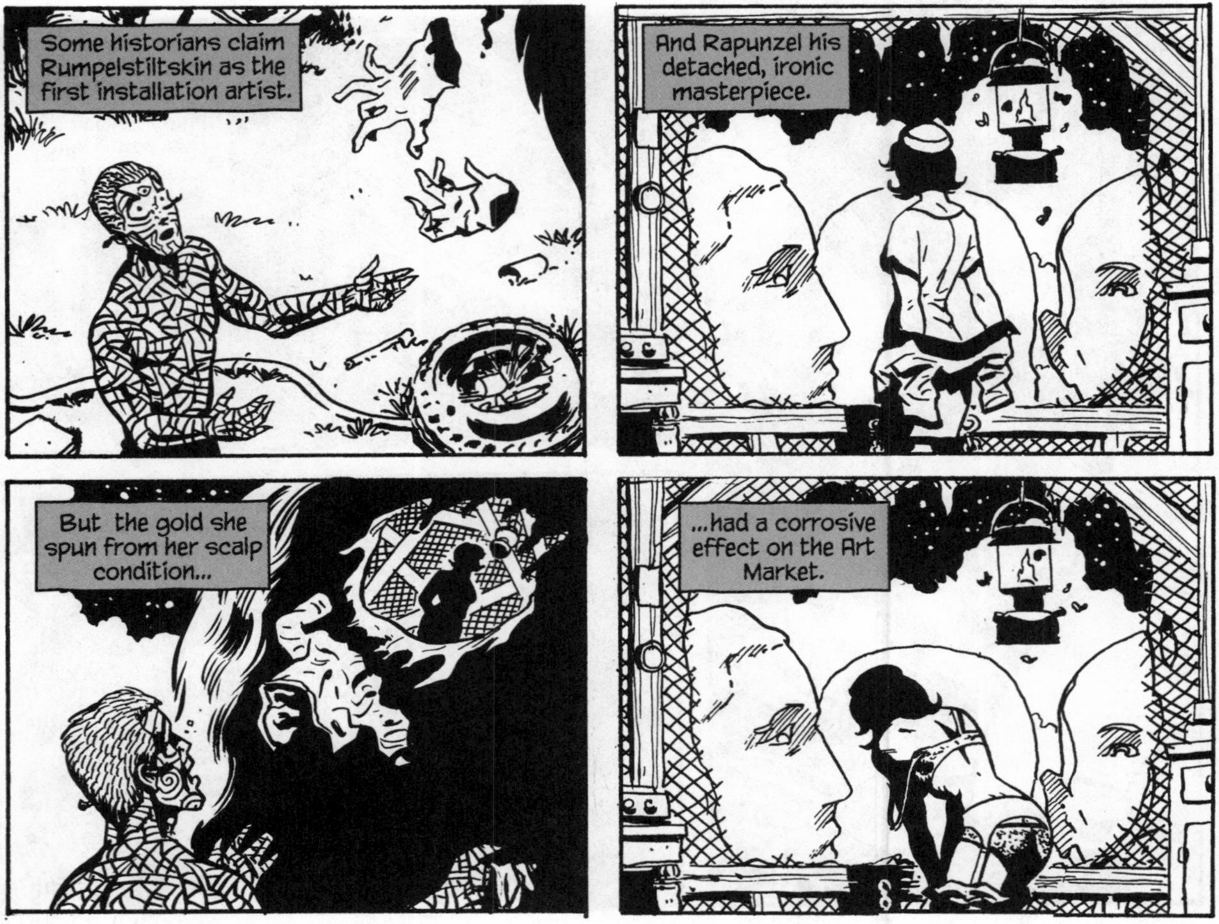
Some historians claim Rumpelstiltskin as the first installation artist.
And Rapunzel his detached, ironic masterpiece.
But the gold she spun from her scalp condition...
...had a corrosive effect on the Art Market.

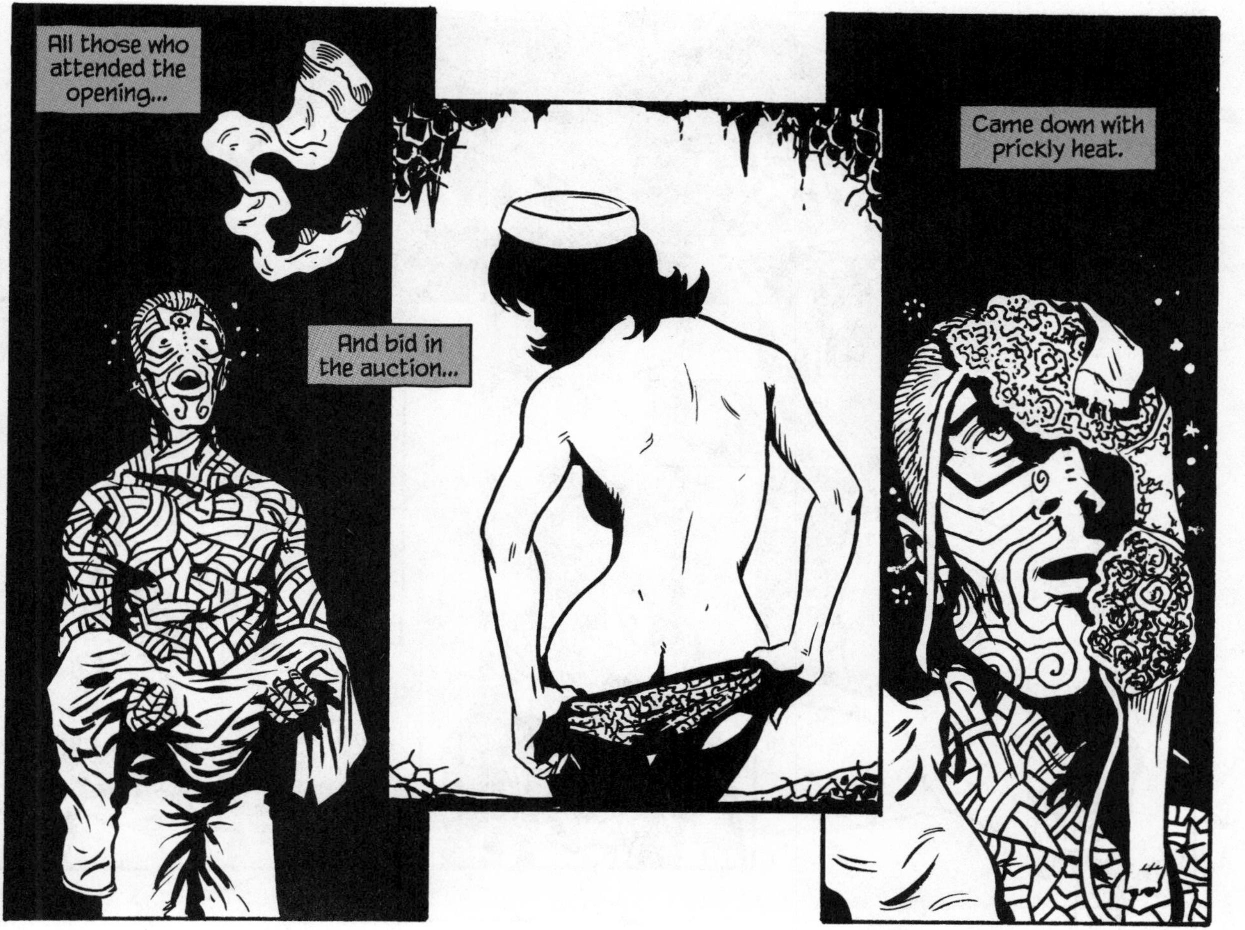
All those who attended the opening...
And bid in the auction...
Came down with prickly heat.

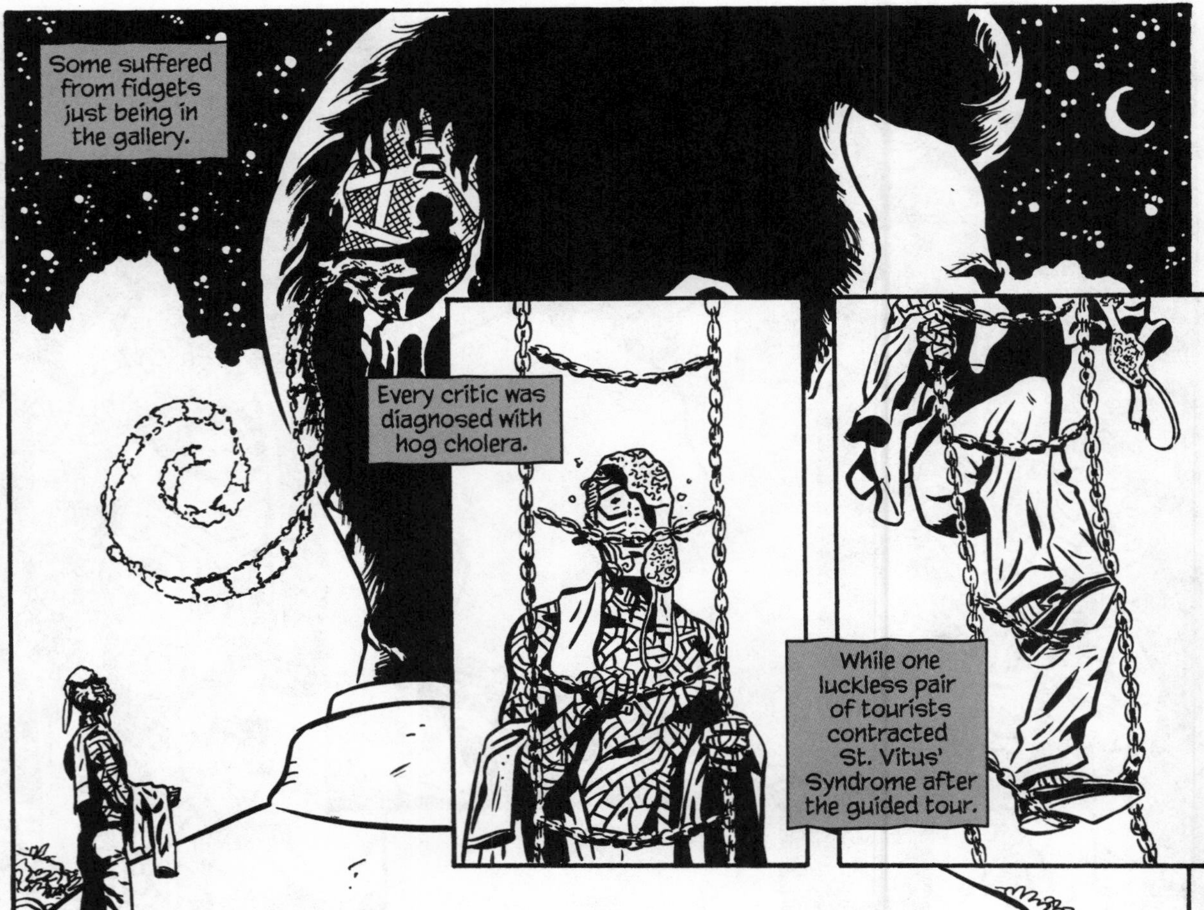
Some suffered from fidgets just being in the gallery.
Every critic was diagnosed with hog cholera.
While one luckless pair of tourists contracted St. Vitus' Syndrome after the guided tour.

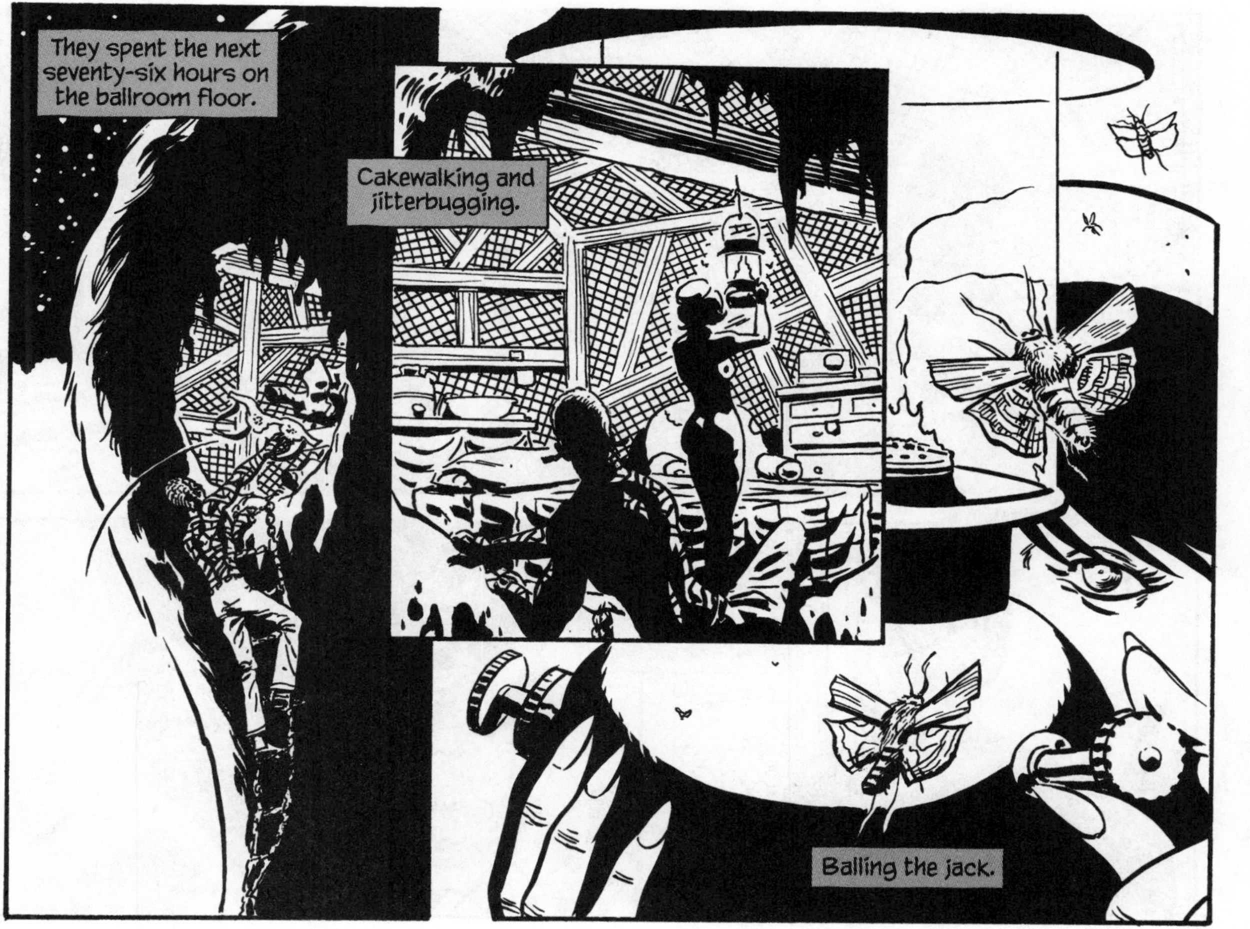
They spent the next seventy-six hours on the ballroom floor.
Cakewalking and jitterbugging.
Balling the jack.

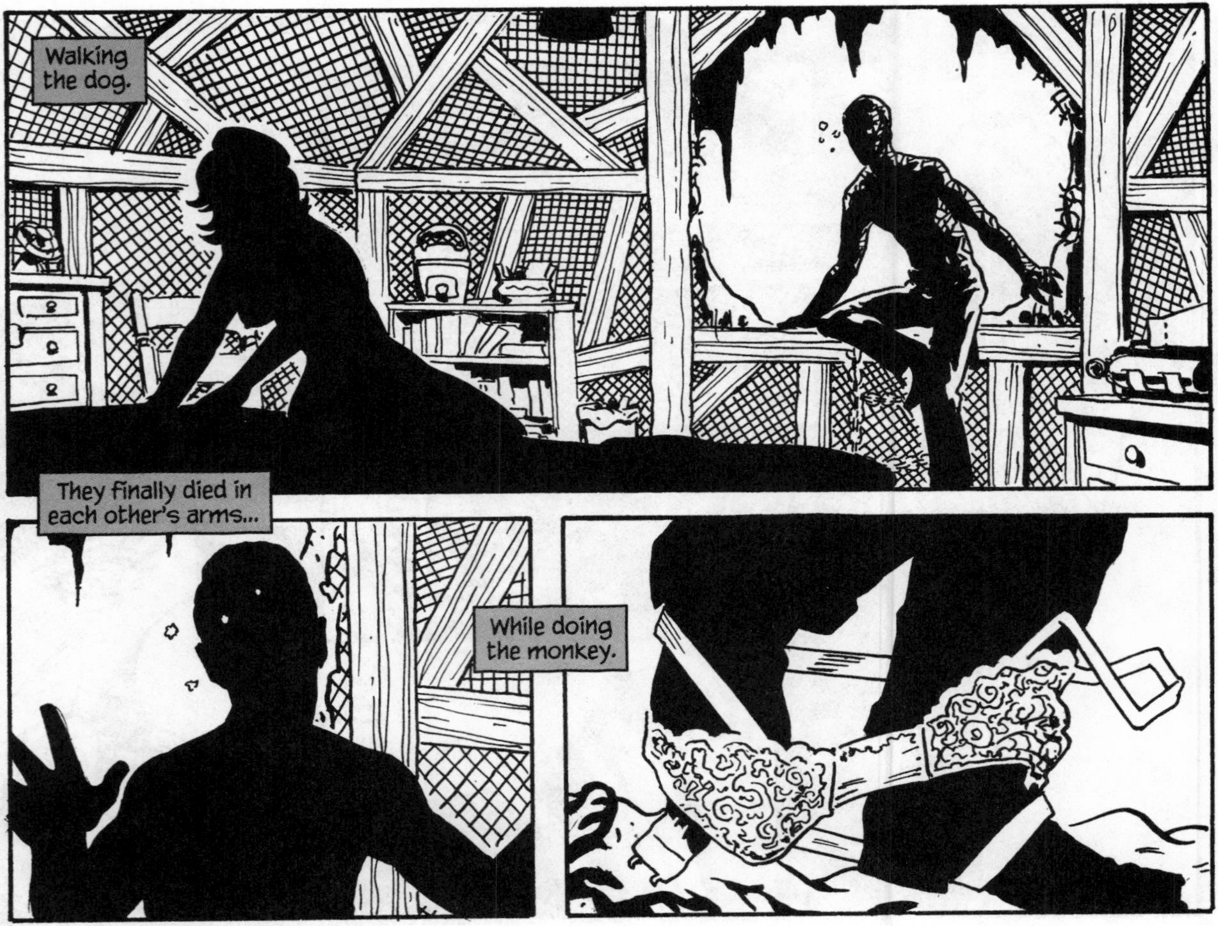
Walking the dog.
They finally died in each other's arms...
While doing the monkey.

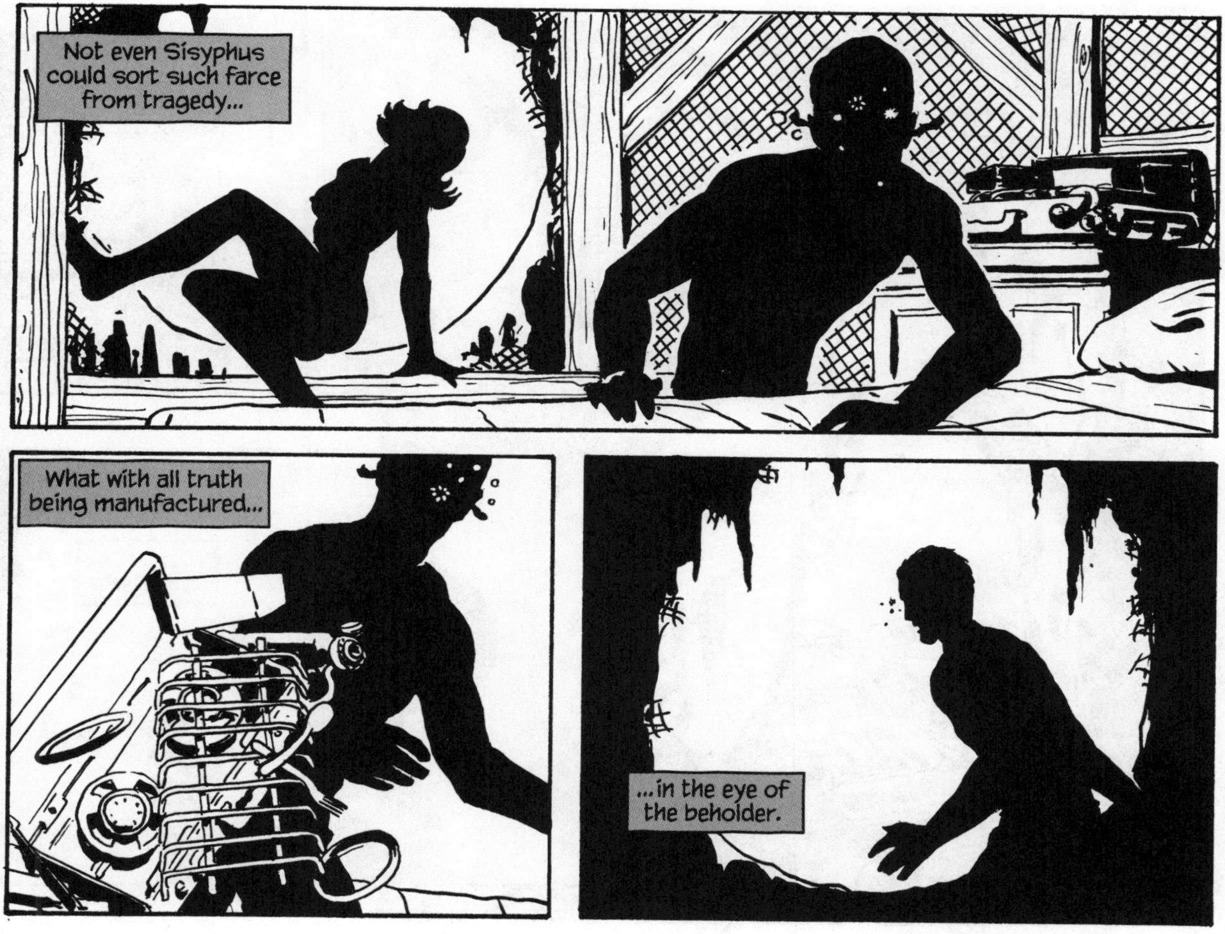
Not even Sisyphus could sort such farce from tragedy...
What with all truth being manufactured...
...in the eye of the beholder.

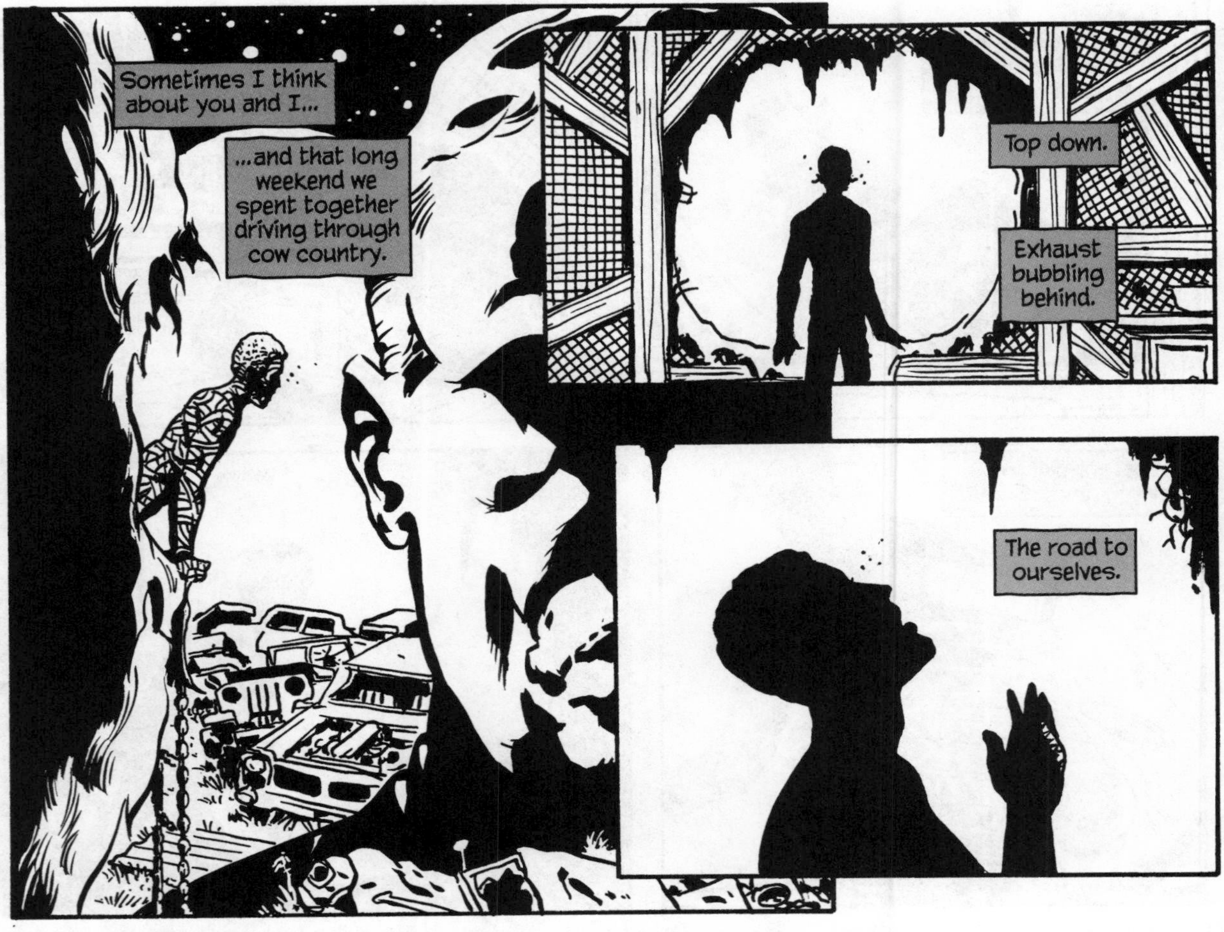
Sometimes I think about you and I...
...and that long weekend we spent together driving through cow country.
Top down.
Exhaust bubbling behind.
The road to ourselves.

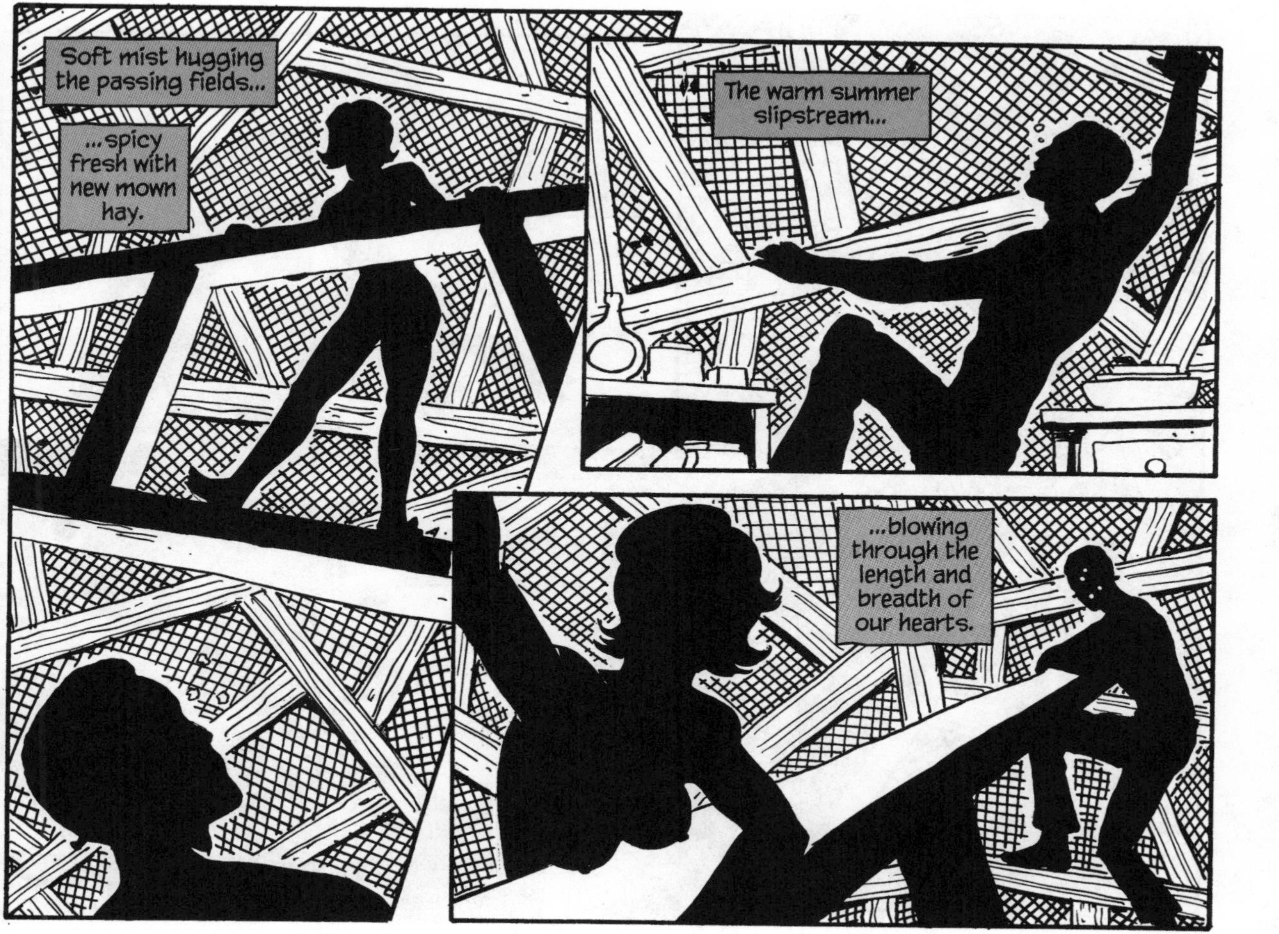
Soft mist hugging the passing fields...
...spicy fresh with new mown hay.
The warm summer slipstream...
...blowing through the length and breadth of our hearts.

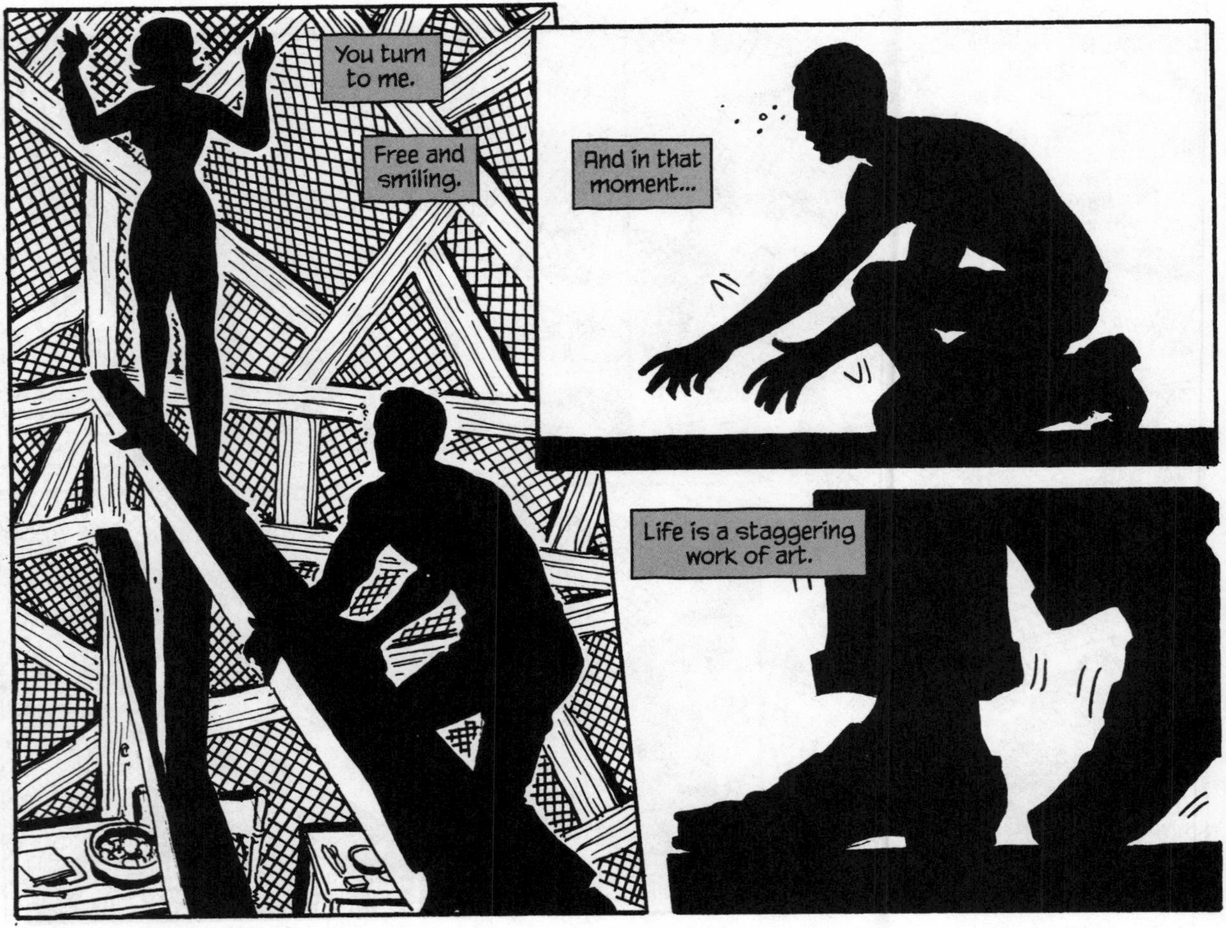
You turn to me.
Free and smiling.
And in that moment...
Life is a staggering work of art.

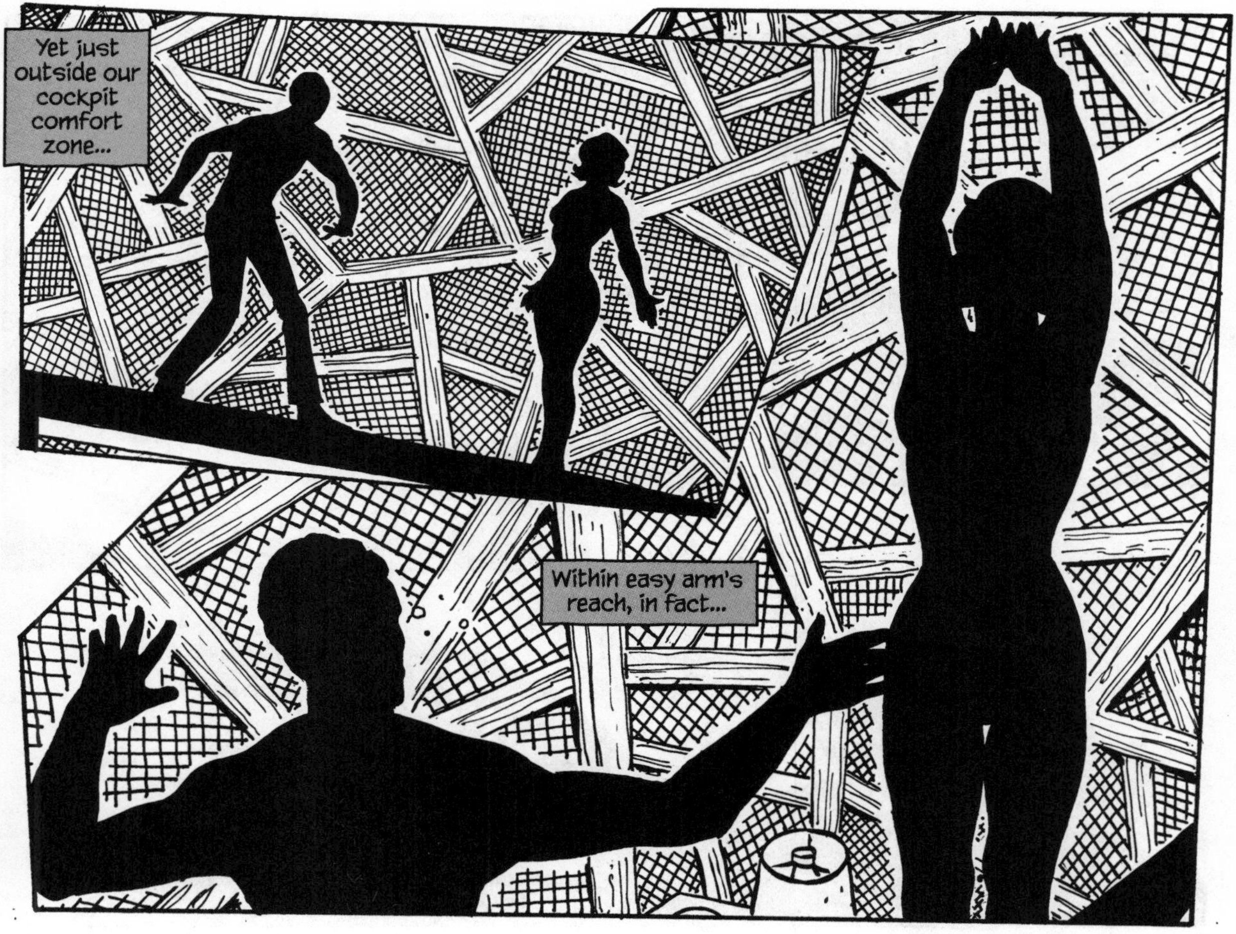
Yet just outside our cockpit comfort zone...
Within easy arm's reach, in fact...

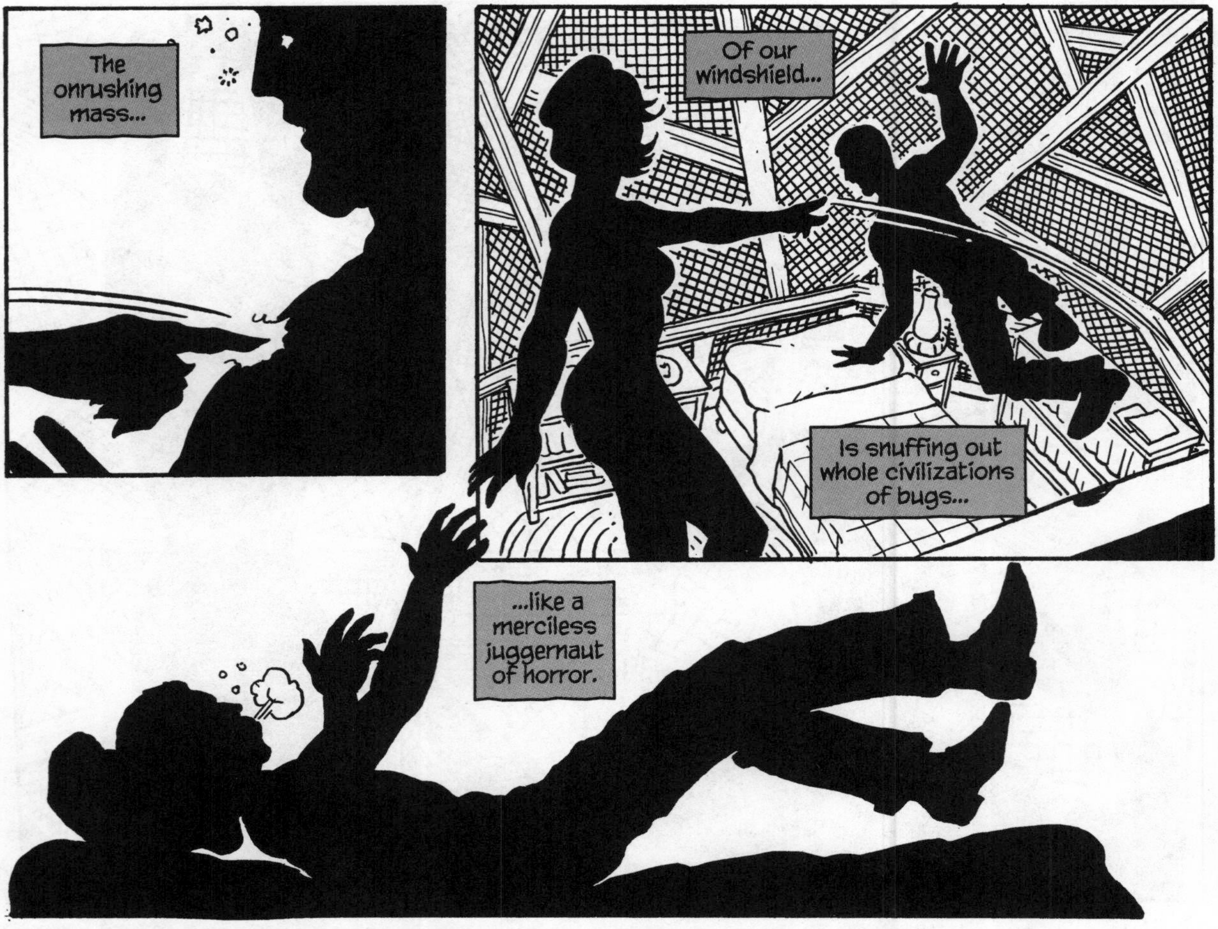
The onrushing mass...
Of our windshield...
Is snuffing out whole civilizations of bugs...
...like a merciless juggernaut of horror.

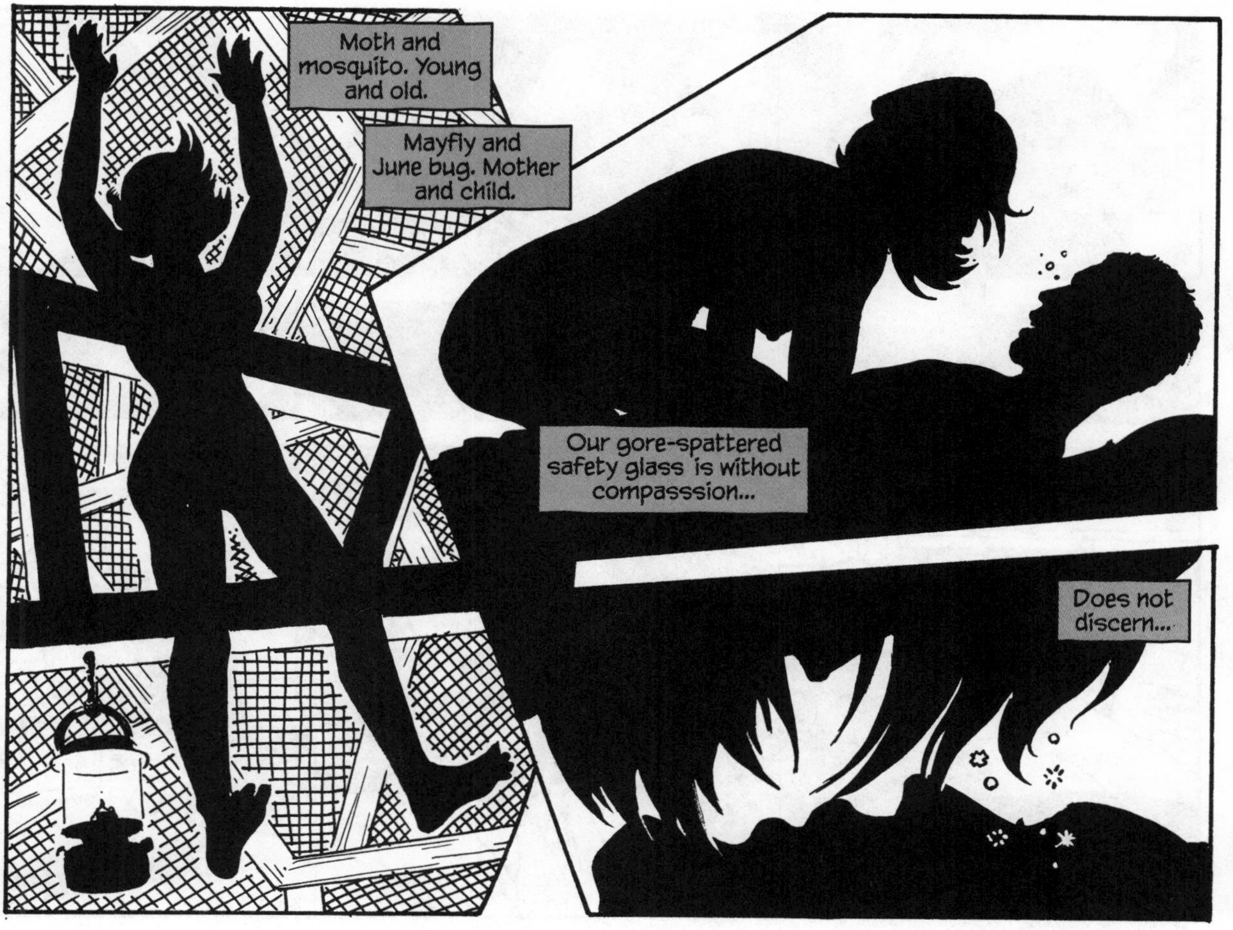
Moth and mosquito. Young and old.
Mayfly and June bug. Mother and child.
Our gore-spattered safety glass is without compasssion...
Does not discern...

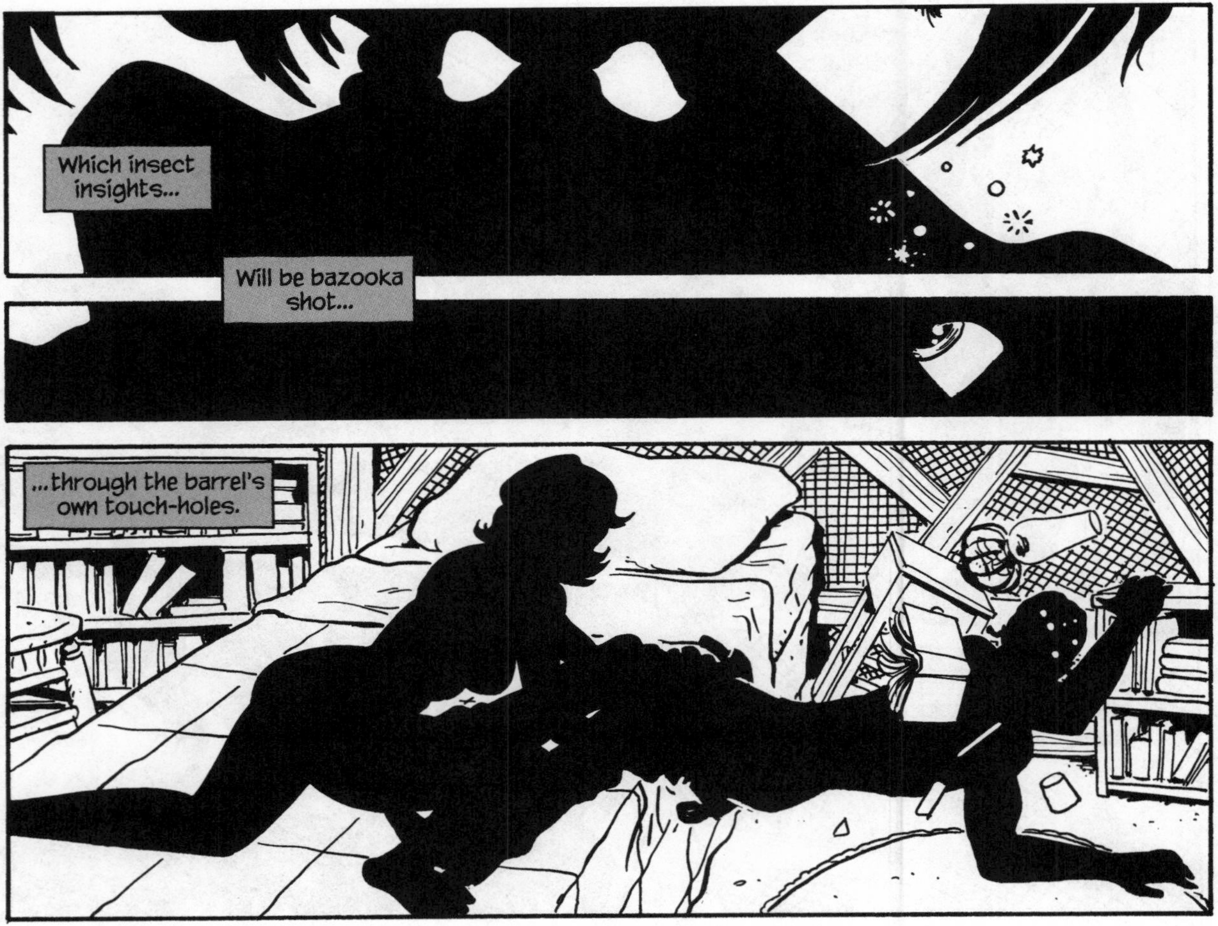
Which insect insights...
Will be bazooka shot...
...through the barrel's own touch-holes.

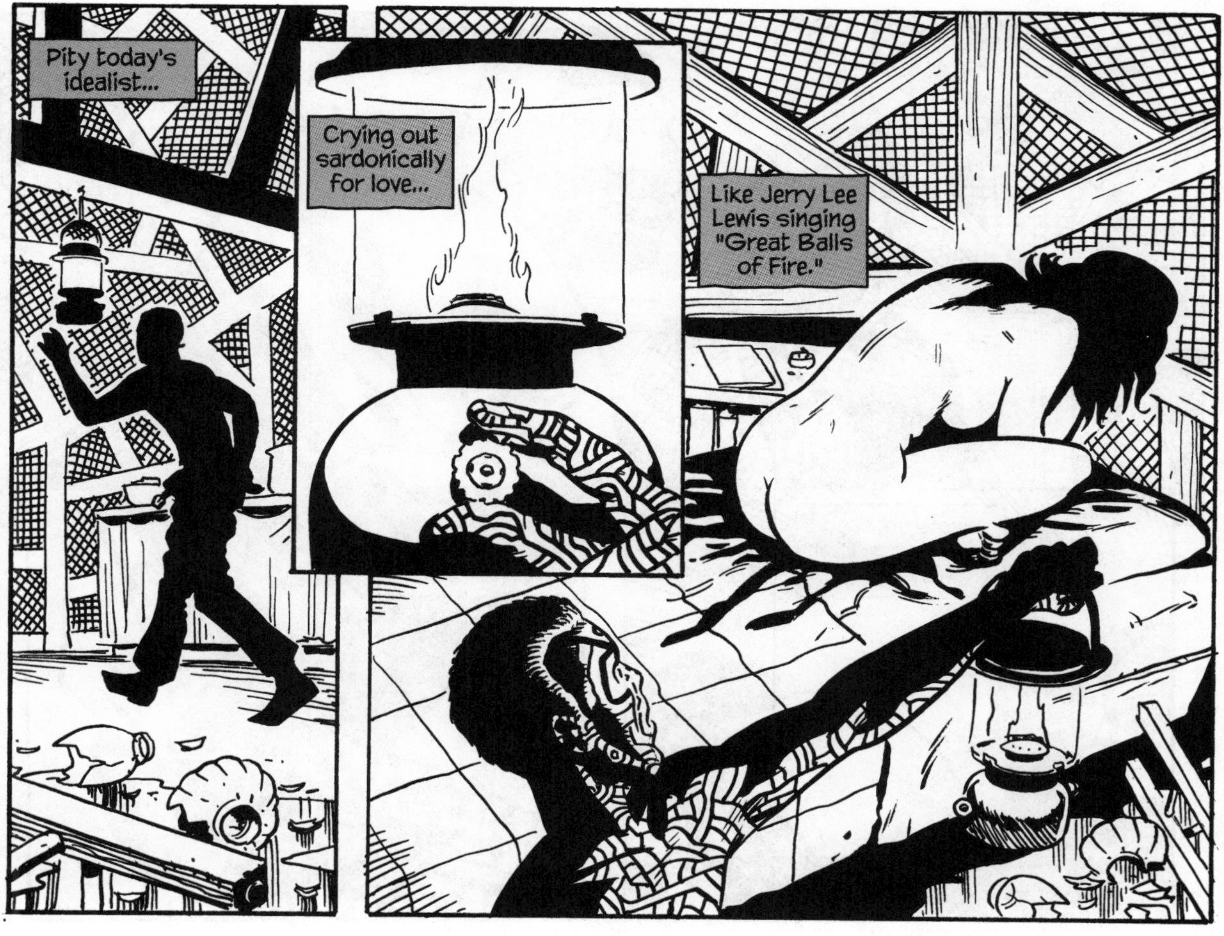
Pity today's idealist...
Crying out sardonically for love...
Like Jerry Lee Lewis singing "Great Balls of Fire."

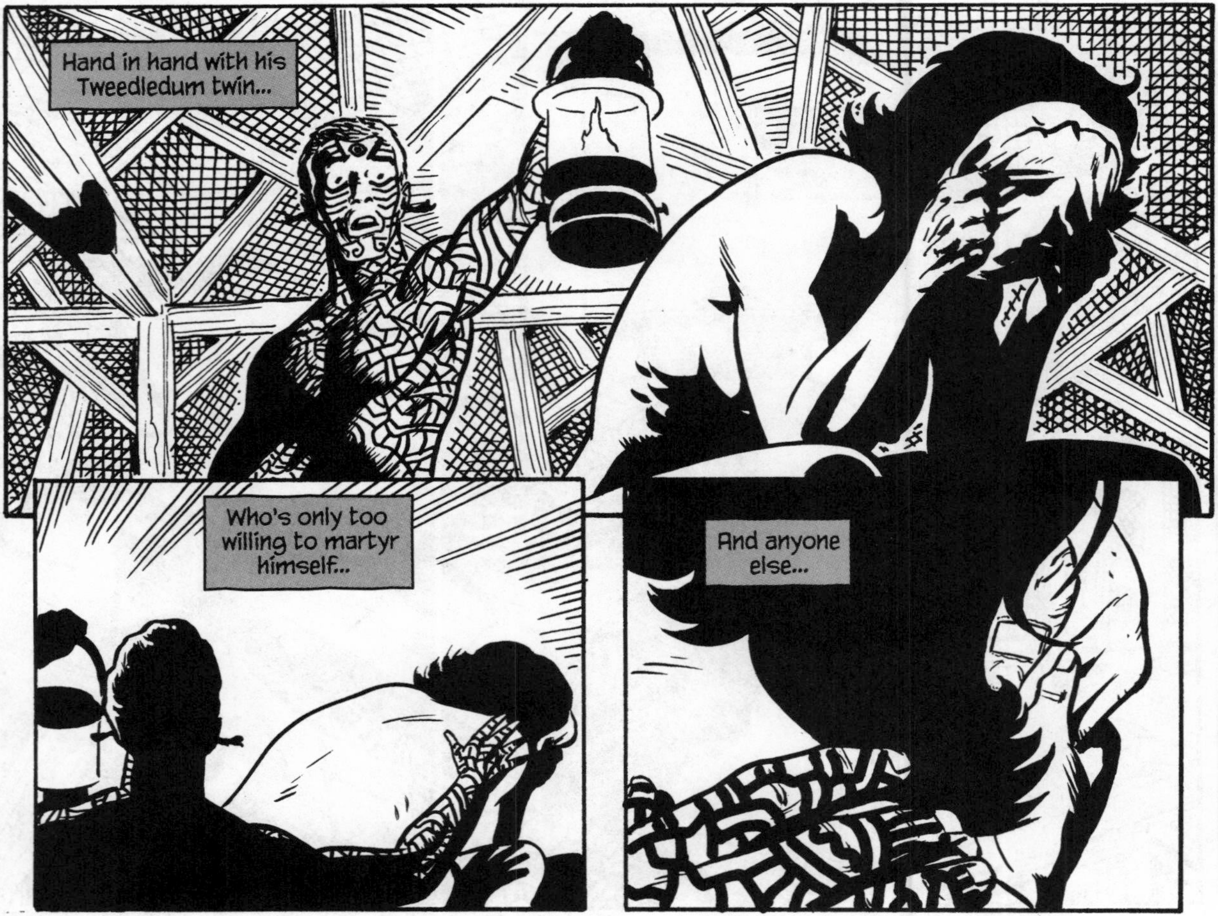
Hand in hand with his Tweedledum twin...
Who's only too willing to martyr himself...
And anyone else...

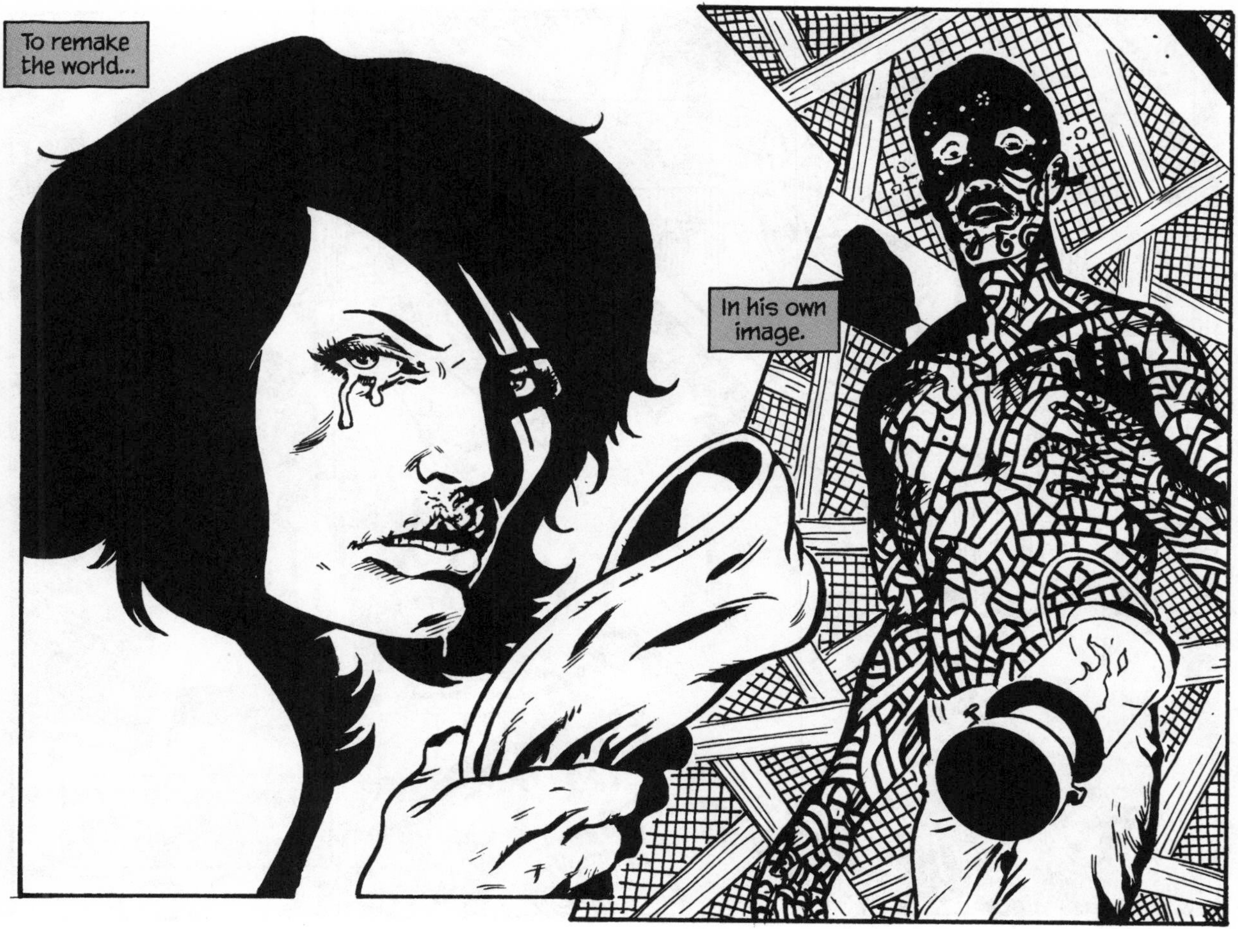
To remake the world...
In his own image.

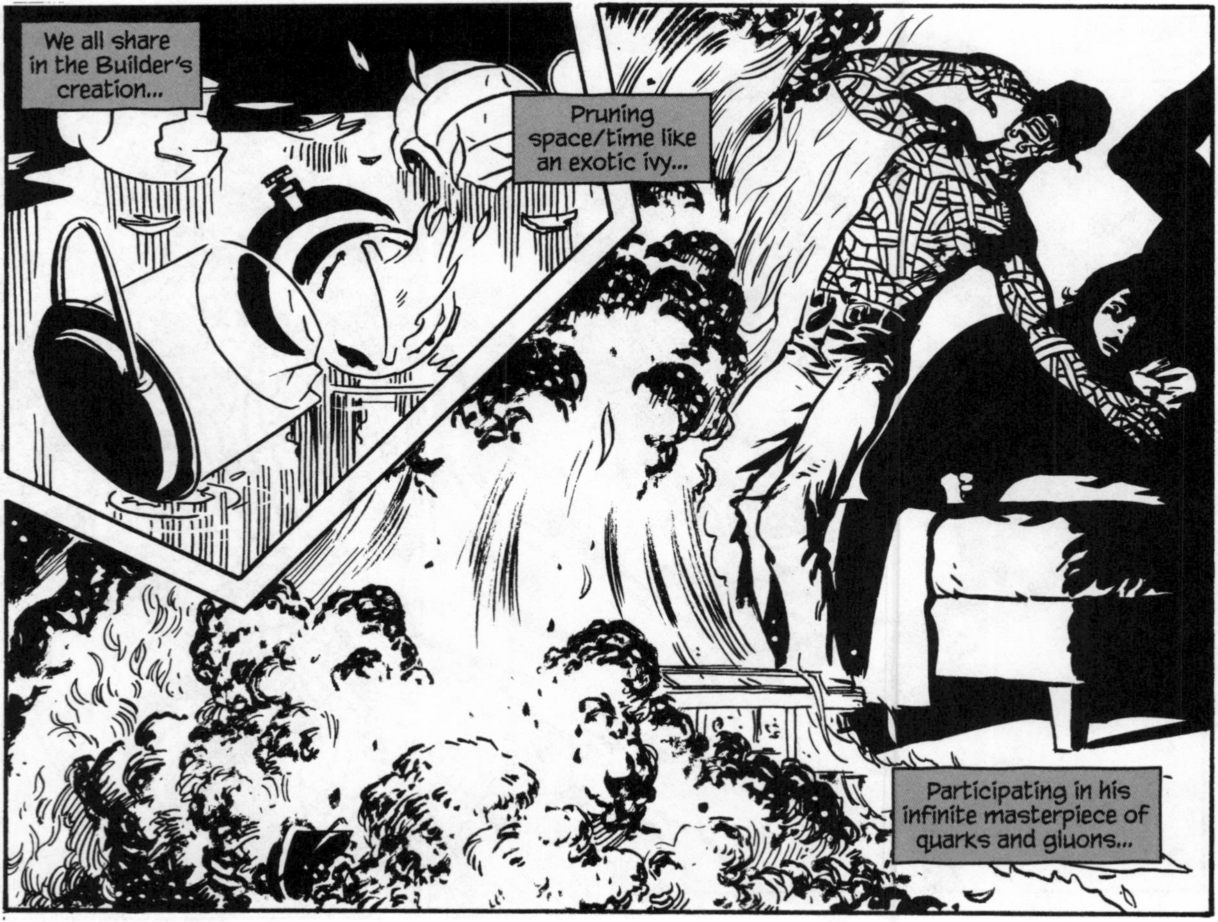

We all share in the Builder's creation...
Pruning space/time like an exotic ivy...
Participating in his infinite masterpiece of quarks and gluons...

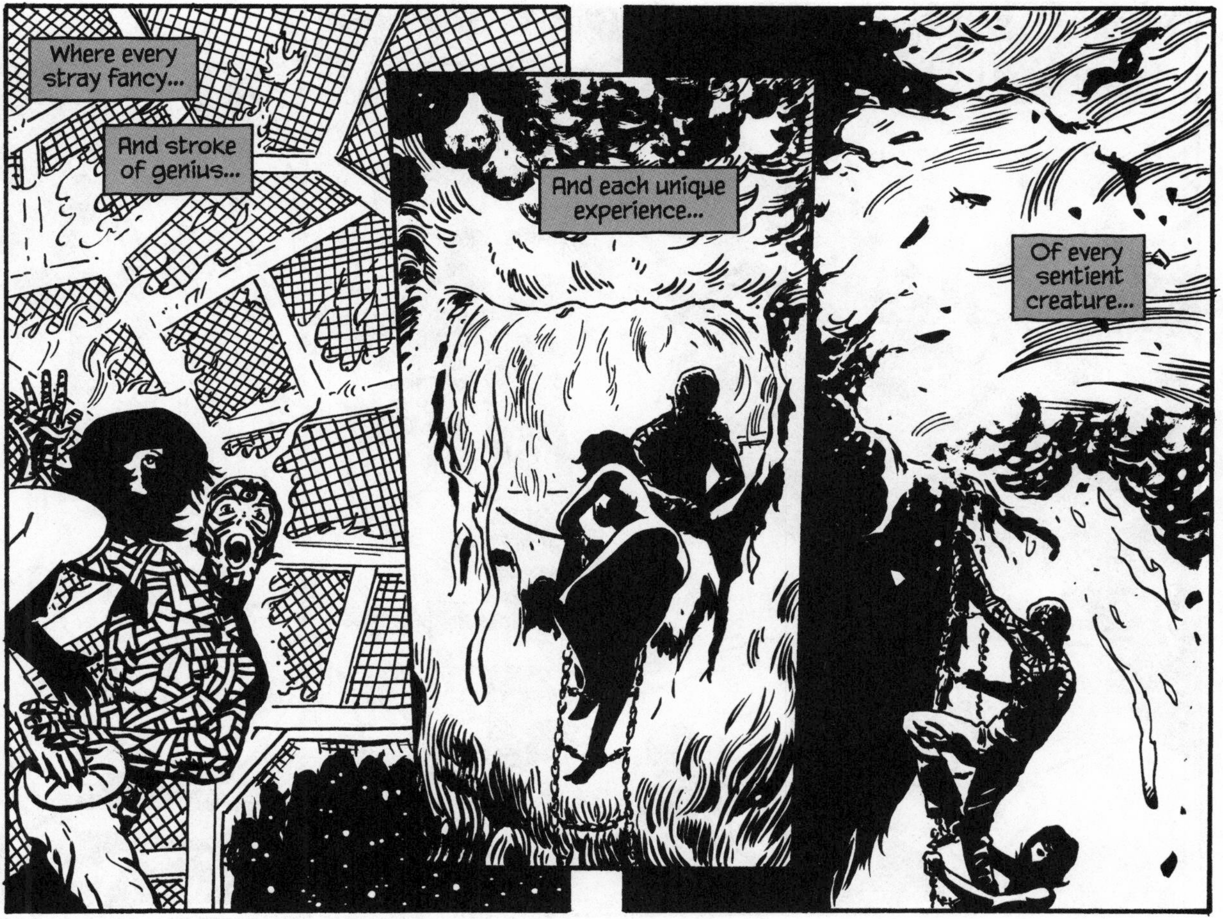
Where every stray fancy...
And stroke of genius...
And each unique experience...
Of every sentient creature...

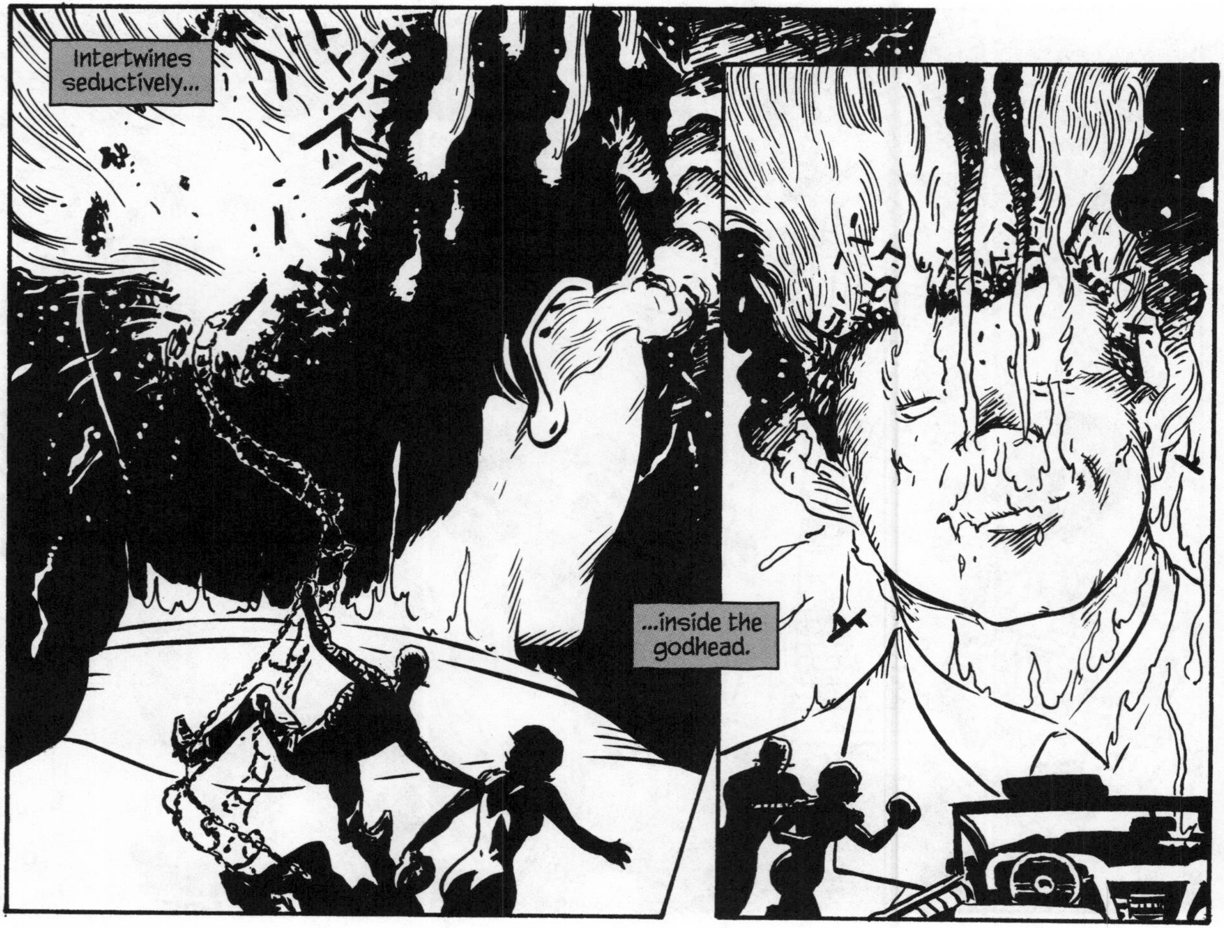
Intertwines seductively...
...inside the godhead.

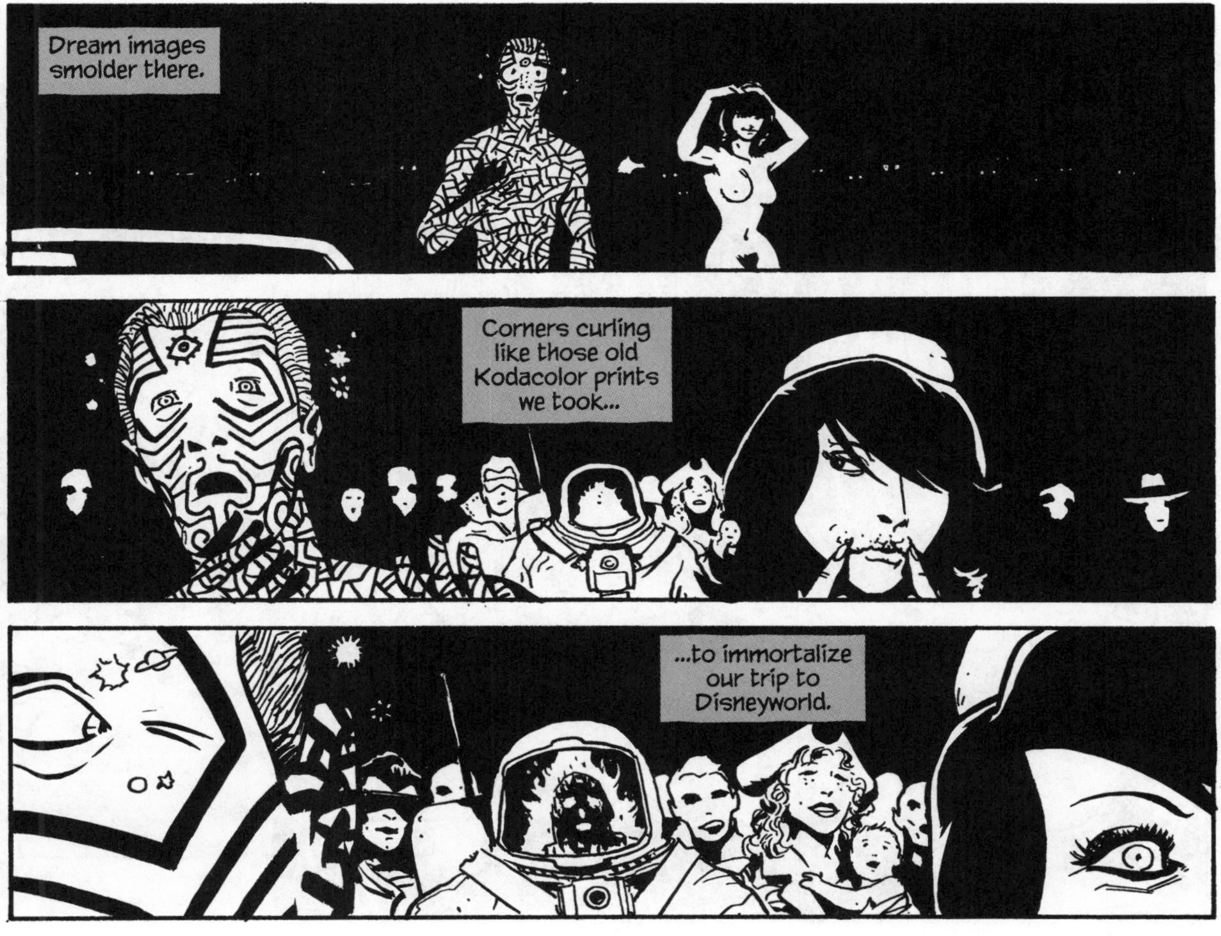
Dream images smolder there.
Corners curling like those old Kodacolor prints we took...
...to immortalize our trip to Disneyworld.

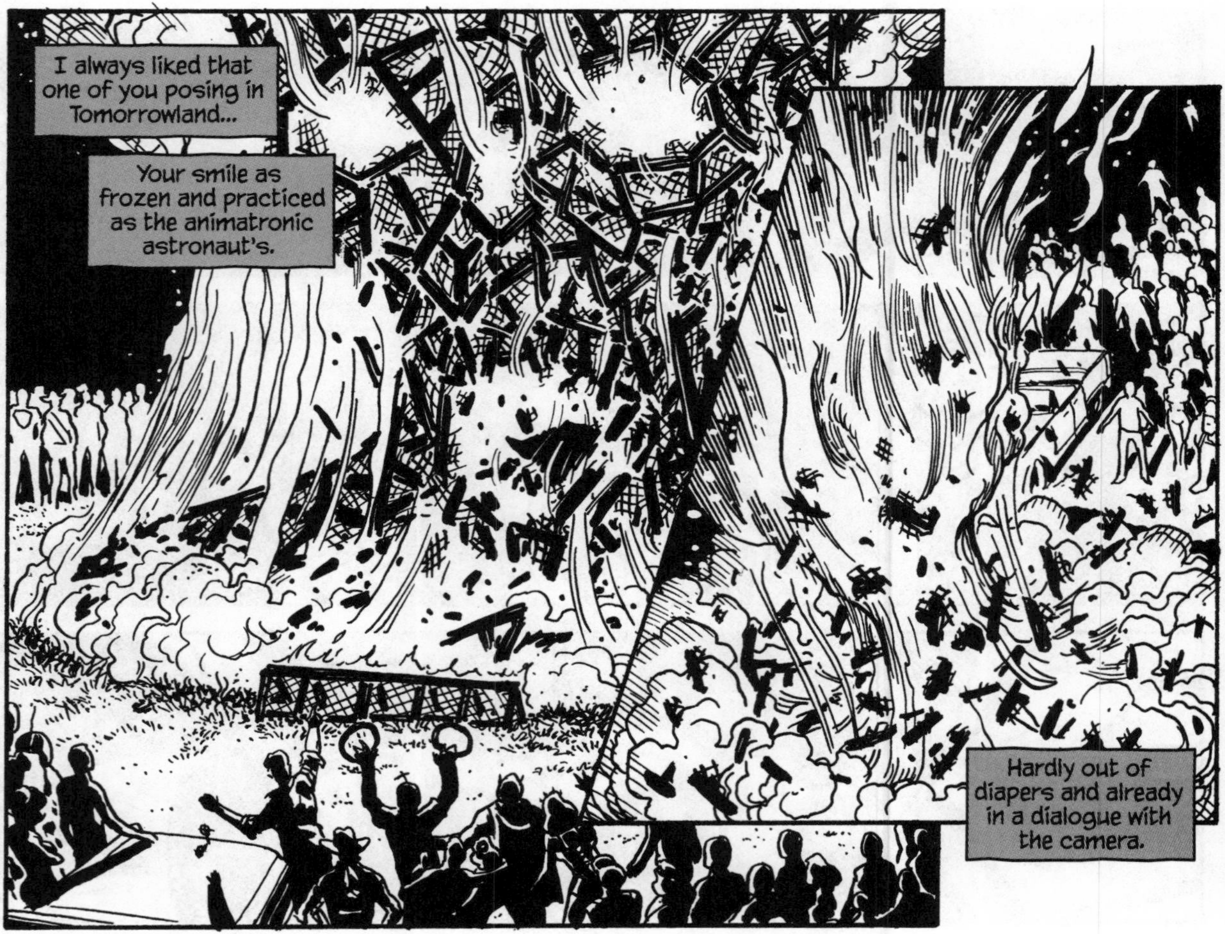
I always liked that one of you posing in Tomorrowland...
Your smile as frozen and practiced as the animatronic astronaut's.
Hardly out of diapers and already in a dialogue with the camera.

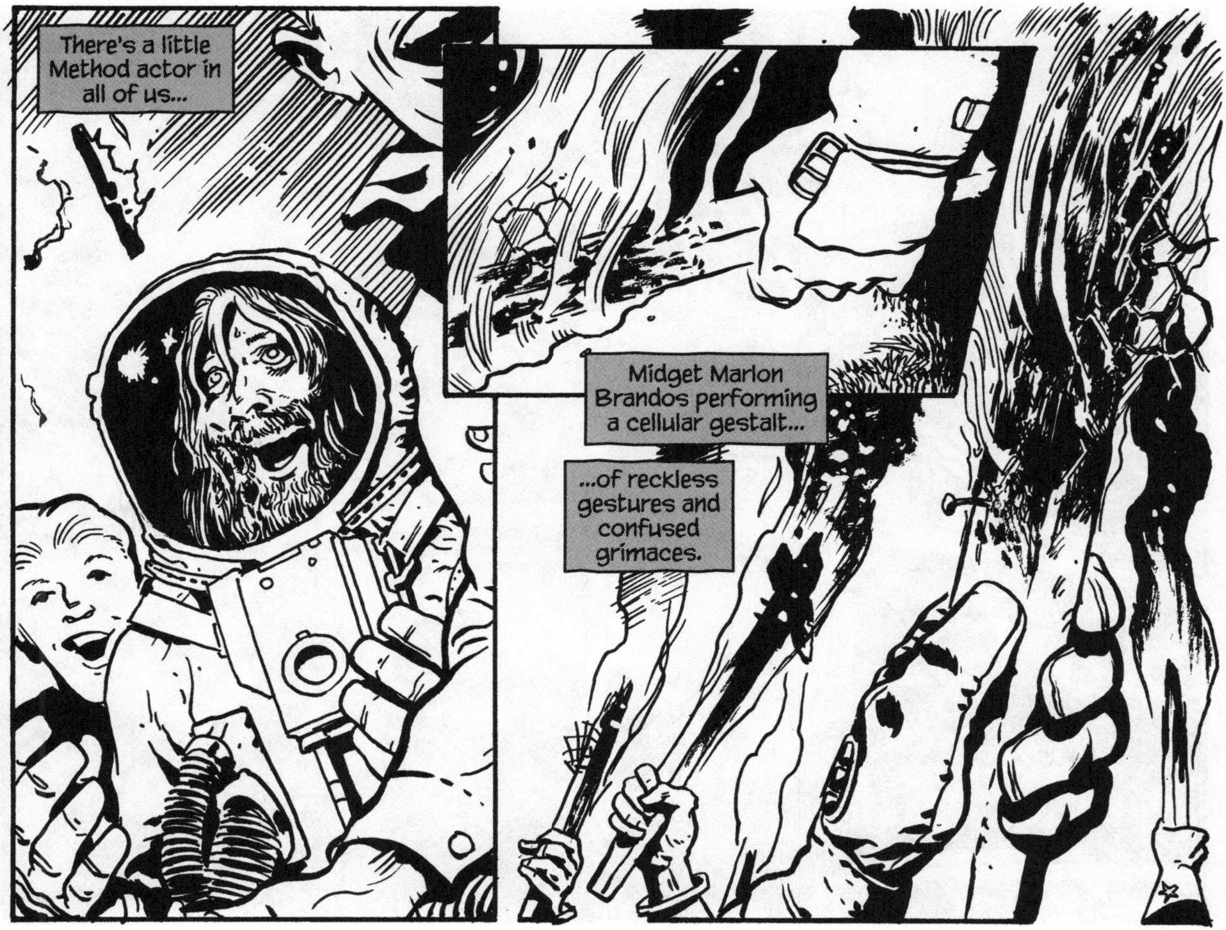
There's a little Method actor in all of us...
Midget Marlon Brandos performing a cellular gestalt...
...of reckless gestures and confused grimaces.

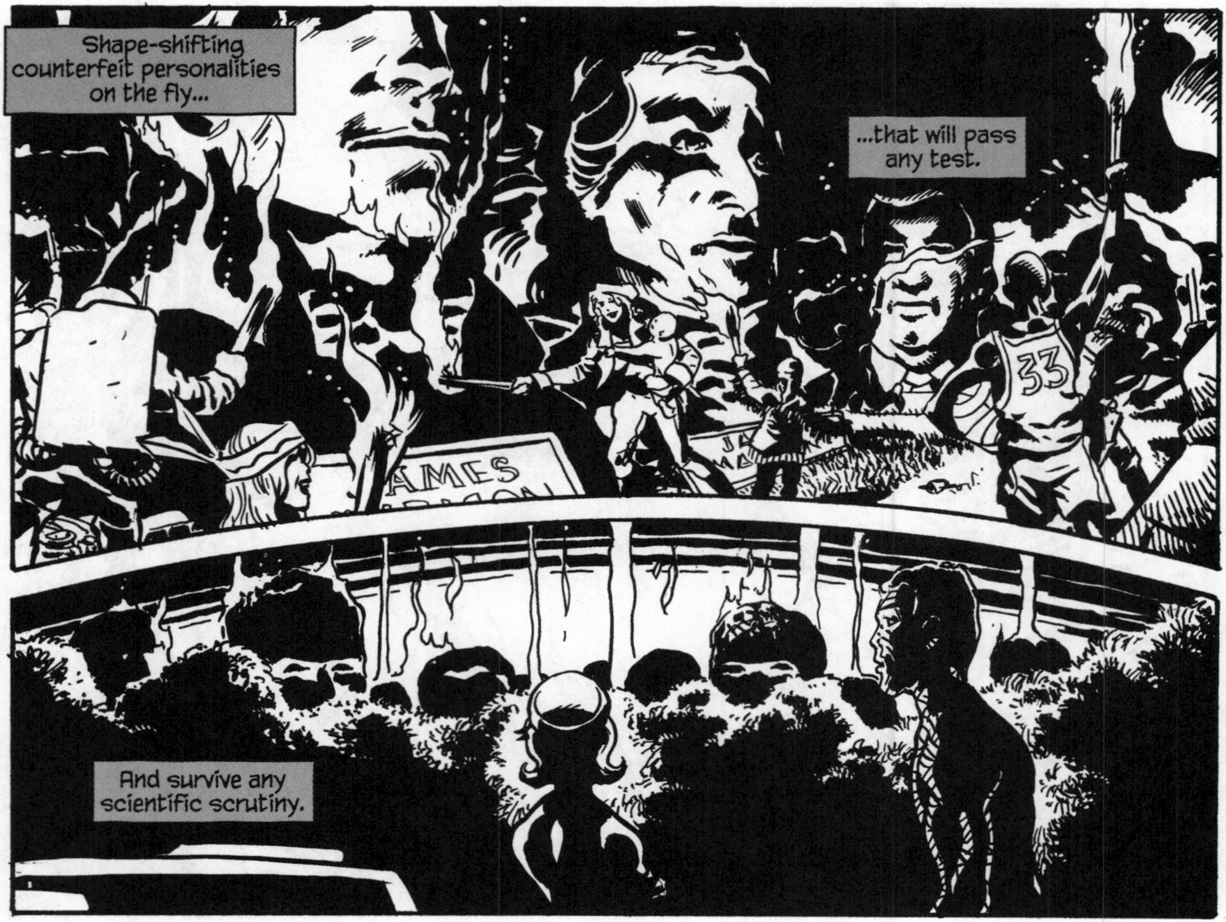
Shape-shifting counterfeit personalities on the fly...
...that will pass any test.
And survive any scientific scrutiny.

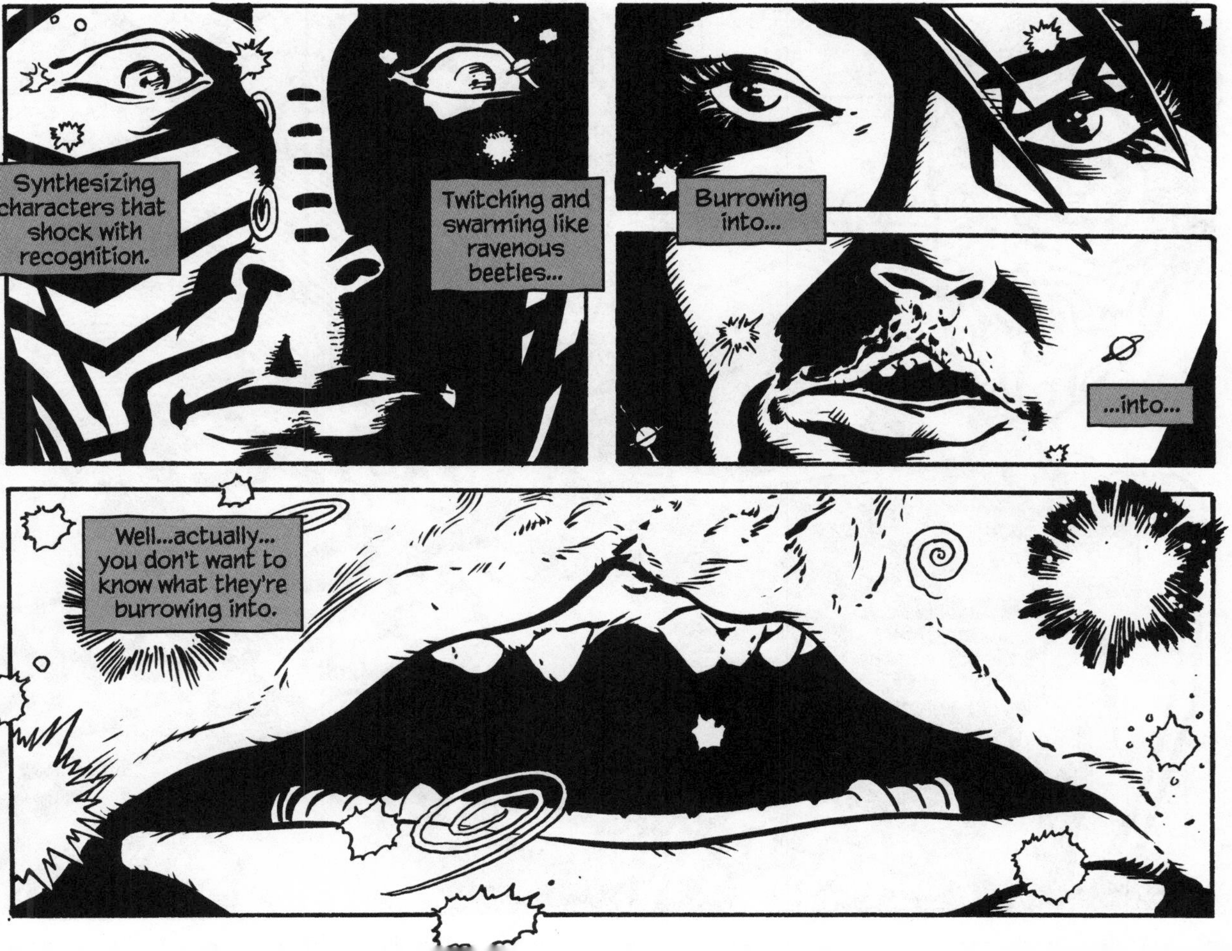
Synthesizing characters that shock with recognition.
Twitching and swarming like ravenous beetles...
Burrowing into...
...into...
Well...actually... you don't want to know what they're burrowing into.

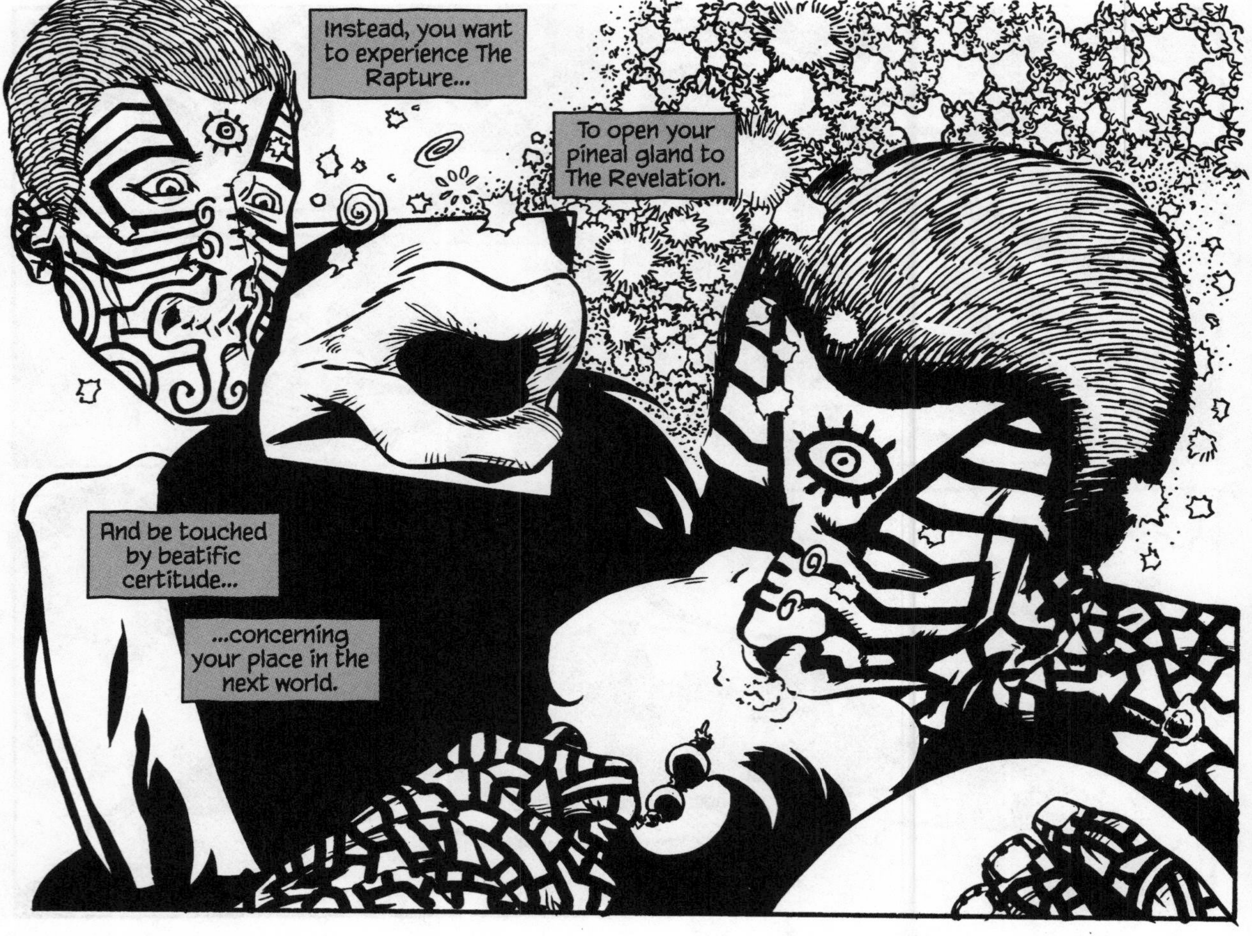
Instead, you want to experience The Rapture...
To open your pineal gland to The Revelation.
And be touched by beatific certitude...
...concerning your place in the next world.

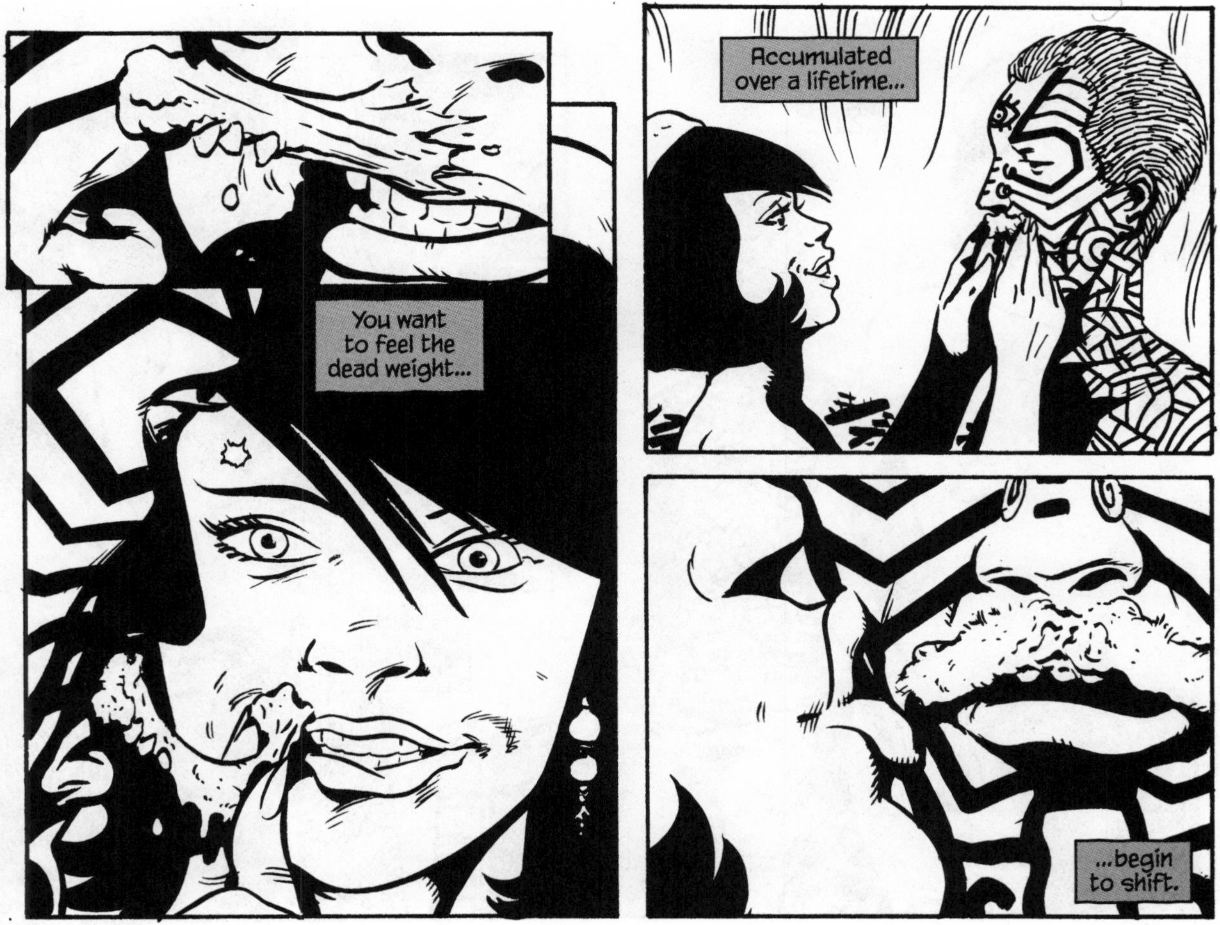
You want to feel the dead weight...
Accumulated over a lifetime...
...begin to shift.

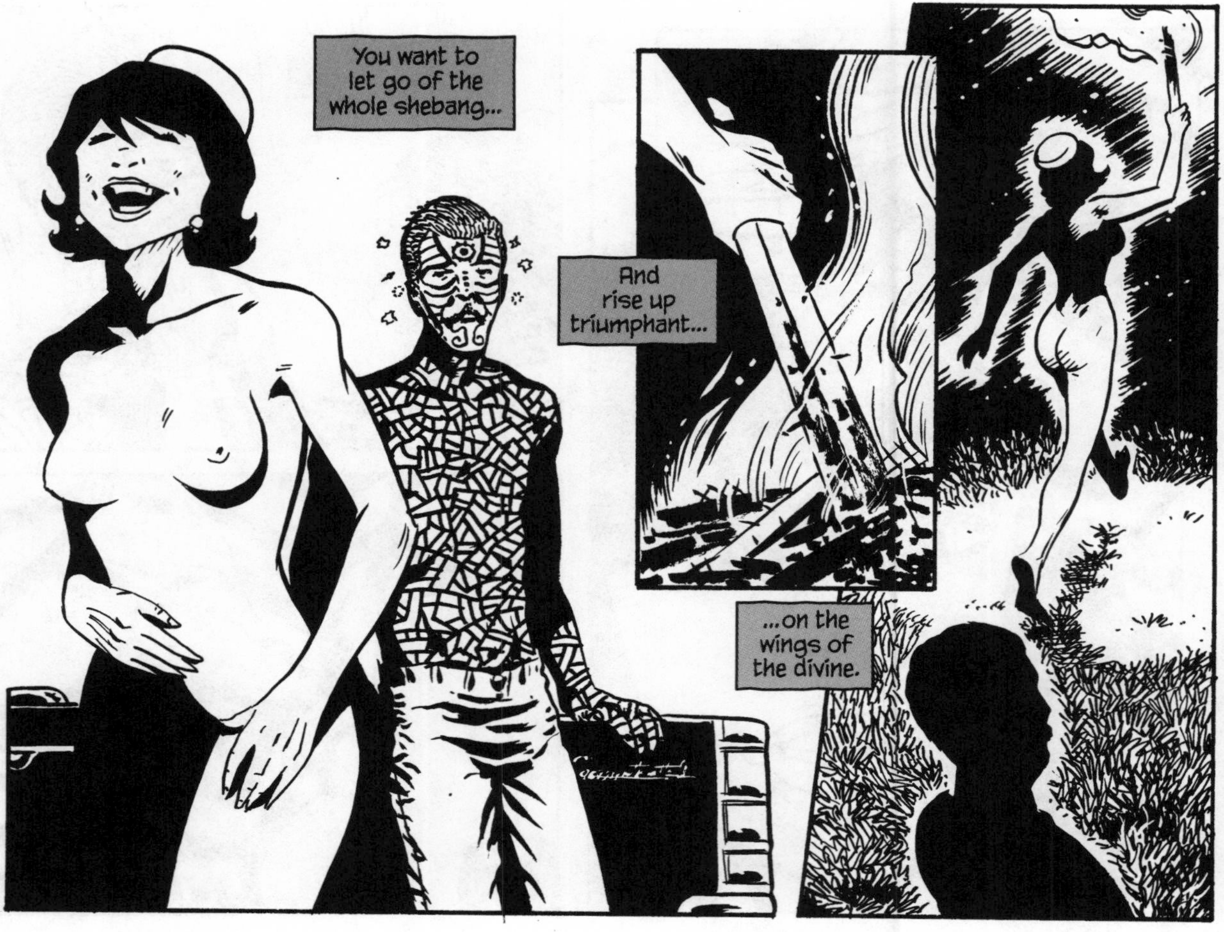
You want to let go of the whole shebang...
And rise up triumphant...
...on the wings of the divine.

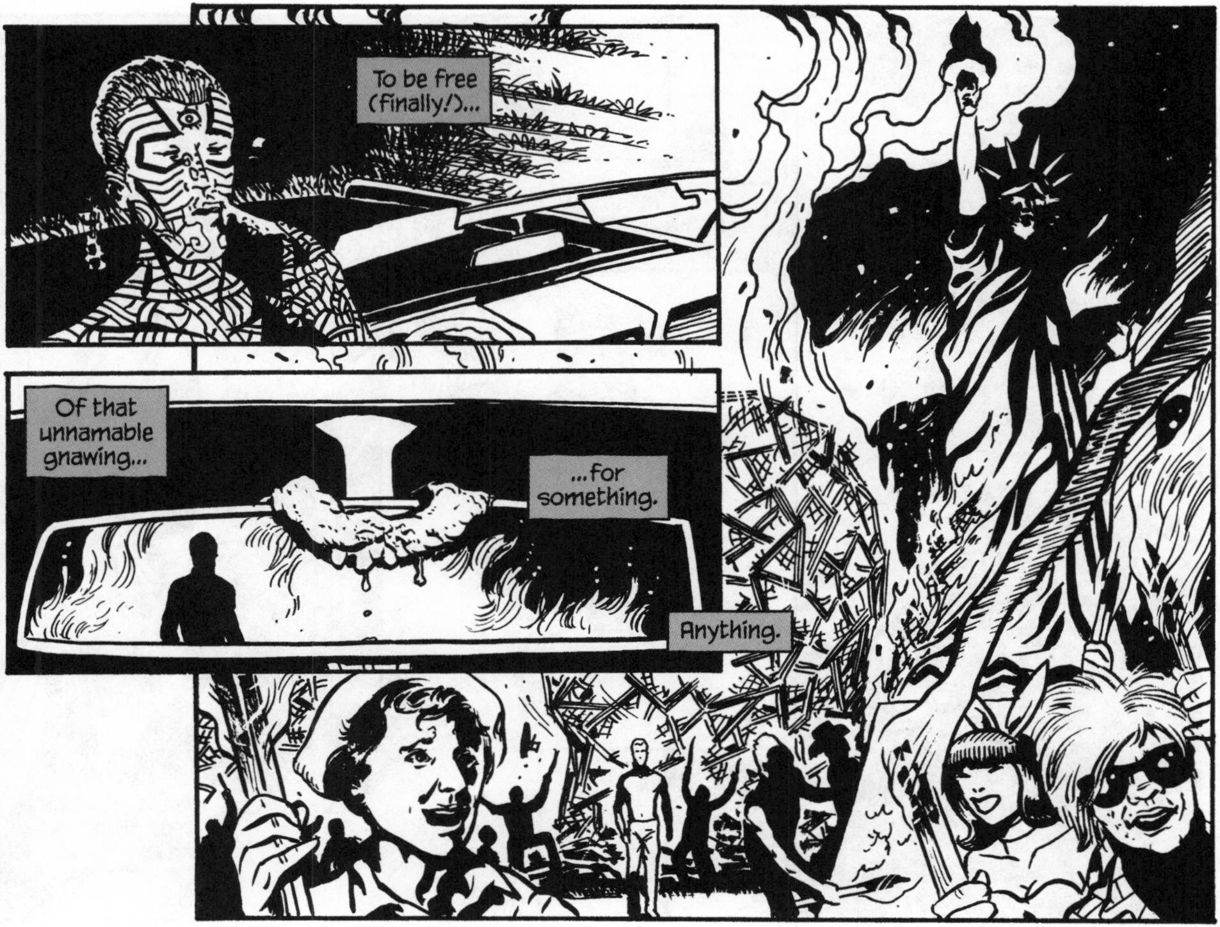
To be free (finally!)...
Of that unnamable gnawing...
...for something.
Anything.

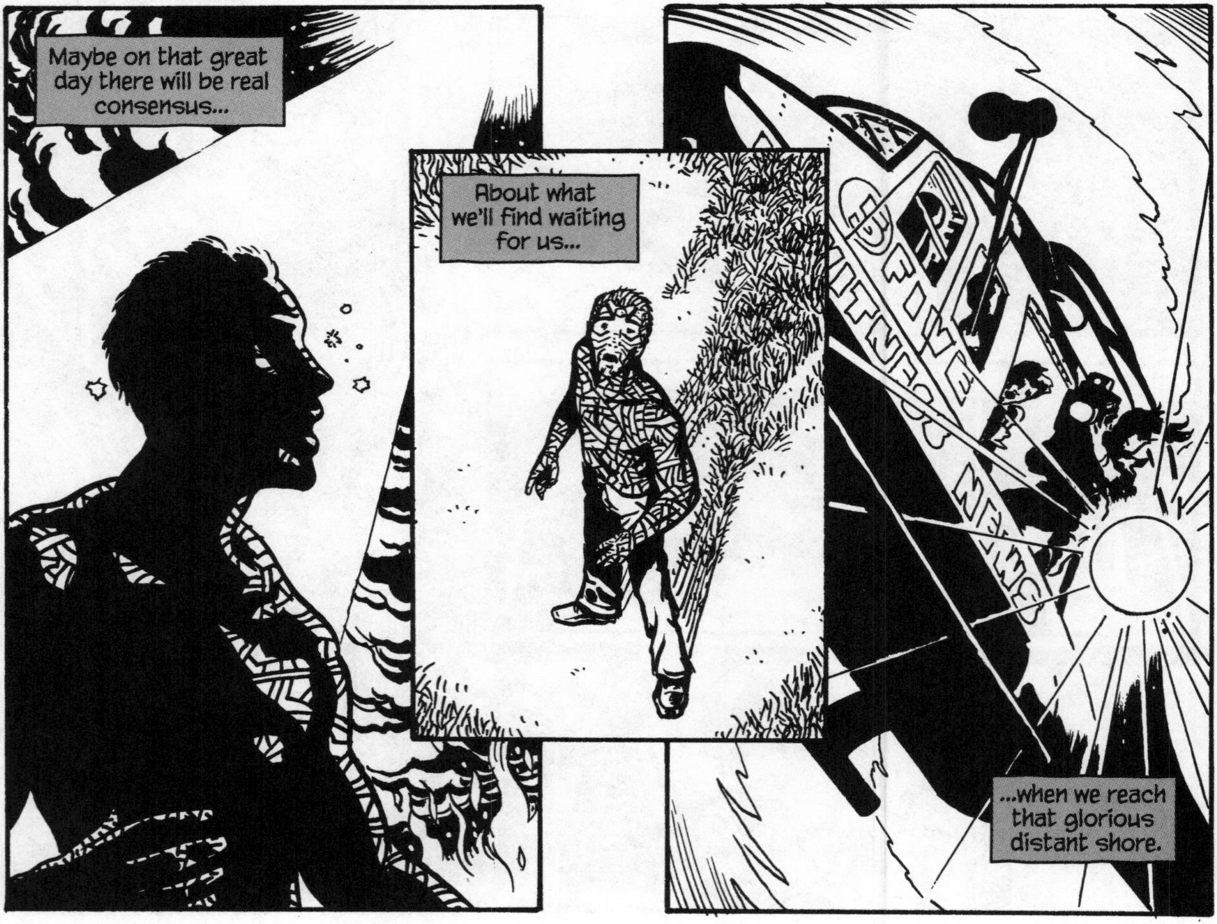
Maybe on that great day there will be real consensus...
About what we'll find waiting for us...
...when we reach that glorious distant shore.

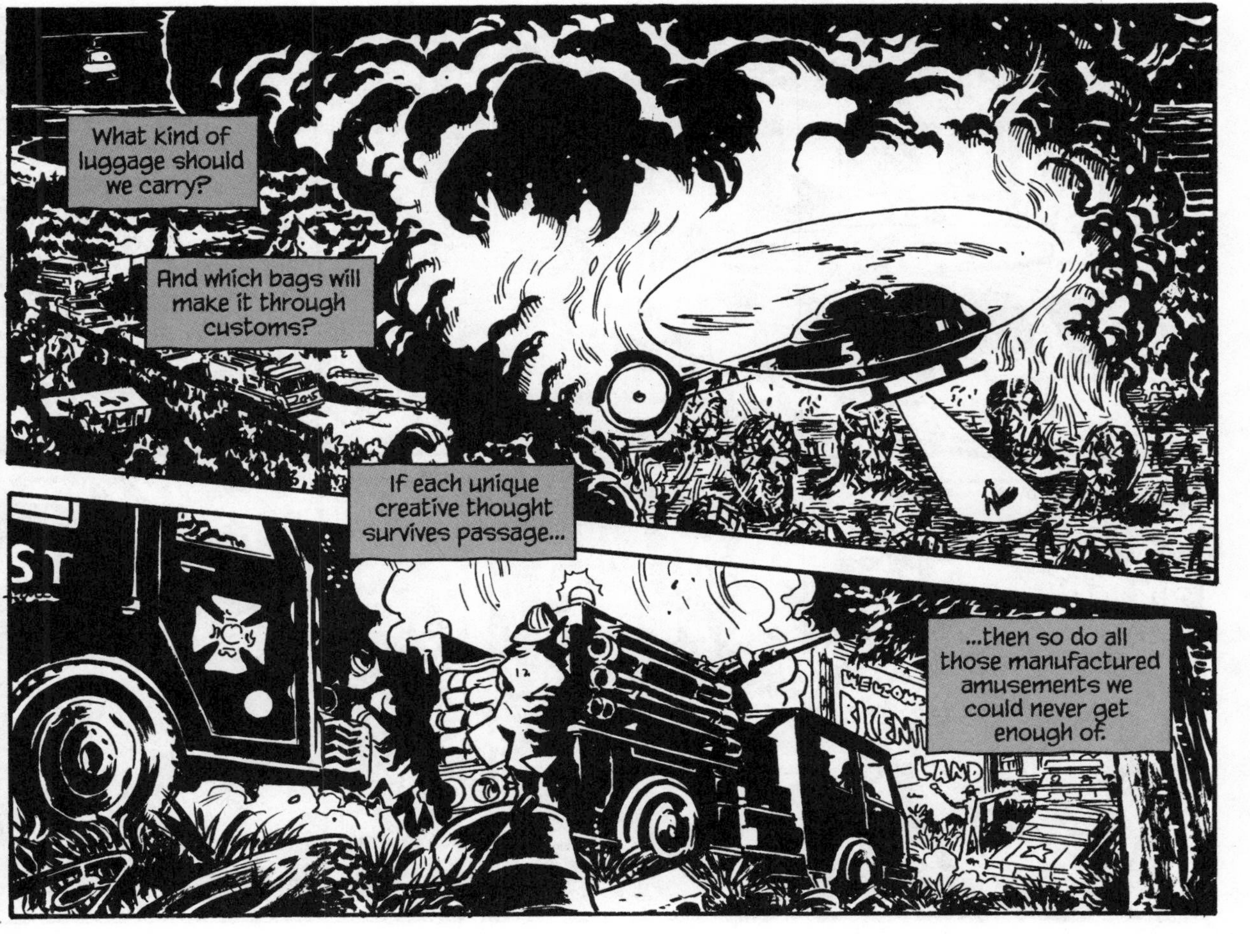
What kind of luggage should we carry?
And which bags will make it through customs?
If each unique creative thought survives passage...
...then so do all those manufactured amusements we could never get enough of.
LAND

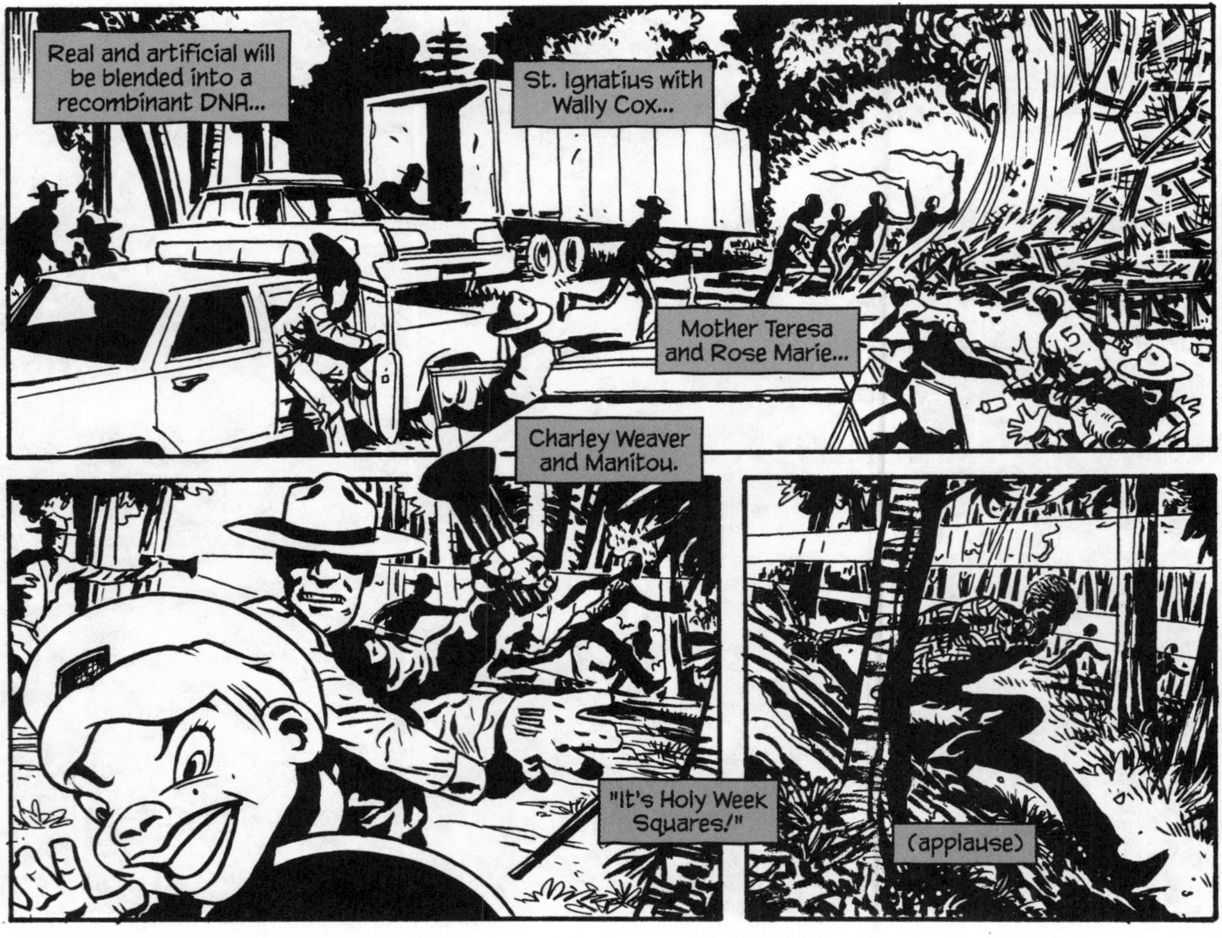
Real and artificial will be blended into a recombinant DNA...
St. Ignatius with Wally Cox...
Mother Teresa and Rose Marie...
Charley Weaver and Manitou.
"It's Holy Week Squares!"
(applause)

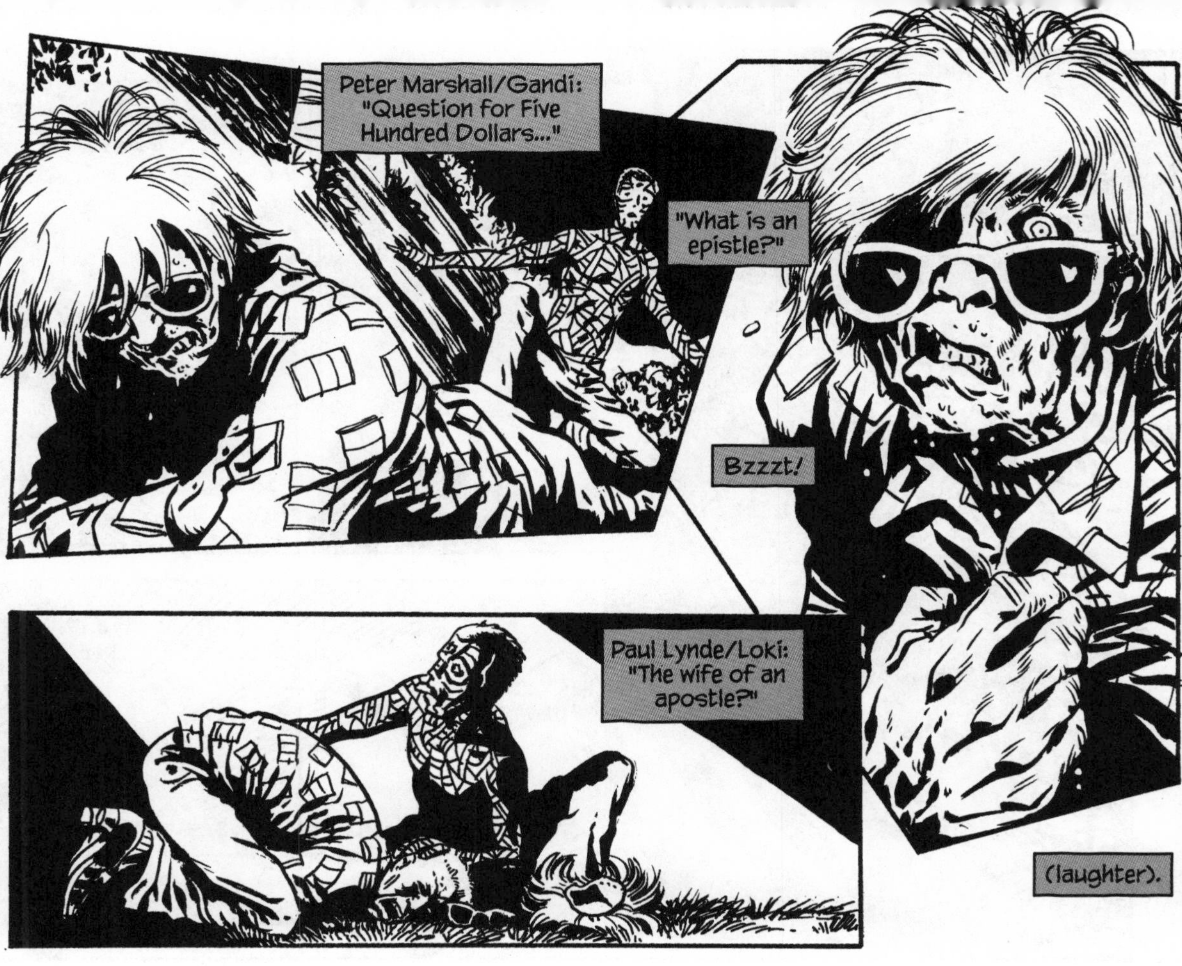
Peter Marshall/Gandi: "Question for Five Hundred Dollars..."
"What is an epistle?"
Bzzzt!
Paul Lynde/Loki: "The wife of an apostle?"
(laughter).

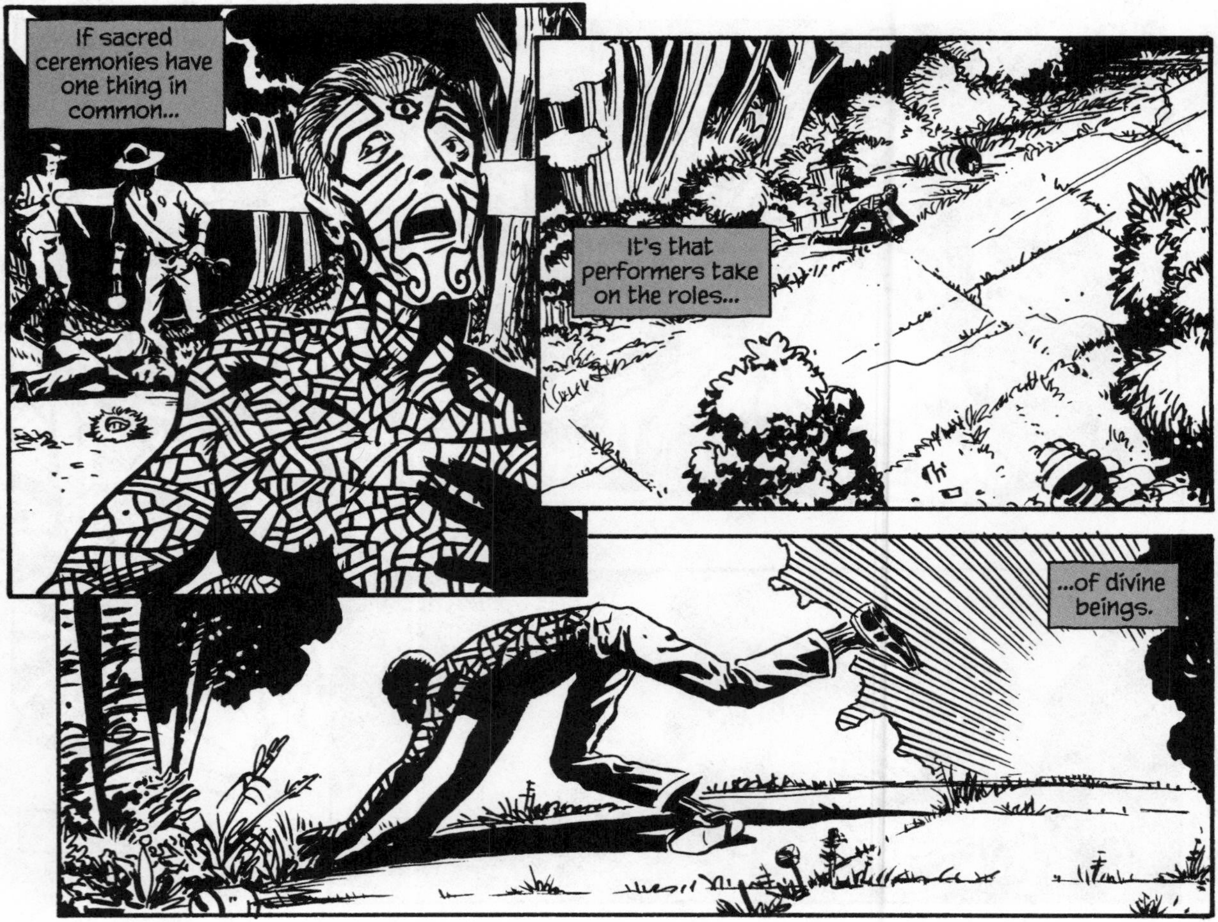
If sacred ceremonies have one thing in common...
It's that performers take on the roles...
...of divine beings.

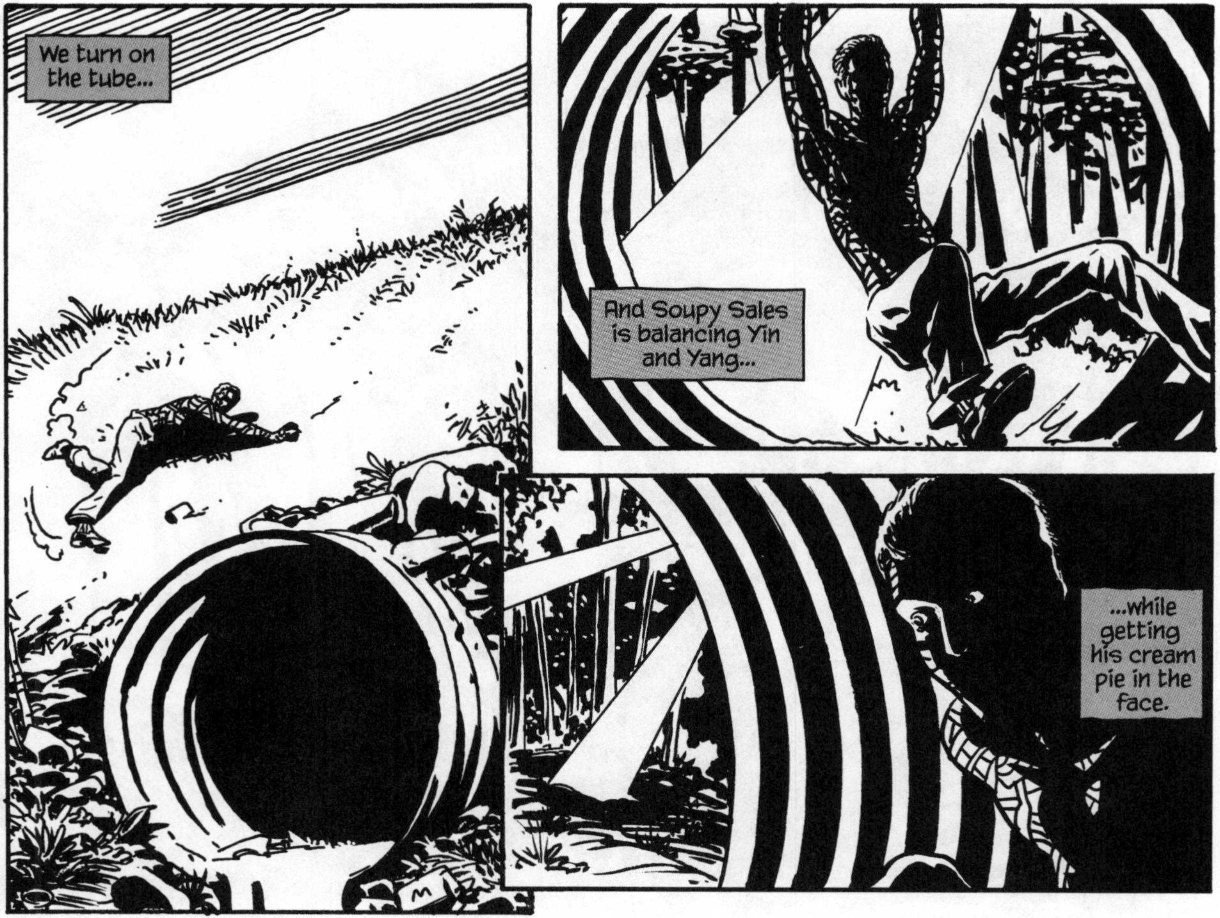
We turn on the tube...
And Soupy Sales is balancing Yin and Yang...
...while getting his cream pie in the face.

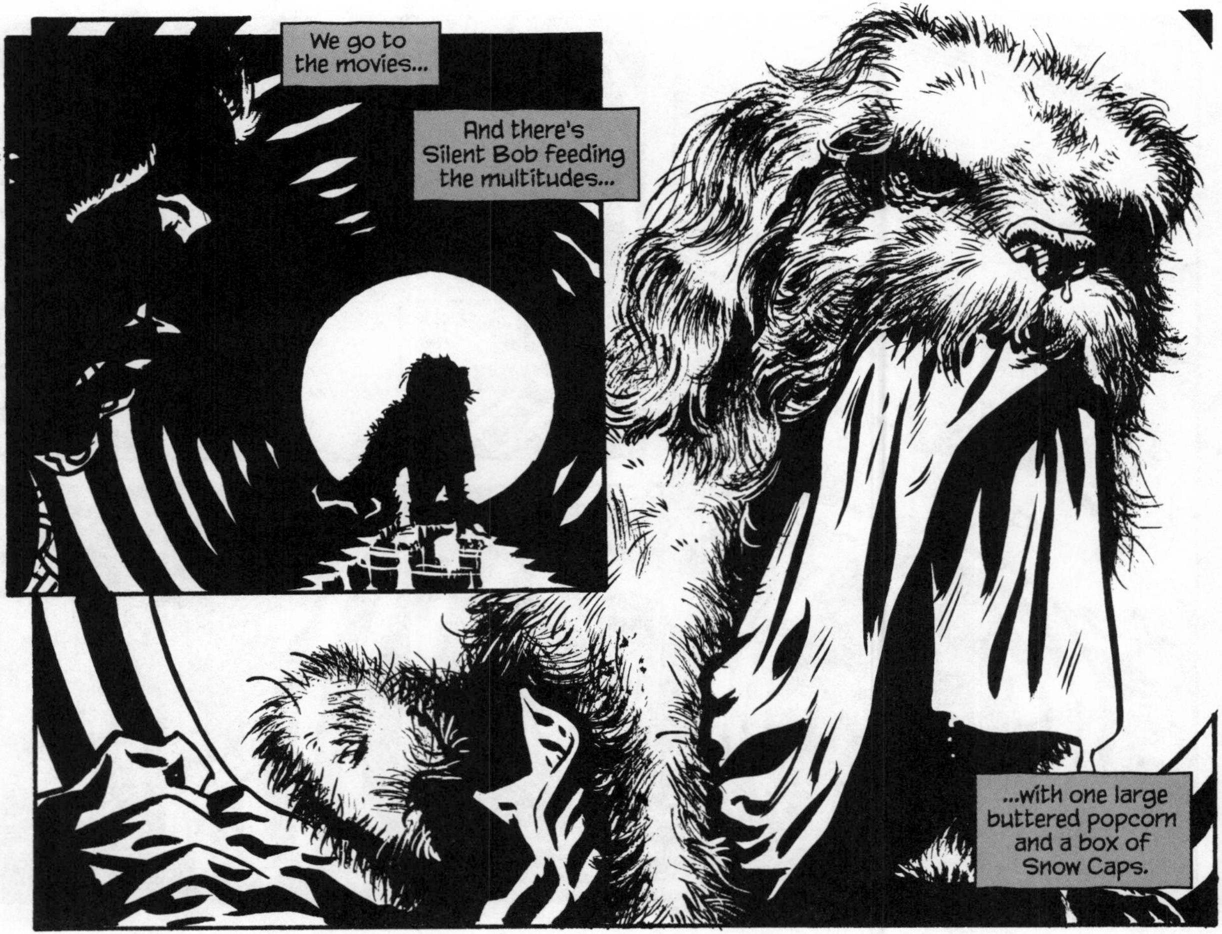
We go to the movies...
And there's Silent Bob feeding the multitudes...
...with one large buttered popcorn and a box of Snow Caps.

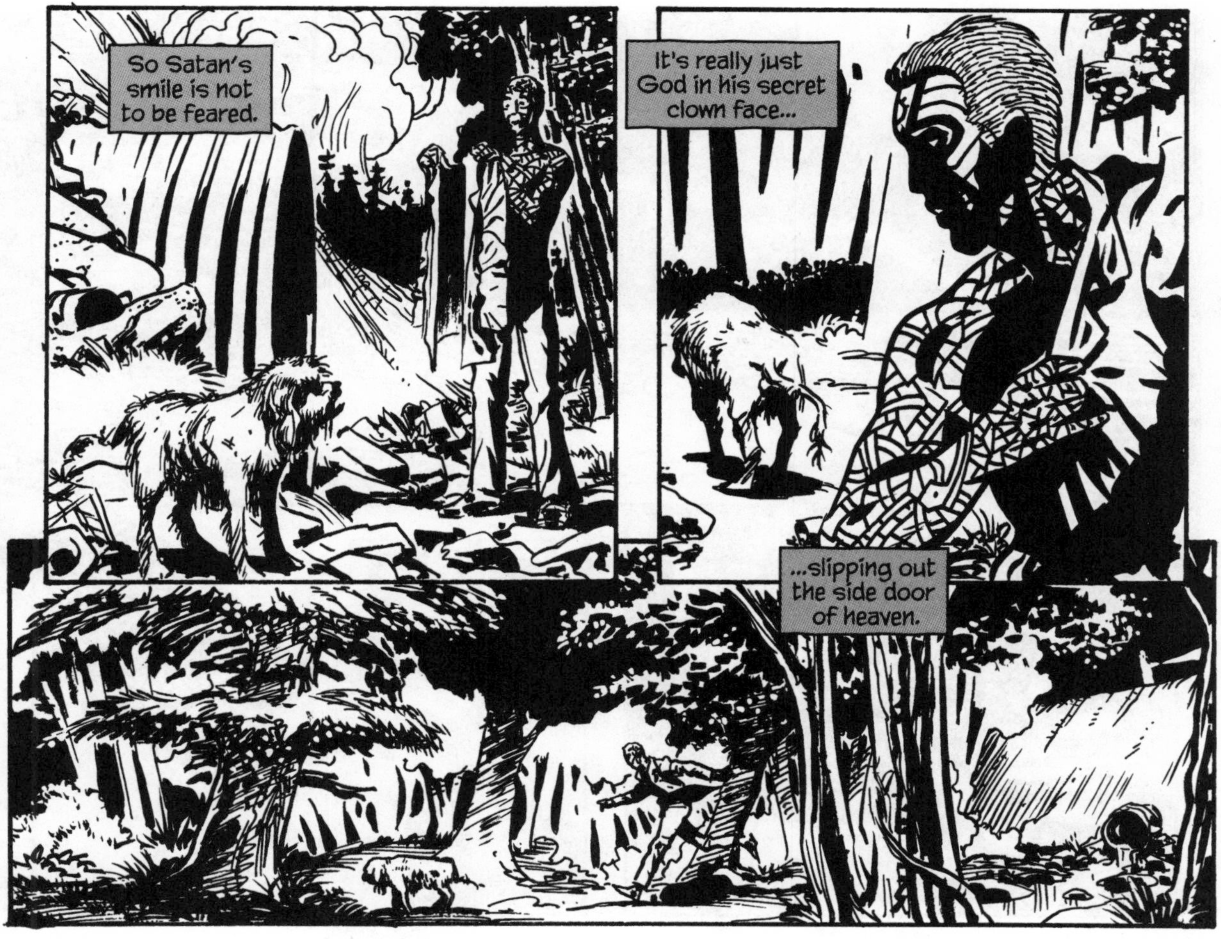
So Satan's smile is not to be feared.
It's really just God in his secret clown face...
...slipping out the side door of heaven.

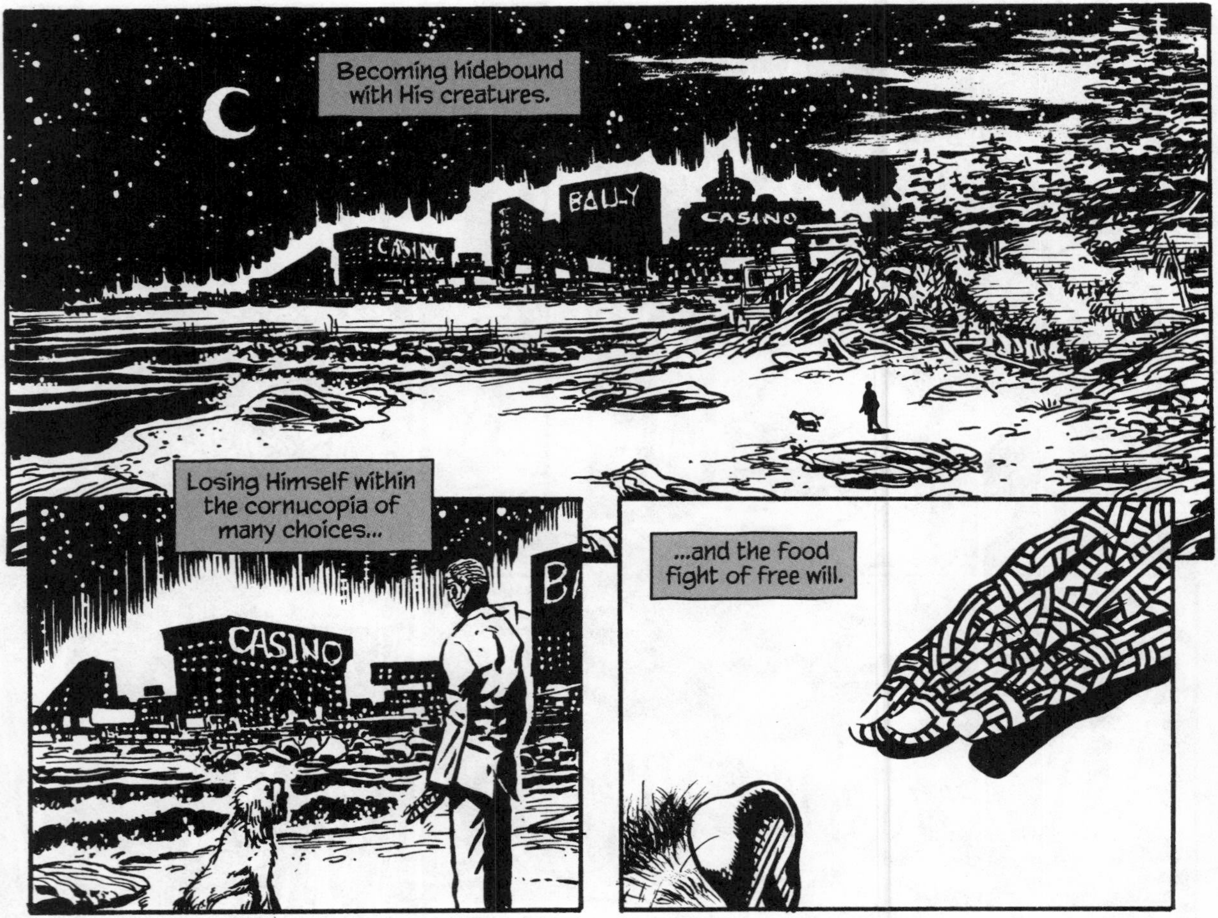
Becoming hidebound
with His creatures.
BALLY
CASINO
CASINO
Losing Himself within
the cornucopia of
many choices...
CASINO
...and the food
fight of free will.

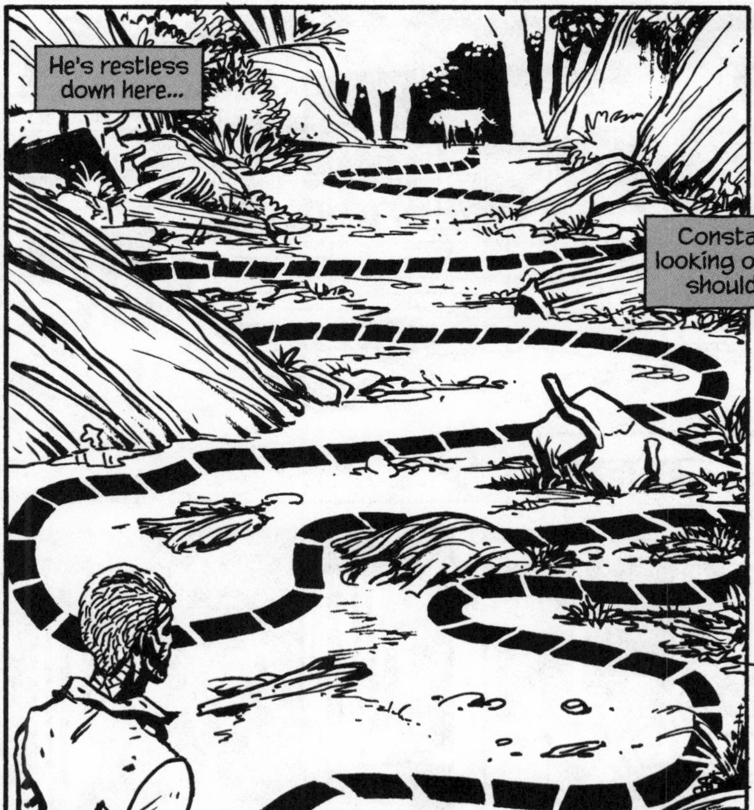
He's restless down here...
Constantly looking over His shoulder...
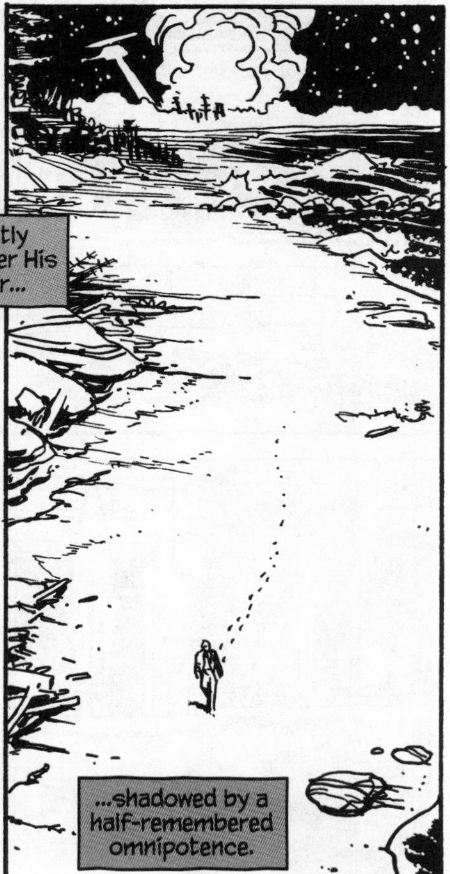
...shadowed by a half-remembered omnipotence.

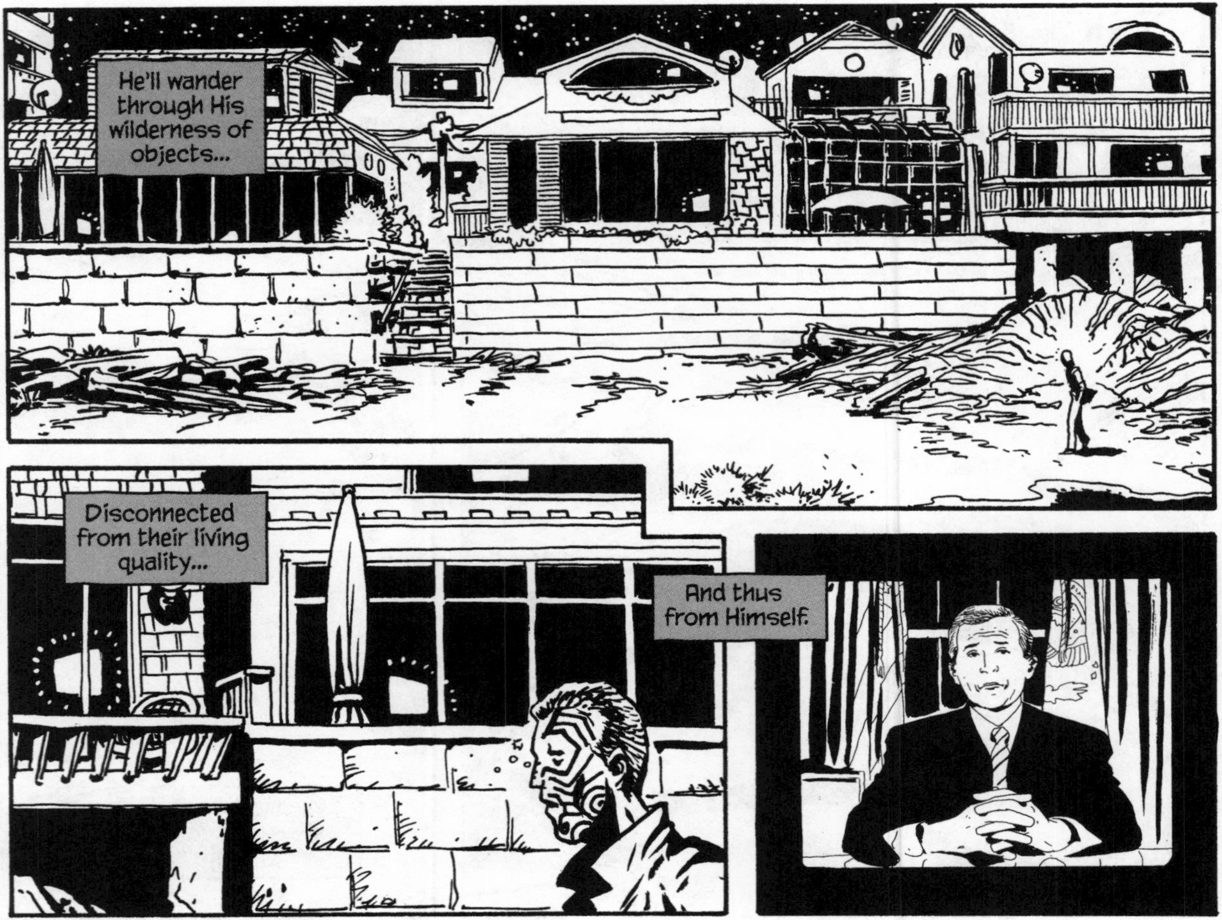

He'll wander through His wilderness of objects...
Disconnected from their living quality...
And thus from Himself.

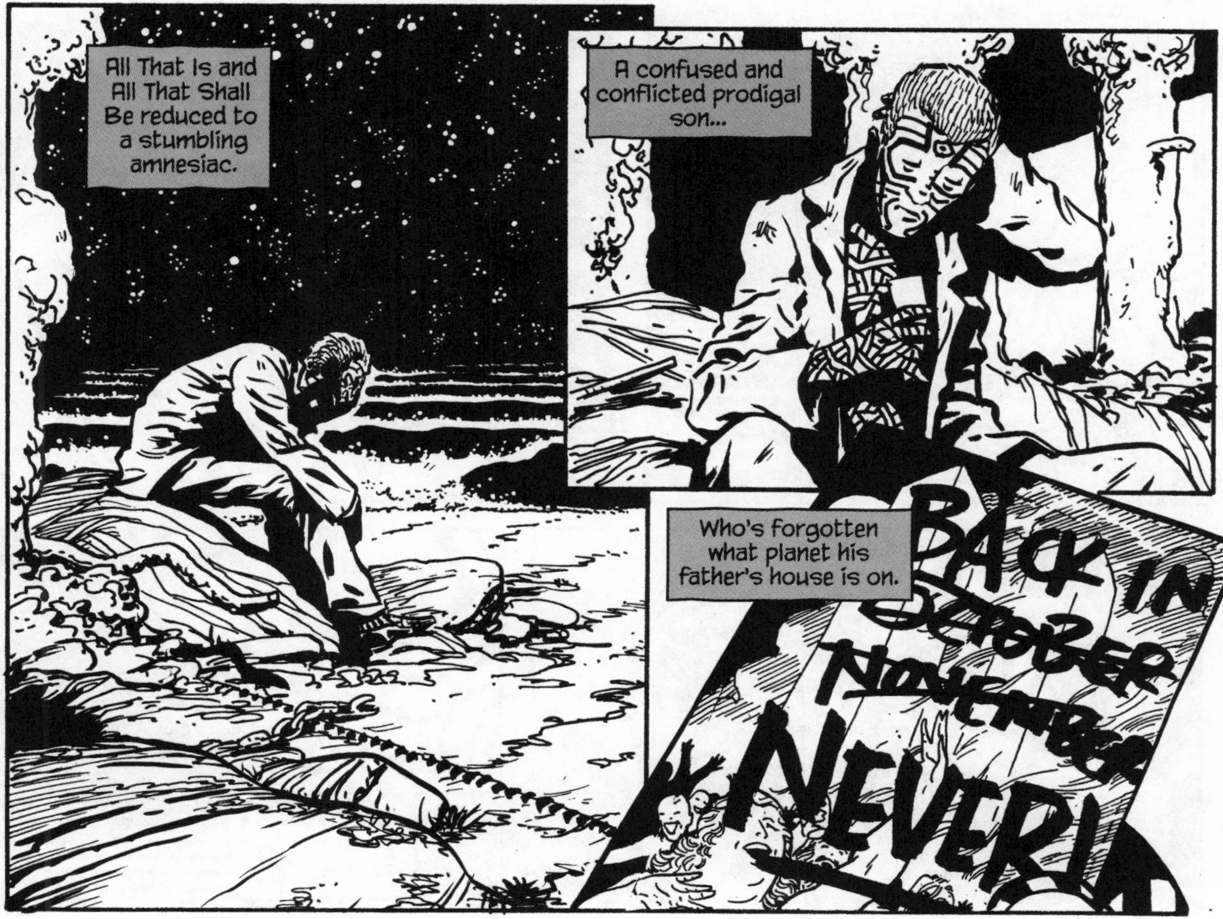
All That Is and All That Shall Be reduced to a stumbling amnesiac.
A confused and conflicted prodigal son...
Who's forgotten what planet his father's house is on.
BACK IN
OCTOBER
NOVEMBER
NEVER!

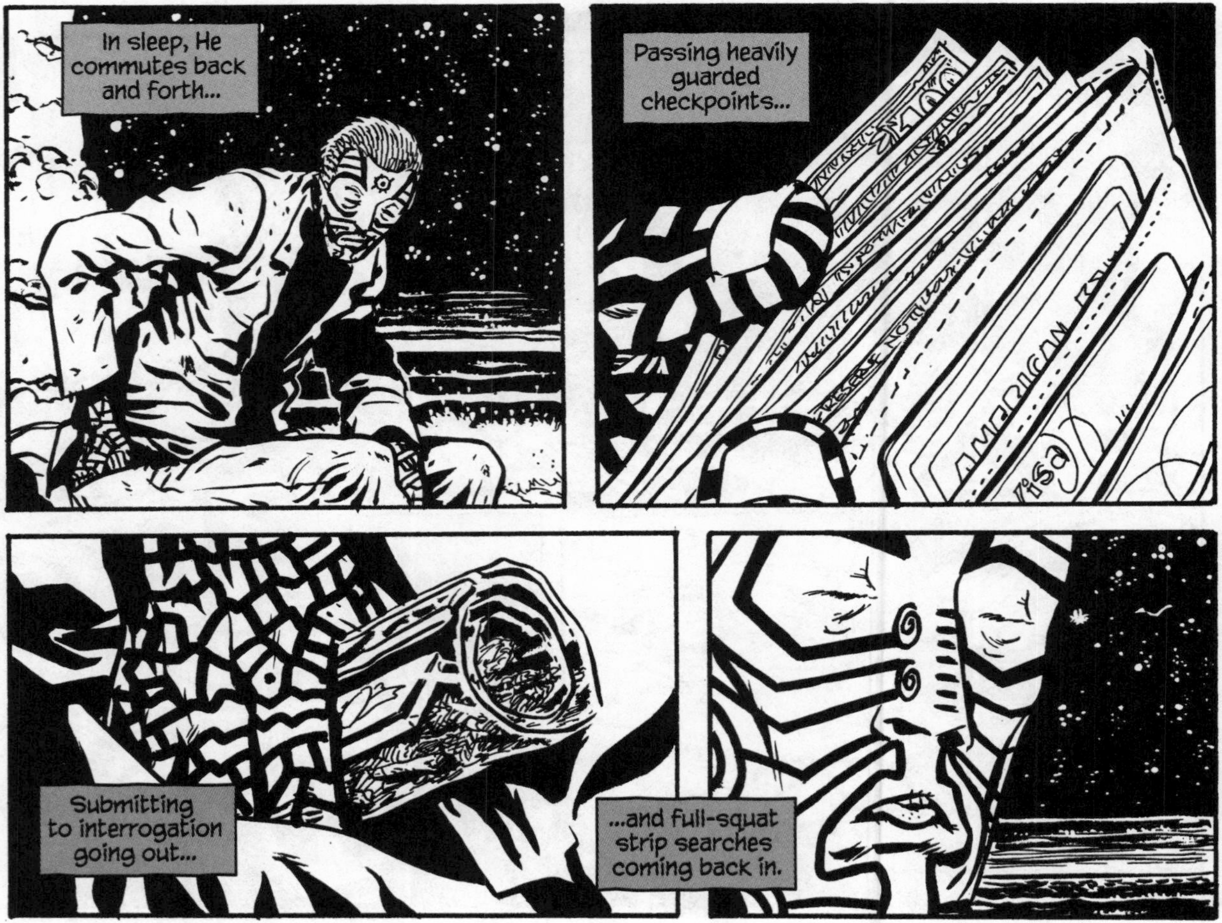
In sleep, He commutes back and forth...
Passing heavily guarded checkpoints...
Submitting to interrogation going out...
...and full-squat strip searches coming back in.

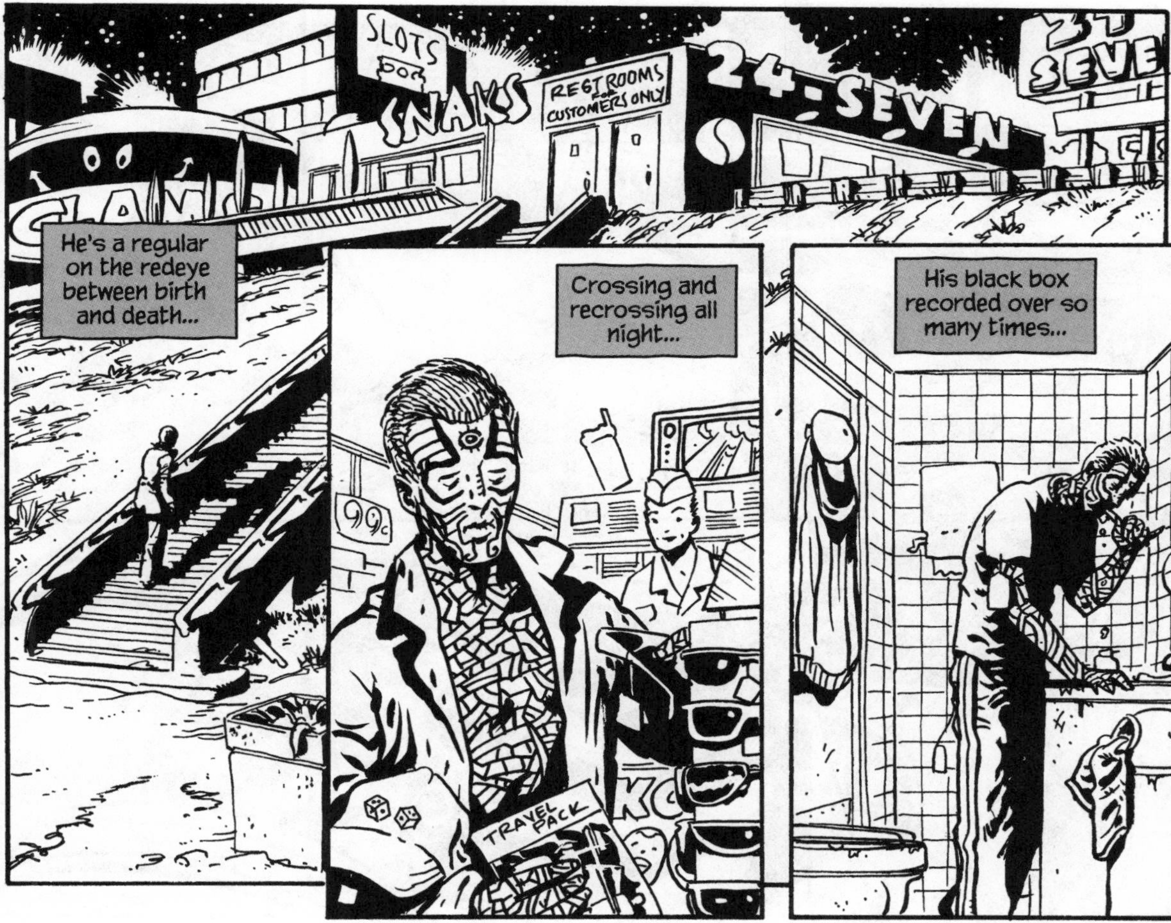
SLOTS
REST ROOMS FOR CUSTOMERS ONLY
24-SEVEN
SEVE
He's a regular on the redeye between birth and death...
Crossing and recrossing all night...
99¢
TRAVEL PACK
His black box recorded over so many times...

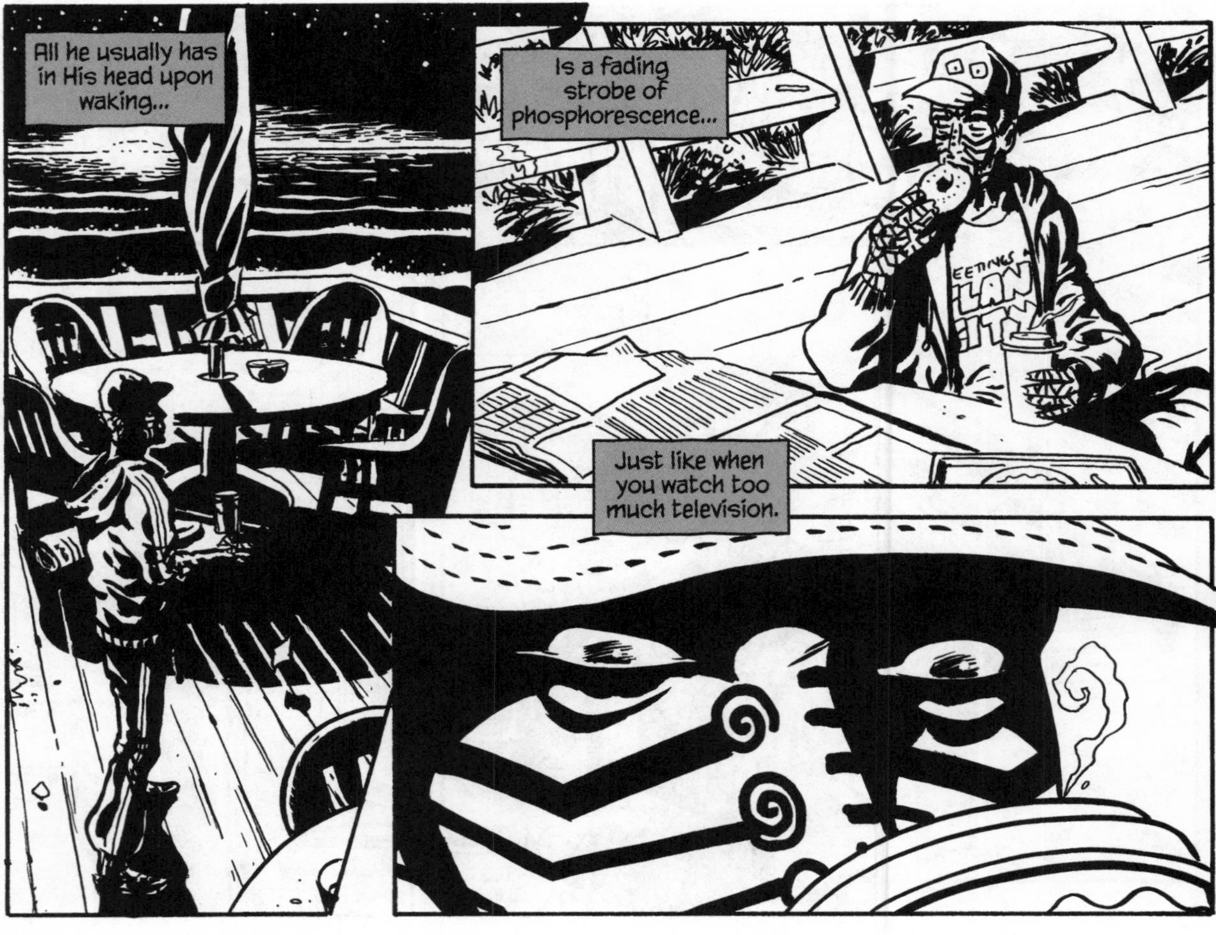
All he usually has in His head upon waking...
Is a fading strobe of phosphorescence...
Just like when you watch too much television.

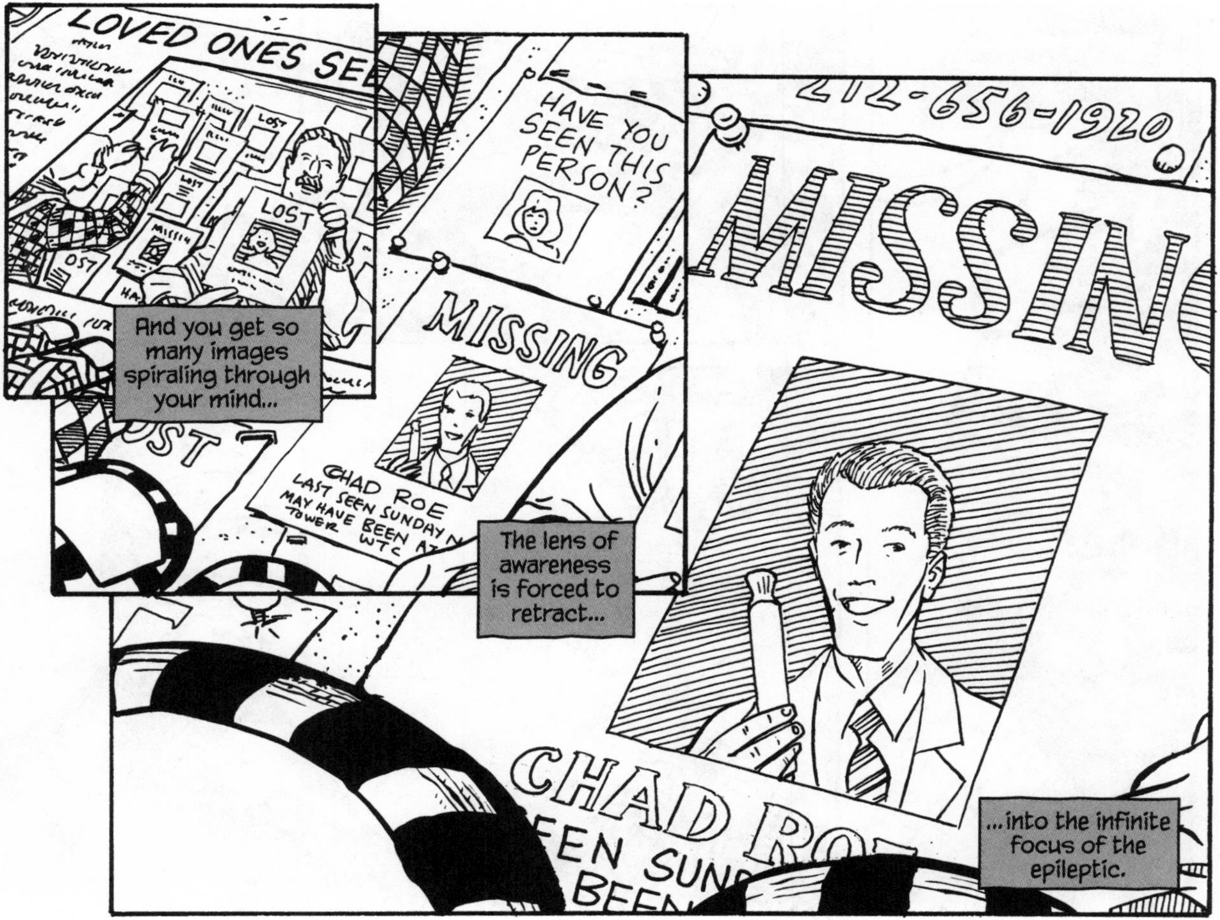

LOVED ONES SE
LOST
MISSING
And you get so many images spiraling through your mind...
HAVE YOU SEEN THIS PERSON?
MISSING
CHAD ROE
LAST SEEN SUNDAY
MAY HAVE BEEN AT
TOWER WTC
The lens of awareness is forced to retract...
212-656-1920
MISSIN
CHAD RO
EEN SUN
BEEN
...into the infinite focus of the epileptic.

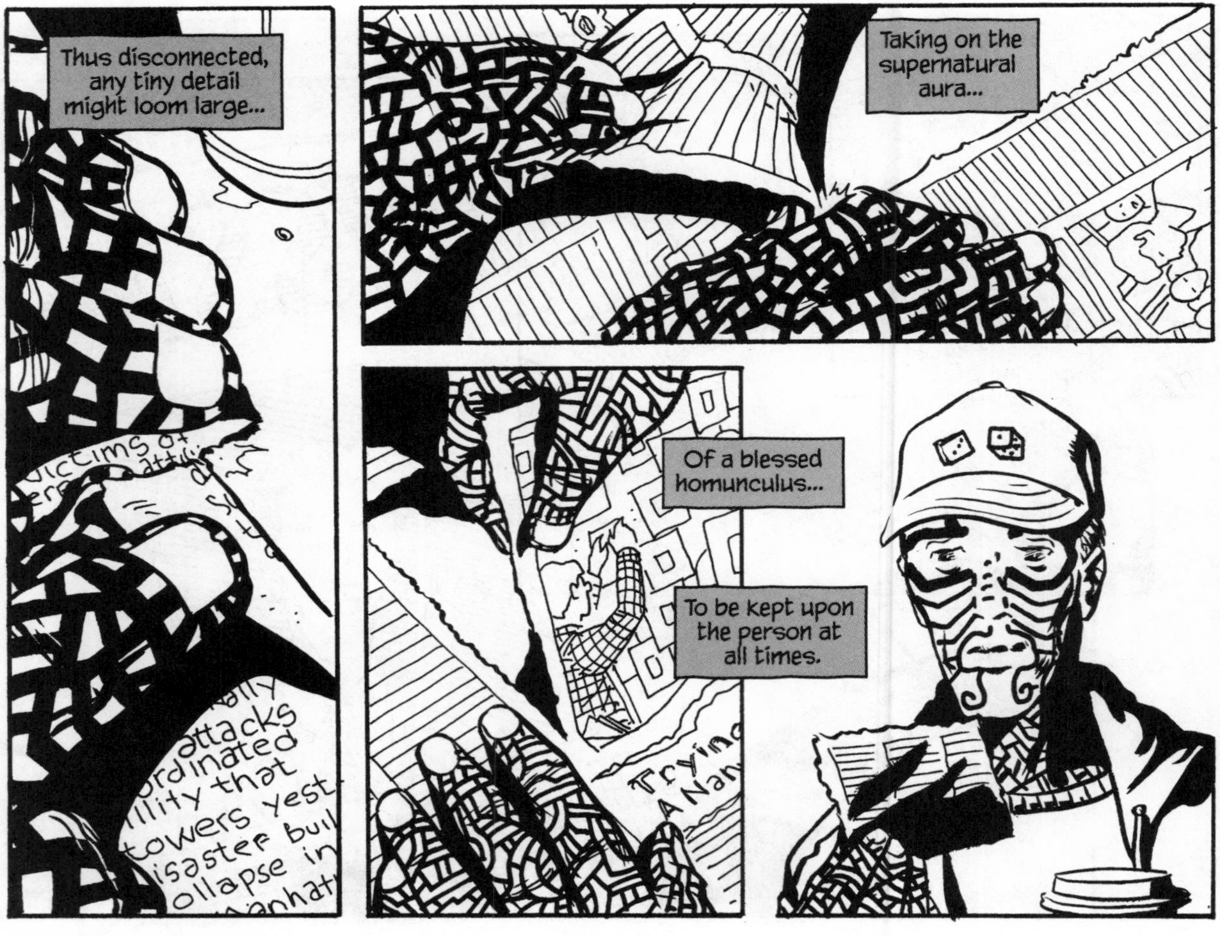
Thus disconnected, any tiny detail might loom large...
Victims of
attacks
ordinated
ility that
towers yest
isaster buil
ollapse in
Taking on the supernatural aura...
Of a blessed homunculus...
To be kept upon the person at all times.

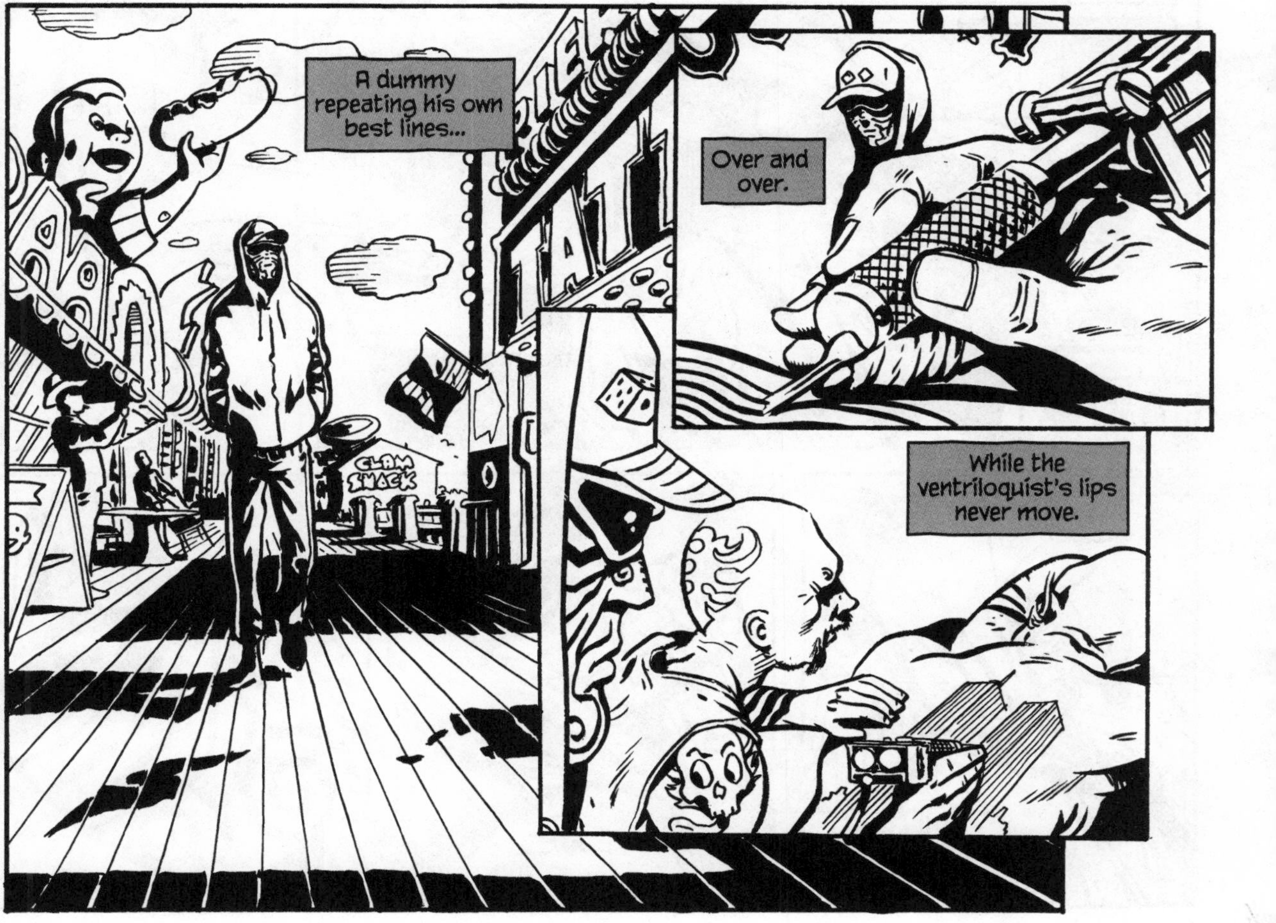
A dummy repeating his own best lines...
CLAM SHACK
Over and over.
While the ventriloquist's lips never move.

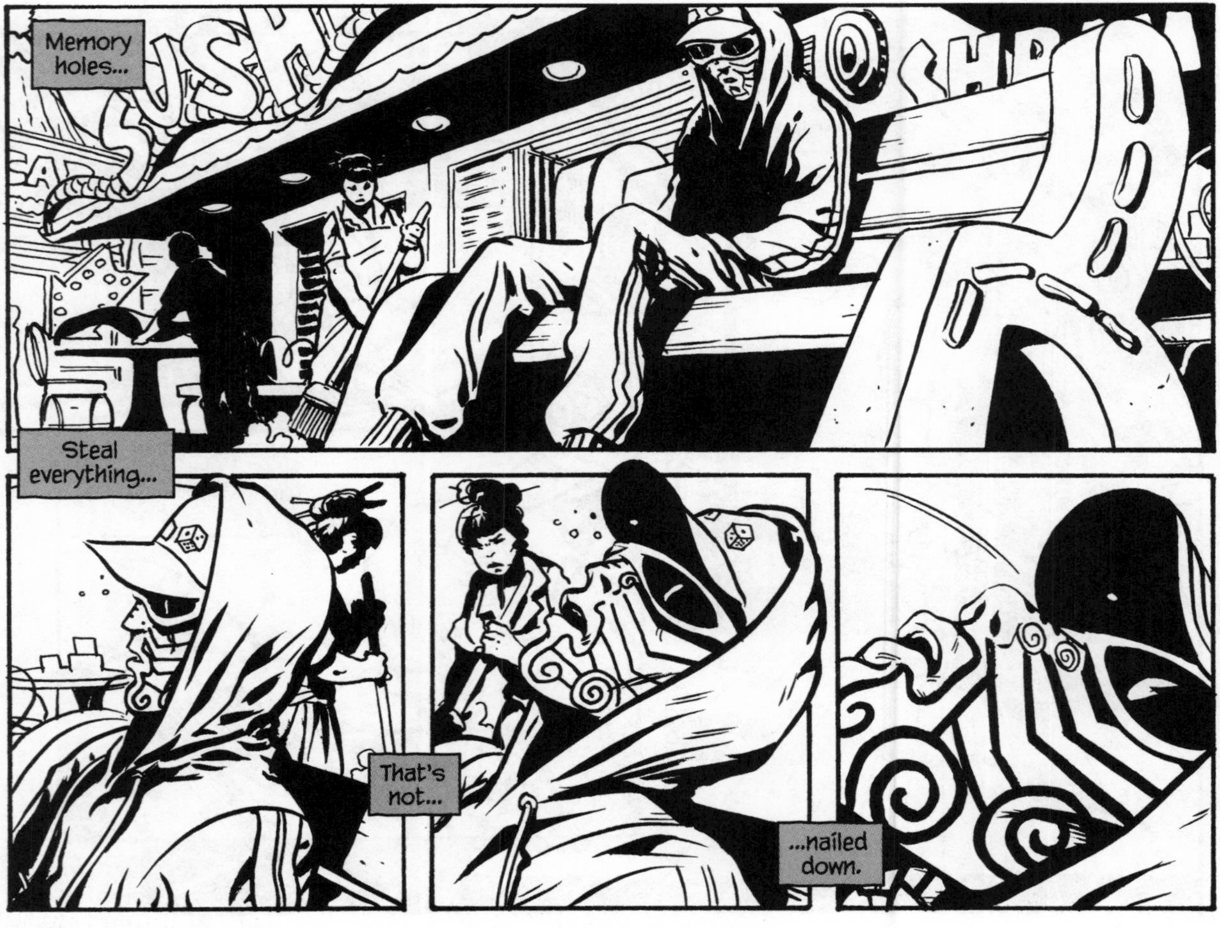
Memory holes...
Steal everything...
That's not...
...nailed down.

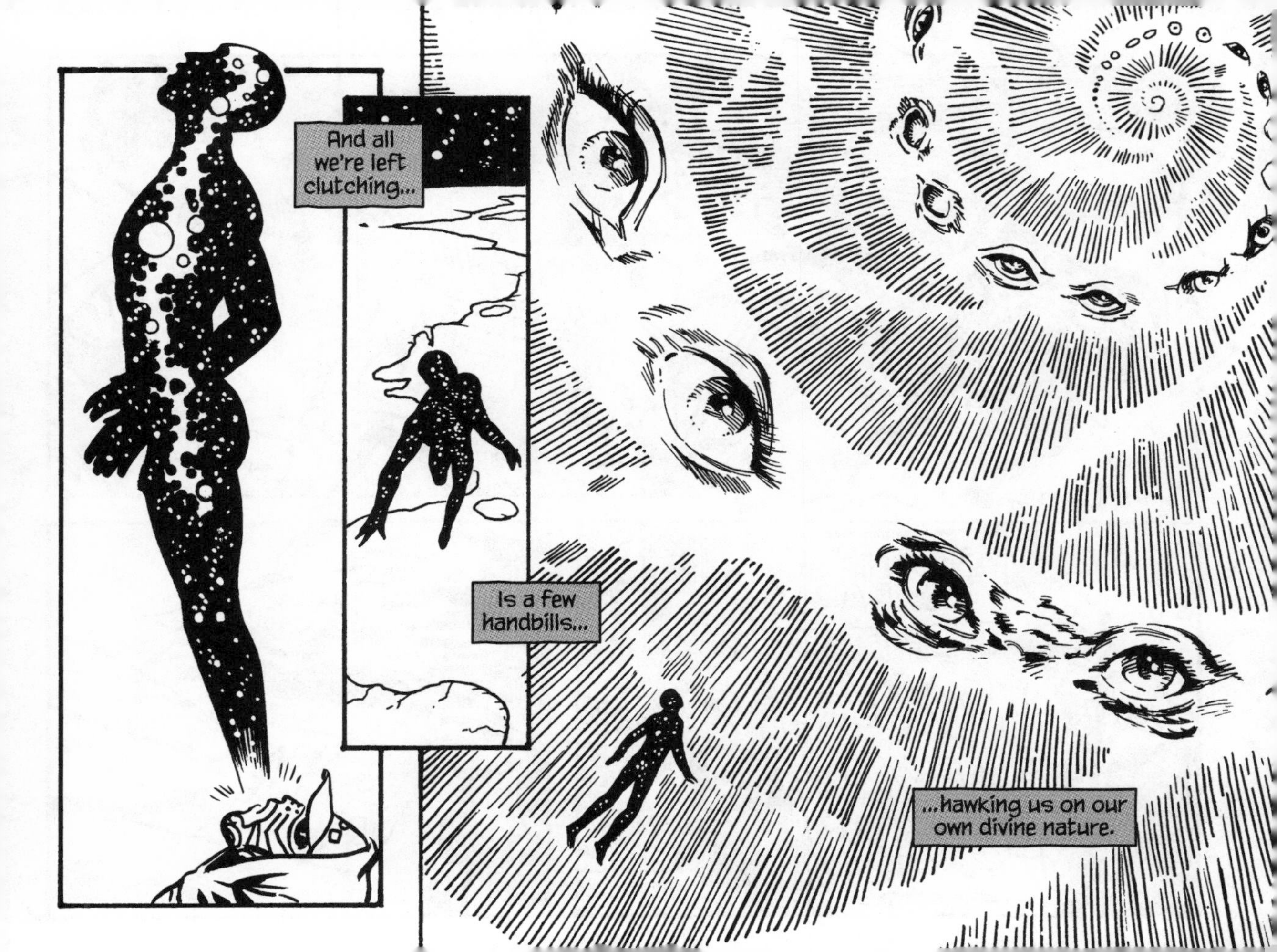

And all we're left clutching...
Is a few handbills...
...hawking us on our own divine nature.

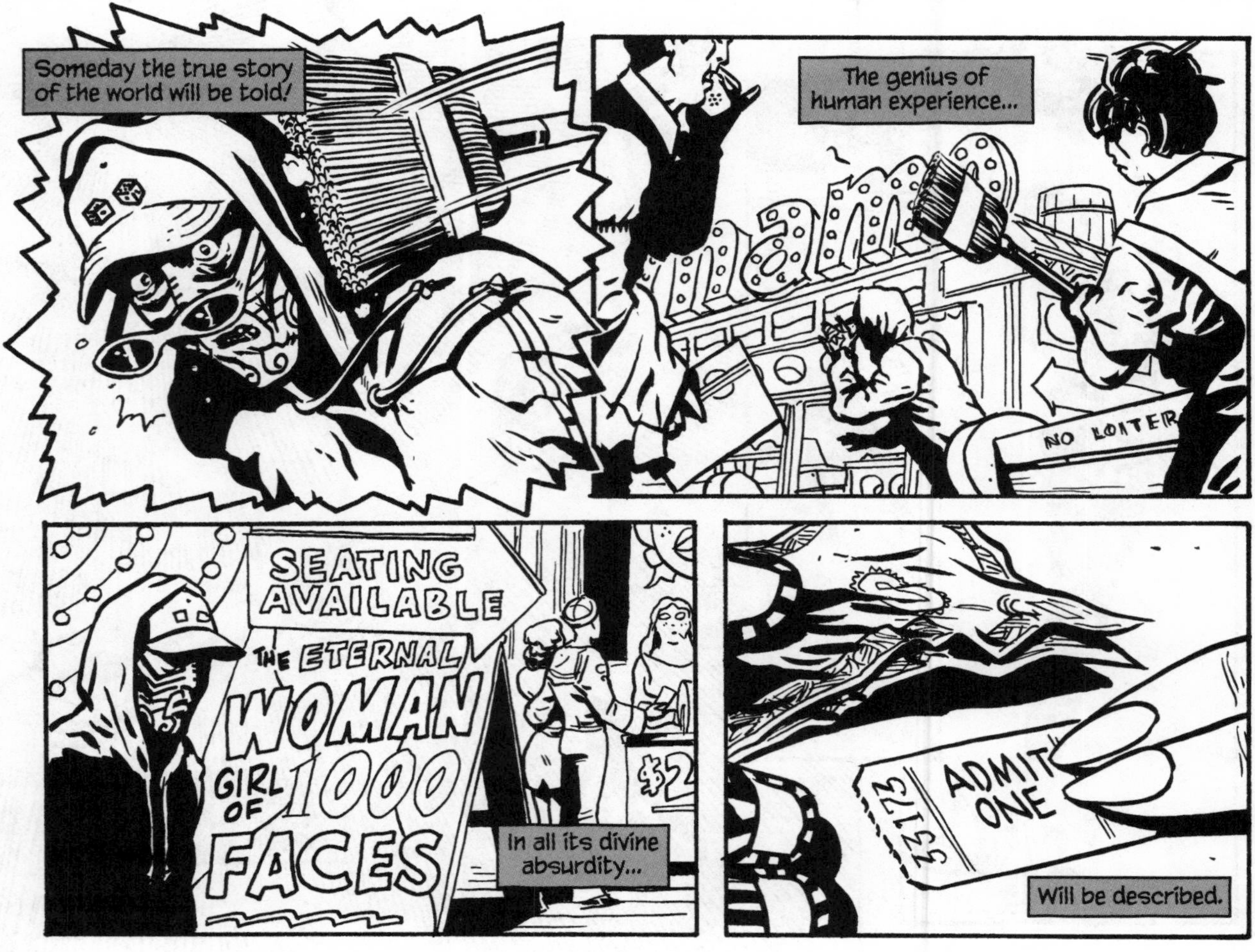
Someday the true story of the world will be told!
The genius of human experience...
NO LOITER
SEATING AVAILABLE
THE ETERNAL WOMAN
GIRL OF 1000 FACES
$2
In all its divine absurdity...
ADMIT ONE
Will be described.

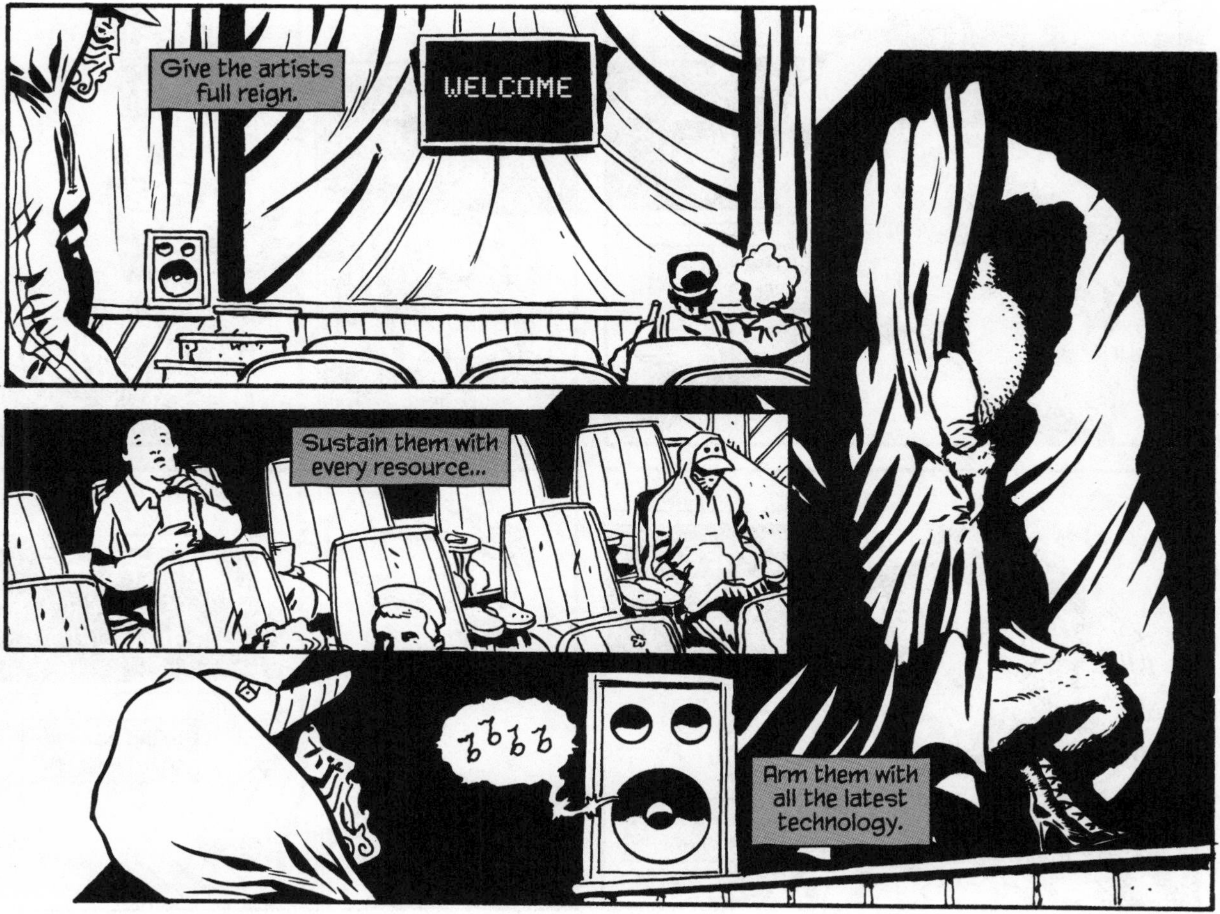
Give the artists full reign.
WELCOME
Sustain them with every resource...
ZZZZ
Arm them with all the latest technology.

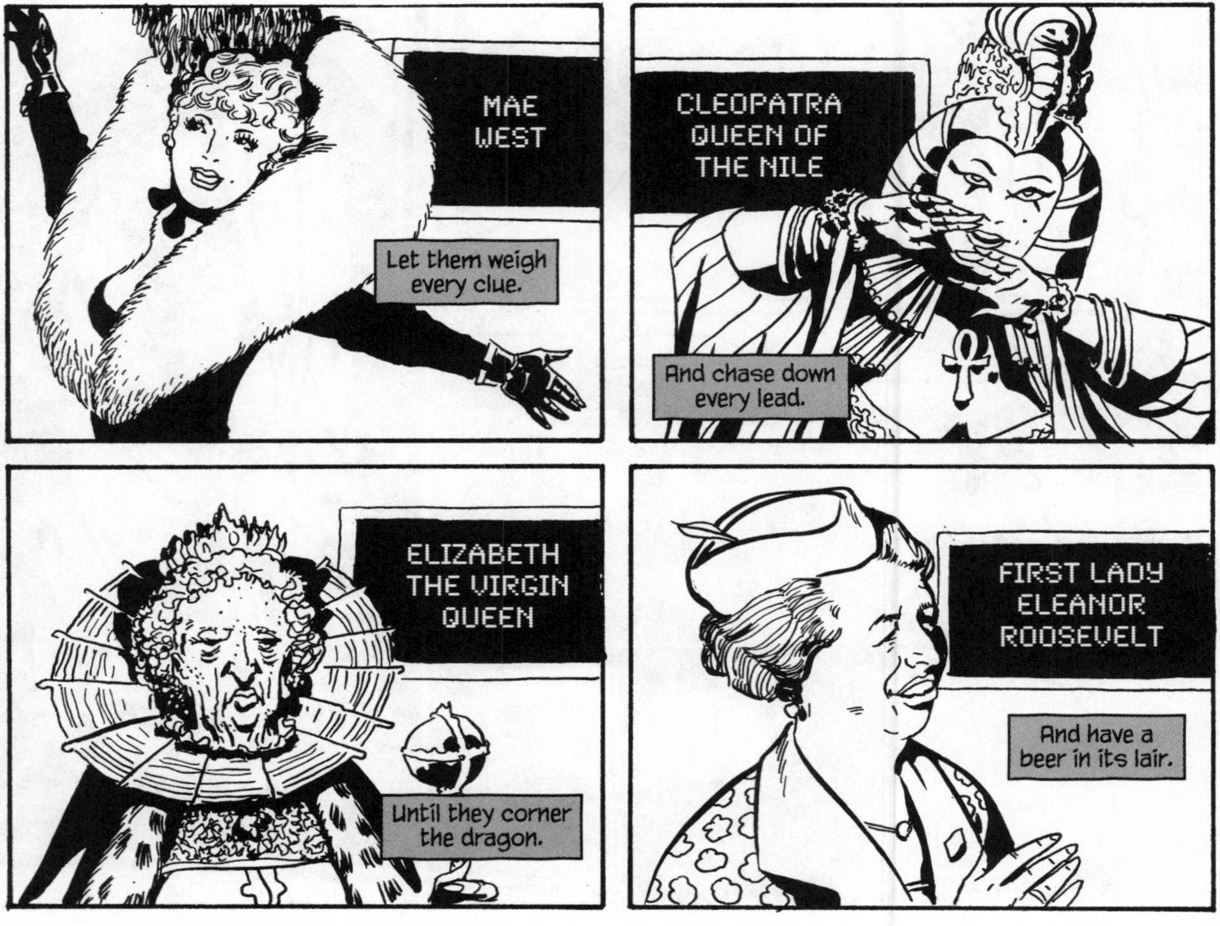
MAE WEST
Let them weigh every clue.
CLEOPATRA QUEEN OF THE NILE
And chase down every lead.
ELIZABETH THE VIRGIN QUEEN
Until they corner the dragon.
FIRST LADY ELEANOR ROOSEVELT
And have a beer in its lair.

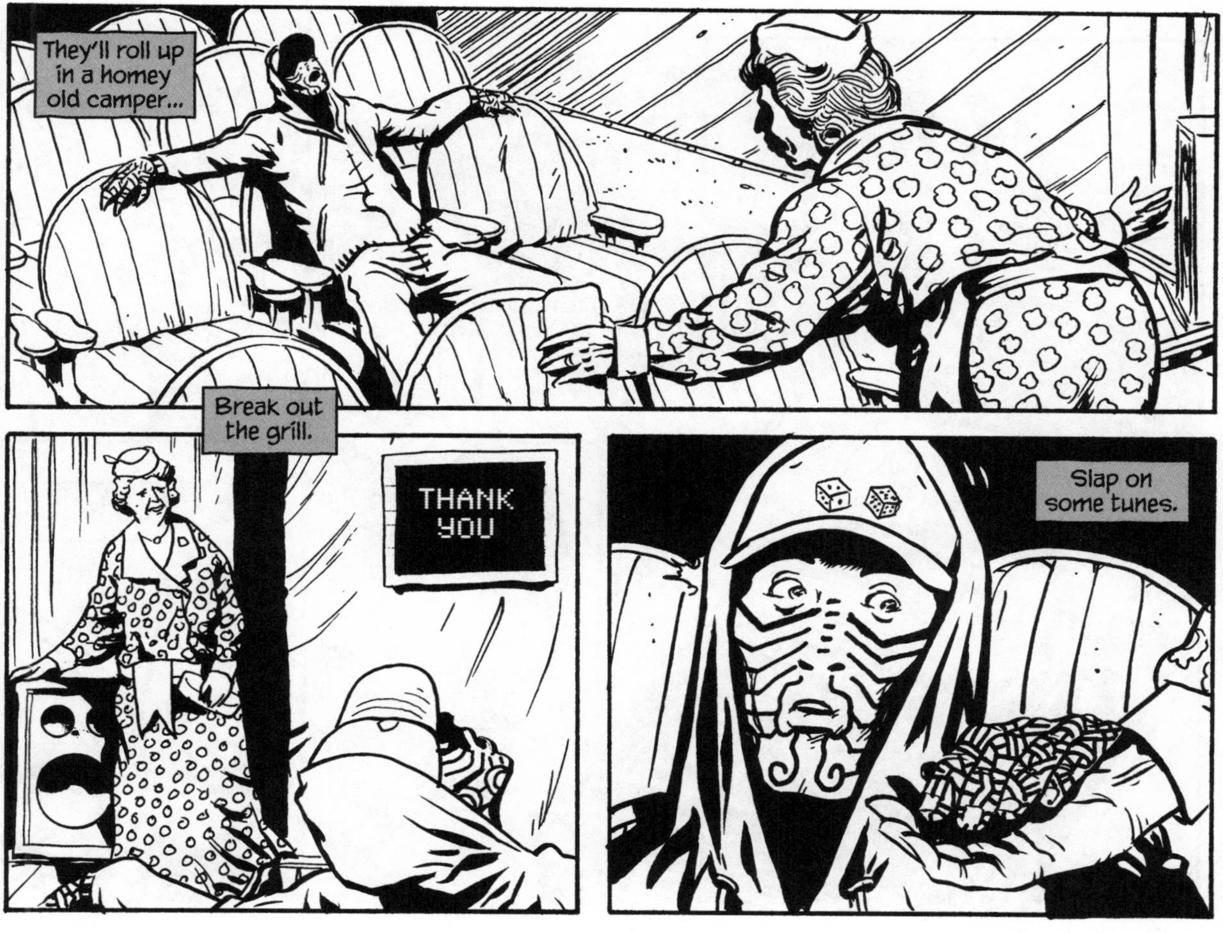
They'll roll up in a homey old camper...
Break out the grill.
THANK YOU
Slap on some tunes.

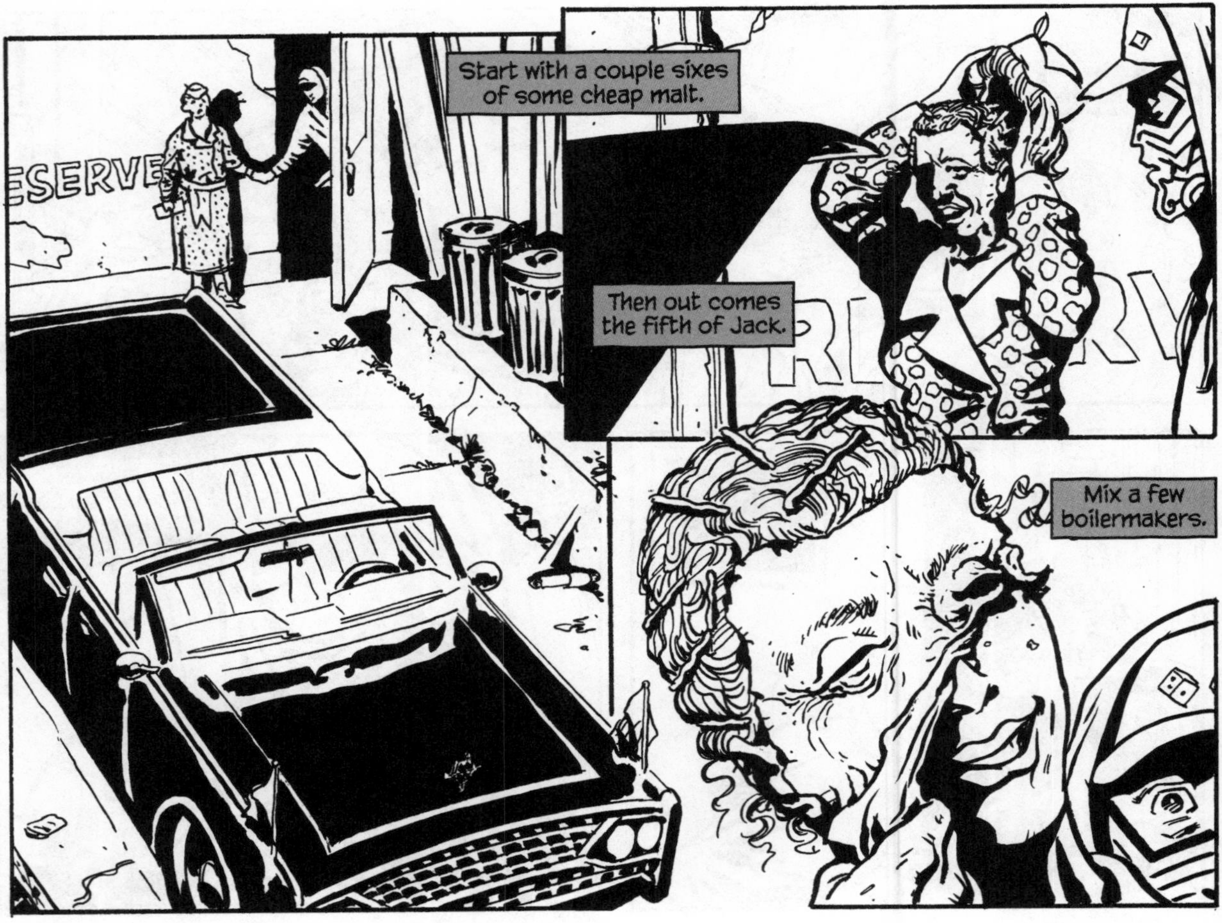
Start with a couple sixes of some cheap malt.
Then out comes the fifth of Jack.
Mix a few boilermakers.

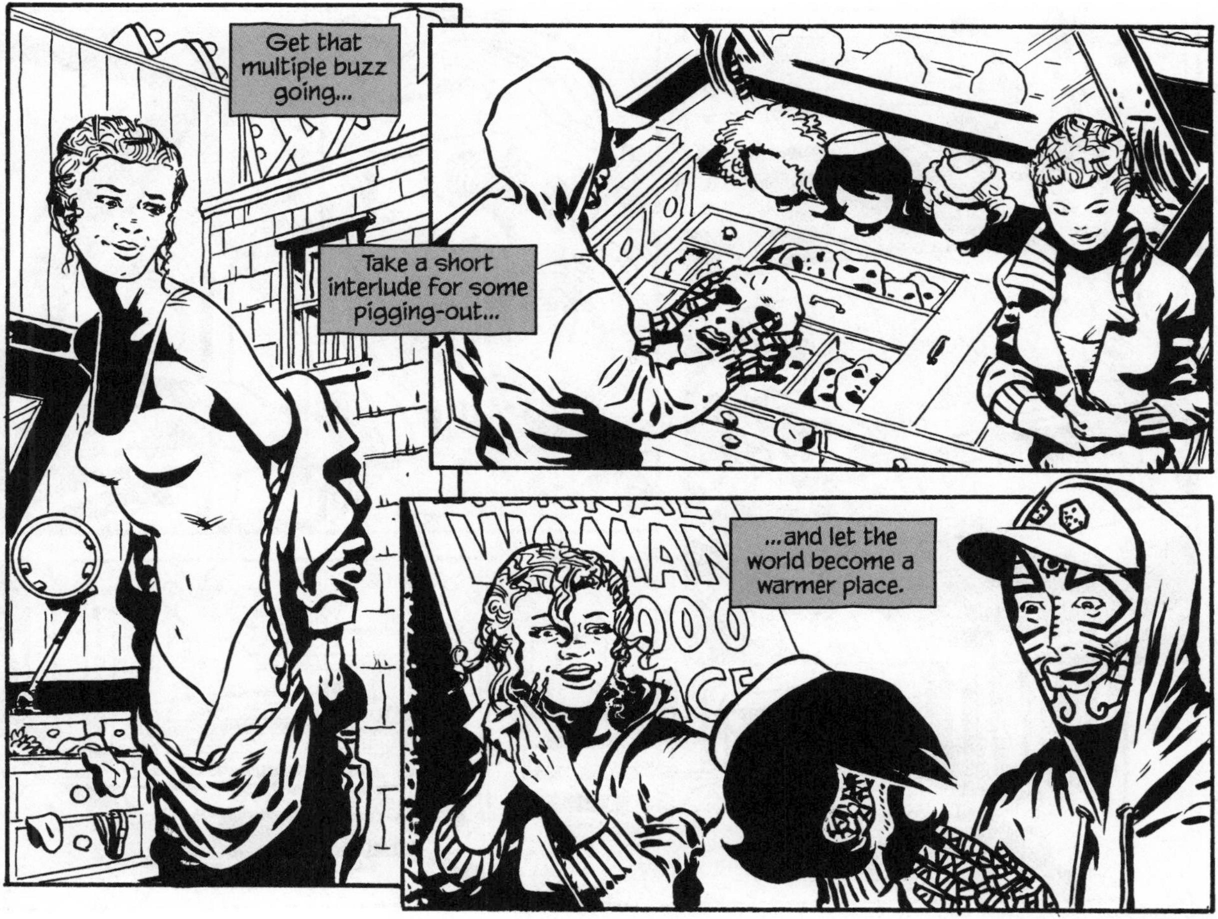
Get that multiple buzz going...
Take a short interlude for some pigging-out...
...and let the world become a warmer place.

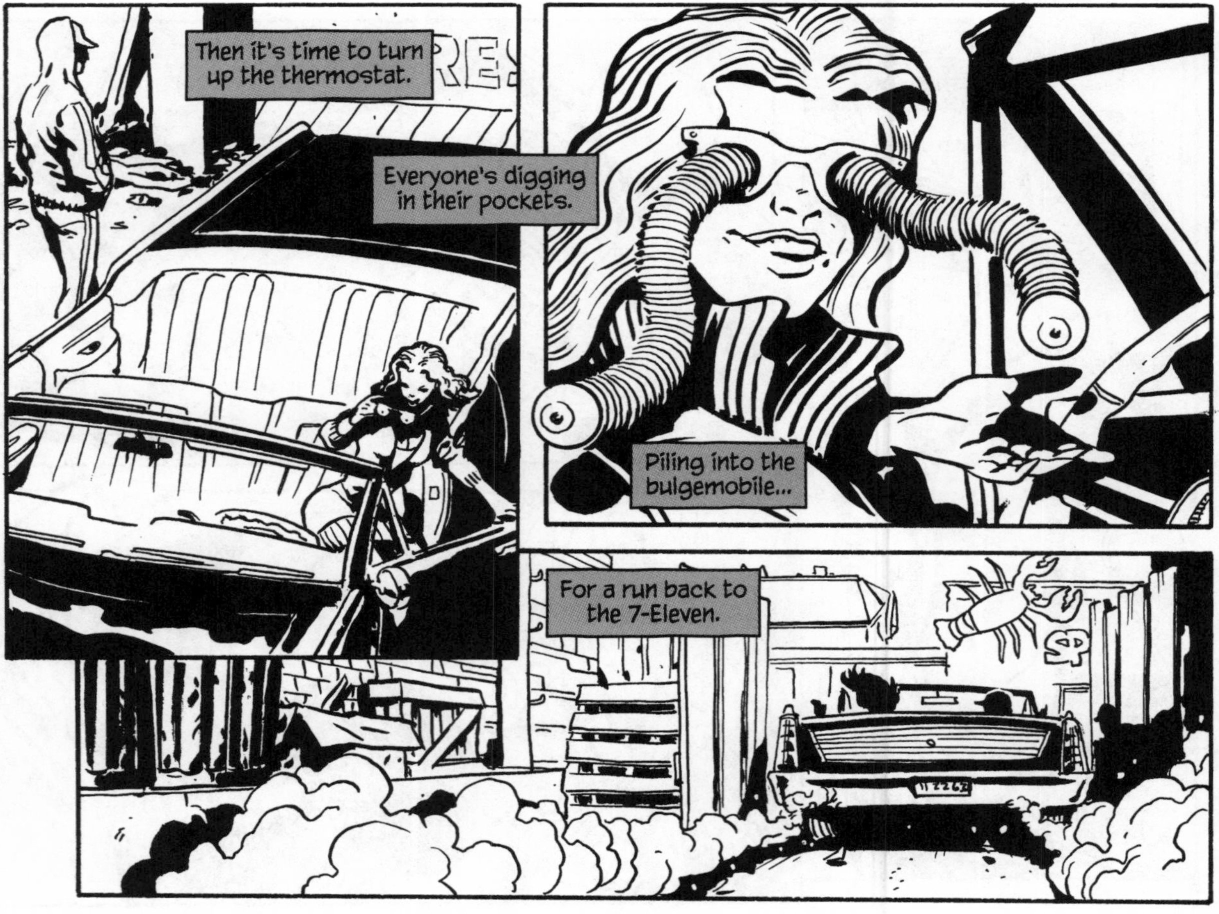
Then it's time to turn up the thermostat.
Everyone's digging in their pockets.
Piling into the bulgemobile...
For a run back to the 7-Eleven.

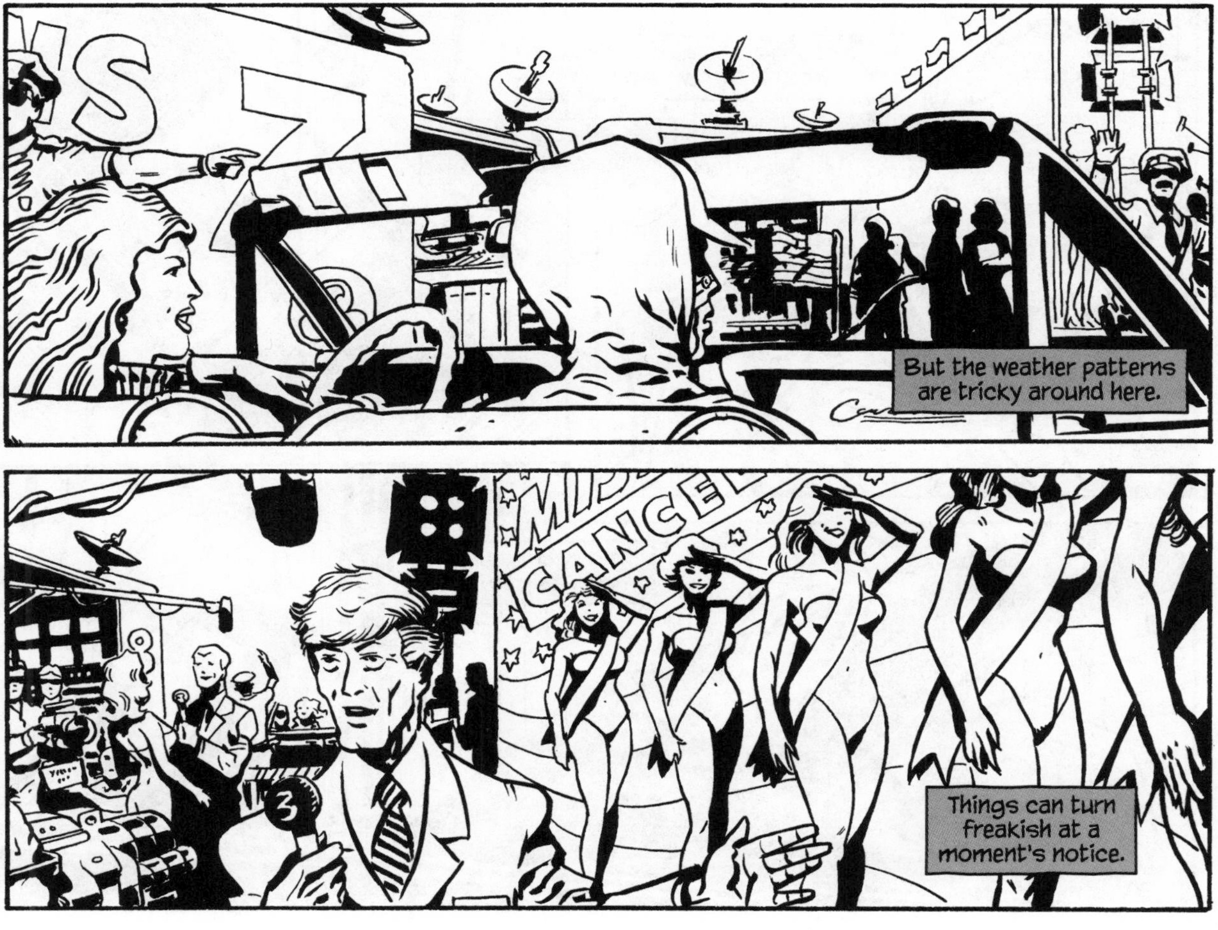
But the weather patterns are tricky around here.
Things can turn freakish at a moment's notice.

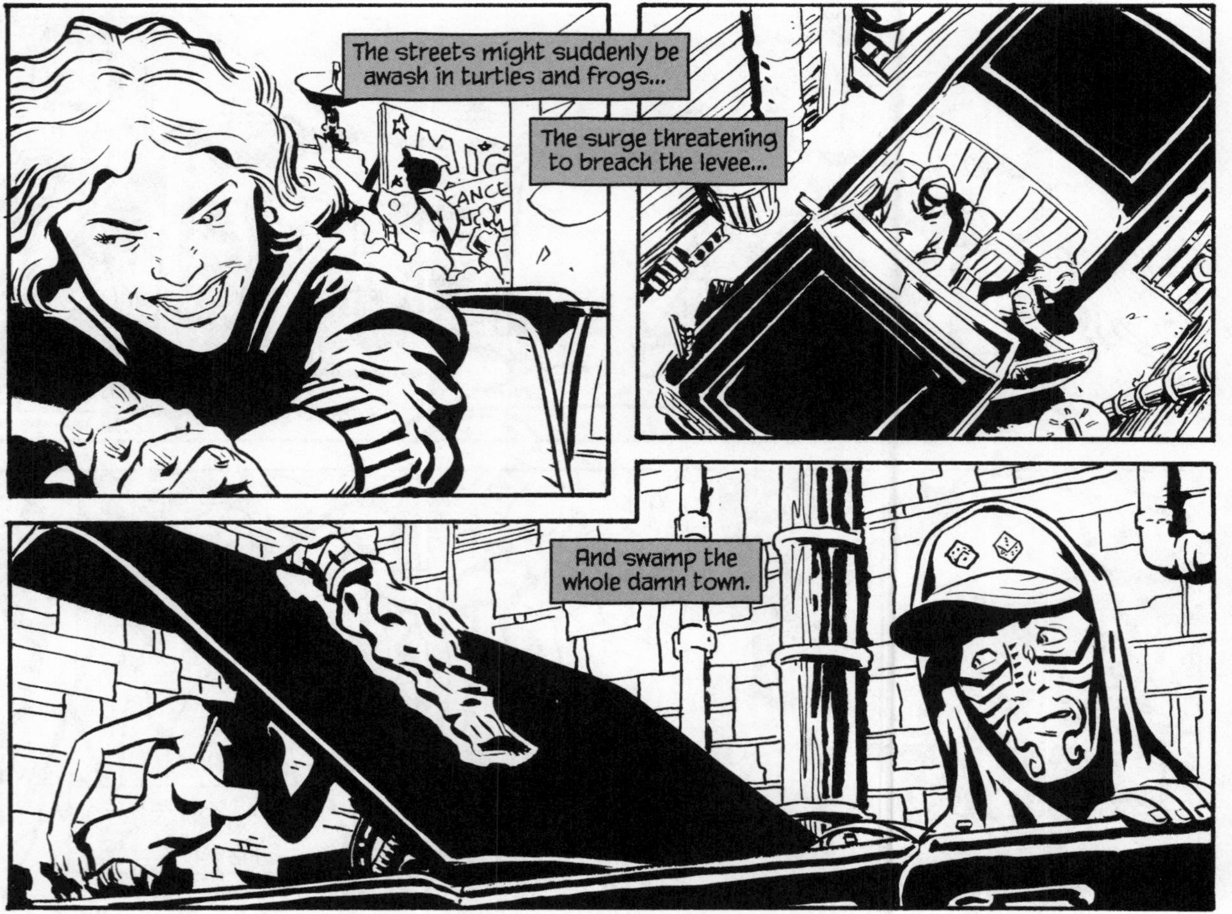
The streets might suddenly be awash in turtles and frogs...
The surge threatening to breach the levee...
And swamp the whole damn town.

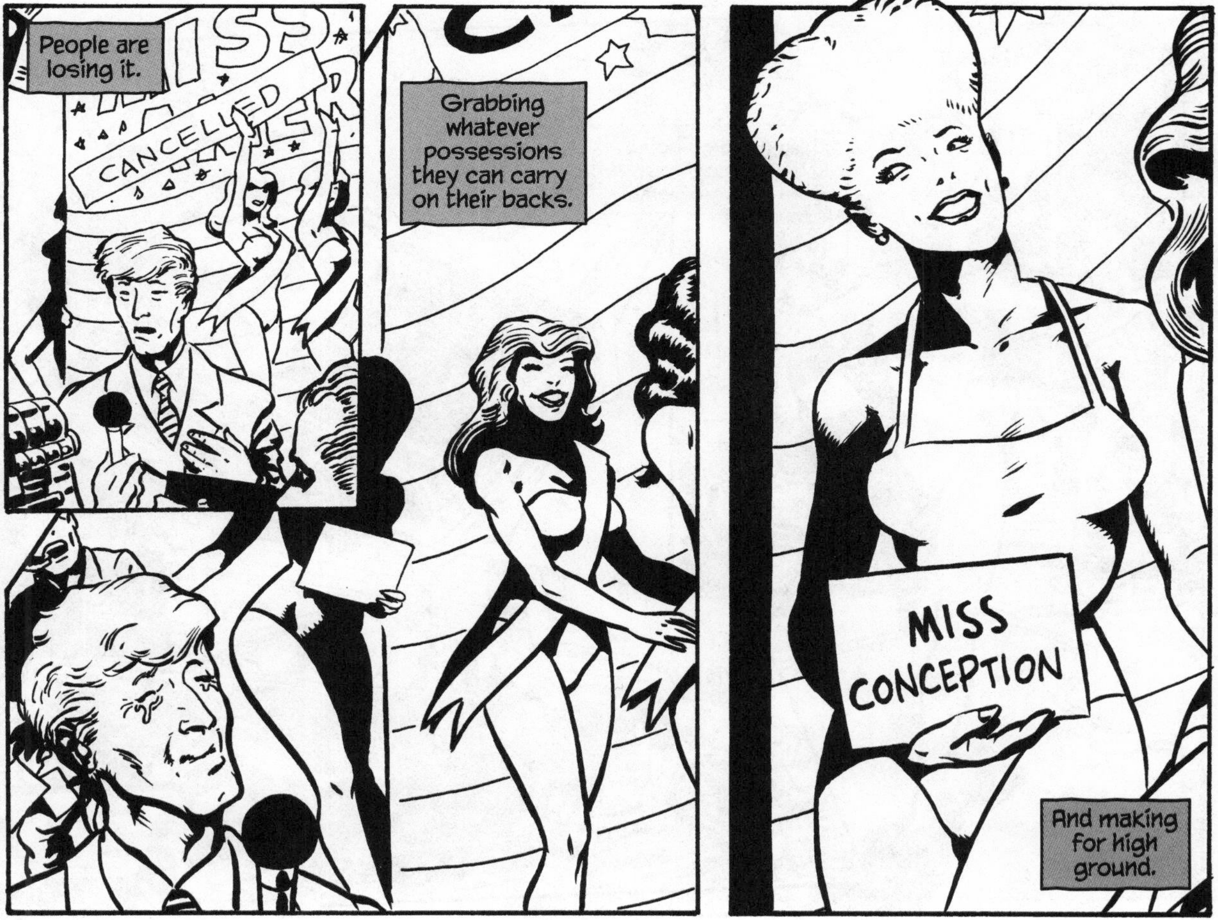
People are losing it.
CANCELLED
Grabbing whatever possessions they can carry on their backs.
MISS CONCEPTION
And making for high ground.

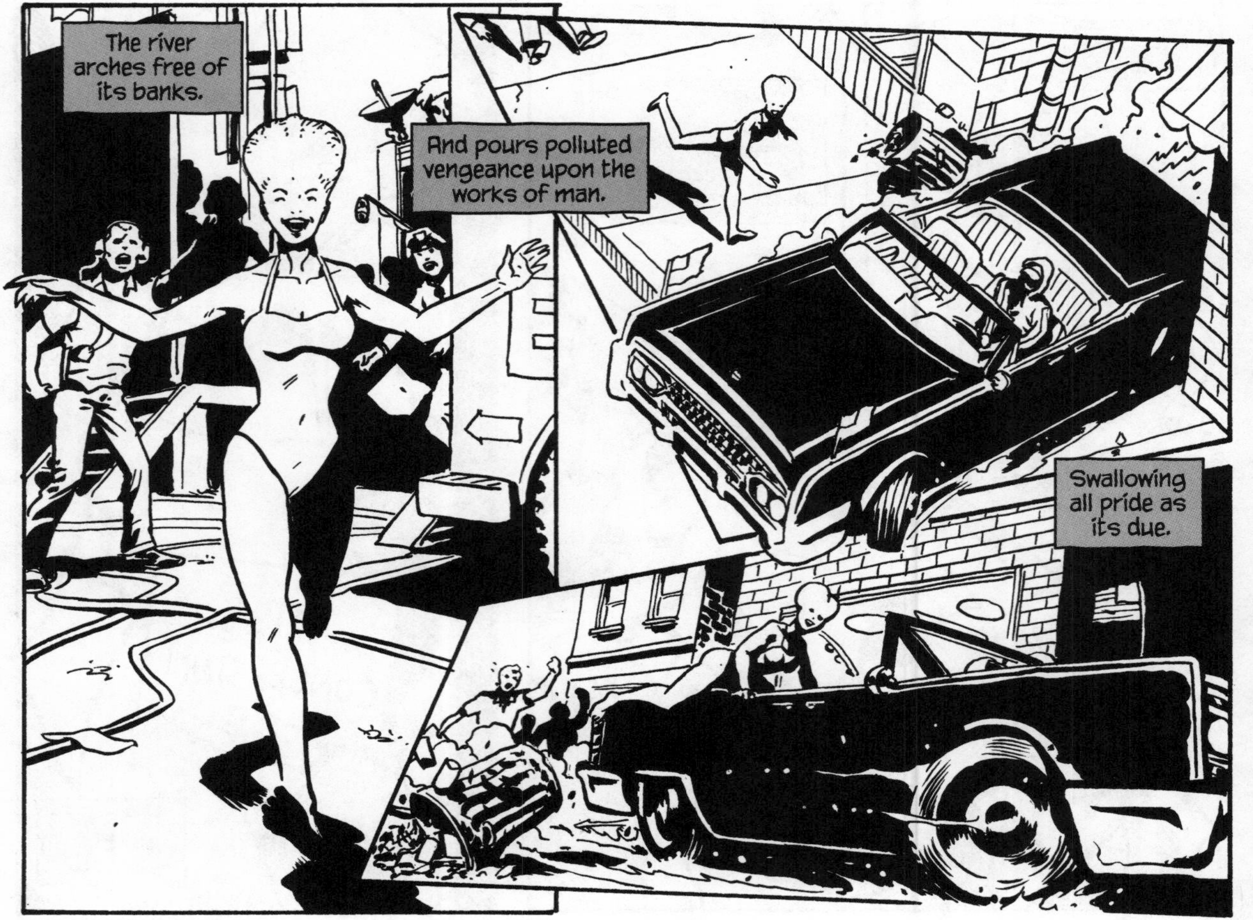
The river arches free of its banks.
And pours polluted vengeance upon the works of man.
Swallowing all pride as its due.

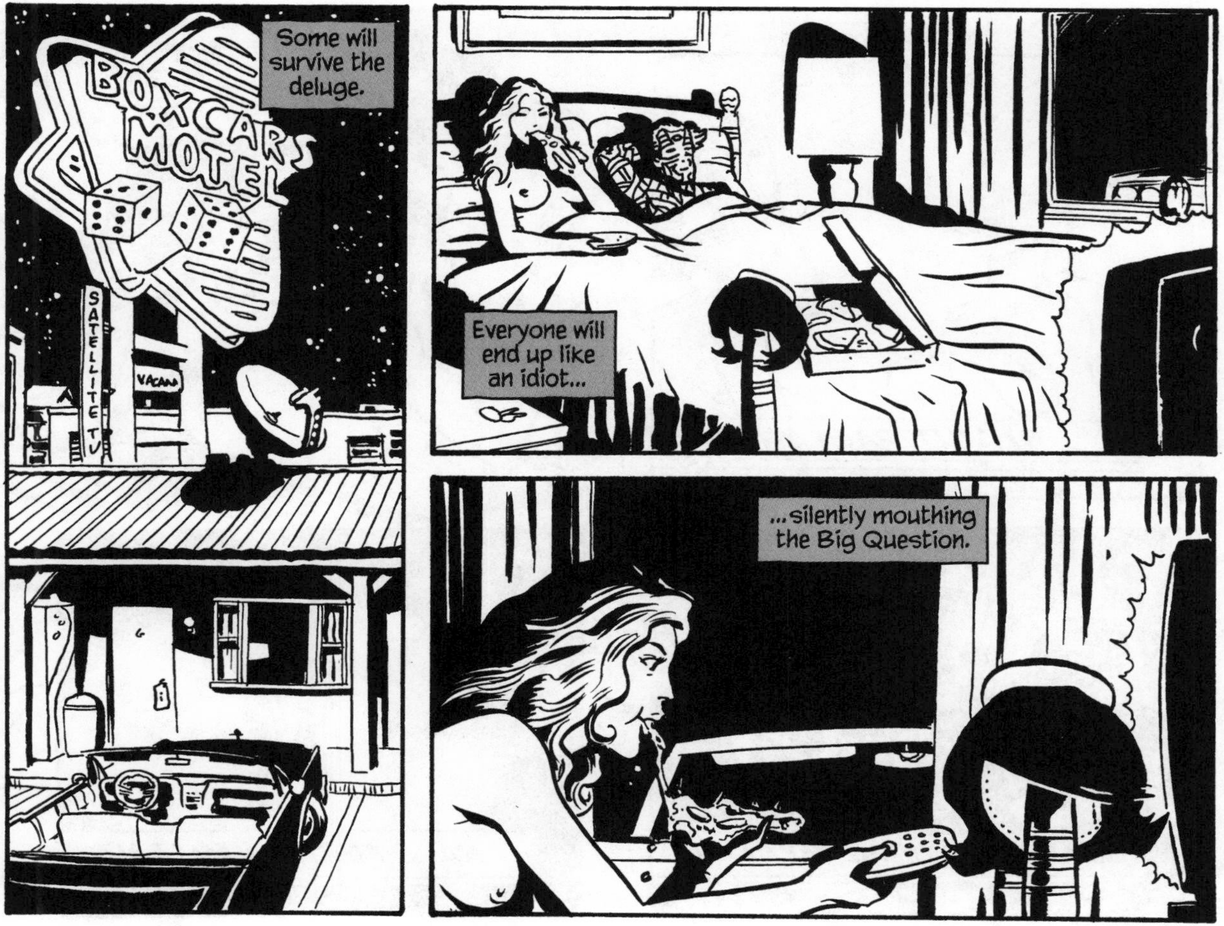
Some will survive the deluge.
BOXCARS MOTEL
SATELLITE TV
Everyone will end up like an idiot...
...silently mouthing the Big Question.

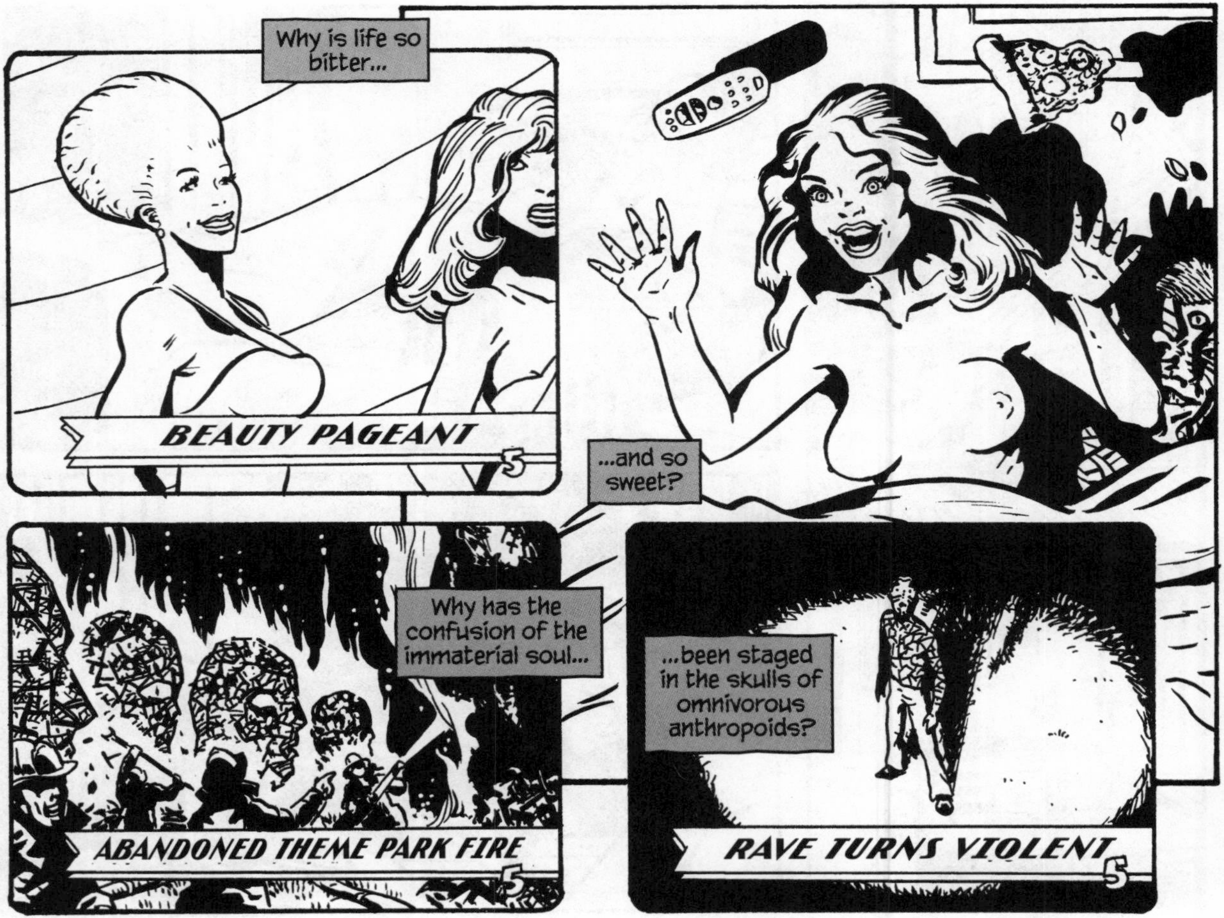

Why is life so bitter...
BEAUTY PAGEANT
5
...and so sweet?
Why has the confusion of the immaterial soul...
ABANDONED THEME PARK FIRE
5
...been staged in the skulls of omnivorous anthropoids?
RAVE TURNS VIOLENT
5

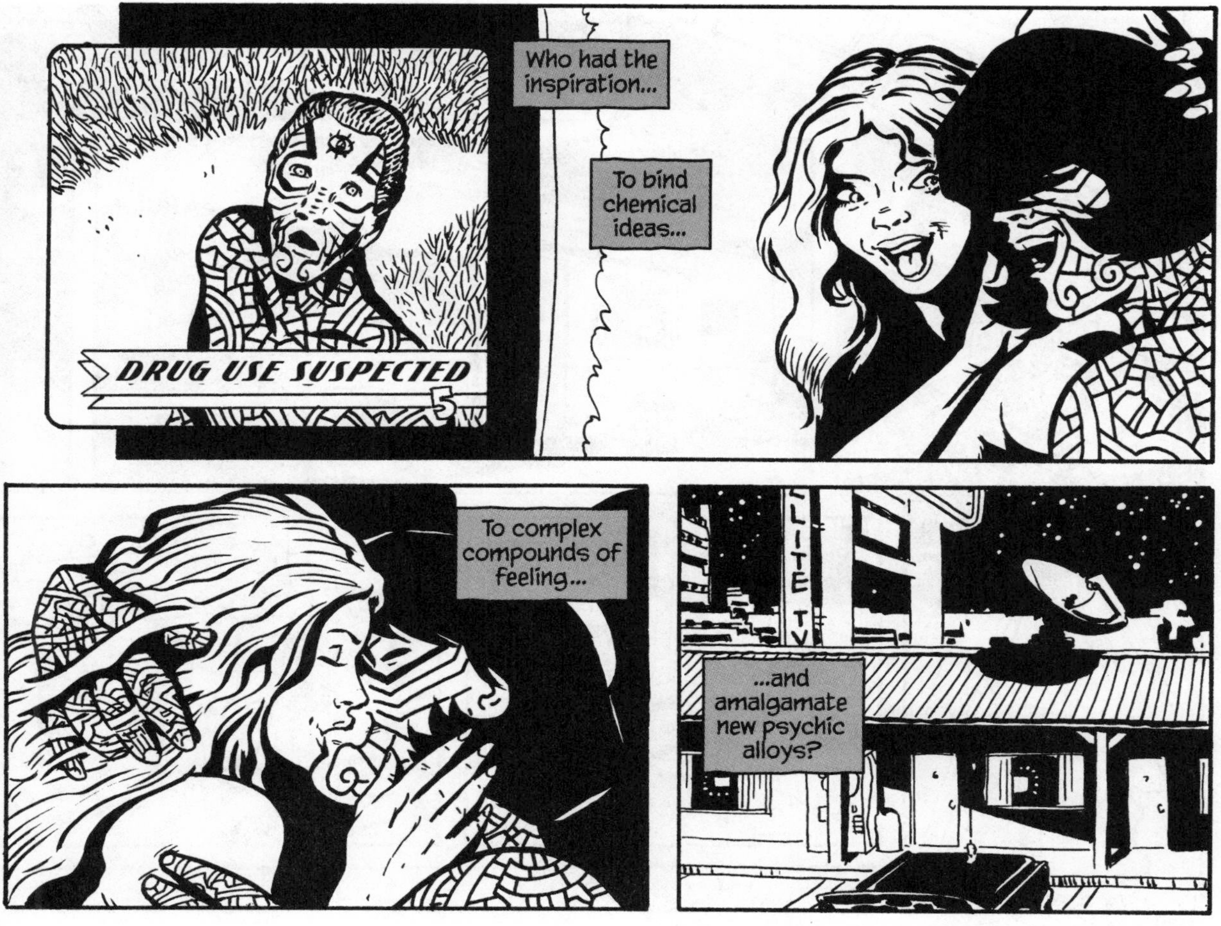

DRUG USE SUSPECTED
5
Who had the inspiration...
To bind chemical ideas...
To complex compounds of feeling...
LLITE TV
...and amalgamate new psychic alloys?

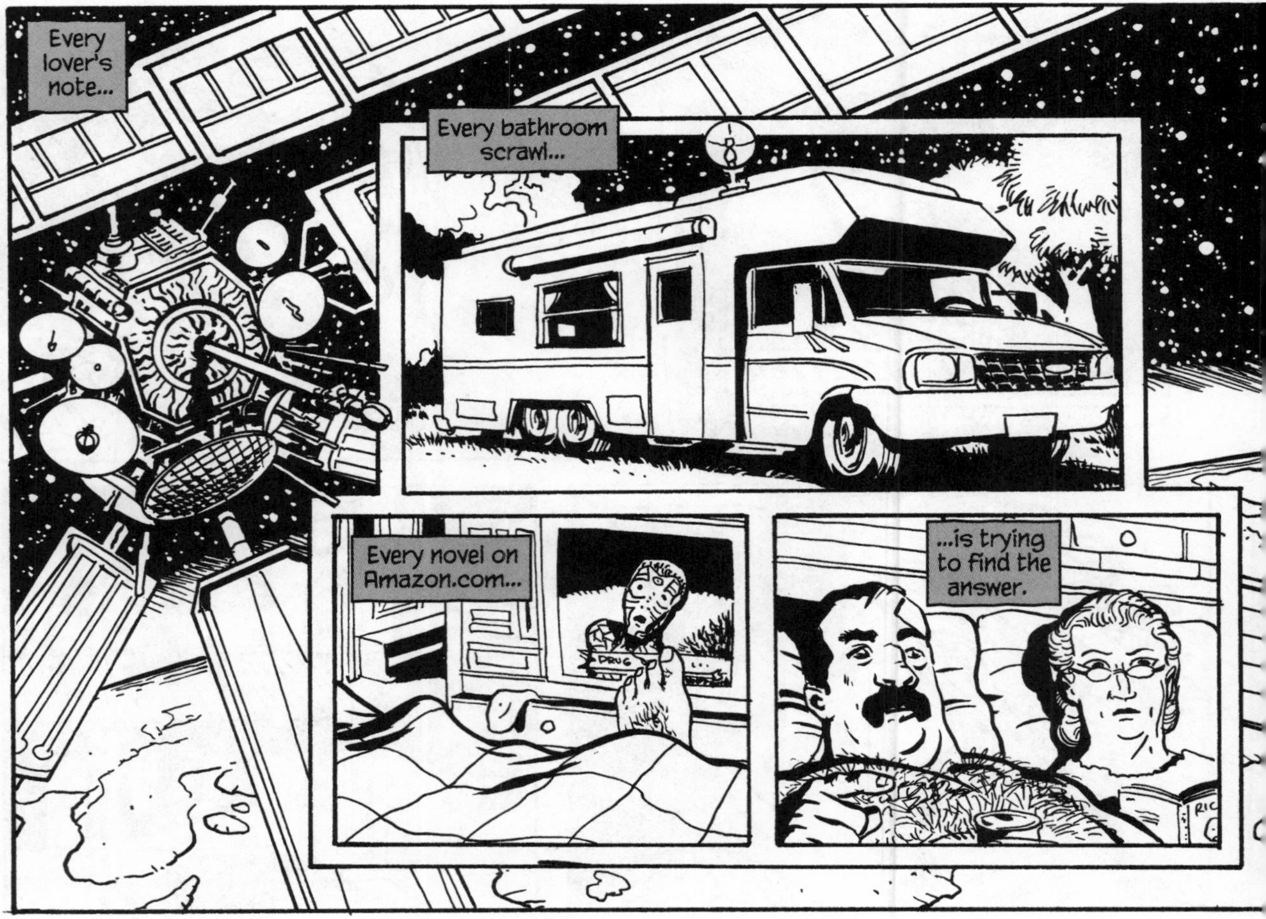
Every lover's note...
Every bathroom scrawl...
Every novel on Amazon.com...
DRUG
...is trying to find the answer.

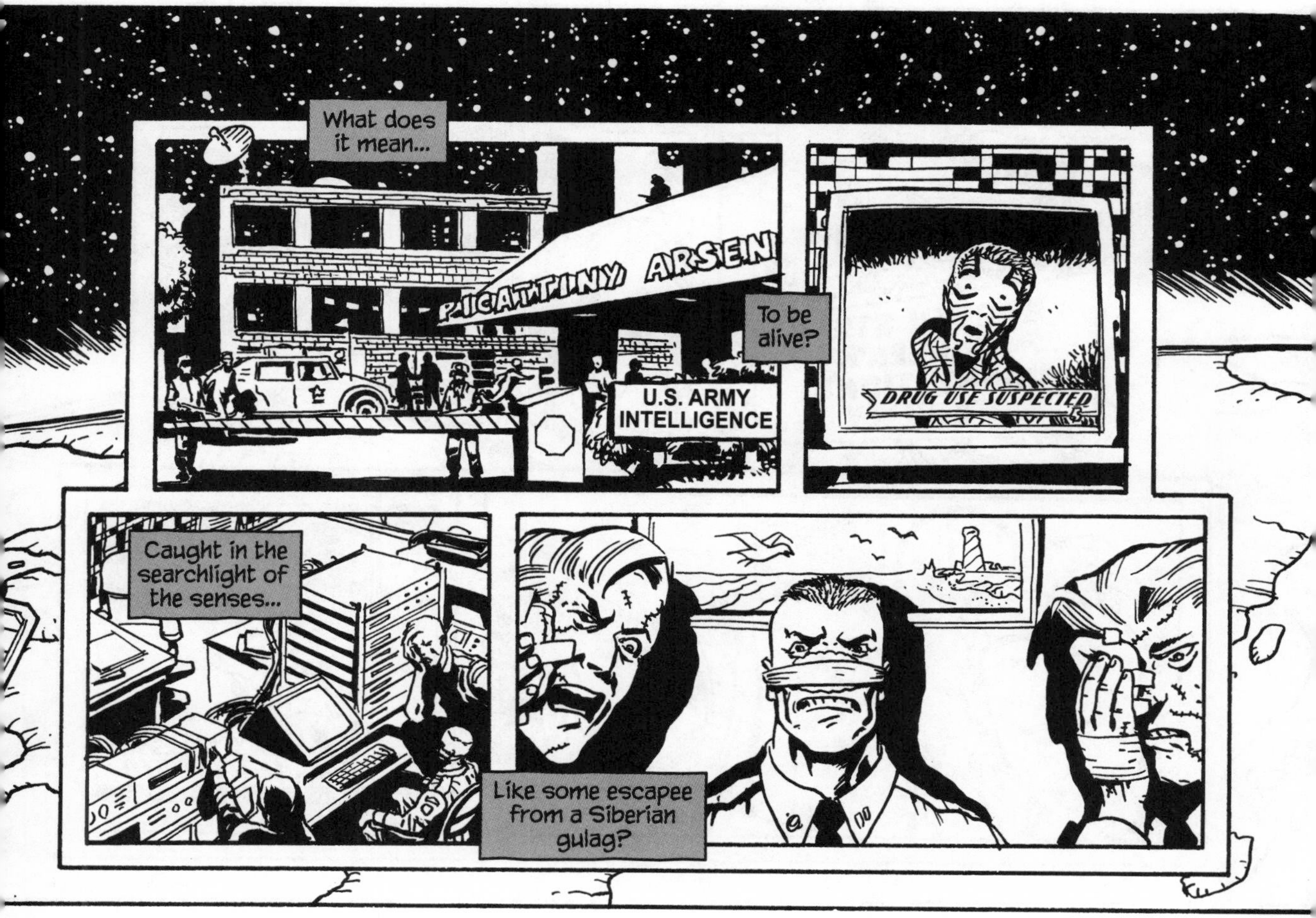

What does it mean...
PICATINNY ARSEN
U.S. ARMY INTELLIGENCE
To be alive?
DRUG USE SUSPECTED
Caught in the searchlight of the senses...
Like some escapee from a Siberian gulag?

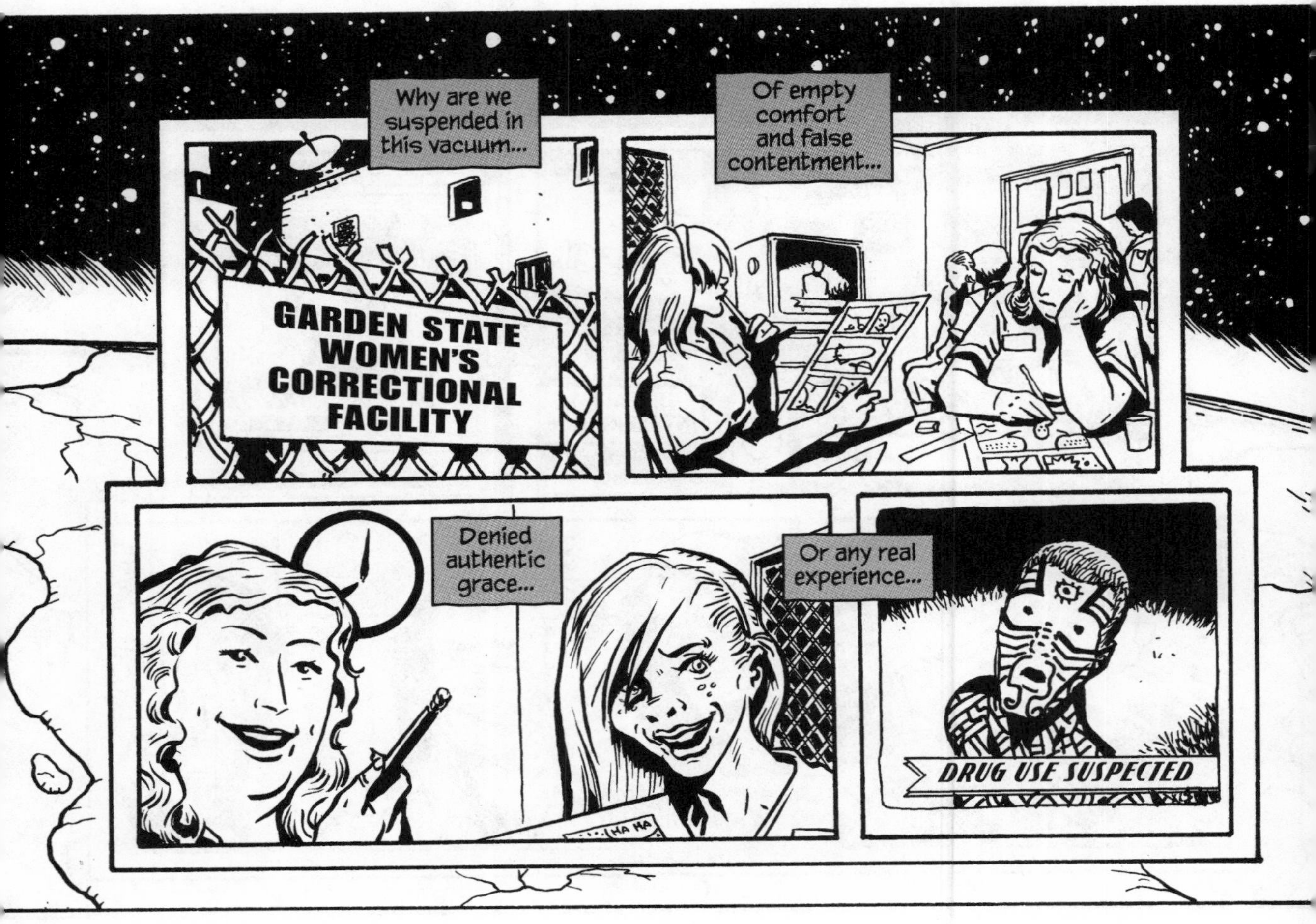
Why are we suspended in this vacuum...
GARDEN STATE WOMEN'S CORRECTIONAL FACILITY
Of empty comfort and false contentment...
Denied authentic grace...
Or any real experience...
DRUG USE SUSPECTED

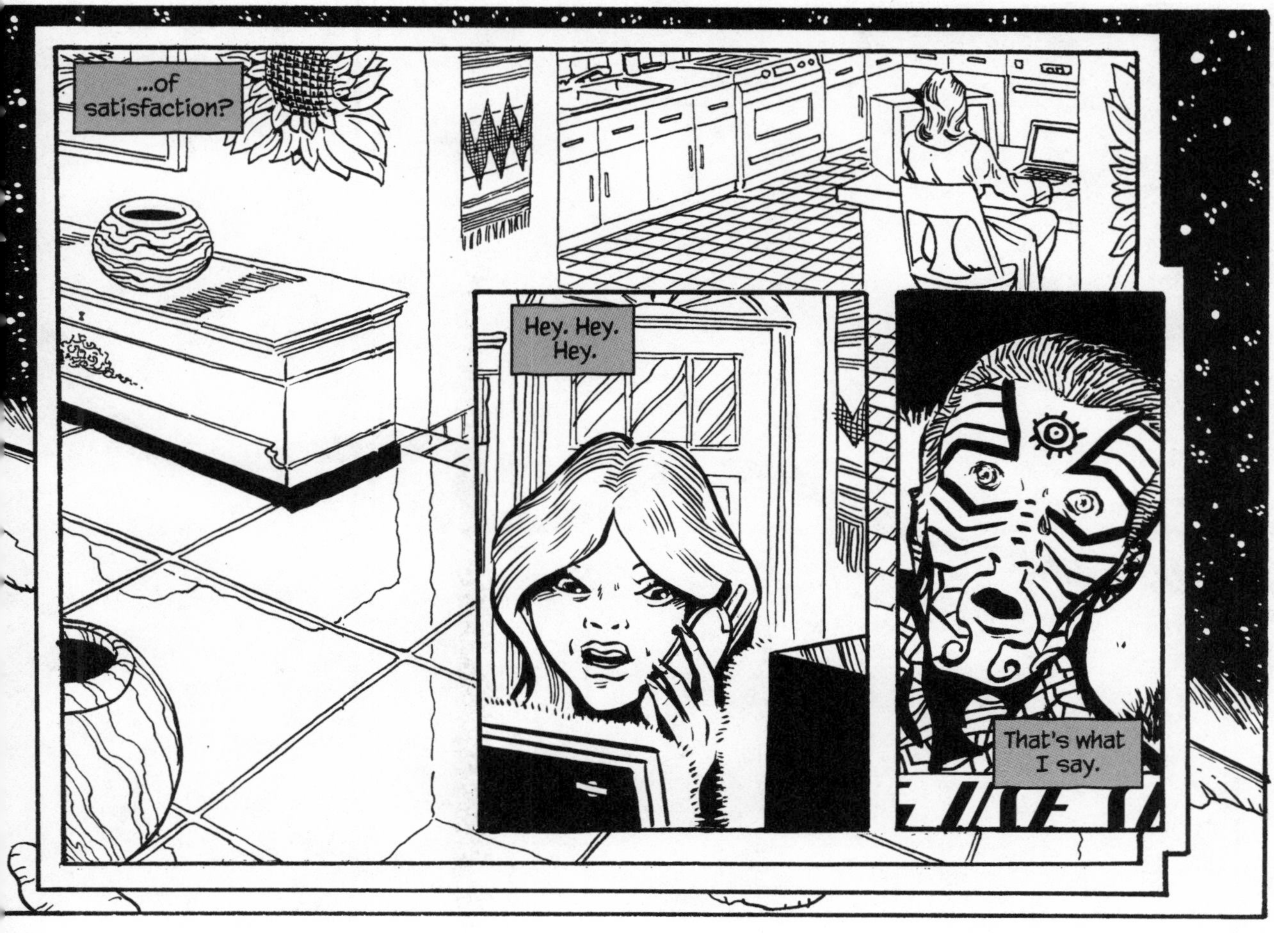
...of satisfaction?
Hey. Hey. Hey.
That's what I say.

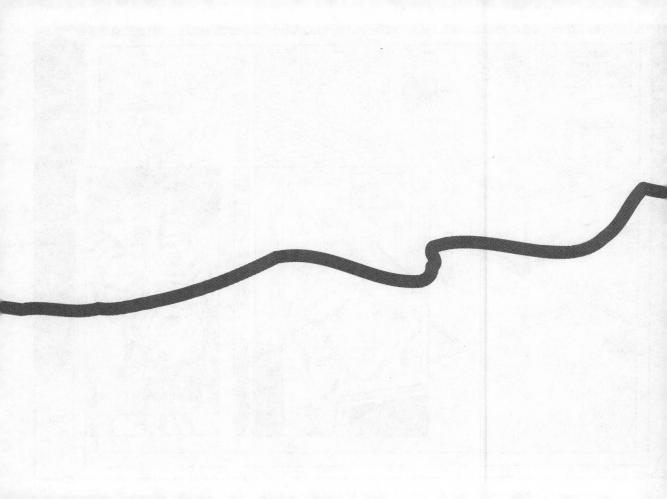

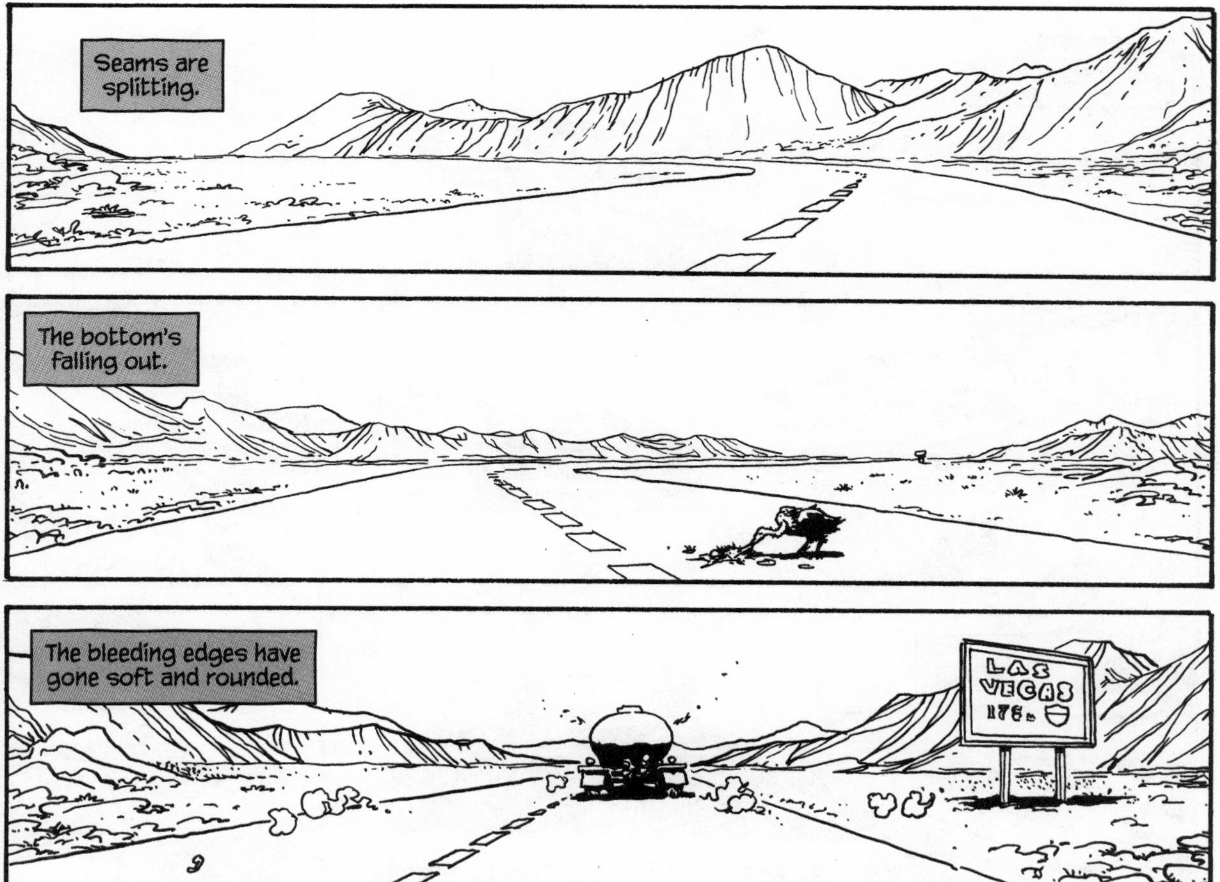
Seams are splitting.
The bottom's falling out.
The bleeding edges have gone soft and rounded.
LAS VEGAS

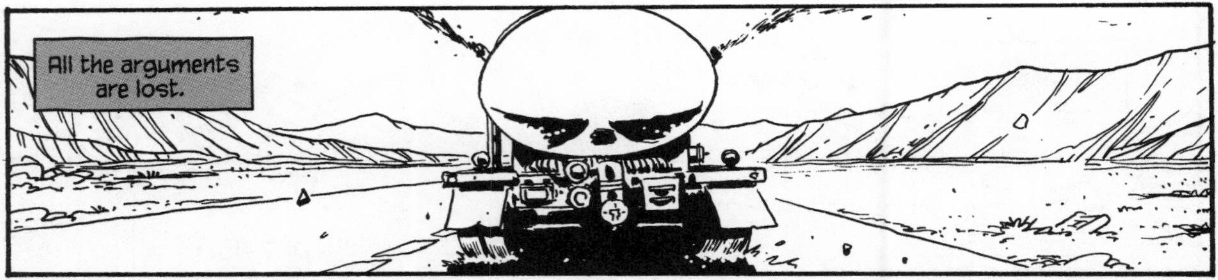
All the arguments are lost.

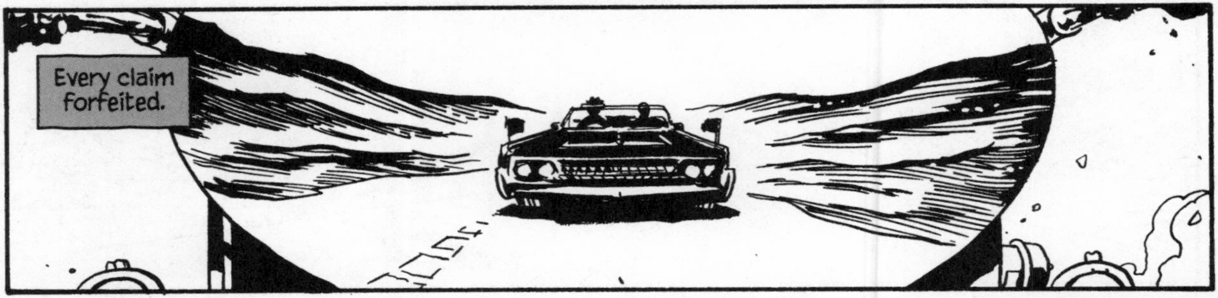
Every claim forfeited.

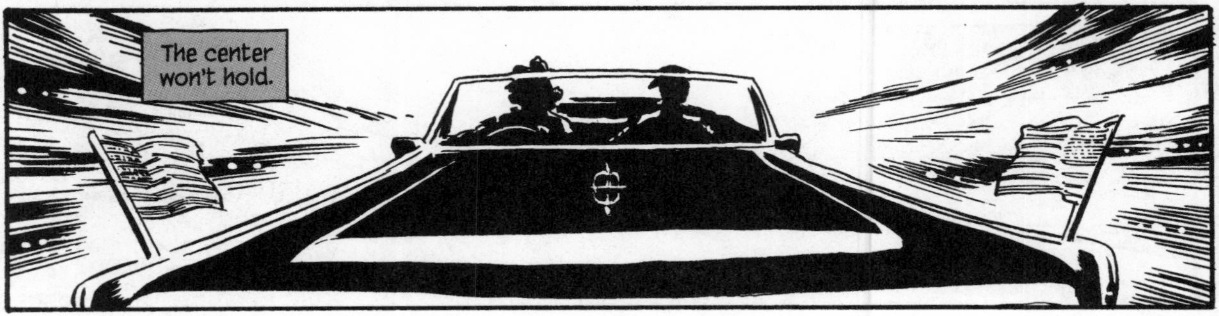
The center won't hold.

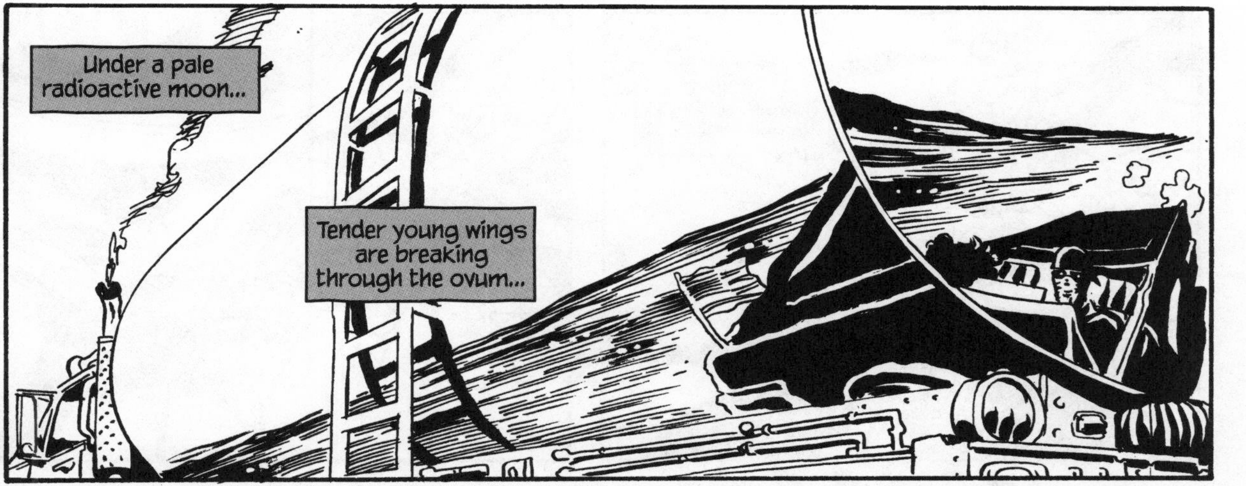
Under a pale radioactive moon...
Tender young wings are breaking through the ovum...

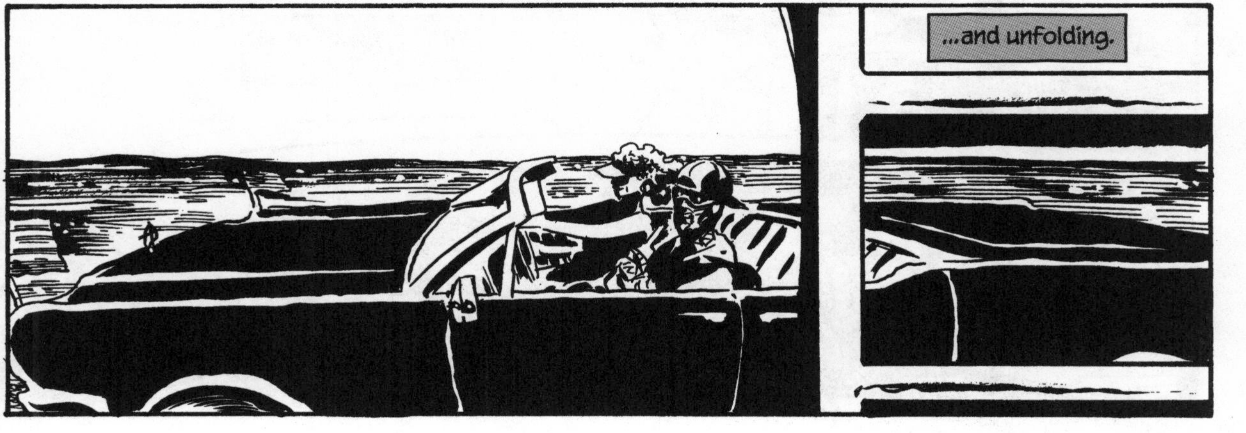
...and unfolding.

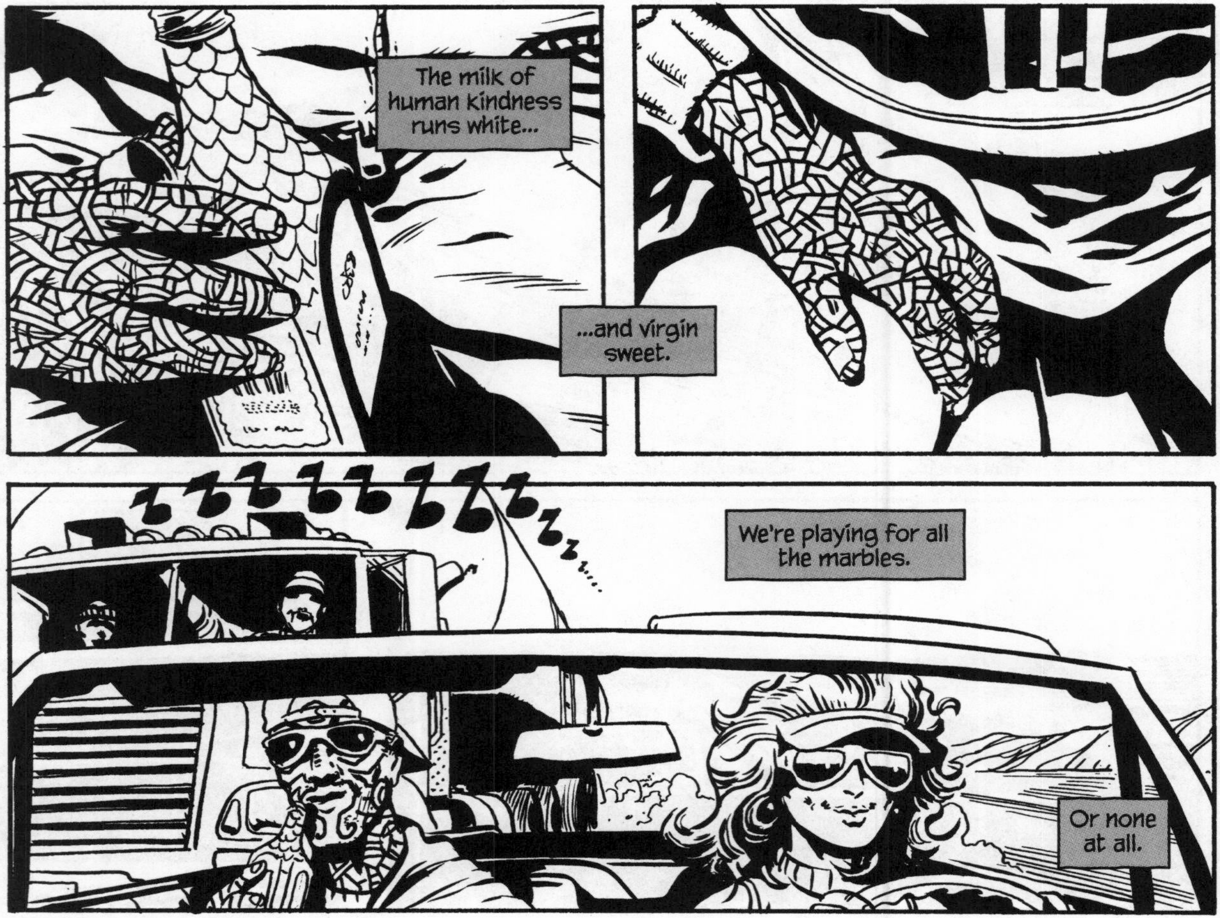
The milk of human kindness runs white...
...and virgin sweet.
ZZZZZZZZZZZZz...
We're playing for all the marbles.
Or none at all.

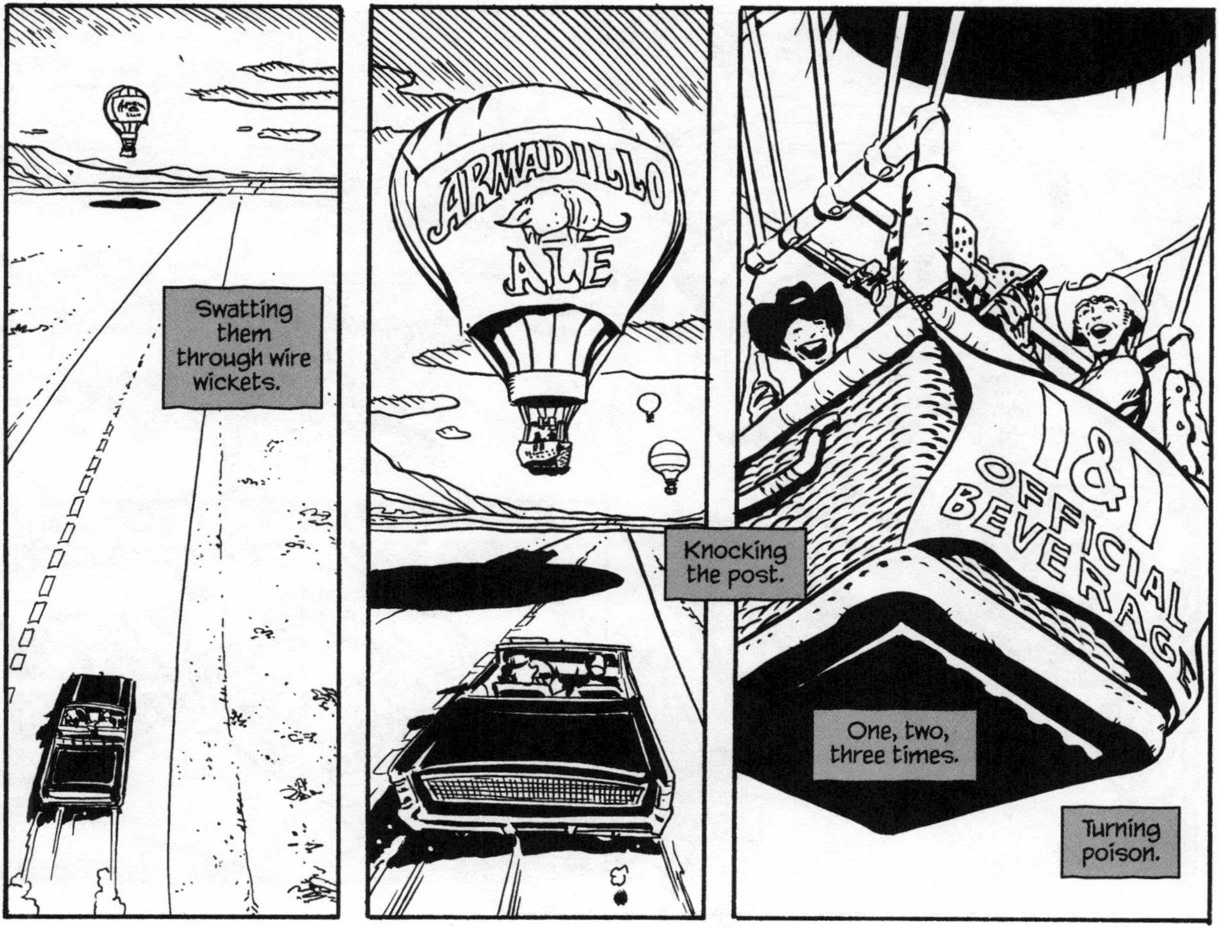
Swatting them through wire wickets.
ARMADILLO
ALE
Knocking the post.
I&D
OFFICIAL BEVERAGE
One, two, three times.
Turning poison.

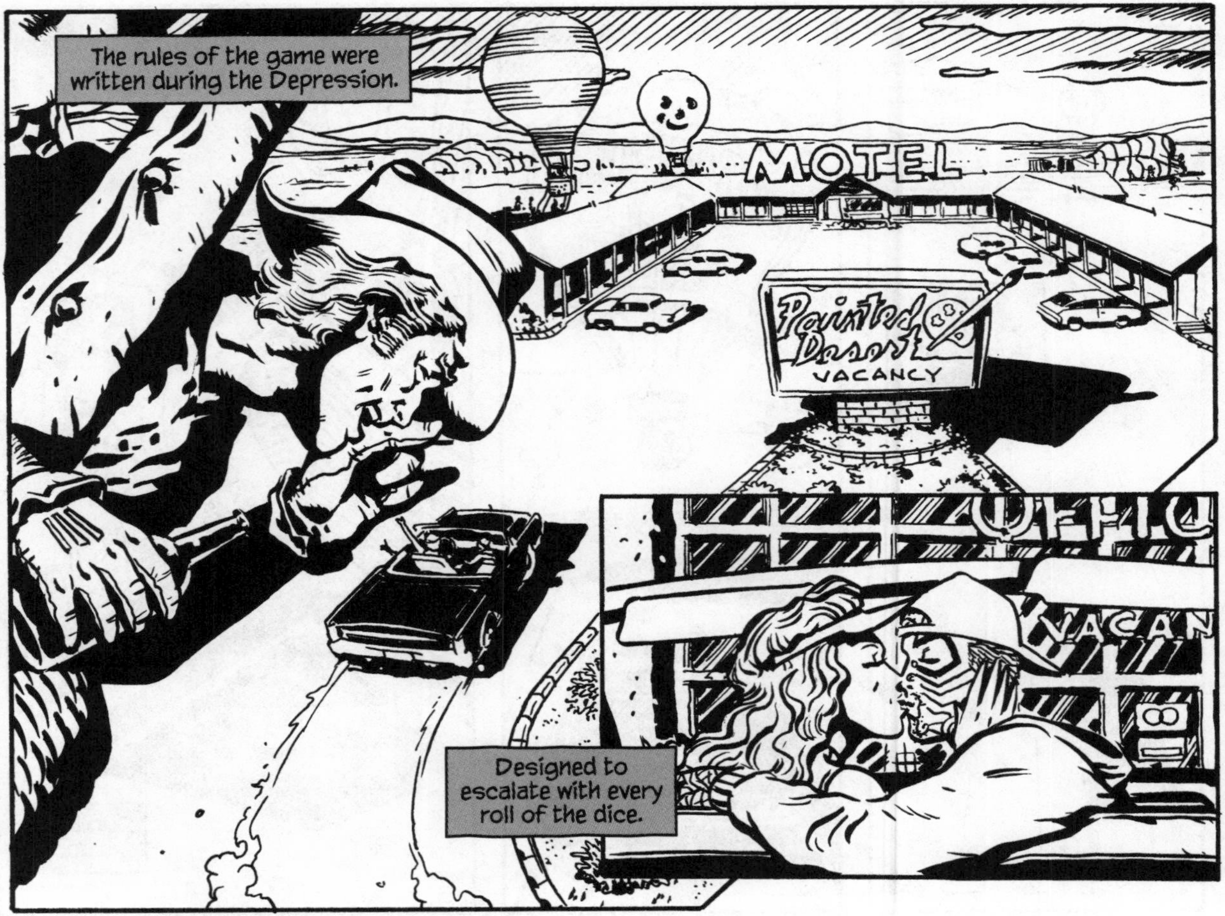

The rules of the game were written during the Depression.
MOTEL
Painted Desert
VACANCY
Designed to escalate with every roll of the dice.

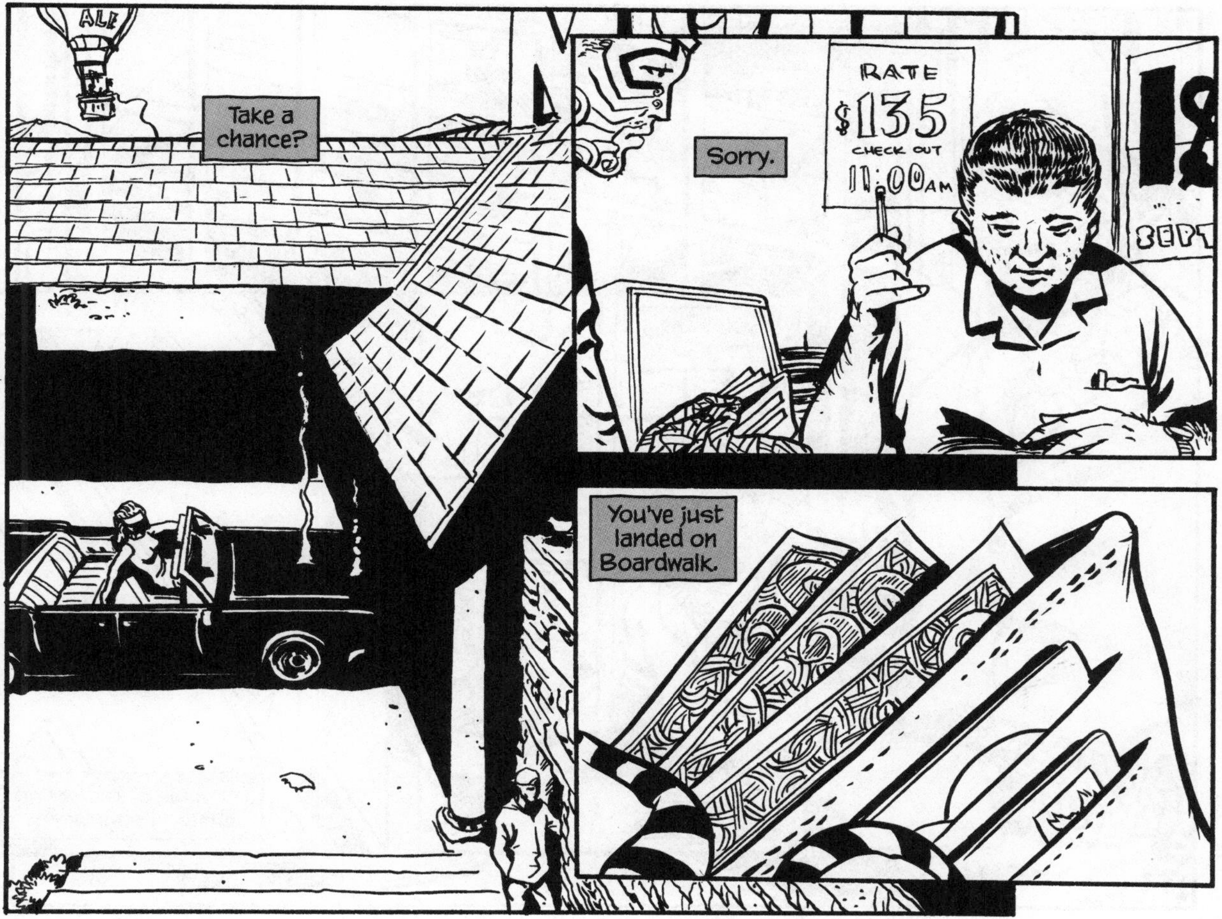

ALE
Take a chance?
Sorry.
RATE
$135
CHECK OUT
11:00AM
You've just landed on Boardwalk.

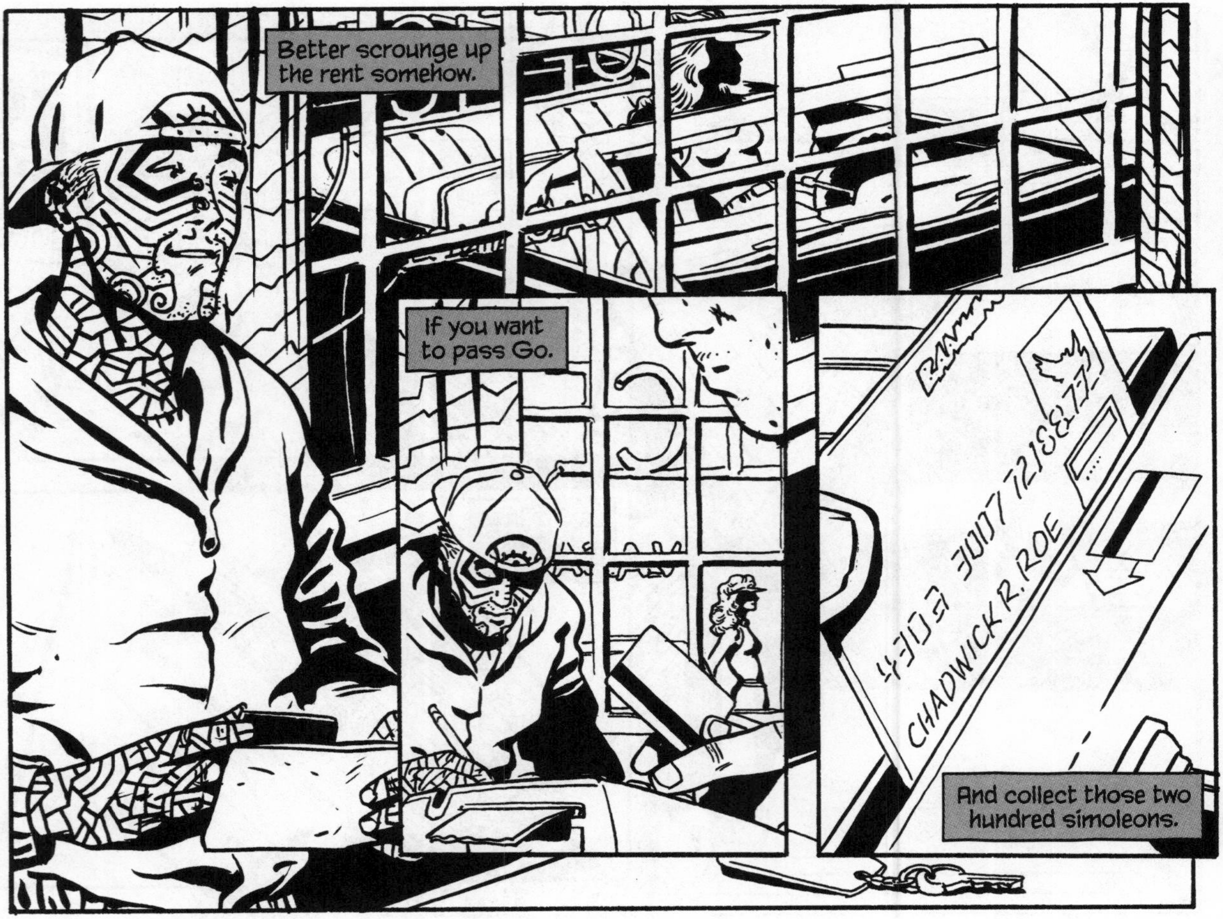
Better scrounge up the rent somehow.
If you want to pass Go.
CHADWICK R. ROE
And collect those two hundred simoleons.

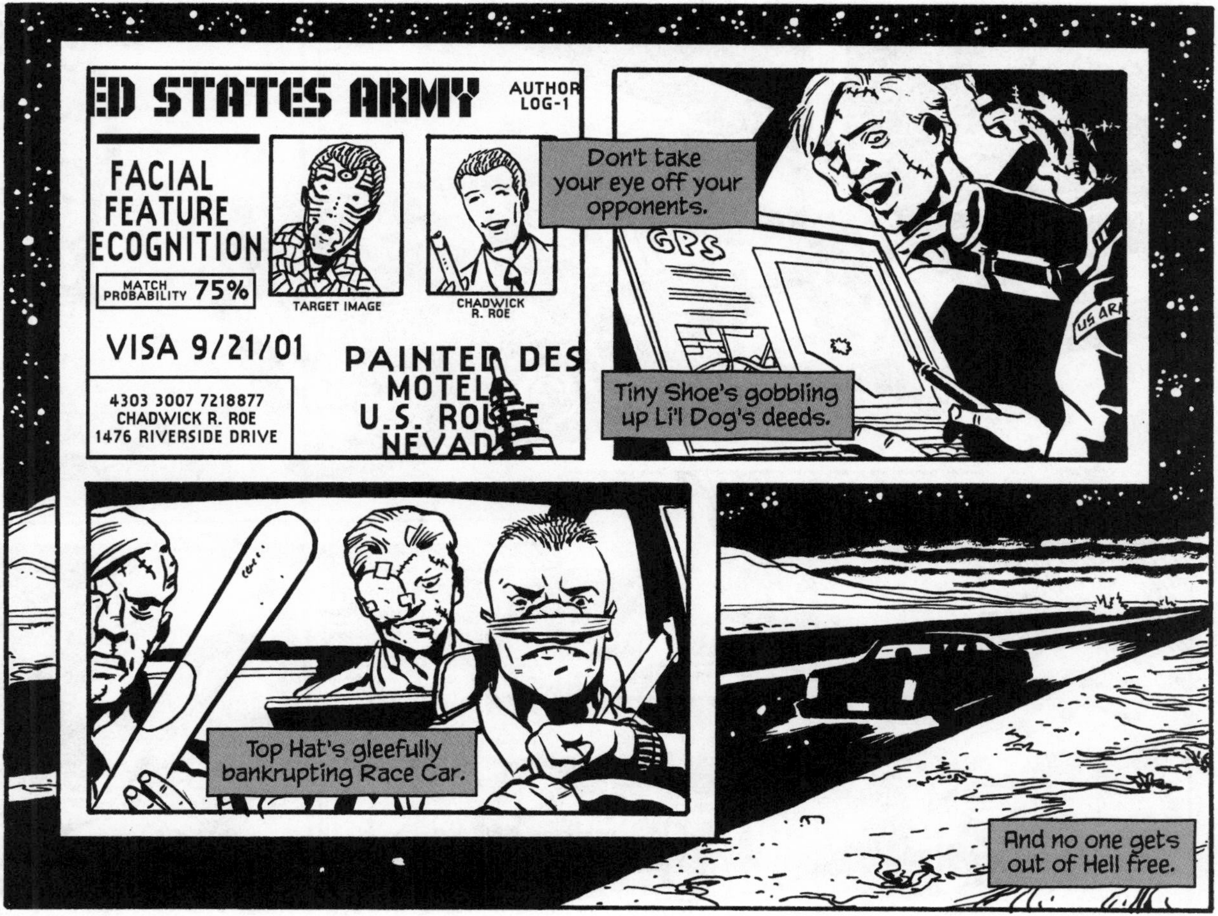

ED STATES ARMY
AUTHOR LOG-1
FACIAL FEATURE ECOGNITION
MATCH PROBABILITY 75%
TARGET IMAGE
CHADWICK R. ROE
VISA 9/21/01
4303 3007 7218877 CHADWICK R. ROE 1476 RIVERSIDE DRIVE
PAINTED DES MOTEL U.S. ROU E NEVAD
Don't take your eye off your opponents.
GPS
US AR
Tiny Shoe's gobbling up Li'l Dog's deeds.
Top Hat's gleefully bankrupting Race Car.
And no one gets out of Hell free.

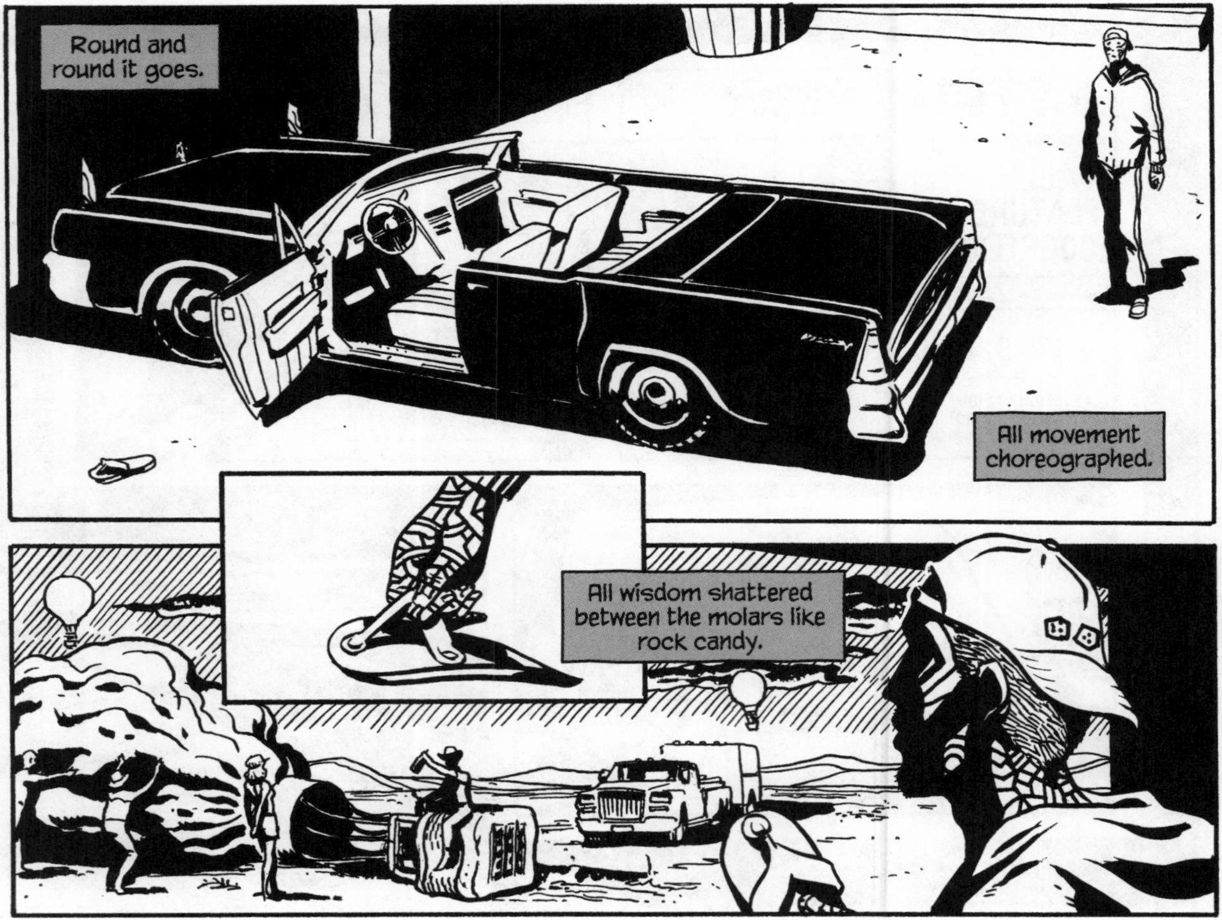
Round and round it goes.
All movement choreographed.
All wisdom shattered between the molars like rock candy.

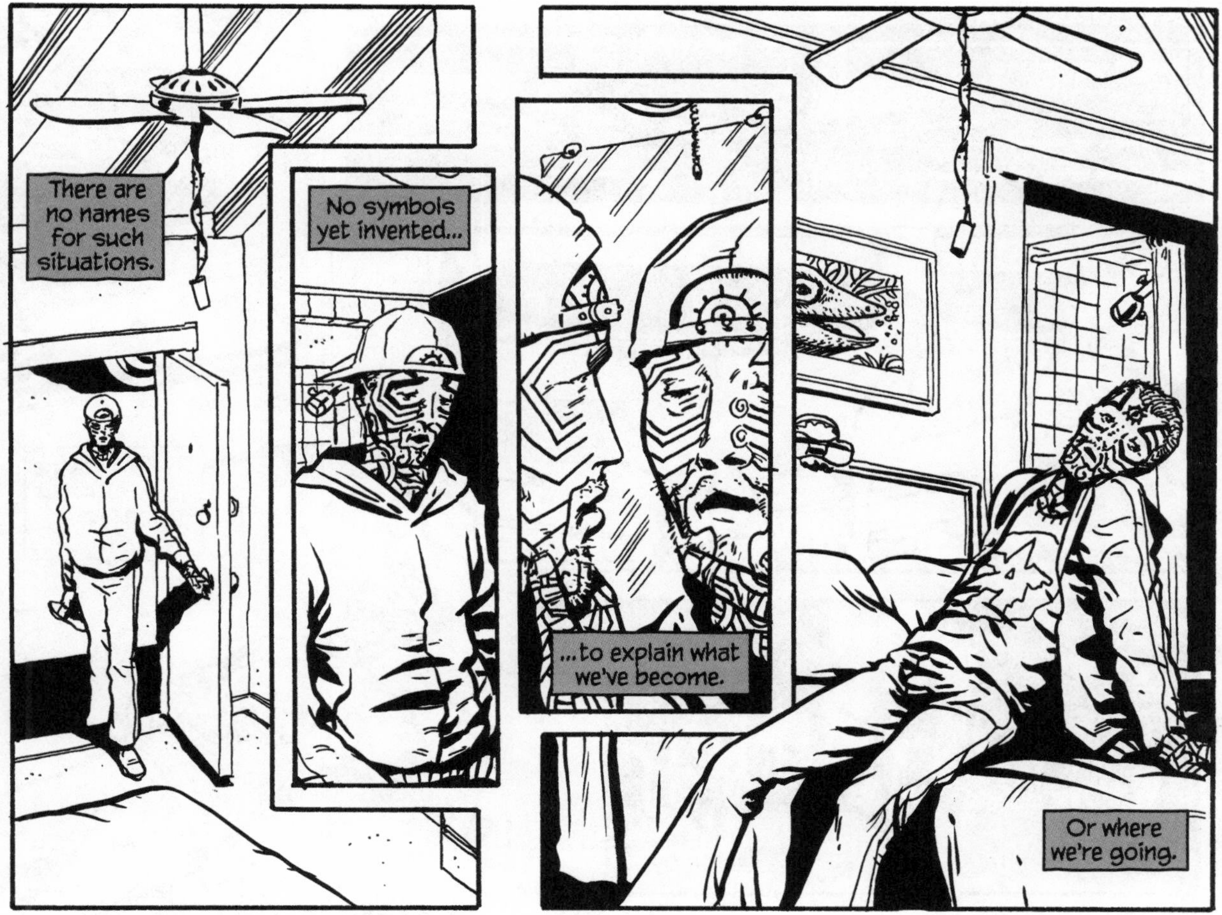
There are no names for such situations.
No symbols yet invented...
...to explain what we've become.
Or where we're going.

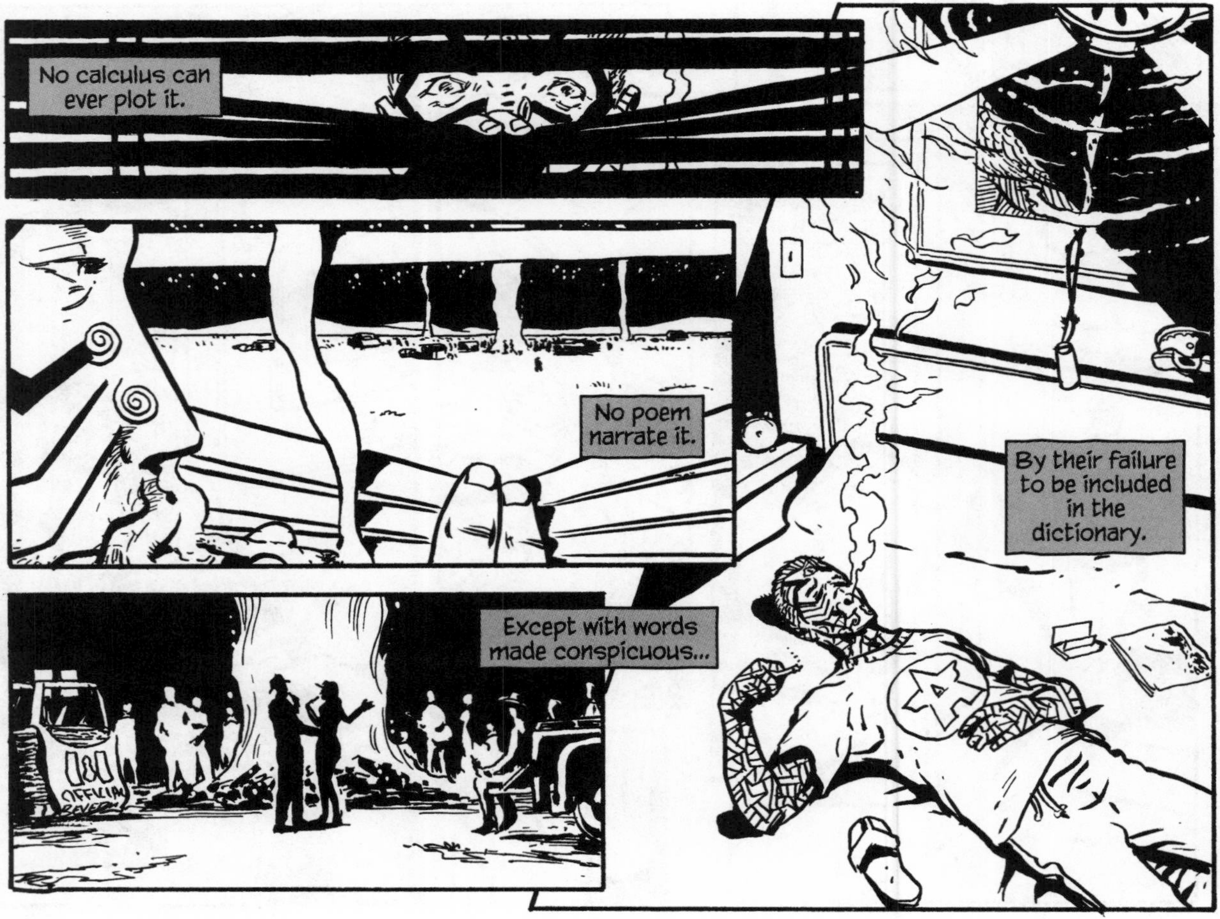
No calculus can ever plot it.
No poem narrate it.
Except with words made conspicuous...
By their failure to be included in the dictionary.

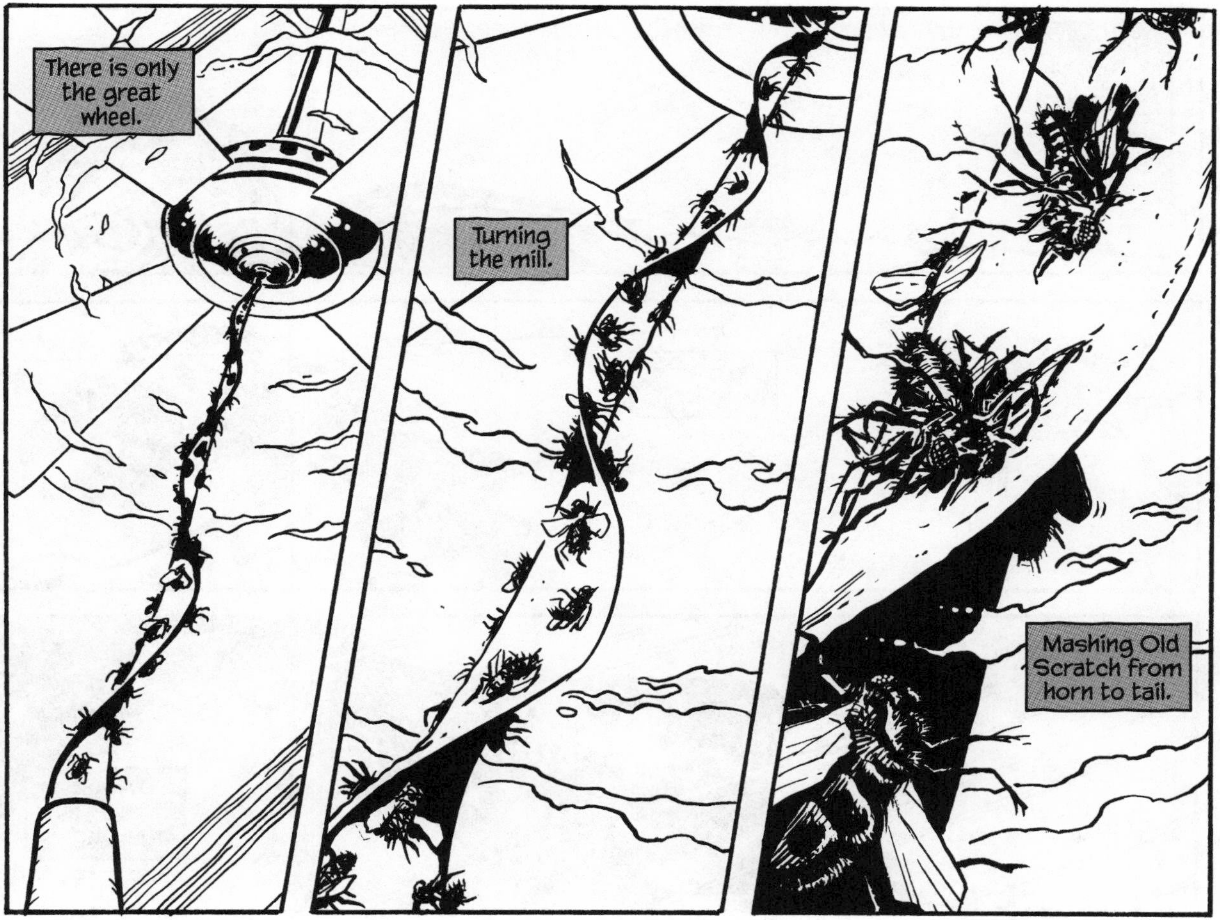
There is only the great wheel.
Turning the mill.
Mashing Old Scratch from horn to tail.

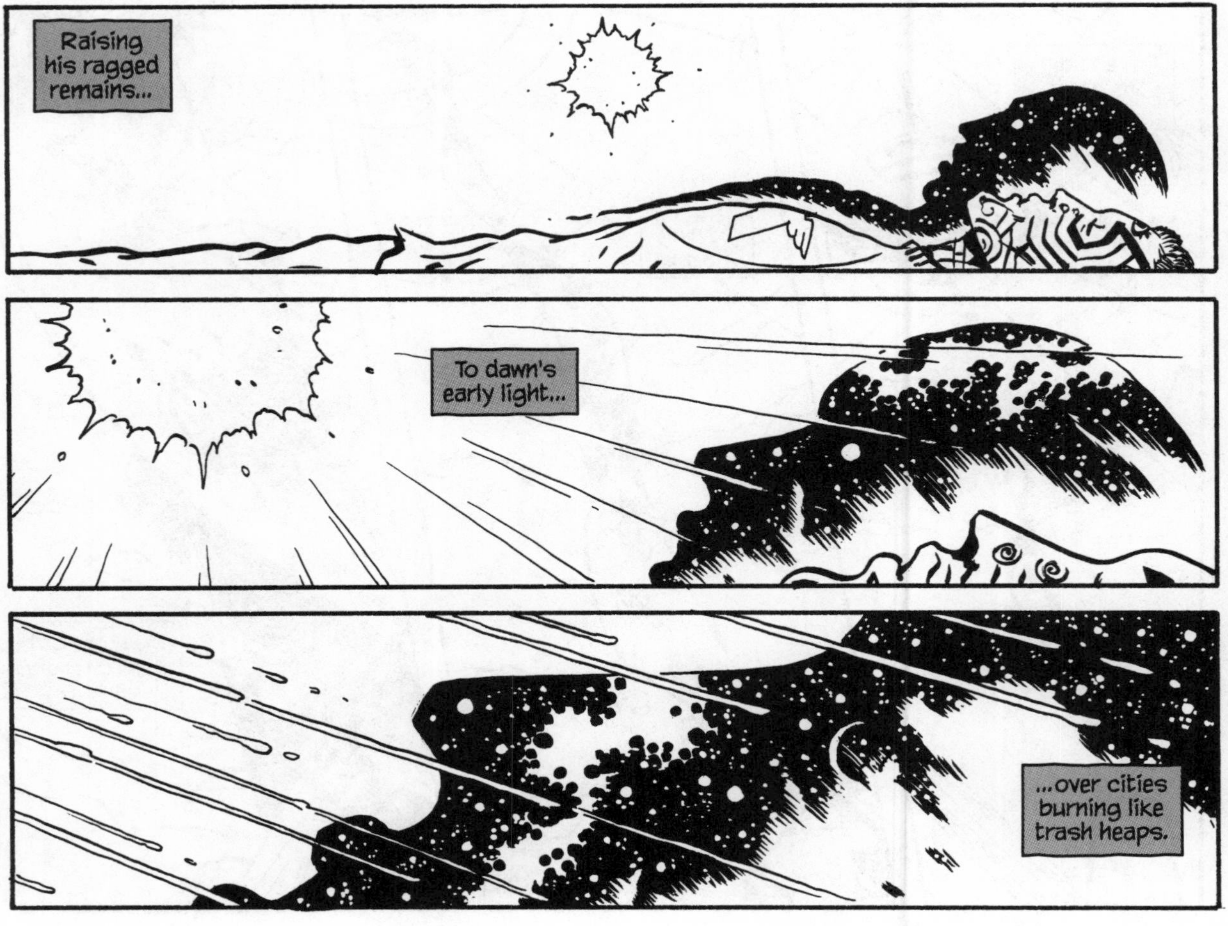
Raising his ragged remains...
To dawn's early light...
...over cities burning like trash heaps.

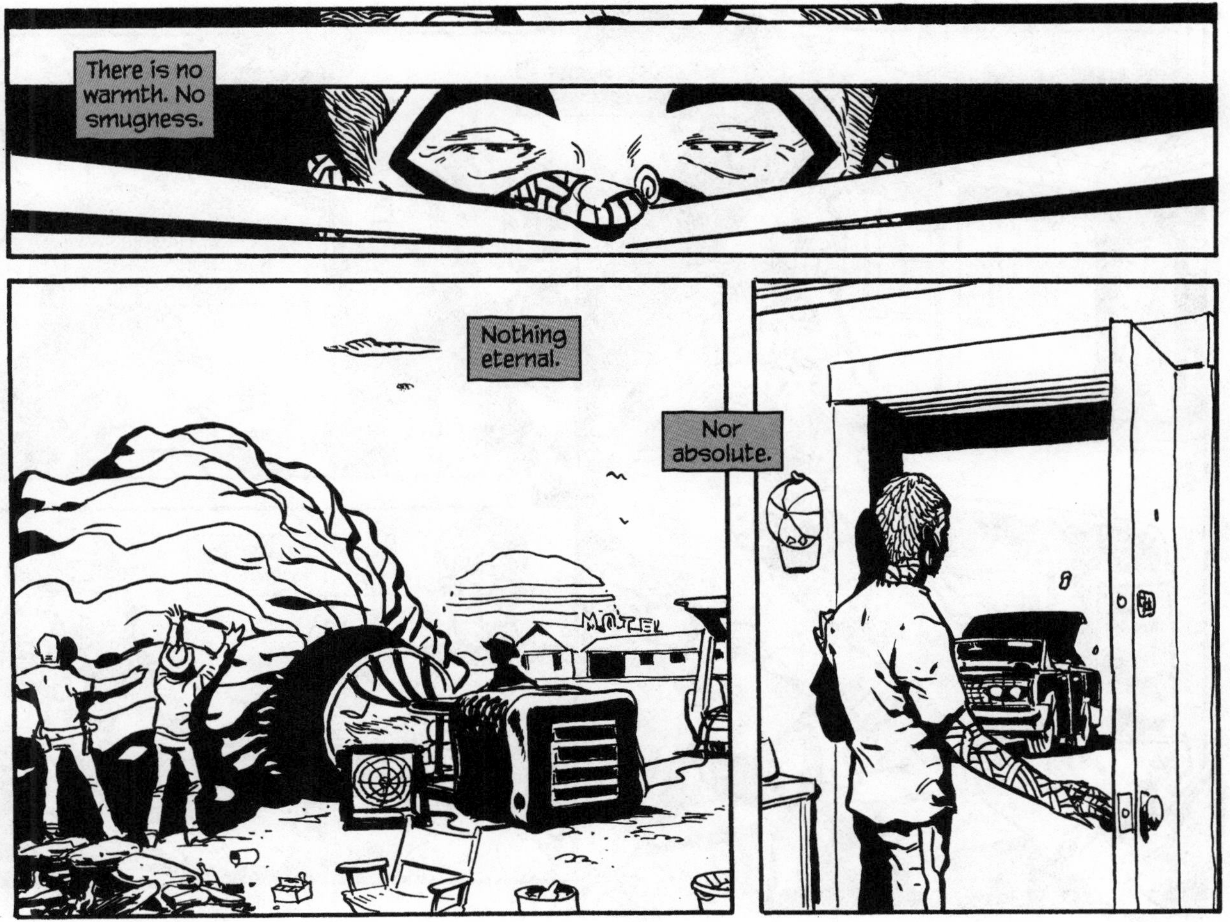
There is no warmth. No smugness.
Nothing eternal.
Nor absolute.

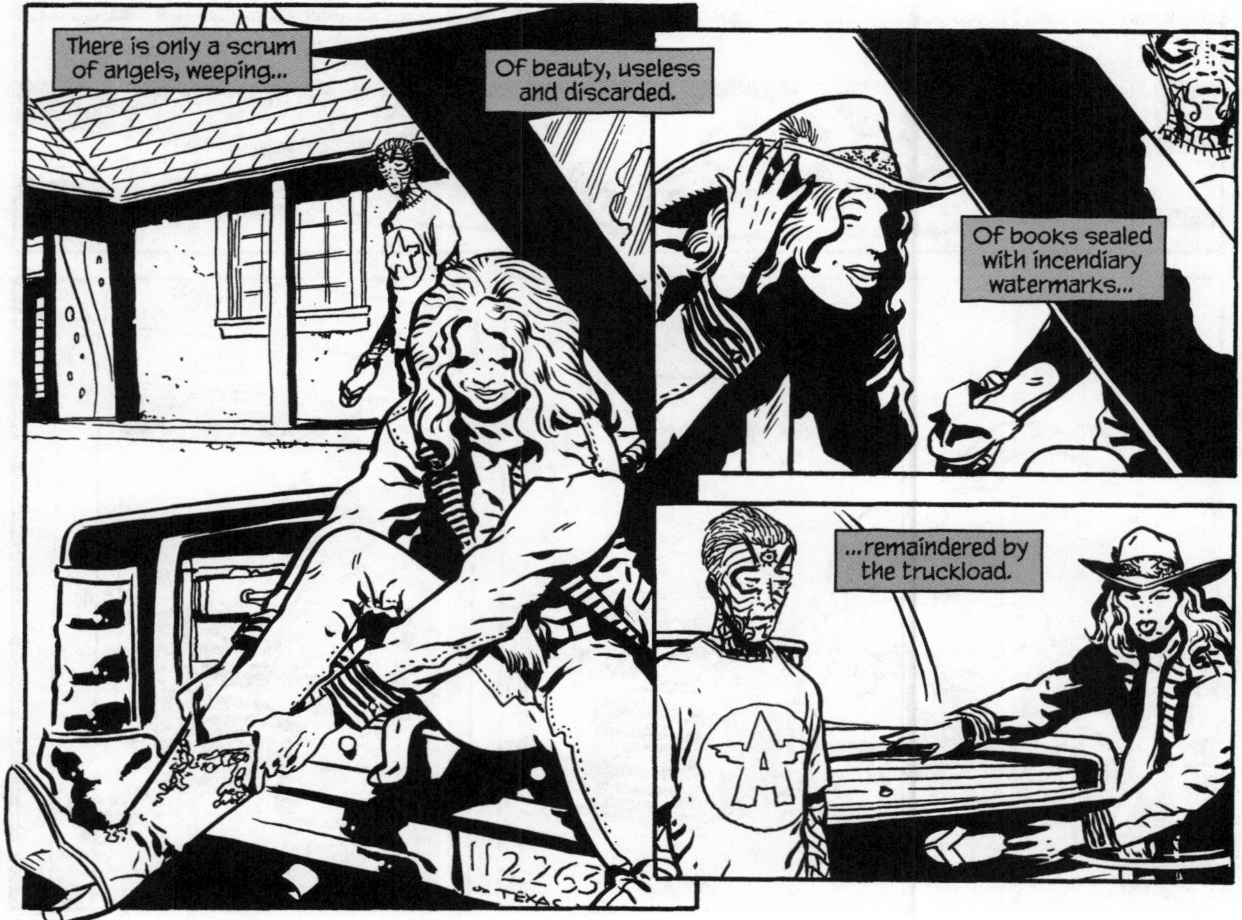
There is only a scrum of angels, weeping...
Of beauty, useless and discarded.
Of books sealed with incendiary watermarks...
...remaindered by the truckload.
TEXAS

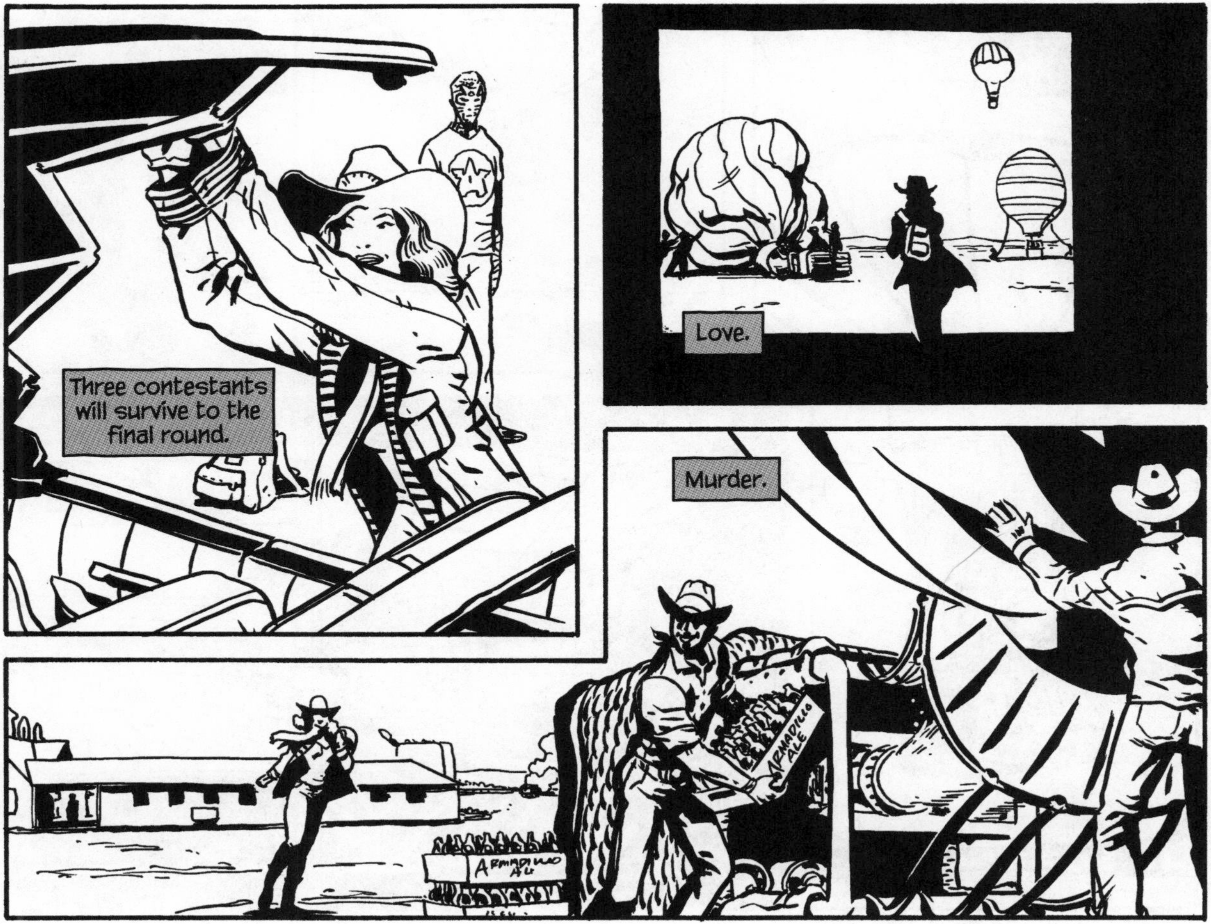
Three contestants will survive to the final round.
Love.
Murder.
ARMADILLO ALE

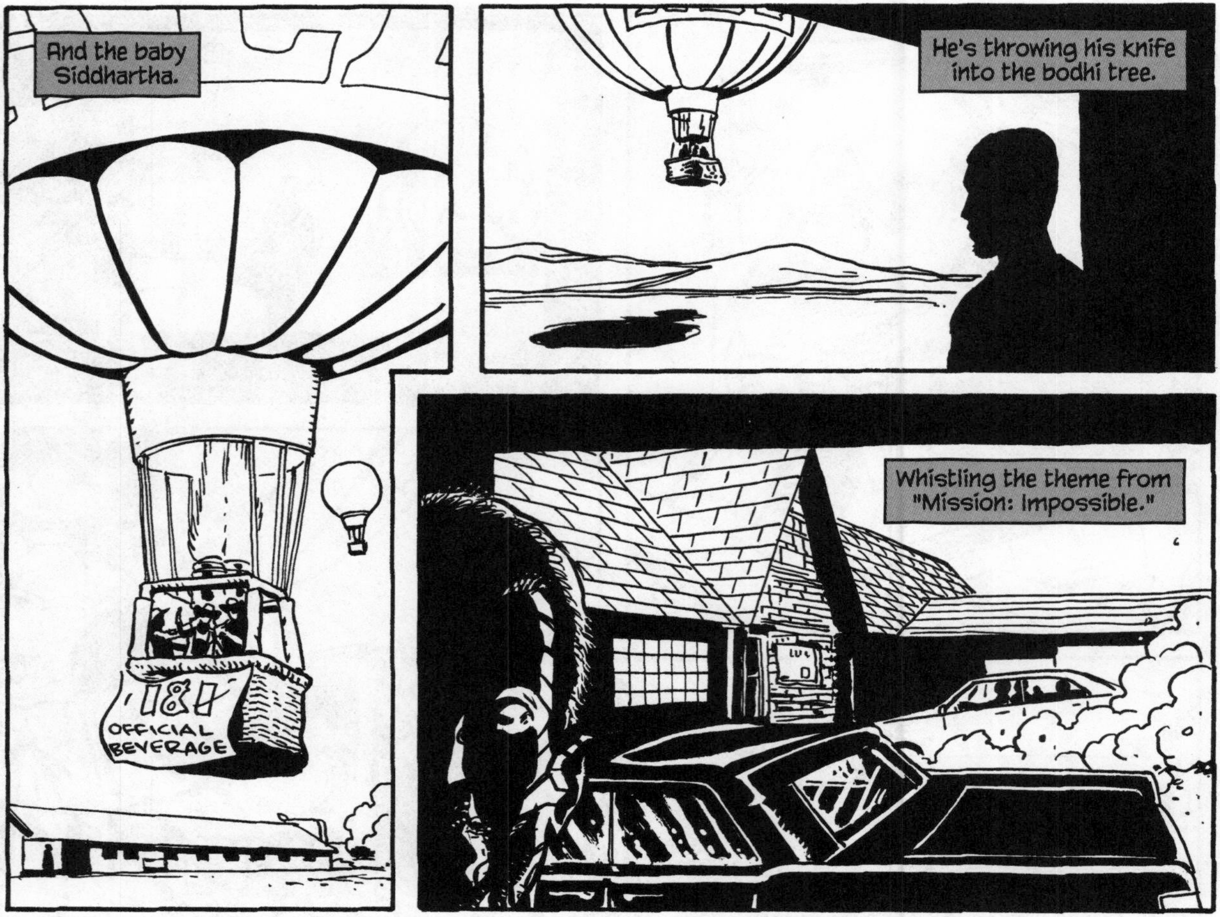
And the baby Siddhartha.
OFFICIAL BEVERAGE
He's throwing his knife into the bodhi tree.
Whistling the theme from "Mission: Impossible."

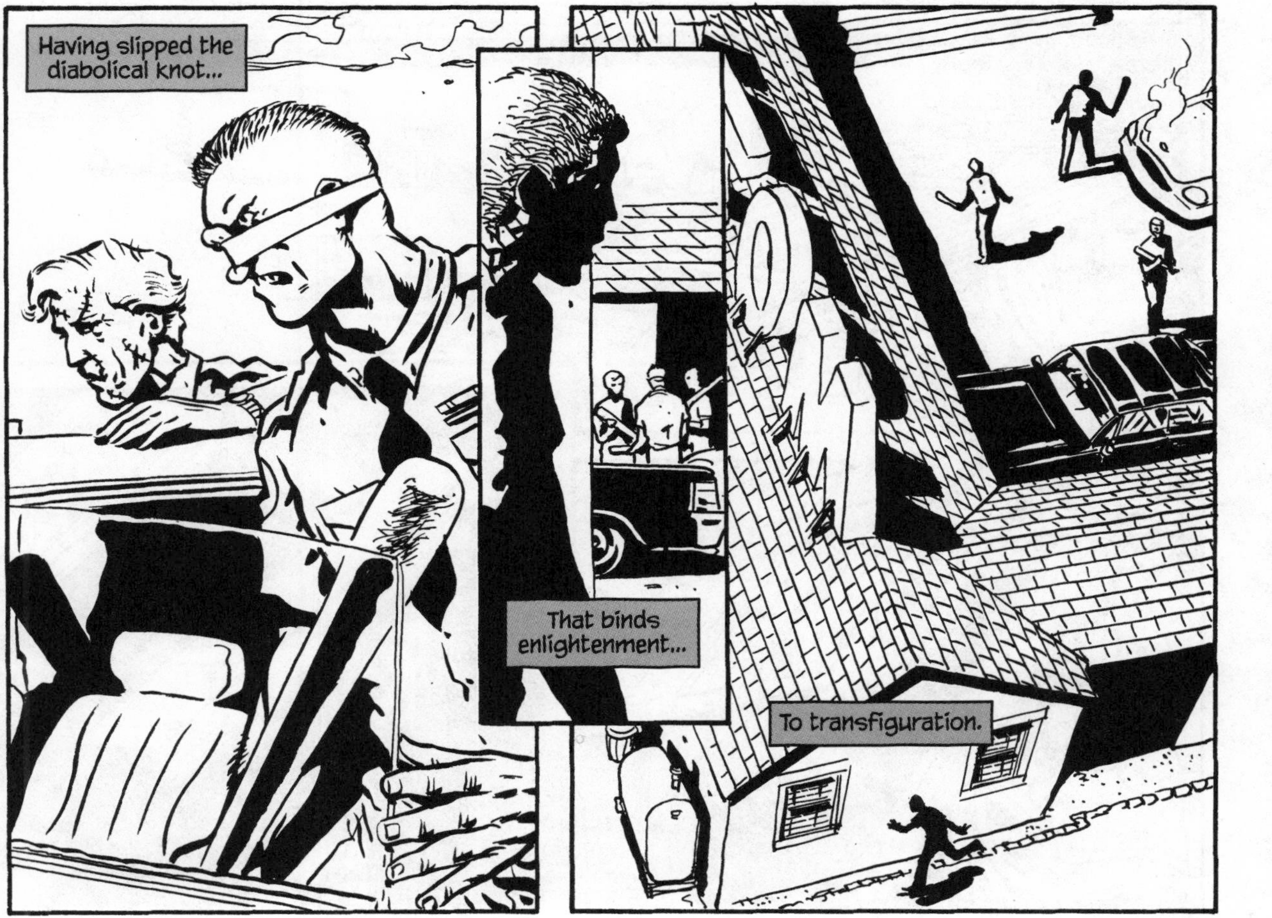
Having slipped the diabolical knot...
That binds enlightenment...
To transfiguration.

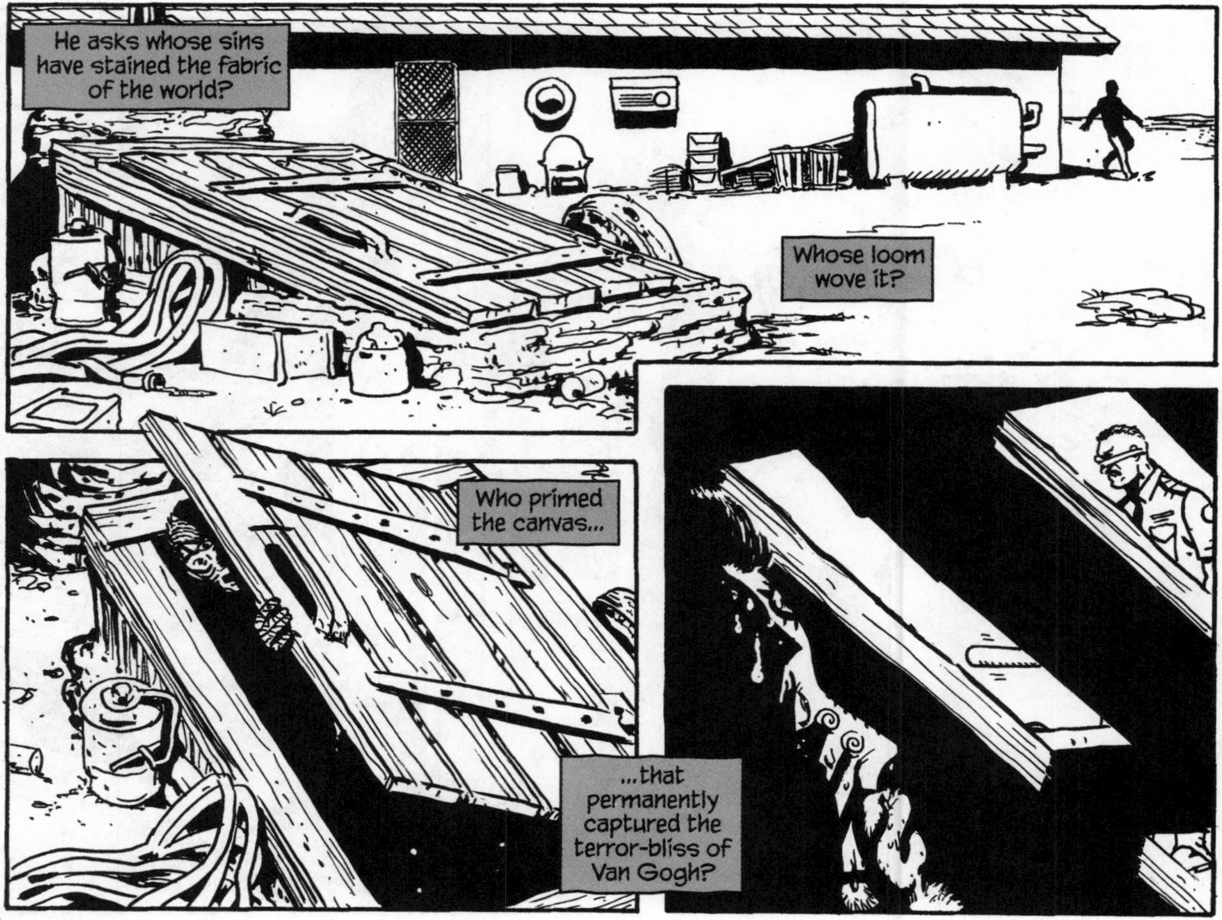
He asks whose sins have stained the fabric of the world?
Whose loom wove it?
Who primed the canvas...
...that permanently captured the terror-bliss of Van Gogh?

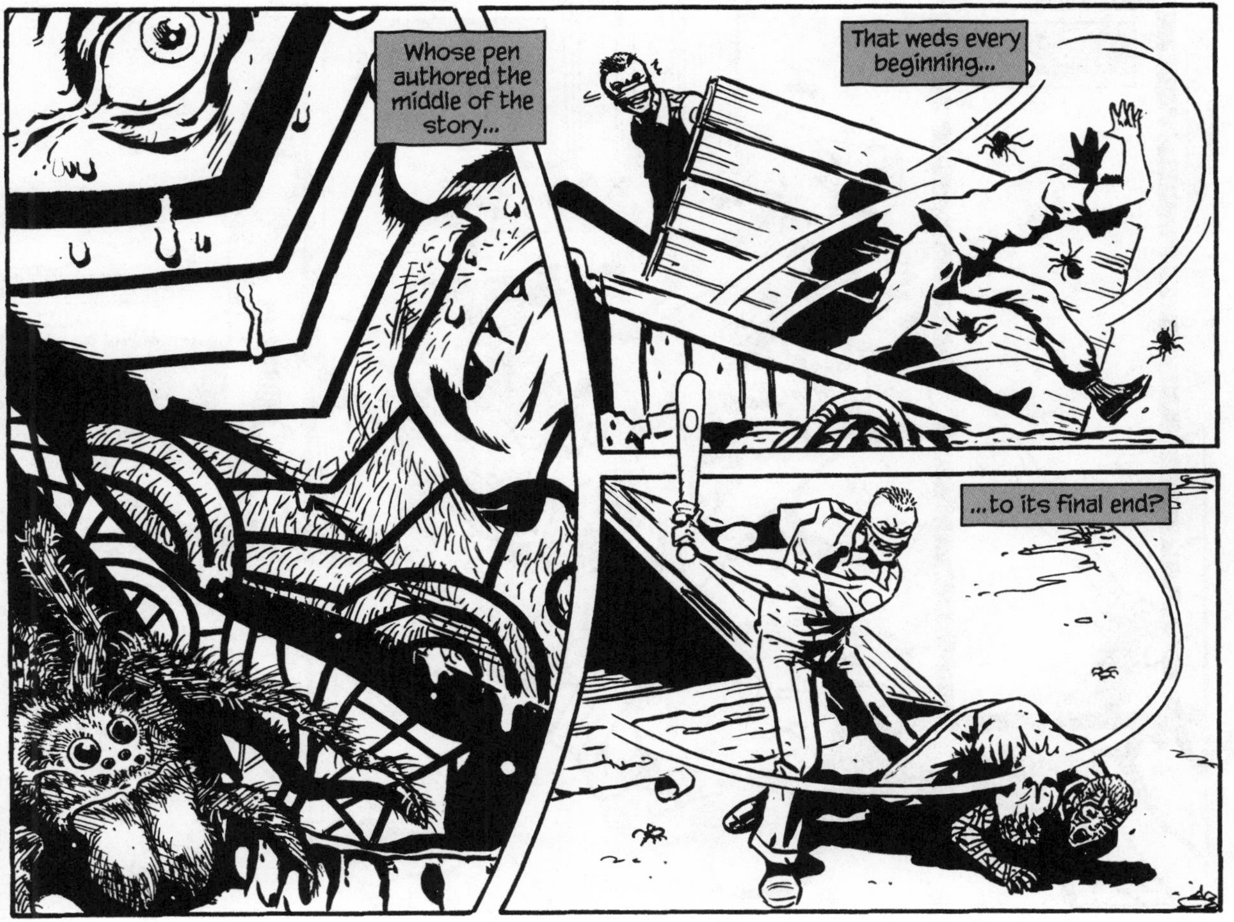
Whose pen authored the middle of the story...
That weds every beginning...
...to its final end?

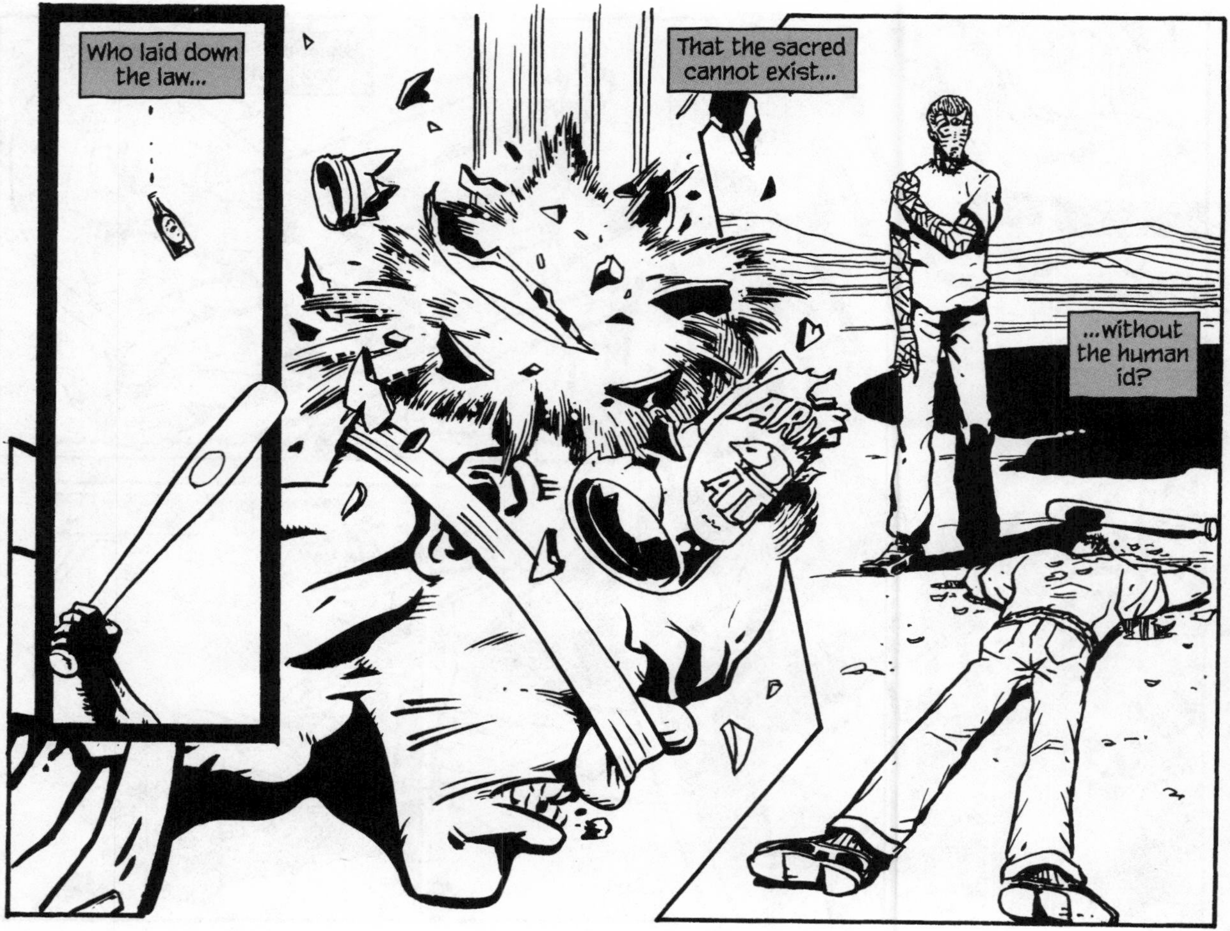
Who laid down the law...
That the sacred cannot exist...
...without the human id?

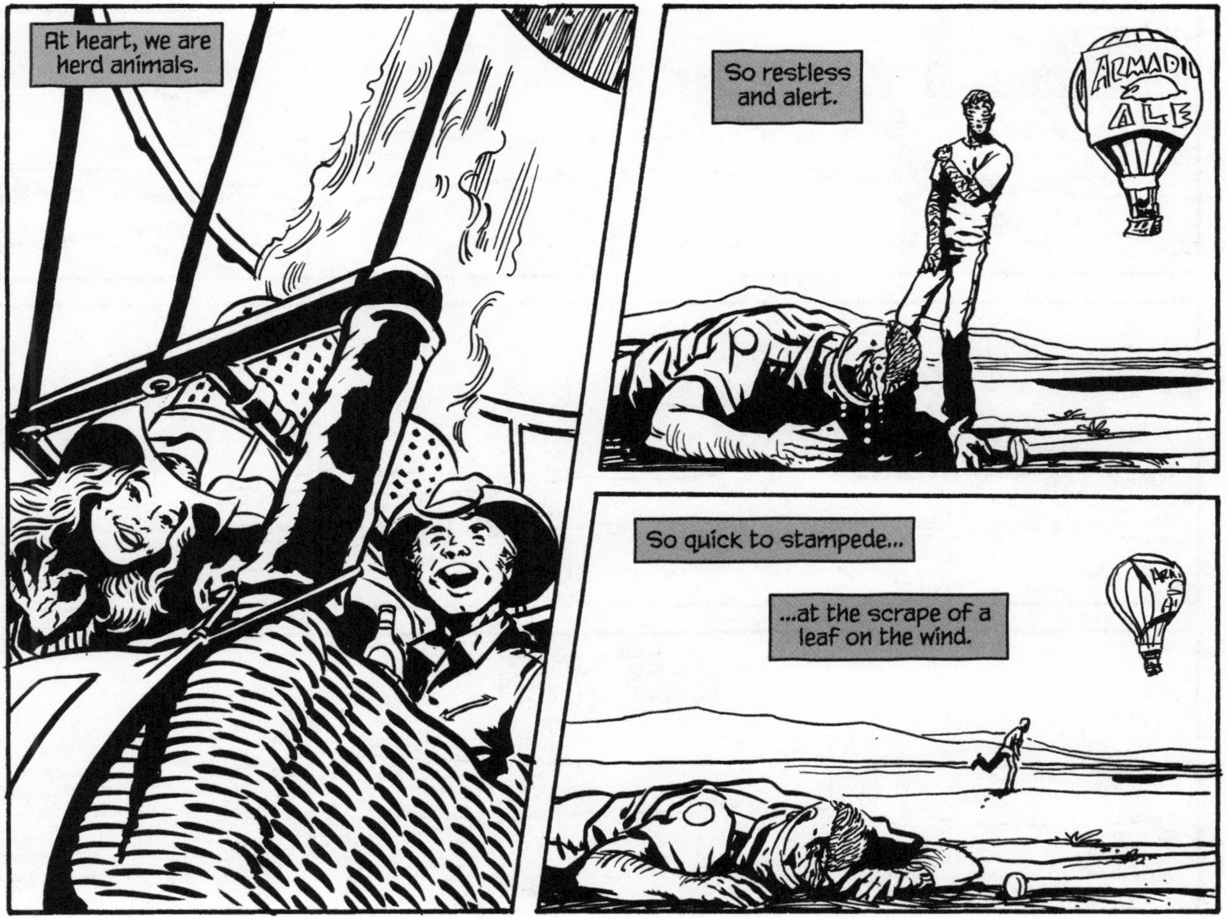
At heart, we are herd animals.
So restless and alert.
ARMADIL
ALE
So quick to stampede...
...at the scrape of a leaf on the wind.

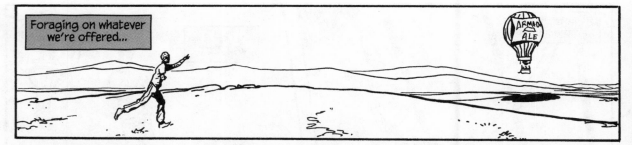

Foraging on whatever we're offered...

Letting life iron out the niggling details...

...in our contracts with God.

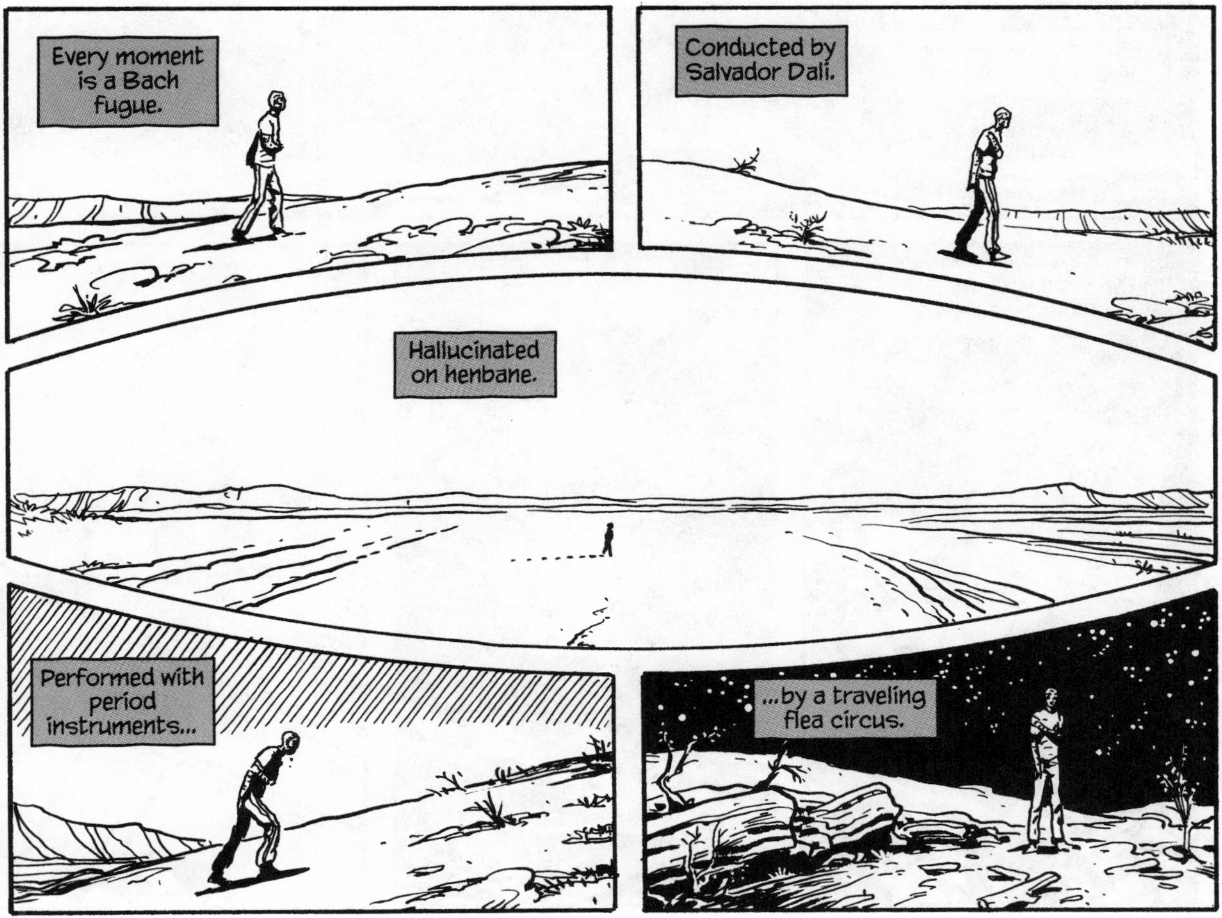
Every moment is a Bach fugue.
Conducted by Salvador Dalí.
Hallucinated on henbane.
Performed with period instruments...
...by a traveling flea circus.

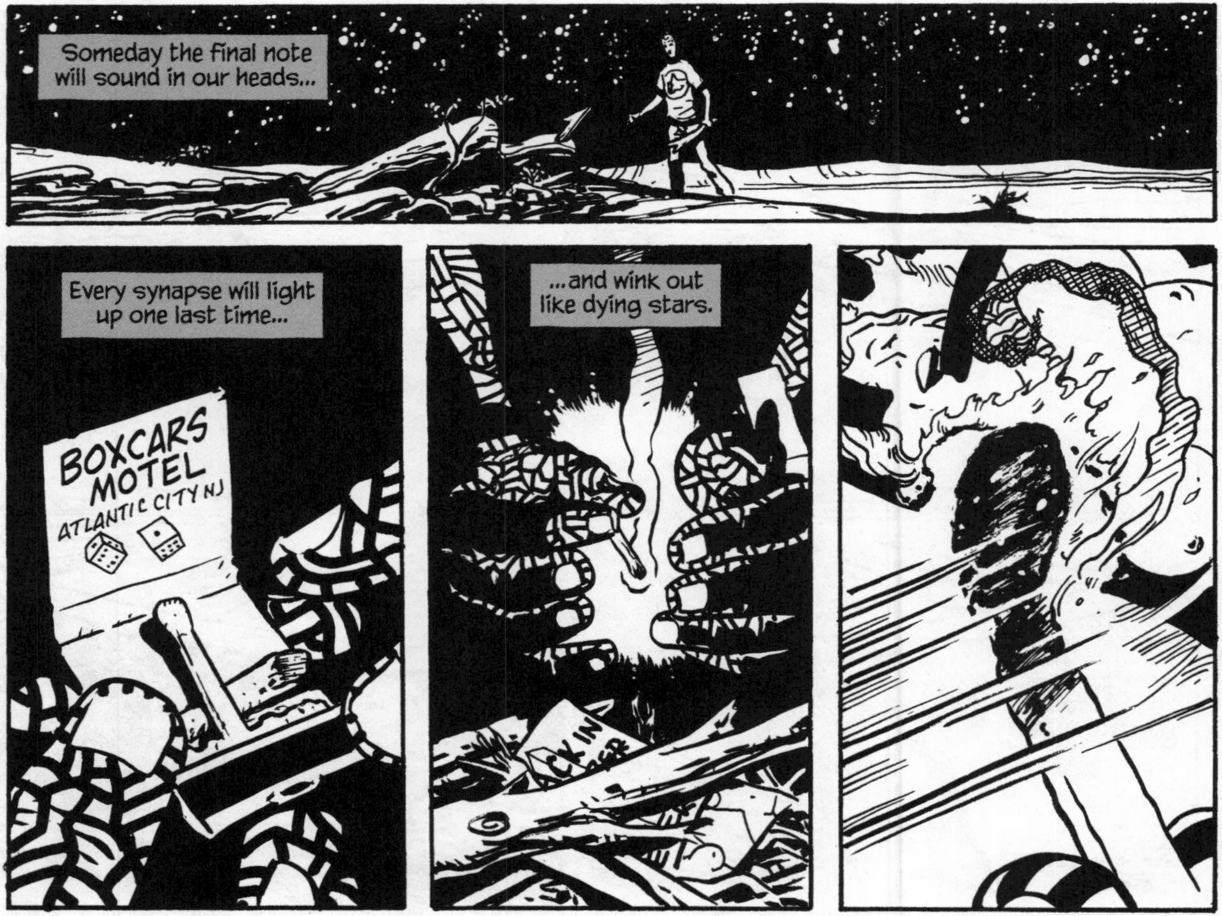
Someday the final note will sound in our heads...
Every synapse will light up one last time...
BOXCARS MOTEL
ATLANTIC CITY NJ
...and wink out like dying stars.

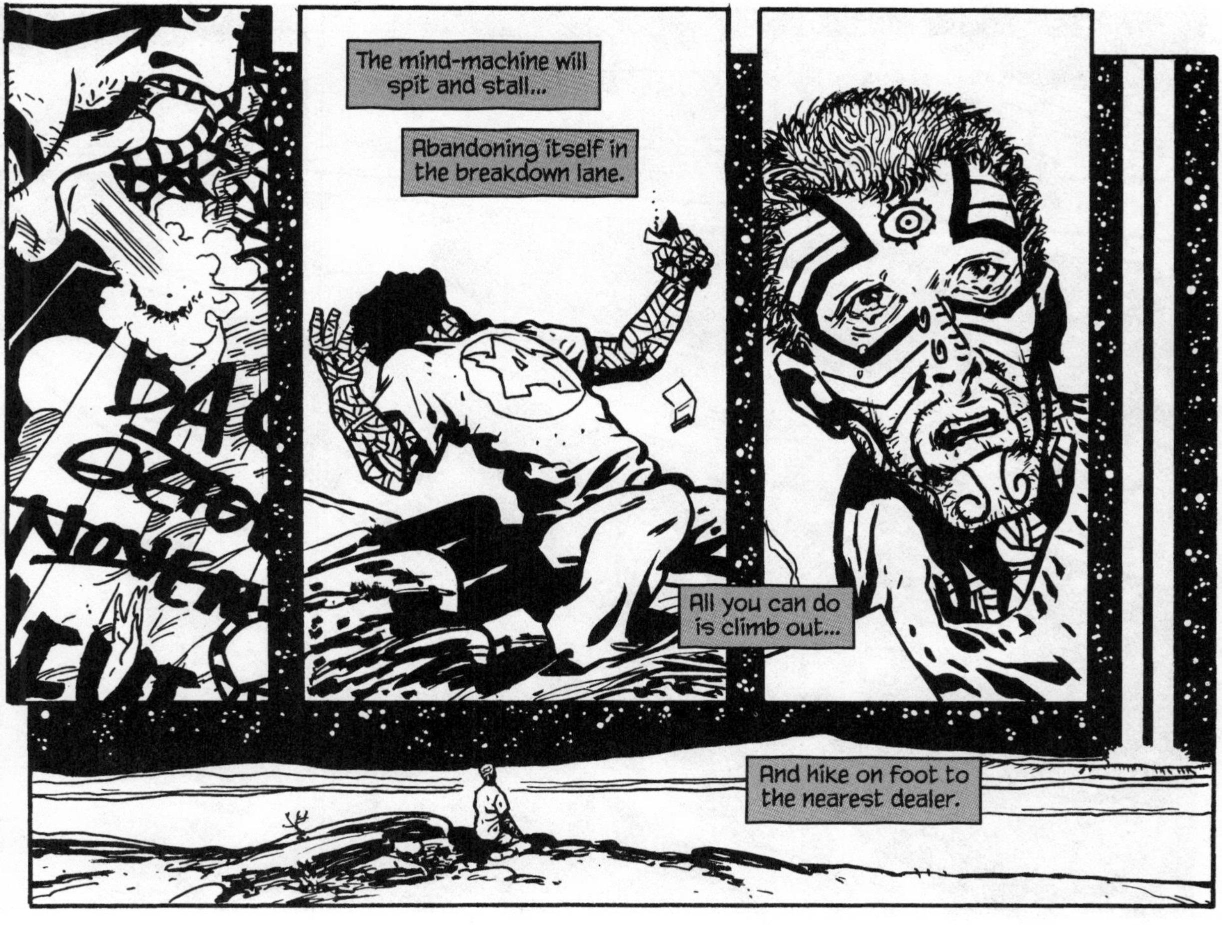
The mind-machine will spit and stall...
Abandoning itself in the breakdown lane.
All you can do is climb out...
And hike on foot to the nearest dealer.

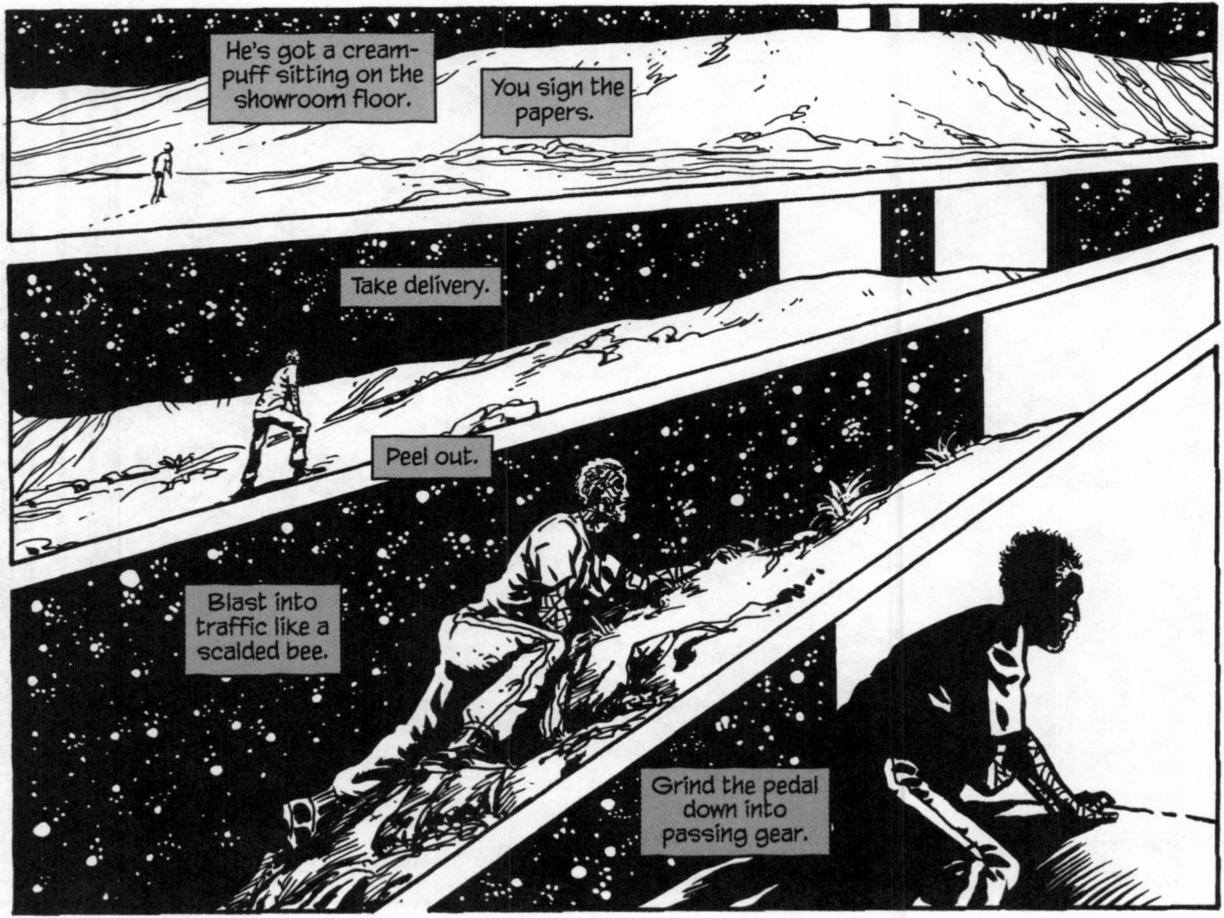
He's got a cream-puff sitting on the showroom floor.
You sign the papers.
Take delivery.
Peel out.
Blast into traffic like a scalded bee.
Grind the pedal down into passing gear.

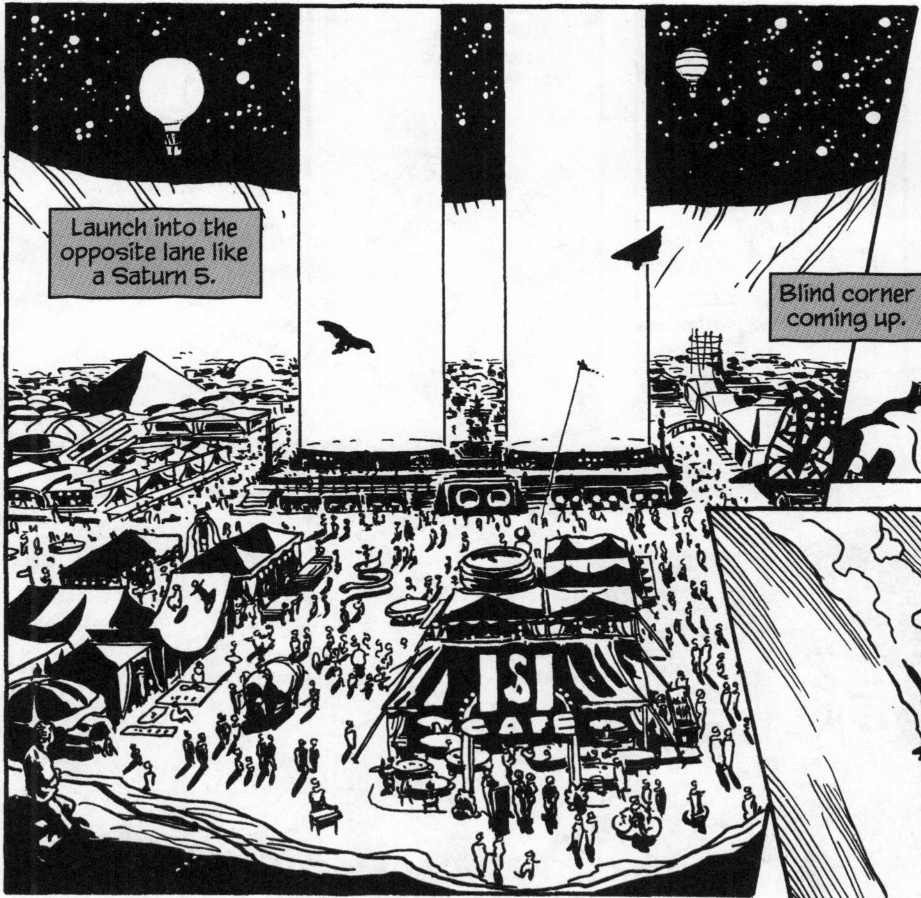
Launch into the opposite lane like a Saturn 5.
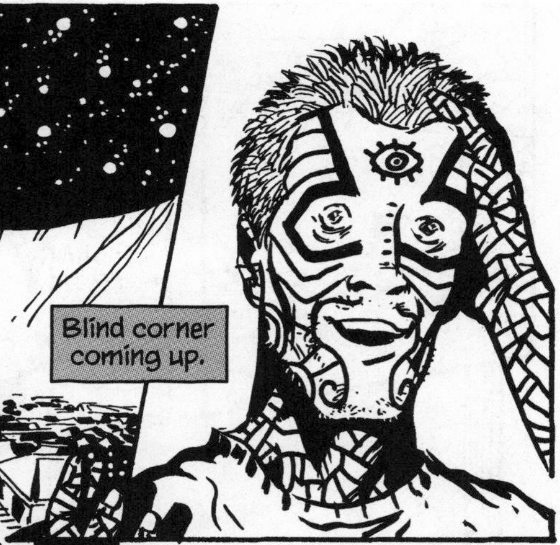
Blind corner coming up.
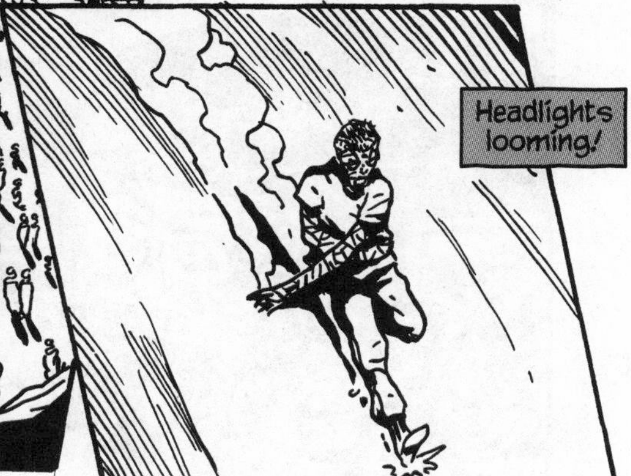
Headlights looming!

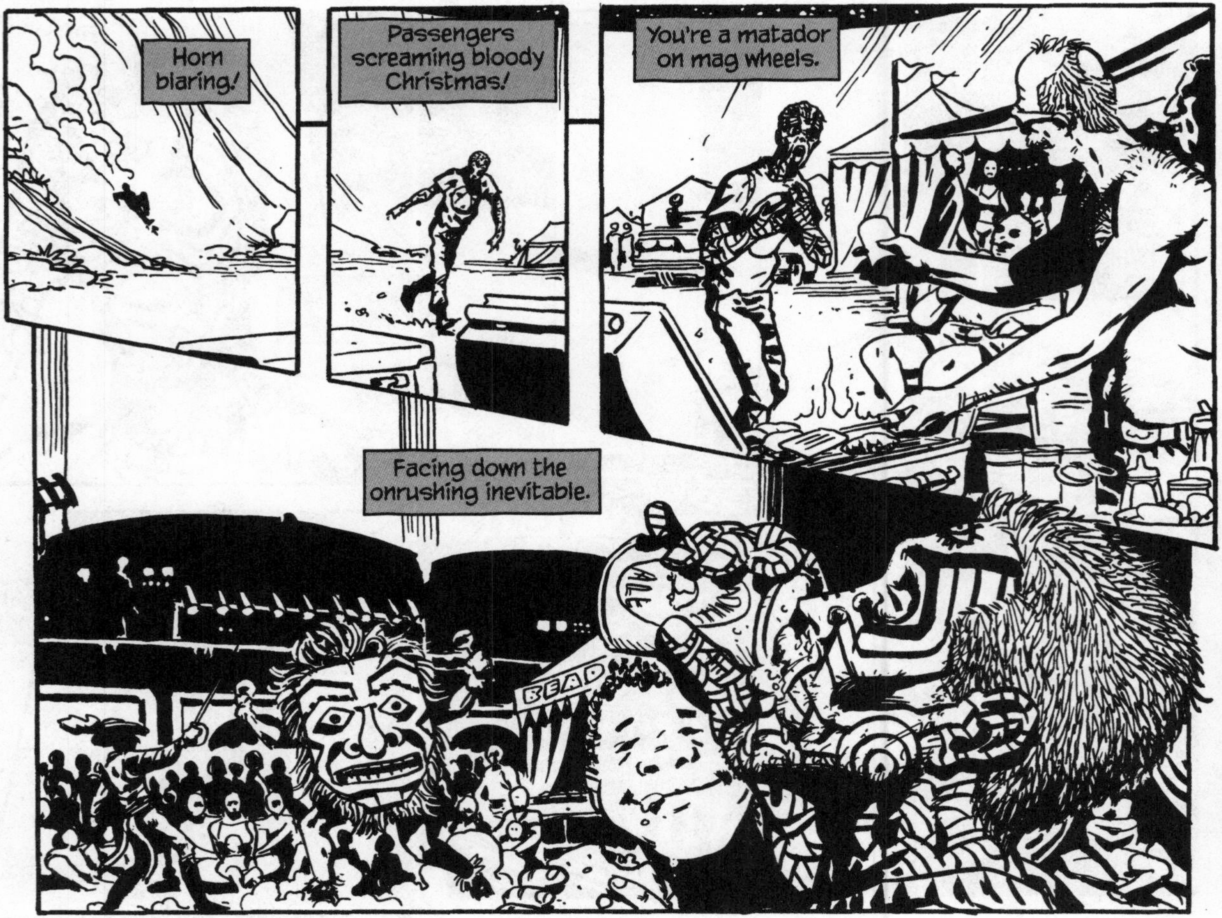
Horn blaring!
Passengers screaming bloody Christmas!
You're a matador on mag wheels.
Facing down the onrushing inevitable.
BEAD

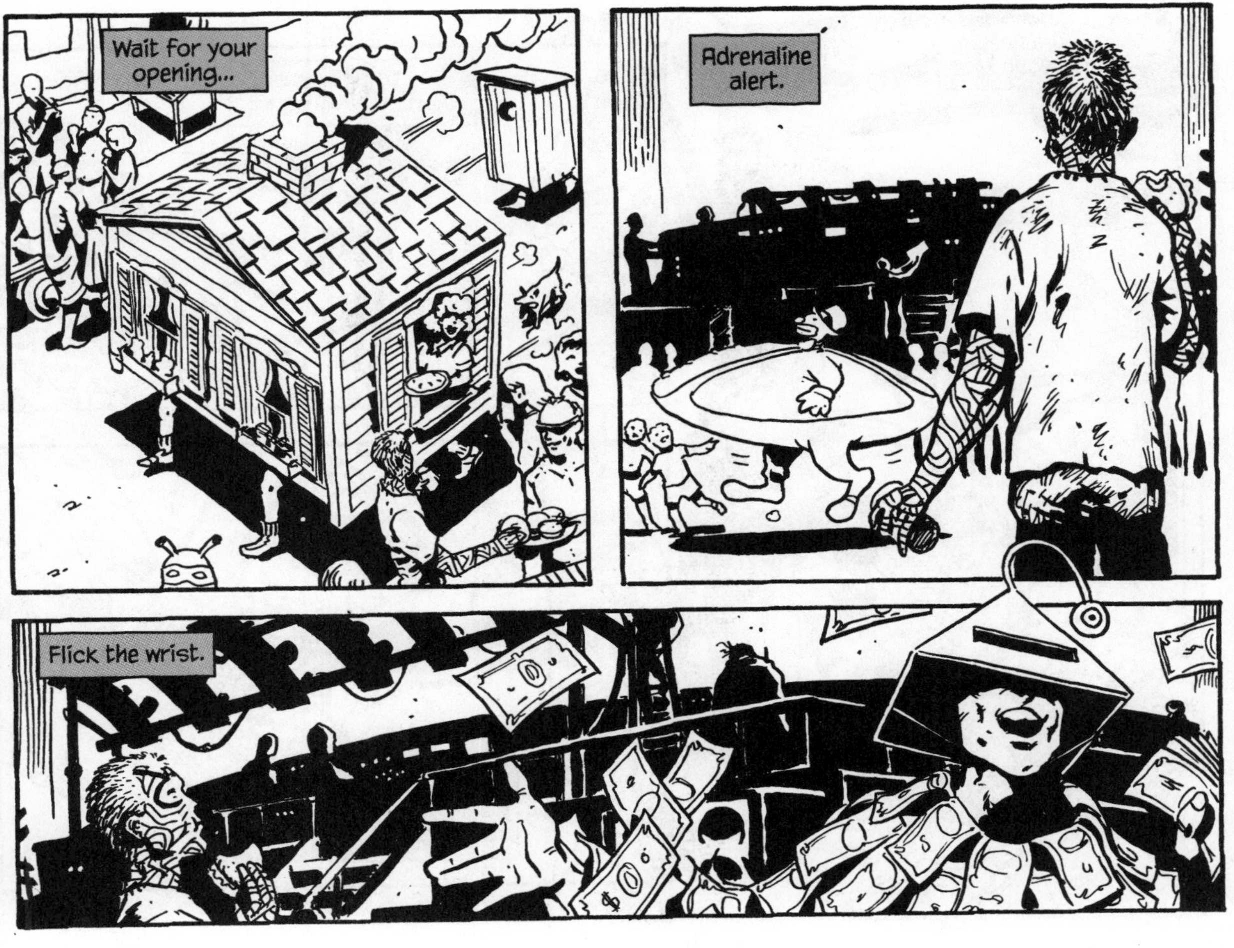
Wait for your opening...
Adrenaline alert.
Flick the wrist.

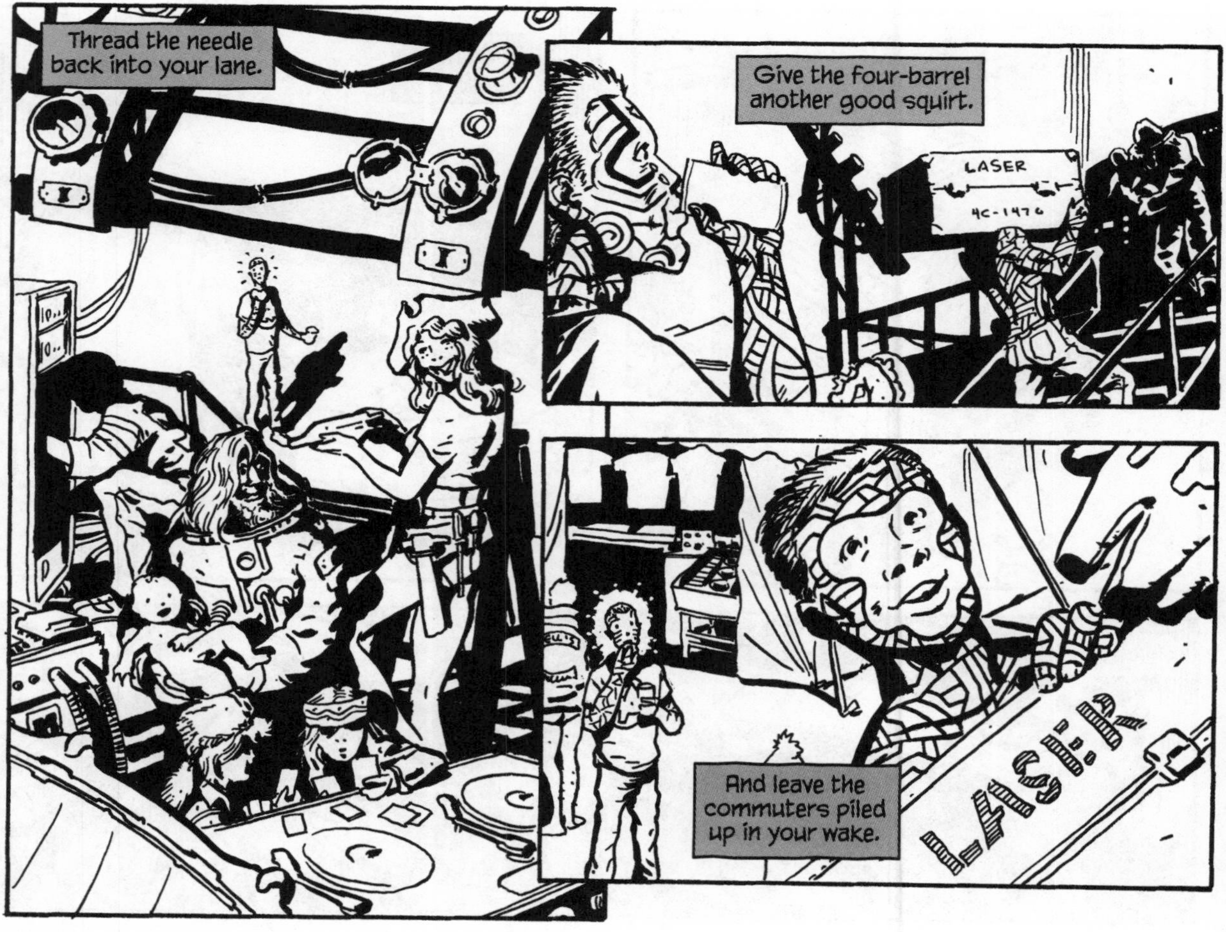

Thread the needle back into your lane.
Give the four-barrel another good squirt.
LASER
4C-1470
And leave the commuters piled up in your wake.
LASER

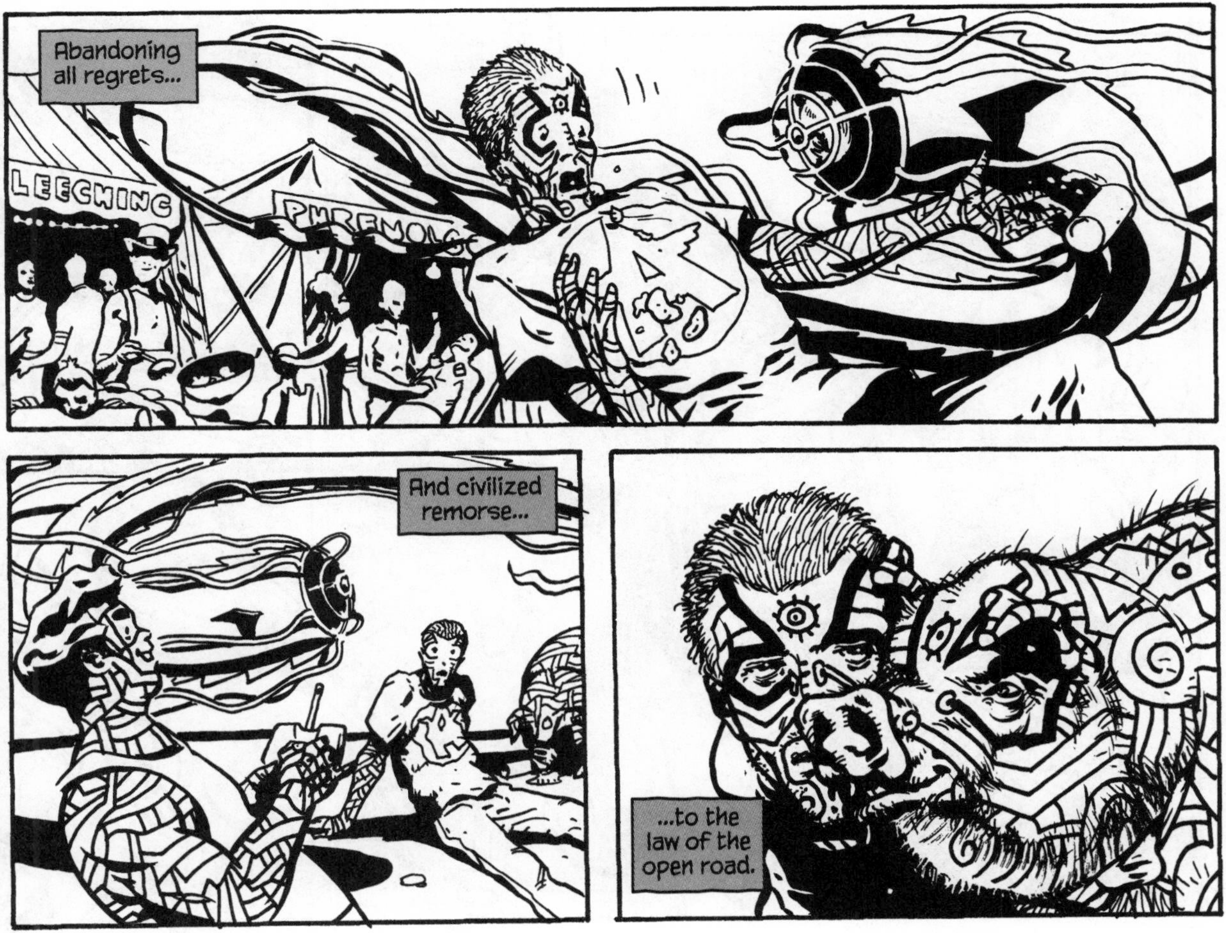
Abandoning all regrets...
LEECHING
And civilized remorse...
...to the law of the open road.

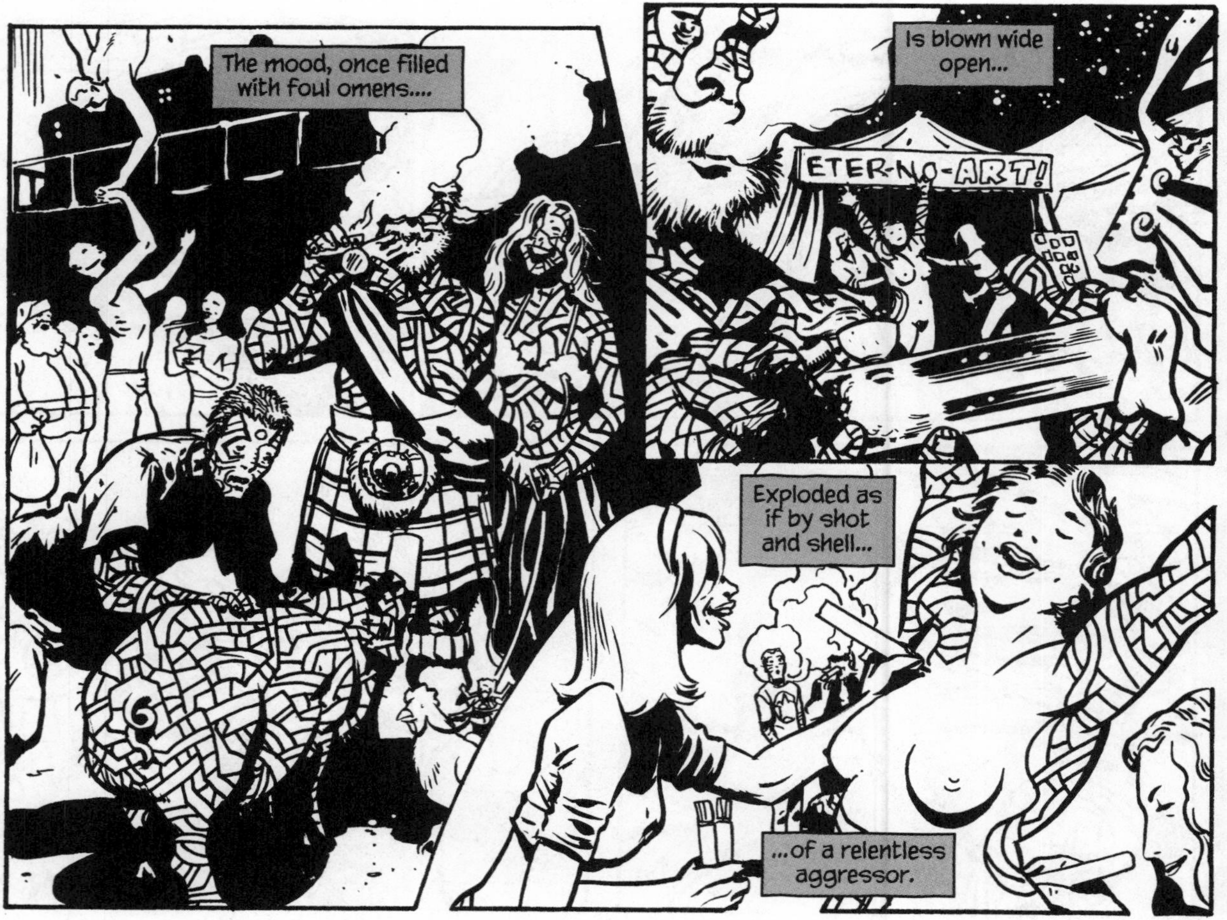
The mood, once filled with foul omens....
Is blown wide open...
ETER-NO-ART!
Exploded as if by shot and shell...
...of a relentless aggressor.

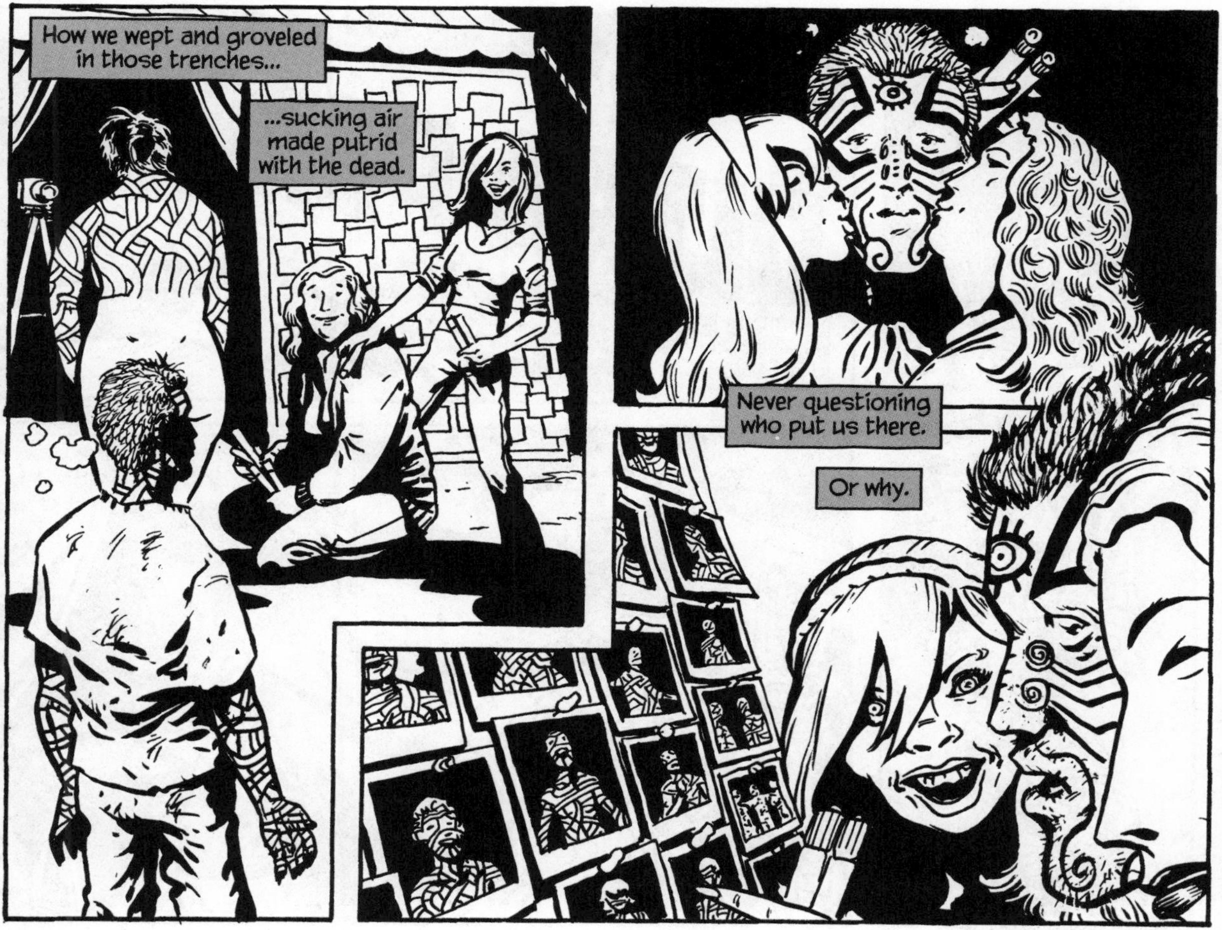
How we wept and groveled in those trenches...
...sucking air made putrid with the dead.
Never questioning who put us there.
Or why.

Thinking only of that magnum of champagne...

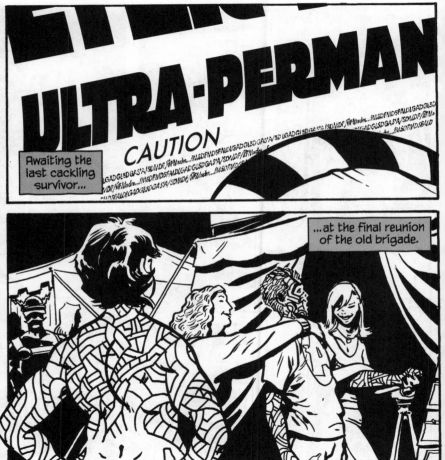

ULTRA-PERMAN

CAUTION

Awaiting the last cackling survivor...

...at the final reunion of the old brigade.

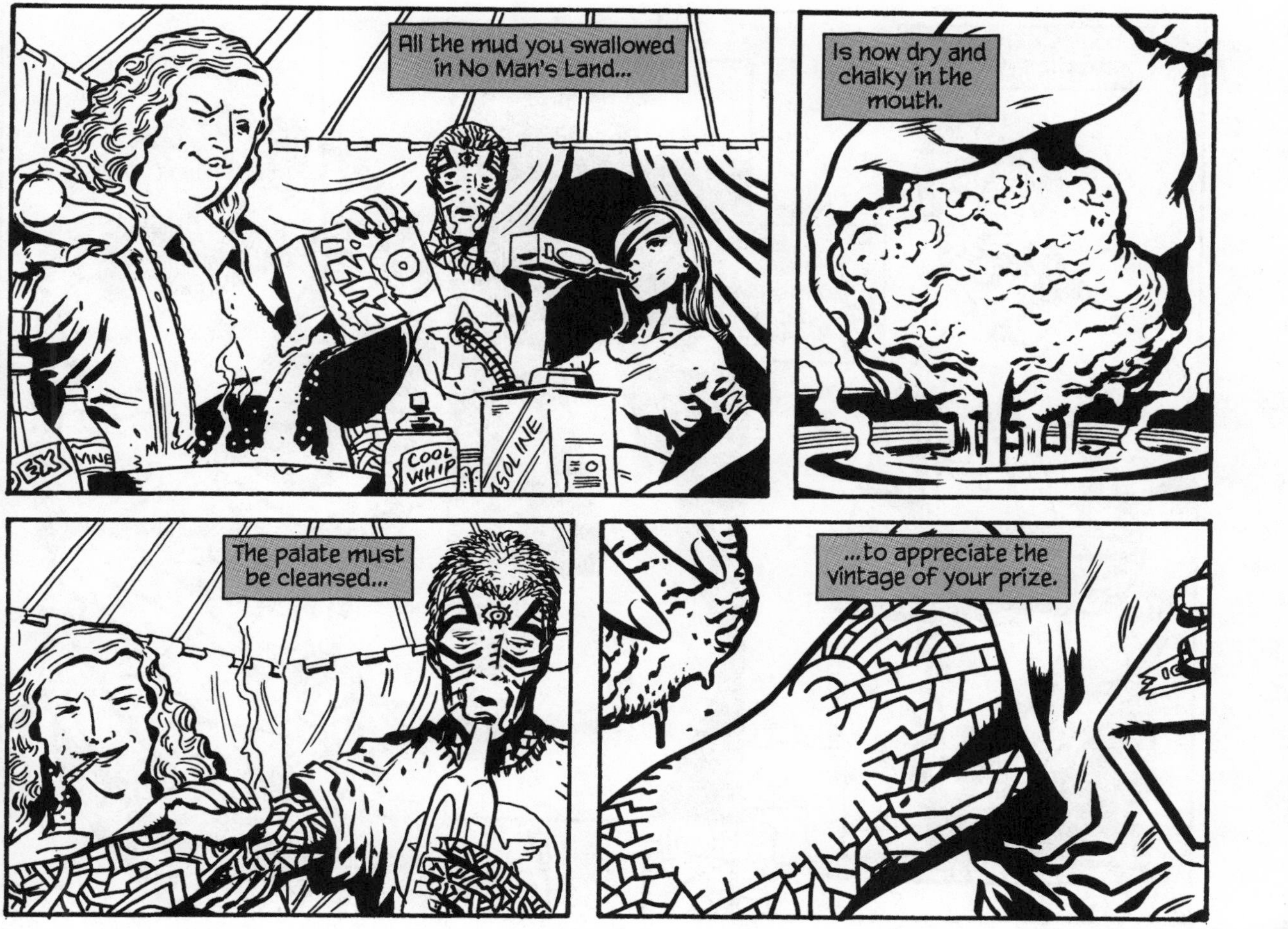
All the mud you swallowed in No Man's Land...
COOL WHIP
Is now dry and chalky in the mouth.
The palate must be cleansed...
...to appreciate the vintage of your prize.

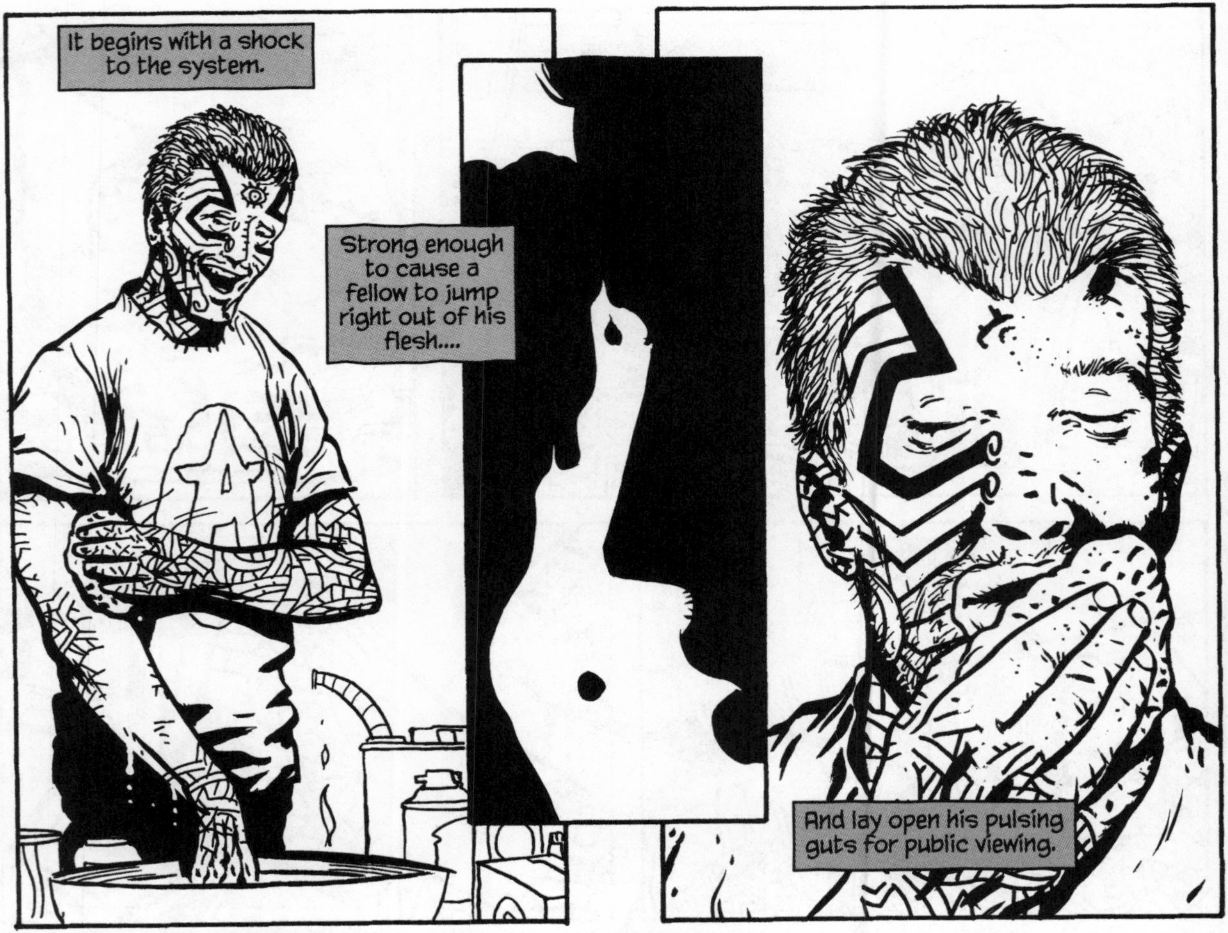
It begins with a shock to the system.
Strong enough to cause a fellow to jump right out of his flesh....
And lay open his pulsing guts for public viewing.

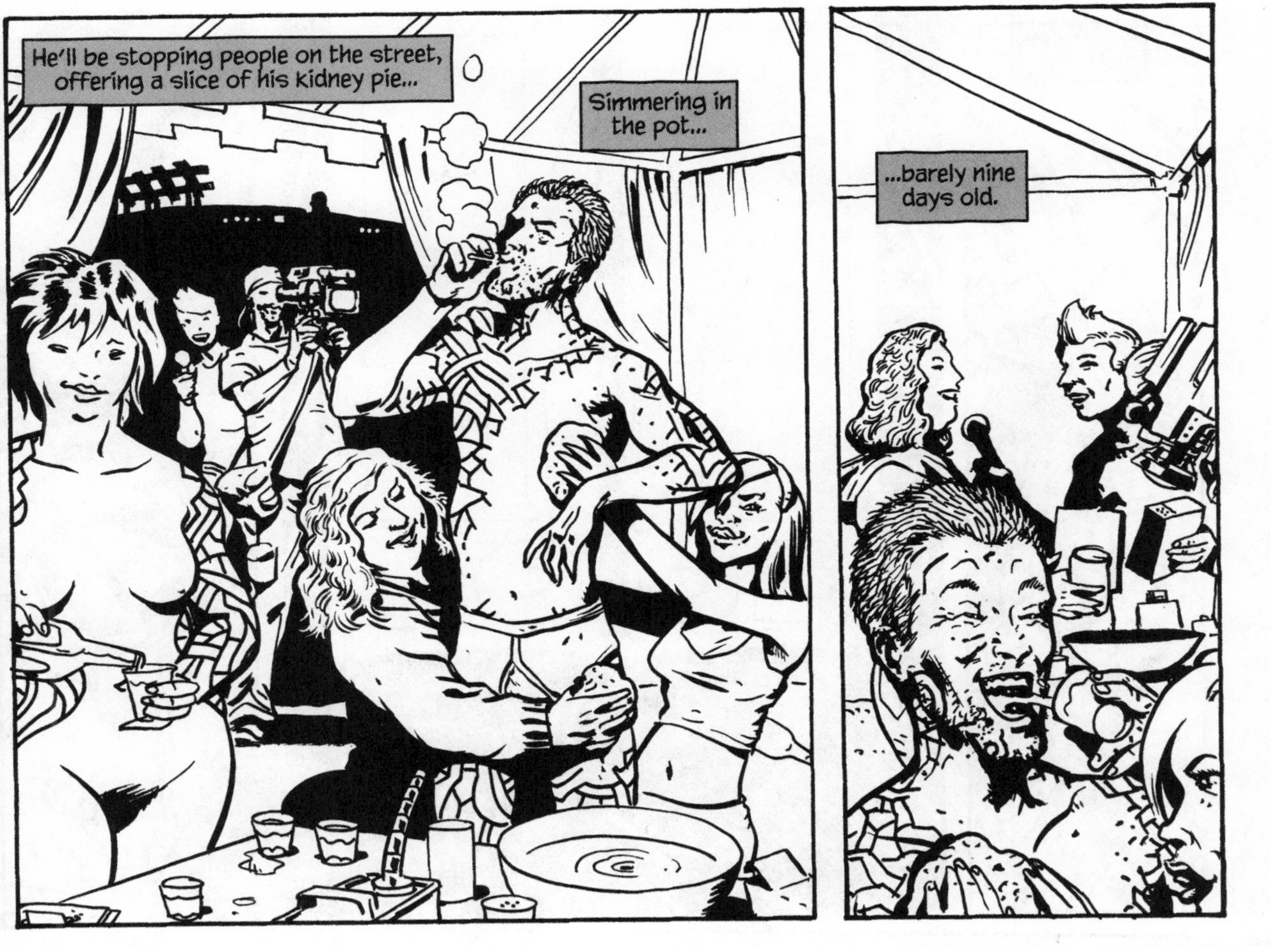
He'll be stopping people on the street, offering a slice of his kidney pie...
Simmering in the pot...
...barely nine days old.

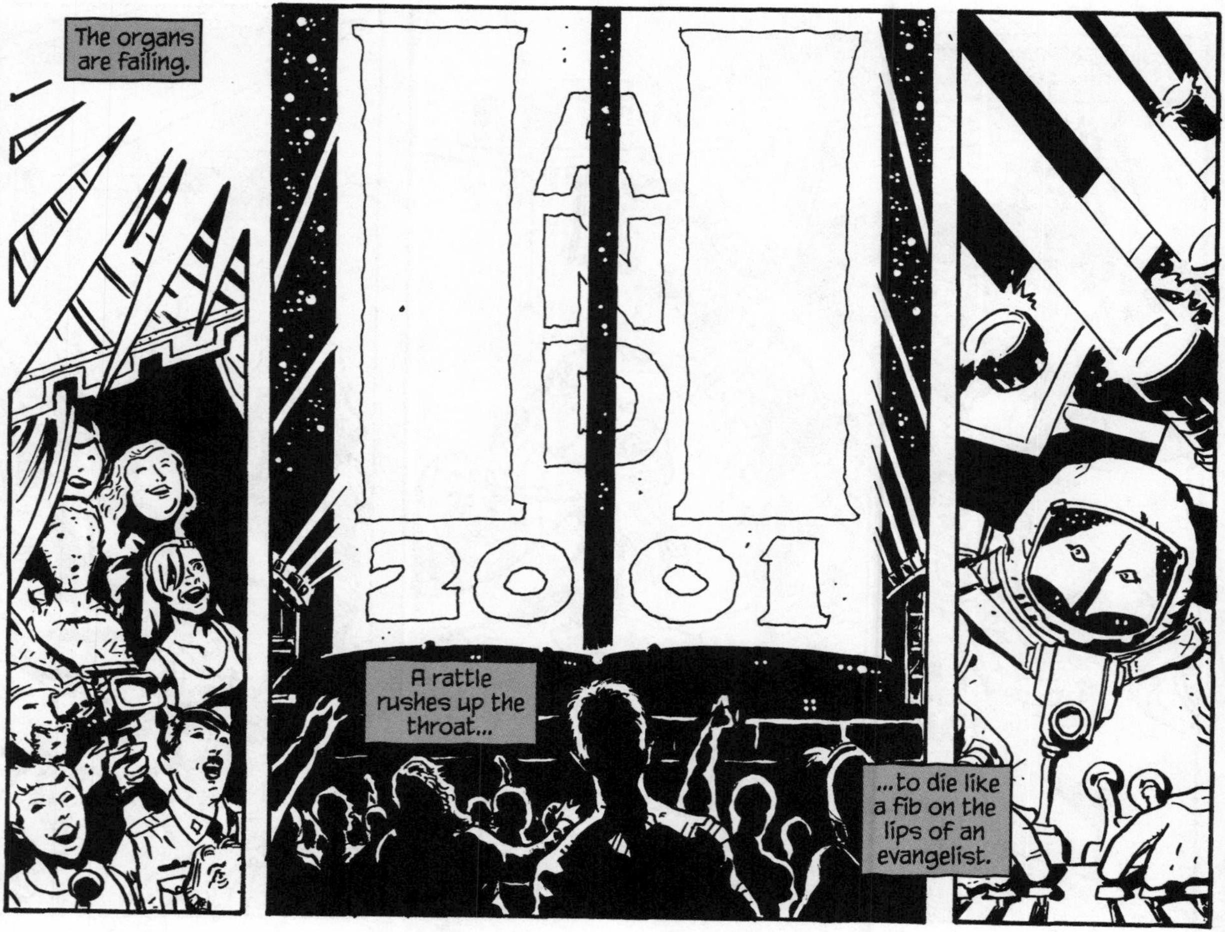
The organs are failing.
AND
2001
A rattle rushes up the throat...
...to die like a fib on the lips of an evangelist.

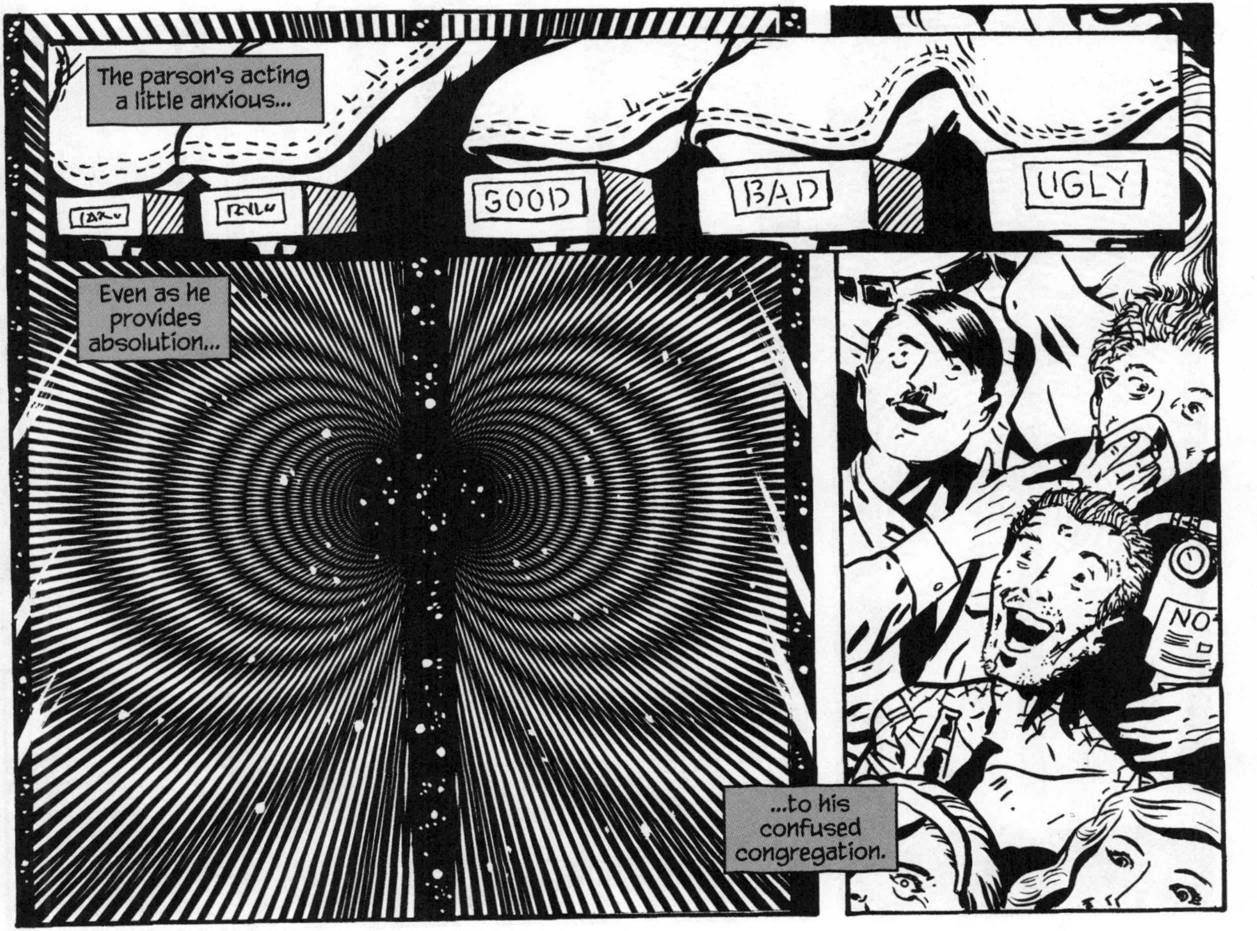
The parson's acting a little anxious...
GOOD
BAD
UGLY
Even as he provides absolution...
...to his confused congregation.

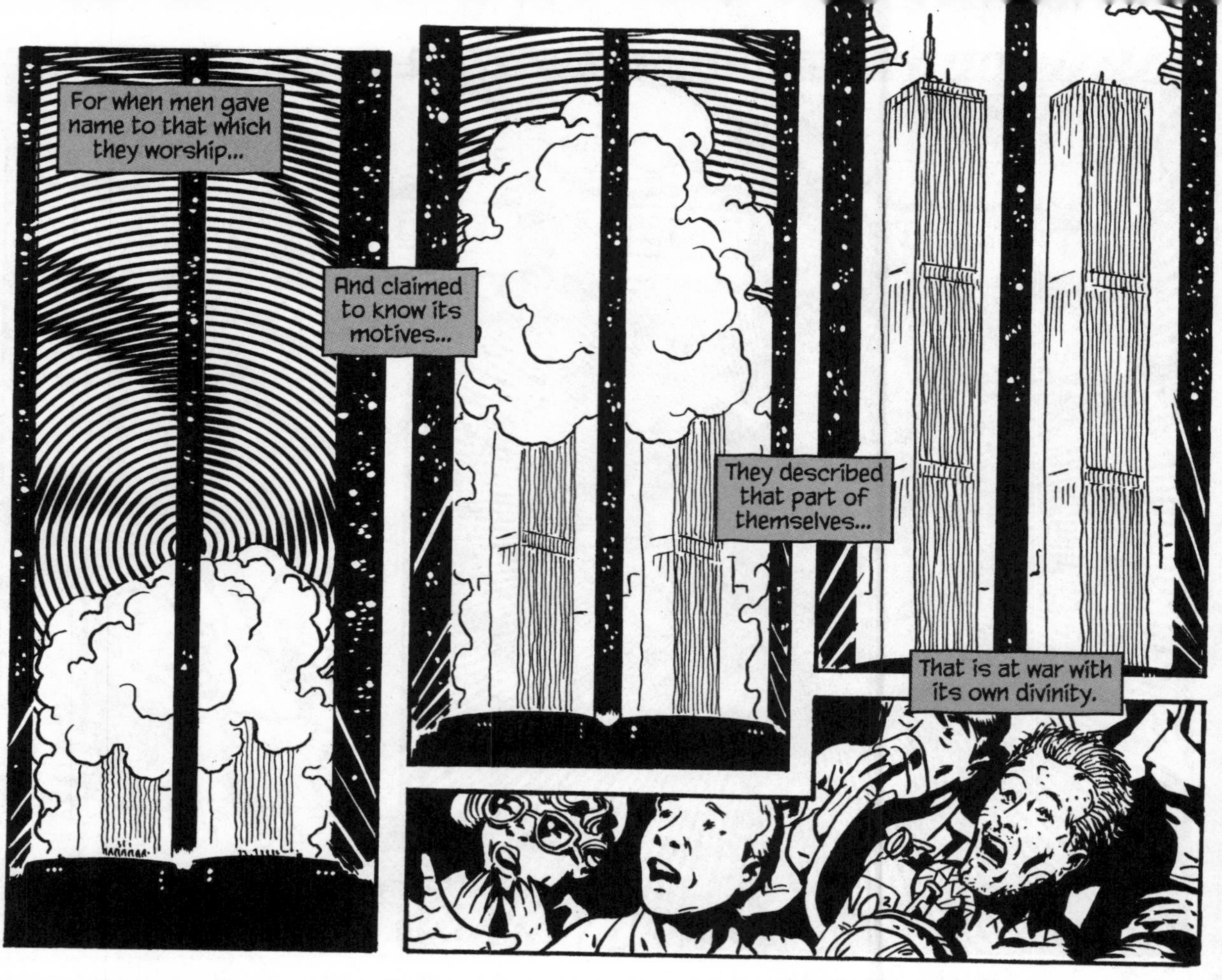
For when men gave name to that which they worship...
And claimed to know its motives...
They described that part of themselves...
That is at war with its own divinity.

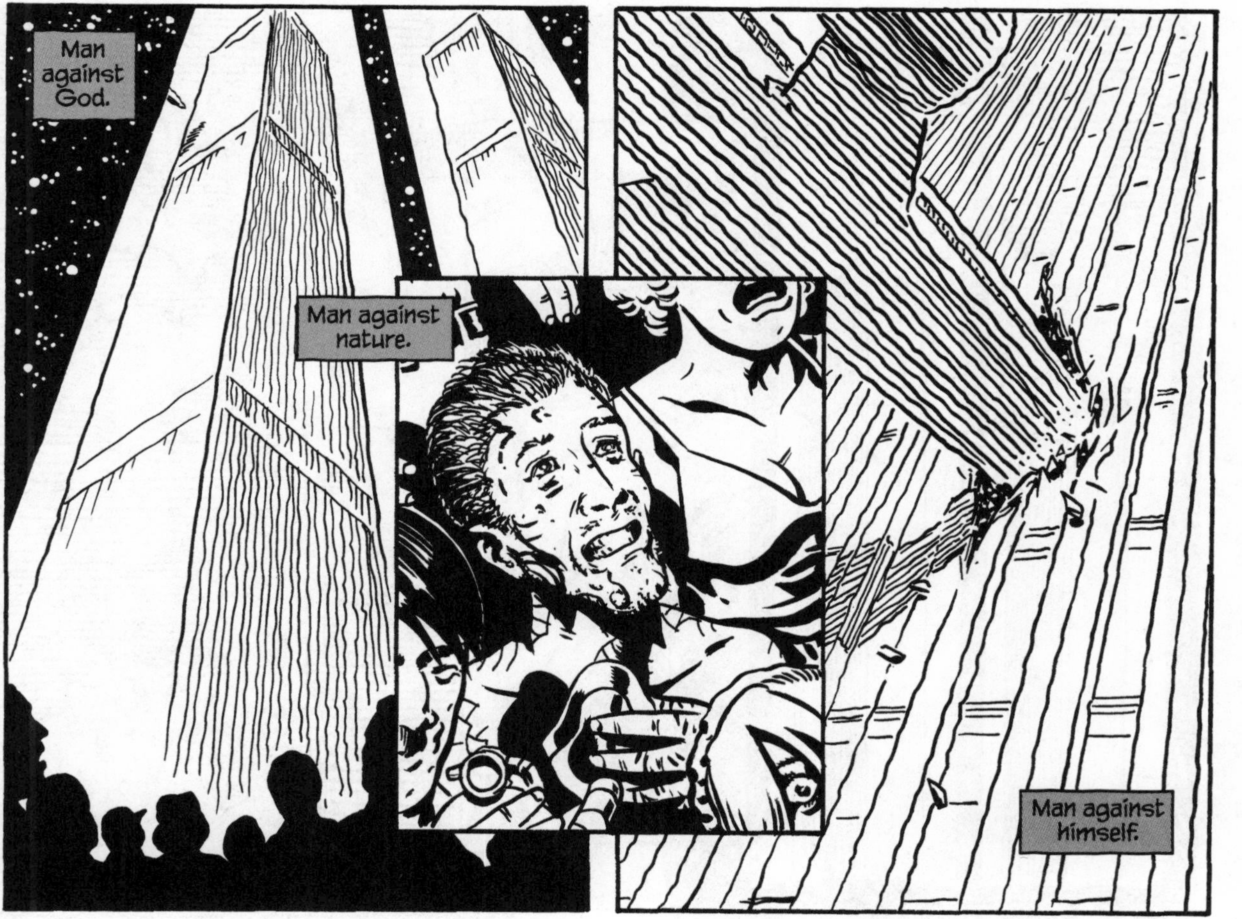
Man against God.
Man against nature.
Man against himself.

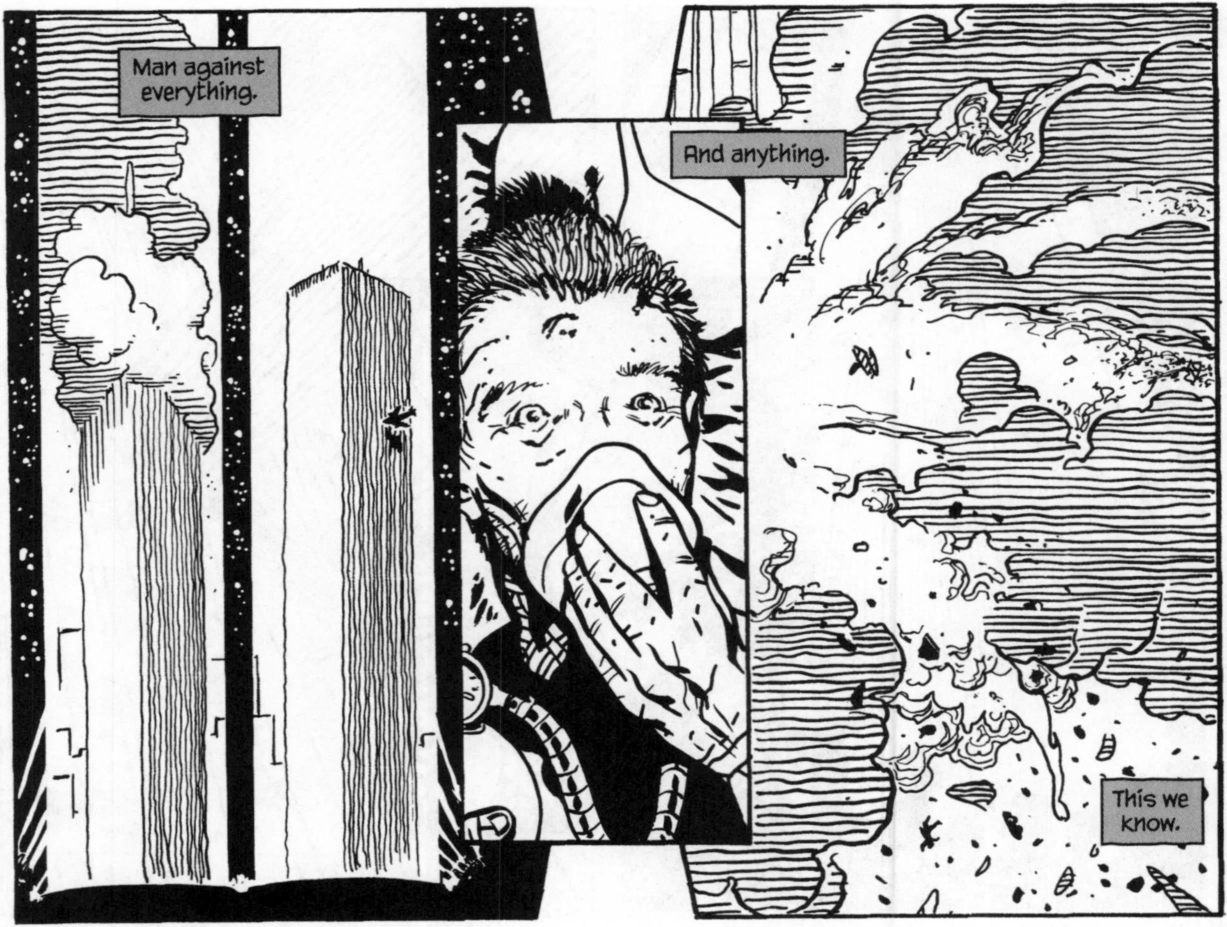
Man against everything.
And anything.
This we know.

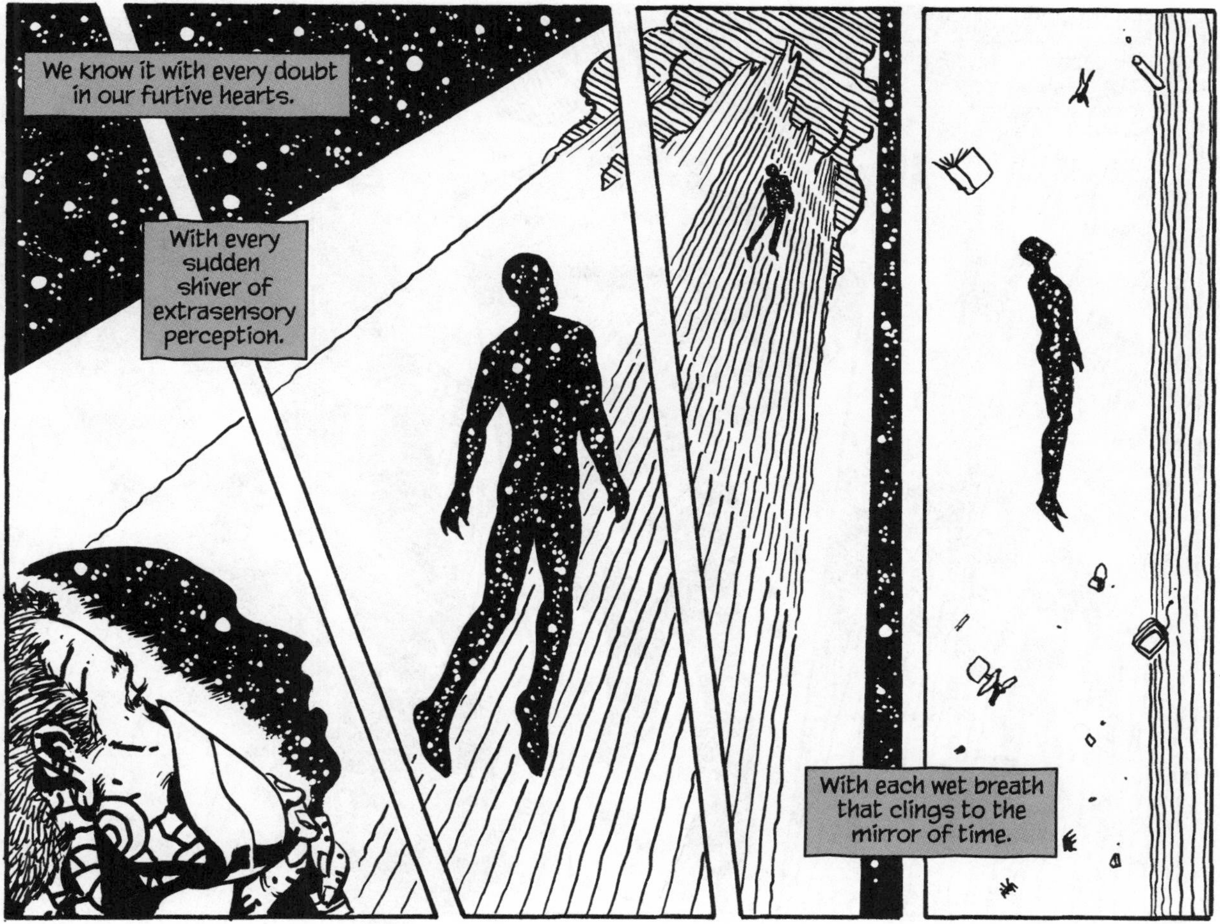
We know it with every doubt in our furtive hearts.
With every sudden shiver of extrasensory perception.
With each wet breath that clings to the mirror of time.

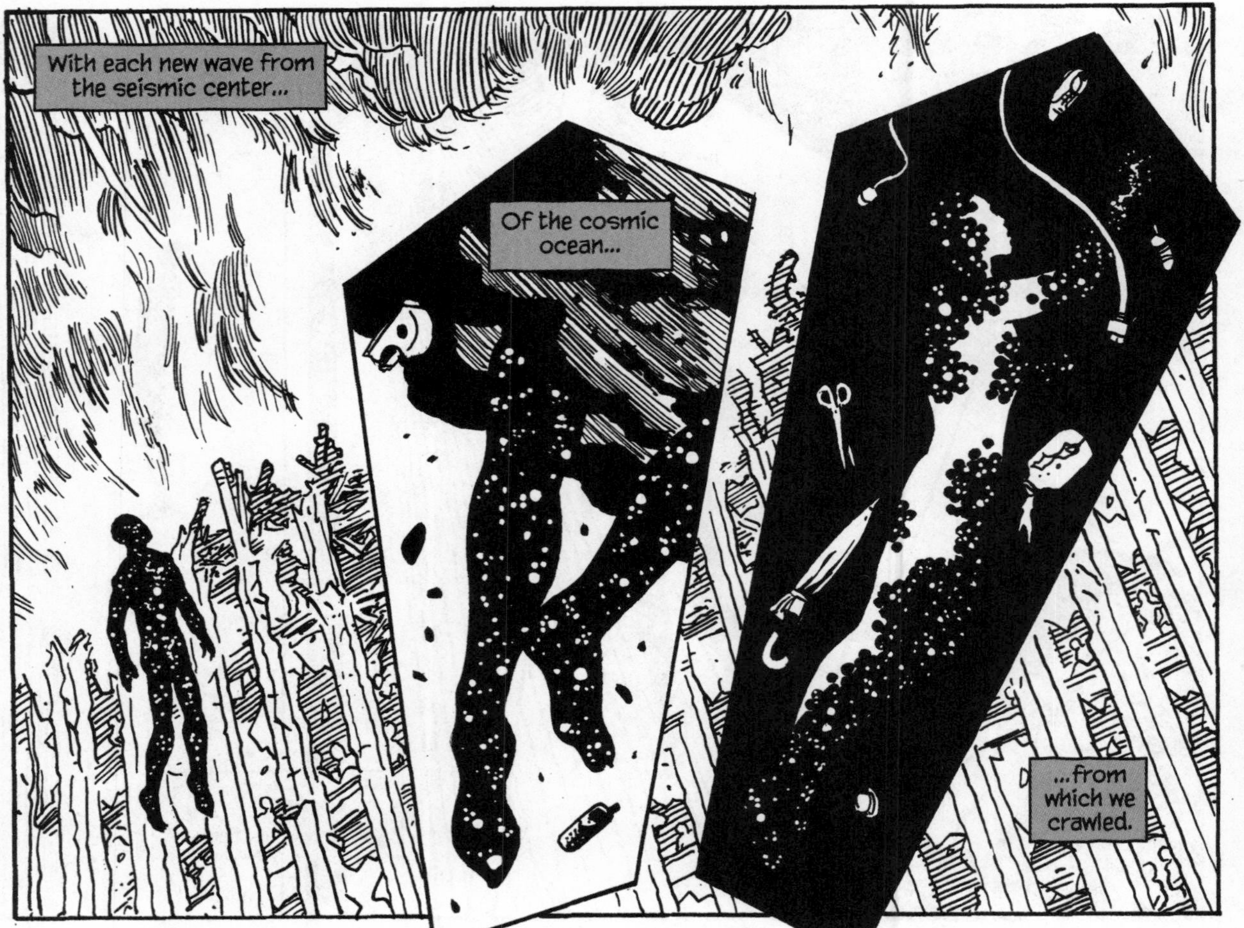
With each new wave from the seismic center...
Of the cosmic ocean...
...from which we crawled.

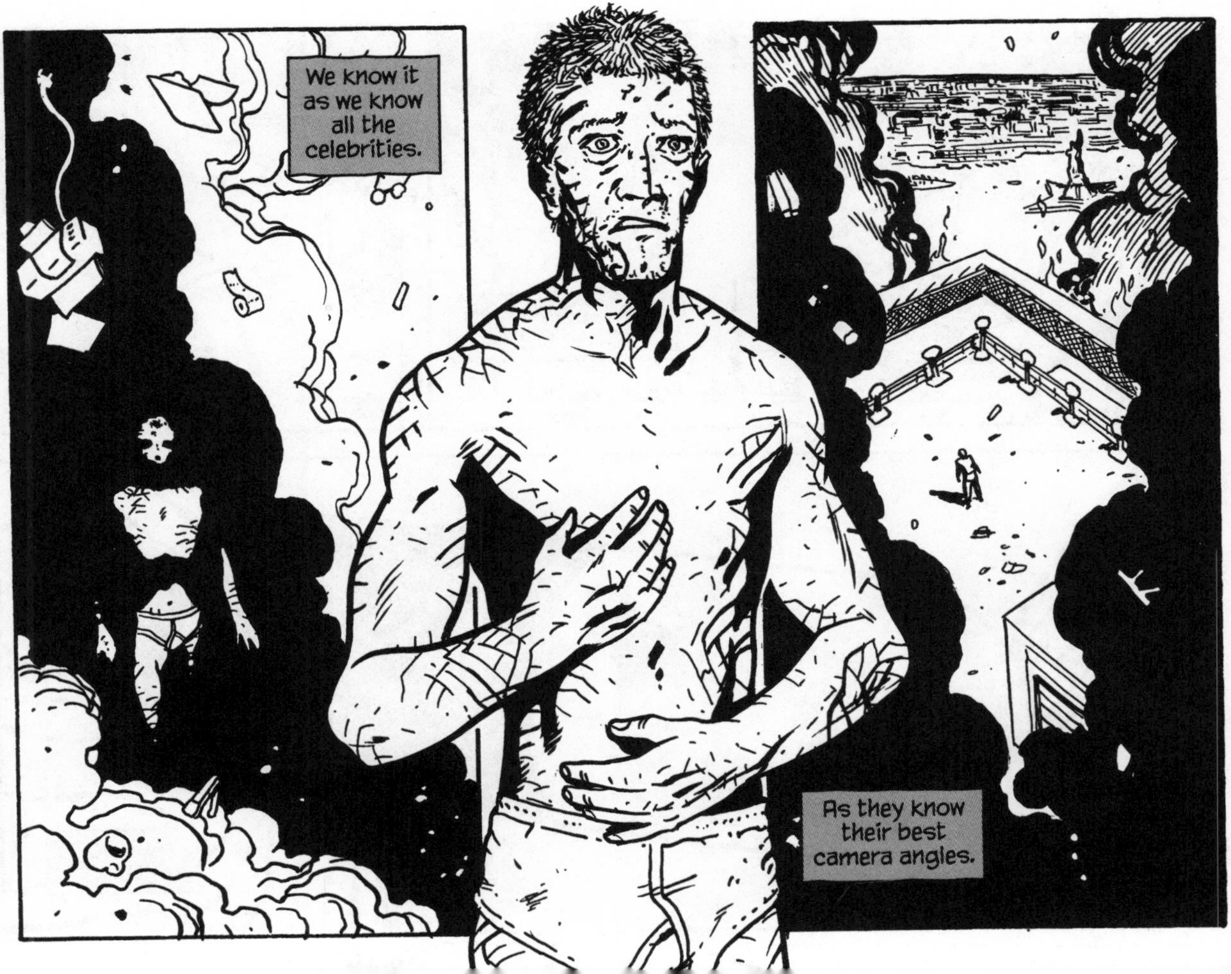
We know it as we know all the celebrities.
As they know their best camera angles.

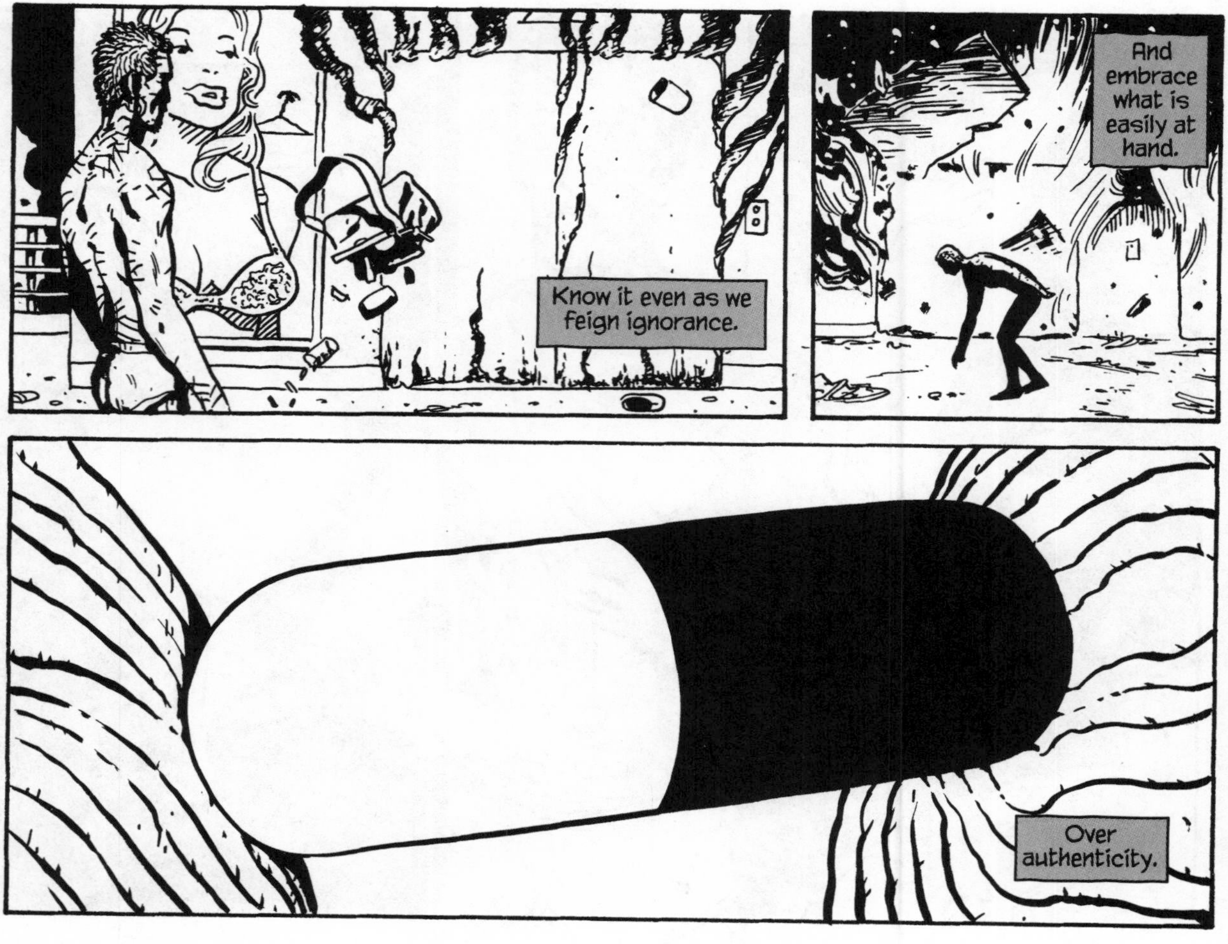
Know it even as we feign ignorance.
And embrace what is easily at hand.
Over authenticity.

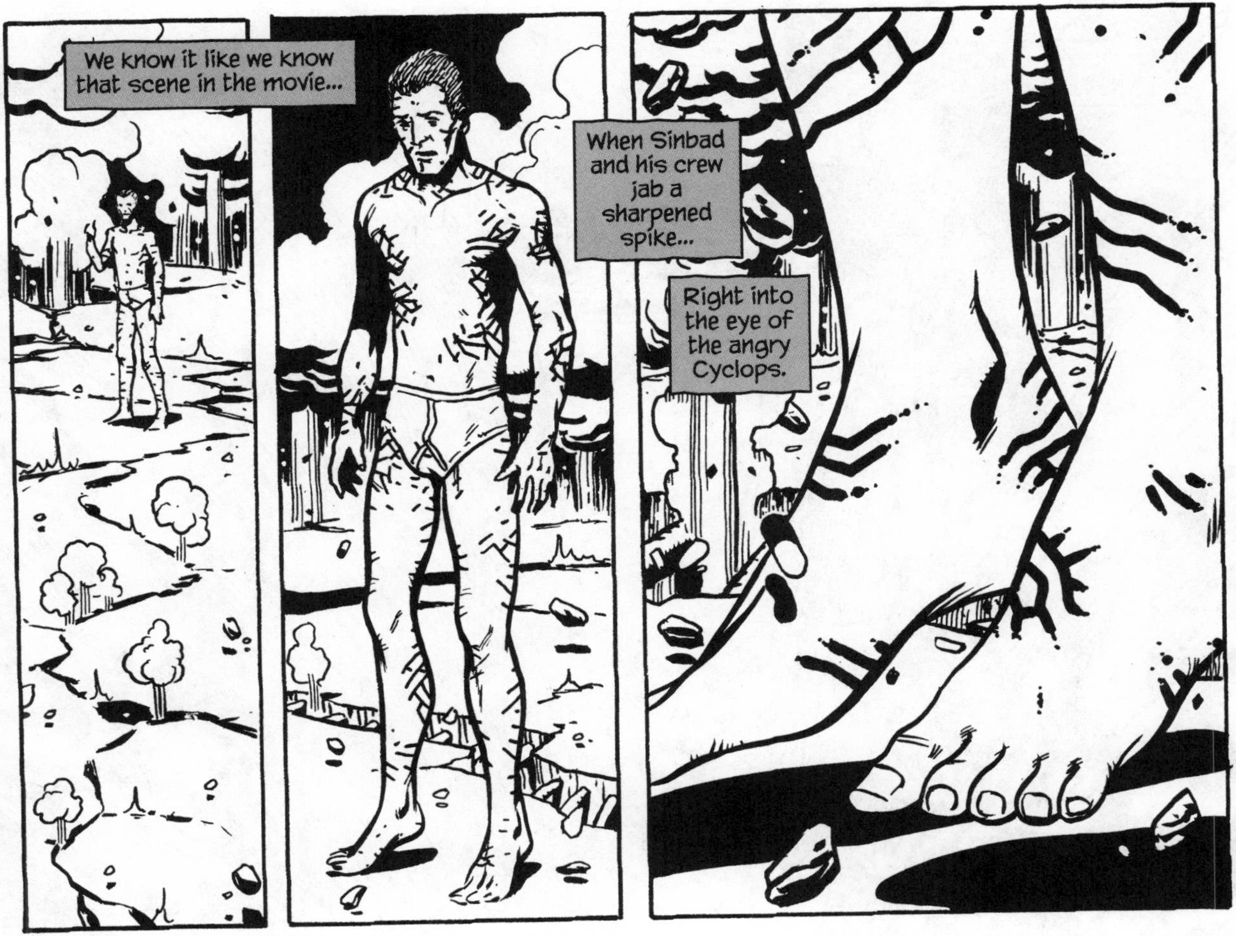
We know it like we know that scene in the movie...
When Sinbad and his crew jab a sharpened spike...
Right into the eye of the angry Cyclops.

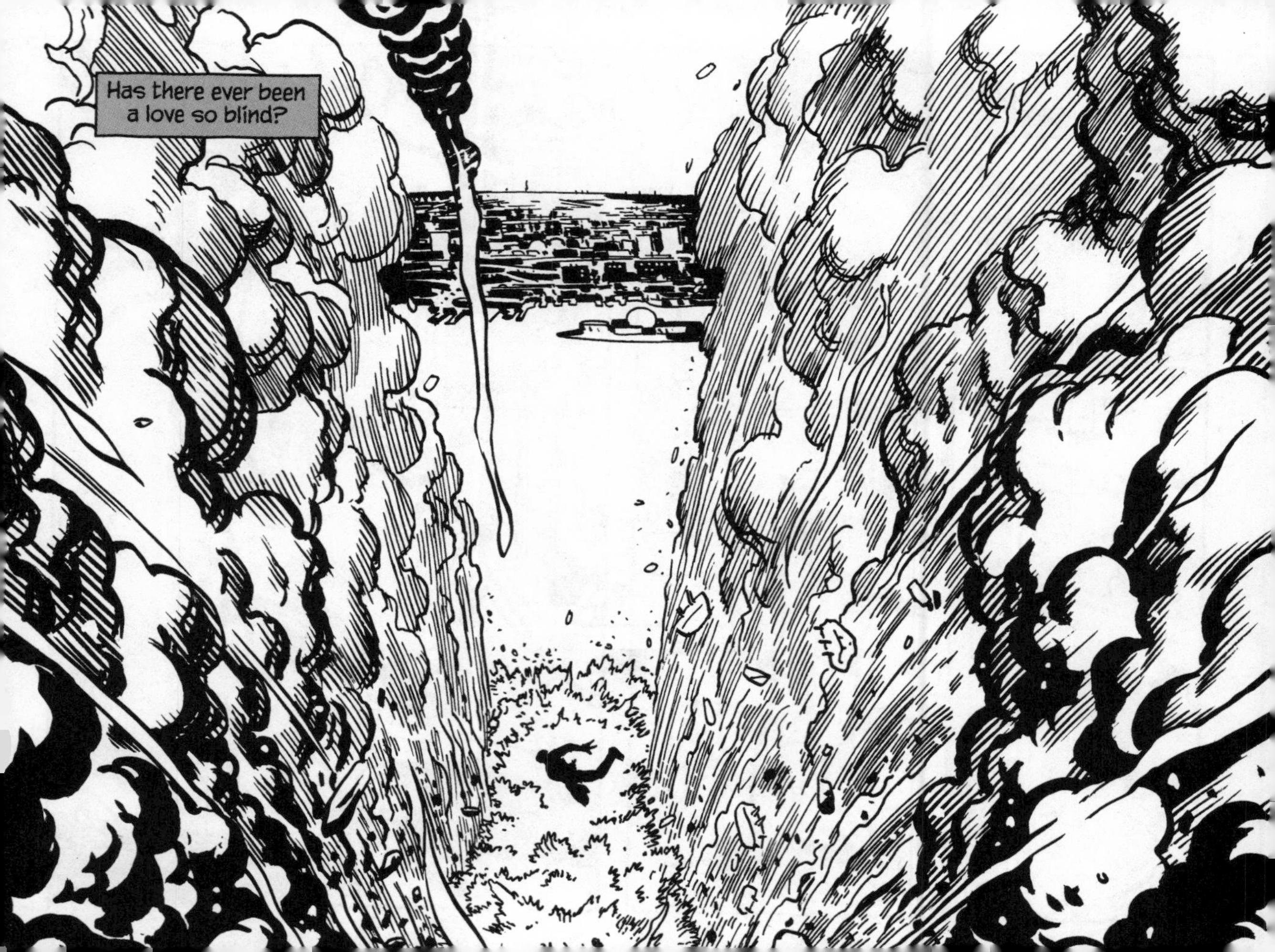
Has there ever been a love so blind?

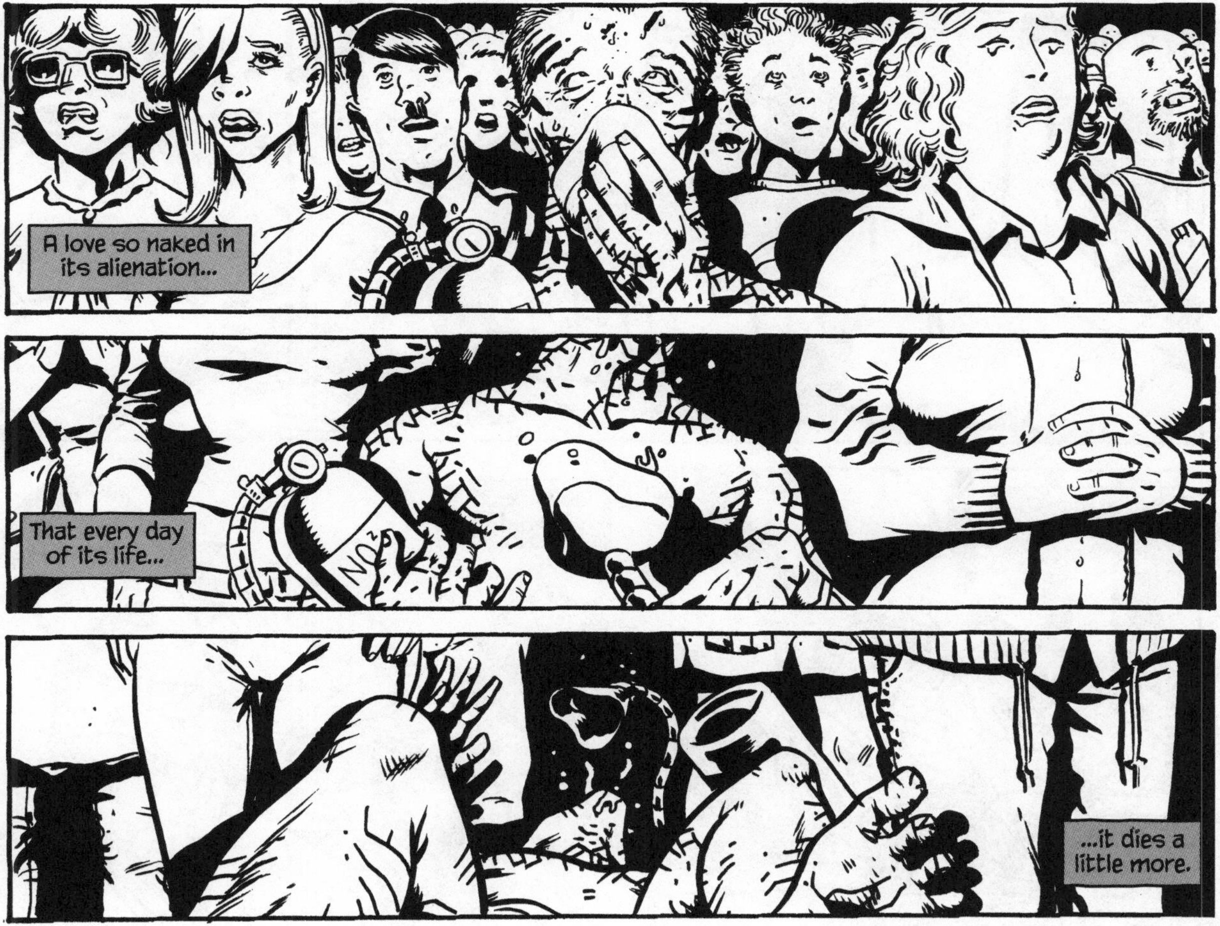
A love so naked in its alienation...
That every day of its life...
...it dies a little more.

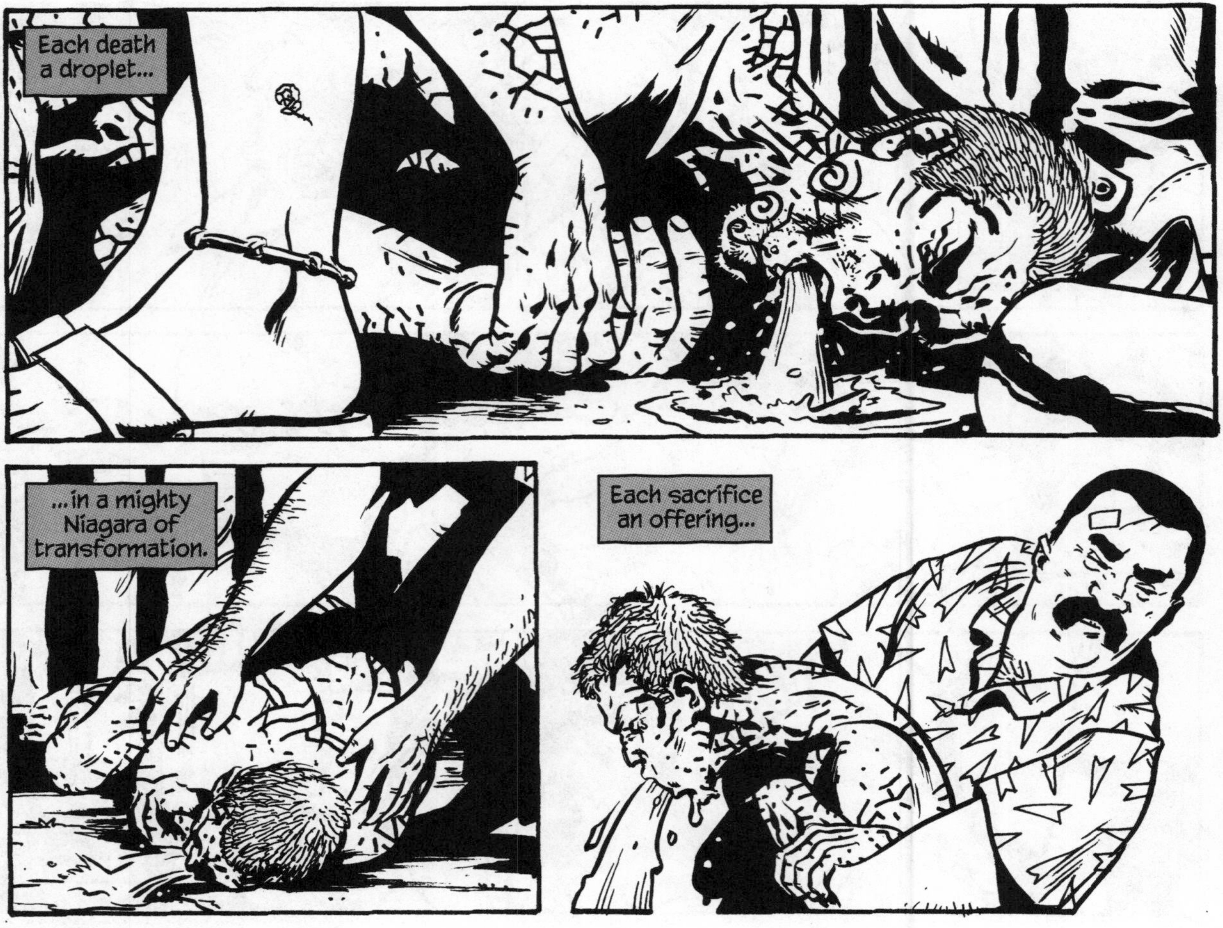
Each death a droplet...
...in a mighty Niagara of transformation.
Each sacrifice an offering...

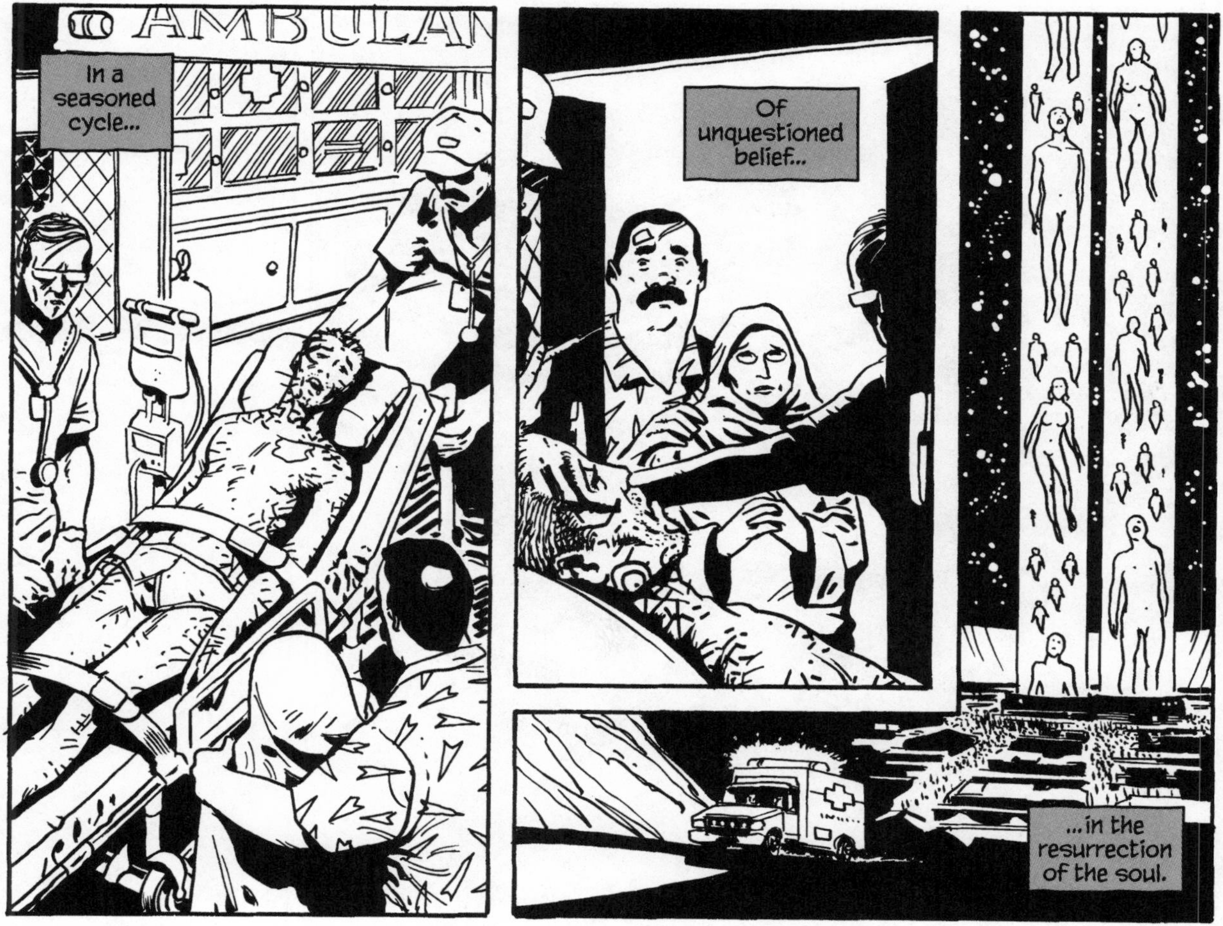
AMBULAN
In a seasoned cycle...
Of unquestioned belief...
...in the resurrection of the soul.

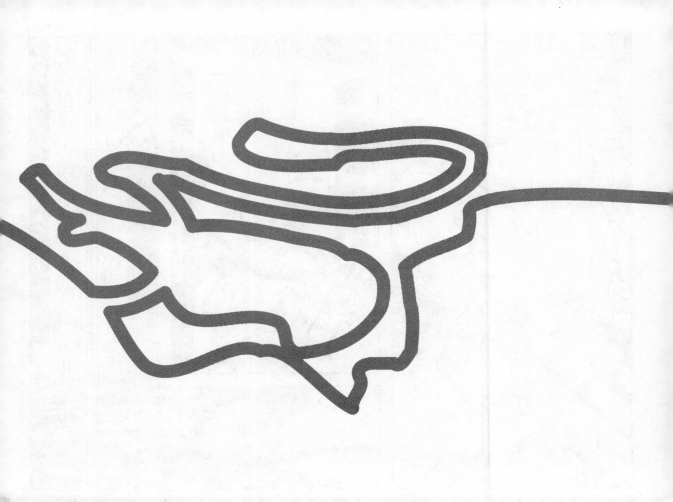

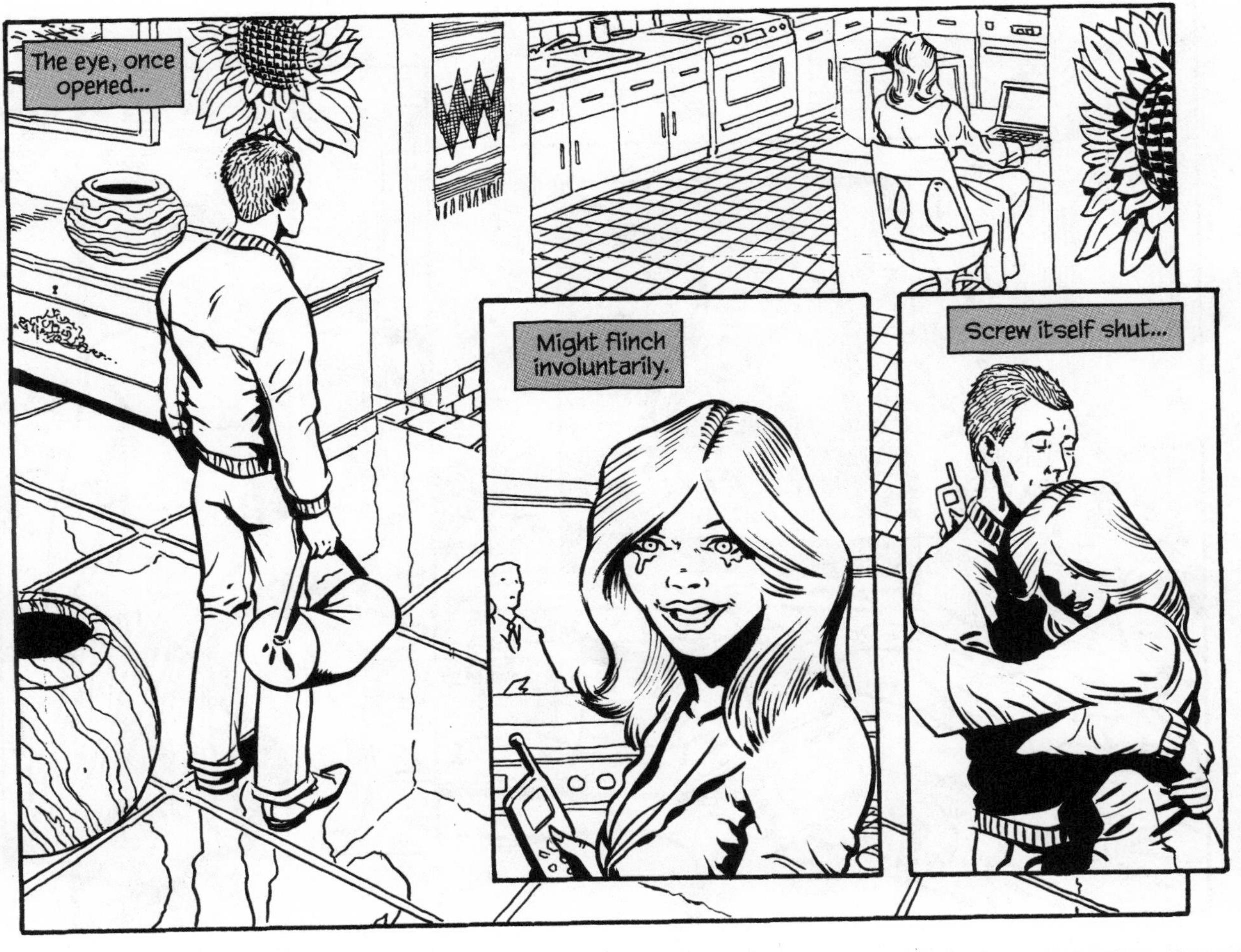
The eye, once opened...
Might flinch involuntarily.
Screw itself shut...

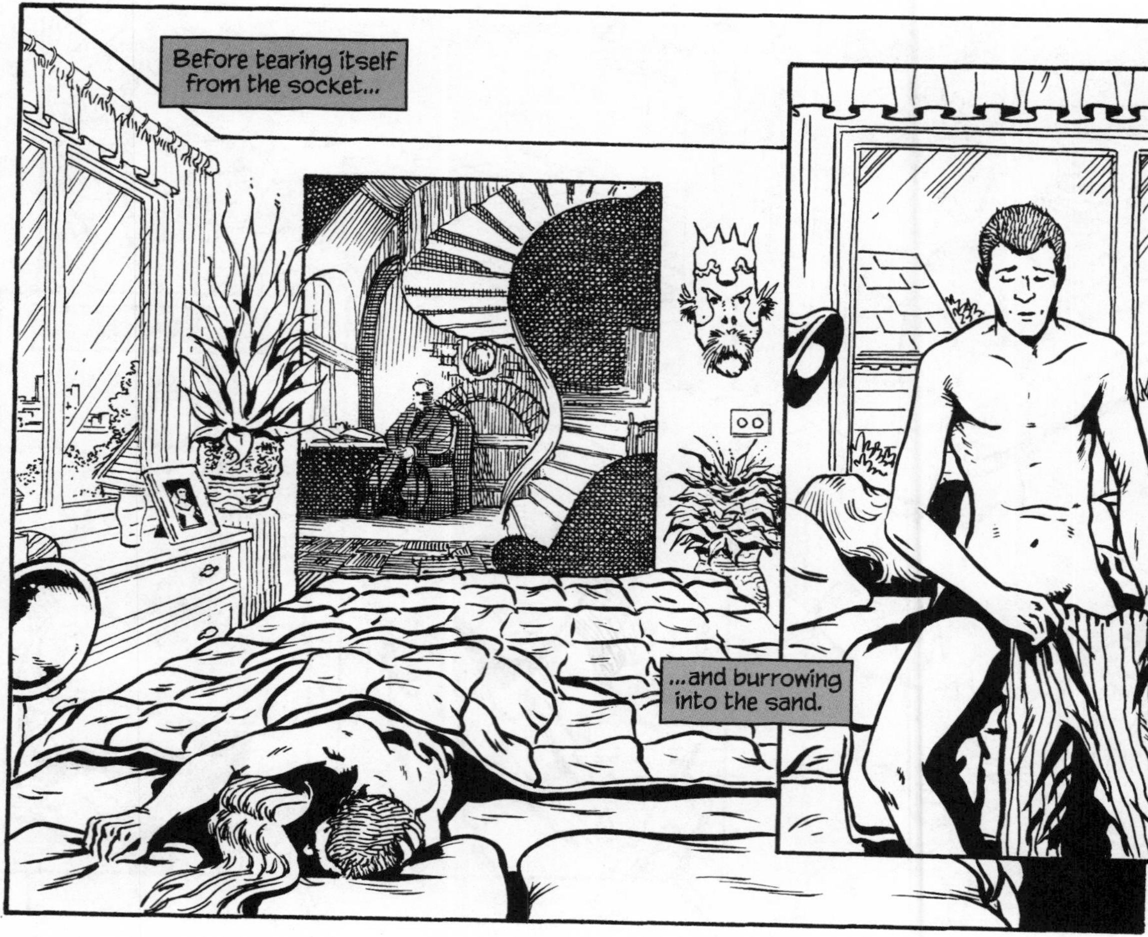
Before tearing itself from the socket...
...and burrowing into the sand.

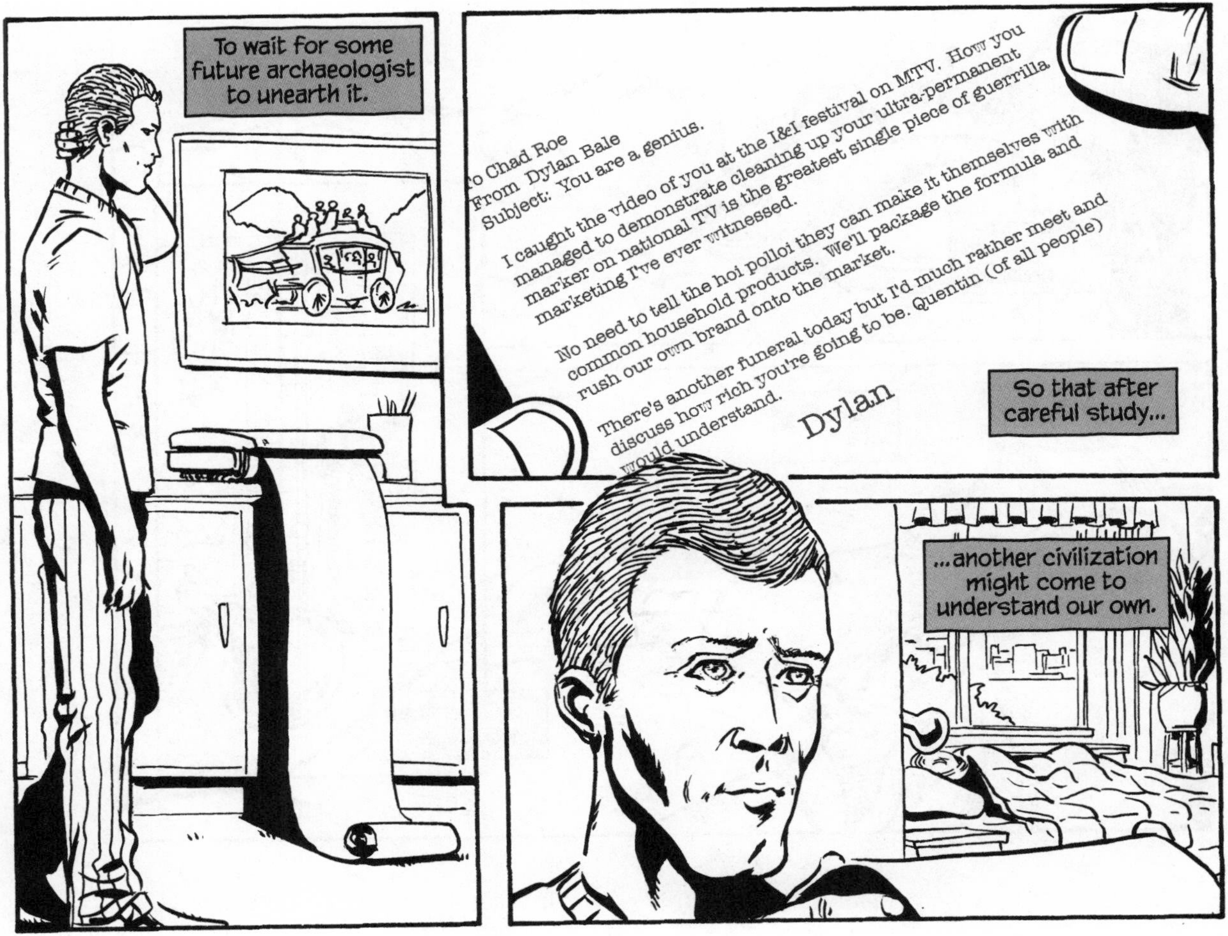
To wait for some future archaeologist to unearth it.
o Chad Roe
From Dylan Bale
Subject: You are a genius.
I caught the video of you at the I&I festival on MTV. How you managed to demonstrate cleaning up your ultra-permanent marker on national TV is the greatest single piece of guerrilla marketing I've ever witnessed.
No need to tell the hoi polloi they can make it themselves with common household products. We'll package the formula and rush our own brand onto the market.
There's another funeral today but I'd much rather meet and discuss how rich you're going to be. Quentin (of all people) would understand.
Dylan
So that after careful study...
...another civilization might come to understand our own.

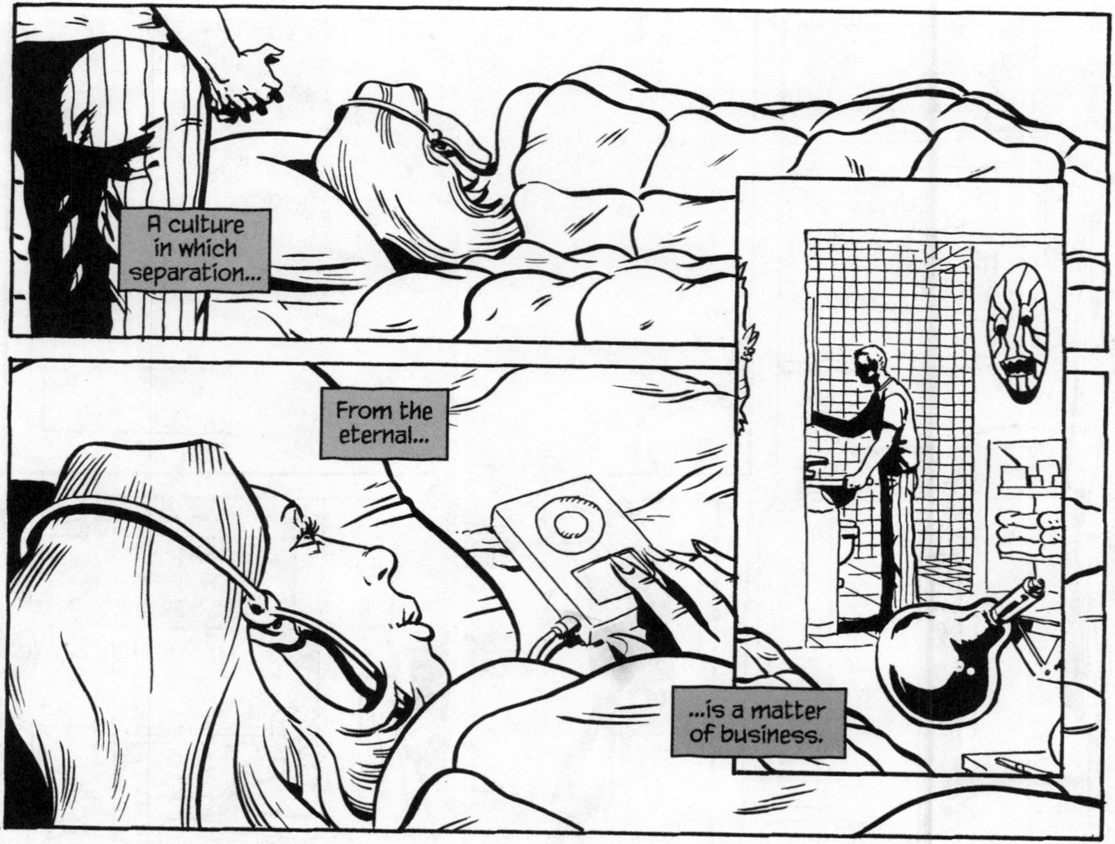

A culture in which separation...
From the eternal...
...is a matter of business.

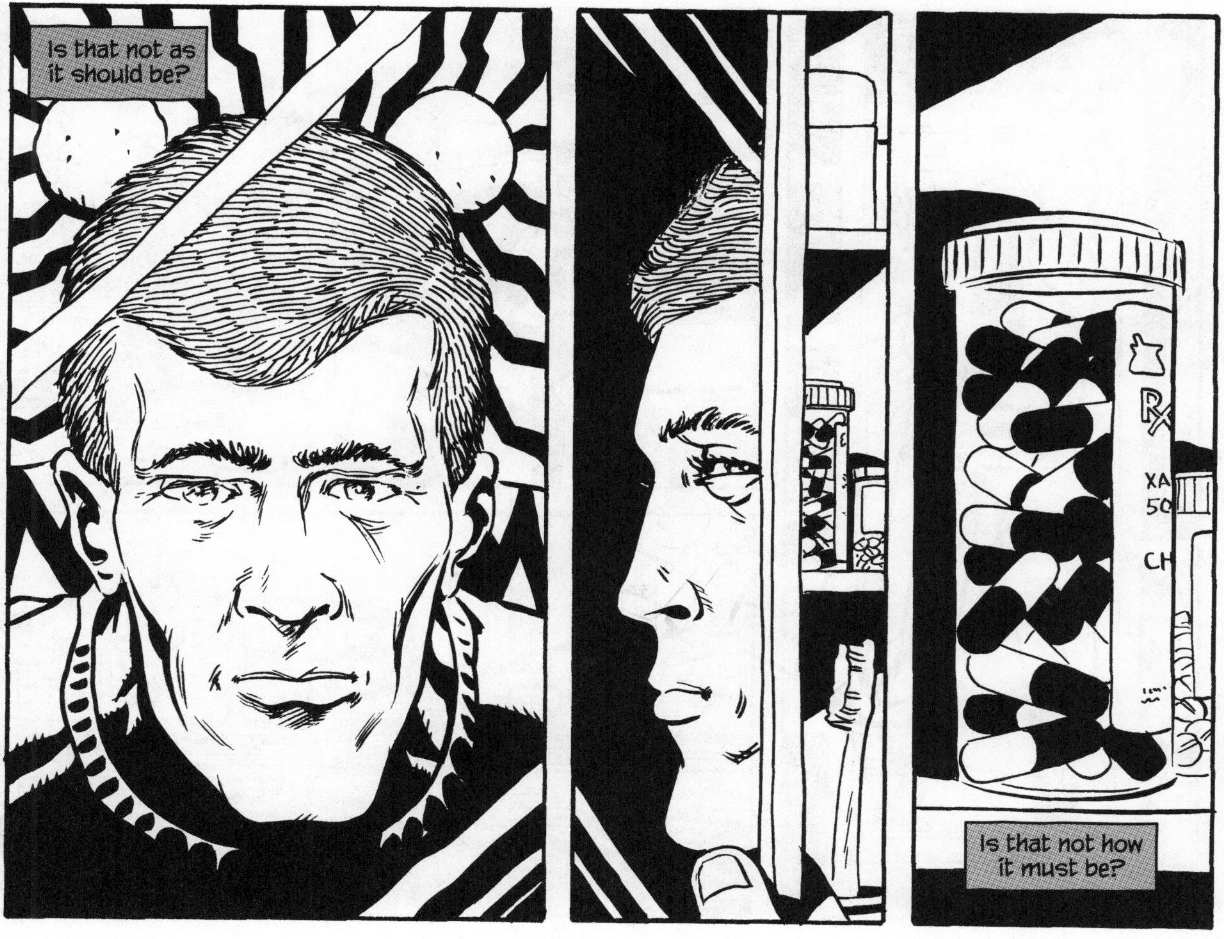
Is that not as it should be?
Is that not how it must be?

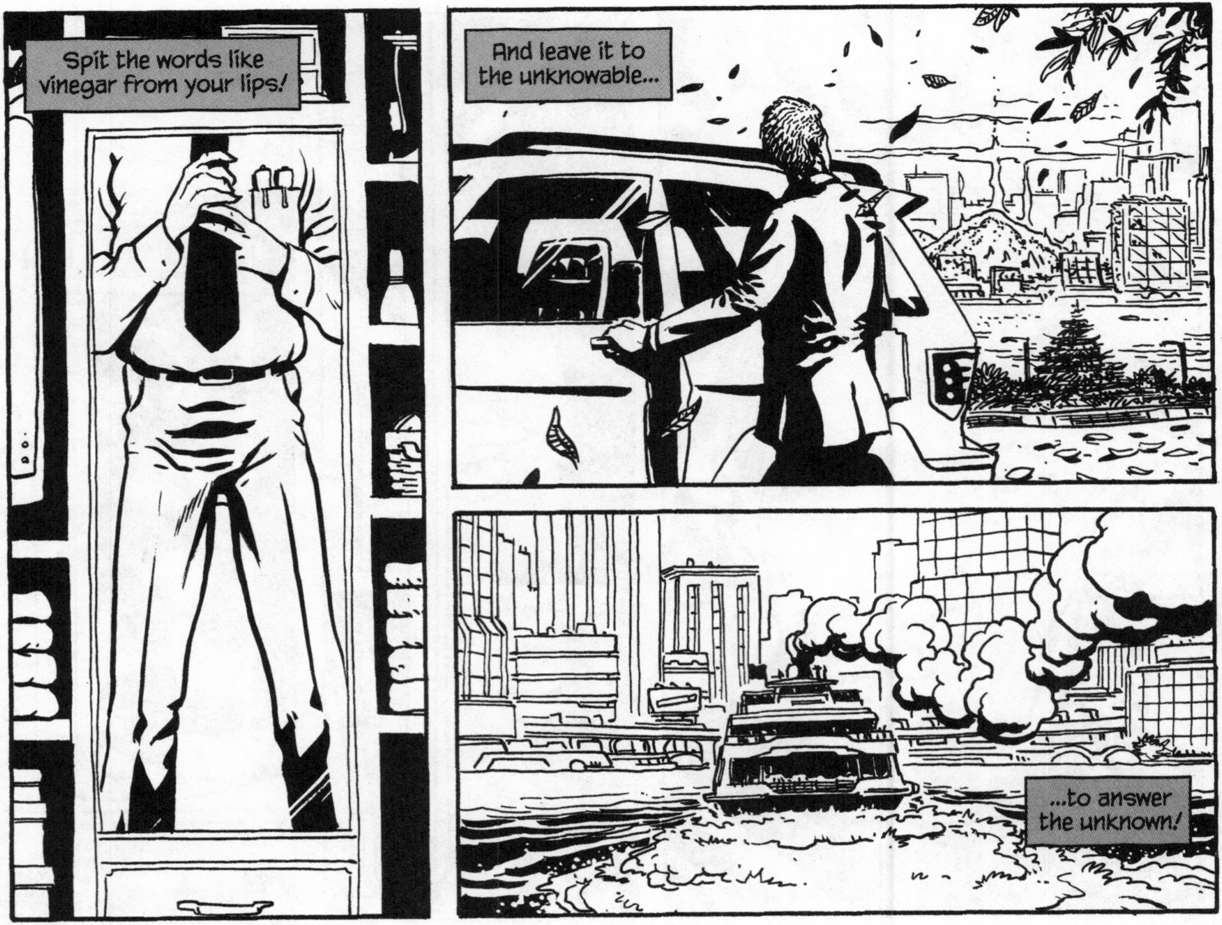
Spit the words like vinegar from your lips!
And leave it to the unknowable...
...to answer the unknown!

Rick Veitch is a lifelong cartoonist who was an early contributor to *Epic* and *Heavy Metal* magazines. He collaborated with Alan Moore and Alfredo Alcala on **Swamp Thing** before taking over the writing as well as pencilling on that series. His first year as writer and artist can be found in the Vertigo collections **Swamp Thing: Regenesis** and **Swamp Thing: Spontaneous Generation**. Veitch was one of the founding artists of the America's Best Comics line, co-creating Greyshirt for **Tomorrow Stories**. The character was later spun off into the graphic novel **Greyshirt: Indigo Sunset**.

Veitch's other graphic novels include *Abraxas and the Earthman, Heartburst, The One, Brat Pack, The Maximortal, Rabid Eye, Pocket Universe,* and *Crypto Zoo*. He is currently writing and pencilling a new monthly ongoing series for Vertigo.

He is the co-founder, with Steve Conley, of the Internet comics site Comicon.com. He lives in Vermont with his wife Cindy and two sons, Kirby and Ezra.

Special Thanks to Heidi MacDonald and Ezra Veitch.

Karen Berger VP — Executive Editor **Pornsak Pichetshote** Associate Editor **Louis Prandi** Art Director **Paul Levitz** President & Publisher **Georg Brewer** VP — Design & DC Direct Creative **Richard Bruning** Sr. VP — Creative Director

Patrick Caldon Executive VP — Finance & Operations **Chris Caramalis** VP — Finance **John Cunningham** VP — Marketing **Terri Cunningham** VP — Managing Editor **Stephanie Fierman** Sr. VP — Sales & Marketing **Alison Gill** VP — Manufacturing

Rich Johnson VP — Book Trade Sales **Hank Kanalz** VP — General Manager, WildStorm **Lillian Laserson** Sr. VP & General Counsel **Jim Lee** Editorial Director — WildStorm **Paula Lowitt** Sr. VP — Business & Legal Affairs

David McKillips VP — Advertising & Custom Publishing **John Nee** VP — Business Development **Gregory Noveck** Sr. VP — Creative Affairs **Cheryl Rubin** Sr. VP — Brand Management **Jeff Trojan** VP — Business Development, DC Direct **Bob Wayne** VP — Sales

YA GRAPHIC NOVEL 7/06